Chris Donlay
A Grammar of Khatso

Mouton Grammar Library

Edited by
Georg Bossong
Bernard Comrie
Patience L. Epps
Irina Nikolaeva

Volume 77

Chris Donlay

A Grammar of Khatso

DE GRUYTER
MOUTON

ISBN 978-3-11-073529-1
ISSN 0933-7636

Library of Congress Control Number: 2018963363

Bibliographic information published by the Deutsche Nationalbibliothek
The Deutsche Nationalbibliothek lists this publication in the Deutsche Nationalbibliografie;
detailed bibliographic data are available in the Internet at http://dnb.dnb.de.

© 2020 Walter de Gruyter GmbH, Berlin/Boston
This volume is text- and page-identical with the hardback published in 2019.
Printing and binding: CPI books GmbH, Leck

www.degruyter.com

Acknowledgements

No project of this size and scope can be accomplished alone. Many people on both sides of the Pacific helped shape the project with their ideas, encouragement and support during the years of planning, research and writing. I would like to acknowledge their contributions here.

First, I sincerely thank the people of Xingmeng who so generously welcomed me to their village. Their warmth, enthusiasm and good humor made my work enjoyable from the first day. $k^huɛi^{44}\ lai^{31}t^hua^{31}$ 奎来团, head of the Tonghai Mongolian Nationality Cultural Research and Inheritance Protection Center, was especially supportive of the project, providing me with a desk at the Center and regularly inviting me to village events to better understand Khatso culture. Two other members of the Center, $xua^{24}\ p^hɛi^{33}xo^{31}$ 华丕和 and $p^hɣ^{33}\ z\underset{\textstyle\smile}{\gamma}^{33}li^{31}$ 普汝林, also routinely dropped by to help out and answer my questions. By far the most important assistance the Center provided was the introduction of $k^huɛi^{44}\ li^{24}$ 奎丽, who became my primary consultant and project assistant. "Professor" $k^huɛi^{44}$ quickly became indispensable, and without her the project would not have succeeded. I thank her for the intelligence, enthusiasm and laughter she brought to our long days of research. Many other residents of Xingmeng actively participated in various aspects of this project. I cannot thank them all individually here, but they are listed in § 1.9 with my gratitude.

The academic community in China also provided invaluable assistance. Prof. Zhou Decai 周德才 of the School of National Cultures at Yunnan University of Nationalities generously agreed to serve as my local sponsor. He, along with Dr. Liu Jinrong 刘劲荣, chair of the School of National Cultures, and Prof. Liu Xun 刘勋 of the International Affairs Department, provided crucial help in securing permission to conduct a year's research in Xingmeng. Our mutual friend, Dr. Li Yongxiang 李永祥 of the Yunnan Academy of Social Sciences, also provided much appreciated insight and support throughout the year, as did two American linguists in Kunming, Cathryn Yang and Keith Slater of SIL. Prof. Melody Chang 张雅音, now at Yunnan University, was the first to urge me to consider researching Khatso. And I send special thanks to Profs. Xu Xianming 许鲜明 and Bai Bibo 白璧波 of the Research Centre for Endangered Languages at Yuxi Normal University, for their friendship, advice and convivial dinners.

I would also like to express my gratitude to the National Science Foundation and the Mellon Foundation/American Council of Learned Societies for validating the importance of documenting Khatso through their generous financial support. Without their assistance, this project would not have been possible.

I have been fortunate to study with some of the most talented linguists in the field. They helped me turn a dream into a dissertation and ultimately this book. I thank my advisor at the University of California, Santa Barbara, Carol Genetti, for her indefatigable support, wise words and good humor, as well as the other esteemed members of my dissertation committee – Bernard Comrie and Marianne Mithun of UCSB and David Bradley of La Trobe University – for giving so generously of their time, insight and guidance. Prof. Bradley, in particular, has earned my undying gratitude for introducing me to so many new colleagues in China as well as steering my education into the Ngwi family and its structures. And Patience Epps, my editor, kindly and gently helped me improve the final draft.

The rest of the faculty at UCSB also deserves thanks for not only providing me with an excellent education but also for their ongoing contributions to the study and documentation of endangered languages. Special thanks also go to Roula Svorou and Dan Silverman at San Jose State University, who gave me a good start, and to Arienne Dwyer at the University of Kansas for her enthusiasm and advice about research in China. In addition, I thank the faculty and students I met at InField 2008 in Santa Barbara and InField 2010 in Eugene for providing inspiration and training to all of us who are dedicated to language documentation and preservation.

Contents

Acknowledgements —— v

List of Tables —— xvi

List of Figures —— xvii

List of Maps —— xviii

List of Photos —— xix

Abbreviations —— xx

1	Overview of Khatso —— 1	
1.1	How to Use this Grammar —— 2	
1.2	Names of the People, Language and Village —— 3	
1.3	The People and Their Past —— 5	
1.4	Language Vitality —— 12	
1.5	History, Contact and Borrowing —— 14	
1.6	Classification —— 18	
1.7	Previous Research —— 20	
1.7.1	A First Exploration of the Yunnan Mongolian Language (Hasieerdun 1976) —— 20	
1.7.2	A Study of Yunnan Mongolian Gazhuo (Dai, Liu and Fu 1987) —— 20	
1.7.3	Yunnan Mongolian and the Classification Question (He 1989) —— 21	
1.7.4	A Tibeto-Burman Lexicon (Huang 1992) —— 22	
1.7.5	About the Formation of Yunnan Mongolian Kazhuo (He 1998) —— 22	
1.7.6	A Study of Kazhuo (Mu 2002) —— 23	
1.7.7	Language Use and Its Evolution Among the Yunnan Mongolian Kazhuo People (Dai 2008) —— 25	
1.7.8	Yunnan Tonghai Xingmeng Mongolian Kazhuo (Wang 2008) —— 26	
1.7.9	Publications in English —— 27	
1.8	Methodology —— 27	
1.9	Language Consultants —— 29	
1.10	Typological Sketch —— 32	
1.11	Photos of Xingmeng —— 34	
2	Consonants and Vowels —— 40	
2.1	Consonants —— 41	
2.1.1	Stops —— 44	

2.1.1.1	Voiceless Bilabial Stops /p, pʰ/ —— 46	
2.1.1.2	Voiceless Alveolar Stops /t, tʰ/ —— 46	
2.1.1.3	Voiceless Velar Stops /k, kʰ/ —— 47	
2.1.2	Nasals —— 47	
2.1.2.1	Bilabial Nasal /m/ —— 48	
2.1.2.2	Alveolar Nasal /n/ —— 48	
2.1.2.3	Palatal Nasal /ɲ/ —— 48	
2.1.2.4	Velar Nasal /ŋ/ —— 49	
2.1.3	Fricatives —— 49	
2.1.3.1	Labio-Dental Fricatives /f, v/ —— 51	
2.1.3.2	Alveolar Fricatives /s, z/ —— 52	
2.1.3.3	Voiceless Alveolo-Palatal Fricative /ɕ/ —— 52	
2.1.3.4	Velar Fricatives /x, ɣ/ —— 53	
2.1.4	Affricates —— 54	
2.1.4.1	Voiceless Alveolar Affricates /ts, tsʰ/ —— 55	
2.1.4.2	Voiceless Alveolo-Palatal Affricates /tɕ, tɕʰ/ —— 56	
2.1.5	Approximants —— 56	
2.1.5.1	Lateral Approximant /l/ —— 57	
2.1.5.2	Palatal Approximant /j/ —— 57	
2.1.5.3	Labio-Velar Approximant /w/ —— 57	
2.2	Vowels —— 58	
2.2.1	Monophthongs —— 58	
2.2.1.1	High Front Unrounded Vowel /i/ —— 62	
2.2.1.2	High Central Apical Vowel /ʅ/ —— 63	
2.2.1.3	High Central Fricative Vowel /v/ —— 64	
2.2.1.4	High Back Unrounded Vowel /ɯ/ —— 67	
2.2.1.5	Mid Front Unrounded Vowel /ɛ/ —— 67	
2.2.1.6	Mid Back Unrounded Vowel /ɤ/ —— 68	
2.2.1.7	Mid Back Rounded Vowel /o/ —— 68	
2.2.1.8	Low Front Unrounded Vowel /a/ —— 69	
2.2.2	Diphthongs —— 70	
2.2.2.1	Diphthong /iɛ/ —— 70	
2.2.2.2	Diphthong /io/ —— 70	
2.2.2.3	Diphthong /ia/ —— 71	
2.2.2.4	Diphthong /uo/ —— 71	
2.2.2.5	Diphthong /ua/ —— 71	
2.2.2.6	Diphthong /ɛi/ —— 72	
2.2.2.7	Diphthong /ai/ —— 72	
2.2.2.8	Diphthong /au/ —— 73	
2.2.3	Triphthongs —— 73	
2.2.3.1	Triphthong /iau/ —— 74	
2.2.3.2	Triphthong /uɛi/ —— 74	

2.2.3.3	Triphthong /uai/ —— 74	
2.2.4	The n̪a³²³ka⁵³ Accent —— 75	
3	**Tone System —— 77**	
3.1	Tones —— 77	
3.1.1	Tone 55 —— 81	
3.1.2	Tone 44 —— 82	
3.1.3	Tone 33 —— 83	
3.1.4	Tone 35 —— 83	
3.1.5	Tone 24 —— 84	
3.1.6	Tone 53 —— 84	
3.1.7	Tone 31 —— 84	
3.1.8	Tone 323 —— 85	
3.1.9	Tone Variation —— 86	
3.2	Tone Change —— 86	
3.2.1	Numerals 'Three', 'Four' and 'Nine' —— 87	
3.2.2	Verb Collocations with li^{323} 'to come' and i^{323} 'to go' —— 90	
3.2.3	Reduplication in Adjectival Constructions —— 90	
3.2.4	Marked Pattern —— 91	
3.2.4.1	Non-Final Phrases in Discourse —— 92	
3.2.4.2	Imperatives —— 96	
3.2.4.3	Aspect Marker wa^{33} —— 97	
3.2.5	Focus Tone Change —— 99	
3.2.6	Tone Fusion —— 102	
3.2.6.1	Fusion of Grammatical Particles —— 103	
3.2.6.2	Fusion in Echo Questions —— 104	
3.2.7	Tone Contours 242 and 353 in Discourse —— 105	
3.2.8	Lexicalized Tone Change in Causatives —— 107	
4	**Syllable, Word and Intonation Unit Structures —— 108**	
4.1	Syllable Structure —— 108	
4.2	Word Structure —— 110	
4.2.1	Defining the Word —— 110	
4.2.2	Phonological Structure of Words —— 113	
4.2.3	Morphological Structure of Words —— 115	
4.2.3.1	Compounds of Bound Morphemes —— 115	
4.2.3.2	Noun Suffixes —— 116	
4.2.3.3	Compounds of Free Morphemes —— 117	
4.2.4	Stress —— 118	
4.3	Homophony —— 119	
4.4	Intonation Units and Prosody —— 120	
4.4.1	Pause —— 121	

4.4.2	Lag —— 122
4.4.3	Rush —— 123
4.4.4	Intensity —— 124

5	Nouns —— 126
5.1	Common Nouns —— 128
5.2	Proper Nouns —— 132
5.2.1	Personal Names —— 132
5.2.2	Place Names —— 135
5.3	Pronouns —— 136
5.3.1	Personal Pronouns —— 136
5.3.2	Demonstrative Pronouns —— 141
5.3.3	Interrogative Pronouns —— 144
5.3.3.1	Interrogative Pronoun $xa^{33}jo^{35}$ 'who' —— 146
5.3.3.2	Interrogative Pronoun $xa^{33}ma^{44}$ 'what', 'which' —— 147
5.3.3.3	Interrogative Pronouns $xa^{33}tɕʰa^{55}kʰy^{33}$, $xa^{33}sau^{33}$ and $xa^{33}tsɛi^{35}$ 'when' —— 148
5.3.3.4	Interrogative Pronoun $xa^{33}n̥a^{53}$ 'where' —— 149
5.3.3.5	Interrogative Pronoun $xa^{33}ma^{35}li^{33}li^{323}$ 'why' —— 150
5.3.3.6	Interrogative Pronoun $xa^{33}ni^{33}$ 'how', 'how many' —— 151
5.3.3.7	Combining Interrogative Pronouns —— 155

6	Quantification and Classifiers —— 156
6.1	Numerals —— 158
6.2	Classifiers —— 164
6.2.1	The Use of Classifiers —— 165
6.2.2	Types of Classifiers —— 170
6.2.2.1	Sortal Classifiers —— 170
6.2.2.2	Mensural Classifiers —— 172
6.2.2.3	Collective Classifiers —— 173
6.2.2.4	Human Classifiers —— 176
6.2.2.5	Family Group Classifiers —— 176
6.2.2.6	Partitive Classifiers —— 183
6.2.2.7	Temporal Classifiers —— 183
6.2.2.8	Monetary Classifiers —— 188
6.2.2.9	Adverbial Classifiers —— 189
6.2.2.10	The Classifier Inventory —— 191
6.3	Lexical Quantifiers —— 197
6.4	Universal Quantification Construction —— 198

| 7 | Noun Phrases —— 201 |
| 7.1 | Constituent Order —— 201 |

7.2	Adjectival Function of Nouns and Stative Verbs —— 204	
7.2.1	Nouns Modifying Nouns —— 204	
7.2.2	Adjectival Stative Verbs —— 205	
7.3	Indefinite Constructions —— 207	
7.3.1	Specific Indefinite Construction —— 208	
7.3.2	Non-Specific Indefinite Constructions —— 210	
7.3.2.1	Indefinite Realis Constructions —— 210	
7.3.2.2	Indefinite Free Choice Construction —— 211	
7.3.2.3	Indefinite Conditional Construction —— 213	
7.3.2.4	Indefinite Comparison Construction —— 213	
7.3.3	Negative Indefinite Constructions —— 214	
7.3.4	Multiple Indefinite Constructions —— 217	
7.4	Possession —— 218	
7.5	Relativization —— 222	
7.6	Nominalization —— 229	
7.7	Coordination and Disjunction —— 232	
7.7.1	Juxtaposition —— 232	
7.7.2	Coordination with Conjunctions —— 234	
7.7.3	Coordination through Disjunction —— 236	

8 Verbs —— 239
8.1	Intransitive Verbs —— 241	
8.1.1	Dynamic Intransitive Verbs —— 242	
8.1.2	Stative Verbs —— 242	
8.1.2.1	Attributive Stative Verb Construction —— 244	
8.1.2.2	Reduplicated Stative Verb Constructions —— 250	
8.2	Transitive Verbs —— 255	
8.3	Ditransitive Verbs —— 257	
8.4	Ambitransitive Verbs —— 260	
8.5	Copula η^{33} —— 261	
8.6	Existential Verb tso^{323} —— 265	
8.7	Auxiliary Verbs —— 268	
8.8	Serial Verb Constructions —— 273	
8.8.1	One-Event Constructions —— 274	
8.8.1.1	Directional Constructions —— 274	
8.8.1.2	Resultative Constructions —— 281	
8.8.1.3	Manner Constructions —— 285	
8.8.1.4	Complex Stative Constructions —— 286	
8.8.2	Two-Event Constructions —— 287	

9 Verb Modifiers —— 290
9.1	Negation —— 290	

9.1.1	General Negator ma^{31} —— 290
9.1.2	Prohibitive Marker ta^{31} —— 293
9.2	Aspect —— 296
9.2.1	Perfective —— 300
9.2.2	Currently Relevant State —— 304
9.2.3	Progressive —— 307
9.2.4	Continuous —— 311
9.2.5	Iterative —— 313
9.2.6	Perfective Irrealis —— 316
9.2.7	Imperfective Irrealis —— 317
9.2.8	Inceptive —— 319
9.2.9	Future —— 320
9.2.10	Experiential —— 323
9.3	Adverbs —— 324
9.3.1	Time Adverbs —— 325
9.3.2	Frequency Adverbs —— 330
9.3.3	Locative Adverbs —— 331
9.3.4	Manner Adverbs —— 333
9.3.5	Degree Adverbs —— 335
9.3.6	Sentential Adverbs —— 338

10	**Argument Structure** —— 340
10.1	Topic-Comment Information Structure —— 340
10.2	Grammatical Relations —— 344
10.3	Word Order —— 347
10.4	Pragmatic Agentivity —— 351
10.5	Pseudo-Passives —— 359
10.6	Oblique Arguments —— 361
10.6.1	Instrumental Arguments —— 361
10.6.2	Locative Arguments —— 363
10.6.3	Temporal Arguments —— 365

11	**Valency-Changing Constructions** —— 369
11.1	Applicative Construction —— 369
11.2	Causative Constructions —— 372
11.2.1	Lexical Causatives —— 372
11.2.2	Periphrastic Causative Constructions —— 374
11.2.2.1	Causative Construction with $la^{33}ta^{55}...mo^{55}$ —— 374
11.2.2.2	Causative Construction with ky^{33} —— 377
11.2.2.3	Causative Construction Formed Only with kw^{31} —— 380
11.2.2.4	Multiple Causation —— 383

12	Basic Clause Types —— 385
12.1	Declarative Clauses —— 385
12.2	Imperatives —— 386
12.2.1	Imperative Marker $jɛ^{24}$ —— 387
12.2.2	Imperative Marker pa^{31} —— 388
12.2.3	Optative Marker $pa^{323}jɛ^{24}$ —— 389
12.2.4	Prohibitive Auxiliary Construction $ma^{31}\,jo^{33}$ —— 390
12.2.5	Imperatives Formed through Tone Change —— 390
12.3	Reciprocal Constructions —— 393
12.4	Questions —— 394
12.4.1	Polar Questions —— 395
12.4.2	Content Questions —— 399
12.4.3	Choice Questions —— 403
12.4.4	Tag Questions —— 404
12.4.5	Interrogative Interjections —— 408
12.4.6	Echo Questions —— 409
12.4.7	Question Markers —— 410
12.4.7.1	'Still' Question Marker sa^{31} —— 410
12.4.7.2	Topic Question Marker ni^{35} —— 411
12.4.7.3	Certainty Question Marker sa^{44} —— 413
12.4.7.4	Irrealis Question Marker la^{31} —— 415
12.4.7.5	Confirmation Question Marker $pɛi^{33}$ —— 416
12.4.7.6	Rhetorical Question Marker ta^{31} —— 416
12.5	Comparative Constructions —— 417
12.5.1	Comparisons of Equality —— 418
12.5.2	Comparisons of Extent —— 422
12.5.3	Comparisons of Superiority/Inferiority —— 424
12.5.4	Quantitative Comparisons —— 426
12.5.5	Implicit Comparative Constructions —— 427
12.5.5.1	Contrastive Comparisons —— 427
12.5.5.2	Temporal Comparisons —— 429
12.5.5.3	Superlative Construction —— 430
12.6	Emphasis —— 433
12.6.1	Imperfective Emphatic Marker ja^{33} —— 433
12.6.2	Perfective Emphatic Marker ja^{323} —— 434
12.6.3	Copular Emphatic Marker $ȵa^{33}$ —— 435
12.6.4	Irrealis Emphatic Marker $lɛi^{31}$ —— 436
12.6.5	Strong Assertion Marker $ŋɛi^{33}$ —— 437
12.6.6	Epistemic Emphatic Particle po^{53} —— 440
12.6.7	Epistemic Emphatic Particle na^{31} —— 440
12.6.8	Stative Emphatic Particle $tɤ^{44}$ —— 441
12.6.9	Discourse Emphatic Particle $mɛi^{44}$ —— 443

13	**Basic Clause-Linking** —— 446	
13.1	Simple Clause-Linking —— 448	
13.1.1	Parallel Clause-Linking —— 449	
13.1.1.1	Parallel Clause-Linking through Juxtaposition —— 449	
13.1.1.2	Parallel Clause-Linking with to^{33} —— 451	
13.1.2	Disjunctive Clause-Linking —— 453	
13.1.3	Adversative Clause-Linking —— 456	
13.1.3.1	Adversative Clause-Linking with $\eta^{44}li^{33}$ and $\eta^{33}na^{44}li^{33}$ 'but' —— 456	
13.1.3.2	Adversative Clause-Linking with to^{33} 'also' —— 458	
13.1.3.3	Contrastive Focus with la^{35} and Related Tone Change —— 458	
13.1.3.4	Borrowed Adversative Conjunction —— 460	
13.2	Temporal Constructions —— 461	
13.2.1	Temporal Construction with $sɛi^{44}$ —— 461	
13.2.2	Constructions with Borrowed Temporal Adverbs —— 463	
13.2.3	Simultaneous Events —— 464	
13.2.3.1	Simultaneous Constructions with wa^{24} $xɛi^{35}$ and jo^{35} —— 464	
13.2.3.2	Simultaneous Construction with $ni^{31}nɛ^{323}$ —— 466	
13.2.3.3	Simultaneous Construction with $sɛi^{44}$ —— 467	
13.2.3.4	Simultaneous Construction with $tɤ^{44}$ —— 467	
13.2.4	Sequential Events —— 469	
13.2.4.1	Sequential Linking with $tɕo^{35}$ —— 469	
13.2.4.2	Sequential Linking with ja^{53} ni^{323} —— 471	
13.2.4.3	Sequential Linking with ta^{31} ni^{323} —— 473	
13.2.4.4	Sequential Linking with ni^{31} —— 474	
13.2.4.5	Sequential Linking with $sa^{24}kɛi^{33}$ 'until' —— 476	
14	**Specialized Clause-Linking Constructions** —— 478	
14.1	Reason Strategies —— 478	
14.1.1	Reason Strategy with ni^{323} and ta^{31} ni^{323} —— 478	
14.1.2	Reason Strategy with $tɕi^{44}$ ni^{31} —— 480	
14.1.3	Reason Strategy with la^{35} or Related Tone Change —— 481	
14.1.4	Borrowed Reason Conjunction —— 482	
14.2	Cause and Effect Strategies —— 483	
14.2.1	Cause and Effect Strategy with $tɕo^{35}$ and ja^{53} ni^{323} —— 484	
14.2.2	Cause and Effect Strategy with $tɤ^{44}$ —— 485	
14.2.3	Cause and Effect Strategy with la^{35} or Related Tone Change —— 486	
14.2.4	Borrowed Cause and Effect Conjunction —— 487	
14.3	Concessive Strategies —— 488	
14.3.1	Concessive Strategy with to^{33} —— 488	
14.3.2	Borrowed Concessive Conjunction —— 490	
14.4	Conditional Constructions —— 491	
14.4.1	Conditional Construction with ni^{31} —— 491	

14.4.2	Universal Conditional Construction —— 495	
14.4.3	Concessive Conditional Construction —— 495	
14.4.4	Comparative Conditional Construction with $i^{24}fa^{33}$, $i^{31}kɯ^{35}$, $to^{33}i^{31}$ —— 496	
14.4.5	Borrowed Conditional Conjunction —— 497	
14.5	Manner Constructions with $tɤ^{44}$ and $sɛi^{44}$ —— 498	
14.6	Purpose Construction with $tɤ^{44}$ —— 500	
15	**Complementation** —— 506	
15.1	Complementation Strategies with $sɛi^{44}$ —— 506	
15.2	Complementation Strategies without $sɛi^{44}$ —— 520	
15.3	Complementation Strategies for Reported Speech —— 523	
16	**Summary of Clause-Linking Particles** —— 531	
16.1	to^{33} —— 533	
16.2	ni^{323} —— 536	
16.3	ni^{31} —— 538	
16.4	la^{35} —— 541	
16.5	$tɤ^{44}$ —— 544	
16.6	$sɛi^{44}$ —— 547	

Appendix A: Grammatical Particles in Khatso —— 551

Appendix B: Khatso Lexicon —— 554

Appendix C: Texts —— 575
C.1   History —— 576
C.2   Sewing —— 582

References —— 589

Index —— 595

List of Tables

Table 1.1: Khatso Language Consultants —— 29
Table 2.1: Ten speakers representing a cross-section of Khatso pronunciation —— 40
Table 2.2: Khatso consonant inventory —— 42
Table 2.3: Consonant and rhyme combinations in Khatso —— 43
Table 2.4: Differences in vowel transcription in previous research on Khatso —— 61
Table 2.5: Comparison of Khatso diphthongs and triphthongs in transcription —— 62
Table 2.6: Examples of $n_{z}a^{323}ka^{53}$ pronunciation —— 75
Table 3.1: Tone and rhyme combinations in Khatso —— 78
Table 3.2: Frequency of the eight tones in Khatso —— 79
Table 3.3: Classifiers that trigger obligatory sandhi in numerals —— 87
Table 3.4: Classifiers that Trigger Optional Sandhi in 'Three', 'Four' and 'Nine' —— 88
Table 4.1: Syllable structure in Khatso —— 109
Table 4.2: Syllable structure frequency in Khatso —— 109
Table 5.1: Personal pronouns in Khatso —— 137
Table 5.2: Interrogative pronouns in Khatso —— 145
Table 6.1: Khatso's two numeral systems —— 159
Table 6.2: Family group classifiers in Khatso —— 177
Table 6.3: Months in Khatso —— 186
Table 6.4: The zodiac year in Khatso —— 187
Table 6.5: Classifier inventory in Khatso —— 192
Table 6.6: Universal indefinite Constructions in Khatso —— 199
Table 7.1: Khatso indefinite constructions —— 208
Table 7.2: Non-specific indefinite pronouns in Khatso —— 212
Table 7.3: One type of negative indefinite construction in Khatso —— 215
Table 8.1: Attributive stative verbs in Khatso —— 246
Table 8.2: Auxiliary verbs in Khatso —— 268
Table 8.3: Directional verbs in serial constructions —— 275
Table 8.4: Verbs in serial resultative constructions —— 282
Table 9.1: Aspect markers in Khatso —— 297
Table 9.2: Aspect combinations in Khatso —— 299
Table 9.3: Days of the week in Khatso —— 326
Table 9.4: Day and year ordinals in Khatso —— 328
Table 9.5: Sentential adverbs in Khatso —— 339
Table 10.1: Verbs of carrying in Khatso —— 362
Table 10.2: Locative and directional particles in Khatso —— 363
Table 11.1: Lexical causatives in Khatso —— 373
Table 12.1: Interrogative pronouns in Khatso —— 400
Table 15.1: Complement-taking verbs in Khatso —— 506
Table 15.2: Patterning of $sɛi^{44}$ with complement-taking verbs —— 510
Table 16.1: Clause-combining particles and their functions —— 531
Table A.1: Grammatical particles in Khatso —— 551

List of Figures

Fig. 2.1: Spectrogram of voiceless stop —— 44
Fig. 2.2: VOT comparison of voiceless stops —— 45
Fig. 2.3: VOT comparison of voiceless aspirated stops —— 45
Fig. 2.4: Comparison of voiced fricatives /v/ and /z/ —— 50
Fig. 2.5: Comparison of voiceless fricatives /f/ and /s/ —— 51
Fig. 2.6: Spectrograms of omitted and fully realized /ɣ/ —— 54
Fig. 2.7: Representative tokens of /ts/ and /tsʰ/ —— 55
Fig. 2.8: Khatso monophthong vowel inventory —— 58
Fig. 2.9: Vowel space for five female speakers of Khatso —— 59
Fig. 2.10: Vowel space for five male speakers of Khatso —— 60
Fig. 2.11: Comparison of onsets in [ʔi³³] and [ji³³] —— 63
Fig. 2.12: Spectrogram showing friction in /ɿ/ —— 64
Fig. 2.13: Comparison of /v/ as vowel and consonant —— 65
Fig. 2.14: Vowel /v/ with greater friction —— 66
Fig. 2.15: /v/ as independent nucleus —— 67
Fig. 3.1: A schematic representation of the eight tones in Khatso —— 77
Fig. 3.2: Pitch traces of the eight tones —— 78
Fig. 3.3: Frequency of the eight tones in Khatso —— 80
Fig. 3.4: Comparison of relative tone length in minimal octuplet —— 81
Fig. 3.5: Tone fusion producing contour 335 —— 103
Fig. 3.6: Tone fusion producing contour 555 —— 104
Fig. 4.1: Syllable structure frequency in Khatso —— 110
Fig. 4.2: The use of pauses to mark IU boundaries —— 121
Fig. 4.3: Pause duration marking different clausal IUs —— 122
Fig. 4.4: Lag in IUs —— 123
Fig. 4.5: Rush versus lag in an IU —— 124
Fig. 4.6: Intensity changes across constituents in an IU —— 125
Fig. 13.1: Degree of integration across clause-combining strategies —— 447

List of Maps

Map 1.1: Yunnan's location in China —— 5
Map 1.2: Xingmeng and nearby towns in Yunnan —— 6
Map 1.3: The five historical villages within Xingmeng —— 7

List of Photos

Photo 1.1: View from the government building —— 34
Photo 1.2: Farms —— 34
Photo 1.3: Traditional homes —— 35
Photo 1.4: Narrow lanes —— 35
Photo 1.5: Locally grown produce —— 36
Photo 1.6: Old doorway —— 36
Photo 1.7: Traditional clothing —— 37
Photo 1.8: Three Beliefs Temple —— 37
Photo 1.9: Three Saints Temple —— 38
Photo 1.10: Holiday feast —— 38
Photo 1.11: Bilingual Chinese and Mongolian signs —— 39
Photo 1.12: Village statue —— 39

Abbreviations

In accordance with the Leipzig Glossing Rules, the following abbreviations are used in the interlinear glossing that parses the examples of spoken Khatso. Individual speakers are also identified by abbreviations; these are listed in Table 1.1 (see § 1.9).

1 2 3	first, second, third person
A	agent (semantic role)
ADJSV	adjectival stative verb
ADV	adverb, adverbial
AGT	agent marker
ANM	animal
ASP	aspect
ASRT	strong assertion
B	beneficiary (semantic role)
BDG	building
BKGD	backgrounding particle
BNCH	bunch
CAUS	causative
CFRM	confirmatory
CL	classifier
CLNK	clause linker
CMP	comparative marker
CNT	content
COL	collective
CONJ	conjunction
CONT	continuous aspect
COP	copula
CRS	currently relevant state aspect
CRTN	certain
CSC	complex stative construction
DEM	demonstrative
DIM	diminutive
DSC	discourse
ECHO	echo question
EMP	emphatic
EPIS	epistemic
EXIST	existential
EXP	experiential aspect
F	female
FILL	filler
FAMGP	family group

FOC	clausal focus marker	
FUT	future aspect	
GEN	general	
HNDL	handle	
HSY	hearsay	
HUM	human	
IMP	imperative marker	
INCP	inceptive aspect	
INS	instrumental marker	
INDR	indirect	
INTJ	interjection	
INTR	intransitive	
IPFV	imperfective aspect	
IPRO	interrogative pronoun	
IRR	irrealis aspect	
ITER	iterative aspect	
IU	intonation unit	
M	male	
MACH	machine	
MNY	money	
MSR	measure	
N	noun	
NEG	negative	
NMLZ	nominalizer	
NUM	numeral	
OPT	optative	
ORD	ordinal	
P	patient (semantic role)	
PART	particle	
PCE	piece	
PFV	perfective aspect	
PHR	phrase	
PL	plural	
POSR	possessor	
POSS	possessive	
PROG	progressive aspect	
PROH	prohibitive	
Q	question	
R	recipient (semantic role)	
RECP	reciprocal	
REL	relative clause marker	
RELC	relative clause	

RHET	rhetorical
S	subject (semantic role)
SEC	section
SFP	sentence-final particle
SG	singular
SOL	solicitative
STAT	stative
TMP	temporal
TOP	topic marker
UNK	unknown
V	verb
VOL	volume

1 Overview of Khatso

Khatso (pronounced $k^ha^{55}tso^{31}$) is an endangered minority language spoken in a single farming village in southwestern China. The 5600 speakers are ethnic Mongolians who descend from troops Kublai Khan brought to Yunnan in the 13th century as part of his campaign to conquer China (Gao 2001: 5–6; Huang 2009: 8). Today they live in the village of Xīngměng 兴蒙 in Tōnghǎi County 通海县, Yùxī Prefecture 玉溪市, Yúnnán Province 云南省 in the People's Republic of China. Khatso likely evolved from contact between the Mongols and local minorities, most specifically the Ngwi (Yí 彝) but perhaps also including the Bai and more recently the majority Han (Dai, Liu and Fu 1987: 174; He 1989: 11–12; Mu 2002: 134).[1] Because Khatso is similar to languages in the Ngwi family, and very unlike Mongolian, the Chinese government considers Khatso to be a dialect of the standard Ngwi language Nuosu, even though the two are mutually unintelligible (Dai, Liu and Fu 1987: 175; Mu 2002: 27). Linguists consider Khatso to be a separate language within the Ngwi family, which is a branch of the Burmese-Ngwi group within the Tibeto-Burman phylum (Bradley 1997; Dai, Liu and Fu 1987: 175; He 1989: 1; Lewis, Simons and Fennig 2013; Mu 2002: 26).

The recent pace of modernization in China has been incredibly rapid. Most noticeable in urban centers, it is also changing life in rural villages. In Yunnan, huge investments in infrastructure over the past twenty years have made formerly remote minority villages much more accessible. This is certainly the case for Xingmeng, which now sits on the highway that connects the county seat of Tonghai with the prefectural seat of Yuxi. The highway not only makes transporting and selling local crops easier, but it also regularly brings tourists, both Chinese and foreign, who often stop for lunch and a stroll through the village market. Xingmeng has, in fact, become a rather prosperous village over the past decade.

These changes are also affecting the linguistic landscape. Khatso is spoken by nearly all of the inhabitants of Xingmeng village (Dai 2008:3). However, the villagers are also by necessity bilingual in Chinese in order to communicate with outsiders. Thus, Khatso is now mainly used at home, while Chinese is used in public domains such as hospitals, government offices and schools. Children continue to learn Khatso at home, but many are taught Chinese first by their parents, since it is required to pursue an education or find employment outside the village. Furthermore, because

---

1 The name of the Ngwi branch of the Tibeto-Burman family has undergone several changes over the decades. Early sources used Lolo, which is now considered pejorative. In China, the term Yí 彝 is now used and this term is also found elsewhere. Western linguists, following the proposal put forth in Bradley 2005a, increasingly use Ngwi, a reconstruction of a common autonym in this family. This book follows that usage throughout, except where an older form occurs in a proper name or title.

Khatso is not officially recognized as an independent language, there is no writing system, nor is it supported by media or technology. As a result, there is an intergenerational decline in language ability, causing UNESCO to list Khatso as 'definitely endangered' (Moseley 2010). Villagers are well aware of these changes, but unsure of how best to maintain their traditional language. In an effort to help them, this grammar presents a comprehensive description of the Khatso language.

More specifically, the aim of this work is to detail, to the greatest extent possible, the features, structures and systems that interact to comprise this unique language. The description of the language is presented in sixteen chapters. The current chapter presents a sociolinguistic and historical profile of the people and the language. Chapter 2 describes the consonant and vowel inventories, and Chapter 3 the tone system. Chapter 4 focuses on word, syllable and intonation unit structures. In Chapter 5, nouns are discussed; quantification and classifiers are described in Chapter 6 and noun phrases in Chapter 7. Verbs are investigated in Chapter 8, and verb modifiers in Chapter 9. Chapter 10 outlines basic argument structure, and Chapter 11 explores valency-changing constructions. Basic clause types are detailed in Chapter 12, and basic clause-linking is described in Chapter 13. More specialized clause-combining structures are explored in Chapter 14 and complementation strategies are investigated in Chapter 15. Chapter 16 provides an overview of clause-linking particles with a focus on those with multiple functionality. Three appendices also provide helpful information. Appendix A presents an index of the grammatical particles found in Khatso. Appendix B offers a trilingual lexicon in English, Chinese and Khatso. Appendix C contains two selected Khatso texts, one a narrative and the other a conversation. Additional texts with recordings can be found at www.khatso.net.

The profile of Khatso presented in this chapter is broken down as follows. Instructions on how to use the grammar are presented in § 1.1. The language name and a description of the Khatso people are introduced in § 1.2 and § 1.3, followed by a discussion of language vitality in § 1.4. The history and classification of Khatso are then presented in § 1.5 and § 1.6. Previous research on Khatso, most of which is in Chinese, is reviewed in § 1.7. In § 1.8 and § 1.9 the linguistic methodology of the project is described and the consultants who participated are introduced. Finally, key typological points about Khatso are summarized in § 1.10.

1.1 How to Use this Grammar

The goal of the grammar is to detail, to the greatest extent possible, the features, structures and systems that interact to comprise Khatso. It is written for multiple audiences, from students and linguists to native speakers. As such, only basic linguistic terminology is employed. Using a discourse functional framework that emphasizes natural speech, the language data presented throughout include examples from spontaneous discourse; the name of the Khatso speaker who produced each utterance is cited for each example. The information in the grammar is organized in ascending fashion – moving from phonetics and phonology to syntax and discourse – which suits the structure of this largely analytic language.

Khatso language data throughout the grammar are presented in the International Phonetic Alphabet (IPA). In examples, the data are accompanied by word-for-word glosses in both English and Chinese and grammatical particles are labeled following the Leipzig Glossing Rules. Abbreviations for the latter can be found on page xx. The glosses also include free translations in both English and Chinese. As just mentioned, for each example the originating text and the speaker are cited. A list of language consultants is presented in § 1.9, and selected texts are included in Appendix C. Following Khatso and Chinese practice, surnames precede given names throughout the grammar. Additional texts along with recordings may be found at www.khatso.net.

Information in this book may be accessed in several ways. For those who want to learn the language or research it step by step, it may be read from beginning to end. Those who are interested in specific topics, say tone change or complementation, will find the detailed table of contents and the index of most help. There is extensive cross referencing throughout the grammar so that readers are easily able to access all relevant discussions of a given topic. A list of grammatical particles is provided in Appendix A.

The word Khatso is used to describe both the people of Xingmeng and their language. In addition to Khatso, the villagers also speak the local Tonghai variety of Southwestern Mandarin 西南官话, a dialect of the national language Pǔtōnghuà 普通话, which they also speak. In this volume, the local variety is called Hànyǔ 汉语, following Khatso practice, and Putonghua is used to refer to Mandarin. The umbrella term Chinese is used when referring to both simultaneously, and also to the written form of the language. Chinese characters are provided for names and key terms throughout the volume. Pinyin with tone marking is provided at the first mention, but frequently used words, such as proper names, are presented without tones after that. The term Han is used to distinguish the ethnic Chinese from the other ethnic groups in Yunnan.

1.2 Names of the People, Language and Village

The Khatso people and their language are known by different names to different people. Native speakers refer to themselves as $k^ha^{55}tso^{31}p^ha^{31}$ 'Khatso man' or $k^ha^{55}tso^{31}ma^{33}$ 'Khatso woman' and their language as $k^ha^{55}tso^{31}tɕ^hi^{31}$ 'Khatso language'. Earlier generations pronounced the first syllable as ka^{55}, but this pronunciation began to fall out of favor in the 1980s. Today, only a few older speakers still use it.

These changes are reflected in the various Chinese versions of these names. Early publications used *Gāzhuó* 嘎卓 (e.g. Dai, Liu and Fu 1987; Huang 1992), which later became *Kǎzhuó* as the autonym changed. The latter was originally rendered in

Chinese characters as 卡卓 (e.g. He 1989; He 1998; Mu 2002), but today the community prefers *Kǎzhuó* 喀卓 (e.g. Dai 2008; Wang 2008). Most people in Yunnan, however, simply refer to the Khatso as the Tonghai Mongolians 通海蒙古族.

The language has no writing system, and so IPA is used throughout to transcribe the data. For simplicity, the name of the language and people is anglicized as Khatso. The spelling Katso, drawn from the earlier pronunciation, can also be found in a few English-language publications, most notably *Ethnologue* (Lewis, Simons and Fennig 2013). *The Sino-Tibetan Etymological Dictionary and Thesaurus* (STEDT) refers to the language by the older Chinese term Gazhuo.

After the Mongols conquered China and established the Yuán 元 Dynasty (1271–1368), Mongol soldiers were stationed in Yunnan near the modern Xingmeng area. After the Yuan Dynasty fell, some of these soldiers settled there with their families, over time founding five "natural" villages 自然村, as the Chinese call them, which still exist today. Their Khatso names differ quite a bit from their names in Putonghua: $ṇa^{323}ka^{53}$ / Zhōngcūn 中村, $pɛi^{323}ko^{53}$ / Báigé 白阁, $kʰa^{55}tsɿ^{33}$ / Xiàcūn 下村, $pɛi^{323}pa^{323}$ / Jiāoyǐwān 交椅湾 and $sɿ^{24}tsʰɿ^{33}xo^{35}$ / Táojiāzuǐ 陶家嘴. Amongst themselves, villagers still distinguish their homes according to the original villages, even though all but $sɿ^{24}tsʰɿ^{33}xo^{35}$ are now geographically contiguous (see Map 1.3). In 1951 they were grouped into a larger administrative unit called Xinmeng Mongolian Autonomous Village 新蒙蒙古族自治乡 (Huang 2009: 10); Xīnměng in Putonghua means 'new Mongolian'. During the collectivization period of the late 1950s, 'Xinmeng' was dropped from the name. It was not until 1980 that the village name again referred to its Mongolian roots, taking the new name Xīngměng 兴蒙, which means 'prosperous Mongolians'. In Khatso, the unified village is called either $kʰa^{55}tso^{31}kʰua^{55}$ 'Khatso village' or the Hanyu loanwords $si^{33}mo^{323}$ or $si^{44}mo^{31}$ 'Xingmeng'.

The etymology of the name Khatso is not well understood. Based on conversations with Mongolian scholars who visited the village decades ago, the Khatso believe the name evolved from the Mongolian word for 'self'. The names for the five original villages are likewise considered to have Mongolian origins. Two Mongolian scholars who visited Xingmeng in 2013 also believe the names have Middle Mongolian roots. However, their work, which is still in progress, points to a different semantic analysis. A competing theory (He 1998: 1) suggests that the name Khatso $kʰa^{55}tso^{31}$ shares an origin with $kʰa^{21}dzo^{55}$, the name of a Ngwi village in Luquan County north of Kunming. Written 卡柱 (Kǎzhù) in Chinese and composed of *kǎ* 'village' and *zhù* 'back, support' or 'in between', the name is interpreted to mean 'center village'. However, without systematic phonological correspondences between Khatso and these languages, all hypotheses remain inconclusive.

1.3 The People and Their Past

Xingmeng 兴蒙 village is located in Yunnan Province in China's southwest corner (see Map 1.1).[2] To the north of Yunnan lies Sichuan, and to the east the provinces of Guizhou and Guangxi. Myanmar shares its western border, and Laos and Vietnam are to the south. The village itself is in central Yunnan. It is located in Tonghai County 通海县, and is only 15 kilometers west of the county seat Tōnghǎi 通海. Kūnmíng 昆明, the provincial capital, lies approximately 100 kilometers to the north (see Map 1.2).

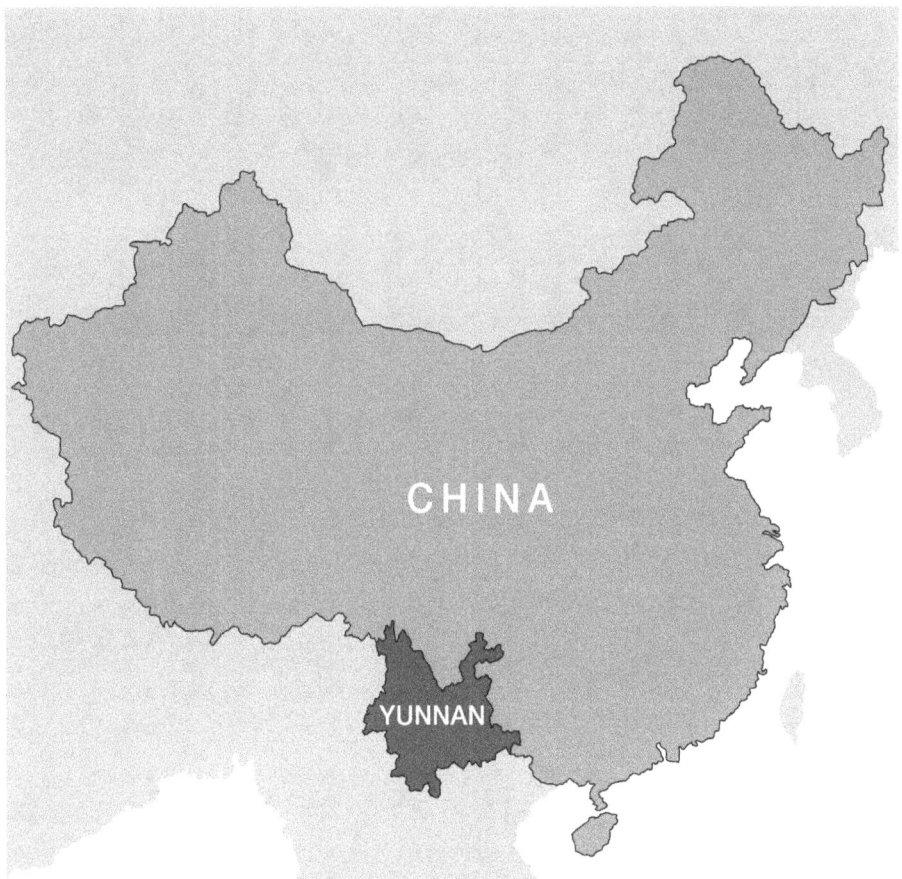

Map 1.1: Yunnan's location in China (Map design: Colin Kent)

---

[2] Maps 1.1 and 1.2 adapted from public domain material via Wikipedia Commons; Map 1.3 adapted from Wang 2008.

The village lies in a flat valley to the west of Qīlù Lake 杞麓湖, one of the province's largest freshwater lakes. It hugs the southern foot of Phoenix Mountain 凤凰山 and is surrounded by Han and Muslim Hui villages. Within Xingmeng itself are five historical villages which are, from west to east: ȵa³²³ka⁵³ or Zhōngcūn 中村, pɛi³²³ko⁵³ or Báigé 白阁, kʰa⁵⁵tsɿ³³ or Xiàcūn 下村, pɛi³²³pa³²³ or Jiāoyǐwān 交椅湾 and sɿ²⁴tsʰɿ³³xo³⁵ or Táojiāzuǐ 陶家嘴 (see Map 1.3). Until recently, these villages, except for pɛi³²³ko⁵³ and kʰa⁵⁵tsɿ³³, were separated by open fields. Today four of the five are contiguous; only sɿ²⁴tsʰɿ³³xo³⁵ remains geographically separate.

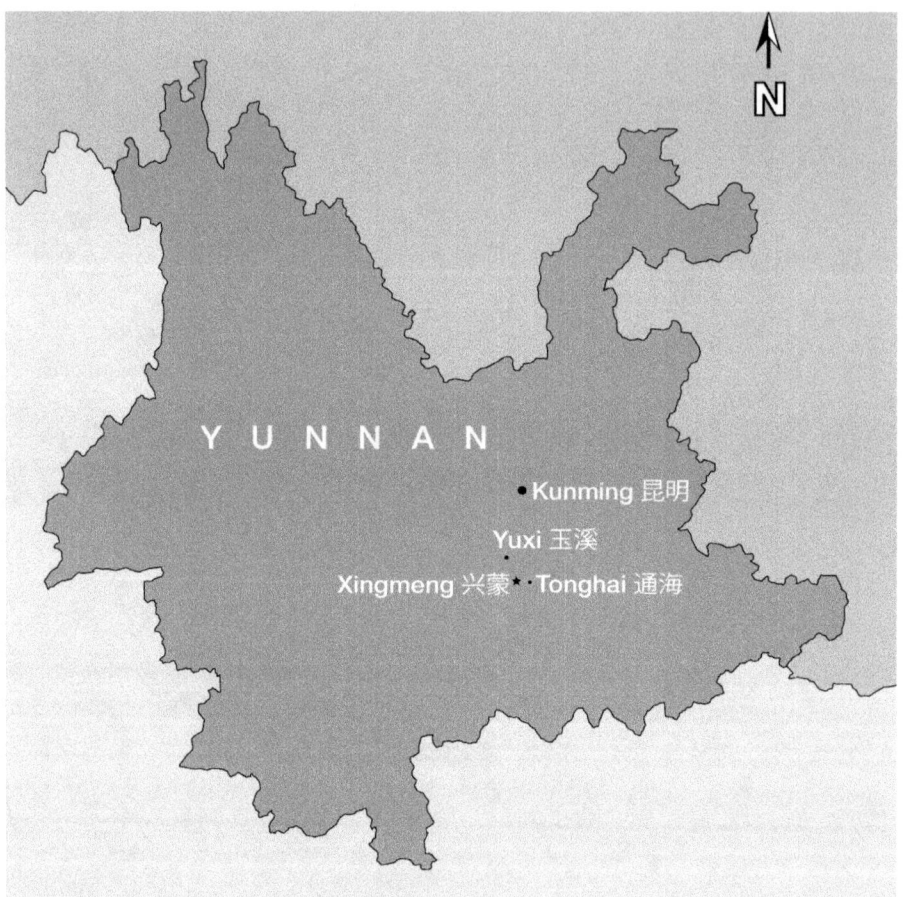

Map 1.2: Xingmeng and nearby towns in Yunnan (Map design: Colin Kent)

Until the 1990s, when highway S304 was built connecting Tonghai and the prefectural capital Yuxi, Xingmeng was rather remote. In a change from the traditional roadways, the highway now cuts through the center of the valley and for several kilometers skirts most of Xingmeng's southern edge (see Map 1.3). As a result, a new part of the village has sprung up on the opposite side of the highway, and now features a large tourist-oriented restaurant, an outdoor market and several multi-story buildings that house shops, restaurants, a hotel and a handful of karaoke clubs.

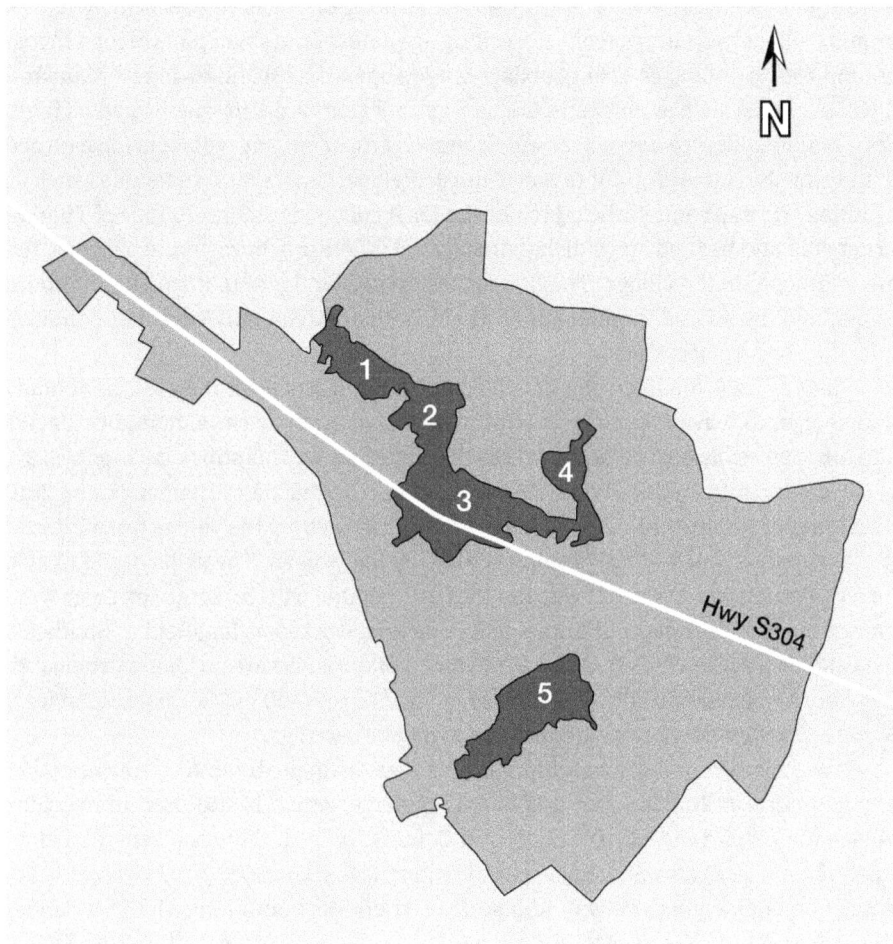

Map 1.3: The five historical villages within Xingmeng (numbered sections indicate buildings, the larger section includes fields); 1 ȵa³²³ka⁵³ 中村, 2 pɛi³²³ko⁵³ 白阁, 3 kʰa⁵⁵tsɿ³³ 下村, 4 pɛi³²³pa³²³ 交椅湾, 5 sɿ²⁴tsʰɿ³³xo³⁵ 陶家嘴. (Map design: Colin Kent)

According to 2010 data (Tōnghǎixiàn Xīngměngxiāng 2010 nián tǒngjì niánjiàn), Xingmeng has a population of 5609 people. The village is fairly homogeneous; 96% percent of its residents are Khatso. The remaining people represent a number of other ethnicities including Han Chinese, Ngwi, Hani, Dai, Hui and others. The largest group, the Han, is mostly composed of government workers, teachers, doctors and their staffs who live and work in the village. A minority of the Han, and the rest of the other ethnicities, are spouses of local Khatso residents. People from Xingmeng can also be found living and working in nearby towns and cities such as Tonghai, Yuxi and Kunming.

Despite the urban feel of the new neighborhood on the highway, Xingmeng is a farming village. Seventy percent of working age adults farm small plots of land in and around the five villages (Tōnghǎixiàn Xīngměngxiāng 2010 nián tǒngjì niánjiàn). Small livestock, such as chickens, ducks, pigs and goats are also raised by some farmers. Traditionally, rice and wheat were common crops, but now villagers have turned to the more lucrative crops of tobacco, musk melons, canola, and vegetables such as cauliflower, beans and garlic. Much of the local cuisine is similar to that of Yunnan in general, and hot and spicy dishes are favored. There are, however, two dishes that are traditional in the village. The first is roast duck, similar to that made in northern China, and the second is small stir-fried eel. Both are frequently served at banquets and other special occasions.

Since at least the late Qīng 清 era (1644–1912), it has been the custom of many Khatso men to leave the village to find work, most often as carpenters, bricklayers and other types of construction workers (Huang 2009: 9). This still occurs today; 23% of the adults in the village work in construction (Tōnghǎixiàn Xīngměngxiāng 2010 nián tǒngjì niánjiàn 2010). These workers may be away from the village for months or years, and thus much of the farming is done by the women. The skills of the Khatso men have achieved some renown, and they are credited with constructing some well-known buildings throughout China, and have even worked as far afield as Southeast Asia and Africa (Lin 1976: 3). While their woodworking skills are no longer in demand, there are a number of traditional houses in the village – 100 or 200 years old at least – that still retain doorways with intricate symbolic carvings.

There are two primary cultural markers that distinguish the Khatso from other ethnic groups in Yunnan. The first is the language, which is still used in everyday village life despite widespread fluency in Chinese. Indeed, there is a general feeling that to be a true Khatso one must speak the language (Dai 2008: 40). However, modernization is changing the way Khatso is used and its continuing vitality is under threat (see § 1.4). The second ethnic marker is the traditional clothing of Khatso women. Modified somewhat from the old days, it now consists of three layers of an undershirt, a blouse and a vest, worn with trousers. A black turban tied with pink yarn, completely concealing the hair, completes the outfit. Older women, age 60 and above, still wear this clothing every day. Younger women typically wear modern clothing and only don the traditional costume for holidays and other special occasions. There is no traditional costume for men. Judging by old photos, they seemed to have adopted Chinese clothing long ago. Because of recent cultural exchanges with Inner Mongolia, some men now wear traditional northern Mongolian robes on special occasions.

In other aspects, Khatso culture mirrors that of traditional Chinese culture. Village residents observe the customs surrounding Mid-Autumn Festival, Dragon Boat Festival, Ancestor Day and the Lunar New Year. International Women's Day, which is an official holiday in China, has been adapted to a traditional local practice called $na^{53}tɕ^hɛ^{55}$ in Khatso or *tiàolè* 跳乐 in Putonghua. Other local minority groups are invited to Xingmeng for a day-long song and dance festival, which includes polished performances as well as traditional folk dancing for everyone. This practice has been going on for centuries, and most local groups know one another's songs and steps, making it easy for them to dance together. Every three years Xingmeng also celebrates Naadam 那达慕, the traditional northern Mongolian dance and sports festival, which is called $na^{323}ta^{323}mo^{323}$ in Khatso. In Xingmeng, the village-wide event lasts several days and includes song and dance performances, games, athletic contests, banquets and night-time bonfire parties.

While the majority of villagers are atheists, there has been a revival in restoring Xingmeng's temples. Some are Buddhist, such as Guanyin Temple 观音寺 in $ṇa^{323}ka^{53}$ and North Sea Temple 北海寺 in $sɿ^{24}tsʰɿ^{33}xo^{35}$, and some are Confucian such as Dragon King Temple 龙王庙 in $pɛi^{323}pa^{323}$. Three Beliefs Temple 三教寺 in $kʰa^{55}tsɿ^{33}$ combines elements from Buddhism, Confucianism and Daoism. The grandest and most impressive is the very recently rebuilt Three Saints Temple 三圣宫 in $kʰa^{55}tsɿ^{33}$, which is now the tallest building in the village. This temple commemorates Genghis Khan and his two grandsons Möngke and Kublai, the eponymous saints, who are worshipped as ancestors. It also contains a permanent exhibition on modern Khatso culture and houses a collection of the centuries-old steles that mention Mongolians in Yunnan history.

From the 1949 revolution on, there have been a number of political, educational and cultural exchanges between Xingmeng and Inner Mongolia (Ma 2000: 310–18). Initial contact began in the 1950s, but it was not until the 1970s that firm ties between the two were established. In 1976 several professors from the Inner Mongolia Teacher's College visited Xingmeng, resulting in the first academic publication describing the Khatso people (Yúnnán měnggǔzú 1976; see § 1.7.1). In the 1980s, several groups of Khatso students were sent to Inner Mongolia to study, some learning traditional song and dance, others focusing on Mongolian language and literature. At the same time, Khatso experts in construction visited Inner Mongolia to exchange technical knowledge. Mongolian instructors were also sent to Xingmeng in 1985 to teach their language to the villagers. This effort did not succeed, but it is the custom now for all public signage in Xingmeng to include Mongolian alongside Chinese. These exchanges continue today and, in fact, Inner Mongolia has become a common vacation destination for Khatso villagers.

The history of the Khatso people is not well documented. Their presence in Yunnan begins with Kublai Khan's invasion of Yunnan in 1253 (Ma 2000: 4–5). The Mongols had previously failed in their attempts to conquer China, and so they devised a strategy in which they would first take Yunnan and then use it as a base from which to attack China from the south. At the time Yunnan was independent of China and contained many different ethnic tribes such as the Ngwi, Hani and Dai. They were ruled by an ethnic Bai dynasty based in Dàlǐ 大理 in northern Yunnan. The Mongols invaded with 100,000 soldiers and quickly conquered the Dali Kingdom, placing troops in strategic spots around the province. Eventually, China fell to the Mongols, and the Yuan Dynasty was established in 1271.

One of the places of strategic importance in central Yunnan was Qūtuóguān 曲陀关, a mountain pass that connected southern Yunnan with points north (Du and Chen 1976: 11; Huang 2009: 6; Ma 2000: 12–13). Today the highway between Yuxi and Tonghai still passes through modern day Qutuoguan. In the Yuan Dynasty, the spot was both a military camp and the governmental seat for much of southern Yunnan. In addition to guarding the pass, the soldiers were also responsible for growing their own food. They farmed in the valley below and raised sheep and cavalry horses on nearby Phoenix Mountain above modern Xingmeng (Huang 2009: 6). Many settled permanently, marrying local women to start families. When the Yuan Dynasty fell in 1368, the Mongol forces in Yunnan continued to resist the new Ming Dynasty army until 1381. At that point, the surviving Mongols fled. Some made their way back to their northern homeland, others hid among various local ethnic tribes. A group from Qutuoguan, said to be the relatives of the last commander and his troops, fled to the marshy western edge of Qilu Lake, which was much larger then than it is today. They are considered to be the ancestors of the Khatso.

The settlements they established became Shàngcūn 上村 (literally 'upper village' in Putonghua), Zhōngcūn 中村 ('middle village') and Xiàcūn 下村 ('lower village') in what is now Xingmeng. Availing themselves of Qilu Lake and its tributaries, the former soldiers became fishermen as well as farmers (Huang 2009: 8). Eventually, they became quite skilled at this new livelihood and invented a variety of tools and methods for harvesting fish, shrimp and snails. They were also able to escape ongoing persecution by hiding in the marshes or rowing boats out into the lake (Lin 1976: 3). As a result, in local historical records the settlements are referred to as the Three Fishing Villages *sānyúcūn* 三渔村, and the Khatso themselves were simply called 'the fishermen' *yúfū* 渔夫. As the population grew, three other villages sprang up (Gao 2001: 12–13). $ṇa^{323}ka^{53}$ and $kʰa^{55}tsɿ^{33}$ (Zhongcun and Xiacun in Chinese) were joined by $pɛi^{323}ko^{53}$ (Báigé 白阁), which was founded by families from $kʰa^{55}tsɿ^{33}$, and $pɛi^{323}pa^{323}$ (Jiāoyǐwān 交椅湾, literally 'armchair bay' in Chinese), which grew around a natural inlet that no longer exists. In 1631 seventeen families from $pɛi^{323}ko^{53}$ moved to another spot on the water where they founded $sɿ^{24}tsʰŋ^{33}xo^{35}$ (Táojiāzuǐ 陶家嘴 in Putonghua); they were later joined by an influx of families from $ṇa^{323}ka^{53}$. At some point long ago Shangcun became a Han village (Mu 2002: 18), and is today known as Lùxīcūn 碌溪村, leaving only five small Khatso villages.

The Míng 明 era (1368–1644) was a time of persecution for many ethnic groups and especially for the remaining Mongols (Mu 2002: 8; Sneath 1999: 125). As Chinese influence spread, many ethnic groups slowly assimilated with Han culture. Most of the remaining pockets of Mongols did as well or, if not, they assimilated into other ethnic groups such as the Ngwi and the Bai (He 1998: 4; Huang 2009: 8). It is also reported that Mongol families from elsewhere eventually found their way to the Khatso villages (Du and Chen 1976: 14). Apparently only the Khatso developed their own independent language and culture over time. How this came about is not clear, but they were no doubt aided by the fact that they were a very small group living in a remote area. Simply known as 'the fishermen', perhaps outsiders were not aware of their Mongolian heritage. Traditionally they practiced female endogamy, meaning that daughters would only marry Khatso men (Dai 2008: 39). Sons were allowed to bring home wives from other ethnic groups, though the women were expected to assimilate into Khatso culture. Through some combination of these factors, the villagers were largely able to keep to themselves.

Over time, as Qilu Lake began to recede, the Khatso reclaimed the former marshland and created rice paddies (Huang 2009: 9). At some point the newly productive land attracted the attention of the local ruling elite. They confiscated much of the land, forcing the Khatso to become tenant farmers in service to landowners and local temples. The bulk of each harvest was returned as rent; what remained was often not enough to support a family. Thus the Khatso continued to fish for a living, or traveled to find work outside the village. According to information recorded in 1950, before the Communist Revolution more than 80% of peasant households in the village were tenant farmers (Huang 2009: 9–10). The Khatso benefitted enormously from the agricultural reforms of Máo Zédōng 毛泽东 and later from the economic liberalization policies of the 1980s. Today, Xingmeng is a relatively prosperous rural village.

With no writing system, the Khatso left few historical records of their own. However, we know that knowledge of their Mongol heritage remained alive through the years due to several memorial tablets written in Chinese that were erected in the 19th and early 20th centuries. This was during the Qing Dynasty, and although the ruling elite were culturally Chinese, they were ethnically Manchu. They also often intermarried with the northern Mongol nobility. Because of this association, Mongolians were no longer considered an inferior group (Sneath 1999: 129), which no doubt encouraged the Khatso to publically proclaim their own Mongol ancestry. For example, a tsa^{33} 旀 clan tablet dating from 1806 says "my family's native place is Mongolia, [we] entered China with the Great Yuan ... [our] earliest ancestor was Altemür who was appointed commander [of Qutuoguan] in 1360..." (Huang 2009: 5). A tablet erected by the same clan in 1813 repeats the narrative saying "Since the Yuan Dynasty, [our] ancestral home is Zhongcun for many generations..." (Huang 2009: 5). A tsa^{33} family memorial on Phoenix Mountain from 1840 states "my family... entered Yunnan from Mongolia, lived in Xia[cun] fishing village..." A later tablet from 1903 states "[our] original home was Mongolia, in the Yuan era [we] followed Zandan [son of Altemür] who was appointed commander of southern Yunnan guarding Qutuoguan..." (Huang 2009: 5).[3]

1.4 Language Vitality

In 2008, a language use survey of the Khatso people was published (Dai 2008). The survey notes that although the village population is small – approximately 5620 in 2006 – more than 99% of the residents are proficient in the language (2008: 3). And despite the fact that all residents are bilingual in Chinese, Khatso remains the language of everyday life in the village. The author points to four main factors that account for the survival of the language.

First, Xingmeng has a high population density (Dai 2008: 2). Xingmeng only occupies 4.77 square kilometers or 1.84 square miles. With a population of 5620 in 2006, 96.5% of whom are Khatso, this translates to 1137 people per square kilometer (2008: 39). The geography thus creates a concentrated linguistic environment in which Khatso is used all day every day. Second, the Khatso traditionally practiced endogamy, in which daughters were married to Khatso men although Khatso men were allowed to take wives from other groups (2008: 39). This limited the number of non-Khatso spouses, and those outsiders who did marry Khatso husbands were expected to live in the village and learn the language. Third, the language is an important part of the Khatso ethnic identity (2008: 40). Because it is their mother tongue, speakers prefer to use Khatso when they can. Even students who board at schools outside the village will use it with Khatso classmates and when they come home for the weekend. Likewise, laborers who go outside the village in small groups continue to speak Khatso every day with their workmates. Fourth, Khatso use in the home provides a strong "fortress" for the preservation of Khatso (2008: 41). Because husbands are often absent for long periods working outside the village, women do much of the farming in the village in addition to running their households. Children are thus typically cared for by their grandparents and hear Khatso all day.

Despite these factors, over the past several decades bilingualism in Chinese has changed the use of Khatso in the village. Now, in certain village domains Chinese may be more commonly used than Khatso, such as government services or medical clinics. Education has been a major driving force in the spread of bilingualism, since only Chinese is used in the classroom. And attending junior high, which is obligatory in China, requires all Khatso students to leave the village for boarding schools where they live in all-Chinese environments. As Dai (2008: 112) points out, in the 1980s

---

3 The inscriptions use the Chinese names of Khato locations: Qutuoguan is a village near Xingmeng that was the Mongol headquarters during the Yuan era; Zhongcun is $na^{323}ka^{53}$ and Xiacun is $k^ha^{55}ts^{33}$, both of which are historical villages that are part of modern Xingmeng. The Chinese to English translations here are my own.

teachers in the local school began urging parents to teach their children Chinese before they started school. Today, many parents now purposely teach children Chinese as their first language. Khatso is then learned in a more informal fashion while playing with friends and listening to the everyday conversation of adults. As a result, the Khatso of the younger generations is increasingly limited since its use is mainly restricted to a few domains.

Therefore, even though Khatso continues to be learned by children, both *Ethnologue* (Lewis, Simons and Fennig 2013) and UNESCO (Moseley 2010) classify it as endangered. A major contributing factor not explored by the survey is the fact that Khatso lacks a writing system. There are consequently no written media in Khatso, neither books nor newspapers. Village signs, notes or even shopping lists must all be written in Chinese. Naturally, new technologies, such as mobile phones and computers, require written Chinese. Nor are there any recorded media in Khatso. Movies and television shows, of course, use Chinese since they are produced for a national audience. The Khatso-language radio station mentioned by Dai (2008: 37) is no longer in operation. In fact, there is little traditional entertainment available in Khatso. There are no longer folk songs sung in Khatso; these disappeared a long time ago. Older villagers can still recall a handful of patriotic songs that were translated into Khatso in the 1970s, but again these have not been written down. Traditional ceremonies, such as weddings and funerals, and even chanting at the local temples are all conducted in Hanyu. Moreover, modernization has nearly ended a lifestyle in which villagers made everyday items by hand in traditional ways, and the language surrounding these items is already slipping away. Thus, even in the home Chinese is becoming increasingly important.

The survey predicts that Khatso will continue to maintain a fairly stable language environment for at least three to five more generations (Dai 2008: 114). This outlook seems incredibly optimistic. Khatso is facing the same inexorable forces felt by every minority language around the world, modernization and bilingualism. Naturally, the villagers want a better way of life for themselves and their children. Unfortunately, as so often happens, their efforts are also eroding the very factors that have kept Khatso vital until now. As more Khatso children learn Chinese as their first language, reinforced not only by school but the seductive call of television, movies and the internet, they may come to view Khatso as limiting and unnecessary. More and more Khatso students are testing into higher education and pursuing careers outside the village. Living outside the village from junior high onwards, these graduates typically marry non-Khatso spouses and, living full-time in a Chinese-only environment, their children never learn Khatso. Thanks to the dramatic improvement in transportation, even those villagers with only minimal education can find day jobs in the nearby towns of Hexi and Tonghai as sales clerks, waitresses, mechanics or factory workers. As these better-paying jobs become more accessible to Khatso youth, the future of farming in the village is also uncertain. Indeed, as ongoing construction expands the boundaries of both Xingmeng and the neighboring towns, it is not inconceivable that in twenty or thirty years the village may become just another suburb, losing the geographical center that anchors the people and their language.

The trends endangering Khatso are not likely to change anytime soon, which adds to the urgency of the current project. The Khatso are very proud of their language, and they are aware that it is under pressure, but they have not been able to make much headway in preserving it. It is my hope that the large corpus of recorded Khatso created for this project, along with this grammar, will provide the people of Xingmeng with useful tools to help keep Khatso a healthy and vital language well into the future.

1.5 History, Contact and Borrowing

Khatso is likely a relatively young language, no older than 750 years. It presumably arose through language contact that came about after the Mongols invaded Yunnan in 1253. Many of the Mongol soldiers settled permanently in Yunnan and found wives from among the local ethnic groups, predominately the Ngwi but perhaps also including the Bai, the Hani and more recently the Han. Exactly how Khatso evolved from this beginning is not well understood. Several linguists have discussed these issues, but none have done the systematic analysis required to determine Khatso's evolutionary path.

What is known is that today Khatso most resembles languages in the Ngwi family in phonology, morphology, vocabulary and syntax (Mu 2002: 142–155). There are quite a few languages in this family and individually they differ to varying degrees, but typologically they are quite similar (Bradley 2012). Khatso shares these similarities. In terms of phonology, the phonemic inventories are largely alike. The main differences in Khatso are a lack of voiced consonants and tensed vowels and a much more elaborate tone inventory. Khatso and the Ngwi languages have very little morphology; it mainly consists of a few noun suffixes that indicate the sex of the referent. The vocabularies are comparable across many semantic domains, from livestock and anatomy to verbs, numerals and personal pronouns. Syntactically, they are all analytic languages with largely APV word order. There is neither case marking nor verb inflection; aspect is marked with a variety of grammatical particles. Based on comparative data, the consensus among linguists is that Khatso is an independent language within the Ngwi family.

There is little sign of Mongolian in Khatso today. As Mù Shìhuá 木仕华 (2002: 135–141) notes, modern Mongolian is an agglutinative stress accent language with vowel length distinctions, vowel harmony and an extensive case system. None of these features exist in Khatso. Inner Mongolian scholars who visited Xingmeng in the 1970s reported a short list of seemingly related words, including some nouns and a few grammatical particles (Hasieerdun 1976: 17–18). However, these similarities are mainly superficial, as Mu demonstrates in a broader comparison of Khatso and

Mongolic languages. Mu concludes that there is no Mongolian substrate in Khatso. However, he does not attempt to find systematic correspondences nor does he look at Middle Mongolian, the language presumably spoken by Kublai Khan's soldiers. Middle Mongolian is not vastly different from its modern day counterpart (Rybatzki 2003: 49), so there is no doubt that Khatso differs significantly from the Mongolic languages. However, the issue of whether it retains Mongolian elements, perhaps greatly modified, remains open.

Because of differences in the phonology of Khatso and many Ngwi languages, Hé Jírén 和即仁 (1989: 33–36, 1998: 54) suggests that the early generations of Mongols in Yunnan began to speak Bai before the latter was displaced by influence from Ngwi. Comparing Khatso and the Dali dialect of Bai spoken in northern Yunnan, he notes that the consonant and vowel inventories are nearly identical, and that Bai has seven tones compared to Khatso's eight; most Ngwi languages have three to five tones. Moreover, a lexical comparison shows that 25% of basic Khatso vocabulary is cognate with Bai. Historically, the Mongols in Yunnan would have had considerable contact with Bai speakers. The ruling elite of the conquered Dali Kingdom were ethnic Bai, and the language was the lingua franca of the region. Moreover, historical records show that there was a sizable population of Bai in and around Tonghai in the Yuan and early Ming eras, along with Ngwi and Hani (He 1989: 11–12, Mu 2002: 134). However, Mu (2002: 266–281) shows that a number of Ngwi languages also have similar cognates, influence one would expect from the local high-status language, and thus there is no reason to claim a unique relationship between Bai and Khatso. Furthermore, as Mu (2002: 255) notes, the status of Bai itself is unclear; it may be either a Sinitic language or a highly Sinicized Tibeto-Burman language (Wang 2005). Thus, the similarity between Khatso and Bai can be explained by competing hypotheses – direct contact or mutual inheritance. Ongoing documentation of Ngwi languages also sheds potential new light on the origin of Khatso's eight-tone system. Sāmù 撒慕, a language spoken in Kunming, contains seven tones and may be closely related to Khatso (Lama 2012: 141).

Khatso also contains a great many loanwords from Chinese. These loans come from Southwestern Mandarin (Mu 2002: 35), the dialect of the national language that is spoken throughout Sichuan, Yunnan, Guizhou and Hubei. Southwestern Mandarin itself has been divided into twelve dialect groups (Kurpaska 2010: 66–67), but local speakers attest to pronunciation differences even from town to town. Indeed, Khatso villagers note that the varieties spoken in Tonghai and Hexi are distinguishable, even though the two towns are separated by only 15 kilometers. Which local variety has most influenced Khatso has yet to be investigated.

These loanwords make up a great deal of Khatso vocabulary and can be found in every word class. Dai (2008: 97) estimates that as much as 40% of the vocabulary is Chinese in origin. Borrowing has not only expanded the vocabulary, it has also impacted Khatso phonology over time (Dai 2008: 78–91; Mu 2002: 34–46). There were at least two stages of borrowing. The first occurred earlier in history, and these loans show greater phonological change than newer loans. No doubt because villagers are now equally fluent in Chinese, loanwords from the past few decades tend to undergo fewer phonetic changes. Unsurprisingly, these later loans mainly deal with new social concepts from the domains of technology, politics and culture. In some cases, loanwords have superseded the original vocabulary, such as the cardinal directions and many kin terms. In other cases, the loans co-exist with native terms. For example, numerals borrowed from Hanyu are used for times and dates, while Khatso numerals are used for counting. Khatso syntax has also been influenced by Chinese (Dai 2008: 92–96, Mu 2002: 124–128). A number of grammatical constructions use loanwords or patterns borrowed from Hanyu, such as reflexive expressions, some comparative phrases and conjunctions marking certain dependent clauses. Bilingualism is further changing Khatso, especially among younger speakers (Dai 2008: 97–101; see § 1.4).

There are two key questions about the evolution of Khatso that have not been answered. The first is which specific variety (or varieties) of Ngwi served as the parent of modern Khatso. Most linguists have sidestepped the question, perhaps wisely. Many varieties of Ngwi are undocumented or underdocumented, making it difficult to find the data needed to perform a comprehensive comparison, although this situation is slowly improving. Though, as Bradley points out (personal communication), it may be that the Ngwi variety spoken by the ancestors of the Khatso no longer exists today. The historical movement of these groups across Yunnan is likewise not well understood. It is generally accepted that the Nánzhào 南诏 Kingdom (734–902), which ruled over much of modern Yunnan, was a Ngwi society (Wu 2001: 31–32; Wuni et al. 2009: 73–92). During the subsequent Dali Kingdom (937–1253), ruled by an ethnic Bai elite, the Ngwi continued to be numerous and widespread (Mu 2002: 257; Wu 2001: 32; Wuni et al. 2009: 93–105). Under the Mongols, Ngwi and Bai nobility both continued to rule their particular tribes on a local level, reporting to Mongol military commanders (Mu 2002: 4; Wuni et al. 2009: 106–118). The fall of the Mongol Yuan Dynasty led to the xenophobic Ming Dynasty, which brought an ever-increasing influx of Han Chinese into the region. Their arrival forced many Ngwi groups to migrate across Yunnan, often pushing them into remote forest and mountain areas (Wu 2001: 34). Thus, there were many opportunities for the ancestors of the Khatso to interact with various Ngwi groups.

The Mongols invaded Yunnan from the north, first conquering Dali and then proceeding down through Kunming to parts farther south (Ma 2000: 4–5). It is thus possible that soldiers found wives among the Ngwi who lived along this path through Yunnan. Villagers claim as ancestors Altemür and his son Zandan, the last two Mongol commanders at nearby Qutuoguan, and their soldiers. It is known that Altemür came to Yunnan directly from a post in Shǎnxī 陕西 Province in central China (Du and Chen 1976: 12; Huang 2009: 5). Thus, those among his entourage who married in Yunnan would have likely taken wives from among those living close to Qutuoguan. Today, the closest Ngwi communities are Lǐshān 里山, a village south of Tonghai, and Éshān 峨山, the capital of Eshan Yi Autonomous County to the west of Tonghai

County. Northward in Yuxi Prefecture there are also the Sādū 撒都 and the Hlersu or Shānsū 山苏. The phonology, morphology, vocabulary and syntax of Khatso and Lishan Ngwi are compared in Dai, Liu and Fu 1987. There are similarities, but also many differences, making the results inconclusive. Sadu and Hlersu are only just now being documented (e.g. Bai 2012; Xu 2012), and so no comparison has yet been conducted. Interestingly, results from a recent computational study of 34 Ngwi languages suggest that the variety most closely related to Khatso is Sāmù 撒慕, also known as Sāmǎdào 撒马涛, spoken in Zǐjūn Village 子君村 on the outskirts of Kunming (Lama 2012). Also closely related are Lìsù 傈僳 (see Bradley 2003 for a description) and Nísū 尼苏. The computational study, however, does not include the Ngwi varieties that are geographically closest to the Khatso area. Xingmeng villagers say they do not understand the varieties spoken nearby, but there are a few anecdotes about limited intelligibility with Lisu. This line of inquiry clearly needs further research.

The other key question surrounding Khatso's origin is its relationship to Mongolian, if there is a relationship at all. On the surface, the modern language seems to be a product of language shift, which occurs when a population replaces its own language with another; the replacement is often more widely spoken or associated with a higher social position (e.g. Matras 2009; Thomason 2001). But is the story this simple, or are there Mongolian elements in the language?

The soldiers brought to Yunnan by Kublai Khan spoke some form of Middle Mongolian (Janhunen 2012: 2). The land they conquered contained many tribes with different languages, but the elite spoke Bai and it was used as a lingua franca (He 1989: 11). Some of the elite may have also spoken Chinese, since there had already been ongoing contact with China for several centuries (Mackerras 1988: 53). Continually employed as soldiers, rank and file Mongols would likely have spoken Mongolian amongst themselves. The language they spoke at home with local wives and their children is unknown. Did they retain the use of the more prestigious Mongolian, at least during the short-lived Yuan Dynasty? Did they quickly shift to the Ngwi of their wives, or were their homes bilingual? If sons became soldiers like their fathers, Mongolian may have been kept alive into the next generations. On the other hand, both Chinese and Mongolian were used officially during the Yuan Dynasty, and the Mongolian elite embraced many aspects of Chinese culture (Man 2007: 148–49). The last Mongol commander at Qutuoguan, a reputed ancestor of the Khatso, is described as knowing the Confucian classics and poetry, which points to a thorough Chinese education (Du and Chen 1976: 12). His soldiers presumably had no formal schooling, but it is possible that Chinese superseded Mongolian as the language spoken in the military. The persecution of the Mongols after the Ming defeated the Yuan would have been great incentive to shift to another language, at least in public. If language shift had not yet occurred, then repeated Ming reprisals may have been what tipped the scales. Perhaps a late shift to a Ngwi language helped the ancestors of the Khatso blend in with their neighbors and avoid detection. The Mongols ruled Yunnan for 128 years, 31 years longer than they ruled China proper, enough time for more than one language shift to occur. Unfortunately, the historical record is not able to solve the question for us.

There are no obvious Mongolic features in modern Khatso; it resembles others in the Ngwi language family in almost every aspect (Mu 2002: 142–155). However, there has yet to be a truly comprehensive study comparing Khatso and Middle Mongolian. Moreover, because of changes in the livelihood of the Khatso people, the semantic domains where Mongolian would have likely had a longer hold, such as weaponry or horsemanship, may have been lost early on. It is entirely possible that Khatso still contains some Mongolian elements; the simple analysis done to date does not rule this out. Likewise, identifying the Ngwi parent of Khatso would also go a long way towards resolving the problem. If a thorough comparison between the two showed few differences or mostly systematic changes, then a simple shift would be the clear answer. If the differences were great or impossible to explain without outside influence, then Mongolian may have left an imprint. It is my hope that the thorough investigation of Khatso presented in this grammar sets the stage for a more systematic investigation into its past.

1.6 Classification

The genealogical classification of minority languages in Yunnan is confused and confusing. In large part this is due to dissonance between the classification scheme used by the Chinese government on one hand and that of Western linguists on the other. After the Communist Revolution in 1949, the new regime proudly promoted equality for all ethnic minorities and set about officially recognizing these groups. However, they favored a lumping strategy. Minorities with similar languages and cultures were deemed a single ethnicity, even if their languages were mutually unintelligible. The language spoken by the most numerous group was labeled the standard while the other varieties were considered something like dialects (Bradley 2001a: 198–199; Bradley and Bradley 2002: 81; Mullaney 2011: 112–117; Poa and LaPolla 2007: 345). One consequence of this system is that resources for education or local language media are only allocated to the officially-designated standard, permanently disadvantaging the other varieties. An empirically-based linguistic analysis, by contrast, would split these families into separate languages or dialect chains. Thus, the Chinese government recognizes 125 minority languages across the nation (Sun 2001: 3, cited in Poa and LaPolla 2007: 337) while *Ethnologue*, which favors a splitting approach, lists more than 250 (Lewis, Simons and Fennig 2013). Furthermore, new varieties are still being identified, such as Sadu and Lawu, changing what we know about these language groups (Bradley 2015). As a result, the classification of minority languages in Yunnan remains a work in progress.

Because Khatso is similar to Ngwi languages in terms of phonology, vocabulary and syntax, and contains no obvious Mongolian elements, linguists place it in the

Ngwi family. Belonging to the Burmic branch of the Tibeto-Burman family, this group is traditionally called Lolo-Burmese in many Western sources. Because the Chinese feel that Lolo carries pejorative connotations, they now use the name Burmese-Yi 缅彝. Citing reconstructed autonyms, Bradley (1995: 1, 2005a) proposes the name Mran-Ngwi for the group.[4] Khatso's place within this language family is less clear. The Chinese officially consider Khatso a dialect of Nuòsū 诺苏, the language they consider to be standard Yi, which is spoken in northern Yunnan and southern Sichuan. The Khatso people, on the other hand, are officially recognized as ethnic Mongolians. Khatso and Nuosu are mutually unintelligible, and in fact Khatso does not seem to be mutually intelligible with any Ngwi variety (Dai, Liu and Fu 1987: 175; Mu 2002: 27). As a result, the Chinese linguists who have researched Khatso consider it to be a separate language in the Burmese-Ngwi group rather than a dialect of any particular variety (Dai, Liu and Fu 1987: 175; Mu 2002: 256), but this position is not officially recognized. In addition, Western linguists view the Ngwi family differently. Matisoff (2003: 697) places Khatso (which he calls Gazhuo) in the Northern Loloish branch of the Lolo-Burmese family, along with Lalo, Nasu and a number of other Ngwi varieties. Bradley (1997: 39) places Nasu and Khatso in the northern Ngwi branch, and situates Lalo, Lipo and Lisu in the central branch. Based on a 2012 field visit to Xingmeng during my own time there, Bradley now believes Khatso belongs in the central branch (personal communication).

Given Khatso's history and its similarity to languages in the Ngwi family, the crucial question related to classification is which Ngwi variety (or varieties) served as the parent language. Khatso would then logically belong to the same branch as the parent. This is not an easy question to answer, however, since many likely candidates are either undocumented or underdocumented. Most of the Chinese linguists who have studied Khatso sidestep the issue, choosing to address the general similarities between Khatso and the entire Ngwi family. The first attempt at answering this question is a paper that explores the relationship between 37 languages in the Ngwi family (Lama 2012). Using a computational phylogenetic model, Lama compares 300 core words across the languages. He determines that the language closest to Khatso is Samu, known as Samadao in Putonghua, which is spoken in a southern suburb of Kunming. In his model Khatso and Samu form a small branch of a subgroup that also includes Lìsù 傈僳 and Nàsū 纳苏. However, Lama notes that the Khatso-Samu pairing is not strong, and few details are provided for independent evaluation. Moreover, the data sample is not large and the results cut across the branches accepted by Western linguists. A much more rigorous comparison needs to be done to clarify the relationship, but these data bring to light a new line of inquiry.

---

4 Following recent practice in this field, the term Ngwi is used throughout this book except where an older form is part of a proper name or title.

1.7 Previous Research

Because of its unique history, Khatso has been the focus of a number of academic studies over the years. Scholars coming to the village include historians, sociologists and linguists. Almost all of the scholarship to date has been done by Chinese researchers, though there are several publications about the village in English. In this section, each of the linguistic studies is introduced and briefly evaluated. The issues they raise around language vitality, language contact and classification are discussed in more detail in § 1.4, § 1.5 and § 1.6 respectively.

1.7.1 A First Exploration of the Yunnan Mongolian Language (Hasieerdun 1976)

In the summer of 1976, several professors from Inner Mongolia Normal College 内蒙古师范学院 visited Xingmeng, one of the first of many educational and cultural exchanges between northern and southern Mongolians. In September of that year the school published an edited volume in Chinese and Mongolian titled *Yunnan Mongolians* 云南蒙古族. The book contains articles on the history, folklore and language of the Khatso people. The article on linguistics, *A first exploration of the Yunnan Mongolian language* 云南蒙古族语言初探 written by Hāsīěěrdūn 哈斯额尔敦, is a brief sketch of the basics. Vowels, consonants, tones and syllable structure are presented in the first section. Nouns and noun phrases are touched on in the second section, along with verbal aspect and word order. The third section discusses a short list of Khatso words and their likely Mongolian cognates. Also included is a vocabulary list of nearly 660 Khatso words with Chinese and Mongolian translations.

The results provide a glimpse of Khatso through northern Mongolian eyes. It is noted that the language is tonal, but only four tones are identified and they are described as identical to those in Putonghua. For the most part, however, tone marking is omitted for the vocabulary transcribed. Noun classifiers are also considered as either case endings or part of the nouns themselves. Of more interest is the section on Mongolian cognates. Impressionistic rather than the result of comparative analysis, these data are not conclusive. They do suggest, however, that Khatso may still retain traces of its Mongolian roots.

1.7.2 A Study of Yunnan Mongolian Gazhuo (Dai, Liu and Fu 1987)

Published in the Chinese journal *Studies in Language and Linguistics* 语言研究, the article *A study of Yunnan Mongolian Gazhuo* 云南蒙古族嘎桌语研究 was written by linguists Dài Qìngxià 戴庆夏, Liú Júhuáng 刘菊黄 and Fù Àilán 傅爱兰. The article presents a systematic overview of the language as well as a comparison with a Ngwi language. The overview begins with a section on phonology which discusses phonemes, presents the eight-tone system and touches on syllable structure. The syntax section identifies ten word classes, which are listed as nouns, pronouns, adjectives, verbs, numerals, classifiers, adverbs, conjunctions, particles and interjections. This section also discusses the structure of short constructions, such as noun and verb phrases, argument structure, and the differences between declarative, interrogative and imperative clauses. The third section delves into vocabulary, discussing the structure of individual words, the simple derivational morphology, and loanwords from Chinese. Every section is exemplified with Khatso data presented in IPA along with translations in Chinese.

The other major topic explored is the relationship between Khatso and Lishan Ngwi 里山彝, a variety spoken in the area south of Tonghai not far from Xingmeng. The phonology, vocabulary and syntax of both are compared and contrasted in successive sections, supplemented with lists of comparative data. Noting that there are similarities as well as key differences, the authors state that Khatso certainly belongs to the Ngwi family, but should be considered an independent language within it.

The article presents the first systematic analysis of Khatso linguistic structure. The comparison of Khatso and Lishan Ngwi is instructive, but inconclusive in terms of determining Khatso's place in the larger Ngwi family. For a more detailed discussion on the issues surrounding classification, see § 1.6.

1.7.3 Yunnan Mongolian and the Classification Question (He 1989)

The article *Yunnan Mongolian and the classification question* 云南蒙古族语言及其系属问题, written by linguist Hé Jírén 和即仁, appeared in the Chinese journal *Minority Languages of China* 民族语文 in 1989. The structure of the piece is similar to that of Dai, Liu and Fu 1987, though it is apparently based on He's own fieldwork. There are two main topics: language structure and the relationship of Khatso to other local minority languages.

In terms of language structure, the article describes the basics: phonology, morphology and syntax. The section on phonology introduces phonemes and tones, and also touches on syllable structure. Unlike the analysis in Dai, Liu and Fu 1987, only seven tones are presented; tones 44 and 323 are not included, but tone 12 is identified. The transcription method for vowels also differs somewhat from the earlier work. On morphology, the article is brief; describing monomorphemes and compounds. The section on syntax discusses ten word classes in succession: nouns, pronouns, adjectives, verbs, numerals, classifiers, adverbs, conjunctions, particles and interjections. Following this is a discussion of phrases, their elements and word order.

The second part of the article focuses on the issue of Khatso's evolution. First, Khatso is compared to Sāní Ngwi 撒尼彝, which is spoken in Shílín County 石林县 to the northeast of Xingmeng. A good deal of overlap in the phonology of the two is observed, though Sani only has five tones. In a discussion of vocabulary, it is noted that

44% of 850 basic words are cognates in the two languages. In terms of syntax, both languages have the same word classes, nominal morphology is similar, and both are SOV languages. Next, Khatso is compared with the Dali dialect of Bai, which was the lingua franca of the region before the Mongol invasion. In this discussion, the phonological similarities are discussed, especially the point that Khatso has eight tones, one more than the seven reported for Bai. The lexicon and syntax are rather different though. Of 821 basic words, only 25% were deemed cognate. Word order is cited as a major difference in the syntax of the two languages, since Bai is an SVO language. The author argues that Khatso must have originally been influenced by Bai, because its phonology is more similar to that of Bai than the phonology of Sani Ngwi. Later, through intermarriage with speakers of Ngwi, Khatso vocabulary and syntax were greatly influenced by the latter language, leaving only a trace of the earlier Bai influence.

This article raises an important point about the influence of Bai on the evolution of Khatso. The Mongols who came to Yunnan undoubtedly had contact of some kind with speakers of Bai. However, the analysis presented here is inconclusive about the result of that contact. Discrepancies in the basic linguistic description of Khatso, such as those on tone, raise questions about the data used in the analysis. A discussion of the comparative methods used would have also helped clarify the conclusions drawn. Nonetheless, the article adds a new layer to the investigation of the Khatso language. For a more detailed discussion on the issues surrounding language contact, see § 1.5.

1.7.4 A Tibeto-Burman Lexicon (Huang 1992)

This book, *A Tibeto-Burman Lexicon* 藏缅语族语言词汇, presents a comparative word list of 1822 common vocabulary items for 50 Tibeto-Burman languages. The data are transcribed in IPA with translations in Chinese and English. Edited by Huáng Bùfán 黄布凡, the Khatso data were provided by the authors of *A study of Yunnan Mongolian Gazhuo* (Dai, Liu and Fu 1987) and presumably come from their earlier fieldwork in Xingmeng.

Although a Khatso equivalent is not provided for every lexeme, more than 1460 Khatso words are included, making this the first extensive vocabulary list published for the language. And since entries are listed adjacent to their counterparts in other languages, Khatso can be readily compared and contrasted with vocabulary from elsewhere within the Tibeto-Burman family, including a handful of Ngwi languages.

1.7.5 About the Formation of Yunnan Mongolian Kazhuo (He 1998)

About the formation of Yunnan Mongolian Kazhuo 关于云南蒙古族卡卓语的形成 appeared in the Chinese journal *Minority Languages of China* 民族语文 in 1998 and was authored by linguist Hé Jírén 和即仁. This brief article largely reiterates the points made in the author's previous article (see § 1.7.3), along with more historical detail on the region. The phonological similarities between Bai and Khatso are noted, as are the lexical and syntactic similarities between Khatso and several varieties of Ngwi, namely Sāní 撒尼, Sāméi 撒梅 and Nièsū 聂苏. Again it is argued that the Mongols first intermarried with the Bai in the Dali area, and then later with the Ngwi in Kunming and eventually in Xingmeng.

Other than additional historical data on the region, no new information is brought to bear on the Bai hypothesis. Data from two new varieties of Ngwi are used to show Khatso's similarities with this language family, but the uncertainties raised by the earlier article are not addressed.

1.7.6 A Study of Kazhuo (Mu 2002)

A Study of Kazhuo 卡卓语研究, written by linguist Mù Shìhuá 木仕华, is the first book-length analysis of the language and its structure. Based on fieldwork carried out in 1999, and numbering 337 pages, the volume is divided between linguistic description and comparative analysis. In addition, the appendices include a lexicon of more than 1870 words and the texts of three traditional stories.

The description of the Khatso language is the smaller portion of the book, comprising four chapters that span 128 pages. The first chapter presents an overview of the Khatso people, their history and culture. The second chapter describes Khatso phonology, confirming the eight contour tones found earlier by Dai, Liu and Fu 1987, and outlines the phonology of Chinese loan words. These loans, which came from Hanyu, were borrowed at different times throughout Khatso's history. They also altered Khatso's phonology, introducing diphthongs for example. Chapter 3 is an exploration of the Khatso lexicon and its origins as well as word morphology. It notes that there are many Chinese loans in the language as well as vocabulary from Ngwi, but very few Mongolian cognates. The various ways that Chinese loans are made to conform to Khatso phonology are also analyzed. Finally, there is a discussion of how the cultural history of Xingmeng, including the change from soldiering to fishing to farming, has influenced the language.

The fourth chapter, the last on language structure, covers the topic of syntax. First, the word classes are defined and described in considerable detail; they are given as nouns, pronouns, verbs, adjectives, numerals, classifiers, adverbs, particles, conjunctions and interjections. Next is an analysis of compound words, their morphology and semantics. The structure of simple phrases is explored, with a discussion of coordinate constructions and various types of modifying constructions. The section on sentence structure discusses the SOV pattern and which elements may serve as verbal arguments. Complex sentences are also briefly described. Finally, there is a discussion of the influence of Chinese on Khatso grammatical particles and syntactic structure.

The last two chapters, which span 161 pages and thus make up the majority of the book, focus on the relationship of Khatso to other minority languages and what this says about its origins. Chapter 5 contains sixteen sections in which various comparative notions are explored in turn. The first section reviews the basic history of the region as well as the previous linguistic research. Next, Khatso is compared with modern Mongolian and other Mongolic languages, demonstrating that the handful of Khatso words previously believed to be Mongolic cognates (see Hasieerdun 1976 in § 1.7.1) are much more similar to their counterparts in the Ngwi family. Khatso consonants and basic vocabulary are then compared to those found in varieties of Ngwi as well as in Hani, Naxi and Lisu, showing close similarities across a variety of lexemes. A short list of vocabulary is compared between Khatso and Tibeto-Burman languages outside the Ngwi branch, again showing similarities. An exploration of the putative relationship with Bai (He 1989; see § 1.7.3) shows that similar correspondences exist in a number of Ngwi languages and thus there is no reason to claim a unique relationship between Bai and Khatso. The rest of the sections further compare Khatso and the Ngwi family, looking at onsets, vowels, numerals, tones, word order, grammatical particles, verb reduplication, causatives, interrogative pronouns and sentence final particles. In each discussion the data show similarities in form and function between Khatso and a variety of Ngwi languages, though rarely are the correspondent languages identical. Finally, the chapter concludes that Khatso is an independent language that evolved within the Ngwi family.

Chapter 6 presents a longer view, looking at history and language contact. The first section compares the results of the linguistic analysis in the previous chapter to what is known about the history of Yunnan at the time the Mongols arrived. The conclusion is that the ancestors of the Khatso shifted to some variety of Ngwi rather quickly, also absorbing some loan words from Bai and, to a much greater degree, Chinese. The second section explains that there is no Bai substrate in Khatso to indicate a deep relationship between the two. Instead, there are loanwords from Bai that are also found in other Ngwi languages, reflecting the relatively high status Bai had in Yunnan before and after the Mongol invasion. Likewise, the notion of a Mongolian substrate is rejected; the few Khatso words that seem similar to Mongolian are also borrowed since it too was a high-prestige language for a time. Finally, the idea of Khatso as a mixed language is explored. Because the language looks in every respect like a Ngwi language, and there is neither a Bai nor Mongolian substrate, the mixed language hypothesis is rejected.

This volume considerably expands the information previously published on Khatso. The structure of the language is described in more detail and instantiated with many examples. However, the data presented are rather basic; the primary focus is on phonology, vocabulary and word classes. Only 13 pages are devoted to sentence structure, focusing mainly on simple clauses followed by a brief discussion of clause coordination. The study would benefit from a discussion of several key areas, such as tone change, the aspectual system and clause combining. There are also discrepancies in transcription, especially with regard to tones 323 and 24.

The second half of the book provides a broader analysis of the comparative issues than the more anecdotal approach previously used. The wealth of data presented from the Ngwi family clearly shows Khatso's close relationship to those languages. Perhaps because many of the relevant languages were undocumented at the time, there is no analysis of phonological correspondences nor an attempt to determine which language is the parent of Khatso. The discussion on Mongolian is the most complete to date, but again there is no attempt to find correspondences between Khatso and Middle Mongolian or to disprove their existence. In sum, the volume is a useful introduction to Khatso, but does not answer all of the questions surrounding the language.

1.7.7 Language Use and Its Evolution Among the Yunnan Mongolian Kazhuo People (Dai 2008)

In 2008, linguist Dài Qìngxià 戴庆夏, who co-authored the 1987 article on Khatso (see § 1.7.2), published a book-length study of Khatso language vitality entitled *Language Use and its Evolution among the Yunnan Mongolian Kazhuo People* 云南蒙古族喀卓人语言使用现状及其演变. Over the course of two months in 2007, Dai and his team surveyed the use of Khatso among villagers age six and older. Villagers were asked in interviews whether they were "proficient", had "partial understanding" or "did not speak" Khatso. Approximately 89% of the 5620 villagers were so ranked. In addition, a random sample of villagers of various ages was asked to take two different oral vocabulary tests. The first consisted of 400 words; the second consisted of a more difficult list of 100 words.

The results show that 99.9% of the villagers can speak Khatso proficiently, including almost all of the outsiders who have married into Khatso families. In addition, 99.8% of the population also speak Chinese, either Hanyu or Putonghua. Khatso remains the language of everyday life, although even in the village certain domains – such as the government, the medical clinics and the market – may require using Chinese to speak with non-Khatso staff. Education, of course, also requires fluency in Chinese, even in the village's own elementary school. And students who attend junior high and high school must leave Xingmeng to board at school, living in Chinese-only environments. Young children in the village continue to learn Khatso, but most parents now primarily speak to them in Chinese to prepare them for school. They pick up Khatso on their own listening to adult conversation and through playing with friends, but their vocabularies are increasingly limited since they only use Khatso in a few domains. Consequently, the vocabulary test results show a strong correlation between age and a fluent grasp of vocabulary.

In addition to the discussion of bilingualism and frequency of Chinese use, the book also discusses the ways in which Chinese has influenced the structure of Khatso itself. Loanwords and their impact on Khatso phonology are discussed, as is the impact Chinese syntax has on a number of Khatso constructions. The volume also includes a lexicon of 2200 Khatso words written in IPA with Chinese translations. The list is broader and more refined than that printed in Huang 1992, which came from fieldwork that Dai and his colleagues conducted in the 1980s.

While there is little doubt about the general trends outlined in the survey, it may overstate the health of the language. Basic proficiency, for example, is measured through simple interviews, which invite participant embellishment. Moreover, the category "proficient" is rather broad, and ignores differences in the use of borrowed words and constructions as well as code switching. Furthermore, the lack of a Khatso writing system and how this makes the language more susceptible to erosion and change is not addressed. A deeper discussion of these issues is presented in § 1.4.

1.7.8 Yunnan Tonghai Xingmeng Mongolian Kazhuo (Wang 2008)

Khatso villagers are well aware that the Khatso lexicon is changing due to language endangerment, especially the vocabulary related to more traditional ways of life. As a result, the village's Tonghai Mongolian Nationality Cultural Research and Inheritance Protection Center 通海蒙古民族文化研究传承保护中心, founded in 2007, created a project to preserve the language. A committee of elders compiled a lexicon of Khatso, including a great deal of traditional vocabulary. The resulting book, *Yunnan Tonghai Xingmeng Mongolian Kazhuo* 云南通海兴蒙蒙古族喀卓语 published in 2008, was edited by *wa^{31} li^{31}tsʰɛi^{31}* (王立才 Wáng Lìcái), one of the members of the committee. The more than 2000 lexemes are organized by semantic categories, from animals and plants to clothing, architecture and cultural objects. Each item is presented in three ways. First, there is a Chinese translation. Second, because Khatso has no writing system, Chinese characters are used to approximate Khatso pronunciation in Hanyu. Third, each word is transcribed in IPA.

There is no doubt that the content of this book provides valuable linguistic and cultural information. And using the local pronunciation of Chinese characters to represent Khatso is a clever solution. Unfortunately, this system does not seem easy to use for those not involved in the project. The IPA is also problematic. Seemingly borrowed from a number of sources with differing standards, it is not consistent and also includes quite a few errors. Nevertheless, as a first step by the community to address language endangerment, it is an important and laudable effort.

1.7.9 Publications in English

There are two academic publications in English about the Khatso people. The first, *Some notes on the Mongols of Yunnan*, appeared in *Central Asiatic Journal* in 1984. The author, Henry G. Schwarz, notes that the content is drawn from Chinese sources rather than original research. The short section on the Khatso language is a summary of the information presented in Hasieerdun 1976. A summary translation of Schwarz article appeared in the Chinese journal *World Nationalities* 世界民族 in 1987, and an expanded translation appeared in 1995 in the Chinese *Journal of Inner Mongolia Teacher's College for Nationalities* 内蒙古民族师院学报.

The second article, *Some notes on a visit to a 'Mongolian' village in Yunnan, China* by David D. Sneath, was published in the journal *Inner Asia* in 1999. Although this article only mentions linguistic matters in passing, it is included here because of the paucity of information on the Khatso in English. The author explains that it is not an academic study, but rather written to convey his observations after a brief visit to Xingmeng. The majority of the piece is devoted to the history of Mongols in Yunnan, and effectively conveys the pride the villagers feel for their Mongolian heritage.

1.8 Methodology

Because language loss is irrevocable, a project that seeks to document an endangered language must create a comprehensive record of the language in question (see Bowern 2008; Gippert, Himmelmann and Mosel 2006; Newman and Ratliff 2001). In addition to capturing the basic building blocks of a language – phonetics, phonology, morphology, syntax and lexicon – there must also be an emphasis on recording natural speech from a variety of speakers. Indeed, in order to fully understand a language, it is crucial to analyze discourse because many constructions are only apparent in extended stretches of speech (e.g. Chafe 1980, Du Bois 1987, Hopper and Thompson 1984, Thompson and Hopper 2001). Thus my project had two main goals: create a comprehensive corpus of the language and write a grammar based on the corpus.

The corpus data were collected during a year of fieldwork in Xingmeng from April 2012 to April 2013. My Khatso assistant $k^hu\varepsilon i^{44}\ li^{24}$ 奎丽 (Ms. Kui) and I recorded more than 50 hours of Khatso in audio and video format. These recordings include both elicited data and natural discourse. The elicited data comprise phonetic and phonological material, vocabulary and short phrases from more than 25 speakers. A number of discourse genres were captured, featuring more than 30 speakers, from instructions and personal anecdotes to spontaneous conversation and traditional narratives. Supplementary data were obtained between April 2013 to May 2015, through regular online conversations via email and Skype with $k^hu\varepsilon i^{44}\ li^{24}$, and by extension other speakers in the village, as well as a follow-up visit to Xingmeng in October 2014.

Language data were captured in different technological formats as recommended by best practice (e.g. Bowern 2008; E-MELD 2006; Good 2011; OLAC 2009; Thieberger and Berez 2012). Elicited data and accompanying linguistic and cultural notes were written in notebooks in the field and later digitally scanned; the language data were also entered into the linguistic analysis program FieldWorks. Elicitation sessions were recorded using a Roland R-26 audio recorder and a Shure SM10A microphone. Conversation was recorded using a Zoom H2 audio recorder and its built-in microphone as well as the Roland R-26 and a Rode NT4 X/Y stereo tabletop microphone. Videos were captured using a JVC GY-HM100 HD Camcorder and either an Audio Technica BP4029 stereo shotgun microphone or the Rode tabletop microphone. Transcriptions were typed into word processing software. Praat was used to analyze the phonetics, and SoundForge used to listen to and edit audio recordings. Ceremonies, events, cultural objects and everyday life in the village were also captured in digital photo format using a Nikon Coolpix S3100 camera.

A combination of data elicitation and discourse analysis was used in the project, following best practice (Mithun 2009). Elicitation was used early on to investigate the phonemic inventory of the language, test morphology and sketch out basic syntactic patterns. This information was transcribed using IPA, and glossed in Putonghua and English. Once the basics were understood, the transcription of spontaneous discourse began. In these transcriptions, which follow the Santa Barbara method (Du Bois 2013), Khatso was written using a Romanized orthography devised for that purpose. The Khatso was translated into Chinese by Ms. Kui and myself, and may consequently have a local Yunnan flavor. English translations were added later by myself. The transcription process also included a certain amount of ad hoc testing via elicitation, as new vocabulary or grammatical patterns were discovered and assessed. These transcriptions were used to analyze the use of grammatical constructions and discourse patterns. Additional texts along with recordings may be found at www.khatso.net.

The grammar was written between April 2013 and May 2015 in Palo Alto, California. Because of the recent resurgence of language documentation, there has been a renewed interest in the theory of grammar writing. The latest literature (e.g. Ameka, Dench and Evans 2006; Payne and Weber 2007; Nakayama and Rice 2014) provides a series of guidelines about the collection, organization and presentation of data. These practices informed my own approach to planning and writing the current volume.

From start to finish, this project was a collaborative one. Thus, the ethical treatment of speakers and their language data was paramount (e.g. Bowern 2008; Dwyer 2006; Rice 2006). Participation in the project was voluntary and speakers gave their informed consent before any recording took place. During this process, mutual rights and responsibilities were explained and consent was recorded either orally or in written form, in accordance with the protocol approved by the Human Subjects Committee at the University of California, Santa Barbara. Participants were also paid for their time. In order to thank the participants for their generous assistance, and to highlight the validity of the information presented, all language data in this volume are gratefully attributed to the Khatso men and women who provided them.

1.9 Language Consultants

The people of Xingmeng were very supportive of this project, and I was able to work with dozens of language consultants during my year in Xingmeng. The primary consultant, who also served as project assistant, is $k^huɛi^{44}$ li^{24} 奎丽 (Kui Li). Ms. Kui was born and raised in $k^ha^{55}tsɿ^{33}$, and Khatso is her native language; she is also fluent in both Hanyu and Putonghua. As primary consultant, she participated in all of the early elicitation work and some of the recorded conversations, and later served as interviewer in a number of the video recordings. As project assistant, she helped with all planning and logistics, such as identifying cultural topics to explore and introducing me to other consultants, and also helped with transcription. She made many of the recordings and transcriptions on her own, significantly expanding the Khatso corpus.

Many other residents of Xingmeng participated in the project. And because their individual contributions may not be specifically cited in the following chapters, I would like to acknowledge their assistance here. Table 1.1 lists these people, their demographic information and their contributions to the project, which range from recording Khatso to demonstrating various aspects of traditional culture. The abbreviations, which are used to identify language examples from individual speakers in the grammar, are based on their Chinese names. And, following Khatso practice, surnames precede given names here and throughout this volume.

Table 1.1: Khatso language consultants

Name		Abbrev.	Sex	Village	Contribution
$ja^{31}\,ai^{24}jɛ^{44}$	杨爱英	YAY	F	$pɛi^{323}ko^{53}$	Elicitation, Stories
$ja^{31}\,ɕo^{24}li^{24}$	杨秀丽	YXL	F	$sɿ^{24}ts^hɿ^{33}xo^{35}$	Conversation; Demonstration (farming; firewood)
$ja^{31}\,fa^{31}jɛ^{44}$	杨发英	YFY	F	$k^ha^{55}tsɿ^{33}$	Demonstration (clothing)
$ja^{31}\,jɛ^{31}fɛi^{44}$	杨莹芬	YYF	F	$ȵa^{323}ka^{53}$	Conversation; Demonstration (baskets)
$ja^{31}\,jɛ^{24}fɛi^{44}$	杨应芬	YYF2	F	$ȵa^{323}ka^{53}$	Elicitation
$ja^{31}\,li^{31}wi^{24}$	杨立位	YLW	M	$pɛi^{323}ko^{53}$	Conversation; Demonstration (qin; dance)
$ja^{31}\,pi^{31}fɛi^{44}$	杨必芬	YBF	F	$pɛi^{323}pa^{323}$	Conversation
$ja^{31}\,po^{44}$	杨波	YB	M	$ȵa^{323}ka^{53}$	Elicitation
$ja^{31}\,tɕɛ^{24}jo^{31}$	杨建荣	YJR	M	$sɿ^{24}ts^hɿ^{33}xo^{35}$	Conversation

Name		Abbrev.	Sex	Village	Contribution
ja³¹ tʰi³¹kua⁴⁴	杨廷光	YTG	M	n̠a³²³ka⁵³	Conversation
ja³¹ tsau²⁴jɛ⁴⁴	杨赵英	YZY	F	pɛi³²³pa³²³	Elicitation
ja³¹ tsi²⁴fɛi⁴⁴	杨进芬	YJF	F	n̠a³²³ka⁵³	Conversation
ja³¹ tsua³³jɛ³¹	杨转元	YZY2	M	pɛi³²³ko⁵³	Conversation
kʰuɛi⁴⁴ i³¹	奎漾	KY	F	kʰa⁵⁵tsŋ³³	Conversation; Recording assistance
kʰuɛi⁴⁴ jɛ³¹fɛi⁴⁴	奎元芬	KYF	F	kʰa⁵⁵tsŋ³³	Conversation; Demonstration (clothing)
kʰuɛi⁴⁴ lai³¹tʰua³¹	奎来团	KLT	M	kʰa⁵⁵tsŋ³³	Demonstration (dance); Stories
kʰuɛi⁴⁴ li²⁴	奎丽	KL	F	kʰa⁵⁵tsŋ³³	Conversation; Demonstration (dance); Elicitation; Project assistance
kʰuɛi⁴⁴ li²⁴xua³¹	奎丽华	KLH	F	sŋ²⁴tsʰŋ³³xo³⁵	Conversation
kʰuɛi⁴⁴ tsʰau³¹zɣ³³	奎朝汝	KCR	M	kʰa⁵⁵tsŋ³³	Elicitation
kʰuɛi⁴⁴ vɛi³¹jɛ⁴⁴	奎文英	KWY	F	kʰa⁵⁵tsŋ³³	Elicitation
kʰuɛi⁴⁴ si⁴⁴tsʰɛi³¹	奎新财	KXC	M	pɛi³²³pa³²³	Conversation
kua⁴⁴ sau²⁴tsʰo⁴⁴	官绍聪	GZC	M	kʰa⁵⁵tsŋ³³	Elicitation
kua⁴⁴ tʰi³¹ɕo²⁴	官廷秀	GTX	M	sŋ²⁴tsʰŋ³³xo³⁵	Conversation
kua⁴⁴ tsʰɛi³³suɛi²⁴	官彩顺	GCS	F	pɛi³²³ko⁵³	Conversation
kua⁴⁴ tsŋ²⁴xo³¹	官继红	GJH	M	sŋ²⁴tsʰŋ³³xo³⁵	Demonstration (firewood)
kua⁴⁴ jo³³si⁴⁴	官有兴	GYX	M	n̠a³²³ka⁵³	Conversation
pʰɣ³³ fa³¹tɕʰa³¹	普发祥	PFX	M	sŋ²⁴tsʰŋ³³xo³⁵	Elicitation
pʰɣ³³ tsʰua³¹vɛi³¹	普传文	PCW	M	sŋ²⁴tsʰŋ³³xo³⁵	Demonstration (firewood)
pʰɣ³³ tsŋ²⁴ɕɛ⁴⁴	普自仙	PZX	F	sŋ²⁴tsʰŋ³³xo³⁵	Demonstration (dance)
pʰɣ³³ zŋ²⁴ɕɛ⁴⁴	普玉仙	PYX	F	n̠a³²³ka⁵³	Conversation
pʰɣ³³ zɣ³³li³¹	普汝林	PRL	M	sŋ²⁴tsʰŋ³³xo³⁵	Demonstration (stools); Stories
tsau²⁴ ɕɛ³¹li²⁴	赵雪丽	ZXL	F	pɛi³²³pa³²³	Conversation; Demonstration (dance)
tsau²⁴ i³¹jo³³	赵云有	ZYY	M	pɛi³²³pa³²³	Demonstration (tools; dance)
tsau²⁴ jɛ²⁴	赵艳	ZY	F	kʰa⁵⁵tsŋ³³	Elicitation
tsau²⁴ mi³¹mɛi³¹	赵明媚	ZMM	F	pɛi³²³ko⁵³	Conversation
tsau²⁴ mo²⁴fɣ³¹	赵茂福	ZMF	M	kʰa⁵⁵tsŋ³³	Conversation
tsau²⁴ jo³¹fɛi⁴⁴	赵荣芬	ZRF	F	sŋ²⁴tsʰŋ³³xo³⁵	Conversation; Demonstration (dance; farming; firewood)
tsau²⁴ pɛi³³ɕɛ⁴⁴	赵本仙	ZBX2	F	sŋ²⁴tsʰŋ³³xo³⁵	Conversation
tsau²⁴ pɛi³³ɕo²⁴	赵本秀	ZBX	F	sŋ²⁴tsʰŋ³³xo³⁵	Conversation; Demonstration (*qin*); Elicitation
tsau²⁴ sɣ²⁴ mɛi³¹	赵树梅	ZSM	F	sŋ²⁴tsʰŋ³³xo³⁵	Demonstration (firewood)
tsau²⁴ tɕɛ²⁴jo³³	赵建勇	ZJY	M	pɛi³²³ko⁵³	Demonstration (firewood)

Name		Abbrev.	Sex	Village	Contribution
tsau^{24} tʰua^{31}fɛi^{44}	赵团芬	ZTF	F	sʅ^{24}tsʰʅ^{33}xo^{35}	Conversation; Demonstration (dance)
tsau^{24} vɛi^{31}jɛ^{44}	赵文英	ZWY	F	kʰa^{55}tsʅ^{33}	Elicitation
tsau^{24} xo^{31}fa^{31}	赵鸿发	ZHF	M	pɛi^{323}ko^{53}	Conversation; Demonstration (*qin*; dance)
tsau^{24} xo^{31}si^{44}	赵红星	ZHX	M	pɛi^{323}ko^{53}	Demonstration (wedding)
tsau^{24} zʅ^{44}tsʰi^{31}	赵依琴	ZYQ	F	sʅ^{24}tsʰʅ^{33}xo^{35}	Demonstration (wedding)
tsʰʅ^{44} jo^{33}tɕʰa^{31}	期永祥	QYX	M	kʰa^{55}tsʅ^{33}	Elicitation
tsʰʅ^{44} li^{31}jɛ^{44}	期玲英	QLY	F	kʰa^{55}tsʅ^{33}	Demonstration (clothing)
tsʰʅ^{44} vɛi^{31}jɛ^{44}	期文英	QWY	F	sʅ^{24}tsʰʅ^{33}xo^{35}	Conversation; Demonstration (dance; farming; firewood)
wa^{31} fɛi^{33}ɕɛ^{44}	王粉仙	WFX	F	sʅ^{24}tsʰʅ^{33}xo^{35}	Demonstration (dance)
wa^{31} fo^{24}jɛ^{44}	王凤英	WFY	F	pɛi^{323}ko^{53}	Elicitation
wa^{31} li^{24}tɕʰɛ^{31}	王利全	WLQ	M	ȵa^{323}ka^{53}	Elicitation
wa^{31} lʮ^{24}sa^{44}	王露莎	WLS	F	ȵa^{323}ka^{53}	Elicitation
wa^{31} sʅ^{44}zʅ^{33}	王思禹	WSY	M	ȵa^{323}ka^{53}	Conversation
wa^{31} tʰi^{31}piau^{44}	王廷彪	WTB	M	pɛi^{323}pa^{323}	Elicitation
wa^{31} tsʰi^{31}fɛi^{44}	王琼芬	WQF	F	kʰa^{55}tsʅ^{33}	Elicitation
wa^{31} tsi^{24}tsʰɛi^{31}	王进才	WJC	M	ȵa^{323}ka^{53}	Elicitation
wa^{31} tsʅ^{24}xuɛi^{24}	王智慧	WZH	F	ȵa^{323}ka^{53}	Elicitation
wa^{31} vɛi^{31}jɛ^{44}	王文英	WWY	F	sʅ^{24}tsʰʅ^{33}xo^{35}	Demonstration (dance)
wa^{31} vɛi^{31}li^{24}	王文利	WWL	M	pɛi^{323}pa^{323}	Elicitation
wa^{31} xɛi^{33}pi^{44}	王海宾	WHB	M	pɛi^{323}pa^{323}	Elicitation
wa^{31} xɛi^{33}tsɛi^{44}	王海珍	WHZ	F	pɛi^{323}pa^{323}	Elicitation
wa^{31} xo^{31}sɛi^{44}	王红生	WHS	M	ȵa^{323}ka^{53}	Elicitation
wa^{31} zʅ^{24}ɕɛ^{44}	王玉仙	WYX	F	ȵa^{323}ka^{53}	Conversation
wa^{31} zʅ^{24}jɛ^{44}	王玉英	WYY	F	pɛi^{323}ko^{53}	Conversation; Demonstration (sewing)
wa^{31} zʅ^{24}tɕi^{44}	王玉金	WYJ	M	sʅ^{24}tsʰʅ^{33}xo^{35}	Elicitation
wa^{31} zʅ^{33}fɛi^{44}	王禹芬	WYF	F	ȵa^{323}ka^{53}	Demonstration (stools); Stories
wa^{31} zʮ^{33}fɛi^{44}	王汝芬	WRF	F	pɛi^{323}pa^{323}	Elicitation
xua^{24} fʮ^{24}fɛi^{44}	华富芬	HFF	F	kʰa^{55}tsʅ^{33}	Demonstration (dance)
xua^{24} xuɛi^{24}tɕʰa^{31}	华惠祥	HHX	M	kʰa^{55}tsʅ^{33}	Demonstration (tools; dance; firewood)
xua^{24} pʰɛi^{33}xo^{31}	华丕和	HPH	M	kʰa^{55}tsʅ^{33}	Conversation; Demonstration (dance); Stories
xua^{24} tʰi^{31}fɛi^{44}	华庭芬	HTF	F	kʰa^{55}tsʅ^{33}	Elicitation
xua^{24} tsau^{24}sʅ^{33}	华兆喜	HZX	M	kʰa^{55}tsʅ^{33}	Demonstration (dance)

Name		Abbrev.	Sex	Village	Contribution
ja³¹ fa³¹jɛ⁴⁴	杨发英	YFY	F	kʰa⁵⁵tsɿ³³	Demonstration (clothing)
ja³¹ jɛ³¹fɛi⁴⁴	杨莹芬	YYF	F	n̠a³²³ka⁵³	Conversation; Demonstration (baskets)

1.10 Typological Sketch

Khatso is a tonal, morphosyntactically-simple language that shares many features with its sister Ngwi languages as well as more distant relatives on the Sinitic side of the family. For example, it is an isolating language with almost no morphology, except for a few nominal suffixes (see § 4.2.3). There are no consonant codas; syllable structure is mainly CVT, although some vowels and nasals may also be syllabic (see § 4.1). Discourse is organized around a topic-comment information structure (see § 10.1) and zero anaphora is extremely common (see § 10.4). The most pervasive feature is the multifunctionality of its grammatical particles and constructions, which makes verbal semantics and pragmatics crucial to understanding any given clause in discourse (see § 10.4).

In terms of phonology, features more specific to Khatso include a lack of a tense/lax vowel distinction, as found in other Ngwi languages (see § 2.2). Khatso is also unusual in the family for its large inventory of eight contour tones (see § 3.1). There are a number of tone sandhi patterns, but most are restricted to specific syntactic or pragmatic environments (see § 3.2). For example, the numerals 3, 4, 9 change tone when followed by a classifier, as in other Ngwi languages (see § 3.3.1). Tone fusion may also occur when a grammatical particle is omitted but its tone latches onto that of the preceding syllable (see § 3.2.6). In addition, intonation unit boundaries are determined by non-pitch-based cues (see § 4.4).

Nouns do not encode number. Instead, bare classifiers mark number and specificity (see § 6.2.1); there are no articles. Similarly, nouns are not marked for syntactic role, but there is an agent marker that is mainly used to clarify ambiguous constructions (see § 10.4). The classifier system itself is large and robust (see § 6.2), including family group classifiers, which are unique to the Ngwi family (see § 6.2.2.5). Numerals require the use of classifiers, and two systems are used, one traditional and the other borrowed from Chinese (see § 6.1). Nominalization is not widely productive, unlike other languages in the family, but possible in specific environments (see § 7.6). There is no a separate adjective class; attributes are conveyed by stative verbs, though some may directly modify nouns (see § 8.1.2). Relative clauses are generalized noun-modifying constructions, a common pattern in Asian languages (see § 7.5).

Verbs are invariant, showing neither agreement nor inflection. Instead, there is an aspectual system of particles, which includes separate continuous and iterative markers (see § 8.5). The copula is employed only for equational phrases, and is often omitted in discourse (see § 8.5). A single verb conveys location, possession and existence; context is required to clarify its meaning (see § 8.6). Serial verb constructions are frequent and they may describe one- and two-event situations (see § 8.8). Question formation typically centers on verbs, and occurs via reduplication, question words, and interrogative particles (see § 12.4)

Basic word order can be described as SV and APV, although it is flexible and context dependent (see § 10.3). Simple noun modifiers follow nouns (see § 7.1), but relative clauses precede nouns (see § 7.5). Aside from almost all adverbs, verb modifiers follow verbs (see § 10.3). Because of zero anaphora, many clauses have few or no overt arguments (see § 10.4).

More specialized formulations include an applicative construction that adds a core argument to clauses, which may be a recipient, beneficiary or causee depending on context (see § 11.1). Three causative constructions reflect different types of causation (see § 11.2). There is no true passive in Khatso, though in discourse P may be fronted for emphasis which requires overt agent marking on A (see § 10.5). Khatso has a variety of emphatic markers, some of which also convey aspect or epistemic information (see § 12.6).

Clause combining often relies on a semantic or pragmatic linkage rather than syntactic integration (see § 13). In fact, clause-combining particles often have multiple functions, and thus require context to clarify which relationship is relevant (see § 16). For example, the basic topic marker is also used in conditional constructions and to convey a sequential temporal relationship between clauses (see § 14.4). Complementation does not involve subordination; a different type of topic-comment structure is used instead (see § 15). In addition, quotative verbs introduce both direct and indirect speech, but the hearsay particle marks only indirect speech (see § 15.3)

Other specific details of Khatso may be located through the table of contents and the index as well as through the list of grammatical particles presented in Appendix A.

1.11 Photos of Xingmeng

Photo 1.1: View from the government building of the bus stop, the highway and the new part of Xingmeng

Photo 1.2: Vegetables such as cabbages are grown in open fields, muskmelons are grown in covered sheds (in background)

Photos of Xingmeng — 35

Photo 1.3: Most villagers live in traditional homes, though newer houses, such as the one in white, are being built in every corner of the village

Photo 1.4: Walking the narrow lanes of the village provides a better view of the traditional mud-brick homes. The lanes are too narrow for cars, but motorcycles are common

Photo 1.5: Locally grown produce for sale at the village market

Photo 1.6: An old doorway in $sɿ^{24}tsʰɿ^{33}xo^{35}$ with intricate carvings above the lintel; doors were carved to reflect the interests or livelihoods of the resident who built the house

Photo 1.7: Traditional clothing worn by $kʰuɛi^{44}$ $jɛ^{31}fɛi^{44}$ 奎元芬, $tsʰɣ^{44}$ $li^{31}jɛ^{44}$ 期玲英, ja^{31} $fa^{31}jɛ^{44}$ 杨发英 (L to R); originally, different costumes were worn by women of different ages, but today only older women dress this way on a daily basis, typically donning some version of the costume on the left

Photo 1.8: There are a number of temples scattered throughout the village; presented here is a view of the main hall inside the Three Beliefs Temple in $kʰa^{55}tsɣ^{33}$

Photo 1.9: The newly renovated Three Saints Temple in Xingmeng also serves as a cultural center

Photo 1.10: Midday feast served in *pɛi³²³ko⁵³* on *Lǎorénjié* 老人节 to celebrate the village's senior citizens

Photo 1.11: Bilingual Chinese and Mongolian signs on the government building (L) and at a local restaurant (R); the Mongolian script is to the left of the Chinese characters

Photo 1.12: Village statue erected in 2003 to commemorate the 750th anniversary of the Mongols settling in Yunnan; the bilingual dedication includes both Chinese and Mongolian

2 Consonants and Vowels

Together, Chapters 2 through 4 explore the phonetics, phonology and prosody of the Khatso language. Despite its small population of speakers, the language does not have a common standard of pronunciation. There is, in fact, a noticeable amount of phonetic variation throughout the village. In addition, the western-most of the five historical villages, $na^{323}ka^{53}$, is well-known among villagers for its special "accent" (see § 2.2.4). The variation is not great, however, and mainly involves several predictable vowel alternations; it does not hinder mutual intelligibility.

Most of the data analyzed in these three chapters come from ten people who represent a cross-section of Khatso speakers. A man and a woman from each of the five historical villages in Xingmeng were randomly chosen to record a list of 316 lexical items (see § 1.2 and § 1.3 for more on the villages). To avoid pronunciation overly influenced by Hanyu, only speakers age 60 and older participated. Most of these speakers were monolingual Khatso speakers until they began school at age seven or eight, and a few did not learn Hanyu until their teenage years. These ten speakers are listed in Table 2.1. Data from these speakers were augmented by elicited words and phrases from Ms. Kui and tokens from other speakers in spontaneous discourse. See § 1.9 for a complete list of the Khatso speakers who served as language consultants on this project.

Table 2.1: Ten speakers representing a cross-section of Khatso pronunciation

Name		Abbrev.	Sex	Village
$ja^{31}jɛ^{24}fɛi^{44}$	杨应芬	YYF2	F	$ɳa^{323}ka^{53}$
$ja^{31}li^{31}wi^{24}$	杨立位	YLW	M	$pɛi^{323}ko^{53}$
$k^huɛi^{44}ts^hau^{31}zv^{33}$	奎朝汝	KCR	M	$k^ha^{55}tsʅ^{33}$
$tsau^{24}pɛi^{33}ɢo^{24}$	赵本秀	ZBX	F	$sʅ^{24}ts^hʅ^{33}xo^{35}$
$tsau^{24}vɛi^{31}jɛ^{44}$	赵文英	ZWY	F	$k^ha^{55}tsʅ^{33}$
$wa^{31}fo^{24}jɛ^{44}$	王凤英	WFY	F	$pɛi^{323}ko^{53}$
$wa^{31}t^hi^{31}piau^{44}$	王廷彪	WTB	M	$pɛi^{323}pa^{323}$
$wa^{31}tsi^{24}ts^hɛi^{31}$	王进才	WJC	M	$ɳa^{323}ka^{53}$
$wa^{31}zʅ^{24}tɕi^{44}$	王玉金	WYJ	M	$sʅ^{24}ts^hʅ^{33}xo^{35}$
$wa^{31}zv^{33}fɛi^{44}$	王汝芬	WRF	F	$pɛi^{323}pa^{323}$

In order to represent Khatso faithfully as it is spoken today, a phonetic approach is taken in transcribing the language in the grammar, and this approach also influences the phonological analysis. As an organizing principle, the pronunciation produced by a majority of the ten speakers is taken as the standard here, but common variations are also described. Segments are considered phonemes if they exist in minimal pairs. In a few cases, segments in complementary distribution are deemed separate phonemes because they are phonetically different and judged separate by Khatso speakers. A maximal approach is also taken among diphthongs and triphthongs, where there is a great deal of overlap. If a diphthong or triphthong serves as a phoneme for an individual speaker, then it is considered one for the language as a whole. These factors are discussed in the sections on each segment below where relevant.

In addition, a large portion of the Khatso lexicon consists of loan words from Hanyu. Mu (2002: 57) and Dai (2008: 70–72) agree that there were at least two phases of borrowing. The first occurred in the more distant past when few Khatso spoke Hanyu, and these loans have become an integral part of the lexicon — speakers do not think of them as foreign. These loan words have also influenced Khatso phonology. Certainly the triphthongs and some of the diphthongs discussed below have Hanyu origins, and there are likely other influences opaque to us now. The second phase of borrowing began in the last century, which has brought a wealth of new social, political and technological concepts to Xingmeng, and coincides with the rise of near-universal bilingualism among the villagers. In both phases the loans largely conform to Khatso phonology; tones change, codas are dropped and other segments may change as well. However, newer loans more faithfully reproduce the original Hanyu pronunciation. In fact, Dai (2008: 82) notes that some younger speakers nasalize vowels in Khatso to better approximate nasal codas in Hanyu. For the purposes of this grammar, loan words are considered no different from native words since the two types co-exist in the lexicon for all Khatso speakers.

This chapter presents information on the consonant and vowel inventories in Khatso. The tone system and the many tone change patterns found in the language are described in Chapter 3. And structure beyond the segment, including that of the syllable, the word and the intonation unit, is discussed in Chapter 4.

2.1 Consonants

Khatso has 24 consonants. The consonant inventory distinguishes six places of articulation, including bilabials, labio-dentals, alveolars, alveolo-palatals, palatals and velars. There are six manners of articulation, which include stops, nasals, fricatives, affricates, a lateral, and approximants. Three voicing types exist in the language — voiceless unaspirated, voiceless aspirated and voiced — but no more than two contrast in any given consonant series. The consonant inventory is shown in Table 2.2.

Table 2.2: Khatso consonant inventory

	Bilabial	Labio-Dental	Alveolar	Alveolo-Palatal	Palatal	Velar
Stop	p pʰ		t tʰ			k kʰ
Nasal	m		n		ɲ	ŋ
Fricative		f v	s z	ɕ		x ɣ
Affricate			ts tsʰ	tɕ tɕʰ		
Lateral			l			
Approximant					j	w

Consonants only occur singly; there are no clusters in the language. All but two serve as syllable onsets only. In addition to occurring as onsets, the nasals /m/ and /ŋ/ also serve as syllable nuclei. There are no consonant codas in the language. Consonants do not co-occur with the full array of vowels, as Table 2.3 shows. For example, the bilabial consonants never occur with high back monophthongs or with diphthongs and triphthongs that begin with those vowels. Similarly, the velar consonants never occur with the high front monophthong, nor with diphthongs and triphthongs that begin with that vowel. Many gaps, however, are random, especially among the borrowed diphthongs and triphthongs.

The description of consonants is highly consistent across the previous publications on Khatso (Dai, Liu and Fu 1987: 151–52; He 1989: 25; Mu 2002: 30–32; Dai 2008: 78–80). The main difference revolves around the status of /ʐ/ as a phoneme, which is omitted in the earlier two publications, but included in the latter two. My own data suggest that this segment only occurs as an epenthetic onset in words that consist solely of the vowel /i/, and then only for some speakers. The approximant [w] is also omitted from He's inventory; he uses the vowel /u/ instead. In addition, Dai, Liu and Fu (1987: 152) and Mu (2002: 31) both observe that alveolar consonants sometimes have a retroflex quality. My own data do not provide evidence for this, but given the wide latitude in pronunciation found among the vowels, it is possible that consonants vary as well.

Consonants — 43

Table 2.3: Consonant and rhyme combinations in Khatso

Onset											Nucleus										
	ø	i	ɿ	ʅ	v	ɯ	ɛ	ɤ	o	a	iɛ	io	ia	uo	ua	ɛi	ai	au	iau	uɛi	uai
ø		i						ɤ	o	a								au			
p		pi			pv			pɤ	po	pa	piɛ					pɛi	pai	pau	piau		
pʰ		pʰi			pʰv			pʰɤ	pʰo	pʰa	pʰiɛ					pʰɛi		pʰau	pʰiau		
t		ti			tv			tɤ	to	ta	tiɛ			tuo	tua	tɛi	tai	tau	tiau	tuɛi	
tʰ		tʰi			tʰv			tʰɤ	tʰo	tʰa	tʰiɛ				tʰua	tʰɛi	tʰai	tʰau	tʰiau	tʰuɛi	
k					kv	kɯ		kɤ	ko	ka				kuo	kua	kɛi		kau		kuɛi	kuai
kʰ					kʰv	kʰɯ		kʰɤ	kʰo	kʰa				kʰuo	kʰua	kʰɛi	kʰai	kʰau		kʰuɛi	kʰuai
m̥		m̥i																			
m		mi						mɤ	mo	ma	miɛ					mɛi		mau	miau		
n̥		n̥i																			
n		ni			nv			nɤ	no	na					nua	nɛi		nau			
ɳ							nɛ̊		nɤ̊	nå											
ŋ										ŋa						ŋɛi					
f					fv			fɤ	fo	fa						fɛi					
v		vi						vɤ		va						vɛi					
s		si	sɿ		sv			sɤ	so	sa				suo	sua	sɛi		sau		suɛi	
z		zi	zɿ		zv			zɤ	zo	za					zua	zɛi		zau		zuɛi	
ɕ		ɕi					ɕɛ		ɕo	ɕa								ɕau			
x						xɯ		xɤ	xo	xa					xua	xɛi	xai	xau		xuɛi	
ɣ						ɣɯ		ɣɤ	ɣo	ɣa								ɣau			
ts		tsi			tsv			tsɤ	tso	tsa				tsuo	tsua	tsɛi		tsau		tsuɛi	tsuai
tsʰ		tsʰi			tsʰv			tsʰɤ	tsʰo	tsʰa					tsʰua	tsʰɛi		tsʰau		tsʰuɛi	
tɕ		tɕi					tɕɛ		tɕo	tɕa								tɕau			
tɕʰ		tɕʰi					tɕʰɛ		tɕʰo	tɕʰa								tɕʰau			
l		li			lv			lɤ	lo	la	liɛ	lio	lia	luo	lua	lɛi	lai	lau	liau	luɛi	
j							jɛ		jo	ja								jau			
w		wi								wa						wɛi	wai				

2.1.1 Stops

Khatso has six stops: /p, pʰ, t, tʰ, k, kʰ/. The stops can be organized into three pairs, each representing the bilabial, alveolar and velar places of articulation. All stops are voiceless in the language; the pairs are distinguished by aspiration. The spectrogram for /t/ in Figure 2.1 illustrates the voiceless quality of the stop series.

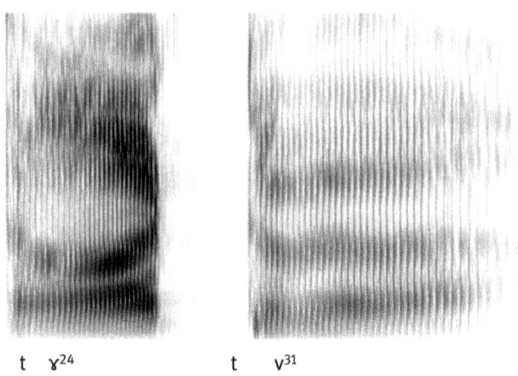

t ɣ²⁴   t v³¹

Fig. 2.1: Spectrogram of voiceless stop /t/ in *tɣ²⁴ tv³¹* 'cloud CL:ITEM' (WJC-Elicitation)

Voice onset time (VOT), the interval between the release of a stop and the beginning of voicing, varies considerably among the stops. Cross-linguistically, VOT typically increases the farther back articulation occurs (Cho and Ladefoged 1999: 208). Based on an analysis of two words each from the ten speakers, we find that the pattern in Khatso differs slightly. While the velar stop /k/ has the longest average VOT at 34 milliseconds, the shortest occurs with the alveolar /t/ at an average of 13 milliseconds. VOT for the bilabial stop is also not long; the average is 17 milliseconds. Figure 2.2 compares waveforms of representative tokens of /p/, /t/ and /k/ from a single speaker.

Aspiration is contrastive among the stops in Khatso, and it tends to be quite pronounced. Although there is considerable variation among the ten speakers, aspiration is greatest in the bilabial stop /pʰ/ which has an average VOT of 123 milliseconds. The average is shortest in the alveolar /tʰ/ at 83 milliseconds; the velar /kʰ/ has average VOT of 103 milliseconds. Figure 2.3 compares waveforms of representative tokens of /pʰ/, /tʰ/ and /kʰ/ from a single speaker. See § 2.1.4 for a comparison of VOT among alveolar stops and affricates.

Because length may be manipulated at the prosodic level (see § 4.4), differences in VOT and aspiration vary widely in natural speech.

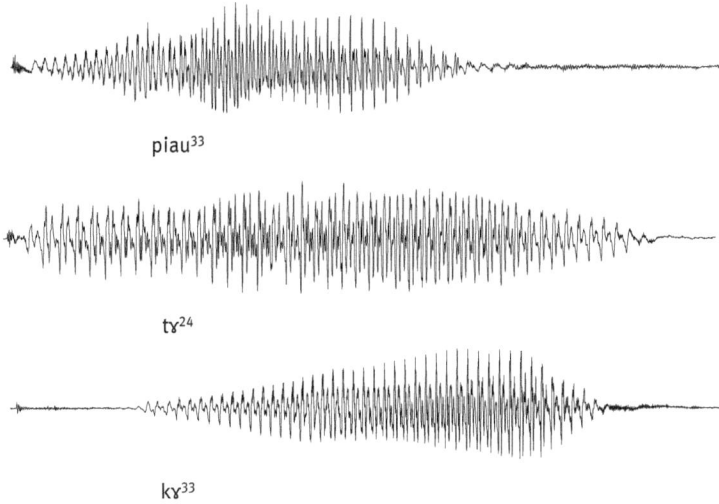

Fig. 2.2: VOT comparison of voiceless stops in *piau³³* 'to climb (pole)' 抱着爬, *tɤ²⁴* 'cloud' 云彩 and *kɤ³³* 'to pick up' 捡 (WFY-Elicitation)

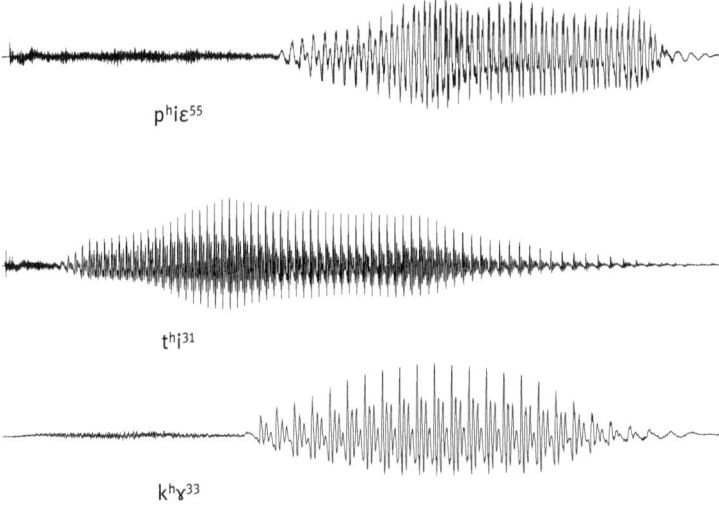

Fig. 2.3: VOT comparison of voiceless aspirated stops in *pʰiɛ⁵⁵* 'to be steep' 陡, *tʰi³¹* 'to braid (hair)' 编织 and *kʰɤ³³* 'thread' 线 (YLW-Elicitation)

2.1.1.1 Voiceless Bilabial Stops /p, pʰ/

The two bilabial stops in Khatso, /p, pʰ/, are produced by a closure of the lips behind which air pressure is built up and then quickly released. Both are voiceless; /pʰ/ is aspirated and /p/ is not. The minimal pairs shown in (1) provide evidence for the distinction. The bilabial stops only occur as syllable onsets in Khatso, and are followed by the monophthongs /i, v, ɤ, o, a/, the diphthongs /iɛ, ɛi, ai, au/ and the triphthong /iau/. The bilabials never co-occur with high back vowels, such as /ɯ/ and the diphthongs and triphthongs that begin with /u/.

(1) pi⁵⁵ 'to shine' 照 　　　　　　　　pʰi⁵³ 'to spit' 吐
　　　pv³¹ 'to carry on one's back' 背　　pʰv³¹sa³⁵ 'caterpillar' 毛虫
　　　pɤ⁵⁵pɤ⁵⁵ 'to be mute' 哑巴 　　　　pʰɤ⁵⁵ 'to break off with fingers' 掰
　　　po³⁵ 'to explode' 爆 　　　　　　　pʰo³⁵ 'to split (wood)' 劈
　　　pa³⁵ 'bowl' 碗 　　　　　　　　　pʰa³⁵ 'handkerchief' 帕
　　　piɛ³⁵ 'pen' 笔 　　　　　　　　　pʰiɛ³⁵ 'to trick' 骗
　　　pɛi³²³ 'mountain' 山 　　　　　　pʰɛi⁵³ 'to swell' 肿
　　　pai³²³ko⁵³ (one of the five historical
　　　　villages in Xingmeng) 白阁
　　　pau³³ 'bundle' 包 　　　　　　　　pʰau³³ 'to be crisp' 脆
　　　piau³³ 'to climb (pole)' 抱着爬 　　pʰiau³³ 'to float' 浮

2.1.1.2 Voiceless Alveolar Stops /t, tʰ/

The alveolar stops are produced by a closure at the alveolar ridge created by the tongue. The resulting build up of air pressure is then quickly released. The stops are voiceless, but distinguished by aspiration; /t/ is unaspirated and /tʰ/ is aspirated. Minimal pairs are shown in (2), providing evidence for the difference. Alveolar stops only serve as syllable onsets in the language, and may be followed by the monophthongs /i, v, ɤ, o, a/, the diphthongs /iɛ, uo, ua, ɛi, ai, au/ and the triphthongs /iau, uɛi/. The alveolar stops never co-occur with the high back /ɯ/, but may occur with diphthongs and triphthongs that begin with /u/.

(2) ti³¹ 'to hibernate' 蛰 　　　　　　　tʰi³¹ 'to weave' 编制
　　　tv³¹ 'to gamble' 赌 　　　　　　　tʰv³¹ 'bucket' 桶
　　　tɤ⁵⁵ 'to boast' 吹牛 　　　　　　　tʰɤ⁵⁵ 'to splash' 溅
　　　to³³ 'also' 也 　　　　　　　　　　tʰo³³ 'to pull' 拉
　　　ta⁵⁵ 'to be a type' 样 　　　　　　tʰa⁵⁵ 'to be sharp' 剪
　　　tiɛ³³ 'to be bumpy' 颠 　　　　　　tʰiɛ²⁴ 'dipper' 舀子
　　　tuo³⁵ 'to judge' 判
　　　tua³³ 'to cup in both hands' 捧 　　tʰua³¹ 'group, club' 团
　　　tɛi³¹ 'one' 一 　　　　　　　　　　tʰɛi³¹ 'to lift' 抬
　　　tai³⁵ 'generation' 代 　　　　　　tʰai³⁵ to delay (treatment)' 拖

tau³³ 'to scold' 骂
tiau³³ 'to toss' 抛
tuɛi³⁵liɛ³²³ 'couplet' 对联

tʰau³³ 'to pull out with hands' 掏
tʰiau³³ 'to embroider' 绣
tʰuɛi³⁵ 'to retreat' 后退

2.1.1.3 Voiceless Velar Stops /k, kʰ/

There are two velars stops in Khatso, /k/ and /kʰ/. They are produced by a closure at the velum made by the root of the tongue. This allows pressure to build up behind the closure, which is then quickly released. Like the rest of the series, both of these stops are voiceless and differ in aspiration; /k/ is unaspirated while /kʰ/ is aspirated. The minimal pairs shown in (3) provide evidence for the distinction. Like the other stops, the velars only appear in syllable onsets. They may be followed by the monophthongs /v, ɯ, ɣ, o, a/, the diphthongs /ɛi, uo, ua, ai, au/ and the triphthongs /uɛi, uai/. The velar consonants never co-occur with the front vowel /i/ nor with the diphthongs and triphthongs that begin with this vowel.

(3)   kɣ̩³³ 'nine' 九   kʰɣ̩³³ 'braid' 辫子
      kɯ³³ 'to enter' 进   kʰɯ³³ 'to rake' 刨
      kɣ³³ 'to pick up' 捡   kʰɣ³³ 'hook' 钩
      ko⁵³ 'to cross, pass' 过   kʰo⁵³ 'year' 年
      ka⁵³ 'to drive (livestock)' 赶   kʰa⁵³ 'card' 卡
      kuo³²³ 'to be crazy, wild' 癫   kʰuo³³ 'to tie, bundle' 捆
      kua²⁴ 'to shave' 刮   kʰua⁵⁵ 'village' 村
                                         kʰai³³ 'to drive (a car)' 开
      kɛi³³ AGT   kʰɛi³³ 'to drive (car)' 开
      kau³⁵ 'to sue' 告   kʰau³⁵ 'to lean against' 靠
      kuɛi³³ 'to be well-behaved' 乖   kʰuɛi³³ 'loss' 亏
      kuai³¹ 'to turn' 拐   kʰuai³¹ 'to have a large physique'
                                            个头大

2.1.2 Nasals

Khatso distinguishes four nasal consonants, /m, n, ɲ, ŋ/, which represent four places of articulation respectively: bilabial, alveolar, palatal and velar. All are voiced, and differ only in place of articulation. A minimal quadruplet, shown in (4), provides evidence for the distinction.

(4)   ma³¹ NEG   ɲa³¹ 'to speak' 说
      na³¹ 'to rest' 休息   ŋa³¹ 'fish' 鱼

2.1.2.1 Bilabial Nasal /m/

The voiced bilabial nasal /m/ is produced by a closure of the lips while the velum is lowered, allowing air flow to exit through the nose. When serving as a syllable onset, it is followed by the monophthongs /i, ɤ, o, a/, the diphthongs /iɛ, ɛi, au/ and the triphthong /iau/. Examples are shown in (5). Like the other labial consonants, /m/ never co-occurs with the high back vowels, such as /ɯ/ and the diphthongs and triphthongs that begin with /u/.

(5) mi³³ 'to be ripe' 熟   miɛ³⁵ 'side' 面
     mɤ³³ 'to be dizzy' 晕   mɛi⁴⁴ 'very' 很
     mo⁵⁵ 'to want' 要   mau³³liɛ³³ 'donkey' 毛驴
     ma⁵⁵ 'to teach' 教   miau³²³ 'to be stubborn' 固执

The bilabial nasal is also one of two consonants that may serve alone as a syllable nucleus, as shown in (6).

(6) m̩⁵³ 'to blow' 吹   m̩³¹ 'horse' 马
     m̩³³ 'to do, make' 做   m̩³²³ 'field' 田

2.1.2.2 Alveolar Nasal /n/

The voiced alveolar nasal /n/ is produced by a closure made by the blade of the tongue against the alveolar ridge while the lips are open and the velum is lowered, allowing air to exit through the nose. The segment only appears in syllable onsets, and may be followed by the monophthongs /i, v, ɤ, o, a/ and the diphthongs /ɛi, ua, au/. Examples are presented in (7). Like the alveolar stops, /n/ does not occur with the high back vowel /ɯ/, but does occur with at least one diphthong that begins with /u/.

(7) ni³⁵ 'to fasten' 系   na⁵³ 'black' 黑
     nv³⁵ 'to hold between the fingers' 捏   nua³²³ 'girl' 女儿
     nɤ³¹ 'to be near' 近   nɛi³³ 2SG 你
     no⁵³ 'bean' 豆   nau³⁵ 'to die of poison' 药

2.1.2.3 Palatal Nasal /ɲ/

The voiced palatal nasal /ɲ/ is produced by a closure made by the body of the tongue against the hard palate. At the same time, the velum is lowered, allowing air to exit through the nose; the lips remain open throughout. The segment only occurs in syllable onsets and is followed by only three vowels, /ɛ, o, a/, as shown in (8). It co-occurs with no diphthongs or triphthongs.

(8) ȵɛ³²³ 'to be sweet' 甜   ȵa³¹ 'to speak' 说
     ȵo³⁵ 'hair' 毛

2.1.2.4 Velar Nasal /ŋ/

The voiced velar nasal /ŋ/ is produced by a closure made by the tongue root against the velum while the lips are open. The velum is also lowered, allowing air to exit through the nose. The segment appears in syllable onsets, but is only followed by a few vowels, including the monophthongs /a/ and /ɤ/ and the diphthong /ɛi/, as shown in (9). It never co-occurs with high vowels.

(9) ŋa³³ 1SG 我   ŋɛi³³ ASRT
     ŋa³¹ 'fish' 鱼   ŋɤ²⁴ 'to defecate' 屙屎
     ŋa²⁴ 'to push' 推

The velar nasal is one of two consonants that may also serve alone as a syllable nucleus, as shown in (10).

(10) ŋ³³ COP 是   ŋ³¹ 'to sell' 卖
     ŋ²⁴ 'to be red' 红   ŋ³²³ 'day' 天

2.1.3 Fricatives

There are seven fricatives in Khatso, /f, v, s, z, ɕ, x, ɣ/, comprising the largest consonant category in the language. They involve four places of articulation: labio-dental, alveolar, alveolo-palatal and velar. A distinction is made between voiceless and voiced production. An eighth fricative, the voiced alveolo-palatal /ʑ/, is proposed in earlier publications, but it appears to be a phonetic variation rather than a separate phoneme (see § 2.1.3.3).

Like aspiration, friction tends to be fairly pronounced in Khatso. Based on an analysis of two words each from the ten speakers listed above, we find that average fricative duration varies considerably among the participants. Among the voiced segments, the differences are not great; /v/, /z/ and /ɣ/ have average durations of 97, 90 and 88 milliseconds respectively. Voiceless fricatives are noticeably longer; the fricatives /f/, /s/, /ɕ/ and /x/ have average durations of 131, 196, 171 and 164 milliseconds respectively. The spectrograms in Figure 2.4 illustrate the similarity in duration among voiced fricatives with representative tokens of /v/ and /z/ from a single speaker. Those in Figure 2.5 compare /f/ and /s/ from the same speaker, showing the longer duration of the latter. Because syllable length is manipulated at the prosodic level (see § 4.4.2), differences in fricative duration vary widely in natural speech.

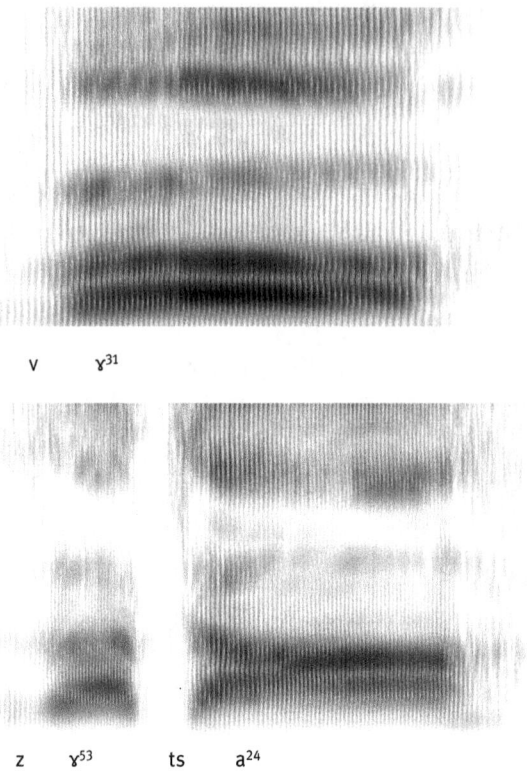

Fig. 2.4: Comparison of voiced fricatives /v/ and /z/ in $vɤ^{31}$ 'to sift' 筛 and $zɤ^{53}$ tsa^{24} 'mat CL:ITEM' 席子 (KCR-Elicitation)

Consonants — 51

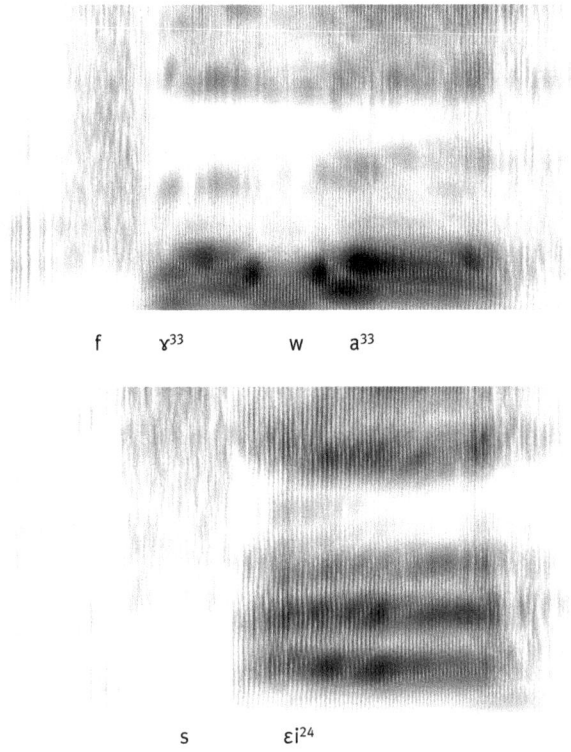

Fig. 2.5: Comparison of voiceless fricatives /f/ and /s/ in fɤ⁴⁴ wa³³ 'dry CRS' 干了 and sɛi²⁴ 'to be astringent' 涩 (KCR-Elicitation)

2.1.3.1 Labio-Dental Fricatives /f, v/

The labio-dental fricatives in Khatso are produced by creating a narrow opening between the lower lip and the upper teeth. Air is forced through the two articulators creating a turbulent or fricative flow. Khatso has both voiceless /f/ and voiced /v/ labio-dental fricatives. The minimal pairs shown in (11) provide evidence for the distinction. The fricatives occur in syllable onsets, but they do not pattern identically. Both are followed by the monophthongs /ɤ, a/ and the diphthong /ɛi/. The voiced /v/ alone co-occurs with the vowel /i/ as in vi⁵³ 'to wear' 穿. Likewise, it is only /f/ that co-occurs with /o/, as in fo³³ 'envelope' 封, and the vowel /v/, as in fv³³ 'egg' 蛋. The vocalic /v/ is discussed in § 2.2.1.3.

(11) vɤ³³ 'to be round' 圆   fɤ³³ 'to be dry' 干
      va³⁵ 'ten thousand' 万   fa²⁴ 'to distribute' 发
      vɛi³²³tʰɛi³¹ 'shoulder pole' 担子   fɛi³²³ 'to be long (of hair)' 长

2.1.3.2 Alveolar Fricatives /s, z/

The alveolar fricatives are produced by creating a narrow opening between the blade of the tongue and the alveolar ridge. Air is then forced through the two articulators creating a turbulent flow. Khatso distinguishes between voiceless /s/ and voiced /z/ counterparts. Minimal pairs, shown in (12), provide evidence for the difference. Both fricatives occur only in syllable onsets, where they are followed by the monophthongs /ɿ, v, ɤ, o, a/, the diphthongs /ɛi, uo, ua, au/ and the triphthong /uɛi/. The one phontactic difference between them is that /z/ never co-occurs with the high front vowel /i/.

(12) si⁵³ 'to kill' 杀
 sɿ³¹ 'seven' 七 zɿ³¹ 'to be far' 远
 sv⁵⁵ 'book' 书 zv³³ 'barley' 大麦
 sɤ²⁴ 'yellow' 黄 zɤ⁵³ 'mat' 席子
 so²⁴ 'to learn' 学 zo³²³ to be 'weak' 弱
 sa³¹ 'meat' 肉 za³¹ 'son' 儿子
 suo³⁵ 'to calculate' 算
 sua²⁴sua³³ 'brush' 刷子 zua²⁴ 'to rub with hands' 搓揉
 sɛi³¹ 'again' 又 zɛi³¹ 'to use' 用
 sau³³ 'to be dissolute' 骚 zau³¹ 'to freeload a meal' 蹭饭
 suɛi³²³kuo³¹ 'fruit' 水果 zuɛi³⁵ 'to be moist' 润

2.1.3.3 Voiceless Alveolo-Palatal Fricative /ɕ/

The voiceless alveolo-palatal fricative /ɕ/ is produced by creating a narrow opening with the blade and body of the tongue against the alveolar ridge and hard palate respectively. Air is forced through the articulators creating a fricated flow. This fricative only occurs in syllable onsets, followed by the monophthongs /i, ɛ, o, a/ and the diphthong /au/. It never co-occurs with high back vowels, such as /ɯ/ or diphthongs and triphthongs that begin with /u/. Examples are presented in (13).

(13) ɕi⁵³ 'eight' 八 ɕa³¹ 'to think' 想
 ɕɛ⁵⁵fɤ³⁵ 'to be furious' 气愤 ɕau⁵³tsʰɿ³⁵ 'to be stingy' 小气
 ɕo²⁴ 'to be fragrant' 香

Mu (2002: 30) and Dai (2008: 78–79) identify the voiced alveolo-palatal fricative /ʑ/ as a phoneme in Khatso. As Mu describes, it primarily occurs before vowels and he standardizes his transcriptions accordingly. However, in my own data it appears only in the speech of a few speakers before syllabic /i/, occasionally alternating with an epenthetic palatal approximant /j/, and thus seems to be a phonetic variation of /ʔi/ rather than phonemic (see § 2.2.1.1 for a discussion of the high vowel).

2.1.3.4 Velar Fricatives /x, ɣ/

The velar fricatives /x, ɣ/ are produced by creating a narrow opening between the tongue root and the velum. Air is forced through the two articulators creating a fricated flow. These two fricatives differ in voicing; /x/ is voiceless while /ɣ/ is voiced. Minimal pairs, shown in (14), provide evidence for the distinction.

(14)   xɯ⁵³ 'to stand' 站   ɣɯ⁵³ 'needle' 针
       xɣ³⁵ 'apricot' 杏子   ɣɣ³⁵ 'to preserve in salt' 腌
       xa⁵⁵ 'rat' 老鼠   ɣa⁵⁵ 'to be loose' 松

Both fricatives occur only in syllable onsets. And like the other velars in the language, they co-occur with the high back /ɯ/ but never with the high front vowel /i/. Despite these similarities, the two velar fricatives do not pattern identically. The voiceless /x/ may be followed by the monophthongs /ɯ, ɣ, a/, the diphthongs /ua, εi, au/ and the triphthong /uεi/; examples are shown in (15).

(15)   xɯ³⁵ 'to hate' 恨   xεi³⁵ 'still' 还
       xɣ³³ 'four' 四   xai³⁵ 'still' 还
       xa³³ 'to send' 送   xau³⁵ 'number' 号
       xua⁵⁵ 'snow' 雪   xuεi³³ 'gray' 灰色

The voiced /ɣ/ is much more restricted. It only co-occurs with the monophthongs /ɯ, ɣ, a/ and the diphthong /au/; examples are presented in (16).

(16)   ɣɯ³²³ 'to cut, slice' 切   ɣa⁵³ 'chicken' 鸡
       ɣɣ³¹ 'to be big' 大   ɣau³²³ 'to boil (medicine)' 熬

Unlike its voiceless counterpart, the voiced /ɣ/ typically has little friction. It appears that the articulators generally do not come together closely enough to form a tight constriction. As a result, the segment often seems more like an approximant than a fricative, making it difficult to distinguish from the following vowel. This is no doubt why some speakers omit it altogether. Dai (2008: 80) notes that the elision of /ɣ/ occurs mainly in the speech of younger speakers, and believes it is a result of Hanyu influence. However, I find the phenomenon in the speech of speakers of all ages. For example, in the first spectrogram shown in Figure 2.6 below the 70-year old speaker omits /ɣ/ in ɣɯ³³ 'to feel'; by contrast, the consonant is very noticeable in the second word ɣɯ⁵³ mεi⁴⁴ 'duck CL:GEN'.

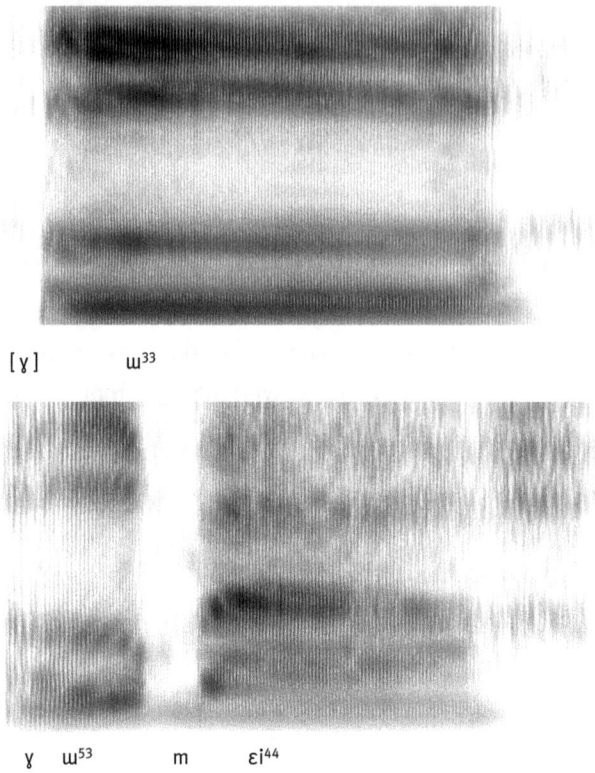

Fig. 2.6: Spectrograms of omitted and fully realized /ɣ/ in *[ɣ]ɯ³³* 'to feel' 摸 and *ɣɯ⁵³ mɛĩ⁴⁴* 'duck CL:GEN' 鸭 (WRF-Elicitation)

2.1.4 Affricates

The language has four affricates, an alveolar pair /ts, tsʰ/ and an alveolo-palatal pair /tɕ, tɕʰ/. All are voiceless, and aspiration is contrastive within each pair.

VOT among the affricates also varies. Again based on an analysis of two words from each of the ten speakers listed above, average VOT is roughly the same for the unaspirated affricates; VOT for /ts/ is 67 milliseconds and for /tɕ/ it is 69 milliseconds. As already observed, aspiration extends VOT considerably. The VOT for /tsʰ/ is 126 milliseconds and for /tɕʰ/ it is 161 milliseconds, and the difference is entirely due to aspiration. If aspiration is excluded from the measurements, the VOT of the two are almost identical, the same pattern is found among the unaspirated affricates. The spectrograms in Figure 2.7 show these features in representative tokens of /ts/ and /tsʰ/.

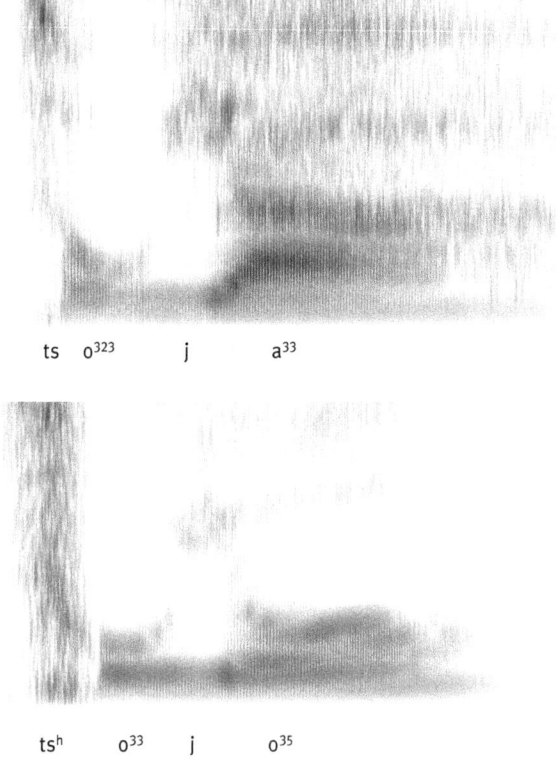

Fig. 2.7: Representative tokens of /ts/ and /tsʰ/ in *tso³²³ ja³³* 'have IPFV.EMP' 有呀 and *tsʰo³³ jo³⁵* 'person CL:HUM' 人位 (ZWY-Elicitation)

The VOT of the affricates also contrast meaningfully with their alveolar stop counterparts. As mentioned in § 2.1.1, the average VOT of /t/ in the sample is 13 milliseconds, while that of /tʰ/ is 83 milliseconds. The VOT of the unaspirated affricates /ts, tɕ/ is much longer than /t/ but still noticeably shorter than the aspirated stop. In contrast, the VOT of the aspirated affricates /tsʰ, tɕʰ/ are the longest by far. Thus, VOT provides another cue for distinguishing between the alveolar consonants.

2.1.4.1 Voiceless Alveolar Affricates /ts, tsʰ/

The voiceless alveolar affricates /ts, tsʰ/ are produced by first blocking air flow using the blade of the tongue at the alveolar ridge. Upon release, only a narrow opening is formed which forces air through the articulators in a turbulent fashion. In Khatso, there is a distinction between the unaspirated /ts/ and the aspirated /tsʰ/. Minimal pairs provide evidence for the difference; they are shown in (17). The affricates only appear in syllable onsets, and are followed by the monophthongs /i, ɿ, v, ɤ, o, a/, the diphthongs /ɛi, uo, ua, au/ and the triphthongs /uɛi, uai/. Like the alveolar consonants, the affricates never co-occur with the high back vowel /ɯ/, though they do occur with diphthongs and triphthongs that begin with /u/.

(17)   tsɿ³¹ 'sore' 疮   tsʰɿ³¹ 'dog' 狗
       tsi⁵³ 'to cut (with scissors)' 剪   tsʰi³³ 'ten' 十
       tsv³³ 'to cover' 盖   tsʰv³³ 'to be fat' 胖
       tsɤ³³ 'to believe' 信   tsʰɤ³³ 'lard' 猪油
       tso³¹ 'should' 应该   tsʰo³¹ 'ginger' 姜
       tsa³³ 'to be dirty' 脏   tsʰa³³ 'to be hot' 热
       tsɛi²⁴ 'to be sour' 酸   tsʰɛi²⁴ 'to be short' 短
       tsuo⁵³tsuo⁵³ 'claw, paw' 爪子
       tsua³⁵ 'to drill' 钻   tsʰua³⁵ 'to pay a call' 串门
       tsau³⁵ CL:MACH 台   tsʰau³⁵ 'to swear' 咒
       tsuai³³ 'gizzard' 砂囊
       tsuɛi³³tsɿ³¹ 'awl' 锥   tsʰuɛi³⁵ 'to be crisp' 脆

2.1.4.2 Voiceless Alveolo-Palatal Affricates /tɕ, tɕʰ/

The voiceless alveolo-palatal affricates /tɕ, tɕʰ/ are produced by first blocking air flow with the blade and body of the tongue against the alveolar ridge and hard palate respectively. Upon release, only a narrow opening is formed at the hard palate, forcing air through the articulators in a fricated fashion. The two are distinguished by aspiration; /tɕ/ is unaspirated and /tɕʰ/ is aspirated. There are minimal pairs, shown in (18), which provide evidence for the difference. The affricates only occur in syllable onsets and are followed by the monophthongs /i, ɛ, o, a/ and the diphthong /au/. Like the other affricates and their alveolar stop counterparts, the affricates /tɕ, tɕʰ/ never co-occur with the high back vowels, such as /ɯ/ or the diphthongs and triphthongs that begin with /u/.

(18)   tɕi³¹ 'to be quick' 快   tɕʰi³¹ 'language' 话
       tɕɛ³³ 'to be full' 满   tɕʰɛ³³ 'to invite' 请
       tɕo³⁵ 'then' 就   tɕʰo³⁵ 'to run' 跑
       tɕa³¹ 'bee' 蜜蜂   tɕʰa³¹ 'to crawl' 爬
       tɕau³³au³⁵ 'to be proud' 骄傲   tɕʰau³³tɕʰau³³ 'spoon' 勺子

2.1.5 Approximants

Khatso has three approximants, the lateral /l/, the palatal /j/ and the labio-velar /w/. The latter two may also be described as semivowels, since they are acoustically similar to the prototypical vowels /i/ and /u/ respectively. However, differences between semivowels and vowels have been found in a number of languages (e.g. Maddieson and Emmorey 1985) and they exist in Khatso as well. The semivowels tend to be longer in duration, lower in intensity and have lower F1 values than their corresponding vowels. As a result, they are considered separate phonemes here, an approach that is also consistent with the previous literature on the language. For a discussion of the corresponding vowels in diphthongs and triphthongs, see § 2.2.2 and § 2.2.3 respectively.

2.1.5.1 Lateral Approximant /l/

The lateral approximant /l/ is produced by touching the blade of the tongue against the alveolar ridge. The sides of the tongue remain free, allowing air to flow laterally around the tongue body. In Khatso the approximant is voiced; there is no voiceless counterpart as in some other Ngwi languages. This segment only occurs in syllable onsets, followed by the monophthongs /i, v, ɤ, o, a/, the diphthongs /iɛ, io, ia, uo, ua, ɛi, ai, au/ and the triphthongs /iau, uɛi/. Examples are shown in (19).

(19) li^{323} 'to know how' 会 luo^{35} 'to be a mess' 乱
lv^{55} 'green' 绿 lua^{323} 'to take turns' 轮
lɤ^{53} 'to lick' 舔 lɛi^{35} 'to sun-dry' 晒
lo^{31} 'dragon' 龙 lai^{35} 'to be rough' 粗糙
la^{33} 'to compare' 比 lau^{33} 'to pull out with a hand' 掏
wa^{53}pʰi^{31}tsɿ^{55}liɛ^{55} 'cricket' 蟋蟀 liau^{33} 'to toss' 抛
lio^{323}xua^{323} 'sulfur' 硫磺 luɛi^{35} 'to be tired' 累
lia^{35} 'to measure (with a ruler)' 量

2.1.5.2 Palatal Approximant /j/

The palatal approximant /j/ is produced by raising the middle of the tongue towards the hard palate but without contact so there is no turbulence. The approximant occurs with the monophthongs /ɛ, o, a/ and the diphthong /au/, as shown in (20). It never co-occurs with the high back vowels, such as /ɯ/ and the diphthongs and triphthongs that begin with /u/. And rarely does it occur with the high front vowel /i/, although some speakers may produce it epenthetically in this environment (see § 2.2.1.1).

(20) jɛ^{31} 'to flow' 流 ja^{35} 'to wash' 洗
jo^{323} 'sheep' 绵羊 jau^{33} 'to be angry' 生气

2.1.5.3 Labio-Velar Approximant /w/

The labio-velar approximant /w/ is produced by raising the tongue root towards the velum but without contact so there is no turbulence; at the same time the lips are rounded. The approximant occurs with the monophthongs /i, a/ and the diphthongs /ɛi, ai/. Examples are shown in (21). It never co-occurs with back vowels.

(21) wi³²³ 'to be listless' 委靡   wɛi³²³na³²³ 'to embarrass' 为难
      wa⁵³ 'pig' 猪   wai³⁵kuo³²³ 'foreign' 外国

2.2 Vowels

There are eight monophthong vowels in Khatso. The vowel inventory distinguishes three levels of vowel height (high, mid and low), three tongue positions (front, central and back) and lip rounding. There are no phonemically nasal vowels, nor are there the laryngeally-constricted tense vowels found in many Ngwi languages. The inventory also includes nine diphthongs and three triphthongs.

2.2.1 Monophthongs

The eight monophthong vowels in Khatso are /i, ɿ, v, ɯ, ɛ, ɤ, o, a/. They are distinguished by three levels of vowel height (high, mid and low), three tongue positions (front, central and back) as well as lip rounding. A vowel chart is presented in Figure 2.8.

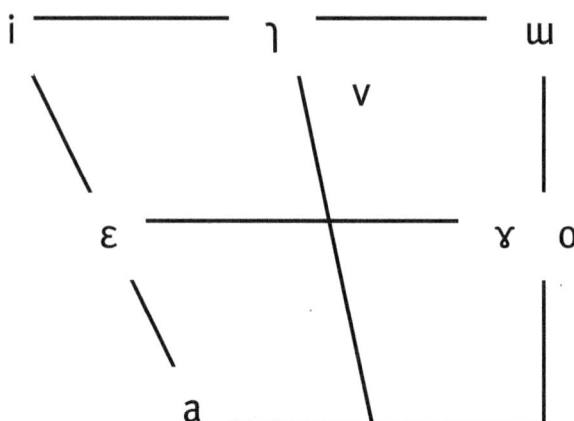

Fig. 2.8: Khatso monophthong vowel inventory

When vowels occur in onsetless syllables in careful speech, a glottal stop is produced before the vowel – a common pattern in many languages (Garellek 2012: 92–94). The low vowel /a/ often begins with creaky phonation in this environment. In natural speech, the glottal stop is often replaced by an epenthetic glide, which may retain some creak, or is omitted altogether, especially when the syllable follows another. Because they are phonetic rather than phonological effects, the glottal stop and creakiness are neither considered phonemic nor represented in transcription.

While it is helpful to identify phonemes in a language, there is often considerable variation in how any given vowel is produced in actual speech. To provide a snapshot of this variation, the eight monophthong vowels are plotted in the vowel space. Two tokens of each vowel, produced in different words, were selected for each of the ten speakers (see Table 2.1). The first (F1) and second (F2) formants of each vowel, which correlate to height and backness respectively, were identified using a Praat script that takes average measurements for vowels. Since the vocal ranges of women and men vary, the results are grouped separately. Figure 2.9 shows the former, and Figure 2.10 the latter. There are ten tokens of each vowel except /ɯ/, which does not exist in the n̪a³²³ka⁵³ accent spoken by two of the participants (see § 2.2.4).

In both figures, the front vowels /i, ɛ, a/ occur where expected, and the lower the vowel the more back it is. The back vowel space is more complex. The vowels /ɯ/ and /ɤ/ roughly share the same degree of backness, but the rounded vowel /o/ is the most back of them all. The fricative vowels /ɿ/ and /v/ are not as front as /i/; rather they are more central in the vowel space, and /v/ is not as high as /i/ or /ɿ/. Some of the fricative vowel tokens converge with /ɤ/, which occurs when they are produced with a more open aperture and less friction, a common variation in the language.

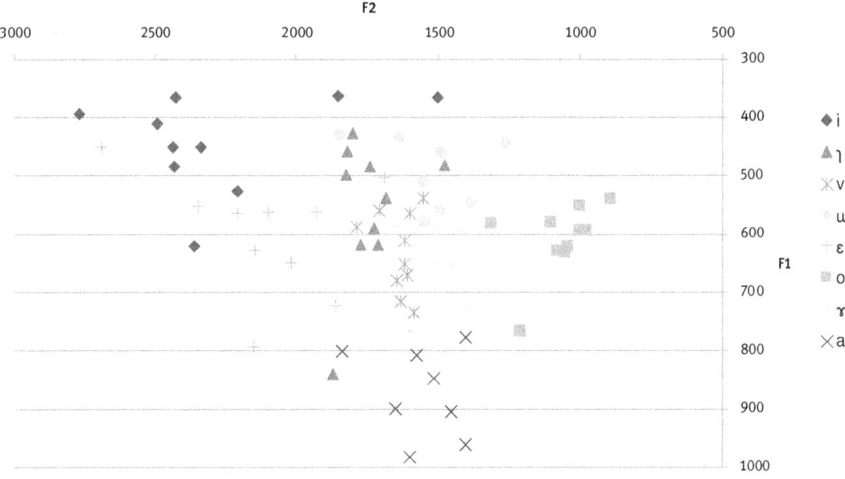

Fig. 2.9: Vowel space for five female speakers of Khatso

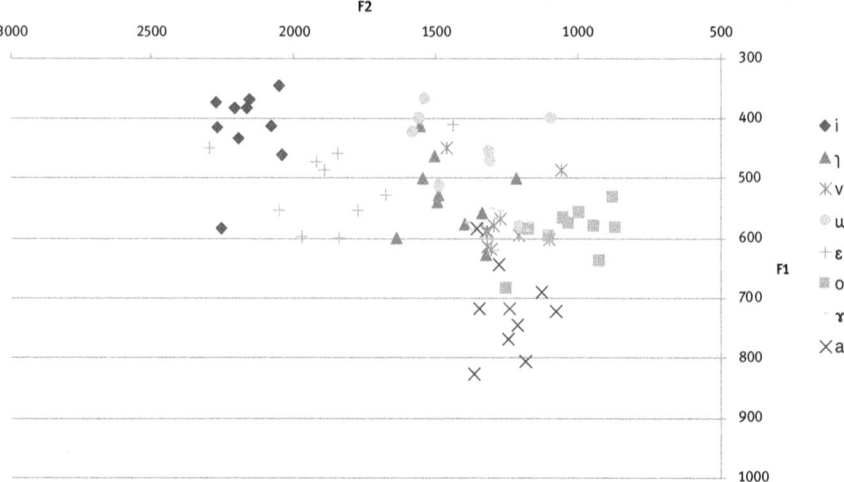

Fig. 2.10: Vowel space for five male speakers of Khatso

It should be noted that vowels are often lengthened in phrase-final syllables, a process that may change the phonetic value of the vowel. For example, high vowels may be lowered, so that /i/ becomes [ɪ] and /ɛi/ becomes [ɛ] or [æ]. Articulatory constrictions may also open to a greater degree. Thus, fricative vowels such as /v/ and /ʅ/ include an open finish similar to an epenthetic [ɤ]. This process is discussed further in the section on intonation unit lag (see § 4.4.2).

Variation in vowel production is undoubtedly one of the reasons that descriptions of the vowel inventory differ across the previous publications on Khatso (Dai, Liu and Fu 1987: 152–53; He 1989: 26; Mu 2002: 32–33; Dai 2008: 80–81). These linguists apparently only worked with a few speakers and had no recourse to phonetic analysis software, so such differences are not surprising. Other discrepancies, especially among the diphthongs and triphthongs, appear to be caused mainly by differences in transcription. Table 2.4 summarizes the differences; note that Chinese linguists traditionally consider /ʅ/ a high front vowel.

Table 2.4: Differences in vowel transcription in previous research on Khatso

	Dai, Liu & Fu 1987		He 1989			Mu 2002		Dai 2008	
	Front	Back	Front	Central	Back	Front	Back	Front	Back
High	i ɿ	ɯ v	i ɿ		ɯ u v	i ɿ	ɯ v	i ɿ	ɯ u
Mid	ɛ	ɤ o	e	ə	o	ɛ	ɤ o	ɛ	ɤ o
Low	a		æ		ɑ	a	ɑ	a	
Diphthongs	iɛ ia io oi oɛ oɤ oa ao		Ie iɑ iə ui uæ uɑ uə			iɛ ia iɑ io oɤ ua uɑ uɛ ɑo		iɛ ia io ui uɛ uɤ ua au	

My own analysis differs somewhat from these data. I identify the same monophthongs as Dai, Liu and Fu 1987. Dai (2008) later conflates /u/ and /v/, stating that the latter only occurs in onsetless syllables; however my own data show that /v/ is widely used with consonant onsets and /u/ is not phonemic as a monophthong, although when /v/ follows labial stops it may lose enough friction to resemble /u/. He (1989: 26) also distinguishes /u/ and /v/, however the only example of /u/ shown is as the onsetless syllable [u³³] 'nest' 窝, which in my data is [o³³]. Some speakers produce /o/ with a low F1, creating a segment that seems to be halfway between cardinal /u/ and /o/, but they reject the pronunciation of a prototypical [u] in these words. He (1989: 26) also identifies the mid vowel /ə/, but in the data it is identical to the /ɤ/ found by the other linguists and myself. Likewise He uses /e/ for the vowel the others transcribe as /ɛ/, both of which correspond to the diphthong /ɛi/ in my data. There are two low vowels /æ/ and /ɑ/ in He 1989, but in my own data I find only the front vowel /a/, although /æ/ may occur as an allophone in phrase-final position. Mu also proposes two low vowels in the language, /a/ and /ɑ/, but again my data only provide evidence for /a/ in the words cited.

A cursory glance at the diphthongs and triphthongs listed in the table above is enough to see that many discrepancies are due to different transcription conventions. For example the diphthong I write as /ua/ is written by some as /uæ/ or /oa/. Other discrepancies follow from the different analyses of monophthongs already described, so Dai, Liu and Fu identify /ia/, He has /iɑ/ and Mu includes both; in my data they are all /ia/. Table 2.5 maps these different transcriptions to those used in my own analysis. Note that the diphthong /ɛi/ is transcribed with a monophthong in the earlier publications; likewise the triphthong /uɛi/ appears as a diphthong in those same sources.

Table 2.5: Comparison of Khatso diphthongs and triphthongs in transcription

Dai, Liu & Fu 1987	He 1989	Mu 2002	Dai 2008	Donlay
iɛ	ie	iɛ	iɛ	iɛ
ia	iɑ	ia, iɑ	ia	ia
io	iə	io	io	io
(ɛ)	(e)	(ɛ)	(ɛ)	ɛi
oɤ	uə	oɤ	uɤ	uo
oa	uæ, uɑ	ua, uɑ	ua	ua
oi	ui	–	ui	ui
ao	–	ao	au	au
iao	–	iao	iau	iau
oɛ	–	uɛ	uɛ	uɛi

2.2.1.1 High Front Unrounded Vowel /i/

The vowel /i/ is produced by positioning the tongue as high and as forward in the mouth as possible without touching another articulator or creating friction. The lips remain unrounded. This vowel co-occurs with most of the consonants in the inventory. These include the stops /p, pʰ, t, tʰ/, the nasals /m, n/, the fricatives /v, s, ɕ/, the affricates /ts, tsʰ, tɕ, tɕʰ/ and the approximants /l, w/. It never occurs with a velar onset, however, nor the voiced fricative /z/. The vowel may also serve as an independent nucleus without an onset. Examples are shown in (22).

(22) pi⁵⁵ 'to reflect' 照   ɕi⁵³ 'eight' 八
      pʰi⁵³ 'to spit' 吐   tsi⁵³ 'to cut with scissors' 剪
      ti⁵⁵ 'pestle' 擂   tsʰi³³ 'ten' 十
      tʰi³¹ 'to braid (hair)' 编织   tɕi³³ 'to speak, do' 说, 做
      mi³³ 'to be ripe' 熟   tɕʰi⁵³ 'to bite' 咬
      ni³⁵ 'to fasten' 系   li⁴⁴ 'in' 里
      vi⁵³ 'to wear' 穿   wi³²³ 'to be listless' 委靡
      si³³ 'three' 三   i³²³ 'to go' 去

When the vowel occurs without a consonantal onset in careful speech, it is often preceded by a glottal stop /ʔ/ or palatal approximant /j/. In rapid speech an epenthetic /j/ may be inserted between a syllabic /i/ and the previous vowel coda. A few speakers produce an epenthetic fricative /ʐ/ before an onsetless /i/, which is also common for some native speakers of Hanyu. Earlier research on the language suggests that a syllabic /i/ always has an onset (Mu 2002: 31), but my own data show that this phenomenon only occurs in the speech of a few speakers and that /ʔi/ is the more common pronunciation. The spectrograms shown in Figure 2.11 compare [ʔi³³] *i*³³ 3SG 他, uttered by a Khatso speaker, and [ji³³], uttered by me. The Khatso word is representative of syllabic /i/ in my data. It begins cleanly with a glottal stop and transitions immediately into the vowel – very different from the initial friction visible in the syllable [ji³³] caused by the palatal approximant, which is shown in the second spectrogram. Because these phonetic variations are sporadic and not contrastive, they are not included in the transcription system used here.

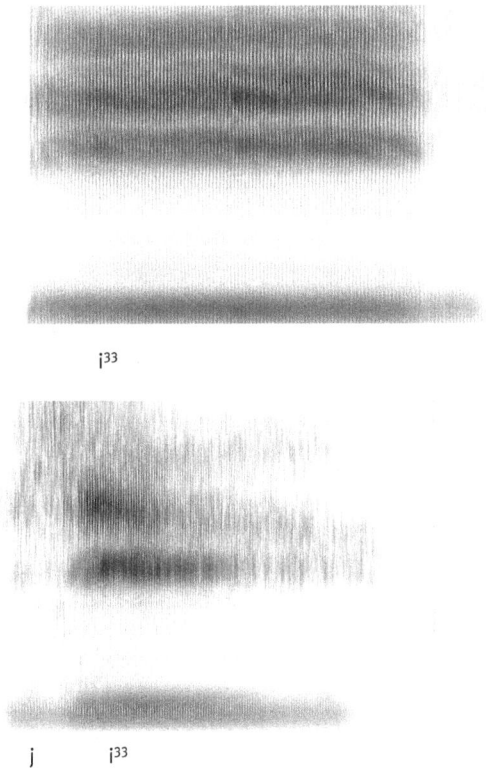

Fig. 2.11: Comparison of onsets in [ʔi³³] and [ji³³]

2.2.1.2 High Central Apical Vowel /ɿ/

The high central apical vowel /ɿ/ is produced by creating a narrow opening between the blade of the tongue and the alveolar ridge while the lips are unrounded and the teeth only slightly apart. Air is then forced through the two articulators creating a turbulent flow which sounds much like the fricative /z/. The tradition among Sinologists is to consider /ɿ/ a high front vowel (e.g. the phoneme inventories listed in Ju 1996), but in Khatso it is produced centrally (see Figures 2.9 and 2.10). Because of its turbulence, the vowel is also called a fricative vowel by some linguists (Ladefoged and Maddieson 2008: 314) and is sometimes written as /z̩/. I follow the tradition among Sino-Tibetan scholars of using the grapheme <ɿ>.

The vowel /ɿ/ only occurs after consonants with an alveolar fricative finish, specifically /s, z, ts, tsʰ/, as shown in (23).

(23) sɿ⁵⁵ 'to know' 知道   tsɿ³⁵ 'to dare' 敢
      zɿ²⁴ 'snake' 蛇   tsʰɿ³¹ 'dog' 狗

In Putonghua the vowel /ɿ/ is considered to be an allophone of /i/ (Ladefoged and Maddieson 2008: 314), but in Khatso the two are contrastive, as shown by the minimal pairs in (24).

(24) sɿ³³ 'to die' 死   si³³ 'three' 三
      tsɿ⁵³ 'basket' 谷箩   tsi⁵³ 'to cut with scissors' 剪
      tsʰɿ³³ 'to arrive' 到   tsʰi³³ 'ten' 十

In fact, in Khatso there is enough friction to distinguish it from a prototypical vowel, as the spectrogram of *sɿ³³wa³²³* 'die PFV' in Figure 2.12 illustrates. Although the first and second formants of /ɿ/ are distinct enough to indicate it is a vowel, the friction where the higher formants would be shows that the segment is not as fully resonant as a cardinal vowel, such as /a/ in the following syllable.

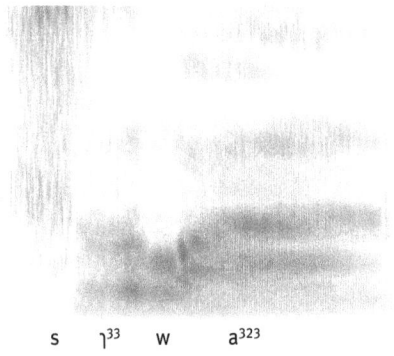

Fig. 2.12: Spectrogram showing friction in /ɿ/ (YYF2-Elicitation)

2.2.1.3 High Central Fricative Vowel /ʋ/

In Khatso the segment /ʋ/ may serve as either a vowel or a consonant (see § 2.1.3.1). Both are produced in essentially the same way, with air being forced through a narrow opening between the lower lip and the upper teeth, and in speech they often sound nearly identical. However, the vowel /v/ is generally produced with the articulators more open than its consonant counterpart, allowing for more perceptible resonance to emerge. As He (1989: 26) also notes, the sound may approach the labiodental approximant [ʋ]. The spectrograms in Figure 2.13 compare the vowel and the consonant. In the first, the final vowel in $tɛi^{31}\ tv^{24}$ 'one thousand' has noticeable formants along with friction at the higher frequencies, indicating a more approximant-like production. By contrast, the consonant /v/ in $vʁ^{31}$ 'to sift' has obvious friction but no formants due to its tighter constriction.

Moreover, the degree of openness in the vowel /v/ varies considerably among Khatso speakers. Older speakers often produce it with little friction, while middle-aged and younger speakers tend to produce a more prototypically fricated [v]. For example, in the spectrogram shown in Figure 2.14, the vowel in tsv^{323} 'chopsticks' shows heavy friction between the formants indicating a narrower aperture and tighter constriction. For all speakers, however, the vowel is most open after bilabial consonants as well as in sentence final position (see § 4.4.2).

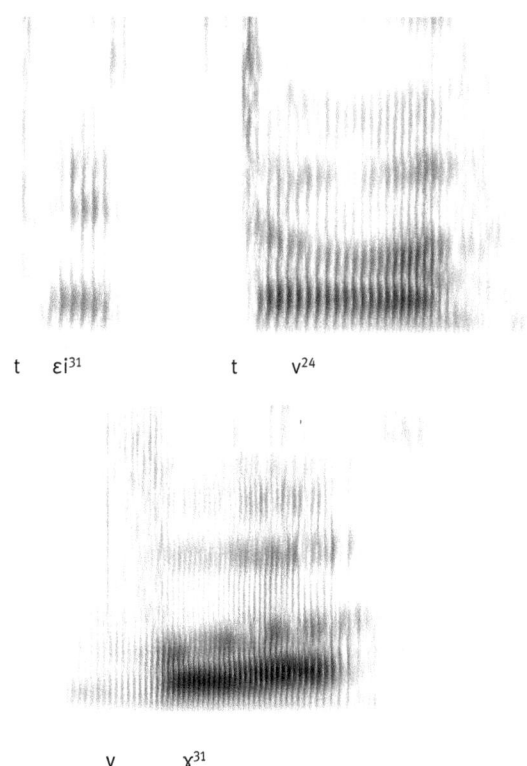

Fig. 2.7: Comparison of /v/ as vowel and consonant (WTB-Elicitation)

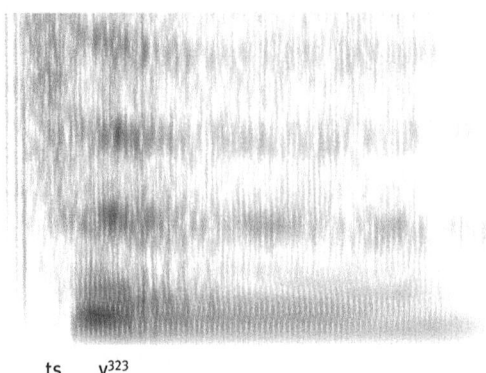

ts   v³²³

Fig. 2.8: Vowel /v/ with greater friction in tsv³²³ 'chopsticks' 筷子 (KL-Elicitation)

The vowel /v/ co-occurs with the stops /p, pʰ, t, tʰ, k, kʰ/, the nasal /n/, the fricatives /f, s, z/, the affricates /ts, tsʰ/ and the lateral approximant /l/. Examples are shown in (25).

(25)   pv⁵³ 'can, jar' 罐子   fv³³ 'egg' 蛋
       pʰv³¹sa³⁵ 'caterpillar' 毛虫   sv⁵⁵ 'book' 书
       tv²⁴ 'thousand' 千   zv³³ 'barley' 大麦
       tʰv³¹ 'bucket' 桶   tsv³²³ 'to call' 叫
       kv⁵⁵ 'to kneel' 跪   tsʰv³³ 'to be fat' 胖
       kʰv³¹ 'to steal' 偷   lv⁵⁵ 'green' 绿
       nv³⁵ 'to hold between the fingers' 捏

The segment also serves as an independent nucleus without an onset, as the examples in (26) demonstrate. The status of /v/ in this environment is unclear. Comparing the spectrogram in Figure 2.15 below with those in Figure 2.13 above, we see that the independent /v/ blurs the lines between consonant and vowel. It is not as constricted as the prototypical consonant /v/, but also not as open as the vocalic /v/. Though weak, there are formants, and so it is considered a vowel in this analysis. Moreover, no other fricative serves as an independent nucleus in the language.

(26)   v²⁴ 'to be called' 叫   v³²³ 'to hold, take' 拿
       v³¹ 'to be crazy' 疯

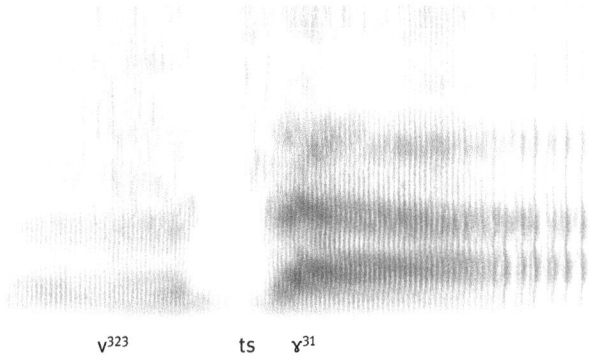

v³²³ ts ɣ³¹

Fig. 2.9: /v/ as independent nucleus in v³²³ tsɣ³¹ 'hold CONT' (YYF2-Elicitation)

2.2.1.4 High Back Unrounded Vowel /ɯ/

The high back unrounded vowel /ɯ/ is produced by positioning the tongue as high and as back in the mouth as possible without touching another articulator or creating friction. The lips and teeth are open slightly and the lips are unrounded; the opening created changes little during production. This vowel is unusual in that it only occurs after the velar consonants /k, kʰ, x, ɣ/, placing it in complementary distribution with the high front vowel /i/. However, these two vowels are acoustically quite different and speakers treat them as different vowels. So, in order to represent spoken Khatso as faithfully as possible, they are treated separately in this analysis. Examples are presented in (27).

(27) kɯ³¹ 'to give' 给   xɯ³³ 'to groan' 哼
      kʰɯ³³ 'hook' 钩   ɣɯ³¹ 'lotus' 藕

The phoneme /ɯ/ does not exist for many speakers born in the historical village of ȵa³²³ka⁵³, where it is typically replaced by the diphthong /εi/. This change is the primary difference between the ȵa³²³ka⁵³ accent and the pronunciation found in the rest of Xingmeng (see § 2.2.4).

2.2.1.5 Mid Front Unrounded Vowel /ε/

The mid front unrounded vowel /ε/ is produced by positioning the tongue as far forward as possible at a mid-point between the roof of the mouth and its resting position without touching another articulator or creating friction. The lips are open and unrounded. The monophthong occurs only after the palatal consonants /ȵ, ɕ, tɕ, tɕʰ, j/. In this regard, it is in complementary distribution with the diphthong /εi/ which occurs with the other consonants. However, in order to represent the language faithfully as it is spoken, the two are considered separate in this analysis. Examples are shown in (28).

(28) ȵɛ³²³ 'to be sweet' 甜   tɕʰɛ⁵⁵ 'to kick' 踢
      ɕɛ³⁵ 'to toss' 仍   jɛ³¹ 'to flow' 流
      tɕɛ²⁴ 'to read aloud' 念

2.2.1.6 Mid Back Unrounded Vowel /ɤ/

The mid back unrounded vowel /ɤ/ is produced by positioning the tongue as back as possible at a mid-point between the roof of the mouth and its resting position without touching another articulator or creating friction. The lips and teeth are open slightly, creating an aperture slightly larger than that of /ɯ/, and the lips are unrounded. During production, the teeth may open somewhat and the lower lip often moves downward slightly. The vowel co-occurs with most of the consonants, including the stops /p, pʰ, t, tʰ, k, kʰ/, the nasals /m, n, ŋ/, the fricatives /f, v, s, z, x, ɣ/, the affricates /ts, tsʰ/ and the lateral approximant /l/. The vowel may also serve as an independent nucleus without an onset. Examples are shown in (29).

(29) pɤ⁵³ 'to play stringed instrument' 弹   vɤ⁵³ 'to write' 写
      pʰɤ³³ 'to be hot and spicy' 辣   sɤ²⁴ 'yellow' 黄
      tɤ⁵⁵ 'to pluck (hair)' 拔   zɤ⁵³ 'mat' 席子
      tʰɤ⁵⁵ 'to splash' 溅   xɤ³⁵ 'apricot' 杏子
      kɤ³¹ 'to run' 跑   ɣɤ⁵³ 'to row a boat' 划
      kʰɤ⁵⁵ 'to comb' 梳   tsɤ³¹ 'to be opinionated' 自以为是
      mɤ³³ 'to be dizzy' 晕   tsʰɤ⁵⁵ 'to pinch' 掐
      nɤ³⁵ 'to tease' 捉弄   lɤ³³ 'to be late' 迟
      ŋɤ²⁴ 'to defecate' 屙屎   ɤ⁵⁵za³¹ 'grandson' 孙子
      fɤ³³ 'to be dry' 干

2.2.1.7 Mid Back Rounded Vowel /o/

The mid back rounded vowel /o/ is the only rounded monophthong in the language. It is produced by positioning the tongue as far back as possible at a mid-point between the roof of the mouth and its resting position without touching another articulator or creating friction. Unlike with its counterpart /ɤ/, the lips are fully rounded and they do not move during production. The vowel co-occurs with a great many of the consonants, such as the stops /p, pʰ, t, tʰ, k, kʰ/, the nasals /m, n, ȵ/, the fricatives /f, s, z, ɕ, x/, the affricates /ts, tsʰ, tɕ, tɕʰ/ and the approximants /l, j/. It may also serve as an independent nucleus without an onset. Examples are presented in (30).

(30) po³¹ 'to be deaf' 耳聋   zo³²³ 'to be weak' 弱
      pʰo³³ 'to shelter from' 躲   ɕo³²³ 'to be handsome' 帅
      to³³ 'to be flat' 平   xo³³ 'to wait' 等
      tʰo³³ 'to pull' 拉   tso³²³ 'to have' 有
      ko⁵⁵ CL:PL 些   tsʰo³³ 'person' 人
      kʰo³¹ 'to spread, unfold' 铺   tɕo³⁵ 'then' 就
      mo³¹ 'to be old' 老   tɕʰo⁵³ 'six' 六
      no⁵³ 'bean' 豆   lo³¹ 'dragon' 龙
      n̠o³⁵ 'body hair' 毛   jo³²³ 'sheep' 绵羊
      fo³³ 'envelope' 封   o³¹ 'vegetable' 菜
      so²⁴ 'to learn' 学

In some cases, /o/ is produced with a relatively low F1, creating a vowel higher than the prototypical [o]. At times it seems to approach the high back vowel /u/. However, speakers reject the use of the cardinal vowel [u] in these words. Since /u/ is not a phoneme in the language, this variation does not cause homophony.

2.2.1.8 Low Front Unrounded Vowel /a/

The low front unrounded vowel /a/ is produced by positioning the tongue as low and as forward as possible without touching another articulator. The lips are unrounded and the jaw opens significantly to keep the tongue low. The vowel occurs with every consonant in the inventory, the only vowel to be so widely distributed. It may also serve as an independent nucleus without an onset. Examples are presented in (31).

(31) pa²⁴ 'to change' 换   za³¹ 'son' 儿子
      pʰa³⁵ 'handkerchief' 帕   ɕa²⁴ 'to rest' 休息
      ta⁵⁵ 'to put' 放   xa⁵⁵ 'rat' 老鼠
      tʰa³²³ 'candy' 糖   ɣa⁵³ 'to knit' 针织
      ka³²³ 'to walk' 走   tsa³²³ 'rice' 饭
      kʰa³¹ 'to be bitter' 苦   tsʰa³³ 'to be hot' 热
      ma⁵⁵ 'to teach' 教   tɕa³⁵ 'to be coarse' 粗
      na³⁵ 'to be deep' 深   tɕʰa³¹ 'leaf' 叶子
      n̠a³⁵ 'to be oily' 腻   la³¹ 'tiger' 老虎
      ŋa⁵⁵ 'to borrow, lend' 借   ja³⁵ 'to wash' 洗
      fa²⁴ 'to distribute' 发   wa²⁴ 'to winnow' 簸
      va³⁵ 'ten thousand' 万   a³³ 'that' 那
      sa⁵⁵ 'to be difficult' 难

2.2.2 Diphthongs

Diphthongs occur when two vowels are produced within a single syllable, causing the tongue to move once during production. In Khatso nine diphthongs are attested: /iɛ, io, ia, uo, ua, ɛi, ai, au/. They are especially frequent in words borrowed from Hanyu (Dai, Liu and Fu 1987: 153; Mu 2002: 33; Dai 2008: 81), and some may have entered the language some time ago through those loans.

There is a great deal of variation in the production of diphthongs, especially among Hanyu loan words. For example, the verb 'to judge' may be pronounced as [tuo³⁵], [tuɔ³⁵] and [tua³⁵], and 'to be tired' may be produced as [li³⁵], [lɛi³⁵] and [lui³⁵]. These variations appear to largely depend on speaker preference. They also account for many of the phonotactic gaps associated with diphthongs in the language (see Table 2.3 above). Mu (2002: 33) corroborates this variation, noting that the phonetic structure of newer loan words is not firmly established and often varies from person to person, likely depending on a speaker's familiarity with the original Hanyu. If a diphthong that frequently occurs as an alternant also appears in words that do not alternate, then it is considered phonemic in this analysis.

Regardless of vowel quality, the prominence of the component vowels in a diphthong, as measured by duration, is predictable. The second vowel is always longer and thus more prominent than the first, and this is true for diphthongs in both medial and final syllables. Sonority, or amplitude, does not vary across the components of a diphthong and thus does not play a role in differentiating prominence in Khatso.

As mentioned in § 2.1.5, the approximants /j/ and /w/ sound similar to the corresponding vowels /i/ and /u/ in speech, but there are measurable acoustic differences. The approximants tend to be longer in duration, lower in intensity and have lower F1 values than the vowels. Thus, words such as /kuo/ consist of a consonant and a diphthong rather than a consonant cluster and a monophthong (i.e. /kwo/). As previously described, there are no consonant clusters in Khatso.

2.2.2.1 Diphthong /iɛ/
The diphthong /iɛ/ occurs after four stops /p, pʰ, t, tʰ/, the nasal /m/ and the lateral approximant /l/. Examples are presented in (32).

(32) piɛ³⁵ 'pen' 笔   tʰiɛ²⁴ 'dipper' 舀子
      pʰiɛ⁵⁵ 'to be steep' 陡   miɛ³²³ 'kernel' 核
      tiɛ³³ 'to be bumpy' 颠   wa⁵³pʰi³¹tsɿ⁵⁵liɛ⁵⁵ 'cricket' 蟋蟀

2.2.2.2 Diphthong /io/
The diphthong /io/ is relatively rare, occurring only after the lateral approximant /l/ in a handful of Hanyu loan words. Examples include *lio³³lio³³tɕʰo³²³* 'yo-yo' 溜溜球, *lio³⁵*

'tumor' 肿瘤, *lio³²³xua³²³* 'sulfur' 硫磺, *ja³²³lio³¹* 'willow' 杨柳 and the Han surname *lio³²³* 刘.

2.2.2.3 Diphthong /ia/

The diphthong /ia/ is also infrequent in the lexicon. It occurs only after the lateral approximant /l/ and mainly in Hanyu loan words. Examples include *lia³⁵* 'to measure (with a ruler)' 量, *lia³⁵* 'to be bright' 亮 and *sa³³lia³³* 'to consult, discuss' 商量.

2.2.2.4 Diphthong /uo/

The diphthong /uo/ is attested after the stops /t, k, kʰ/, the fricative /s/, the affricate /ts/ and the approximant /l/. Like all diphthongs that begin with /u/ in Khatso, /uo/ never co-occurs with labial consonants. The second vowel /o/ is usually realized as the lower mid back rounded vowel [ɔ], much as it is in Putonghua. Examples are shown in (33).

(33) tuo³⁵ 'to judge' 判   suo³⁵ 'to calculate' 算
      kuo³²³ 'to be wild, crazy' 癫 tsuo⁵³tsuo³³ 'claw, paw' 爪子
      kʰuo³¹ 'to hit' 打   luo³⁵ 'to be a mess' 乱

In some cases, the second vowel /o/ is lowered even farther to [a], especially in Hanyu loan words, making the diphthong an alternant of /ua/. As a result, some words may be pronounced in two ways, such as *luo³²³* and *lua³²³*, which both mean 'to take turns' 轮, and *tuo³⁵* and *tua³⁵*, which both mean 'to judge' 判. The two are not identical, however. The diphthong /ua/ occurs with a wider range of consonants (see § 2.2.2.5). Moreover, some words only allow one of these pronunciations, underscoring the difference of the two diphthongs.

2.2.2.5 Diphthong /ua/

The diphthong /ua/ appears after the stops /t, tʰ, k, kʰ/, the nasal /n/, the fricatives /s, z, x/, the affricates /ts, tsʰ/ and the lateral approximant /l/. Like all diphthongs that begin with /u/ in Khatso, /ua/ never co-occurs with labial consonants. Examples are shown in (34).

(34) tua³³ 'to hold in both hands' 端   zua²⁴ 'to rub with hands' 搓揉
      tʰua³¹ 'group, club' 团   xua⁵⁵ 'snow' 雪
      kua²⁴ 'to shave' 刮   tsua³⁵ 'to drill' 钻
      kʰua⁵⁵ 'village' 村   tsʰua³⁵ 'to drop in on someone' 串门
      nua³²³ 'girl' 女儿   lua³²³ 'to take turns' 轮
      sua²⁴sua³³ 'brush' 刷子

As mentioned above, in some cases this diphthong alternates with /uo/, because the second vowel in the latter is often lowered to [a] in certain Hanyu loan words. Thus some words may be pronounced with either diphthong, such as *luo*³²³ and *lua*³²³ 'to take turns' 轮, and *tuo*³⁵ and *tua*³⁵ which mean 'to judge' 判. However, the two are not identical. The diphthong /ua/ occurs with a wider range of consonants than /uo/ (see § 2.2.2.4), and some words only take one form or the other.

2.2.2.6 Diphthong /ɛi/

The diphthong /ɛi/ is one of the most frequently encountered syllable nuclei in the language. It occurs after the stops /p, pʰ, t, tʰ, k, kʰ/, the nasals /m, n, ŋ/, the fricatives /f, v, s, z, x/, the affricates /ts, tsʰ/ and the approximants /l, w/. It never follows the palatal series /ɲ, ɕ, tɕ, tɕʰ, j/, which co-occur with the monophthong /ɛ/ instead; thus, the two are in complementary distribution. Because the two are acoustically different, they are treated separately in this analysis, which also results in a more faithful representation of Khatso pronunciation. Examples are presented in (35).

(35) pɛi³²³ 'mountain' 山　　　　　fɛi³²³ 'to be long (of hair)' 长
　　　pʰɛi⁵³ 'to swell' 肿　　　　　vɛi³²³tʰɛi³¹ 'shoulder pole' 担子
　　　tɛi⁵³ 'to bear (fruit)' 结　　　　sɛi²⁴ 'to be sleepy' 困
　　　tʰɛi³⁵ 'to delay (treatment)' 拖　zɛi³¹ 'to use' 用
　　　kɛi³³ AGT　　　　　　　　　xɛi³⁵ 'still' 还
　　　kʰɛi³³ 'to drive (a car)' 开　　tsɛi⁵⁵ 'to occupy' 占有
　　　mɛi³³ 'to hold in the mouth' 含　tsʰɛi³³ 'rice seedling' 稻谷
　　　nɛi³¹ 'to smell' 闻　　　　　lɛi³⁵ 'to sun-dry' 晒
　　　ŋɛi³³ ASRT　　　　　　　　　wɛi³²³na³²³ 'to embarrass' 为难

The diphthong /ɛi/ often alternates with /ai/ in Hanyu loan words (see § 2.2.2.6), but /ɛi/ is much more common in the lexicon. In addition, the diphthong /ɛi/ occurs in place of the high back unrounded monophthong /ɯ/ in the *ɲa*³²³*ka*⁵³ accent (see § 2.2.4).

2.2.2.7 Diphthong /ai/

As already mentioned, the diphthong /ai/ frequently alternates with /ɛi/ (see § 2.2.2.6). Thus, /ai/ may co-occur with a wide range of consonants. This alternation occurs most often in words borrowed from Hanyu. And even though the two diphthongs are contrastive in Putonghua, villagers rarely distinguish between the two in Khatso words. For example, the verb 'to drive (a car)' 开 may be pronounced as either kʰai³³ or kʰɛi³³. However, there are a few words in which only /ai/ is used, such as *wai*³⁵*kuo*³²³ 'foreign' 外国, and thus the diphthong is considered phonemic in this analysis.

2.2.2.8 Diphthong /au/

The diphthong /au/ is one of the most frequent vowel nuclei in the language. It co-occurs with the stops /p, pʰ, t, tʰ, k, kʰ/, the nasals /m, n/, the fricatives /s, z, ɕ, x, ɣ/, the affricates /ts, tsʰ, tɕ, tɕʰ/ and the approximants /l, j/. The diphthong is also one of the few that occurs without an onset. Examples are presented in (36).

(36) pau³³ 包
pʰau³³ 'to be crisp' 脆
tau³³ 'to scold' 骂
tʰau³³ 'to pull out with hands' 掏
kau³⁵ 'to sue' 告
kʰau³⁵ 'to lean against' 靠
mau³³liɛ³³ 'donkey' 毛驴
nau³⁵ 'to die of poison' 药死
sau³³ 'to be dissolute' 骚
zau³¹ 'to freeload a meal' 蹭饭

ɕau⁵³tsʰŋ³⁵ 'to be stingy' 小气
xau³⁵ 'number' 号
ɣau³³ 'to boil (medicine)' 熬
tsau³⁵ CL:MACH 台
tsʰau³⁵ 'to swear' 咒
tɕau³³au³⁵ 'to be proud' 骄傲
tɕʰau³³tɕʰau³³ 'spoon' 勺子
lau³³ 'to pull out with a hand' 掏
jau³³ 'to be angry' 生气
au³⁵ 'to measure (with a scoop)' 用斗量

2.2.3 Triphthongs

Triphthongs occur when three vowels are produced within a single syllable, causing the tongue to move twice during production. Three triphthongs are attested in Khatso: /iau, uɛi, uai/. They occur almost exclusively in Hanyu loan words (Dai, Liu and Fu 1987: 153; Mu 2002: 33; Dai 2008: 81), and thus are not frequent in the lexicon. As a result, there are a great many phonotactic gaps associated with them in the language (see Table 2.3 above).

As with the diphthongs, the prominence of the component vowels in triphthongs, measured by duration, is predictable. The final vowel is always longer and thus more prominent than the second, which is in turn more prominent than the first. Sonority, or amplitude, does not vary across the components in Khatso and thus does not play a role in differentiating prominence in triphthongs.

And as mentioned in § 2.1.5, although the approximants /j/ and /w/ sound similar to the corresponding vowels /i/ and /u/ in speech, there are measurable acoustic differences. The approximants tend to be longer in duration, lower in intensity and have lower F1 values than the vowels. Thus, words such as /kuɛi/ consist of a consonant and a triphthong rather than a consonant cluster and a diphthong (i.e. /kwɛi/). As previously stated, there are no consonant clusters in Khatso.

2.2.3.1 Triphthong /iau/

The triphthong /iau/ follows the stops /p, pʰ, t, tʰ/, the nasal /m/ and the approximant /l/. Examples are presented in (37). Like the monophthong /i/, it never co-occurs with velar consonants.

(37) piau³³ 'to climb (pole)' 抱着爬   tʰiau³³ 'to embroider' 绣
      pʰiau³³ 'to float' 浮   miau³²³ 'to be stubborn' 固执
      tiau³³ 'to toss' 抛   liau³⁵ 'flee' 撒腿

2.2.3.2 Triphthong /uɛi/

The triphthong /uɛi/ occurs following the stops /t, tʰ, k, kʰ/, the fricatives /s, z, x/, the affricates /ts, tsʰ/ and the lateral approximant /l/. Like the diphthongs, triphthongs that begin with /u/ in Khatso never co-occur with labial consonants. Examples are shown in (38).

(38) tuɛi³⁵liɛ³²³ 'couplet' 对联   zuɛi³⁵ 'to be moist' 润
      tʰuɛi²⁴ 'to evade, shirk' 推脱   xuɛi³³ 'gray' 灰色
      kuɛi³³ 'to be well-behaved' 乖   tsuɛi³³tsʅ³¹ 'awl' 锥
      kʰuɛi³³ 'loss' 亏   tsʰuɛi³⁵ 'to be crisp' 脆
      suɛi³²³ko³¹ 'fruit' 水果   luɛi³⁵ 'to be tired' 累

As previously mentioned, the diphthong /ɛi/ often alternates with /ai/ in Khatso (see § 2.2.2.7). The triphthongs /uɛi/ and /uai/ may also do so. For example, the verb 'to blame' 怪 may be pronounced as either *kuɛi³⁵* or *kuai³⁵* with no difference in meaning. Nonetheless, there are words that take one but not the other, and so the two are considered phonemic.

The triphthong /uɛi/ also alternates with /ui/ for some speakers, so that words such as *xuɛi³³* 'gray' 灰色 and *zuɛi³⁵* 'to be soft, moist' 润 may also be pronounced *xui³³* and *zui³⁵* respectively. The diphthong /ui/ is not contrastive, however; it does not seem to occur outside these alternations. It is therefore not considered a phoneme in this analysis.

2.2.3.3 Triphthong /uai/

The triphthong /uai/ occurs mainly in loanwords following the velar stops /k, kʰ/, as shown in (39). As already noted, the diphthong /ai/ frequently alternates with /ɛi/ in Khatso words (see § 2.2.2.6). The triphthong also alternates with /uɛi/ in some words, but in others the alternation is not possible. Thus, /uai/ is considered a separate phoneme in the language.

(39) kuai³¹ 'to turn' 拐
      kʰuai³¹ 'to have a large physique' 个头大

2.2.4 The n̪a³²³ka⁵³ Accent

Small variations in vowel production have been discussed in the preceding sections. A more systematic variation pattern is found in the accent spoken in n̪a³²³ka⁵³, the western-most of the five historical Khatso villages (see § 1.3). As Mu (2002: 38–39) notes, the differences in n̪a³²³ka⁵³ pronunciation involve only a few vowels. There does not seem to be a difference among the consonants.

The main difference is that the n̪a³²³ka⁵³ accent lacks the high back vowel /ɯ/. The diphthong /ɛi/ is typically used in its place. Thus 'duck' 鸭, which is pronounced ɣɯ³⁵ by most Khatso speakers, is said ɣɛi³⁵ in n̪a³²³ka⁵³. Additional examples of this substitution are listed in Table 2.6.

However, some n̪a³²³ka⁵³ speakers may replace /ɯ/ with /ʏ/. Thus, in n̪a³²³ka⁵³ the word kɯ³¹ 'to give' is sometimes rendered as kɛi³¹ and sometimes as kʏ³¹. In addition, some speakers also replace phonemic /ɛi/ with /ʏ/, especially in the frequently-used words tɛi³¹ 'one' and tɛi³³ 'this', which are then pronounced as tʏ³¹ and tʏ³³ respectively. Although not uncommon, these two patterns do not seem to be employed by all n̪a³²³ka⁵³ speakers.

Table 2.6: Examples of n̪a³²³ka⁵³ pronunciation

Majority Pronunciation	n̪a³²³ka⁵³ Pronunciation	English	Chinese
kɯ³³	kɛi³³	'to enter'	进
kɯ²⁴	kɛi²⁴	'to get hurt'	硌
kɯ⁵³	kɛi⁵³	'to step on'	踩
kʰɯ³³	kʰɛi³³	'to rake'	刨
xɯ³³	xɛi³³	'to groan'	哼
xɯ³⁵	xɛi³⁵	'to hate'	恨
xɯ⁵³	xɛi⁵³	'to stand'	站
ɣɯ³³	ɣɛi³³	'to feel'	摸
ɣɯ⁵³	ɣɛi⁵³	'needle'	针
ɣɯ³²³	ɣɛi³²³	'to cut, slice'	切

Because Xingmeng is small and intermarriage with people from other parts of the village is common, most residents of n̪a³²³ka⁵³ interact daily with people who speak with the majority accent. Thus, some n̪a³²³ka⁵³ residents are not consistent in their use of these vowel differences, and may even make use of /ɯ/ sporadically in their speech. This is an idiolectic pattern and highly unpredictable, although it likely correlates to the degree of exposure a n̪a³²³ka⁵³ resident has to the majority accent.

In addition, the newest of the historical villages, sɿ²⁴tsʰŋ³³xo³⁵, was partially populated by families from n̪a³²³ka⁵³. Although this minor migration occurred more than a century ago at the latest, some modern residents produce n̪a³²³ka⁵³ pronunciations from time to time; this does not seem to be widespread, however.

3 Tone System

Khatso is a tonal language, which means that pitch is used to differentiate meaning at the syllable level. The language has eight distinct tonal contours. Such a large tone inventory is unusual for languages in the Ngwi family, and its origin in Khatso is unclear. It is thus one of the most noticeable features of the language.

The previous publications on Khatso largely agree on the eight tones in the inventory. Dai, Liu and Fu (1987: 153), Mu (2002: 33–34) and Dai (2008: 81) find the same inventory presented below in § 3.1. He (1989: 26) describes a seven-tone inventory, in which tone 44 is omitted and a tone 12 is identified instead of tone 323. The reason for these discrepancies is not clear, although some speakers truncate the initial fall of tone 323, producing something closer to 23, which may explain his tone 12.

This chapter begins with a discussion of each of the eight tones in § 3.1, followed by a description of the various tone change patterns in § 3.2.

3.1 Tones

Khatso has eight tones: three level tones (55, 44, 33), two rising tones (35, 24), two falling tones (53, 31) and a low falling-rising tone (323). Every syllable in the language carries a lexical tone, including clitics and grammatical particles. Toneless syllables are not attested in the language. A schematic diagram of the eight tones, presented in Figure 3.1, provides a simplified view of the paradigm. Figure 3.2 presents spectrogram pitch traces of each tone, providing a comparative snapshot of their contours.

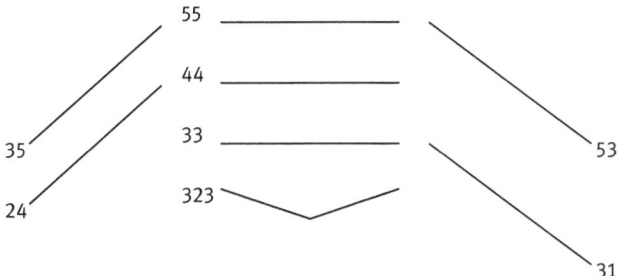

Fig. 3.1: A schematic representation of the eight tones in Khatso

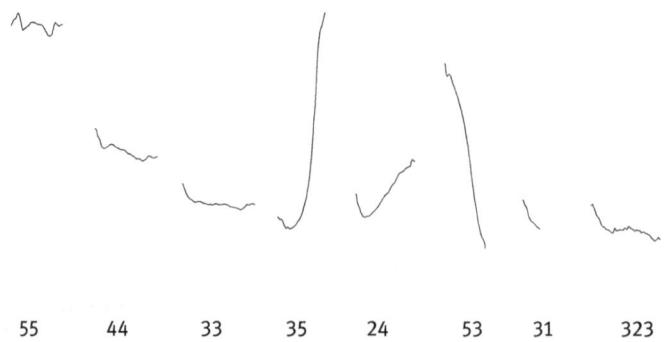

| 55 | 44 | 33 | 35 | 24 | 53 | 31 | 323 |

Fig. 2.2: Pitch traces of the eight tones produced with the syllable /sɛi/ (KL-Elicitation)

The eight tones occur with every simplex rhyme, including all of the monophthongs and both of the nasal nuclei /m, ŋ/. They also occur with most of the diphthongs and triphthongs, although there are gaps in these series. This is most likely due to the fact that most complex vowels seem to have entered the language through Hanyu loans (see § 2.2.2 and § 2.2.3), a random historical process. The one noticeable exception to this robust distribution is tone 44, which is found in only a few words in the lexicon, as discussed below. Table 3.1 presents the tone and rhyme combinations found in Khatso.

Table 3.1: Tone and rhyme combinations in Khatso

Rhyme	Tone							
	55	44	33	35	24	53	31	323
i	•	•	•	•	•	•	•	•
ɿ	•		•	•	•	•	•	•
v	•		•	•	•	•	•	•
ɯ	•		•	•	•	•	•	•
ɛ	•		•	•	•	•	•	•
ɣ	•		•	•	•	•	•	•
o	•		•	•	•	•	•	•
a	•	•	•	•	•	•	•	•
iɛ	•		•	•	•	•	•	•
io			•	•			•	•
ia			•	•				•
uo			•	•	•	•	•	•

Rhyme	Tone							
	55	44	33	35	24	53	31	323
ua	•		•	•	•	•	•	•
εi	•	•	•	•	•	•	•	•
ai			•	•	•		•	•
au	•		•	•	•	•	•	•
iau	•		•	•		•	•	•
uεi			•	•	•	•	•	•
uai			•	•			•	
m	•		•	•	•	•	•	•
ŋ	•	•	•	•	•	•	•	•

In fact, none of the tones are distributed evenly in the lexicon. Tabulating the frequency of tones in 1954 syllables in the basic vocabulary, comprising 678 monosyllabic words and 638 disyllabic words, we find that a quarter of the lexemes carry tone 33. The next most frequent tones are the low falling tone 31 (19%) and the high rising tone 35 (16%). Tone 44 is the rarest; with a token count of only six, it occurs in less than 1% of the sample. The frequency data are shown in both table and pie chart form in Table 3.2 and Figure 3.3 respectively.

Table 3.2: Frequency of the eight tones in Khatso

Tone	# of Tokens	Percentage
55	149	8%
44	6	0%
33	477	24%
35	305	16%
24	226	12%
53	179	9%
31	378	19%
323	234	12%
Total:	1954	100%

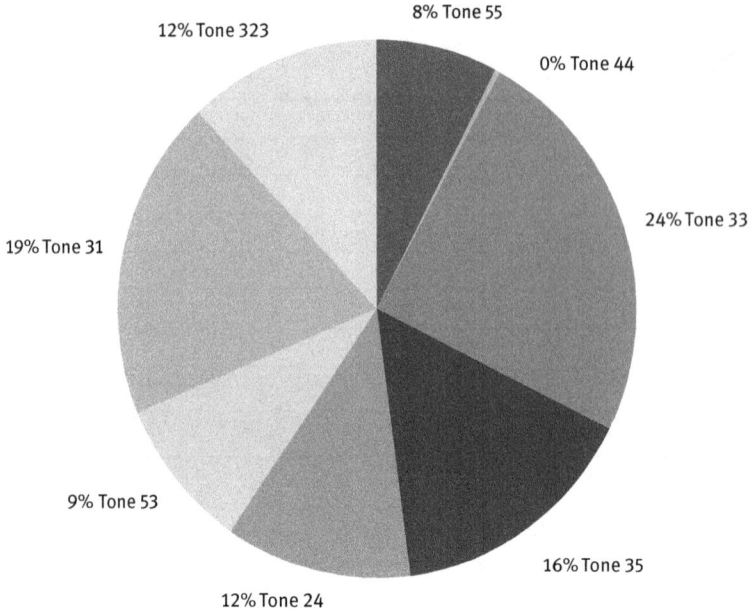

Fig. 3.3: Frequency of the eight tones in Khatso

The paucity of tone 44 is overstated in these data. The data set, which consists of lexemes from the basic vocabulary, includes few modern borrowings. These loans often contain tone 44, as Dai also notes (2008: 81). Moreover, proper names frequently contain borrowed morphemes with this tone (see Table 1–1), and these nouns are also excluded from the set. There is no question, however, that tone 44 is by far the rarest tone in the inventory. However, it is clear tone 44 is not merely an allotone of another tone; the lexemes which carry tone 44 in citation form are invariant (see § 3.1.2).

Because tone 44 occurs in few core lexemes, only two minimal tone octuplets are attested in Khatso. The monosyllables /sɛi/ and /li/ occur with all eight tones, as shown in (40). Excluding tone 44, a great many minimal septuplets can be found.

(40) sɛi^{55} 'to wipe' 擦   li^{55} 'to turn over' 翻
      sɛi^{44} 'family' 家   li^{44} 'in' 里面
      sɛi^{33} 'iron' 铁   li^{33} 'to come' 来
      sɛi^{35} 'to receive' 受   li^{35} 'to remove (clothes)' 脱
      sɛi^{24} 'to be astringent' 涩   li^{24} 'to divorce' 离婚
      sɛi^{53} 'to be gritty (food)' 牙碜 li^{53} 'street' 街
      sɛi^{31} 'peach' 桃子   li^{31} 'li (distance measure)' 里
      sɛi^{323} 'to be unusual' 特别   li^{323} 'to know how' 会

Phonation differences are not phonemic in the tone inventory. However, in citation form there are two noticeable effects linked to particular tones. The falling tones 53 and 31 may include a glottal finish, and tone 323 exhibits a breathy quality. These effects often disappear in rapid speech, except in phrase final position where extended duration may emphasize them.

Duration is also an identifiable feature of tone in citation form. Three recordings of a speaker producing the minimal octuplet /sɛi/ were examined. In each recording the eight tokens are said in the same order and with the same rhythm; there is no intervening material. Several consistent patterns emerge. Tone 323 is the longest, while tone 31 is the shortest. Among the even tones, tone 33 is the longest, tone 55 the shortest, and tone 44 falls in between. Tone 35 is the shorter of the two rising tones, and tone 31 is the shorter of the two falling tones. Pitch trace contours from a single recording, shown in Figure 3.4, illustrate the comparative lengths just described (tones 55, 44, 33 and 323 are represented by dotted lines, 35 and 24 by dashed lines, and 53 and 31 by dark solid lines). However, because length is manipulated at the prosodic level (see § 4.4.2), these differences are minimized in natural speech even to the point of disappearing altogether.

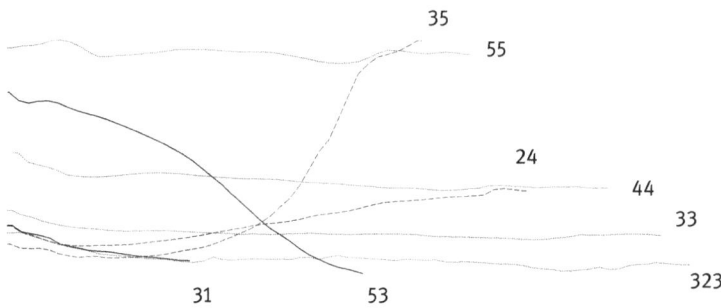

Fig. 3.4: Comparison of relative tone length in minimal octuplet /sɛi/ (KL-Elicitation)

3.1.1 Tone 55

Tone 55 is the highest even tone in the inventory. It is noticeably high, especially among female speakers.[1] In citation form, tone 55 is also the shortest of the three even

---

[1] It is also higher than the high even tone in Putonghua and at least one other Ngwi language. An informal aural comparison of the high even tones in Sadu and Khatso showed that tone 55 in Sadu has approximately the same pitch as tone 44 in Khatso. David Bradley (personal communication) notes that labeling the Khatso tone 66 may better represent its unusual height, but this notably high pitch only occurs among a subset of female speakers.

tones. Examples of words with tone 55, showing a variety of syllable onsets and nuclei, are presented in (41).

(41) ɣa⁵⁵ 'to be loose' 松   pɣ⁵⁵ 'to ferment' 发酵
     kʰɣ⁵⁵ 'to comb' 梳   sa⁵⁵ 'to leak' 漏
     ko⁵⁵ CL:PL 些   sɿ⁵⁵ 'to know, understand' 知道
     kv̩⁵⁵ 'to kneel' 跪   sɣ⁵⁵ 'book' 书
     lɣ⁵⁵ 'to molt' 蜕   tɕʰa⁵⁵ 'to grab' 抓
     m̩⁵⁵ 'to hatch' 孵   tɛi⁵⁵ 'to be thick (of liquids)' 稠
     mo⁵⁵ 'to want' 要   tʰo⁵⁵ 'to peck (at grains)' 啄
     ni⁵⁵ 'to spill' 泼   tsa⁵⁵ 'to feed' 喂
     ŋa⁵⁵ 'to borrow, lend (things)' 借   tsɿ⁵⁵ 'to dare' 敢
     pʰɣ⁵⁵ 'to peel (fruit, etc.)' 剥   xo⁵⁵ 'insect' 虫

Dai, Liu and Fu (1987: 153) state that tone 55 is approximately twice as high as tone 33. My own data show that this difference may occur among female speakers, but not in a consistent way. Moreover, the data show that the distance between the even tones is greater for women than for men.

3.1.2 Tone 44

Tone 44 is the second of the three even tones. And as already mentioned, it is rather rare, as Dai, Liu and Fu (1987: 153) and Mu (2002: 34) also observe. The evidence suggests that despite its rarity, it is not merely an allotone but a toneme of its own accord, a situation Mu corroborates. The words that carry tone 44 in citation form are invariant; the tone never changes in discourse. And because tone 44 occurs in some very basic words and grammatical particles, as shown in (42), it is frequently encountered in natural speech. Moreover, there are tone change patterns that raise lexical tone 33 to tone 44 (see § 3.2.4 and § 3.2.5), further increasing its frequency in discourse. Dai (2008: 81) states that tone 44 mostly appears in Hanyu loan words – it is common in proper names, for example (see Table 1.1) – and this may be one of the reasons it emerged in the language. In many cases, an obvious counterpart in Chinese can be found, providing evidence for borrowing. But, this is not always the case, and thus it is not clear that all words with lexical tone 44 are loans. Some may have evolved through the tone change pattern just mentioned.

(42) li⁴⁴ 'in' 里
 mɛi⁴⁴ CL:GEN 个
 mɛi⁴⁴ 'very' 很
 mɛi⁴⁴ DISC.EMP
 ŋ³³si⁴⁴ 'or' 或
 ŋ⁴⁴li³³ 'but' 但是

 sɛi⁴⁴ 'family' 家
 sɛi⁴⁴ TOP, TMP
 tɤ⁴⁴ CLNK
 tɤ⁴⁴ 'all' 都
 tɤ⁴⁴ STAT.EMP

3.1.3 Tone 33

Tone 33 is the lowest and the longest of the even tones. It is also the most frequent tone in the lexicon (see Table 3.2 above). Examples of words with tone 33, showing a variety of syllable onsets and nuclei, are presented in (43).

(43) a³³ 'that' 那
 ɕo³³ 'to be clean' 干净
 fɤ³³ 'to be dry' 干
 kʐ³³ 'to do, make' 做
 la³³ 'to compare' 比
 mo³³ 'mother' 母亲
 nɛi³³ 2SG 你
 pau³³ 'bundle' 包
 ŋa³³ 1SG 我
 sɛi³³ 'iron' 铁

 sʐ³³ 'to die' 死
 tɕɛ³³ 'to be full' 满
 to³³ 'also' 也
 tʰiau³³ 'to embroider' 绣
 tsʰʐ³³ 'to be fat' 胖
 xa³³ 'to offer as a gift' 送
 pʰɤ³³ 'to be hot and spicy' 辣
 vɤ³³ 'to be round' 圆
 wa³³ 'tile' 瓦
 ɣ³³ 'to count' 数

3.1.4 Tone 35

Tone 35 is the higher of the two rising tones. In citation form it tends to be shorter and rise faster than tone 24. Examples of words with tone 35, showing a variety of syllable onsets and nuclei, are listed in (44).

(44) fɤ³⁵ 'portion' 份
 ɣɯ³⁵ 'duck' 鸭
 kɤ³⁵ 'to dig' 挖
 kʰo³⁵ 'to pound' 拍
 la³⁵ 'to air-dry' 晾
 lo³⁵ 'to herd' 放
 mɛi³⁵ 'to hide (oneself)' 躲
 na³⁵ 'to be deep' 深
 nʐ³⁵ 'to pinch' 捏
 ŋ³⁵ 'to pick up with chopsticks' 夹

 pa³⁵ 'bowl' 碗
 sʐ³⁵ 'to be new' 新
 tɕa³⁵ 'to hoe' 耙
 tʰa³⁵ 'to be hot (of food)' 烫
 to³⁵ 'hole' 洞
 tsʰɛi³⁵ 'scale' 秤
 tsi³⁵ 'to be quiet' 安静
 va³⁵ 'ten thousand' 万
 xɯ³⁵ 'to hate' 恨
 zʐ³⁵ 'hundred million' 亿

3.1.5 Tone 24

Tone 24 is the lower of the two rising tones. In citation form it tends to be longer and change pitch at a slower rate than tone 35. Examples of words with tone 24, showing a variety of syllable onsets and nuclei, are presented in (45).

(45)   ɕo²⁴ 'to be fragrant' 香   sʅ²⁴ 'to choose' 选
        kʰɤ²⁴ 'to carve' 刻   tɕa²⁴ 'to pen (livestock)' 关
        ko³⁵ 'to roast' 烤   tʰi²⁴ 'to paste' 贴
        fa²⁴ 'to distribute' 发   to²⁴ 'to light (lamp)' 点
        lɛi²⁴ 'to strap tight' 勒   tsa²⁴ 'to seek' 找
        m̩²⁴ 'to be tall' 高   tsʰɛi²⁴ 'to guess' 猜
        nɤ²⁴ 'to be low' 低   vɤ²⁴ 'to be horizontal' 横
        ŋ̍²⁴ 'red' 红   xo²⁴ 'box' 盒子
        o²⁴ 'to be ferocious' 凶   xɯ²⁴ 'to dry by a fire' 烘
        po²⁴ CL:ROD 支   zʅ²⁴ 'boat' 船

3.1.6 Tone 53

Tone 53 is the higher of the two falling tones. Its duration also tends to be longer than its lower counterpart. In citation form, it often ends with a glottal stop, though this feature typically disappears in natural speech. Examples of words with tone 53, showing a variety of syllable onsets and nuclei, are listed in (46).

(46)   kʰo⁵³ 'year' 年   tɕa⁵³ 'to be cold' 冷
        ɕi⁵³ 'eight' 八   tɤ⁵³ 'to hold up' 撑
        ɣɤ⁵³ 'to row (boat)' 划   tsʰʅ⁵³ 'goat' 山羊
        ka⁵³ 'to drive out' 赶   tsi⁵³ 'to cut with scissors' 剪
        lo⁵³ 'to be enough' 够   vi⁵³ 'to wear' 穿
        m̩⁵³ 'to blow' 吹   wa⁵³ 'pig' 猪
        ma⁵³ 'to pile' 堆   xɯ⁵³ 'to stand' 站
        n̥a⁵³ 'to paste' 粘   jɛ⁵³ 'to be smooth' 滑
        pʰi⁵³ 'to clean (fish)' 剖   zʅ⁵³ 'to sleep' 睡
        si⁵³ 'to kill' 杀   i⁵³ 'to be drunk' 醉

3.1.7 Tone 31

Tone 31 is the lower of the two falling tones. It is also the shortest tone in the inventory. In citation form it typically ends with a glottal stop, as Dai, Liu and Fu (1987: 153) also observe. In natural speech, however, the glottal stop is often replaced by a creaky-voiced transition to the next syllable or it may disappear altogether. Interestingly, the negative marker *ma³¹* tends to almost always retain the glottal stop in discourse. Examples of words with tone 31, showing a variety of syllable onsets and nuclei, are presented in (47).

(47) ɣɯ³¹ 'lotus' 藕   sa³¹ 'meat' 肉
     kɤ³¹ 'to run' 跑   sɹ̩³¹ 'blood' 血
     kʰa³¹ 'to be bitter' 苦   tɕʰa³¹ 'to crawl' 爬
     n̪a³¹ 'to speak' 说   tʰɤ³¹ 'bucket' 桶
     la³¹ 'tiger' 老虎   ti³¹ 'to hibernate (of insects)' 蛰
     ŋ³¹ 'two' 二   tsʰau³¹ 'to have a fishy smell' 腥
     miɛ³¹ 'destiny' 命运   vɤ³¹ 'to sift' 筛
     na³¹ 'to rest' 休息   xo³¹ 'to be soft' 软
     o³¹ 'vegetable' 菜   jɛ³¹ 'to flow' 流
     pa³¹ 'to be thin (of things)' 薄   zɹ̩³¹ 'to be heavy' 重

3.1.8 Tone 323

Tone 323 is the most complex tone in the inventory, containing both a fall and a rise in the same contour. As a result, in citation form it has the longest duration of all the tones. Often, it is produced with a breathy voice in slow, careful speech. In discourse, however, the contour may be truncated and the breathiness may disappear. Common truncations include clipping the initial fall, producing something closer to 23, or abbreviating the dip, so that the contour is flattened. In both cases, however, the pitch remains lower than either tone 24 or tone 33 and is therefore still audibly contrastive. Examples of words with tone 323, showing a variety of syllable onsets and nuclei, are presented in (48).

(48) tso³²³ 'to have' 有   pɛi³²³ 'mountain' 山
     i³²³ 'to go' 去   sɛi³²³ 'deity' 神
     fɛi³²³ 'to be long (hair)' 长   tɕa³²³ 'road' 路
     ɣɯ³²³ 'to cut' 割   tɛi³²³ 'to be shallow' 浅
     ka³²³ 'to walk' 走   tsʰa³²³ 'silkworm' 蚕
     la³²³ 'gong' 铜锣   tsɹ̩³²³ 'liquor' 酒
     m̩³²³ 'field' 田   vɤ³²³ 'to buy' 买
     mo³²³ 'to see' 看见   xa³²³ 'hundred' 百
     n̪ɛ³²³ 'to be sweet' 甜   zɤ³²³ 'post, pillar' 柱子
     ŋ³²³ 'day' 天   jo³²³ 'sheep' 绵羊

3.1.9 Tone Variation

In Khatso, every syllable carries a lexical tone. There are a handful of words, however, that may occur with more than one tone without a change in meaning. These variations are lexicalized; they are not a result of tone sandhi. For example, the plural human morpheme $tsʰɤ^{33}$ 们 may also be uttered as $tsʰɤ^{31}$. Thus in discourse 'we' 我们 may appear as $nɛi^{33}tsʰɤ^{33}$ or $nɛi^{33}tsʰɤ^{31}$ depending on speaker preference. Likewise, 'day' 天 may be pronounced as either $ŋ^{33}$ or $ŋ^{323}$ in various collocations.

There are also instances where a single morpheme in Hanyu was borrowed into Khatso with different tones, likely because the loans were adopted at different times. For example, the basic word for 'dragon' 龙 in Khatso is lo^{31}. However, in certain borrowed compounds it appears with tones 24 and 323. For example, in 'dragon pool' 龙潭 it may be pronounced with either tone: $lo^{24}tʰa^{33}$ or $lo^{323}tʰa^{33}$. In $tɕo^{31}lo^{323}tsʰŋ^{323}$ 'nine dragon pond' 九龙池, the morpheme takes tone 323. The use of tone 31 in these compounds is ungrammatical.

3.2 Tone Change

Tone sandhi describes the phonological process whereby one lexical tone changes due to the influence of another, usually adjacent, tone (Ladefoged 2006: 252). Khatso has a number of tone change patterns. Some appear to be phonologically motivated and thus may be considered traditional tone sandhi. These are typically restricted to very specific environments in the language, such as in numeral and classifier collocations or in reduplicative constructions. Other tone change patterns, such as tone fusion and the focus pattern, are triggered in part by discourse factors and thus do not easily fit the definition of sandhi. One pattern, found in causative verbs, has been lexicalized and thus can no longer be considered an active phonological process, though it is included below. Lexicalized variation in tone, unrelated to any change process, is discussed in § 3.1.9.

Tone change in Khatso is not fully described in the previous literature. He (1989) does not discuss the topic at all. Dai, Liu and Fu (1987: 153) note that certain verbs change tone to indicate a causative meaning, and that the numerals 'three', 'four' and 'nine' change tone with classifiers, a pattern found in many Ngwi languages (Bradley 2005a). A third pattern mentioned — when the first tone of a disyllabic word is 55 it changes to tone 53 — is not found in my data. Mu (2002: 33) states that tone sandhi occurs in natural speech, but that there is no regular pattern because it is a result of economy in pronunciation. Mu also cites a pattern wherein certain classifiers adopt tone 24 after nouns, such as ma^{24} 只 and $kə^{24}$ 问, but according to my data these are their lexical tones. Dai (2008: 81) repeats the examples mentioned in Dai, Liu and Fu 1987, and notes that in reduplicated noun compounds the second tone may change if it is not tone 33. Examples of the latter are few in my data and there is no discernable pattern, suggesting this phenomenon is lexicalized. Thus, the previous research identifies lexical differences and simple tone sandhi, but largely overlooks the more complex patterns that occur in discourse.

3.2.1 Numerals 'Three', 'Four' and 'Nine'

In Khatso, the numerals si^{33} 'three' 三, xy^{33} 'four' 四 and ky^{33} 'nine' 九 change tone when used with certain classifiers. In citation form and general counting, they retain tone 33, and in fact they are the only numerals below ten that carry this tone. When followed by a classifier with tone 55, 53 or 31, they may take tone 35. While the change may occur with any classifier that carries one of these tones, it appears to be obligatory with only a handful, shown in Table 3.3. Note that this pattern only applies to the numerals below ten; in higher numeral compounds, such as 'thirteen', 'thirty four' and 'seventy nine', these morphemes carry a different lexical tone and thus sandhi is not triggered in that environment.

Table 3.3: Classifiers that trigger obligatory sandhi in numerals

Classifier	English	Chinese	Types of Nouns
ko^{55}	'crowd, group', PL	些, 拨	people, animals in groups; any noun made plural
$tɕi^{55}$	'type, sort', 'phrase', 'item'	种, 句, 件	any noun; audible items: language, speech, noises; incidents: events, accidents
$py̱^{53}$	'can, jar'	罐	liquids: beverages, pickled items, etc.
$nɛi^{31}$	—	个	(alternant of general classifier ma^{24})

This pattern is optional, however, with most classifiers that carry tones 55, 53 or 31. For example, the phrase 'three flowers', shown in (49), is grammatical either way. Table 3.4 below lists the classifiers with which the change is optional; more detail on these and other classifiers is found in Table 3.11.

(49)   *No tone change*   *Tone change*

	$vi^{53}li^{24}$	**si^{33}**	to^{31}		$vi^{53}li^{24}$	**si^{35}**	to^{31}
	flower	three	CL:ITEM		flower	three	CL:ITEM
	花	三	朵		花	三	朵

        'three flowers'   'three flowers'
        三朵花   三朵花
        (KL-Elicitation)

Table 3.4: Classifiers that trigger optional sandhi in 'three', 'four' and 'nine'

Classifier	English	Chinese	Types of Nouns
fy⁵⁵	'pair, set'	副	paired items: couplets, eyeglasses, dentures; items in sets: playing cards, mahjong tiles
ɣɯ⁵³	'household'	户	organized groups of people: families, businesses, institutions
jɛ³¹	'page'	页	page in bound items
jo⁵³	'dose'	剂, 种	items consumed in measured increments: medicine, herbs, spices; languages; school classes
ka³¹	–	枝	long, rigid, smooth items: flagpoles, rifles, sticks
kʰɯ³¹	'lump'	块	mineral pieces: coal, dirt
kʰo⁵³	'year'	年, 岁	(time, age)
kʰuai³¹	'yuan'	块	(money)
kʰuɛi³¹	'bundle'	捆	bundles of larger items: clothes, paper, etc.
la⁵³	'piece', 'face'	块, 面	pieces of larger items: cloth, land, rocks, glass, plastic, metal; flat items: mirrors, signs, cloth, framed pictures, drapes, carpets
li³¹	'li'	里	unit of distance
lo³¹	'ounce'	两	unit of weight
m̩³¹	'6ᵗʰ of an acre'	亩	unit of land
ma⁵³	'pile'	堆	items often piled: grain, coal, clothes, etc.
ma⁵⁵	–	母女	(family groups)
mo³¹	'couple'	对	paired humans (husband & wife)
pa³¹	'roll'	卷	items in rolls: paper, cloth
pa⁵³	'handle', 'stick'	把, 根	items lifted in one hand, such as those with handles: teapots, pitchers, spoons; and those without: firewood, split wood
pa⁵⁵	–	父子	(family groups)
pɛi³¹	'volume'	本	items with bound paper: books, magazines, notebooks, etc.
piɛ⁵⁵liɛ⁵⁵	–	子孙	(family groups)
pɤ³¹	'piece'	块	increments of land: farms, fields
tɕa⁵⁵	'piece'	张	flat paper items: loose paper, newspaper, paintings, stamps

Classifier	English	Chinese	Types of Nouns
tɕɛ³¹	'roll'	卷	items in rolls: paper, cloth
tɕʰa³¹	'leaf', 'slice'	叶, 片	small, thin items: leaves, slices of larger items
tɛi³¹	'ten liters'	斗	unit of weight
tɤ⁵³	'sack', 'womb'	袋, 胎	items traditionally carried in bags: rice, food, things; items in wombs: litter of animals
tʰi̭³¹	'leg'	肘, 只	meat; one of a pair
ti⁵³	'dot, piece, small amount'	点	small things or amounts: small items, portion of food, portion of mass nouns, etc.
tiɛ⁵⁵	'pair'	双	paired items: gloves, couples (human), twins (human and animal)
to³¹	–	朵	flowers
tsɤ³¹	'bundle'	捆	bundles of larger items: clothes, paper, etc.
tsʰŋ³¹	'piece'	块	items that come in pieces: wood, bricks, tiles
tsŋ⁵⁵	'row'	行	items in rows: trees, corn, books, Chinese characters
tɤ̭³¹	–	堵, 朵	walls; clouds
xa⁵³	'night'	夜	unit of time

For a few of these classifiers, one pattern seems to be preferred over the other, although both are acceptable. For example, the tone change is preferred but not obligatory with *li³¹* 'li (distance measure)' 里, *je³¹* 'page' 页 and *pa⁵³* 'stick (of firewood)' 根, while *tsŋ⁵⁵* 'row (of books)' 行 is more likely not to trigger the change. In addition, there are a few classifiers that do not fit this tone pattern. The human classifier *jo³⁵* 位 and the classifiers *pʰɛi³²³* 'row' 排 and *tʰɛi³²³* 'event' 件 optionally trigger sandhi even though they do not carry tone 55, 53 or 31.

A tone sandhi pattern involving the numerals 'three', 'four' and 'nine' is also observed in Lisu, another Ngwi language spoken in northern Yunnan (Bradley 2005b: 226–27). However, in Lisu the change results in a different set of tones. Nonetheless, sharing such a unique feature highlights the close relationship between Khatso and other languages in the Ngwi family.

Numerals are described in § 6.1, and classifiers are discussed in § 6.2.

3.2.2 Verb Collocations with *li³²³* 'to come' and *i³²³* 'to go'

When *li³²³* 'to come' 来 and *i³²³* 'to go' 去 occur as matrix verbs, they retain their lexical tones of 323. But, when they take part in serial verb constructions, where they combine with other verbs to form a unitary predicate (see § 8.8), they must change to tone 33. In these verb serializations, *li³³* and *i³³* are always the last in the series, as (50) and (51) illustrate.

(50) tɕa³²³   ka³²³   za⁵³   i³³   tɤ³⁵   ŋɛi³³.
    road   walk   descend   go   PROG.FOC   ASRT
    路   走   下   去
    '(We) went down (there) by walking.'
    是走路下去的。
    (GCS-Weddings)

(51) i³²³tɕa⁵³   mau³⁵   to⁵³   li³³   tɤ³³ wa³³.
    water   gush   exit   come   INCP
    水   冒   出   来
    'Water began to gush out.'
    水冒出来了。
    (HPH-Horse Dug Well)

This change likely evolved to differentiate the verb *li³²³* 'to go' from the homophonous auxiliary *li³²³* 'to know how' 会. The latter always carries tone 323 and follows the main verb in a phrase. Without the tone change, the resulting homophony would create confusion between the two constructions. Because *i³²³* occurs in the same syntactic environments as *li³²³*, it likely conformed through analogical change.

3.2.3 Reduplication in Adjectival Constructions

Descriptors in Khatso are stative verbs and do not require the use of the copula. For example, *jo³³* translates as 'to be slow' 慢 and thus S alone may create a grammatically complete phrase. When not functioning as predicates, stative verbs may be reduplicated for emphasis. This is, in fact, the basis for the *za³¹ ni³³* construction which has adverbial, adjectival and nominal functions (see § 8.1.2.2). Tone change is often triggered by the reduplication of these verbs. The general pattern is that if the first syllable carries tone 33, 24, 53, 31 or 323, it changes to tone 35. Some words that carry tone 31 show sandhi on the second syllable instead, which takes tone 323. Syllables that carry tone 55 or 35 do not change. Thus, *kʰa³¹* 'to be bitter' 苦 becomes *kʰa³⁵kʰa³¹*, *tsʰɣ³³* 'to be fat' 胖 becomes *tsʰɣ³⁵tsʰɣ³³* and *tɕi³¹* 'to be quick' 快 becomes *tɕi³¹tɕi³²³*, but *tʰa⁵⁵* 'to be sharp' 尖 retains its original tone in $tʰa^{55}tʰa^{55}$. Additional examples for each pattern are provided in (52).

(52) *Tones 33, 24, 53, 31, 323 in first syllable → tone 35*
  ɕo³³ 'to be clean' 干净   ɕo³⁵ɕo³³ 干干净净
  tshʅ³³ 'white' 白   tshʅ³⁵tshʅ³³ 白白
  ŋ²⁴ 'red' 红   ŋ³⁵ŋ²⁴ 红红
  kʰɣ²⁴ 'to be empty' 空   kʰɣ³⁵kʰɣ²⁴ 空空
  na⁵³ 'black' 黑   na³⁵na⁵³ 黑黑
  pʰiɛ³¹ 'to be flat' 平   pʰiɛ³⁵pʰiɛ³¹ 平平
  ȵɛ³²³ 'to be sweet' 甜   ȵɛ³⁵ȵɛ³²³ 甜甜

Tone 31 in second syllable → tone 323
  mo³¹ 'to be old' 老   mo³¹mo³²³ 'to be old' 老老
  ȵa³¹ 'to be many' 多   ȵa³¹ȵa³²³ 'to be many' 多多

Tones 55, 35 unchanged
  lv⁵⁵ 'green' 绿   lv⁵⁵lv⁵⁵ 绿绿
  pʰɣ⁵⁵ 'to be dense (of vegetation)' 茂密   pʰɣ⁵⁵pʰɣ⁵⁵ 茂茂密密
  na³⁵ 'to be deep' 深   na³⁵na³⁵ 深深
  i³⁵ 'to be dirty' 脏   i³⁵i³⁵ 脏脏

Not all reduplicated stative verbs follow this pattern. Some show no sandhi at all, and for others the change is optional. For example, reduplicating *na²⁴* 'to be good' 好 yields *na²⁴na²⁴* rather than the ungrammatical *na³⁵na²⁴. The verb *ɣɤ³¹* 'to be big' 大 has three possibilities. It may follow either pattern or show no change — *ɣɤ³¹ɣɤ³²³*, *ɣɤ³⁵ɣɤ³¹* and *ɣɤ³¹ɣɤ³¹* are all grammatical. These variations are not predictable; rather, they seem to be the result of routinization.

The reduplication of verbs is also employed in the formation of polar questions (see § 12.4.1), but this function never triggers tone change. For example, the questions *tɕi³¹ tɕi³¹?* 'is (it) fast?' 快不快? and *ɕo³³ ɕo³³?* 'are (they) clean?' 干净不干净? show no sandhi even though in the reduplicated adjectival construction these verbs typically change. As a result, the sandhi pattern helps differentiate the two uses in discourse.

Stative verbs are described in more detail in § 8.1.2.

3.2.4 Marked Pattern

There is a tone change pattern that occurs in three different environments. Because it has different functions in each environment, it seems that the change does not have a particular meaning. Rather, it is a marked pattern that is defined by the discourse context in which it appears. This kind of multifunctionality is commonplace in Khatso; many grammatical particles operate in a similar manner (see Appendix A).

The three environments are varied. The first involves the backgrounding particle ni^{323} and its temporal counterpart $ta^{31}ni^{323}$, the topic marker ni^{31} and the clause linker to^{33}, all of which mark non-final phrases in discourse. In the second environment, the pattern has an imperative function, replacing overt imperative particles. The third environment contains the currently relevant state marker wa^{33}, but its purpose is currently unclear.

Regardless of function, the fundamental pattern of change remains the same. Syllables with tone 33 change to tone 44, and those with tones 31 and 323 both change to tone 24. The other five tones are unaffected. Remarkably, the triggers for the change carry a variety of tones and come from all word classes, suggesting that it is the environment rather than a particular tone combination or syntactic category that forces the issue. Moreover, the specifics of each environment determine which syllable changes tone, as outlined in the three sections that follow. The possible historical origin of the pattern is discussed along with the final pattern (see § 3.2.4.3).

3.2.4.1 Non-Final Phrases in Discourse

There are several grammatical particles in Khatso that mark phrases that are non-final in discourse, meaning that the speaker intends to continue providing information. The most frequent markers — the backgrounding particle ni^{323}, its temporal counterpart $ta^{31}ni^{323}$, the topic marker ni^{31} and the clause linker to^{33} 'also, and' — also trigger the marked tone change pattern. The change occurs on the syllable preceding the marker, regardless of whether it is a stand-alone word or part of a multisyllabic word. Note, however, that $ta^{31}ni^{323}$ operates as a unit in triggering tone change; ta^{31} is never affected by its adjacency to ni^{323}. Despite the fact that the four markers have different lexical tones, they all induce the same pattern of change. That is, if the syllable preceding the marker carries tone 33, it changes to tone 44, and if it carries either tone 31 or 323, it changes to tone 24. The other five tones remain unchanged. The pattern ensures that the markers are always preceded by a tone contour higher than the ones they themselves carry, thereby phonologically highlighting their grammatical function of marking non-final phrases in discourse. Examples of the three changes are illustrated in (53). Two examples of tones that do not change before the markers, here tones 55 and 53, are shown in (54).

(53) *Tone 33 tsʰŋ³³ 'to be white' 白 → tone 44 tsʰŋ⁴⁴*
tsʰɛi³³ **tsʰŋ⁴⁴** to³³   ma³¹   ɕi³³   tɕa³³ wa³³.
rice   be.white   also   NEG   be.accustomed   send   CRS
米   白   也   不   习惯   送
'(We) also wouldn't send white rice.'
大米也不送了。
(YJF-Weddings)

Tone 31 ɳa³¹ 'to be many' 多 → tone 24 ɳa²⁴
fv̩³³   **ɳa²⁴**   ni³¹
raise many   TOP
养   多
'(they) were raising a lot'
养多了呢
(YJR-Training)

Tone 323 tʰɛi³²³ 'very' 很 → tone 24 tʰɛi²⁴
lau³³ti³³   pɛi³¹sɻ³⁵   na²⁴   **tʰɛi²⁴**   ni³²³
grandfather basically   be.good very   BKGD
老爹   本事   好   很
'(his) grandfather was basically very good'
爷爷本事很好了呢
(YJR-Grandfather)

(54) *Other tones remain unchanged*
mo³¹ la²⁴ **ko⁵⁵** ni³¹   i²⁴fa³³   ɳa³¹   ma³¹   li³²³.
old   REL   CL:PL   TOP   more   speak   NEG   know.how
老   些   更   说   不   会
'The old ones, (they) are even less able to speak (it).'
那些老的呢，更不会说。
(YAY-Erasers)

xa³³ni³³   **kʰo⁵³**   ni³²³   tsʰŋ³¹ma³³   tsʰŋ³³   ɳa³¹?
what   CL:TMP   BKGD   wife   marry   CNT.Q
什么   岁   太太   娶
'At what age did (he) take a wife?'
几岁结婚的？
(KL-Grandfather)

to³³ 'also, and' has a number of functions in discourse (see Chapter 16), and tone change is triggered in all of them. In its primary use, it is a prototypical adverb that modifies verbs in simple clauses, as shown in (55). It also has a more overtly syntactic function of linking clauses. Occurring at the end of the first clause, as in (56), *to³³* modifies neither the first verb nor the second; it serves only to link the two clauses in a coordination-like construction (see § 13.1.1). The adverbial use of *to³³* clearly has nothing to do with signaling a non-final phrase, yet the tone change pattern almost always occurs in this position. This is likely to be a case of diachronic regularization. Initially linked to one use, for example clause linkage, the tone change pattern has come to be associated with all uses, including the adverbial function.

(55) *to³³ as adverb*
  pʰi²⁴ŋ²⁴tɕʰi³¹   tɕi⁵⁵   **to³³**   lo³¹sŋ²⁴   na²⁴   ma³¹   li³²³.
  Hanyu   CL:TYPE also   much   hear   NEG   know.how
  汉语   种   也   多   听   不   会
  '(I) also couldn't understand much Mandarin.'
  也听不懂很多汉语。
  (YAY-Erasers)

(56) *to³³ as clause linker*
  i³²³tɕa⁵³   ma³¹   tso²⁴   **to³³**,   ta²⁴to³³   tsʰo³³   tso³²³   ŋa³²³   ma³¹   ta³²³.
  water   NEG   EXIST   also   still   people   EXIST   get   NEG   able
  水   不   有   也   还   人   有   得   不   能
  'There was no water, and people still weren't able to live (there).'
  没有水呢，还是不可能居住人。
  (PYX-Dragon Pools)

Regardless of the trigger, tone change and grammatical markers work together to mark non-final phrases. They are, in fact, redundant cues. As a result, the marker itself may be omitted in discourse, leaving the tone change alone to signal a speaker's intent. In spontaneous speech, *to³³* is omitted much more frequently than either *ni³¹* or *ni³²³*. In the phrase shown in (57), three successive intonation units omit *to³³*. The first clause establishes an ability to sew, and each successive clause adds another item that the speaker knows how to make. The adverb 'also' is never spoken, but the tone change in each noun lets us know that it is meant. In fact, speakers routinely add the adverb when translating such phrases into Chinese. Respectively, the changes are: *wi³²³jau³³* → *wi³²³jau⁴⁴*, *tʰo³³pɛi³³* → *tʰo³³pɛi⁴⁴*, and *tʰo³³* → *tʰo⁴⁴*.

(57) ŋa³³   kʰa³¹kʰv̩³³   mɛi⁴⁴   sa³³   tɕi⁵³   li³²³,
      1SG   hat   CL:GEN   sew   wear   know.how
      我   帽子   个   逢   戴   会
      'I can sew hats to wear,'
      我会做帽子戴，

wi³²³**jau⁴⁴** sa³³ li³²³,
apron sew know.how
围腰 逢 会
'(I) can also sew aprons,'
也会缝围腰，

tʰo³³**pɛi⁴⁴** sa³³ li³²³,
Chinese.robe sew know.how
褂子 逢 会
'(I) can also sew Chinese-style robes,'
也会缝褂子，

tʰo⁴⁴ sa³³ li³²³.
clothes sew know.how
衣服 逢 会
'(I) can also sew clothes.'
也会缝衣服。
(WYY-Sewing)

Omitting the marker seems to depend largely on speaker preference. However, there is one very productive construction involving *to³³* in which the marker is almost always omitted. This is a construction that discusses the degree of ability in doing a given task. It is formed by stating the verb, adding *to³³*, repeating the verb and describing the degree, such as in *pʏ⁵³ to³³ pʏ⁵³ ma³¹ xo²⁴* 'plays (a stringed instrument) but plays badly' in which *ma³¹ xo²⁴* 'NEG good' describes the inability 'to play' *pʏ⁵³*. Two additional examples from discourse are shown in (58) and (59). In both, *to³³* is omitted from between the verbs, but the first verb changes tone as if it were there. Note that the pattern here is different from that occurring in the reduplication of stative verbs (see § 3.2.3), and the presence of tone change also differentiates it from the formulation of polar questions (see § 12.4.1).

(58) **ṇa²⁴** ṇa³¹ ma³¹ xo²⁴ mɛi⁴⁴.
speak speak NEG be.correct DSC.EMP
说 说 不 对
'(I) spoke but spoke (it) badly.'
说也说不好。
(YAY-Erasers)

(59) **sa⁴⁴** sa³³ li³²³ tsɣ²⁴ ma³¹ xɛi³⁵ kɣ³³ li³²³ ja³³.
 sew sew know.how everything make know.how IPFV.EMP
 逢 逢 会 什么 做 会
 '(I) sewed and knew how to sew, could make everything.'
 逢也会逢，什么都会做。
 (WYY-Sewing)

3.2.4.2 Imperatives

Imperative phrases — which encompass commands, instructions and suggestions — are typically marked by grammatical particles. However, the marked tone change pattern may replace the particles in certain environments (see § 12.2.5). In this construction, when an imperative particle is omitted, the final syllable remaining in the clause — typically the verb or an aspect marker — changes according to the pattern to signal that it is an imperative expression. That is, tone 33 changes to tone 44 and tones 31 and 323 both change to tone 24; the other five tones do not change. In addition, the classifier phrase *tɛi³¹ tʰɤ⁵⁵* 'awhile' or a similar phrase such as *tɛi³¹ti⁵³* 'a piece, a little', is typically required in these phrases. Examples of the three changes are illustrated in (60). This pattern is not obligatory, but rather seems to be a matter of speaker preference.

(60) *Tone 33 m̩³³ 'to make'* → *tone 44 m̩⁴⁴*
 tsa³²³ tɛi³¹ tʰɤ⁵⁵ **m̩⁴⁴**.
 rice one CL:TMP make.IMP
 饭 一 下 做
 'Cook for a while.'
 做一下饭吧。
 (KL-Elicitation)

 Tone 31 tɕi³¹ 'to be quick' → *tone 24 tɕi²⁴*
 ti⁵³ **tɕi²⁴**. ɣa³¹ tsʰŋ⁵³ n̪a³¹ jo³³ ja³³.
 CL:PCE be.quick.IMP strength exit speak must IPFV.EMP
 点 快 力 出 说 应该
 'Hurry. Use (some) effort to speak up.'
 快点。出点力气说。
 (KL-Grandfather)

Tone 323 pa³²³ 'to help' → tone 24 pa²⁴

ŋ³¹	si³³	ma⁴⁴	tsʰua³³	tsɤ³¹	**pa²⁴**.
two	three	CL:GEN	sew	CONT	help.IMP
二	三	个	穿		帮

'(I'll) help (you) sew two or three.'
帮你穿两三个。
(KL-Sewing)

Other tones remain unchanged

i²⁴tɕʰɛ³²³	tɛi³¹	tʰɤ⁵⁵	**pɤ⁵³**!
qin	one	CL:TMP	play
琴	一	下	弹

'Play (your) qin for a while!'
弹一下琴！
(YAY-Erasers)

Although this pattern is productive in elicitation, in discourse it mainly occurs with four particular morphemes in which the resulting tone is 24 — mirroring the tone of the basic imperative particle *jɛ²⁴*. These four morphemes are frequent in imperatives, which is likely why they are the main recipients of the change. They are the verb *pa³²³* 'to help'; the indirect causative verb *kɯ³¹* 'to give'; the verb *tɕʰɛ³¹* 'to open', which conveys a sense of trial and error; and the continuous aspect marker *tsɤ³¹*, which urges the addressee to proceed with the action. Details on their use in discourse are described more fully in § 12.2.5. By contrast, verbs with tone 33 typically retain the imperative marker in discourse, making the change to tone 44 rather rare with the imperative function. Thus, although the changes are based on the marked tone change pattern, in actual practice it is rather different, employed mainly to replicate the tone of the imperative particle *jɛ²⁴* on a few morphemes frequently involved in imperative expressions.

3.2.4.3 Aspect Marker *wa³³*

The marked tone change pattern also occurs with *wa³³*, which is the currently relevant state aspect marker (see § 9.2.2). In this construction, it is the syllable preceding *wa³³* — which is almost always a verb — that must change according to the pattern. That is, tone 33 changes to tone 44 and tones 31 and 323 both change to tone 24; the other five tones remain unchanged. The pattern is obligatory in this environment, regardless of verbal semantics or discourse context; failing to produce it is considered ungrammatical. No other aspect markers trigger tone change, however, not even the phonologically similar *wa³²³* or *wa³⁵*, respectively the perfective and future particles. Only one other morpheme may occur before *wa³³* — the progressive marker *tɤ³³* which combines with it to form the inceptive aspect — and it neither changes tone nor triggers change in the preceding verb in this environment. Examples of the three changes are illustrated in (61). An example containing $tʁ^{33}$ is presented in (62).

(61)   Tone 33 $kʰai^{33}$ 'to be clean' → tone 44 $kʰai^{44}$
ja^{53} ni^{323} kʰai^{33}tsʅ^{323} ti^{53},   kʰai^{33} **ɕo^{44}**   wa^{33}.
later   eraser   CL:PCE   rub be.clean CRS
然后   橡皮擦   点   擦   干净
'Later, (the) eraser, (it) was rubbed off (by use).'
然后橡皮擦，用完了。
(YAY-Erasers)

Tone 31 $zʅ^{31}$ 'to be far' → tone 24 $zʅ^{24}$
tɕa^{323} ɕa^{33}ta^{33} **zʅ^{24}**   wa^{33}.
road   fairly   be.far   CRS
路   相当   远
'(It) was fairly far away.'
路特别远了。
(HPH-Family)

Tone 323 ta^{323} 'to be able' → tone 24 ta^{24}
"tso^{24} ko^{53} li^{33} ma^{31} **ta^{24}**   wa^{33}.
turn   cross   come   NEG be.able   CRS
转   过   来   不   能
' "(I still) won't be able to cross." '
"绕不过来了。"
(HPH-Weeds)

Other tones remain unchanged
tɛi^{31} tsʅ^{24} to^{33} ma^{31} **sʅ^{55}**   wa^{33} mɛi^{44},   tɛi^{33}tɕʰa^{55}kʰʅ^{33} ni^{53}.
everything   also   NEG   know   CRS   DSC.EMP   this.time   TOP
什么   也   不   知道   这时侯
'(I) don't know (any), now.'
现在什么也不知道了。
(YJF-Dance Parties)

(62)   i³²³tɕa⁵³   mau³⁵   to⁵³   li³³   tʁ³³ wa³³.
       water   gush   exit   come   INCP
       水   冒   出   来
       'Water began to gush out.'
       水冒出来了。
       (HPH-Horse Dug Well)

The purpose of a tone change in this environment is unclear. It is seemingly unrelated to the two other functions marked by this pattern. The presence of an aspect marker indicates that a clause is complete, and so there is no need to signal an intention to continue speaking. Likewise, there is no omission of a grammatical particle, such as the imperative marker, to warrant the assistance of an accompanying tone change. It is possible that it is a purely phonological pattern with long roots in history. In Nuosu, a Ngwi language spoken in northern Yunnan and southern Sichuan, tone 44 exists solely as an allotone of tone 33, and mainly occurs when two 33 syllables become adjacent in discourse (Bradley 1990: 127–131; Gerner 2013: 28–30). This is identical to one piece of the marked pattern, and it may be that the Khatso change evolved from such a pattern in its own Ngwi parent language. The use with wa^{33} may, in fact, be the original construction, which later developed more specific functions in non-final phrases and imperatives (see § 3.2.4.1 and § 3.2.4.2 respectively). This hypothesis does not, however, explain the changes that occur in syllables with tone 31 and 323. A thorough analysis of historical tone correspondences is needed to fully answer this question.

3.2.5 Focus Tone Change

The focus particle la^{35} serves to pragmatically link a clause to an earlier comment in discourse. Primarily, the clause containing la^{35} provides contrastive information (see § 13.1.3.3), though it may also be interpreted as describing the reason for the previous situation (see § 14.1.3) or its effect (see § 14.2.3). The particle sits in the clause providing the new information, placed between the verb and one of a few phrase-final morphemes, such as the strong assertion particle $\eta\varepsilon i^{33}$, the currently relevant state marker wa^{33}, the epistemic emphatic po^{53}, the discourse emphatic $m\varepsilon i^{44}$ or the affirmative interrogative particle sa^{44}. An example is presented in (63). Because the meaning depends heavily on context, and its corresponding function in English is mainly conveyed through prosody, there is no simple translation for la^{35}. In its contrastive use, it may be interpreted as 'thus', 'just', 'only', 'like that' or 'instead'. For an overview of the multiple functions of la^{35}, see § 16.4.

(63) i³²³tso³³   a³³   ma⁴⁴   ɕo³³   tʰɛi³²³   ja³³   tɛi³³   tsɛi³⁵.
     well   that   CL:GEN be.clean very   IPFV.EMP   this   CL:TMP
     井   那   个   干净   很   这   段
     'That well is very clean, now.'
     现在那口井很干净。

     i²⁴la³¹   ni³⁵?   tsa³³   tʰɛi³²³   **la³⁵**   ŋɛi³³,   i²⁴la³¹.
     past   TOP.Q   be.dirty   very   FOC   ASRT   past
     以前   脏   很   以前
     'In the past? (It) was really dirty, in the past.'
     以前呢，很脏的啦。
     (PYX-Dragon Pools)

The particle *la³⁵* may be replaced by a tone change pattern that likewise focuses the clause. There are two ways in which the change occurs. In the first, the tone of the syllable preceding the position in which *la³⁵* would typically sit changes to tone 35. This pattern tends to mainly occur when the changing syllable has a low tone — such as 24, 33, 323 and 31 — and is a verb or verb-modifying morpheme. For example, in (64) the existential verb *tso³²³* changes to *tso³⁵* before *ŋɛi³³*. When the syllable preceding *ŋɛi³³* has a high tone or is not a verb-related morpheme, then it is *ŋɛi³³* itself that changes to tone 35, as (65) illustrates. This pattern does not appear to be a case of tone fusion (see § 3.2.6), but rather an actual change in tone that replicates that of the original particle *la³⁵*.

(64) *tso³²³ → tso³⁵*

   A: xa³³ni³³   nɛi²⁴   xa³³ni³³   fɤ²⁴   tso³²³   ŋa³¹?
      how.many   CL:ITEM   how.many   CL:ITEM EXIST   CNT.Q
      多少   姐妹   多少   兄弟   有
      'How many brothers and sisters were there?'
      有几个姐妹几个兄弟？

   B: ŋa³³   sɛi⁴⁴   mo³³   sɛi⁴⁴   ni³¹   si³³   nɛi²⁴   **tso³⁵**   ŋ³³   po⁵³.
      1SG   family   mother   family   TOP   three   CL:ITEM   EXIST.FOC   ASRT   EPIS.EMP
      我   家   妈   家   三   姐妹   有
      'My mother's family, there were (only) three sisters!'
      我妈家，只有三个姐妹嘛。
      (KL, YJR-Grandfather)

(65) ŋɛi³³ → ŋɛi³⁵
    A: n̠a³²³ka⁵³pʰa³¹   ko⁵⁵   tɕi³³   tʏ³³   ŋ³³   po⁵³.   ŋ⁴⁴   ŋuo³¹?
         n̠a³²³ka⁵³.M   CL:PL   say   PROG   ASRT   EPIS.EMP   COP   COP.Q
         中村男人   些   说   　　　　　　　　　　　　　　　　　是
         '(They) say (they were) n̠a³²³ka⁵³ men, is that right?'
         说的是中村的男的，是吗？

    B: ma³¹   ŋɛi³³.   kʰa⁵⁵tsɿ³³pʰa³¹   ko⁵⁵   **ŋɛi³⁵**.
         NEG   COP   kʰa⁵⁵tsɿ³³.M   CL:PL   ASRT.FOC
         不   是   下村男人   些
         'No. (They) were kʰa⁵⁵tsɿ³³ men (instead).'
         不是。是下村的男人。
    (KL, PYX-Performing)

Although the tone change patterns are productive in elicitation, in discourse they are employed more sparingly. The first pattern consistently occurs with only a handful of morphemes, including the adverb *sa²⁴* 'perhaps', the copula *ŋ³³*, the existential verb *tso³²³*, the auxiliary *jo³³* 'must' and the progressive marker *tʏ³³*. The example in (64) above demonstrates the pattern with *tso³²³*; those in (66) through (69) illustrate the others. In addition, the progressive marker carrying the tone change, *tʏ³⁵*, may likewise be omitted, causing the verb it modifies to change to tone 35 instead. In discourse, this occurs most often with the quotative verb *tɕi³³* 'to say' and the verb *i³²³* 'to go', which is frequent in serial verb constructions (see § 8.8). Examples are shown in (70) and (71) respectively. By contrast, the use of *ŋɛi³⁵* is comparatively rare in the corpus — it seems that retaining the particle *la³⁵* is generally preferred over this second tone change pattern.

(66) sa²⁴ → sa³⁵
      nɛi³³   ma³¹   sɿ⁵⁵   **sa³⁵**   nɛi³³,   a³³   jo³⁵.
      2SG   NEG   know   perhaps.FOC   ASRT   that   CL:HUM
      你   不   知道   可能   　　　　那   位
      'You probably don't know (him), that one.'
      你可能不知道，那位。
    (YJR-Grandfather)

(67) ŋ³³ → ŋ³⁵
      wa⁵³   a³³   ko⁵⁵   **ŋ³⁵**   sa⁴⁴?
      INTJ   that   CL:PL   COP.FOC   CRTN.Q
      　　　那   些   是
      'Oh, (it) was those (people, right?)'
      哦，是那些人。
    (KL-Performing)

(68) jo^{33} → jo^{35}

tɕo³⁵	tɛi³³	ma⁴⁴	tɕa³¹	**jo³⁵**	ŋɛi³³,	ŋ³³	n̪a³³.
then	this	CL:GEN	speak	must.FOC	ASRT	COP	COP.EMP
就	这	个	讲	因该		是	

'Then (you) should tell that one, that's right!'
就得讲这个吧，是的。
(KL-Performing)

(69) $tɤ^{33}$ → $tɤ^{35}$

tɕo³⁵	xɤ³³pɛi³³	tɛi³³ni³³	kv̩³³	tso²⁴	**tɤ³⁵**	wa³³.
then	home	this.way	do	ITER	PROG.FOC	CRS
就	家	这么	做			

'(He) is at home doing (things) like that now.'
就是在家里这么弄一弄。
(YAY-Erasers)

(70) $tɕi^{33}$ $tɤ^{35}$ → $tɕi^{35}$

to³³	mɛi⁴⁴	na²⁴	kɯ³²³	sa³³	ja³³	**tɕi³⁵**	tsɛi³¹.
also	very	hear	CSC	be.good	IPFV.EMP	say.FOC	HSY
也	很	听		好		说	

'(They) said (it) sounded great!'
说的也很好听啊！
(PYX-Performing)

(71) i^{33} $tɤ^{35}$ → i^{35}

tsʰ1³³pʰa⁵⁵tɕʰa³¹ma³³	tɛi³³ni³³	ɕi³³	za⁵³	**i³⁵**	ŋɛi³³!
bare.foot	this.way	be.accustomed	descend	go.FOC	ASRT
光脚	这么	习惯	下	去	

'(We) were used to going down (there) barefoot!'
是光着脚地这么下去的！
(YJF-Weddings)

3.2.6 Tone Fusion

Some tone change patterns in Khatso involve tone fusion, which occurs when the contour of one tone is combined with that of another in a single syllable. Two consistent patterns of tone fusion are identified in the language. One occurs when grammatical particles are omitted, and the other occurs in echo questions. Both are discussed below.

3.2.6.1 Fusion of Grammatical Particles

In fast speech, it is common for words to be elided. In Khatso, when a key grammatical particle is omitted its tone is often fused with that of the preceding syllable so that the functional information is not lost. This process depends largely on speaker preference, and does not seem to be extremely common in discourse. However, it is a predictable tone change phenomenon and therefore included here.

The fusion process generally consists of appending the tone of the omitted word to that of the syllable before it, creating a complex contour. More specifically, it is the end point of the contour on the omitted word that is fused. For example, the fusion of tone 55 and tone 31 results in a contour of 551, and the fusion of tones 24 and 35 results in 245. If the omitted word and the preceding syllable share the same tonal end point then the resulting contour changes only by becoming longer. That is, if tone 55 and tone 35 are fused, the resulting tone is the contour 555 or, in other words, a tone 55 that is longer than usual. Naturally, the syllable rhyme is lengthened to accommodate the longer tone contour.

The pitch traces in the following diagrams illustrate the process. Figure 3.5 contains two phrases. On the right is $n̪o^{31}\ kv^{33}\ tr^{35}\ po^{53}$, in which the phrase $n̪o^{31}\ kv^{33}$ 'work, make a living' is followed by the progressive aspect marker tr^{33} with focus tone change (see §3.2.5) and the epistemic emphatic marker po^{53}. On the left, the tone 33 of kv^{33} and the tone 35 of the aspect marker fuse, resulting in a contour of 335. The pitch trace for 335, on the right, shows that the initial portion retains an even contour at roughly the same level as the independent tone 33 in the left chart. After this initial even contour, the pitch rises to the final high endpoint of tone 35, which corresponds to that of tr^{35} on the left.

n̪o³¹ kv³³ tr³⁵ po⁵³   n̪o³¹   kv³³⁵   po⁵³

Fig. 3.5: Tone 33 + tone 35 → fused contour 335

The two phrases in Figure 3.6 illustrate a case in which two tones with the same end point fuse. On the left, the phrase $na^{31}ni^{24}za^{31}\ sr^{55}\ tr^{35}\ po^{53}$ contains the phrase $na^{31}ni^{24}za^{31}\ sr^{55}$ 'mind, look after children' followed by the focused progressive aspect marker tr^{35} and the epistemic emphatic marker po^{53}. On the right, the verb sr^{55} fuses with the aspect marker tr^{35}. The resulting contour is 555, or a long tone 55 — it is visibly longer than the single contour of sr^{55} on the left.

na³¹ni²⁴za³¹ sɤ⁵⁵ tɤ³⁵ po⁵³   na³¹ni²⁴za³¹ sɤ⁵⁵⁵ po⁵³

Fig. 3.6: Tone 55 + tone 35 → fused contour 555

Tone fusion may occur with words that exhibit other kinds of tone change. The examples in (72) and (73) below both occur before the temporal clause marker *ta³¹ni³²³* 'after' which triggers the non-final tone change described in the previous section (see § 3.2.4.1). In (72), the stative verb *tɕɛ³¹* 'to be tight' changes to *tɕɛ²⁴* before the marker, and then because the syllable *ta³¹* is omitted *tɕɛ²⁴* becomes *tɕɛ²⁴¹*. In (73) the verb *tsa³¹* 'to eat' likewise becomes *tsa²⁴* before the same marker, which is again omitted, leaving only the fused tone to indicate its function.

(72) Tone 31 → tone 24 + tone 31 → fused contour 241
tso⁵⁵   kɯ³²³   **tɕɛ²⁴¹**   ni³²³,   tso⁵⁵   tɤ⁵⁵   tɤ³³   ŋ³³   tsɛi³¹.
pull   CSC   be.tight   BKGD   pull   be.wrinkled PROG   ASRT   HSY
拉   紧   拉   皱
'Because (I) pull (it) tight, they say (I) make (it) wrinkled.'
说拉得紧，被拉皱了。
(WYY-Sewing)

(73) Tone 31 → tone 24 + tone 31 → fused contour 241
na³²³tsʰɹ̩³¹   ko⁵⁵   vɤ³²³   **tsa²⁴¹**   na³²³tsʰɹ̩³¹   ko⁵⁵   kɛi³³   tʰau³²³   tɤ⁴⁴.
medicine   CL:PL   buy   eat. BKGD   medicine   CL:PL   AGT   insomnia   STAT.EMP
药   些   买   吃   药   些   搉
'(I) went and bought medicine, (but) the medicine (gave me) insomnia.'
买了一些药吃了呢，让药给搉的。
(WYY-Sewing)

3.2.6.2 Fusion in Echo Questions

In conversation, a tonal change may create an echo question. This happens when one participant has not clearly understood another, either through lack of attention or surprise at the content of a given utterance. Phonetically, the change involves fusing a high rising tone, much like tone 35, to the final syllable of the phrase, so that tone 33 becomes 35 and tone 44 becomes 45. If the lexical contour of an interrogative pronoun ends at a high point, such as tones 35 and 55, then the tone is extended even higher. Tone 35 becomes something like 36 and 55 may drop somewhat so that a higher rising tone may be appended, yielding 535.

Though productive with all kinds of words in elicitation, the change often occurs with interrogative pronouns, since they query information in a semantically similar way, as the example in (74) illustrates. It does occur on other words as well, as (75) demonstrates. Unlike the fusion created by the omission of grammatical particles discussed in § 3.2.6.1, in echo questions the appended tone contour is not attached to any lexical item. Rather, it is the contour itself that creates the interrogative sense in discourse.

(74) A: i³³   sɛi⁴⁴   mo³³   sa²⁴kɛi³³   sl̩³³   ja³²³   sɛi³¹.
          3SG   family   mother   just   die   PFV.EMP   still
          她   家   妈   刚才   死   还
          'Her mother just died.'
          她的母亲刚死了。

     B: xa³³**ma³⁵**?!
          what.ECHO
          什么
          'What?!'
          什么？！
          (KL-Elicitation)

(75) A: tɛi³³   ma⁴⁴   xa³³ma⁴⁴   ma⁴⁴   ŋa³¹?
          this   CL:GEN   what   what   CNT.Q
          这   个   什么   么
          'What (is) this?'
          这个是什么？

     B: tɛi³³   **ma⁴⁵**?   ma³¹   xo²⁴   pa³¹.
          this   CL:GEN.ECHO   NEG   be.correct   IMP.SOL
          这   个   不   对
          'This one? (It) isn't right, see?'
          这个不对吧。
          (KL, WYY-Sewing)

3.2.7 Tone Contours 242 and 353 in Discourse

The tonal contours 242 and 353 appear to have special status in Khatso discourse. While they are not phonemic, they are predictably associated with two discourse functions, the vocative use of kin terms and a number of discourse markers.

Like many languages in the Sino-Tibetan family, Khatso has an elaborate kin term system that distinguishes sex, generation, birth order and parental relation. Many of these terms were originally borrowed from Hanyu, but have subsequently become completely assimilated into Khatso. Thus, *tsi³¹tsi³¹* 'elder sister' is morphologically distinct from *nɛ³²³ma³³* 'younger sister', and *ta³⁵ti³³* 'father's older brother' is distinguished from *ta³⁵tɕo³⁵* 'mother's brother'. In a system such as this, one often addresses a relation by the kin term rather than a personal name. When kin terms are used in this vocative way, the final syllable typically adopts a special tonal contour. If the final syllable has a lower tone, such as 31 or 323, it changes to the contour 242. If the final syllable has a higher tone, such as 35, it changes to a 353 contour. The even tone 33 changes to tone 53 in this environment. Thus, in calling out to one's father (*pa³¹pa³¹*) one says *pa²⁴²!*, and for one's mother (*mo³³mo³³*) one says *mo⁵³!* There is some variation about the way these contours are produced in discourse, but the general pattern is fairly consistent. Additional examples are shown in (76).

(76) *Lower tone → 242 contour*
 a³³mi⁵⁵za³¹ 'older brother's wife' 大嫂   mi⁵⁵za²⁴²!
 sv̩³¹sv̩³¹ 'father's younger brother' 叔叔   ta³⁵sv̩²⁴²!
 a³⁵pʰo³²³ 'mother's mother' 外婆   a³⁵pʰo²⁴²!

 Higher tone → 353 contour
 tɕo³⁵tɕo³⁵ 'mother's brother' 舅舅   tɕo³⁵tɕo³⁵³!

 Tone 33 → tone 53
 sa⁵⁵v̩³³ 'older sister's husband' 姐夫   sa⁵⁵v̩⁵³!
 lau³³ti³³ 'paternal grandfather' 爷爷   lau³³ti⁵³!
 nɛi³³nɛi³³ 'paternal grandmother' 奶奶   nɛi³³nɛi⁵³!

The contours 242 and 353 are also employed with discourse markers, especially the former, making them maximally distinct from lexical items. A partial list of these markers and their functions is presented in (77).

(77) mo³⁵³   regret, pity, wonderment
 mɛi²⁴²   surprised reproach, exasperation
 sɛi²⁴²   scolding
 ŋɤ²⁴²   backchannel
 wɛi²⁴²   general vocative
 ʂi²⁴² / ai²⁴²   discourse filler
 m̩²⁴²   discourse filler

3.2.8 Lexicalized Tone Change in Causatives

The previous literature (Dai, Liu and Fu 1987: 153; Mu 2002: 34; Dai 2008: 81) observes that some causative verbs are distinguished from their non-causative counterparts solely by a change in tone. This is not a productive process, however, and is only attested in a few cases, as shown in (78). These forms have clearly become lexicalized, and are therefore not true examples of tone sandhi. The primary process for creating causative expressions is periphrastic (see § 11.2.2).

(78) *Voluntary form*   *Causative form*
      tsa^{31} 'to eat' 吃   tsa^{55} 'to feed' 喂
      to^{323} 'to drink' 喝   to^{33} 'to make drink' 使喝
      tɕo^{53} 'to be afraid' 害怕   tɕo^{35} 'to frighten' 吓唬
      mo^{323} 'to perceive' 见   mo^{33} 'to show' 给看

4 Syllable, Word and Intonation Unit Structures

The previous chapters provide information on the consonant, vowel and tone inventories in Khatso. This chapter explores the way these basic building blocks are combined into more complex phonological configurations. At the syllable level, this structure is rather simple, as most contain a single consonant and vowel. Word structure can be more complex. A large percentage of the lexicon is monosyllabic, but disyllabic and trisyllabic words are not uncommon. Nonetheless, as with most analytic tone languages, lexical homophony is widespread. An analysis of natural language also yields information about discourse structure, which is centered on the intonation unit.

These features are organized according to level of complexity. Syllable structure is outlined in § 4.1. Word structure is described in § 4.2 in both phonological and morphological terms. Lexical homophony is discussed in § 4.3. And the structure of intonation units, which rely on cues unrelated to pitch, is outlined in § 4.4.

4.1 Syllable Structure

As previously mentioned, every syllable carries a lexical tone in Khatso. Thus, in terms of structure a syllable minimally contains a voiced segment that can carry a tone (VdT). The nucleus is most often a vowel — whether monophthong, diphthong or triphthong — either alone or more frequently with a consonant onset. There is an exception to this structure; the nasals /m, ŋ/ may also serve as onsetless nuclei. Onsetless /v/ is considered a vowel (see § 2.2.1.3). Syllable codas are not attested in the language.

The possible syllables in Khatso, with examples, are shown in Table 4.1 where C stands for consonant, V for vowel, N for nasal and T for tone. These data correspond to the structure observed by Dai, Liu and Fu (1987: 153), Mu (2002: 34) and Dai (2008: 81–82). He (1989: 26), however, does not identify triphthongs in his analysis.

When vowels occur in onsetless syllables in citation form or careful speech, a glottal stop [ʔ] occurs before the vowel — a common phonetic phenomenon in the world's languages (Garellek 2012: 92–94). This occurs in Khatso as well, although in discourse the glottal features often change or disappear altogether (see § 2.2.1). Because this is a phonetic rather than phonological effect, and the glottal stop is not a phoneme in the language, this analysis does not differentiate between VT and ʔVT syllable structures.

Table 4.1: Syllable structure in Khatso

Structure	Examples
CVT	k^hv^{31} 'to steal' 偷, vv^{53} 'to write' 写, jo^{33} 'to be slow' 慢
CVVT	$ts\varepsilon i^{24}$ 'to be sour' 酸, $p\varepsilon i^{323}$ 'mountain' 山, $m\varepsilon i^{55}$ 'to be few' 少
CVVVT	$xu\varepsilon i^{33}$ 'gray' 灰色, $liau^{35}$ 'to flee' 撒腿, $kuai^{31}$ 'to turn' 拐
VT	i^{33} 3SG 他, o^{31} 'vegetable' 菜, v^{323} 'to take' 拿
NT	m^{31} 'horse' 马, m^{53} 'to blow' 吹, η^{24} 'red' 红, η^{33} 'to sit' 坐

A look at the basic lexicon shows that the vast majority of syllables in Khatso are CVT in shape. Tabulating the syllable structures found in 1954 syllables[1], from 678 monosyllabic words and 638 disyllabic words, we find that 76% are CVT, while only 18% are CVVT. Only 1% contains triphthongs (CVVVT). Onsetless vowel and nasal syllables are also relatively few, 2% and 3% respectively. The percentage data are shown in both table and pie chart form in Table 4.2 and Figure 4.1 respectively.

Table 4.2: Syllable structure frequency in Khatso

Syllable Structure	# of Tokens	Percentage
CVT	1487	76%
CVVT	351	18%
CVVVT	10	1%
VT	43	2%
NT	63	3%
Total	1954	100%

---

1 These are the same data used to tabulate tone frequency (see § 2.3.1).

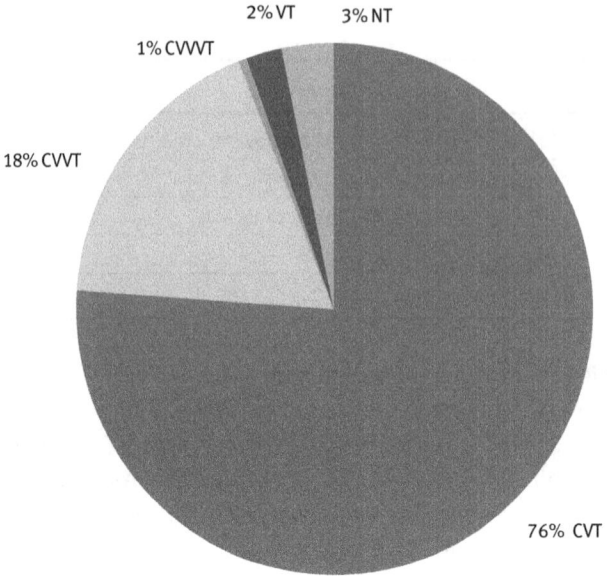

Fig. 4.1: Syllable structure frequency in Khatso

4.2 Word Structure

Deciding what constitutes a word in Khatso is not a straightforward task. Khatso is not a written language nor is it used in any classroom setting. Thus, parsing speech into individual words is not an activity that speakers do with any frequency. During elicitation, in fact, speakers are just as likely to translate a single Chinese word into a Khatso phrase as reply with a single lexeme. In addition, the analytic nature of the language means that there are few morphemic features available to help decide the issue. However, there are enough cues to define a word in Khatso, as described in the following sections.

4.2.1 Defining the Word

The general process of analyzing a word in a language is usually done in two ways, phonologically and grammatically, and then the results are compared. In general, a phonological word can be identified by segmental features, prosodic features and morphophonological rules (Dixon and Aikhenvald 2002. 13–18). While there is variation in pronunciation among Khatso speakers, there is no allomorphy that can help define a word. Consonants and vowels help identify syllable structure, but there is no difference in structure between mono- and multisyllabic words since every syllable has a lexical tone. Tone change does occur in a few nouns containing reduplicated syllables, but the same pattern occurs when words are reduplicated as well. Thus, the only reliable segmental feature that applies to the word in Khatso is the pause, which can identify a word boundary. Pause is not always present in discourse, however, so it is more accurate to state that the potential for a pause is the most useful feature. That is, if a pause may be inserted as a boundary then it can define a phonological word.

The other two types of phenomena that are often employed to define a phonological word are not relevant in Khatso. The first, prosodic features, does not consistently occur within the lexical domain. Stress appears to be assigned at the phrase level rather than at the word level (see § 4.2.4), while tone is assigned at the syllable level (see § 3.1). There are no other phenomena, such as vowel harmony or nasalization, that are restricted to the lexical domain. The second phenomenon, morphophonology, is likewise unhelpful. There is little morphology in the language; words remain largely invariant. Thus, there are no particular internal processes that emerge within a word to help define its boundaries.

The grammatical word is generally defined by three basic features: cohesiveness of form, a fixed order of morphemes, and a coherent meaning (Dixon and Aikhenvald 2002: 18–25). These features are extremely reliable in Khatso. There is no inflection in the language, and there are only a handful of affixes, so units rarely change form. And because of the relative lack of morphological processes, the order of morphemes within a word is reliably fixed. In fact, most Khatso words are monomorphemes. Coherent meaning is also a dependable indicator of a word; in the case of homophonous elements it is the *only* differentiating feature. Thus, almost all of the evidence for defining a word in Khatso comes from syntax and semantics rather than phonology. Syllable duration may vary in disyllabic words, but this is a phrasal process rather than a lexical feature (see § 4.4.2 and § 4.4.3).

In Khatso the phonological and grammatical analyses of words coincide for the most part. That is to say, a pause — the only feature to define a phonological word in the language — will identify the same word boundary as the grammatical criteria of cohesion, fixed morpheme order and coherent meaning. In both elicitation and discourse, however, two types of exceptions are found, and they both involve phonological words that consist of two or more grammatical words. The first is the category of compound words. For example, $o^{31}ma^{33}\eta^{24}$ contains two words that may be used independently, $o^{31}ma^{33}$ 'turnip' 萝卜 and η^{24} 'to be red' 红, but together they mean 'carrot' 胡萝卜. The two independent words have their own coherence and thus are separate grammatical words. Together, however, they create a new form with a separate meaning and a pause cannot be inserted between the elements without altering the meaning, indicating that the compound is a single phonological word. Moreover, compound nouns such as this also only take one numeral classifier, and it is chosen based on the new meaning. Words borrowed from Hanyu compounds are excluded from this group, since their component parts typically cannot be used independently in Khatso. Compounds are discussed in more detail in § 4.2.3.

The second exception is the category of clitics in Khatso. Clitics are morphemes that have a status somewhere between an affix and a word (Dixon and Aikhenvald 2002: 42–43). They may fulfill the definition of a grammatical word, but usually cannot stand alone as a phonological word. In Khatso, most particles fall into this category, including the possessive marker, classifiers, intensifiers, aspect markers and sentence-final particles. For example, the possessive marker *pɣ³²³*, which is placed between the possessor and the possessum as shown in (79), has a coherent meaning of its own in this construction. However, phonologically it is always uttered together with the possessor; a pause may follow but can never intervene between possessor and marker.

(79) i³³ **pɣ³²³** tsʰ\]³¹ mɛi⁴⁴
 3SG POSS dog CL:GEN
 他　　　　狗　个
 'his/her dog'
 他的狗
 (WFY-Elicitation)

Classifiers provide another example. They are grammatical words; each one has a coherent meaning and function that defines or modifies the noun it follows (see § 6.2). In discourse they may either follow a bare noun, such as the example in (79) above, or they may follow a demonstrative or a numeral, as in (80) below. Phonologically, however, they combine with the preceding morpheme if not with the entire preceding phrase. There may be a pause after a classifier, but never between a classifier and the preceding element.

(80) tsʰɛi³³ tɛi³³ **tɛi³⁵**　　　i³²³tɕa⁵³ ŋ³¹ **pʰi³²³**
 rice this CL:MSR　　　water two CL:MSR
 饭　这　袋　　　　　　水　两　瓶
 'this bag of rice'　　　　'two bottles of water'
 这袋米　　　　　　　　两瓶水
 (KL-Elicitation)

Other grammatical particles behave similarly. Intensifiers are clitics that bond with the stative verbs they modify. Aspect markers combine with the verbs they follow, and sentence-final particles bond with the preceding element. These constituent phrases form a single phonological word that contains two or more grammatical words.

4.2.2 Phonological Structure of Words

Now that the word has been defined in Khatso, we can investigate word structure in the language. As already described, syllable structure is fairly restricted, only CVT, CVVT, CVVVT, VT and NT syllables are attested; there are no syllable codas (see § 4.1). This structure does not change at the word level. Thus, a discussion of phonological word structure centers primarily on the number of syllables in a word. A great deal of the lexicon consists of monosyllabic words, though disyllabic words are also common. Words of three or more syllables exist, but they are much rarer. To simplify the discussion, only monomorphemes are considered here; compounds are discussed in § 4.2.3.

Mu (2002: 51) observes that words minimally have one syllable, though words with two, three, four or more syllables exist. He points to the noun category as the most diverse in terms of syllable quantity; though because he treats numeral classifiers as affixes, nouns are minimally disyllabic in his analysis. Verbs, he says, tend to be monosyllabic. These basic observations are borne out by my own data, though I consider classifiers to be separate grammatical words. Nouns commonly contain one or two syllables. Monomorphemic nouns with three syllables also exist, such as $na^{24}po^{24}tɕʰa^{31}$ 'ear' 耳朵 and $si^{53}ma^{33}ko^{31}$ 'stomach' 肚子, but most nouns with three or more syllables are morphologically complex or are compounds borrowed from Hanyu. Examples of nouns containing different numbers of syllables are shown in (81). The mono- and disyllabic nouns are monomorphemic; the trisyllabic nouns are morphologically complex.

(81)   *Monosyllabic nouns*
   wa⁵³ 'pig' 猪   sɿ³¹ 'blood' 血
   tsʰɿ³¹ 'dog' 狗   la⁵⁵ 'trousers' 裤子
   no⁵³ 'bean' 豆   o³¹ 'vegetable' 菜
   tɕa³¹ 'bee' 蜜蜂   tɕɛ³⁵ 'mushroom' 菌
   ʁa³¹ 'physical strength' 力气   ʁɯ⁵³ 'needle' 针

   Disyllabic nouns
   a²⁴ŋ⁵⁵ 'cat' 猫   vi⁵³li²⁴ 'flower' 花
   pa³¹tɛi³⁵ 'chair' 椅子   ŋ³⁵ma³³ 'heart' 心
   pv̩³¹sa³⁵ 'caterpillar' 毛虫   pʰi³²³ta³¹ 'knife' 刀
   xa³⁵tɕʰɛ³²³ 'celery' 芹菜   a²⁴n̪o⁵³ 'monkey' 猴子
   za³¹m̩³¹ 'daughter' 女儿   tɕɛ³⁵ka⁵³ 'arrow' 箭

Trisyllabic nouns

ni³¹tsɣ³³ma³³ 'mud brick' 土坯
tsʰo³³mo³²³tʰɛi³¹ 'funeral' 丧礼
lɛi²⁴pa³³kɣ²⁴ 'rib' 肋骨
tsʰɛi³³tsʰɿ³³po³⁵ 'popcorn' 爆米花
tsʰɿ³³ni³⁵tʰo³³ 'sole (of shoe)' 鞋底

tiɛ³⁵xua³⁵tsɿ³³ 'telephone' 电话机
m̩³³to³⁵pʰɛi³²³ 'brazier' 火盆
lɛi³²³tsʰɿ³¹pa³¹ 'floor' 楼板
ɕa³³tsɛi³⁵fɣ³¹ 'village government' 乡政府

Active verbs tend to be monosyllabic, as shown in (82), though there are a few disyllabic verbs such as ŋ²⁴ka³³ 'to look' 看, na²⁴ŋ²⁴ 'to ask' 问 and m̩³³to³¹ 'to forget' 忘记.

(82) *Monosyllabic active verbs*
       pʰo³⁵ 'to split (wood)' 劈
       tʰo³³ 'to pull' 拉
       tʰiau³³ 'to embroider' 绣
       kʰɯ³³ 'to rake' 刨
       ma⁵⁵ 'to teach' 教
       nɣ³⁵ 'to hold between the fingers' 捏

       ŋa²⁴ 'to push' 推
       fa²⁴ 'to distribute' 发
       si⁵³ 'to kill' 杀
       tsɣ³³ 'to cover' 盖
       ɣɤ³⁵ 'to preserve in salt' 腌
       lɤ⁵³ 'to lick' 舔

Stative verbs may contain either one or two syllables; disyllabic words are more common in this category than among active verbs. Examples are shown in (83).

(83) *Monosyllabic stative verbs*
       ɣ̩³¹ 'to be crazy' 疯狂
       pʰiɛ⁵⁵ 'to be steep' 陡
       ko⁵³ 'to be crooked' 弯
       mɤ³³ 'to be dizzy' 晕

       ȵɛ³²³ 'to be sweet' 甜
       kɯ³⁵ 'to be hard (texture)' 硬
       z̩ɿ³¹ 'to be heavy' 重

       Disyllabic stative verbs
       ɕɛ⁵⁵fɤ³⁵ 'to be furious' 气愤
       pʰɣ³¹lo³²³ 'to be cheap' 便宜
       si³⁵si³³ 'to be confident' 自信
       tsa³¹ȵa²⁴ 'to be delicious' 好吃

       tau³¹ta³³ 'to be gluttonous' 贪食
       si³³si³³ 'to be happy' 高兴
       tsi³⁵sɿ²⁴ 'to be quiet' 安静

Basic numerals, classifiers, adverbs, aspect markers and other grammatical particles are monosyllabic. A few examples of each are shown in (84).

(84) *Numerals*
       tɛi³¹ 'one' 一
       ŋ³¹ 'two' 二
       si³³ 'three' 三

       Classifiers
       ma²⁴ (for animals) 只
       jo³⁵ (for humans) 位
       kɤ²⁴ (for long, thin objects) 条

Adverbs	*Aspect markers*
to³³ 'also' 也	wa³³ CRS
tɕo³⁵ 'then' 就	wa³²³ PFV
xɛi³⁵ 'still' 还	wa³⁵ FUT
Grammatical particles	*Phrase-final particles*
pv̩³²³ POSS	ja³³ IPFV.EMP
la²⁴ REL	sɛi⁴⁴ TMP
kɛi³³ AGT	tsɛi³¹ HSY

4.2.3 Morphological Structure of Words

As already noted, Khatso is analytic in structure, meaning that there is little morphology in the language. Indeed, most words are free monomorphemes that do not change in use. For example, nouns do not change for number or case nor do verbs inflect for agreement or aspect. However, there are three categories in which the underlying morphology is apparent, as noted by Dai, Liu and Fu (1987: 165–66), He (1989: 26) and Mu (2002: 52–56). The first involves words that contain two bound morphemes, as discussed in § 4.2.3.1. The second, presented in § 4.2.3.2, consists of words that contain a root and a suffix. And the third category, outlined in § 4.2.3.3, involves compound words that contain two or more free morphemes.

4.2.3.1 Compounds of Bound Morphemes

Some words in Khatso contain two bound morphemes. These morphemes have identifiable meanings and may have been roots at one point, though today they only occur in compounds. For example, the first syllable of m̩³¹tʰa³³ 'sky' 天空, which appears to have the meaning 'sky', occurs in the temporal nouns m̩³¹lo⁵³ 'noon' 中午 and m̩³¹tsʅ³³ 'evening' 晚上 as well as in the weather terms m̩³¹ma²⁴ 'rain' 雨, m̩³¹tsʅ³³ma³³ 'sun' 太阳, m̩³¹xa³³ 'lightning' 闪电 and m̩³¹kv³³ 'thunder' 雷. Similarly, the first syllable of i³²³tɕa⁵³ 'water' 水 also appears in related compounds such as tsɛi⁵⁵i³²³ 'dew' 露水, i³²³tso³³ 'well' 水井, n̩a⁵³i³²³ 'tear' 眼泪 and tɕa³¹i³²³ 'honey' 蜂蜜. Although these morphemes are still identifiable, they have become lexicalized in compound forms.

Another commonly occurring bound morpheme is the general noun suffix -ma³³. Although it is homophonous with the feminine suffix (see § 4.2.3.2), it occurs in inanimate nouns such as fv³³ma³³ 'lake' 湖 and ŋ³⁵ma³³ 'fruit pit' 核; the language does not have grammatical gender. Matisoff (1973: 117) describes a similar morpheme in Lahu as referring to amounts, and Mu (2002: 55) suggests that its meaning in Khatso is 'big'. This residual sense may still apply in words such as o³¹ma³³ 'turnip' 萝卜, literally 'big vegetable', and wa²⁴ma³³ 簸箕, the largest of the traditional grain sifters. However, in most cases it seems to be analogous to the general nominalizing suffix -*ma* observed in many Ngwi languages (Bradley 2005b: 225). For example, *tsʰo³³o³¹ma³³* 'old person' 老人 contains the words *tsʰo³³* 'person' and *o³¹* 'to be old'; without the suffix this could be interpreted as a clause. In any event, words containing the suffix -*ma³³* are fully lexicalized; the suffix is not part of a productive process. Additional examples include *tʰo³³tso⁵³ma³³* 'button' 纽扣, *tʰo³³piɛ⁵⁵ma³³* 'lapel' 衣襟, *ŋa³¹tɕa³³ma³³* 'fish hook' 鱼钩 and *ni³¹tsʏ³³ma³³* 'brick' 土坯.

The most productive of the bound morphemes are the two demonstratives, the proximal *tɕi³³* 'this' 这 and the distal *a³³* 'that' 那. They freely combine with the more than one hundred classifiers in the language, with or without numerals, but generally do not occur on their own. Examples are shown in (85).

(85) tsʰŋ³¹ **tɕi³³** ma⁴⁴   sʏ⁵⁵ **a³³** pɛi³¹   m³¹ **a³³** ŋ³¹ kʏ²⁴
      dog   this= CL:GEN   book   this= CL:VOL   horse this= two= CL:ANM
      狗   这   个   书   那   本   马   那   二   头
      'this dog'   'that book'   'those two horses'
      这只狗   那本书   那两匹马
      (KL-Elicitation)

Mu (2002: 55) identifies a prefix *kɛi³³*- in a number of words although its use is not explained. This morpheme is actually the agent marker, which also has a pseudo-passive use, and is considered a free morpheme in the current analysis (see § 10.4 and § 10.5 respectively).

4.2.3.2 Noun Suffixes

There are only a handful of productive suffixes — defined as bound morphemes that attach to roots — attested in Khatso. Most of them specify the sex of the noun referent. For example, there is a pair of suffixes for humans, -*pʰa³¹* for men and -*ma³³* for women, which occur primarily with nouns of ethnic heritage, as shown in (86). They also show up in compounds such as *a³¹sŋ⁵⁵pʰa³¹* 'monk' 和尚 and *a³¹sŋ⁵⁵ma³³* 'nun' 尼姑. Language names are expressed with a similar bound morpheme -*tɕʰi³¹* 话, so that 'Hanyu' is *pʰi²⁴ŋ²⁴tɕʰi³¹* 汉语 and 'Ngwi (language)' is *na⁵³tɕʰi³¹* 彝语.

(86) kʰa⁵⁵tso³¹**pʰa³¹** 'Khatso man' 喀卓男人
      kʰa⁵⁵tso³¹**ma³³** 'Khatso woman' 喀卓女人
      na⁵³**pʰa³¹** 'Ngwi man' 彝族男人
      na⁵³**ma³³** 'Ngwi woman' 彝族女人
      pʰi²⁴ŋ²⁴**pʰa³¹** 'Han man' 汉族男人
      pʰi²⁴ŋ²⁴**ma³³** 'Han woman' 汉族女人

The sex of animals is also expressed through suffixes. The suffix -*pa⁵⁵* is used for males; -*ma³³*, identical to the human suffix, is used with females. Another suffix, the diminutive -za^{31}, is used with animate nouns to denote a 'young' referent and with inanimate nouns to denote a 'small' referent. Examples of these three suffixes with animal nouns are shown in (87).

(87) ɣa⁵³ 'chicken' 鸡   m̩³¹ 'horse' 马
      ɣa⁵³**pa⁵⁵** 'rooster' 公鸡   m̩³¹**pa⁵⁵** 'stallion' 公马
      ɣa⁵³**ma³³** 'hen' 母鸡   m̩³¹**ma³³** 'mare' 母马
      ɣa⁵³**za³¹** 'chick' 小鸡   m̩³¹**za³¹** 'foal' 小马

4.2.3.3 Compounds of Free Morphemes

The final group of compounds in Khatso consists of free morphemes. The resulting compounds are typically nouns, and they usually refer to items that are different than the individual components. They also take the classifier appropriate to the new meaning. There are two very common structures found in this type of compound. In the first, two nouns are combined to create a new one, as shown in (88).

(88) *Noun + noun*
      ɣa⁵³ 'chicken' 鸡 + fʏ³³ 'egg' 蛋   ɣa⁵³fʏ³³ 'chicken egg' 鸡蛋
      ɣɯ³⁵ 'duck' 鸭 + fʏ³³ 'egg' 蛋   ɣɯ³⁵fʏ³³ 'duck egg' 鸭蛋
      m̩³¹ 'horse' 马 + tsʰɹ̩³¹ 'manure' 屎   m̩³¹tsʰɹ̩³¹ 'horse manure' 马屎
      i³²³tɕa⁵³ 'water' 水 + zɹ̩²⁴ 'snake' 蛇   i³²³tɕa⁵³zɹ̩²⁴ 'water snake' 水蛇

The second type combines a noun and a stative verb modifying it. The resulting compound is a new noun. Examples are shown in (89).

(89) *Noun + stative verb*
      tsʰɹ̩³¹ 'dog' 狗 + ʏ³¹ 'to be crazy' 疯   tsʰɹ̩³¹ʏ³¹ 'rabid dog' 疯狗
      o³¹ 'vegetable' 菜 + fʏ³³ 'to be dry' 干   o³¹fʏ³³ 'dried vegetable' 干菜
      m̩³²³ 'field' 田 + fʏ³³ 'to be dry' 干   m̩³²³fʏ³³ 'dry farmland' 干田
      o³¹ma³³ 'turnip' 萝卜 + ŋ²⁴ 'red' 红   o³¹ma³³ŋ²⁴ 'carrot' 胡萝卜
      ɣa⁵³fʏ³³ 'chicken egg' 鸡蛋 + sʏ²⁴   ɣa⁵³fʏ³³sʏ²⁴ 'egg yolk' 蛋黄
      'yellow' 黄
      ɣa⁵³fʏ³³ 'chicken egg' 鸡蛋 +   ɣa⁵³fʏ³³tsʰɹ̩³³ 'egg white' 蛋白
      tsʰɹ̩³³ 'white' 白

Collocations such as nouns and classifiers, stative verbs and intensifiers, and serial verb constructions are not derivational and therefore not considered here.

4.2.4 Stress

Stress, or accent, is not contrastive in Khatso at the word level. That is, there are no minimal pairs that are distinguished purely by different lexical stress patterns. Evidence for this conclusion is presented below.

A majority of the scholarship on lexical stress explores non-tonal languages, especially those in which stress is contrastive such as English. Analyses of stress in languages with contour tones tend to focus on Putonghua (e.g. Chen and Gussenhoven 2008, Duanmu 1999, Jongman et al. 2006, Lai, Sui and Yuan 2010). While stress in Putonghua is not completely understood, there is a growing consensus that there are three correlates of stress in the language: pitch, amplitude and duration. Note that pitch is used to indicate stress even though it also differentiates meaning at the lexical level. This is possible because each of the four tones in Putonghua has a distinct contour — even, rising, falling and falling-rising. Thus the register, or the pitch range, of a given tone may change without impacting its shape and, by extension, its meaning. For instance, a stressed falling tone will begin at a higher pitch than usual which makes the pitch change more dramatic. The contour, while longer, still retains the falling shape and thus lexical meaning is not affected. Intensity and duration may also increase, helping to make the stressed syllable stand out from the surrounding material.

Unlike Putonghua, pitch is not a correlate of stress in Khatso. Because contours in different registers are already part of the lexical tone system, changing register alters meaning. For instance, there are two rising tones in Khatso, tone 24 and tone 35, that already overlap somewhat acoustically (see Figure 3.4). Raising the register of a word with tone 24, such as ku^{24} 'to get hurt' 硌, would make it more similar or perhaps even identical to ku^{35} 'to be hard' 硬. And tone 35 already ends at the high end of the range — recall that tone 55 in Khatso is remarkably high — so raising it farther would be difficult. The same challenges exist among the three even tones (33, 44, 55) and the two falling tones (31, 53). It is likely because of these functional pressures that pitch is not involved in the production of stress in Khatso.

Intensity and duration, then, would be the likely potential correlates of stress in the language. However, at the lexical level they do not pattern together. This becomes evident by comparing tokens from two of the speakers described above (see Table 2.1). An analysis of 90 disyllabic and trisyllabic responses obtained through elicitation, which include single as well as multiple word responses, fails to produce a predictable pattern involving the two features at the lexical level. The use of intensity is the most varied. Among disyllabic responses from the female speaker (WRF) we find greater intensity on the first syllable in half of the tokens and on the second in the other half. Responses from the male speaker (KCR) were more heavily weighted towards greater intensity on the second syllable. Trisyllabic responses show even more variation. Moreover, the two speakers often produce different intensity patterns for the same word. None of the differences correlate with a specific lexical feature — segment, tone, syllable shape, syllable weight and word class are all irrelevant.

Syllable duration shows a clearer pattern. In almost all of the responses, both disyllabic and trisyllabic, the final syllable is the longest. However, differences in the way identical words pattern are revealing. For example, in a bare disyllabic noun the second syllable is the longest. If a classifier is postposed, it is the latter that shows lengthening and not the noun. This demonstrates that duration is assigned at a level higher than the lexeme.

Furthermore, intensity and duration are not obliged to pattern together. The syllable with the greatest intensity may not be the longest and vice versa. Moreover, there is no obvious shared element in those instances in which the two features coincide. In responses from the male speaker, intensity and duration coincide in 66% of the tokens, but for the female speaker they converge in only 35%. Such conflicting data again point to a phrasal process. Indeed, further analysis shows that the sample data reflect phrase-initial and phrase-final prosodic patterns (see § 4.4), which the two speakers use randomly during elicitation.

As a result, the three features most likely to be used in lexical stress — pitch, intensity and duration — are not assigned at the word level in Khatso. Manipulating the pitch range of tone contours alters meaning, and thus is not an option for marking lexical stress. The remaining features, intensity and duration, pattern separately and, most importantly, randomly at the word level. Taken together, the evidence indicates that stress is not part of lexical phonology. Intensity and duration are used as intonation unit boundary cues, however, as described in § 4.4.

4.3 Homophony

Given the large number of monosyllabic words in Khatso, there is a great deal of homophony in the language. In practice the homophones are easily differentiated by semantics and function. For example, the three meanings of $t\varepsilon i^{31}$ are distinct because they each belong to a different word class: 'to haul' 拽 is a transitive verb, 'to be blunt, dull' 钝 is a stative verb and 'one' 一 is a numeral. As a result, they appear in different constructions in discourse. Likewise, the four meanings of to^{33} are also used differently in speech: 'mound' 墩 is a noun, 'to make drink' 让喝 is a causative verb, 'to be flat' 平 is a stative verb and 'also' 也 is an adverb.

Homophones that belong to the same word class are usually different enough in meaning to avoid confusion. For example, because the two transitive verbs i^{53} 'to plaster' 糊 and i^{53} 'to reap' 割, belong to different semantic domains, construction and agriculture respectively, the pragmatics of an utterance easily differentiates the two. A similar semantic distinction can be seen in pairs such as p^hi^{53} 'to spit' 吐 and p^hi^{53} 'to clean (fish)' 劈, $p^h\gamma^{31}$ 'to fly' 飞 and $p^h\gamma^{31}$ 'to crank (a handle)' 摇, and na^{24} 'to be good'

好 and *na²⁴* 'to hear' 听. Additional homophones can be identified in the lexicon provided in Appendix B.

4.4 Intonation Units and Prosody

In natural speech, words are uttered in phrases that are embedded in a larger discourse context. These phrases have their own phonological packaging which occurs at a level higher than segments or words. This packaging, called prosody, often invokes phrasal features such as pitch, intensity, tempo and pause. These features are typically used in two ways. First, they help organize speech into manageable chunks called intonation units (IUs) (e.g. Chafe 1987: 22, 1994: 22; Du Bois 2013: 91). IUs coincide with syntactic units such as phrases and sentences, although it is common for longer sentences to be broken into several clausal IUs (Chafe 1994: 38). Second, they allow speakers to express emotion and attitude through speech. Together, these features bring utterances to life with 'rhythm and tunes' and they are crucial to the flow of discourse (Du Bois 2013: 104).

While intonation units are universal, how they are composed and used in speech varies from language to language. The basic set of cues that combine to create a coherent IU includes the following (adapted from Du Bois 2013: 93):

Pause: silence demarcating an IU boundary;
Lag: lengthening of a final syllable to mark the end of an IU;
Rush: accelerated tempo in syllables preceding a lag;
Primary accent: the greatest prominence in an IU;
Boundary tone: lowered pitch to mark the end of an IU;
Pitch reset: pitch change between the end of one IU and the start of the next;
Tune: a unified intonation contour.

Because Khatso is a tonal language and tone contours are part of the lexical tone system, the functional load on pitch is too great to allow it to also play an extensive role in prosody. Thus, boundary tone, pitch reset and tune are not employed in Khatso IUs. Instead, IUs rely on cues that do not involve pitch — that is, pause, lag, rush and intensity. Intensity, divorced from word stress, is not generally considered a cue by itself, but rather part of the prominence created by primary accent. However, in Khatso, which does not have lexical stress (see § 4.2.4), intensity operates independently to help mark IU boundaries.

Of course, it is not necessary for every IU to contain all of the possible cues. Because they are functionally redundant, one may be omitted without undermining the overall coherence of the unit. For example, it is possible for consecutive IUs to run together without pauses, but the lag-rush and intensity patterns will still clearly mark them as separate units.

4.4.1 Pause

A pause is the measurable silence found at the end of a prosodic unit. In Khatso, a pause may be used to define a phonological word (see § 4.2.2). But in discourse, words are typically run together so that word-boundary pauses disappear. Instead, pauses are used to mark intontation unit (IU) boundaries. The delimited IU may contain any amount of lexical material, from a single word to a complex sentence. The spectrogram shown in Figure 4.2 provides several consecutive examples. The first pause, labeled P1, occurs after the filler word i^{31}; P2 marks a dependent clause, and P3 occurs after the main clause which contains a noun, adverb and serial verb construction.

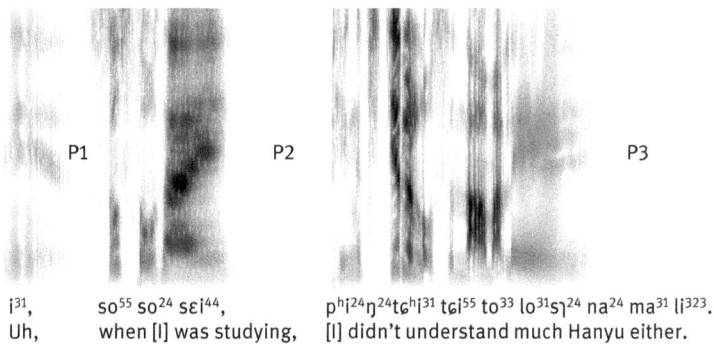

i³¹,   so⁵⁵ so²⁴ sɛi⁴⁴,   pʰi²⁴ŋ²⁴tɕʰi³¹ tɕi⁵⁵ to³³ lo³¹sɿ²⁴ na²⁴ ma³¹ li³²³.
Uh,   when [I] was studying,   [I] didn't understand much Hanyu either.

Fig. 4.2: The use of pauses to mark IU boundaries (YAY-Erasers)

The duration of a pause is variable, largely depending on speaker preference. Speed, pacing and mood may all influence pause duration in discourse. In some cases, the pause may be omitted altogether. However, there is a general tendency for pauses that follow a non-final clausal IU to be shorter than those marking a final IU. An example of this is shown in Figure 4.3, in which a grammatically complete sentence is uttered in three separate clausal IUs. There are only brief pauses following the two non-final IUs, marked as P1 and P2 and measuring 140 milliseconds and 164 milliseconds respectively. By contrast, P3, the pause separating the final clause from the beginning of the next IU, is many times longer, in this case measuring nearly 1.3 seconds (1272 milliseconds) in duration. Although the absolute duration of pauses varies widely in natural speech, the relative difference just described helps mark different clause types.

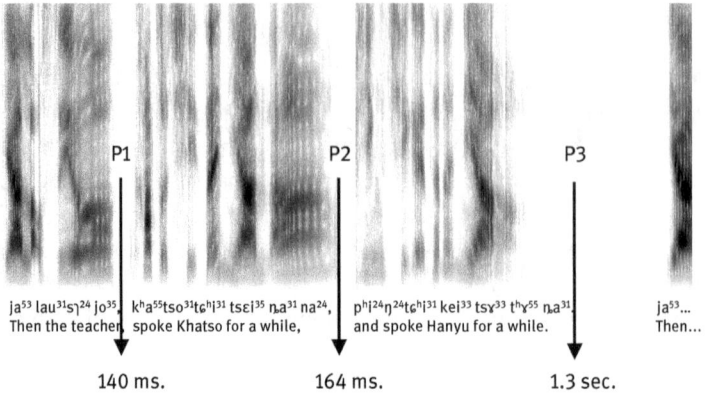

Fig. 4.3: Pause duration marking different clausal IUs (YAY-Erasers)

4.4.2 Lag

Lag refers to the lengthening of the final syllable in an intonation unit (IU). This cue is especially pronounced in Khatso, where it is common for the final syllable to be several times longer than medial syllables. This pattern is highly consistent, and occurs regardless of whether the final syllable consists of an independent word or belongs to a multisyllabic word. The example in Figure 4.4 illustrates this phenomenon with two consecutive IUs separated by a pause. Using vowel duration as a proxy for syllable length, we find that the final vowel in both IUs is much longer by far, 488 milliseconds and 635 milliseconds respectively, than the other vowels in the phrase. Also note that lag in the final IU is longer than that of the non-final IU.

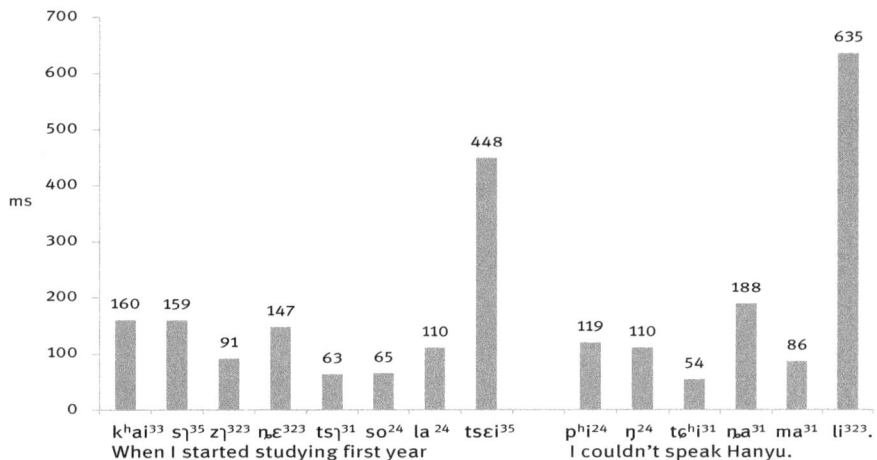

Fig. 4.4: Lag in IUs (YAY-Erasers)

Moreover, lag is also frequently accompanied by a phonetic change in the nucleus of the lengthened syllable. There is variation in how the change is realized, and it does not always occur, but several general patterns are observed. First, vowels are often lowered. This is most noticeable among the high vowels, where /i/ often becomes [ɪ] and /ɛi/ becomes [ɛ] or [æ]. At times the lengthening of /i/ produces the diphthong [iɛ]. Second, articulatory constrictions are opened to a greater degree. Thus, the fricative vowels /v/ and /ʅ/ will often include an open finish that is similar to an epenthetic [ɤ]. The nasal nuclei /m, ŋ/ may likewise take on an epenthetic [ɤ] to accommodate lag.

The final syllable may not be the only element that is lengthened in an IU. It is also common for at least one IU-medial syllable to also show lengthening, although never to the extent of IU-final lag. Typically, this syllable is the verb, or the first syllable of a disyllabic verb, although sometimes it is the initial syllable in an IU. Elements emphasized in pragmatically marked speech may also show lengthening. These patterns can be seen in Figure 4.4 above. In the first IU, the longest syllables besides the final occur in $k^hai^{33}sɿ^{35}$ 'to begin' 开始, which is both a verb and the initial word in the phrase. In the next IU, the second longest vowel occurs in the matrix verb $ȵa^{31}$ 'to speak' 说.

4.4.3 Rush

Rush, also called anacrusis, refers to the relatively quick tempo of speech that occurs at the beginning and middle of an intonation unit (IU), before the lag of the final syllable. Together, rush and lag combine to create a coherent tempo for each IU. Figure

4.5 illustrates the point, again using vowel duration as a proxy for syllable length. The non-final syllables range between 83 milliseconds and 156 milliseconds, or an average of 108 milliseconds — roughly a quarter of the length of the final syllable (585 milliseconds). The large contrast between the rushed and final syllables provides plenty of leeway to lengthen other key words, such as the matrix verb vʁ³²³ 'to buy' (156 milliseconds), without undermining the overall coherence of the tempo.

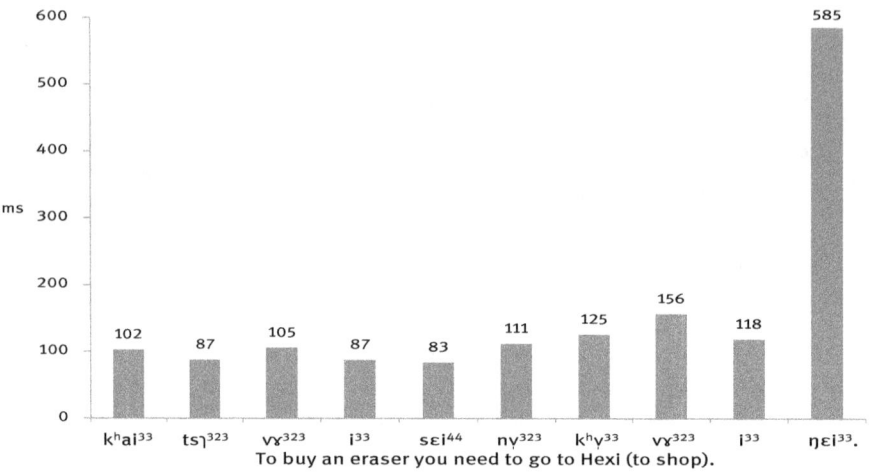

Fig. 4.5: Rush versus lag in an IU (YAY-Erasers)

4.4.4 Intensity

Intensity, or amplitude, is influenced by a number of acoustic factors. Breathing, for example, affects intensity over the course of an intonation unit (IU). Most phonemes are produced with an egressive air stream, meaning that one exhales as one speaks. The longer one speaks the emptier the lungs and the less energy there is for speaking without taking another breath. Speakers, of course, manipulate breathing so that it does not interfere with speech production (e.g. Henderson, Goldman-Eisler and Skarbek 1965), but IUs may also incorporate this natural declination as a defining feature. At the syllable level, intensity is influenced by the acoustics of the vowel (or vowels) in the rhyme. In general, the lower the vowel the greater the intensity is (e.g. Fairbanks, House and Stevens 1950). Breathy phonation, such as that accompanying tone 323 in Khatso, tends to decrease intensity (Gordon and Ladefoged 2001: 387).

That said, intensity does appear to serve as a cue for a coherent IU contour in Khatso. The basic pattern is for the first syllable of an IU to have the greatest intensity, which then decreases over the following syllables. Longer IUs tend to have one or more intensity peaks medially. These peaks may be located on the first syllable of a single syntactic constituent, such as a multisyllabic adverb or noun phrase, or a pragmatically emphasized element. In fact, within IUs most phrasal constituents — such as a noun and classifier or a stative verb and intensifier — follow this pattern, unlike the more random behavior of intensity in elicited phrases (see § 4.2.4). For some speakers the phrase-final drop in intensity may also be accompanied by a glottal or breathy finish, even if the final tone is not 323.

Figure 4.6 illustrates the pattern. In order to simplify the visual contour, the average intensity of each syllable, measured in decibels, is linked together with a schematic trend line. Within the IU we see that the two constituents are distinguished by intensity patterns. The compound noun $pʰi^{24}ŋ^{24}tɕʰi^{31}$ 'Hanyu' 汉语 begins with intensity of 65 decibels and ends at 54 decibels on the final syllable, a drop of 17%. Intensity in the verb construction, $ȵa^{31}\ ma^{31}\ li^{323}$ 'could not speak' 不会说, begins high at 68 decibels and decreases to 60 decibels at end of the IU, a change of 12%.

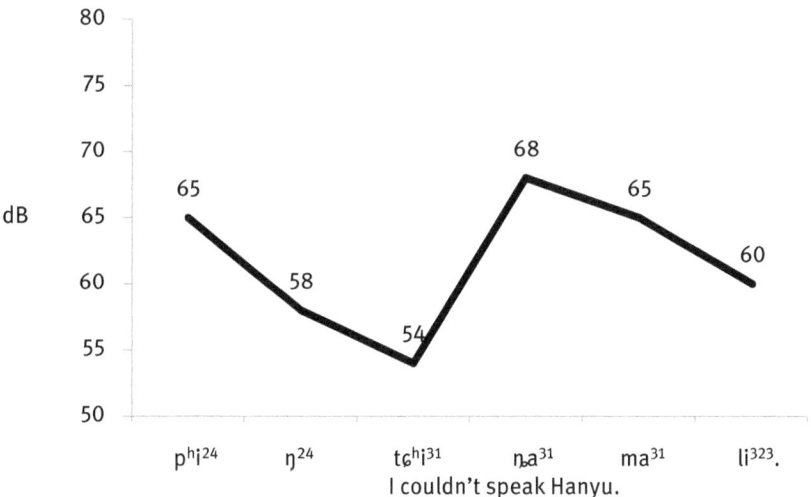

Fig. 4.6: Intensity changes across constituents in an IU (YAY-Erasers)

Furthermore, the fact that intensity peaks occur at the beginning of an IU, or a constituent within it, and lag occurs IU-finally explains why these two cues generally operate separately.

5 Nouns

The Khatso lexicon can be organized into four broad word classes: nouns, verbs, adverbs and grammatical particles. Membership in a class is based on morphosyntactic evidence from the language itself. Given the largely analytic nature of Khatso, most of this evidence is syntactic. Moreover, members of a particular class are rarely uniform; their use, meaning and function often vary to a certain degree. As a result, the evidence provided by the majority of the members of each class is considered decisive in this analysis. In this chapter, the defining data for nouns are explored, along with important variations and exceptions. Noun modifiers, and other elements within noun phrases, are described in Chapters 6 and 7.

This approach differs somewhat from that found in the previous literature on Khatso. All three earlier descriptions (Dai, Liu and Fu 1987: 153; He 1989: 26-27; Mu 2002: 78) identify the same ten word classes: nouns, pronouns, adjectives, verbs, numerals, classifiers, adverbs, conjunctions, particles and interjections. My own analysis shows that some of these groups are best considered as subsets of the others. For example, pronouns and classifiers are shown to be subsets of the noun class. Likewise, adjectives are better thought of as stative verbs, and conjunctions and interjections belong to a broad class of particles.

The noun class in Khatso is one of the largest categories in the lexicon. Nouns are unmarked; there is nothing in the internal structure of nouns that indicates their membership in the class. Indeed, many nouns are monosyllabic with only a consonant onset and vocalic nucleus, the same structure found in verbs, adverbs and particles (see § 4.1). Nouns of more than one syllable are also common; disyllabic nouns are plentiful, and trisyllabic nouns are not unusual. Nouns with more than three syllables can be found, but they are often compounds (see § 4.2.3).

The noun class in Khatso is also an open class, excluding pronouns. That is, the class of common nouns can readily accept new words as members. New nouns are created through compounding, but in Khatso the most common method by far is through borrowing. As has already been mentioned, a great deal of the Khatso vocabulary consists of loans from Hanyu. These include basic terms such as $pei^{33}pei^{33}$ 'cup' and $suei^{323}ko^{31}$ 'fruit' as well as terms for newer concepts such as $sei^{31}tsʅ^{33}$ 'mobile telephone', $tie^{35}sʅ^{35}$ 'television' and $tie^{35}nau^{31}$ 'computer'. It appears that borrowing words from Hanyu has been a productive process for centuries (see § 1.5). Today, the Khatso are all bilingual in Hanyu, if not Putonghua, and the use of loanwords in discourse is very common. In some cases it is unclear if these tokens are truly Khatso lexemes or Hanyu words given Khatso pronunciation on an ad hoc basis.

The evidence for nouns as a class relies mainly on syntactic patterns. First, nouns can serve as heads of possessive constructions. This applies not only to common nouns, as shown in (90) and (91), but to pronouns and proper nouns as well, as in (92) and (93) respectively.

(90)   ŋa³³tsʰɤ³¹   pɤ̰³²³   **ɤ⁵⁵za³¹**
       3PL   POSS   grandson
       我们   孙子
       'our grandsons'
       我们的孙子
       (KL-Sewing)

(91)   ŋa³³   pɤ̰³²³   **ni³¹na²⁴**   mɛi⁴⁴
       1SG   POSS   mouth   CL:GEN
       我   嘴   个
       'my mouth'
       我的嘴
       (YAY-Erasers)

(92)   i²⁴la³¹   pɤ̰³²³   **ŋa³³**
       past   POSS   1SG
       过去   我
       '(the) old me', literally '(the) past's me'
       以前的我
       (KL-Elicitation)

(93)   ŋa³³tsʰɤ³¹   pɤ̰³²³   **fɤ³¹pi³¹li³¹**
       3PL   POSS   Kublai
       我们   忽必烈
       'our Kublai Khan'
       我们的忽必烈
       (HPH-Horse Dug Well)

Second, nouns can similarly serve as heads of relative clauses. This applies to common nouns, as in (94) and (95), as well as to pronouns and proper names, as in (96) and (97) respectively.

(94)   nɛi³³   kɛi³³   sa³³   la²⁴   **tʰo³³pɛi³³**   mɛi⁴⁴
       2SG   AGT   sew   REL   upper.garment   CL:GEN
       你   缝   褂子
       '(the) upper garment that you sewed'
       你缝的褂子
       (WYY-Sewing)

(95) jɛ³²³tsʰau³²³   tʰo³¹z̩²⁴ la²⁴   **tsʰi³²³kʰua³⁵**
Yuan.Dynasty   unite   REL   situation
元朝   统一   情况
'(the) situation of uniting Yuan Dynasty (rule)'
元朝统一的情况
(HPH-Horse Dug Well)

(96) nv̩³²³kʰv̩³³   tso³²³ la²⁴   **i³³**
Hexi   EXIST REL   3SG
河西   有   他
'he who lives in Hexi'
住在河西的他
(KL-Elicitation)

(97) kʰua³¹la³¹   tso³²³ la²⁴   **kʰuɛi⁴⁴ i³¹**
Kunming   EXIST REL   Kui Ying
昆明   有   奎滢
'(the) Kui Ying who lives in Kunming'
住在昆明的奎滢
(KL-Elicitation)

The following sections explore basic types of nouns. Common nouns begin the discussion in § 5.1, followed by proper nouns in § 5.2. Pronouns are described in § 5.3, including personal pronouns, demonstrative pronouns and interrogative pronouns. The quantification of nouns, including the use of classifiers, is examined in Chapter 6. Constructions that modify nouns are described in Chapter 7, which include the qualification of nouns, indefinite constructions, possession, relativization, nominalization, and coordination.

5.1 Common Nouns

Common nouns make up the vast majority of the noun category. And, as already mentioned, this is an unmarked and open class. These are the general terms for "people, places and things" in a broad sense, including abstract entities, such as friendship, time and justice, along with the more prototypical tangible items.

Common nouns can generally be quantified in some fashion. In Khatso, when using numerals with nouns a classifier must also be used, as the examples in (98) and (99) illustrate. Bare classifiers are also often used with nouns in discourse (see § 6.2.1), but since a few bare classifiers also occur with verbs, this is not a reliable test for membership in the common noun category.

(98) kv̩³¹tie³¹ tɛi³¹ **ma²⁴**
story   one   CL:GEN
故事   一   个
'one story'
一个故事
(HPH-Weeds)

(99) tsʰa⁵³ŋa³⁵ ŋ̩³¹ **ma²⁴**
magpie   two   CL:GEN
喜鹊   二   个
'two magpies'
两个喜鹊
(YLW-Qin)

Bare nouns — that is, those that are taken out of a discourse context — do not specify number. Thus, the noun *vi⁵³li²⁴* 'flower' could refer to a specific flower, many flowers or the general category of flowers. In discourse, number is indicated with a classifier. Singular nouns may be accompanied by the numeral *tɛi³¹* 'one' and a classifier, as in (100), a demonstrative and a classifier, as in (101), or a bare classifier, as in (102). The latter, which is frequently used, is always interpreted as if *tɛi³¹* 'one' is omitted. Plurality may be marked by a numeral and a classifier or a bare collective classifier, as shown in (103) and (104) respectively.

(100) so³³mo³³ **tɛi³¹** **tsɤ³²³**
pine.tree   one   CL:PLNT
松树   一   棵
'one pine tree'
一棵松树
(YLW-Qin)

(101) mi³²³tsʰv̩³²³ **tɛi³³** **ma⁴⁴**
ethnic.group   this   CL:GEN
民族   这   个
'this ethnic group'
这个民族
(HPH-Horse Dug Well)

(102) ŋa³¹   **ma²⁴**
      fish   CL:GEN
      鱼   条
      'a/the fish'
      一条鱼
      (KL-Hotpot)

(103) na²⁴po²⁴tɕʰa³¹   xɤ³⁵   **pa⁵⁵**
      tuning.peg   four   CL:ITEM
      耳朵   四   只
      'four tuning pegs'
      四只耳朵
      (YLW-Qin)

(104) mo³²³kv̩³¹   zɛi²⁴   **ko⁵⁵**
      Mongol   people   CL:P
      蒙古   人   些
      'Mongols'
      蒙古人
      (HPH-Horse Dug Well)

In addition to marking number, these constructions also indicate specific reference. In other words, nouns that point to a particular referent in discourse must be marked for both number and specificity. For example, in the directions given in (105), bare classifiers are used to indicate that the nouns *ɣ³¹tʰɛi³²³* 'stage' and *tiɛ³⁵ka³³* 'electric pole' refer to specific entities in the village. The classifiers *ma²⁴* and *mɛi⁴⁴* alternate depending on whether or not a numeral is present (see § 6.2.1). Note that the definite/indefinite opposition apparent in the English translation is not overtly marked in Khatso syntax, but rather determined by context.

(105) i⁴⁴ ni³²³,   ɣ³¹tʰɛi³²³   tɛi³¹   **ma²⁴**   mo³²³.
      then   stage   one   CL:GEN   see
      然后   舞台   一   个   见
      'Then, (you) see a stage.'
      然后就见一个舞台。

      wa²⁴ni³²³,   ɣ³¹tʰɛi³²³   **mɛi⁴⁴**   pɤ³²³   la⁵³   vɤ⁵⁵   pi³¹   li³²³.
      then,   stage   CL:GEN   POSS   hand   left   side   come
      然后   舞台   个   手   左   边   来
      'Then, come to the left side of the stage.'
      然后来舞台的左边。

tiɛ³⁵ka³³   **po²⁴**   tso³²³.
electric.pole   CL:ROD   EXIST
电杆   根   有
'There is an electric pole.'
有电杆。
(KL-Directions)

In contrast, the absence of a classifier marks non-specific reference. For example, in discussing the name of an item in (106), no classifier is needed because the topic is the entire category rather than a particular referent. Likewise, in (107) the topicalized noun ɕɛ³²³so³²³ 'instrument string' refers to the category; only in the following clause are the strings on a particular instrument referenced and a classifier used.

(106) **kʰai³³tsɿ³²³** v̩²⁴ tɤ³³ ŋɛi³³.
eraser   call PROG ASRT
橡皮擦   叫
'(It is) called an eraser.' / '(They are) called erasers.'
叫橡皮擦呀。
(YAY-Erasers)

(107) **ɕɛ³²³so²⁴**   ni³¹, xɤ³⁵ kɤ²⁴ tso³²³.
instrument.string TOP four CL:STRIP EXIST
弦线   四 根 有
琴弦呢，有四根
'As for strings, there are four.'
(YLW-Qin)

In addition, nouns serving as P often lack a classifier in Khatso. In many cases, these nouns are semantically bleached, again referring to a category rather than a specific item. For example, in (108) the compound ȵo³¹ m̩³³, literally 'do things', is the general way of expressing the verb 'to work', which can be used for any kind of job. Thus, the noun ȵo³¹ 'thing' refers to a broad category of possible activities. Similarly, in (109) the phrase i²⁴tɕʰɛ³²³ pɤ⁵³, literally 'play qin' does not involve a specific qin but rather any such instrument.

(108) **ȵo³¹** m̩³³ m̩³³ ta³³ sa³¹?
thing   do do IPFV.IRR still.Q
事   做 做   还
'Does (he) still work?'
还有没有在干活？
(KL-Erasers)

(109) tɕo³⁵ i²⁴tɕʰɛ³²³ pɤ⁵³ so²⁴
       then   qin   play learn
       就   琴   弹   学
       'then (I) learned to play (the) *qin* [a banjo-like instrument]'
       就学弹琴
       (YLW-Learning)

Once nouns are established in discourse, they may be replaced by a pronoun or a demonstrative-classifier construction. They are also likely to be omitted altogether, especially if the referent is A or S — a feature known as zero anaphora. Repeated mentions of the noun, however, will almost always be accompanied by a classifier.

5.2 Proper Nouns

Proper nouns comprise a subset of nouns that point to unique named referents in the world rather than a general category. As a result, they are typically not modified by classifiers, the method usually employed to denote specific reference in common nouns (see § 6.2.1). The proper nouns most commonly encountered in Khatso discourse are personal names and place names.

5.2.1 Personal Names

Personal names in Khatso follow the Chinese convention of surname followed by given name. And, in fact, today all morphemes in Khatso names are Hanyu loans. Surnames are monosyllabic; given names may contain one or two syllables. Most Khatso people have one of a few common surnames — *ja*³²³ 杨, *kʰuɛi*³³ 奎, *kua*³³ 官, *lv̩*³²³ 禄, *pʰɤ*³³ 普, *tsa*³³ 旃, *tsau*³⁵ 赵, *tsau*³³ 招, *tsʰŋ*³³ 期, *wa*³²³ 王 and *xua*³⁵ 华 — a fact also noted by earlier researchers (Huang 2009: 8; Ma 2000: 27; Mu 2002: 19–20).[1] Just as in Chinese culture, women do not change surnames when they marry. For examples of full names in Khatso, see § 1.9 for a list of the language consultants who assisted with this project. It should also be mentioned that in addition to their formal names, many Khatso are known by nicknames within the village.

---

[1] When surnames appear alone they carry different tones than when they are combined with given names. The general pattern seems to be that those with a lexical tone of 33 change to 44 in combination, those with a lexical tone of 35 change to 24, and those with a lexical tone of 323 change to tone 31. However, there are also exceptions: *pʰɤ*³³ is always tone 33, and for some speakers *tsa*⁴⁴ and *tsao*⁴⁴ do not change at all. Compare the list here with the names in § 1.9.

Personal names satisfy the test for nounhood. They can serve as heads in both possessive constructions and relative clauses, as shown in (110) and (111) respectively. The semantics of these constructions is rather particular, however, and so they are not frequently encountered in discourse.

(110) kʰua³¹la³¹ pɣ̩³²³ **kʰuɛi⁴⁴ i³¹**
      Kunming POSS Kui Ying
      昆明   奎滢
      'Kui Ying from Kunming', literally 'Kunming's Kui Ying'
      昆明的奎滢
      (KL-Elicitation)

(111) kʰua³¹la³¹ tso³²³ la²⁴ **kʰuɛi⁴⁴ i³¹**
      Kunming EXIST REL Kui Ying
      昆明   有   奎滢
      '(the) Kui Ying who lives in Kunming'
      住在昆明的奎滢
      (KL-Elicitation)

When occurring as an argument of a verb, personal names generally do not take a classifier, as shown in (112), because they already have specific reference. There are several exceptions, however. For example, when a title accompanies a name, then the generic classifier *mɛi⁴⁴* is used, as shown in (113) and (114). The human classifier *jo³⁵* is not grammatical in this kind of construction.

(112) **kʰuɛi⁴⁴ i³¹** kʰua³¹la³¹ i³²³ wa³²³
      Kui Ying Kunming go PFV
      奎 滢   昆明   去
      'Kui Ying went to Kunming'
      奎滢去了昆明
      (KL-Elicitation)

(113) kʰuɛi³³ sɣ̩³³tsɹ̩³⁵ **mɛi⁴⁴**
      Kui   secretary   CL:GEN
      奎   书记   个
      'Secretary Kui'
      奎书记
      (KL-Elicitation)

(114) xua³⁵ ɕɛ³³sɛi³³ **mɛi⁴⁴**
 Hua mister CL:GEN
 华　　先生　　个
 'Mr. Hua'
 华先生
 (KL-Elicitation)

Two other morphemes may occur with personal names. The first is the noun *sɛi⁴⁴*, which means 'family' and can be used alone or followed by another noun to indicate possession. The possessive marker *pɣ³²³* is not required in the latter construction, making it idiomatic (see § 7.4). Examples are shown in (115) and (116) respectively.

(115) tsau²⁴li³¹ **sɛi⁴⁴** ni³⁵?
 tsau²⁴li³¹ family TOP.Q
 赵力　　　家　呢
 'What about *tsau²⁴li³¹*'s family?'
 赵力家呢？
 (KL-Sewing)

(116) tɕɛ²⁴li³¹ **sɛi⁴⁴** lau³³ti³³ na³²³ka⁵³ tso³²³ la³⁵ tsɛi³¹.
 tɕɛ²⁴li³¹ family grandfather na³²³ka⁵³ EXIST FOC HSY
 建林　　　家　　爷爷　　　　中村　　　有
 '*tɕɛ²⁴li³¹*'s grandfather reportedly lived in *na³²³ka⁵³*.'
 建林家爷爷是中村住的。
 (ZRF-Grandfather)

The second is *tsʰɣ³³*, the morpheme employed in plural personal pronouns, which also serves as an associative plural marker (see § 5.3.1). When used with proper names, it refers to people in close relationships to the focal referent, such as friends or family, as in (117).

(117) ɕa³³pa³¹ko⁵⁵ **tsʰɣ³³** kɛi³³, a³³ ko⁵⁵ ŋɛi³³.
 ɕa³³pa³¹ko⁵⁵ PL CONJ that CL:PL ASRT
 小八哥　　　　们　　和　　　那　　些
 'And *ɕa³³pa³¹ko⁵⁵* and his friends, those people.'
 小八哥们，那些人呀。
 (PYX-Performing)

5.2.2 Place Names

Place names in Khatso can be divided into two groups: those that are native and those that are borrowed from Hanyu. Generally, locations that are in or near Xingmeng have Khatso names, such as the five historical Khatso villages (see § 1.2) as well as *nɣ³²³kʰɣ³³* 'Hexi', *ŋ⁵⁵lo⁵³* 'Tonghai', *ɕi³³ɕi³³* 'Yuxi' and *kʰua³¹la³¹* 'Kunming'. The names of places farther away are loanwords, such as 'Beijing' *pɣ²⁴tɕi³³*, 'Shanghai' *sa³⁵xai³¹* and 'Mongolia' *mo³²³kɣ³¹*. There are two notable exceptions — the borrowed names for Xingmeng itself, *si³³mo³²³* and *si⁴⁴mo³¹*, which are used as alternates to the traditional name *kʰa⁵⁵tso³¹kʰua⁵⁵*, literally 'Khatso village'.

As nouns, place names may serve as heads of possessive constructions and relative clauses, as shown in (118) and (119) respectively.

(118) ŋa³³tsʰɤ³¹   pɣ³²³   **tsʰi³³lɣ³¹fɣ³¹**   mɛi⁴⁴
      3PL   POSS   Qilu.Lake   CL:GEN
      我们   杞麓湖   个
      'our Qilu Lake'
      我们的杞麓湖
      (HPH-Weeds)

(119) ŋa³³   mo⁵⁵   ŋ⁵⁵ka³³   la²⁴   **tɕʰa³¹ma³³**
      1SG   want   see   REL   Qiama.River
      我   要   看   中河
      'The Qia River that I want to see'
      我想看的中河
      (KL-Elicitation)

Like personal names, place names do not generally take classifiers in discourse, as shown in (120). However, those that contain a common noun, such as *tɕʰa³¹* 'river' and *sɛi³¹* 'province', must take the classifier appropriate to that noun, as shown in (121) and (122).

(120) **nɣ³²³kɣ³³**   vɣ³²³   i³³   ŋɛi³³.
      Hexi   buy   go   ASRT
      河西   买   去
      '(You) buy (it in) Hexi.'
      是去河西买的。
      (YAY-Erasers)

(121) tɕo³⁵ **tɕi³³sa³³tɕa³³ kɤ²⁴** li⁴⁴ tsʰŋ³³ li³³ wa³³.
then Jinsha.River CL:STRIP in arrive come CRS
就 金沙江 条 里 到 来
'Then (they) came to the Jinsha River.'
就到了金沙江了。
(KLT-History)

(122) ŋa³³tsʰɤ³¹ **jɛ³²³na³²³sɛi³¹** mɛi⁴⁴ tɕi³³ɲa⁵³ li⁴⁴
3PL Yunnan.Province CL:GEN here in
我们 云南省 个 这里 里
'here in our Yunnan Province'
我们云南省这里
(HPH-Horse Dug Well)

5.3 Pronouns

The pronoun class consists of words that are used as substitutes for common and proper nouns in discourse. They are deictic in nature, which means that their meaning is determined by the immediate context of the utterance in which they appear. For example, the personal pronoun ŋa³³ 1SG or 'I', which points to the person who utters it, can refer to many different people in a single conversation. Three types of pronouns are found in Khatso: personal pronouns, demonstrative pronouns and interrogative pronouns. The latter also take part in certain indefinite constructions (see § 7.3).

5.3.1 Personal Pronouns

Personal pronouns are typically used to refer to humans in Khatso discourse. Occasionally the third person pronoun will refer to an animal or inanimate object, but usually a demonstrative is used for this purpose. In Khatso this is a closed class, containing only six basic members, as shown in Table 5.1. There is some variation in the pronunciation of the plural morpheme; it may be uttered as /tsʰɤ/ or /tsʰɛi/ and take either tone 33 or tone 31 without a change in meaning.

Table 5.1: Personal pronouns in Khatso

Person	Number		
	Singular	Plural	
First	ŋa³³	ŋa³³tsʰɤ³³	ŋa³³tsʰɤ³¹
		ŋa³³tsʰɛi³³	ŋa³³tsʰɛi³¹
Second	nɛi³³	nɛi³³tsʰɤ³³	nɛi³³tsʰɤ³¹
		nɛi³³tsʰɛi³³	nɛi³³tsʰɛi³¹
Third	i³³	i³³tsʰɤ³³	i³³tsʰɤ³¹
		i³³tsʰɛi³³	i³³tsʰɛi³¹

As the table illustrates, the pronouns distinguish person and number, but not sex. Thus, *i³³* 3SG can be translated as either 'he' or 'she' in English. Nor is there an inclusive-exclusive distinction in the language, so using a pronoun such as *ŋa³³tsʰɤ³³* 'we' may be ambiguous as to which participants are included in the action discussed. It should be noted that verbs do not require overt arguments in Khatso. That is, once nouns are established in a discourse context, their participation is understood whether or not a noun or pronoun is present. Although zero anaphora is frequent in natural speech, pronouns are typically employed to clarify ambiguity or signal a change in referent in discourse.

The personal pronouns do not inflect to convey their roles in a clause, so they remain invariant regardless of whether they instantiate A, S, P, R or any other function. Examples are shown in (123), (124), (125) and (126) respectively.

(123) *Pronoun as S*
 xɤ³³ ŋɛi³³ tɕi⁴⁴ to³³ i³³ tɕo³⁵ ma³¹ ɣɤ³⁵ tso²⁴.
 scold ASRT say also 3SG then NEG move ITER
 骂 说 也 他 就 不 动
 '(Although you) scold (him), he doesn't move.'
 骂他，他就是不动。
 (PRL-Education)

(124) *Pronoun as P*
 ŋa³³tsʰɤ³³ i³³ tɕi³¹ ŋ³²³ miau⁵⁵ i³⁵ wa³³.
 3PL 3SG one CL:TMP inspect go.FOC CRS
 我们 他 一 天 观察 去
 'We one day plan to go find him.'
 我们去找他一天了。
 (KL-Erasers)

(125) *Pronoun as R*
 nɛi³³ tɛi³¹ ma²⁴ vɣ³²³ tɣ⁴⁴ ŋa³³ kɯ³¹ li³³ pa³¹.
 2SG one CL:GEN buy CLNK 1SG give come IMP
 你 一 个 卖 我 给 来 吧
 'Buy one for me.'
 你买一个来给我吧。
 (ZRF-Grandfather)

(126) *Pronoun as possessor*
 ŋa³³tsʰɣ³¹ pɣ³²³ ɣ⁵⁵za³¹
 3PL POSS grandson
 我们 孙子
 'our grandsons'
 我们的孙子
 (KL-Sewing)

Personal pronouns do not take classifiers in discourse, unless a numeral is introduced, as shown in (127). They may, however, serve as heads of possessive phrases and relative clauses, as the examples in (128) and (129) show, though this is rather rare in discourse.

(127) **i³³tsʰɣ³¹ ŋ³¹ jo³⁵** i³²³ kɯ³¹ wa³²³ po⁵³.
 3PL two CL:HUM go INDR.CAUS PFV EPIS.EMP
 他们 两 位 去
 'They two were allowed to go, (didn't you know?)'
 让他们两个去了。
 (KL-Competition)

(128) i²⁴la³¹ pɣ³²³ **ŋa³³**
 past POSS 1SG
 过去 我
 '(the) old me', literally '(the) past's me'
 以前的我
 (KL-Elicitation)

(129) kʰua³¹la³¹ tso³²³ la²⁴ **i³³tsʰɣ³³**
 Kunming EXIST REL 3PL
 昆明 有 他们
 'those who live in Kunming'
 住在昆明的他们
 (KL-Elicitation)

The plural morpheme *tsʰɤ³³* is also used with other human nouns. When affixed to common human nouns, it often carries a general meaning of plurality, as in (130), though the classifier *ko⁵⁵* is more usually employed for this purpose (see § 6.2.2.3). More often, it acts as an associative plural — that is, a plural pointing to a heterogeneous set of people who are closely associated with the named referent (Moravcsik 2003). Frequently, these associates are friends or relatives of the referent, as in (131) and (132) respectively. The exact status of the morpheme in Khatso is unclear. It seems to straddle the classifier and noun categories. Its function is similar to a classifier in denoting number, and it can form a demonstrative construction like classifiers, as in (133), but it cannot co-occur with a numeral. And like both common nouns and classifiers, it may serve as head of a relative clause, as shown in (134), but it cannot itself be modified by a classifier like a prototypical noun.

(130) ŋa³³tsʰɤ³¹   ɤ³⁵tɕo³⁵   pv̩³²³   za³¹m̩³¹   **tsʰɤ³³**
       1PL   two.maternal.brother   POSS   daughter   PL
       我们   二舅   女儿   们
       'our second maternal uncle's daughters'
       我们的二舅的女儿们
       (WYY-Sewing)

(131) ɕa³³pa³¹ko⁵⁵   **tsʰɤ³³**   kɛi³³,   a³³   ko⁵⁵   ŋɛi³³.
       ɕa³³pa³¹ko⁵⁵   PL   CONJ   that   CL:PL   ASRT
       小八哥   们   和   那   些
       'And *ɕa³³pa³¹ko⁵⁵* and his friends, those people.'
       小八哥们，那些人呀。
       (PYX-Performing)

(132) ja⁵³   ŋa³³   sɛi⁴⁴   pʰo³²³   **tsʰɤ³³**   ni³⁵?
       FILL   1SG   family maternal.grandmother PL   TOP.Q
       那   我   家   外婆   们
       'So, what about my grandmother's family?'
       那我外婆她们呢？
       (KL-Sewing)

(133) n̩ɛ³²³za³¹   n̩ɛ³²³ma³³   **a³³**   **tsʰɤ³³**   ni³¹
       younger.brother younger.sister   that   PL   TOP
       弟弟   妹妹   那   们
       'as for little brothers, little sisters, those (people)'
       那些小弟弟、小妹妹呢
       (YJF-Childhood)

(134) ti⁵³   so²⁴   kɯ³²³   xɯ³²³   la²⁴   **tsʰɤ³³**
      CL:PCE   learn   CSC   good   REL   PL
      点   学   好   们
      'those who have learned a little more'
      学得好一点的
      (YAY-Erasers)

Khatso does not have a set of reflexive pronouns analogous to the personal pronouns. Instead, there is a reflexive term *tsɿ³¹tɕa²⁴* 'self', a Hanyu loan, which accompanies personal pronouns in a reflexive clause. These are not common in discourse; elicited examples are shown in (135) and (136). In fact, the verbs that would be candidates for reflexive action, such as those involving grooming for instance, are simple intransitive verbs in Khatso (see § 8.1.1). More often, the word *tsɿ³¹tɕa²⁴* functions as an adverb to indicate that the agent performed an action alone, and this is the use most often encountered in discourse. In addition, there is another adverb *mɤ³¹zɛi³²³*, which best translates as 'for oneself' and indicates that an action is done for one's own benefit. For example, in (137), the speaker is talking about a group of girls who have gone out to gather firewood. Although they go as a group, each girl is responsible for finding and bringing home her own bundle of wood.

(135) i³³   **tsɿ³¹tɕa²⁴**   kuai³⁵   tɤ³³   ŋɛi³³
      3SG   self   blame   PROG   ASRT
      他   自己   怪
      'he blames himself'
      他自己怪自己呀
      (KL-Elicitation)

(136) ŋa³³   **tsɿ³¹tɕa²⁴**   pɤ³²³   tʰo³³   vi⁵³
      1SG   self   POSS   clothes   wear
      我   自己   衣服   穿
      'I'm wearing my own clothes'
      我穿我自己的衣服
      (KL-Elicitation)

(137) tɕi³³   li³²³   la²⁴   tsʰɤ³³   ni³¹   tɕo³⁵   **mɤ³¹zɛi³²³**   tɕi³³.
      pack   know.how   REL   PL   TOP   then   for.oneself   pack
      装   会   们   就   自个   装
      'Those who know how to bundle (it), (each) bundles (it) for her own use.'
      会装的那些呢就自己装。
      (YJF-Dance Parties)

There are no possessive pronouns in Khatso. Rather, the possessive particle py^{323} combines with nouns and pronouns alike to form possessive constructions (see § 7.4). In addition, the third person singular pronoun i^{33} appears in a nominalizing construction involving stative verbs (see § 7.6).

5.3.2 Demonstrative Pronouns

Demonstrative pronouns are used to point out particular referents in discourse with regard to the spatial environment, or deictic center, of the utterance. In Khatso, demonstratives have only a two-way distinction. Referents are described as either near to (proximal) or far from (distal) the speaker. These meanings are instantiated by two morphemes, the proximal tei^{33} and the distal a^{33}, and thus this is a closed class. They are also bound morphemes; they must combine with a classifier. These demonstrative-classifier constructions follow the noun. In discourse, demonstrative pronouns are typically used instead of personal pronouns for non-human referents.

The demonstrative pronoun construction may modify a noun, as in (138) and (139), or replace a noun altogether, as in (140) and (141). In the latter use, the classifier, which often describes a salient feature of the noun (see § 6.2), helps clarify the anaphoric reference. For example, in (140) jo^{35} can only be used with human nouns thus making it clear that the demonstrative refers to a human in the narrative. Note that the general classifier ma^{24} idiomatically changes its tone to 44 when combined with a demonstrative, as (138) illustrates.

(138) ka³²³tɕʰi³²³ **tɛi³³** ma⁴⁴
 door this CL:GEN
 门 这 个
 'this door'
 这个门
 (KL-Doors)

(139) ŋa³¹tsɿ³²³ **a³³** ta³²³
 eel that CL:ANM
 鳝鱼 那 条
 'that eel'
 那条鳝鱼
 (ZMF-Fishing)

(140) nɣ³²³kɣ³³ so²⁴   i³³   la²⁴   **tɛi³³**   jo³⁵
Hexi   learn   go   REL   this   CL:HUM
河西   学   去   这   位
'this one who went to Hexi to learn'
去河西上学的 这个
(YAY-Erasers)

(141) tɕo³⁵ **tɛi³³** ma⁴⁴ tɕa³¹ jo³⁵   ŋɛi³³.
then   this   CL:GEN speak must.FOC ASRT
就   这   个   说   应该
'Then (you) should tell that one.'
就是说这个了。
(PYX-Performing)

The demonstrative morphemes are inherently singular. To point out plural referents, two constructions may be employed. First, the demonstratives may combine with the classifier *ko⁵⁵*, which is used to indicate plurality for any type of noun, whether human, animal or inanimate, as the elicited examples in (142) illustrate. Second, a numeral greater than 'one' — *tɛi³¹* 'one' itself cannot combine with the demonstratives — may be inserted between the demonstrative and the classifier, as shown in (143). For clarity, the constructions in the examples below modify overt nouns, but they can also be used as substitutes for the nouns. Thus, a construction such as *tɛi³³ ko⁵⁵* 'these' can serve alone as a pronoun, as the phrase excerpted from discourse shows in (144).

(142) tsʰo³¹pa³⁵ **a³³** **ko⁵⁵**   a³³ŋ⁵⁵ **a³³** **ko⁵⁵**   vi⁵³li²⁴ **a³³** **ko⁵⁵**
friend   that CL:PL   cat   that CL:PL   flower   that CL:PL
朋友   那   些   猫   那   些   花   那   些
'those friends'   'those cats'   'those flowers'
那些朋友   那些猫   那些花
(KL-Elicitation)

(143) tsʰo³¹pa³⁵ **a³³** **ŋ³¹** **jo³⁵**   a³³ŋ⁵⁵ **a³³** **ŋ³¹** **ma²⁴**   vi⁵³li²⁴ **a³³** **ŋ³¹** **to³¹**
friend   that two CL:HUM   cat   that two CL:GEN   flower   that two CL:ITEM
朋友   那   两   位   猫   那   两   个   花   那   两   朵
'those two friends'   'those two cats'   'those two flowers'
那两位朋友   那两只猫   那两朵花
(KL-Elicitation)

(144) **tɛi³³ ko⁵⁵**　sɿ⁵⁵　ma³¹　sɿ³²³.
　　　 this　 CL:PL　know　NEG　be.certain
　　　 这　　 些　　 知道　 不　　 确定
　　　 'I'm not sure about all those (things).'
　　　 不知道这么多了。
　　　 (WYY-Sewing)

Like the personal pronouns, demonstrative contructions may serve as heads of possessive constructions and relative clauses, as shown in (145) and (146) respectively. As a result, they satisfy the tests for nounhood.

(145) tɕʰa³¹　kɤ²⁴　pɤ³²³　**tɛi³³　pi³¹**
　　　 river　CL:STRIP　POSS　this　CL:SIDE
　　　 河　　 条　　　　　　 这　　 边
　　　 'that side of the river', literally 'the river's that side'
　　　 河的这边
　　　 (HPH-Weeds)

(146) piɛ³⁵　po²⁴　ka⁵³la³¹　tɕi³⁵　la²⁴　**a³³　ti⁵³**
　　　 pen　CL:ROD　on　　 carry　REL　that　CL:PCE
　　　 笔　　支　　 上　　　带　　　　　 那　　块
　　　 'that one [eraser] on pens', literally 'carried on a pen that one'
　　　 笔上带的那块
　　　 (YAY-Erasers)

In addition to the demonstrative pronouns just described, which point to particular arguments in discourse, the morphemes *tɛi³³* and *a³³* also appear in several deictic adverbs, such as *tɛi³³ŋa⁵³* 'here' 这里, *a³³ŋa⁵³* 'there' 那里, *tɛi³³ni³³* 'this way' 这样, *a³³ni³³* 'that way' 那样, and *tɛi³³tɕʰa⁵⁵kʰɤ³³* 'this time, now' 这样 and *a³³tɕʰa⁵⁵kʰɤ³³* 'that time, then'. Note that in rapid speech, the demonstrative *tɛi³³* may appear alone. Typically, this is interpreted as a reduction of *tɛi³³ni³³* 'this way', as shown in (147) and in (148), unless context points to an alternative adverbial meaning. Adverbs and the adverbial function are discussed in § 9.3.

(147) tɕo³⁵,　**tɛi³³**　tɕi³³　tɤ³³　wa³³　tsɛi³¹.
　　　 then,　 this　　 speak　PROG　CRS　 HSY
　　　 就　　 这　　　 说
　　　 'So, (it's said they) said it this way.'
　　　 听说就是这么说的。
　　　 (PYX-Performing)

(148) **tɛi³³** kuai³⁵ tso³²³ ma³¹ ta³²³.
 this be.strange EXIST NEG able
 这 怪 有 不 能
 '(It) isn't so strange.', literally '(It) isn't strange (in) this way.'
 不会有这么怪。
 (YAY-Erasers)

Because of the bound status of demonstratives, it is not possible to test them separately for nounhood. However, given their deictic function of pointing to common nouns like pronouns, they are included in this section. A similar problem arises in testing numerals (see § 6.1).

5.3.3 Interrogative Pronouns

Interrogative pronouns are used to question particular elements in a phrase, such as 'who', 'what', 'when' and 'where'. This is a closed class; its members are shown in Table 5.2. As can be seen, in Khatso these words all begin with the interrogative morpheme *xa³³*, which combines with classifiers, such as *jo³⁵* and *ma⁴⁴*, or other morphemes, such as *ȵa⁵³* and *ni³³*. Each pronoun is discussed in a separate section below.

In Khatso, interrogative words appear in situ. That is, they generally occur in the same position of the nouns they replace; there is no special word order for content questions. Two elicited phrases, one declarative and one interrogative, are compared in (149) and (150) below. Note that *xa³³ma⁴⁴* 'what' in (150) appears in the same position as the noun *sɣ⁵⁵* 'book' in (149).

(149) i³³ **sɣ⁵⁵** pɛi³¹ vɣ³²³ ŋɛi³³.
 3SG book CL:VOL buy ASRT
 她 书 本 买
 'She is buying (a) book.'
 她买书呀。
 (KL-Elicitation)

(150) i³³ **xa³³ma⁴⁴** vɣ³²³ ŋa³¹?
 3SG what buy CNT.Q
 她 什么 买
 'what did she buy?'
 她买什么?
 (KL-Elicitation)

Table 5.2: Interrogative pronouns in Khatso

Khatso	Morphology	English	Chinese
xa³³jo³⁵	xa³³ (interrogative morpheme) + jo³⁵ (CL:HUM)	'who'	谁
xa³³ma⁴⁴	xa³³ (interrogative morpheme) + ma⁴⁴ (DEM form of CL:GEN ma²⁴)	'what', 'which'	什么, 哪个
xa³³tɕʰa⁵⁵kʰɣ³³ xa³³tsɛi³⁵ xa³³sau³³	xa³³ (interrogative morpheme) + tɕʰa⁵⁵kʰɣ³³ (part of temporal DEM), tsɛi³⁵ (CL:TMP), sau³³ (CL:TMP)	'when'	什么时候
xa³³n̠a⁵³	xa³³ (interrogative morpheme) + n̠a⁵³ (DEM 'place')	'where'	哪里
xa³³ma³⁵li³³li³²³ xa³³ma³⁵li⁴⁴li³²³ xa³³ma³⁵li⁴⁴li³³ xa³³ma³⁵ta⁵⁵li⁴⁴li³³li³²³ xa³³ma³⁵ta⁵⁵tɣ⁴⁴li³²³ xa³³ma³⁵ta⁵⁵tɣ⁴⁴li³³ xa³³ma³⁵ti³³li³²³ xa³³ma³⁵ti³³li³³ xa³³ma³⁵ti⁴⁴li³²³ xa³³ma³⁵ti⁴⁴li³³ xa³³ma⁴⁴ta³⁵ti³³ xa³³ma⁴⁴ta⁵⁵ta³¹ni³²³li³²³ xa³³ma⁴⁴ta⁵⁵tɣ⁴⁴li³²³ xa³³ma⁴⁴ta⁵⁵ti³³ xa³³ma⁴⁴ti³⁵ti³³	xa³³ (interrogative morpheme) + ma⁴⁴ (DEM form of CL:GEN ma²⁴); the remaining syllables are unanalyzable	'why'	为什么
xa³³ni³³ xa³³ni³³ko⁵⁵	xa³³ (interrogative morpheme) + ni³³ (ADV morpheme), ko⁵⁵ (CL:PL)	'how', 'how many'	怎么, 几, 多少

Questions formed with an interrogative pronoun typically include the sentence-final interrogative marker ŋa³¹ which helps differentiate the interrogative function from the indefinite constructions described in §7.3. An example from discourse is presented in (151).

(151) a³³tɕʰa⁵⁵kʰɣ³³ **xa³³jo³⁵** kɛi³³ nɛi³³ ma⁵⁵ **ŋa³¹**?
       that.time   who   AGT   2SG   teach CNT.Q
       那时   谁   你   教
       'At that time who taught you?'
       那个时候谁教你的？
       (KL-Sewing)

While these interrogative terms may be used independently as pronouns, several also combine with other elements. For example, both *xa³³ni³³* and *xa³³ma⁴⁴* are used with nouns and classifiers; these constructions are explained in the relevant sections below. Naturally, using interrogative pronouns is just one way to form questions in Khatso. Additional interrogative constructions are discussed in § 12.4.

5.3.3.1 Interrogative Pronoun *xa³³jo³⁵* 'who'

The personal interrogative pronoun in Khatso is *xa³³jo³⁵* 'who'. It may be used to question any argument in a clause, as (152), (153) and (154) illustrate. Because the second syllable is the human classifier *jo³⁵*, this pronoun is specifically restricted to human participants in discourse.

(152) **xa³³jo³⁵** kɛi³³ nɛi³³ ma⁵⁵ **ŋa³¹**?
       who   AGT   2SG   teach CNT.Q
       谁   你   教
       'Who taught you?'
       谁教你？
       (KL-Sewing)

(153) **xa³³jo³⁵** ŋa³¹ ni³⁵?
       who   CNT.Q TOP.Q
       谁
       'And who is (she)?'
       她是谁呢？
       (YXL-Competition)

(154) lau³³fɛi⁴⁴ kɛi³³ **xa³³jo³⁵** **xa³³jo³⁵** i³²³ **ŋa³¹**?
       lau³³fɛi⁴⁴ CONJ who   who   go   CNT.Q
       老芬   和   谁   谁   去
       'Who all went with *lau³³fɛi⁴⁴*?'
       老芬和哪位哪位去的？
       (ZRF-Competition)

5.3.3.2 Interrogative Pronoun *xa³³ma⁴⁴* 'what', 'which'

Depending on its use, the interrogative pronoun *xa³³ma⁴⁴* has two meanings, 'what' and 'which'. When occurring as a stand-alone argument, the pronoun means 'what', as shown in (155) and (156). In contrast to *xa³³jo³⁵* 'who', which refers only to humans, *xa³³ma⁴⁴* tends mainly to denote animals and inanimate objects. The second morpheme *ma⁴⁴* is the demonstrative form of the general classifier *ma²⁴* (see § 6.2.1).

(155) a³³ sɛi⁴⁴ **xa³³ma⁴⁴** ɣ²⁴?
that family what call
那 家 什么 叫
'What is that family called?'
那家叫什么？
(YJR-Grandfather)

(156) **xa³³ma⁴⁴** n̪a³¹ ni³⁵?
what speak TOP.Q
什么 说
'And what do (I) say?'
说什么呢？
(YJR-Grandfather)

In its second use, in which the pronoun carries the meaning of 'which', *xa³³ma⁴⁴* precedes either a noun or its classifier to query a specific option among several choices. Examples are shown in (157) and (158). With classifiers, the interrogative word is often shortened to just the question morpheme *xa³³*, as (159) and (160) illustrate.

(157) tɛi³³ tsʏ³²³ **xa³³ma⁴⁴** tsʏ³²³ ŋa³¹?
this CL:PLNT what CL:PLNT CNT.Q
这 棵 什么 棵
'Which tree (is) this?'
这棵是什么树？
(KL-Qin)

(158) nɛi³³ **xa³³ma⁴⁴** xo³¹ko³³ mo⁵⁵ tsa³¹ tʏ³³ ŋa³¹?
2SG what hotpot want eat PROG CNT.Q
你 什么 火锅 要 吃
'Which (kind of) hotpot do you want to eat?'
你想吃什么火锅？
(KL-Hotpot)

(159) **xa³³** **tɕi⁵⁵** kɛi³³?
       what   CL:TYPE INS
       哪   种
       'With which type?'
       跟哪种？
       (WYY-Sewing)

(160) **xa³³** **kʰua⁵⁵** pɣ̩³²³ ko⁵⁵ pɣ³¹ tɣ³³ ŋa³¹?
       What   village   POSS   CL:PL dance PROG CNT.Q
       哪   村   些   跳乐
       '(You) danced (with) those (people) from which village?'
       和哪个村子的人跳？
       (KL-Sewing)

As previously noted, a strong distinction is made between the human and non-human interrogative pronouns, *xa³³jo³⁵* and *xa³³ma⁴⁴*. Thus, *xa³³jo³⁵* is used to mean 'which person' as well as 'who'. The one exception, shown in (161), combines *xa³³ma⁴⁴* with the human noun *tsʰo³³* 'person' in an idiomatic construction meaning 'what kind of person'. This question may be answered by either describing the character of the referents (e.g. 'honest people') or identifying them as a particular group (e.g. 'my friends from work').

(161) **xa³³ma⁴⁴** **tsʰo³³** ko⁵⁵ tso³²³ ŋa³¹?
       what   person   CL:PL EXIST   CNT.Q
       什么   人   些   有
       'What kind of people (will) be there?'
       有一些什么人？
       (KL-Elicitation)

5.3.3.3 Interrogative Pronouns *xa³³tɕʰa⁵⁵kʰy³³*, *xa³³sau³³* and *xa³³tsɛi³⁵* 'when'

There are several temporal interrogatives in Khatso: *xa³³tɕʰa⁵⁵kʰy³³*, *xa³³sau³³* and *xa³³tsɛi³⁵*. All three carry the general meaning of 'when', as shown in (162), (163) and (164). The answer may be fairly general, such as *a³¹ŋ³⁵tha³³* 'last year' or *na³¹tɕi³³ŋ³³* 'tomorrow'. However, context may provide a more specific reading, as in (164), where the reply is expected to include an exact hour. In discourse, *xa³³tsɛi³⁵* is most often used to ask about the particular time of an activity in this way.

(162) tsʰo³¹to⁴⁴ tsɤ⁵³ sɛi⁴⁴ nɛi³³ **xa³³tɕʰa⁵⁵kʰɣ³³** kɛi³³ tsɤ⁵³ tsɹ²⁴ ŋa³¹?
straw.stool make TMP 2SG when from make rise CNT.Q
草墩 打 你 什么时候 从 打 起
'Making straw stools, when did you start making (them)?'
打草墩你是什么开始的？
(KL-Stools)

(163) a³³ŋ³⁵ta³³ tɕi³³ ŋ³³si⁴⁴ **xa³³tsɛi³⁵** tɕi³³ tɤ³³ ŋa³¹?
last.year say or when say PROG CNT.Q
去年 说 或是 什么时候 说
'(They) say last year or when?'
说的是去年呢还是什么时候？
(ZRF-Competition)

(164) **xa³³tsɛi³⁵** sa²⁴kɛi³³ m̥³¹tsʰɹ³¹ lia³⁵?
when until sky light
什么时候 才 天 亮
'When does it get light?'
什么时候天才亮？
(PYX-Performing)

However, constructions involved in asking and telling the time combine the interrogative *xa³³ni³³* 'how many' with a temporal classifier (see §5.3.3.6); the temporal interrogatives are not employed for this purpose.

5.3.3.4 Interrogative Pronoun *xa³³ȵa⁵³* 'where'

The locative interrogative is *xa³³ȵa⁵³* 'where'. It may be used to query any place, regardless of whether it is the semantic location, source or goal. Examples are shown in (165), (166) and (167) respectively. The second syllable, *ȵa⁵³* 'place', is the same morpheme that occurs in the demonstratives *tɕi³³ȵa⁵³* 'here' and *a³³ȵa⁵³* 'there'.

(165) kʰua³¹la³¹ ŋ³³si⁴⁴ **xa³³ȵa⁵³?**
Kunming or where
昆明 或是 哪里
'Kunming or where?'
昆明或是哪里？
(YXL-Tuition)

(166) **xa³³n̠a⁵³** kɛi³³ tsʰa³¹lia³⁵ tso³²³ sa³¹ pa⁵³ ŋa³¹?
where from yield EXIST still.Q FUT CNT.Q
哪里 从 产量 有 还
'Where would there still be (such a) yield?', literally 'From where would there still be (such a) yield?'
哪里还有什么产量？
(HPH-Weeds)

(167) ŋa³³tsʰɤ³³ **xa³³n̠a³¹** tsʰa³⁵ jɛ³³?
3PL where sing go
我们 哪里 唱 去
'Where do we go to sing?'
我们去哪里唱？
(YXL-Plans)

The locative interrogative pronoun is only used alone; it cannot accompany nouns that denote locations. More specific questions about locations are formed with *xa³³ma⁴⁴* 'what' or 'which', or sometimes just *xa³³*, followed by a noun or classifier, as in (168). See § 5.3.3.2 for more on this construction.

(168) **xa³³** kʰua⁵⁵ pɤ³²³ ko⁵⁵ pɤ³¹ tɤ³³ ŋa³¹?
what village POSS CL:PL dance PROG CNT.Q
哪 村 些 跳乐
'(You) danced (with) those (people) from which village?'
和哪个村子的人跳？
(KL-Sewing)

5.3.3.5 Interrogative Pronoun *xa³³ma³⁵li³³li³²³* 'why'

There are a number of ways to pronounce the interrogative adverb of reason in Khatso, such as *xa³³ma³⁵li³³li³²³*, *xa³³ma³⁵ti³³li³²³*, *xa³³ma³⁵ti³³li³³*, *xa³³ma⁴⁴ta³⁵ti³³* and *xa³³ma⁴⁴ti³⁵ti³³*. They all translate as 'why' with no difference in meaning. Their use depends on speaker preference, although older speakers tend to use the longer forms. In quick speech, the reduced term *xa³³ma³⁵liɛ³³¹* is often used, in which the final syllable is omitted but its falling tone is fused onto the preceding tone (see § 3.2.6 for a discussion of tone fusion). This interrogative is typically placed in the prototypical adverbial position between A/S and the verb. And, because given arguments are often omitted in discourse, the interrogative may begin a phrase. Examples are presented in (169) and (170). Aside from the first syllable, which is the content question morpheme, the semantic composition of these words is unclear.

(169) na³¹tɕi³³   m̩³¹tsʰɻ̍⁵³ **xa³³ma³⁵ti⁴⁴li³³** tsʰa³⁵ko³³ tsʰa³⁵ pa⁵³ ŋa³¹?
     tomorrow   evening   why   song   sing   FUT   CNT.Q
     明天   晚上   为什么   歌   唱
     'Why will (you) sing tomorrow evening?'
     明天晚上为什么要歌唱呢？
     (KL-Plans)

(170) **xa³³ma³⁵ti³³li³³** tɕi³³ kuai³⁵   tso³²³ ŋa³¹?
     why   this   be.strange EXIST   CNT.Q
     为什么   这   怪   有
     'Why are (they) so strange as that?'
     为什么会有这么怪？
     (PYX-Dragon Pools)

There are additional forms — such as *xa³³ma³⁵ta⁵⁵tɤ⁴⁴li³²³*, *xa³³ma³⁵ta⁵⁵li⁴⁴li³³li³²³*, *xa³³ma⁴⁴ta⁵⁵ta³¹ni³²³li³²³* — which carry emphasis. The addition of *ta⁵⁵* 'appearance, manner, way' highlights the unknown nature of the queried purpose, so that a closer translation may be 'for what reason?' or 'why in the world?' rather than the neutral 'why?'. Compare the phrase in (171) with the more emphatic use in (172).

(171) i³³   **xa³³ma³⁵li⁴⁴li³³** kʰua³¹la³¹ i³²³ ŋa³¹?
     3SG why   Kunming   go   CNT.Q
     他   为什么   昆明   去
     'Why is he going to Kunming?'
     他为什么去昆明？
     (KL-Elicitation)

(172) i³³   **xa³³ma³⁵ta⁵⁵li⁴⁴li³³li³²³** kʰua³¹la³¹ i³²³ ŋa³¹?
     3SG why   Kunming   go   CNT.Q
     他   为什么   昆明   去
     'Why in the world is he going to Kunming?'
     他为什么去昆明？
     (KL-Elicitation)

5.3.3.6 Interrogative Pronoun *xa³³ni³³* 'how', 'how many'

Mirroring *xa³³ma⁴⁴* 'what', the interrogative pronoun *xa³³ni³³* has two meanings, 'how' and 'how many', depending on its use. As an interrogative relating to manner, it is usually placed between A/S and the verb, which is the prototypical position for adverbs. In clauses in which A or S is omitted, it may begin a question. Examples are shown in (173) and (174). The question in (175) is very common in discourse and has developed a rhetorical meaning. Literally, it asks how a certain procedure is done, corresponding to the English translation of 'how do (you) do it?'. Rhetorically, it is used to describe a situation that cannot be changed, meaning 'what can (you) do (about it)?' or 'what can (you) do?'. The second morpheme of the interrogative pronoun appears to be the adverbial morpheme ni^{33} (see § 9.3.4).

(173) **xa³³ni³³** pɤ⁵³?
 how play
 怎么 弹
 'How do you play (it)?'
 怎么弹？
 (KL-Qin)

(174) tɕʰɛ³²³ tɕi⁵⁵ **xa³³ni³³** kɤ̰³³ zɛi³¹ tɤ³³ ŋa³¹?
 money CL:TYPE how make use PROG CNT.Q
 钱 种 怎么 弄 用
 'How did (you) get the money to pay?'
 钱是怎么弄来用的？
 (KL-Tuition)

(175) **xa³³ni³³** tɕi³³ pa⁵³ ŋa³¹ lɛi³¹?
 how do FUT CNT.Q IRR.EMP
 怎么 弄
 'How do (you) do (it)?' / 'What can (you) do (about it)?'
 要怎么办？
 (WYY-Sewing)

One common collocation contains ta^{55} 'be a type', which yields the question $xa^{33}ni^{33}\ ta^{55}$? 'how, in what way?'. Examples are shown in (176) and (177).

(176) a³³ tɕi⁵⁵ kɤ̰³³ tɤ⁴⁴ **xa³³ni³³ ta⁵⁵** ta³²³ ŋa³¹ lɛi³¹?
 that CL:TYPE do CLNK how be.type able CNT.Q IRR.EMP
 那 种 做 怎么 样 能
 'That type is made in which way?'
 那种能做得怎么样？
 (KL-Sewing)

(177) kʰa⁵⁵tso³¹tɕʰi³¹ ɳa³¹ la³¹? **xa³³ni³³ ta⁵⁵** ŋa³¹?
Khatso speak IRR.Q how be.type CNT.Q
喀卓语 说 怎么 样
'Do (you) speak Khatso? How (good is it)?'
讲喀卓语吗？怎么样？
(KL-Competition)

The pronoun also combines with stative verbs and the verb *tso³²³* to form extentive questions, as shown in (178) and (179). These are described in more detail in § 12.4.2.

(178) **xa³³ni³³** m̩²⁴ tso³²³ ŋa³¹?
how be.tall EXIST CNT.Q
怎么 高 有
'How tall is (he)?'
有多高？
(KL-Elicitation)

(179) tsʰo³¹to³³ tɕi³¹ ma²⁴ ti²⁴ ni³¹, **xa³³ni³³** sɤ²⁴ tso³²³ jo³³ ŋa³¹?
straw.stool one CL:GEN weave TOP how be.long EXIST must CNT.Q
草墩 一 个 编 多么 长 有 应该
'To weave one straw stool, how long must (the straw) be?'
编一个草墩要多长？
(KL-Stools)

When *xa³³ni³³* precedes a classifier, it functions as an interrogative of quantity meaning 'how many', as (180) shows. The plural classifier *ko⁵⁵* can replace a singular classifier, such as *pɛi³¹*, in this construction, as in (181). The meaning of these phrases differs slightly. Using a singular classifier, as in (180), suggests that there are only a few referents. The plural classifier in (181), by contrast, implies that the number is more than a few. Since singular classifiers denote particular types of noun (see § 6.2.1), it is possible to omit the noun without an appreciable change in meaning, as in (182). Examples from discourse are shown in (183) and (184).

(180) sɤ⁵⁵ **xa³³ni³³** **pɛi³¹** vɤ³²³ ŋa³¹?
book how.many CL:VOL buy CNT.Q
书 多少 本 买
'How many books did (you) buy?'
买了多少书？
(KL-Elicitation)

(181) sɣ⁵⁵   **xa³³ni³³**   **ko⁵⁵**   vɤ³²³   ŋa³¹?
book   how.many   CL:PL   buy   CNT.Q
书   多少   本   买
'How many (books) did (you) buy?'
买了多少书？
(KL-Elicitation)

(182) **xa³³ni³³**   **pɛi³¹**   vɤ³²³   ŋa³¹?
how.many   CL:VOL   buy   CNT.Q
几   本   买
'How many (volumes) did (you) buy?'
买了几本？
(KL-Elicitation)

(183) i³³   **xa³³ni³³**   **kʰo⁵³**   so²⁴   ŋa³¹?
3SG   how.many   CL:TMP   study   CNT.Q
他   多少   年   学
'How many years did he study?'
他读了几年？
(KL-Tuition)

(184) **xa³³ni³³**   **nɛi²⁴**   **xa³³ni³³**   **fɤ²⁴**   tso³²³   ŋa³¹?
how.many   CL:ITEM   how.many   CL:ITEM   EXIST   CNT.Q
多少   姐妹   多少   兄弟   有
'How many sisters and brothers were there?'
有几个姐妹几个兄弟？
(KL-Grandfather)

One such construction has become the general plural interrogative pronoun. In *xa³³ni³³ko⁵⁵* the final syllable is the plural classifier *ko⁵⁵*, and it is used when larger quantities are involved. Like *ko⁵⁵*, this interrogative is used with all types of nouns, whether human, animal or inanimate. An example is shown in (185). This form is often used as a stand-alone question in discourse.

(185) ti⁴⁴   tɤ⁴⁴   **xa³³ni³³ko⁵⁵**   li³⁵   tɕʰɛ²⁴   tɤ⁴⁴?
break   CLNK   how.many.CL:PL   leave   finish   STAT.EMP
砸   多少些   离开   完
'How many did (he) finish breaking apart?'
砸开了多少？
(HPH-Toys)

5.3.3.7 Combining Interrogative Pronouns

Multiple interrogative pronouns may be used in a single clause. Following the pattern described above, each pronoun occurs in situ. Thus, it is possible to form questions that query multiple arguments as shown in (186). Naturally, this is not a situation that occurs often in discourse, since context usually makes most details clear.

(186) xa³³   sɛi⁴⁴   xa³³ma⁴⁴ o³¹   tso³²³   ŋa³¹?
      what family   what   vegetable   EXIST   CNT.Q
      哪   家   什么   菜   有
      'Which family has what vegetables?'
      谁家有什么菜？
      (KL-Elicitation)

6 Quantification and Classifiers

As described in Chapter 5, nouns comprise a large portion of the Khatso lexicon. On their own, they do not inherently convey number. In many Sino-Tibetan languages, where this is also true, number need not be marked unless it is vital to the context. In Khatso, however, number is usually indicated in one way or another. The main exception involves common nouns serving as non-specific P of transitive verbs, such as no^{31} 'thing' in no^{31} m^{33} 'to work' which literally means 'to do things'.

There are a number of strategies for indicating number in Khatso. Most involve, at some level, numerals and classifiers. Numerals obviously relate to quantity, but so do classifiers since without a numeral they are considered singular. Even lexical quantifiers and universal constructions include numerals and classifiers in various combinations, as discussed below. There are, however, a few exceptions. For example, the plural morpheme $ts^hɤ^{33}$ in personal pronouns also serves as an associative plural marker (see § 5.3.1). There are a few stative verbs, such as na^{31} 'to be many' and $mɛi^{55}$ 'to be few', which lexically encode quantity. And, indefinite constructions, such as those denoting 'someone' and 'nothing', also inherently refer to quantity (see § 7.3).

Aside from universal quantification, which is a phrasal construction, most of these quantifiers satisfy the noun test. For example, classifiers can appear, without numerals or demonstratives, as heads of both possessive and relative constructions, as shown in (187) and (188). Thus, classifiers are a subset of nouns in Khatso, although their use does not otherwise coincide with that of common nouns.

(187) nɛi³³   pɤ³²³   **tɕi⁵⁵**
      2SG   POSS   CL:TYPE
      你   种
      'your type'
      你的那种
      (KL-Sewing)

(188) mo⁵⁵   pɤ⁵³   so²⁴   la²⁴   **jo³⁵**
      want play learn REL CL:HUM
      要   弹   学   位
      '(the) one who wants to learn to play'
      想要学弹琴的
      (YLW-Learning)

The lexical quantifiers *tɕi³¹ko⁵⁵ma³³* 'many, a lot' and *tɕi³¹ti⁵³za³¹* 'a few, a little' — which are composed of numeral-classifier constructions suffixed by nominal morphemes (see § 4.2.3.2) — also satisfy these tests. They may serve as the head of both possessive constructions and relative clauses, as shown in (189) and (190) respectively. These constructions do not always translate well into English, but they are perfectly grammatical in Khatso.

(189) ŋa³³ i³³ pv̩³²³ **tɕi³¹ko⁵⁵ma³³** vɤ³²³ wa³²³.
 1SG 3SG POSS many buy PFV
 我 他 很多 买
 'I bought a lot from him', literally 'I bought his many.'
 我买他的很多了。
 (KL-Elicitation)

(190) i³³ kɛi³³ m̩³³ la²⁴ **tɕi³¹ko⁵⁵ma³³** tsa³¹n̪a²⁴ tʰɛi³²³ ja³³.
 3SG AGT make REL many be.delicious very IPFV.EMP
 她 做 很多 好吃 很
 'The many she made are delicious.'
 他做的有很多很好吃的。
 (KL-Elicitation)

The status of numerals, however, is less clear. Aside from the act of counting, numerals never occur alone in Khatso. They are bound morphemes that must always attach to classifiers in discourse. Numeral-classifier phrases, like the lexical quantifiers, satisfy the tests for nounhood even without a common noun. The examples in (191) and (192) show them serving as heads of possessive constructions and relative clauses respectively. However, it is uncertain if this is a feature shared by both numerals and classifiers, or a property exclusive to the latter, since classifiers may pattern this way alone. The same problem arises when testing the demonstratives, which are likewise bound morphemes that attach to classifiers, though their pronominal properties suggest that they too are nouns (see § 5.3.2). The ability of numerals to attach to classifiers like demonstratives likewise hints at a nominal status, but it is difficult to prove syntactically because of their bound condition. Nonetheless, given the close functional relationship between numerals and classifiers in quantifying nouns, they are included in this chapter.

(191) sɿ³⁵mɛi³²³xua³³ pv̩³²³ **tɕi³¹ tua³⁵** tɕɛ²⁴ mo³³ ŋa³²³ta³²³ ŋɛi³³.
 sɿ³⁵mɛi³²³xua³³ POSS one CL:SEC read.aloud show be.able ASRT
 细梅花 一 段 念 给听 可以
 '(I) can read out a section of the *sɿ³⁵mɛi³²³xua³³*.'
 可以念一段细梅花给听。
 (KYF-Three Ladies)

(192) tsŋ³²³ tsŋ³¹ sɛi⁴⁴ o²⁴   tʰɛi³²³ la²⁴ **tɛi³¹ jo³⁵** wa³²³.
war fight TOP be.fierce very REL one CL:HUM PFV
战   打   厉害   很   一   位
'When waging war, (he) was a very fierce one.'
打战很厉害的一个了。
(KLT-History)

The following sections describe the various methods of quantification in Khatso. Numerals are described in § 6.1, followed by an explanation of classifiers in § 6.2. Key lexical quantifiers are explained in § 6.3, and universal quantification is described in § 6.4.

6.1 Numerals

There are two cardinal numeral systems that are employed in Khatso. One is the traditional system, which is similar to those found in other Ngwi languages. It is used in counting, buying and selling, and in enumerating common nouns in discourse. The other, newer system is borrowed from Hanyu, likely at the same time that modern time-keeping and currency were adopted. The borrowed system is, in fact, obligatory in constructions involving calendar dates, telling time and discussing prices (see § 6.2.2.7 and § 6.2.2.8 respectively). Commerce is increasingly becoming a Hanyu-only activity. The Khatso often travel to nearby towns to shop, and even in the village market not all merchants speak the language. Thus the newer system is increasingly used in buying and selling, and even in conversation among Khatso speakers. As a result, the newer numerals are now used in syntactic environments where previously only the traditional numerals were used, such as enumerating common nouns in discourse. This change suggests that the traditional numeral system is one of the most endangered parts of the lexicon.

Both systems, listed side-by-side in Table 6.1, are decimal systems. That is, numeral ten is the base and larger numerals are calculated from that base. Numerals of 10,000 and greater, however, operate on a slightly different system. This numeral has its own monomorphemic word va^{35}, and is used as the base for even greater numerals. Thus, 'one hundred thousand' is $tsʰi^{33}va^{35}$, literally 'ten ten-thousands'. Both va^{35} 'ten thousand' and the system that uses it as a base were also borrowed from Hanyu, so even the traditional system shows Chinese influence. Another result of this influence concerns the use of li^{323} 'zero', another Hanyu loan. Larger numbers that lack a numeral in an internal position now require li^{323} in that position, following Chinese practice. Thus 'one hundred one' is typically said as $tɛi^{31}xa^{323}li^{323}tɛi^{31}$ 'one hundred zero one', a rather recent custom. Even the newer system is evolving. For example, the table shows two versions for the numerals 'one', 'two' and 'five'; the older terms are listed first, followed by the newer words. The latter are much closer to the original Hanyu pronunciation and are more often employed by younger speakers who speak Hanyu much more frequently than the older generations. The two versions are interchangeable throughout the system, but for simplicity the table only shows the relevant combinations for numerals one through ten.

Table 6.1: Khatso's two numeral systems

Value	Traditional	New
0	–	li³²³
1	tɛi³¹	zɿ³²³, i³²³
2	ŋ³¹	zɿ³⁵, ɤ³⁵
3	si³³	sa³³
4	xɤ³³	sɿ³⁵
5	ŋa³¹	v̩³³, o³¹
6	tɕʰo⁵³	lv̩³²³
7	sɿ³¹	tsʰɿ³²³
8	ɕi⁵³	pa³²³
9	kv̩³³	tɕo³¹
10	tsʰi³³	sɿ³²³
11	tsʰi³³tsɿ³⁵	sɿ³²³i³²³
12	tsʰi³³ŋ³¹	sɿ³²³ɤ³⁵
13	tsʰi³³si²⁴	sɿ³²³sa³³
14	tsʰi³³xɤ²⁴	sɿ³²³sɿ³⁵
15	tsʰi³³ŋa³¹	sɿ³²³o³¹
16	tsʰi³³tɕʰo⁵³	sɿ³²³lv̩³²³
17	tsʰi³³sɿ³¹	sɿ³²³tsʰɿ³²³
18	tsʰi³³ɕi⁵³	sɿ³²³pa³²³
19	tsʰi³³kv̩²⁴	sɿ³²³tɕo³²³
20	ŋ³¹tsi²⁴	ɤ³⁵sɿ³²³
21	tsi³³tɛi³¹	ɤ³⁵sɿ³²³i³²³
22	tsi³³ŋ³¹	ɤ³⁵sɿ³²³ɤ³⁵
23	tsi³³si²⁴	ɤ³⁵sɿ³²³sa³³
24	tsi³³xɤ²⁴	ɤ³⁵sɿ³²³sɿ³⁵
25	tsi³³ŋa³¹	ɤ³⁵sɿ³²³o³¹
26	tsi³³tɕʰo⁵³	ɤ³⁵sɿ³²³lv̩³²³
27	tsi³³sɿ³¹	ɤ³⁵sɿ³²³tsʰɿ³²³
28	tsi³³ɕi⁵³	ɤ³⁵sɿ³²³pa³²³

Value	Traditional	New
29	tsi³³kv̩²⁴	ɤ³⁵sŋ³²³tɕo³¹
30	si³³tsʰi³³	sa³³sŋ³²³
31	si³³tsʰi³³tɛi³¹	sa³³sŋ³²³i³²³
40	xɤ³³tsʰi³³	sŋ³⁵sŋ³²³
41	xɤ³³tsʰi³³tɛi³¹	sŋ³⁵sŋ³²³i³²³
50	ŋa³¹tsʰi³³	o³¹sŋ³²³
51	ŋa³¹tsʰi³³tɛi³¹	o³¹sŋ³²³i³²³
60	tɕʰo⁵³tsʰi³³	lv³²³sŋ³²³
61	tɕʰo⁵³tsʰi³³tɛi³¹	lv³²³sŋ³²³i³²³
70	sŋ³¹tsʰi³³	tsʰŋ³²³sŋ³²³
71	sŋ³¹tsʰi³³tɛi³¹	tsʰŋ³²³sŋ³²³i³²³
80	ɕi⁵³tsʰi³³	pa³²³sŋ³²³
81	ɕi⁵³tsʰi³³tɛi³¹	pa³²³sŋ³²³i³²³
90	kv̩³³tsʰi³³	tɕo³²³sŋ³²³
91	kv̩³³tsʰi³³tɛi³¹	tɕo³²³sŋ³²³i³²³
100	tɛi³¹xa³²³	i²⁴pɤ³²³
101	tɛi³¹xa³²³tɛi³¹, tɛi³¹xa³²³li³²³tɛi³¹	i²⁴pɤ³²³li³²³i³²³
110	tɛi³¹xa³²³tɛi³¹tsʰi³³	i²⁴pɤ³²³li³²³sŋ³²³
111	tɛi³¹xa³²³tsʰi³³tsŋ³⁵	i²⁴pɤ³²³li³²³sŋ³²³i³²³
120	tɛi³¹xa³²³ŋ³¹tsi²⁴	i²⁴pɤ³²³ɤ³⁵sŋ³²³
121	tɛi³¹xa³²³tsi³³tɛi³¹	i²⁴pɤ³²³ɤ³⁵sŋ³²³i³²³
200	ŋ³¹xa³²³	ɤ³⁵pɤ³²³
201	ŋ³¹xa³²³tɛi³¹, ŋ³¹xa³²³li³²³tɛi³¹	ɤ³⁵pɤ³²³li³²³i³²³
300	si³³xa³²³	sa³³pɤ³²³
1000	tɛi³¹tv̩²⁴	i²⁴tɕʰɛ³³
1001	tɛi³¹tv̩²⁴li³²³tɛi³¹	i²⁴tɕʰɛ³³li³²³i³²³
2000	ŋ³¹tv̩²⁴	ɤ³⁵tɕʰɛ³³
10,000	tɛi³¹va³⁵	i³¹va³⁵
100,000	(tɛi³¹)tsʰi³³va³⁵	sŋ³²³va³⁵
1,000,000	tɛi³¹xa³²³va³⁵	i²⁴pɤ³²³va³⁵
10,000,000	tɛi³¹tv̩²⁴va³⁵	i²⁴tɕʰɛ³³va³⁵
100,000,000	tɛi³¹ɿŋ³⁵	i³¹ɿŋ³⁵

As both He (1989: 28) and Mu (2002: 89) also note, there are two types of abbreviations that are often found in the traditional system. First, η^{31} 'two' 二 is often omitted as the first numeral in the values 21 through 29. Because the morpheme for ten is tsi^{33} rather than ts^hi^{33} in this set, the initial digit is easily omitted without causing confusion. Second, there are shorter forms of the numerals 31 through 99, excluding those that are multiples of ten, which are not shown in the table. Specifically, in these numerals the digit ts^hi^{33} 'ten' is omitted. Thus, 'thirty-one' may be said as $si^{33}tei^{31}$ 'three one' as well as $si^{33}ts^hi^{33}tei^{31}$, and 'seventy-five' is both $sŋ^{31}ŋa^{31}$ 'seven five' and the longer $sŋ^{31}ts^hi^{33}ŋa^{31}$. In addition, there is tone sandhi in the abbreviated forms for 'thirty-three', 'forty-four' and 'ninety-nine'. In this environment the second syllable changes from tone 33 to tone 24, making them $sa^{33}sa^{24}$, $xɤ^{33}xɤ^{24}$ and $kɤ^{33}kɤ^{24}$ respectively. These three numerals often undergo sandhi, a topic discussed in § 3.2.1.

In discourse, numerals are almost always accompanied by a classifier. This occurs regardless of whether the noun is count or mass. Examples are shown in (193), (194) and (195). Note that in the last phrase the newer system is used to discuss prices. For more a detailed discussion of classifiers, see § 6.2.

(193) ɕe³²³so²⁴   ni³¹   **xɤ³⁵**   **kɤ²⁴**   tso³²³.
       instrument.strings TOP   four   CL:STRIP   EXIST
       弦线   四   根   有
       'As for strings, there are four.'
       琴弦呢，有四根。
       (YLW-Qin)

(194) tʰo³³pɛi³³ tɛi³³ ko⁵⁵   to³³   **ŋ³¹**   **jo³⁵**   pɤ³²³   ŋ³³   ja³³.
       shirt   this   CL:PL   also   two   CL:HUM   POSS   COP   IPFV.EMP
       小褂   这   些   也   二   位   是
       'These shirts are also from two people.', literally 'These shirts are also two people's.'
       这些小褂也是两个人的。
       (WYY-Sewing)

(195) **sŋ³⁵sŋ³²³o³¹ kʰuai³¹**   kɛi³³   **o³¹sŋ³²³**   **kʰuai³¹**   kɛi³³   tɛi³³ni³³   ŋ³¹   tɤ³³   ŋɛi³³.
       forty-five CL:MNY   CONJ   five.ten   CL:MNY   CONJ   this.way   sell   PROG   ASRT
       四十五   块   和   五十   块   和   这么   卖
       '45 yuan and 50 yuan, (they) sell (them) this way.'
       四十五块和五十块这么卖的。
       (WYF-Stools)

Numeral-classifier constructions may also be used with pronouns to specify an exact number of participants, such as in (196) and (197). This is a productive process — any numeral may be used — though in discourse round numbers tend to be used above 'ten'.

(196) **i³³tsʰɤ³¹ ŋ³¹ jo³⁵** i³²³ kɯ³¹ wa³²³ po⁵³.
      3PL　　　two　CL:HUM　go　INDR.CAUS　PFV　EPIS.EMP
      他们　　两　　位　　　去
      'They two were allowed to go, (didn't you know?)'
      让他们两个去了。
      (KL-Competition)

(197) **ŋa³³tsʰɤ³³ ŋ³¹ jo³⁵** tsɿ³⁵ ko⁵³ ŋɛi³³.
      1PL　　　two　CL:HUM　fish　EXP　ASRT
      我们　　两　　位　　　捞　　过
      'We two have fished together.'
      我们两个一起捞过。
      (ZMF-Fishing)

Of course, speakers are not always exact in natural speech, and there are several strategies for making numerical approximations. The first is by mentioning two consecutive numerals before the classifier, as in (198), which is identical to the English construction 'three or four', though in Khatso disjunction is unnecessary. In the second strategy, the noncompositional phrase *ma³¹ pa³¹* is placed after the numeral and classifier, as in (199). It means 'approximate' and thus includes amounts that are only slightly less or slightly more.

(198) **si³⁵ xɤ³⁵ kʰo⁵³** za³¹ lo⁵³ ŋɛi³³.
      three　four　CL:TMP　DIM　reach　ASRT
      三　　四　　年　　　　　　到
      '(It) took three or four years.'
      是有三四年了。
      (WYF-Stools)

(199) sɿ³⁵ŋ³⁵tʰa³³, ɛi³¹, **si³⁵ m³¹ ma³¹ pa³¹** v³²³.
      year.before.last　FILL　three　CL:MSR　approximate　buy
      前年　　　　　　　　　　三　　亩　　　左右　　　　　买
      'The year before last, um, (I) bought around half a hectare.'
      前年，嗯，买三亩左右。
      (WYF-Stools)

The third strategy allows speakers to indicate amounts that are more or less than the stated numeral. The first construction involves a negative reduplicative adverb derived from the existential verb *tso³²³*, as shown in (200), which means 'not quite'. When modifying times, a similar adverb *ma³¹ tsʰŋ³³ tsʰŋ³³ za³¹ ni³³*, derived from *tsʰŋ³³* 'to arrive, reach', is used. When the amount is greater, the stative verb *ɳa³¹* 'to be many', modified by by the quantifier *tɕi³¹ti⁵³za³¹*, is employed in an adverbial manner, as shown in (201). Reduplicative adverbial constructions are discussed in § 8.1.2.2.

(200) tɕi³¹va³⁵   **ma³¹ tso³²³ tso³²³ za³¹ ni³³** kɯ³¹ ŋɛi³³.
one.thousand NEG   EXIST   EXIST   DIM   ADV   give ASRT
一万   不   有   有   给
'(I) paid not quite one thousand (yuan).'
给了不到一万。
(KL-Elicitation)

(201) tɕi³¹va³⁵   **tɕi³¹ti⁵³za³¹ n̩a³¹**   kɯ³¹ ŋɛi³³.
one.thousand a.little   be.many give ASRT
一万   一点   多   给
'(I) gave more (than) one thousand (yuan).'
给了一万多一点。
(KL-Elicitation)

Fractions involve a borrowed construction. This construction contains the phrase *fɛi³³ tsʅ³³* which literally means 'divided by' in Hanyu. Thus, the denominator is named first and the numerator last. For example, *sa³³ fɛi³³ tsʅ³³ i³²³* 'one third' is literally 'three divided by one'. Percentages follow the same format, although in this phrase 'hundred' may carry either tone 323 or tone 24, and it is never preceded by *tɕi³¹* 'one'. 'One percent', then, can be said *pɤ³²³ fɛi³³ tsʅ³³ i³²³* or *pɤ²⁴ fɛi³³ tsʅ³³ i³²³*.

The ordinal numeral construction also makes use of a Hanyu loanword. The borrowed morpheme *tiɛ³⁵* is placed before a numeral and a classifier, and the numeral must be from the newer system. However, unlike in Hanyu, the construction follows the noun in Khatso. The construction may be used with an overt noun, as in (202), or replace it as a pronoun, as in (203).

(202) tsʰo³³   **tiɛ³⁵ lɤ³²³ jo³⁵**
person   ORD   six   CL:HUM
人   第   六   位
'the sixth person'
第六个人
(KL-Elicitation)

(203) **tiɛ³⁵ sʅ³⁵ pɛi³²³**   pɤ³²³ **tiɛ³⁵ i³²³ kɤ³⁵**
ORD   four CL:ROW   POSS   ORD   one CL:BDG
第   四   排   第   一   间
'the first (house) in the fourth (street)'
第四排的第一所
(YAY-Erasers)

Comparative constructions that involve numerals and the multiplier classifier *pɛi³⁵* are explained in § 12.5.4. Quantification constructions that do not involve numerals are discussed in § 6.3 and § 6.4.

6.2 Classifiers

Like many languages in the Sino-Tibetan family, Khatso has a rich classifier system. Classifiers are morphemes that modify nouns according to one or more salient features inherent in the noun, such as humanness, shape, size, structure or function (Aikhenvald 2000: 272–274). Linguists make a distinction between noun classifiers, which typically accompany nouns in all contexts, and numeral classifiers, which are generally only obligatory when numerals are employed (Aikhenvald 2000: 90–91). Khatso classifiers straddle the two groups. They behave like prototypical numeral classifiers, but are also often used without a numeral in discourse. Moreover, a few modify verbs rather than nouns. For these reasons, the more general term *classifier* is used here.

The category is a closed class in Khatso, although it is clear that there have been many loans from Hanyu over the years, such as *pʰi³²³* 'bottle', *tsʰuɛi³⁵* 'inch' and *fɛi³³* 'minute'. Because classifiers in Khatso can serve as the heads of possessive constructions or relative clauses, as shown in (204) and (205) respectively, they satisfy the test for nounhood and are thus considered a subset of the noun class. This independent use also suggests that they are syntactically separate words, but in fact they cannot pattern as stand-alone nouns. In natural speech, they are phonologically cliticized to the element that precedes them, whether that is a noun, numeral, demonstrative or grammatical particle.

(204) ŋa³³tsʰʏ̩³³ pʏ³²³ **ko⁵⁵**
      3PL   POSS   CL:PL
      我们   些
      'our many'
      我们的那些
      (ZRF-Competition)

(205) ni³¹tsʏ̩³³pa³³pa³³ mɛi⁴⁴ xɛi⁵³ la²⁴ **jo³⁵**
      millstone   CL:GEN stand REL CL:HUM
      石碾团   个   站   位
      'the one standing on the millstone'
      站在石碾团上那个
      (PYX-Performing)

6.2.1 The Use of Classifiers

Every count noun in Khatso has at least one lexically-assigned classifier. As already mentioned, the classifier typically refers to a specific feature of the noun, and thus the relationship between the two is semantic. For example, *jo³⁵* is the classifier that accompanies all human nouns, and *kɤ²⁴* is used with long, thin and flexible items, such as rope, thread, cable, fishing line and so on. Mass nouns can take a variety of classifiers depending on the relevant measure. For instance, *i³²³tɕa⁵³* 'water' may be modified by *pɛi³³* 'cup', *pʰi³²³* 'bottle' or *sɛi³³* 'liter' as appropriate. Note that some classifiers correspond to nouns in English, but others are untranslatable; see the descriptions presented in Table 6.5 in § 6.2.3.

Classifiers almost always follow nouns in discourse. When numerals and demonstratives are used, they are placed between noun and classifier, as shown in (206) and (207). All three elements can be used together to modify a noun, as the example in (208) illustrates. Some classifiers — especially those relating to money, time and date — require numerals borrowed from Hanyu rather than the traditional Khatso system (see § 6.1).

(206) **ta³⁵kɤ³³mo³³**　　　　**tɛi³¹**　**jo³⁵**　　tso³²³.
　　　big.paternal.aunt　　one　CL:HUM　EXIST
　　　大姑妈　　　　　　　一　　位　　　有
　　　'There is one older paternal aunt.'
　　　有一个大姑妈。
　　　(YJR-Grandfather)

(207) **m̩³²³**　**tɛi³³**　**pɤ²⁴**　　o⁵³　　tɕʰɛ⁵³　ja³³.
　　　field　this　CL:PCE　weed　finish　IPFV.EMP
　　　田　　这　　块　　　薅　　完
　　　'(I want to) finish pulling weeds (in) this field.'
　　　要薅完这块田的。
　　　(HPH-Weeds)

(208) tsɿ³¹to⁵³xo³¹　**jo³⁵**　　la³³　　　　**tɛi³³**　**tɛi³¹**　**jo³⁵**.
　　　leprosy　　　CL:HUM　resemble　this　　one　　CL:HUM
　　　麻风病　　　位　　　像　　　　这　　　一　　　位
　　　'This one resembled a leper.'
　　　像麻风病人一样的一个。
　　　(HPH-Weeds)

Classifier constructions — that is, collocations in which a classifier is modified in some way, whether by demonstrative, numeral, possessor or relative clause — can serve as pronouns in discourse. This occurs when a particular noun is omitted because it is already given information. Examples are shown in (209) and (210). And while personal pronouns may be used for humans, non-human arguments are usually replaced by classifier constructions, which usually provide more semantic information than a personal pronoun. Unmodified classifiers, however, cannot serve as pronouns. In a separate construction, classifiers accompany interrogative pronouns in questions about specific items and amounts (see § 5.3.3.2 and § 5.3.3.6).

(209) **a³³ kɤ²⁴** tʰɤ⁵⁵ tʰi³¹.
that CL:STRIP CL:TMP weave
那 根 下 编
'Weave that strip.'
编一下那根。
(WYF-Dance Parties)

(210) sɛi⁴⁴ tɛi³¹ ŋ³²³ **ŋ³¹ si³³ ma⁴⁴** kɛi³³ tɕɛ⁵⁵ ŋa³²³ ja³³ tsɛi³¹.
person one CL:TMP two three CL:GEN AGT sew able IPFV.EMP HSY
人家 一 天 二 三 个 钉 能
'(They) say a person can sew two or three in one day.'
说人家一天能打两三个的。
(WYY-Sewing)

In addition, there are routinized classifier constructions that have developed idiomatic uses. For example, the quantifier nouns tɛi³¹ko⁵⁵ma³³ 'many' and tɛi³¹ti⁵³za³¹ 'few' are composed of the numeral tɛi³¹ 'one', a classifier relating to quantity and a nominal suffix. These compound nouns are discussed in more detail in § 6.3.

Other idiomatic expressions involve reduplicating the classifier with the numeral one, with the meaning of a few members within a larger group. Thus the phrase in (211), in which the human classifier jo³⁵ is reduplicated, means 'several people within a group', and that in (212) translates as 'several dogs within a pack'. With temporal classifiers, a better interpretation is 'some', as in tɛi³¹xa⁵³xa⁵³ 'some evenings' and tɛi³¹la³³la³³ 'some months'. However, the phrase tɛi³¹ŋ²⁴ŋ³²³, which includes the classifier 'day' and idiosyncratic tone sandhi, has developed the idiomatic meaning of 'every day'.

(211) **tɛi³¹ jo³⁵ jo³⁵**
one CL:HUM CL:HUM
一 位 位
'several people within a group'
一个个
(KL-Elicitation)

(212) tsʰŋ³¹ tɛi³¹ ma²⁴ ma²⁴
dog   one   CL:GEN CL:GEN
狗   一   个   个
'several dogs within a pack'
一只只狗
(KL-Elicitation)

When a reduplicated classifier construction is followed by the adverbial particle *ni³³*, it carries the meaning of 'one after another', as shown in (213) and (214).

(213) tɛi³¹ tɛi³⁵ tɛi³⁵ ni³³ tɕa³¹ tsʰi³³ li⁴⁴ ta³¹
one   CL:TMP CL:TMP ADV talk descend come after
一   代   代   讲   下   来   后
'after coming down one generation after another'
一代代地讲下来呢
(HPH-Horse Dug Well)

(214) tɛi³¹ tɕʰa³¹ tɕʰa³¹ ni³³ vɤ³²³ tɤ³³ ŋ³³ sŋ⁴⁴?
one   CL:BNCH CL:BNCH ADV buy PROG COP COP
一   捆   捆   买   是   是
'Don't you buy (it) bunch by bunch?'
是不是一捆捆地买?
(KL-Stools)

Classifiers serve several functions in discourse. First, they indicate number. Naturally, when a numeral is present, number is clearly marked. But even without a numeral, classifiers convey a numerical meaning. Collective classifiers, such as the all-purpose plural *ko⁵⁵*, make nouns plural. The other classifiers, by contrast, mark nouns as singular. This may be emphasized with a demonstrative, but a bare classifier — likely the result of routine omission of the numeral *tɛi³¹* 'one' — is sufficient to convey the singular meaning, as shown in (215), (216) and (217). Note that bare classifiers may be translated into English with either the indefinite or definite articles; Khatso does not syntactically mark this distinction.

(215) ŋa³³tsʰɤ³³ vɤ⁵³ tɤ⁴⁴ sɤ⁵⁵ pɛi³¹ li⁴⁴ tɕi³³.
3PL   write CLNK book CL:VOL in enter
我们   写   书   本   里   进
'We will write (it) in a book.'
我们写在书里。
(KL-Sewing)

(216) i^{323}xo^{323} mɛi^{44} mo^{55} tɤ^{44} xa^{33}ma^{44} m^{33} ta^{31}?
flat.button   CL:GEN   want   CLNK   what   do   RHET.Q
纽扣   个   要   什么   做
'What (do you) want (to) do with a flat button?'
扁纽扣要了做什么嘛？
(WYY-Sewing)

(217) ɕo^{323}ɕau^{35} mɛi^{44} pγ^{323} wɛi^{323}tɕʰa^{323} mɛi^{44} v̩^{33} tɕa^{33} i^{33} n̩a^{31}.
school   CL:GEN POSS   wall   CL:GEN   count   cross   go   speak
学校   个   围墙   堵   数   过   去   说
'Count over from the wall of the school.'
从学校的围墙数过去。
(YAY-Erasers)

The second purpose of classifiers is to mark the specificity of the referent. That is, the presence of a classifier marks the noun as a unique referent in discourse. And of course, if a referent is specific then it also has number. For example, the nouns modified by bare classifiers in (215), (216) and (217) above are not only singular, they also refer to real items in the world. Because of these important referential functions, bare classifiers are so common in natural speech that speakers often translate single Chinese nouns into noun-classifier constructions in Khatso. As a result, earlier glossaries of the language occasionally mistake the classifier for a part of the noun itself. For a list of classifiers in Khatso, see Table 6.5 in § 6.2.3..

By contrast, the absence of a classifier indicates that the noun has non-specific reference, pointing to the entire category rather than a particular member within it. For instance, the vegetables listed in (218) refer to possible types of ingredients rather than to individual items on a kitchen counter. Likewise, the classifier-less nouns in the first three intonation units in (219) instantiate types of clothing rather than particular garments.

(218) xa^{35}tɕʰɛ^{323}, tɕɛ^{35},   ŋ^{24}tɕa^{323},   no^{53}tsɿ^{31},   wa^{53}sa^{31},   tɛi^{31} tiɛ^{55} tiɛ^{53} ni^{33}
celery   mushroom   other   tofu   pork,   one   slice   slice   ADV
芹菜   菌   别的   豆腐   猪肉   一   片   片
so^{35} pa^{31}.
chop   be.thin
切   薄
'Celery, mushrooms, other (vegetables), tofu, pork, chop (them) into thin slices.'
芹菜，菌，别的，豆腐，猪肉，一片片地切成薄片。
(KL-Hotpot)

(219) **wi³²³jau⁴⁴** sa³³ li³²³,
belt sew know.how
围腰 逢 会
'(I) also know how to sew belts,'
也会缝围腰，

tʰo³³pɛi⁴⁴ sa³³ li³²³,
upper.garment sew know.how
褂子 逢 会
'(I) also know how to sew upper garments,'
也会缝褂子，

tʰo⁴⁴ sa³³ li³²³,
clothing sew know.how
衣服 逢 会
'(I) also know how to sew clothes,'
会缝衣服，

la⁵⁵ tsa²⁴ sa³³ ma³¹ ko⁵³ la³⁵ ŋɛi³³.
trousers CL:ITEM sew NEG EXP FOC ASRT
裤子 件 逢 不 过
'(I) have never sewn a pair of trousers.'
就是没有缝过裤子。
(WYY-Sewing)

Items serving as P in transitive and ditransitive phrases often lack classifiers, especially in contexts where it is the least important element of the discussion. Not only are these nouns non-specific, in many constructions they are so bleached of meaning that they arguably have no referent whatsoever. For example, *tsa³²³ tsa³¹* 'rice eat' is the basic term for eating even if rice is not part of the meal. Similarly, *sɣ⁵⁵vɣ⁵³* 'book write' is the basic term for writing Chinese characters even if one is writing on a blackboard or typing on a computer. The nouns in (220) and (221) have non-specific reference, referring to entire categories rather than individual items. These compounds also approximate non-specific indefinite constructions, which are discussed in § 7.3.2.

(220) **tsʰo³¹to³³** **tsɣ⁵³** xɛi³¹ pv̩³¹ sɻ⁴⁴ xua²⁴ ma³¹ tʰɣ⁵⁵.
straw.stool weave still NEG COP expense NEG achieve
草墩 打 还 不 是 划 不 着
'Making straw stools is not worth the expense.'
打草墩也不划算。
(WYF-Stools)

(221) tɕo³⁵ i²⁴tɕʰɛ³²³ pɤ⁵³ so²⁴
       then   qin   play   learn
       就   琴   弹   学
       'then (I) learned to play (the) *qin*'
       就学弹琴
       (YLW-Learning)

This pattern is consistent with agency hierarchies (e.g. Dixon 1979: 85-86; Du Bois 1987: 840–843; Silverstein 1976), which state that animate participants are typically more relevant in discourse than inanimate objects, and there may thus be morphosyntactic differences in how they are treated. Indeed, if P is the topic of a narrative in Khatso, it will usually be introduced separately and explicitly early on in discourse. In later constructions it will be omitted altogether; interlocutors rely on pragmatics to follow key participants in discourse. Mentioning new P in transitive phrases underscores their relative unimportance in the discourse.

6.2.2 Types of Classifiers

The classifier inventory in Khatso is broad and varied. At a high level, classifiers can be divided into two general types, sortal and mensural. Sortal classifiers accompany count nouns and highlight salient features inherent in the noun, such as humanness, shape, size, texture, structure or function. Some classifiers combine several features for even greater specificity. Mensural classifiers modify mass nouns, and define the relevant measure of quantity. At a lower level, however, we find a great deal of variation in type and function across these two groups. For example, collective classifiers are used to mark nouns as plural, temporal classifiers establish clausal time frames, and other classifiers perform adverbial functions. These subtypes are explored in this section along with the broader types of sortal and mensural classifiers. A list of classifiers is presented in Table 6.5 in § 6.2.3 below.

6.2.2.1 Sortal Classifiers

As mentioned above, sortal classifiers accompany count nouns and denote a salient feature of the noun. The highlighted feature typically relates to physical properties such as shape, size, internal structure or arrangement. Some classifiers combine several of these meanings. In Khatso, a few classifiers also highlight the function of a noun. In addition, one classifier, ma^{24}, is used with such a wide variety of nouns that no single feature is implied, as described below.

There are a number of classifiers that relate to shape. One such is la^{53} which accompanies nouns that are flat, such as mirrors, framed pictures, cloth, sheets, drapes, carpets, signs and banners. There are two mensural classifiers that are specifically differentiated by size — $tsɤ^{35}$ denotes a bunch of smaller items, such as vegetables or pens, and $tsɤ^{31}$ describes bunches of larger items, such as clothing or paper. In addition, some classifiers encode multiple features. For example, $kɤ^{24}$ refers to long, thin and flexible items, such as thread, rope, cable and fishing line. Another classifier, po^{24}, refers to long and thin items that do not bend, such as pens, sticks, canes and poles.

For other nouns, structure is more salient. For example, the classifier $pɛi^{31}$ is used with all items made of bound paper, such as books, notebooks and magazines, and $jɛ^{31}$ denotes a page within such an item. Some classifiers highlight noun function, such as tsa^{33}, which is used with implements that can be held in the hand, such as knives, oars and tools of all types. The classifier ta^{323} denotes animals that wriggle, such as snakes, eels, worms and dragons.

There is one sortal classifier that refers to more than one feature or category. This classifier is ma^{24}, and it is used with small, round items — such as rice, corn, beans and seeds — as well as with smaller animals, fish and birds. It is also serves a variety of inanimate nouns such as furniture, airplanes, poems, bags, bottles, ghosts, demons and the generic noun $ņo^{31}$ 'thing'. It is unclear if this is a general classifier, much like gè 个 in Chinese, or two or more homophonous yet distinct classifiers. Unlike the Chinese classifier, however, ma^{24} cannot replace other classifiers in discourse, which is often the case in spoken Putonghua.

The ma^{24} classifier is also the only one that has alternants in various constructions. When a numeral greater than two accompanies ma^{24} the classifier becomes $nɛi^{31}$, as shown in (222). When combined with the demonstrative morphemes, the classifier carries tone 44, as in (223), but if a numeral is also present then $nɛi^{31}$ is again required, as in (224). And when used as a bare classifier, it typically takes the form $mɛi^{44}$, as (225) illustrates. The latter cannot, in fact, co-occur with a demonstrative or numeral, and is the only classifier to be so restricted.

(222) tɛi³¹ **ma²⁴**   ŋ³¹ **ma²⁴**   sɛi³⁵ **nɛi³¹**   xɤ³⁵ **nɛi³¹**
      one   CL:GEN   two CL:GEN   three CL:GEN   four   CL:GEN
      一   个   二   个   三   个   四   个
      (KL-Elicitation)

(223) tɛi³³ **ma⁴⁴**   a³³   **ma⁴⁴**
      this   CL:GEN   that CL:GEN
      这   个   那   个
      'this one'   'that one'
      这个   那个
      (KL-Elicitation)

(224) tɕi³³ ŋa³¹ **nɛi³¹**   a³³ ŋa³¹ **nɛi³¹**
      this five CL:GEN   that five CL:GEN
      这   五   个   那   五   个
      'these five'   'those five'
      这五个   那五个
      (KL-Elicitation)

(225) tsʰŋ̩³¹ **mɛi⁴⁴**   ŋa³¹ **mɛi⁴⁴**   tsɤ²⁴tsŋ̩³²³ **mɛi⁴⁴**   ʐŋ̩²⁴ **mɛi⁴⁴**
      dog   CL:GEN   fish CL:GEN   desk   CL:GEN   boat CL:GEN
      狗   个   鱼   个   桌子   个   船   个
      'a/the dog'   'a/the fish'   'a/the desk'   'a/the boat'
      狗   鱼   桌子   船
      (KL-Elicitation)

6.2.2.2 Mensural Classifiers

The mensural classifiers are measure words that define the relevant quantity of a noun. They are most often used with mass nouns, such as i³²³tɕa⁵³ 'water' and tsa³²³ 'rice'. And because there is no single measure dedicated to each mass noun, there is considerable freedom in pairing these nouns with classifiers. Moreover, mensural classifiers may also modify count nouns, since the latter can also be grouped in certain quantities. The inventory of mensural classifiers may be loosely divided into three groups: traditional measures, modern measures and containers.

Traditional measures include classifiers that appear to have been borrowed from Hanyu some time ago. They include length measures such as tsʰuɛi³⁵ 'inch' and tsʰŋ̩²⁴ 'foot', weight measures such as tsŋ̩²⁴ 'jīn (half a gram)', distance measures such as li³¹ 'lǐ (half a kilometer)', and surface measures such as m̩³¹ 'mǔ (one-sixth of an acre)'. The category also includes more specialized measures such as lɛi³²³ 'length of arm span', mɛi³³ 'mouthful', tsʰau³³ 'cupped handful' and jo⁵³ 'dose of medicine'. Modern measures refer to the metric system now used in China, and they copy the same structure as the original Chinese. That is, they include the initial borrowed morpheme ko³³ 'public' which is combined with traditional measures. For example, 'kilogram' is ko³³tsŋ̩²⁴ and 'kilometer' is ko³³li³¹.

There are also mensural classifiers that denote containers. These include tɕi³⁵ '(small) bag', tɤ⁵³ '(large) sack', kɤ²⁴ŋ³³ 'basket', tɕɛ³²³ 'pitcher', pʰi³²³ 'bottle', pɤ⁵³ 'jar, can', pa³⁵ 'bowl', xo²⁴ 'box' and tʰy̩³¹ 'bucket'. These classifiers are often closely related to the common nouns for these items. In some cases, they are identical, such as those shown in (226). In others, the common noun consists of a reduplicated form of the classifier, as shown in (227).

(226) o³¹   tɕi³¹   **kɤ²⁴ŋ³³**   **kɤ²⁴ŋ³³**   tɕi³¹   pa²⁴
     vegetable one   CL:MSR   basket   one   CL:HNDL
     菜   一   箩   箩   一   把
     'one basket of vegetables'   'one basket'
     一箩筐菜   一只箩筐

     i³²³tɕa⁵³   ŋ³¹   **tʰɤ³¹**   **tʰɤ³¹**   ŋ³¹   pa²⁴
     water   two   CL:MSR   bucket   two   CL:HNDL
     水   二   桶   桶   二   把
     'two buckets of water'   'two buckets'
     两桶水   两只水桶
     (KL-Elicitation)

(227) i³²³tɕa⁵³ tɕi³¹   **pɛi³³**   **pɛi³³pɛi³³** tɕi³¹   ma²⁴
     water   one   CL:MSR   cup   one   CL:GEN
     水   一   杯   杯   一   个
     'one cup of water'   'one cup'
     一杯水   一个杯子

     tsʅ³²³   ŋ³¹   **pʰi³²³**   **pʰi³²³pʰi³²³** ŋ³¹   ma²⁴
     wine   two   CL:MSR   bottle   two   CL:GEN
     酒   二   瓶   瓶子   二   个
     'two bottles of liquor'   'two bottles'
     两瓶酒   两个瓶子
     (KL-Elicitation)

6.2.2.3 Collective Classifiers

One group of classifiers is collective in nature, meaning that they mark accompanying nouns as plural without a numeral. Because of this plural sense, they typically do not co-occur with numerals greater than one. Doing so indicates that there are multiple groups rather than multiple individuals. For example, the most common collective classifier is *ko⁵⁵*, which can be used with any kind of noun, whether count or mass, human, animal or inanimate. Used as a bare classifier or with a demonstrative, it provides a general plural meaning, as shown in (228) in (229). When the numeral one is introduced, it denotes a smaller quantity and is interpreted as 'some' or 'several', as in (230) and (231). When it co-occurs with a numeral greater than one the classifier is interpreted as 'group', as the example in (232) demonstrates.

(228) na³¹ni²⁴za³¹ **ko⁵⁵** to³³ tɕo³⁵ sʅ⁵⁵.
child CL:PL also then know
小孩 些 也 就 知道
'The children also knew (about it).'
小孩也就知道。
(KL-Childhood)

(229) **tɛi³³ ko⁵⁵** sʅ⁵⁵ ma³¹ sʅ³²³.
this CL:PL know NEG be.certain
这 些 知道 不 确定
'I'm not sure about all these (things).'
不知道这么多了。
(WYY-Sewing)

(230) m̥²⁴tʰei³³ **tɛi³¹ ko⁵⁵** kʰɤ²⁴ ta⁵⁵
wood one CL:PL carve put
木头 那 些 刻 放
'some of the wood is carved'
刻得这些木头放着
(KL-Doors)

(231) m̥³²³ ma³¹ n̥a³¹ ma³¹ mɛi⁵⁵ **tɛi³¹ ko⁵⁵** tso³²³ ni³¹
field NEG be.many NEG be.few one CL:PL EXIST TOP
田 不 多 不 少 一 些 有
'there were several fields, neither many nor few'
田不多不少有一些呢
(GCS-Childhood)

(232) tsʰo³³ **si³³ ko⁵⁵** kʰua³¹la³¹ i³²³ wa³²³.
person three CL:PL Kunming go PFV
人 三 些 昆明 去
'Three groups of people went to Kunming.'
三拨人去昆明了。
(KL-Elicitation)

Another classifier, *tɕi⁵⁵*, has also taken on a general pluralizing function. When used with a numeral or demonstrative, it means 'type, sort', as shown in (233). This meaning also holds when it is used as a bare classifier, as in (234). However, often the latter usage is interpreted simply as plural, perhaps because semantically a 'type' implies multiple members. Examples of this additional interpretation are shown in (235) and (236); note that *tɕa⁵³* 'toothgrass' is a countable noun in Khatso. Context often determines which sense is most relevant, although note that in (235) *tɕi⁵⁵* may be interpreted in either way. In (236) the plural sense is more logical.

(233) tɕa⁵³ m̩³²³ a³³ **tɕi⁵⁵** n̪a³¹ tʏ⁴⁴.
toothgrass field that CL:TYPE be.many STAT.EMP
牙齿草 田 那 种 多
'That type of toothgrass field was plentiful.'
牙齿草田那么多。
(HPH-Weeds)

(234) pʏ⁵⁵ to⁵³ li³³ la²⁴ tsʐ³²³ tsʰʐ³³ **tɕi⁵⁵**
ferment exit come REL liquor white CL:TYPE
酿 出 来 酒 白 种
'(that) type of fermented clear liquor'
酿出来的白酒
(HPH-Horse Dug Well)

(235) tɕa⁵³ **tɕi⁵⁵** tɛi³³tɕʰa⁵⁵kʰʏ³³ kʏ³³ tsuɛi²⁴ wa³³.
toothgrass CL:TYPE this.time make cut CRS
牙齿草 种 这时候 弄 绝
'Now (they were able) to cut the toothgrass.' / 'Now (they were able) to cut that type of toothgrass.'
牙齿草现在弄绝了。
(HPH-Weeds)

(236) m̩³¹ to³⁵tsʐ³¹ **tɕi⁵⁵** kɛi³³ ŋ³¹ si³³ to³⁵tsʐ³¹ ŋ³³ n̪a³³ tsɛi³¹.
horse pack CL:TYPE INS two three pack COP COP.EMP HSY
马 驮子 种 用 二 三 驮子 是
'(They) say (they did it) with horse packs, two or three loads.'
说是用马驮子驼两三驮子的。
(YJR-Grandfather)

The other collective classifiers are more restricted semantically. For example, *o³³* is usually only used for groups of non-human animates, such as animals, birds, fish and insects — there are no specialized terms in Khatso corresponding to 'flock', 'school', 'swarm', etc. Collective classifiers such as *tsʏ³⁵* 'bunch', *ma⁵³* 'pile' and *tsʐ⁵⁵* 'row' describe the shape or arrangement of the collected nouns in addition to plurality.

Khatso has several classifiers that refer to nouns that come in pairs. For example, *tsɛi²⁴* is used with socks, shoes, chopsticks and scissors; *kʰʏ³³* with earrings and pairs of bracelets; *fʏ⁵⁵* is used with eyeglasses and dentures; and *tiɛ⁵⁵* with pairs of humans, such as twins and married couples.

In addition, there are collective classifiers that uniquely refer to humans and family groups. They are discussed in § 6.2.2.3 and § 6.2.2.5 respectively.

6.2.2.4 Human Classifiers

There is a small group of classifiers that specifically refer to humans. The classifier jo^{35} is singular, and is used with any noun that points to a human referent, such as man, child, father, sister, teacher, farmer, mayor, etc. By contrast, the general classifiers ma^{24} and $mɛi^{44}$ are used with human nouns to denote the occupation rather than the person. Compare $lau^{323}sɿ^{33}\ jo^{35}$ 'a teacher (person)' and $lau^{323}sɿ^{33}\ mɛi^{44}$ 'a teacher position'. Note, however, that when personal names are accompanied by a title the classifier $mɛi^{44}$ is used rather than jo^{35} (see § 5.2.1).

The other human classifiers are collective in nature. For example, $sɛi^{44}$ 'family' denotes a family group and is often used in possessive constructions (see § 7.4), while yu^{53} 'household' refers to families as well as businesses and institutions — i.e., places full of people. The classifier $tɛi^{35}$ refers to a generation of people, and mo^{31} refers to a couple in a relationship. Khatso also has a set of classifiers that are used specifically for family groupings such as 'father and son' and 'mother and daughter'; these are described in the next section.

6.2.2.5 Family Group Classifiers

Like many languages in the Ngwi family (Bradley 2001b: 1), Khatso has an unusual set of deictic family group classifiers. These specifically refer to combinations of people within an immediate family, such as 'father and son' and 'mother and daughter', though their meaning varies considerably due to context. Given their very specific semantic content, they are not frequent in discourse and, in fact, they are falling out of use among speakers. Even older speakers now mainly use periphrastic expressions to describe family relationships. Technically, they are a subset of human collective classifiers (see § 6.2.2.4), but because they are so typologically unusual, they are given their own section here.

The classifiers are listed in Table 6.2, along with a rubric for their use. *Relation* points to the family relationship the classifier instantiates, *referent* means the person denoted by the pronoun or noun the classifier modifies, and *meaning* defines the interpretations possible for each referent. Given the semantics, all but one of these classifiers must be accompanied by a numeral of two or greater. The exception is $pʰa^{31}$, which requires a numeral of three or greater, since it minimally includes two parents and a child. The classifiers for mother, father and the two together are related to the human suffixes described in § 4.2.3.2. And, except for those involving siblings, these classifiers trigger tone 35 sandhi in the numerals si^{33} 'three', $xʏ^{33}$ 'four' and $kʏ^{33}$ 'nine' (see § 3.2.1).

Table 6.2: Family group classifiers in Khatso

Classifier	Relation	Referent	Meaning
pa⁵⁵	father	man	father & referent, referent & son/daughter
		woman	father & referent
ma⁵⁵	mother	man	mother & referent
		woman	mother & referent, referent & daughter/son
pʰa³¹	father & mother	man	father, mother & referent
		woman	father, mother & referent
piɛ⁵⁵liɛ⁵⁵	grandparent	man	grandparent & referent, referent & grandchild
		woman	grandparent & referent, referent & grandchild
fɤ²⁴	brother, brother-in-law	man	brother & referent, brother-in-law & referent
nɛi²⁴	sister, sibling	man	sister & referent, siblings & referent
		woman	sister & referent, brother & referent, siblings & referent
tsɿ⁵⁵miɛ⁵⁵	sister-in-law	man	sister-in-law & referent (but first person not possible)
		woman	sister-in-law & referent

As the table indicates, each classifier refers to a combination of family members, so that a phrase containing *ma⁵⁵* will refer to a mother and a child, and *piɛ⁵⁵liɛ⁵⁵* will refer to a grandparent and a grandchild. The exact interpretation will also be influenced by the number, age and sex of a particular referent. For example, the phrase in (237) may mean 'my father and I' for any speaker regardless of the situation, but when spoken by an adult male it may also mean 'my child and I'. Likewise, if the phrase is spoken by people who do not have children — for example, teenagers or those who are unmarried — it can only mean 'my father and I'. An adult female cannot use this phrase to refer to her own children; she uses *ma⁵⁵* instead. Examples from discourse are presented in (238), (239) and (240). Note that if the numeral is greater than two, the noun *sɛi⁴⁴* 'family' often follows the referent, as in (240), where it has a possessive meaning (see § 7.4).

(237) ŋa³³ ŋ³¹ pa⁵⁵
1SG two CL:FAMGP¹
我 二
'my father and I' (for all referents) / 'my child and I' (for male referents)
我们父子俩
(KL-Elicitation)

(238) ŋ³¹ pa⁵⁵ tɤ⁴⁴ i³²³ wa³³.
two CL:FAMGP all go CRS
二 都 去
'My father and I both went.'
父子俩都去了。
(HPH-Family)

(239) ŋ³¹ ma⁵⁵ ŋ³¹ ma⁵⁵ tɤ⁴⁴ i³²³ la²⁴
two CL:FAMGP two CL:FAMGP all go REL
二 二 都 去
'mother and daughter, mother and daughter both went'
母女俩，母女俩都去的
(HPH-Family)

(240) ŋa³³ sɛi⁴⁴ ŋa³¹ piɛ⁵⁵liɛ⁵⁵ tɤ⁴⁴ tɕo³⁵ xɯ³³pɛi³³ ta⁵⁵ ta⁵⁵.
1SG family five CL:FAMGP all then home be.at be.at
我 家 五 都 就 家里 在 在
'My family's grandmother, my three brothers (and) I were all at home.'
我家祖孙五人就在家里。
(HPH-Family)

In the case of the parental classifiers, increasing the numeral, as in (241), restricts the possible interpretations. Because no person has more than one father, this phrase can only refer to a man and his two children, who may be of either sex. In contrast, the classifier *piɛ⁵⁵liɛ⁵⁵* allows for a greater variety of interpretations. The phrase in (242) may mean 'your three grandchildren and you' for older referents of either sex, or 'your three grandparents and you' for any referent. In addition, the intervening generation may also be included, so that another interpretation is 'your father, two grandparents and you'. Again, the grandchildren and grandparents may be of either sex. An example from discourse is shown in (243).

---

1 Chinese does not have family group classifiers. Thus, they are not translated in the word-for-word glosses and compound nouns convey their meaning in the free translations.

(241) i³³ **si³⁵** **pa⁵⁵**
 他 三
 3SG three CL:FAMGP
 'he and his two children' (for male referents)
 他们父子三人
 (KL-Elicitation)

(242) nɛi³³ sɛi⁴⁴ **xɤ³⁵** **piɛ⁵⁵liɛ⁵⁵**
 3PL family four CL:FAMGP
 你 家 四
 'your three grandchildren and you' / 'you three siblings/cousins and your grandparent' / 'you two grandparents and your two grandchildren' / 'you two siblings/cousins and your two grandparents' (for any referent)
 我们祖孙四个人
 (KL-Elicitation)

(243) si³⁵ **piɛ⁵⁵liɛ⁵⁵** tɤ⁴⁴ sʅ³¹ ɕi⁵³ tsʰi³³ kʰo⁵³ za³¹ lo⁵³ ja³²³ sɛi³¹,
 three CL:FAMGP all seven eight ten CL:TMP DIM reach PFV.EMP still
 三 都 七 八 十 岁 到 还
 a³³tɕʰa⁵⁵kʰv̩³³ ŋa³³tsʰɤ³³.
 that.time 3PL
 那时候 我们
 'My grandmother and (we) two grandchildren, at that time we were only about seven, eight, ten years old.'
 祖孙三人，那时候我们才有七、八、十岁。
 (GTX-Doctor)

The sibling classifiers, *fɤ²⁴* and *nɛi²⁴*, pattern in a slightly different manner. When they do not modify a personal pronoun, as in (244) and (245), they serve as simple sortal classifiers. When a pronoun is present, they are interpreted as family group classifiers, as the phrases in (246) and (247) demonstrate. In both constructions the male classifier *fɤ²⁴* is only used to refer to brothers of male referents. The birth order of the brothers is irrelevant; *fɤ²⁴* may refer to older or younger brothers. The female classifier *nɛi²⁴* is used for all other combinations. Thus, the phrase in (247) may refer to two sisters or a mixed group of siblings of a male speaker. For female speakers, the additional referents may be two sisters, two brothers or a mixed group of siblings. In discourse this ambiguity is resolved by context. *tsʅ⁵⁵miɛ⁵⁵* 'sister-in-law' is unusual in that it may function as either a family classifier or a noun, as shown in (248), the only classifier in this group to do so. However, in the latter use it has an idiomatic meaning of '[numeral] sister(s)-in-law among many', as the translation shows. There does not seem to be an analogous classifier for brothers-in-law; *fɤ²⁴* is employed instead.

(244) ŋ³¹ si³³ fɤ²⁴ tɤ⁴⁴ tsʰɿ³¹ma³³ tsʰɿ³³ tɕi³³ wa³²³.
two three CL:ITEM all wife marry enter PFV
二 三   都   妻子   娶   进
'Two or three brothers (of mine) all got married.'
兄弟两三个都结了婚。
(HPH-Family)

(245) si³³ fɤ²⁴ kɛi³³ nɛ³²³ma³³ jo³⁵ kɛi³³ sɛi⁴⁴,
three CL:ITEM CONJ younger.sister CL:HUM CONJ TOP
三   和   妹妹   位   和
xɤ³³ nɛi²⁴ tso³²³ sɛi⁴⁴
four CL:ITEM EXIST TOP
四   有
'three brothers and a younger sister, there are four siblings'
三兄弟和一妹妹呢，有四个兄妹呢
(HPH-Family)

(246) i³³ si³³ fɤ²⁴
3SG three CL:FAMGP
他 三
'he and his two brothers' (for male referents)
他们兄弟三个
(KL-Elicitation)

(247) ŋa³³ si³³ nɛi²⁴
1SG three CL:FAMGP
我 三
'my two sisters and I' / 'my brother and sister and I' (for male speakers) / 'my two sisters and I' / 'my two brothers and I' / 'my brother and sister and I' (for female speakers)
我们姐妹三个
(KL-Elicitation)

(248) ŋ³¹ tsɿ⁵⁵miɛ⁵⁵   tsɿ⁵⁵miɛ⁵⁵ ŋ³¹ jo³⁵
two CL:FAMGP   sister-in-law two CL:HUM
二   妯娌   二 位
'[referent] and a sister-in-law'   'two sisters-in-law among many'
两个妯娌   妯娌当中的两个
(KL-Elicitation)

Cultural knowledge helps in deciphering the intended meaning of the classifiers in discourse. For example, it was traditional for boys to accompany their fathers to learn farming or a trade while girls would remain with their mothers to learn domestic chores. As a result, *pa^{55}* and *ma^{55}* are typically assumed to involve two generations of the same sex. Thus, the phrase in (241) above would historically be understood as 'he and his two sons', absent context to the contrary. Similarly, children were traditionally tended by their paternal grandmothers. Thus, although *piɛ^{55}liɛ^{55}* may semantically point to any grandparent, combinations involving this classifier are assumed to refer to one grandmother and several grandchildren, as the translation in (243) above attests.

These classifiers may also refer to relatives outside the nuclear family, though this is not their primary function. In this use, the same generational combination must be retained. Thus, *pa^{55}*, which often means 'father and son', may also refer to 'uncle and nephew', and the sibling classifiers are employed to refer to cousins on either side of the family. There are, in fact, no common nouns that mean 'cousin' in Khatso; they are called 'brothers' or 'sisters' in discourse. The example in (249) illustrates another possibility; *ma^{55}* points to a pair consisting of mother-in-law and daughter-in-law. Similarly, these classifiers may also be employed to refer to close friends of the family. Thus, *ma^{55}* may refer to a mother's best female friend and *piɛ^{55}liɛ^{55}* may refer to friends of a grandparent. Consequently, interpreting these classifiers depends heavily on context as well as traditional culture. Knowledge about the family situation of the speaker is also helpful, and because the village population is relatively small, most residents are very familiar with the family history of their friends and neighbors.

(249) ta^{24}to^{33} tɕo^{35} **ŋ^{31}**   **ma^{55}**   tɤ^{44},
      still   then   two CL:FAMGP all
      还   就   二   都
      'Then mother-in-law and daughter-in-law both,'
      还是婆媳俩都,

      sua^{35} tɤ^{44} tɕi^{33} tʰɛi^{31} ti^{33} i^{33}.
      lead   CLNK this   pick   PROG go
      带   这   挑   去
      '(they) went to go pick (firewood).'
      这么带着去挑。
      (HPH-Family)

Because the classifiers specifically refer to two or more people, they can never attach to the numeral *tɛi^{31}* 'one'. Likewise, they cannot be used with the demonstratives, which are considered singular, unless a numeral is interposed between them. Nor can they modify nouns as bare classifiers. They are the only classifiers to be restricted in these ways. They often occur without an overt referent, as the examples above illustrate. If a referent is present, it is more likely to be a singular personal pronoun than a noun; plural pronouns are dispreferred in this construction. If the referent is plural, then the noun sɛi⁴⁴ 'family' will usually be added to the pronoun. This is also the case if the referent is a proper name, as shown in (250). The use of sɛi⁴⁴ is very common with the family group classifiers, and it is almost always present if the numeral is three or greater, as in (251) and (252).

(250) kʰuɛi⁴⁴ li²⁴   sɛi⁴⁴   ŋ³¹   ma⁵⁵
      Kui Li   family   two   CL:FAMGP
      奎丽   家   二
      'Kui Li and her mother' / 'Kui Li and her daughter'
      奎丽家母女两个
      (KL-Elicitation)

(251) i³³   sɛi⁴⁴   si³⁵   pʰa³¹
      3SG   family   three   CL:FAMGP
      他   家   三
      'he and his two children'
      他家父子三个
      (KL-Elicitation)

(252) ŋa³³   sɛi⁴⁴   ŋ³¹   si³³   fɣ²⁴,
      1SG   family   two   three   CL:ITEM
      我   家   两   三
      'The two or three brothers in my family,'
      我家兄弟两三个，

      ŋa³³   sɛi⁴⁴   pv̩³¹   sl̩⁴⁴,
      1SG   family   NEG   COP
      我   家   不   是
      'My family,'
      我家不是，

      si³³   fɣ²⁴   li³³   n̻ɛ³²³ma³³   tɛi³¹   jo³⁵   tso³²³.
      three   CL:ITEM   plus   younger.sister   one   CL:HUM   EXIST
      三   和   妹妹   一   位   有
      'There are three brothers and one younger sister.'
      有三兄弟和一个妹妹。
      (HPH-Family)

There seems to be only one common noun that may be modified by a family group classifier, and that is the generic noun tsʰo³³ 'person', as (253) demonstrates. No other nouns may be so modified, including human nouns such as za³¹ni²⁴za³¹ 'girl' or any of the common nouns denoting kin. If the flow of discourse requires that referents be instantiated by common nouns, they are usually preposed, as in (254), or even topicalized, so that the classifiers do not directly modify a noun. A pronoun may be inserted, as in (254), but none is required.

(253) tsʰo³³ ŋ³¹ ma⁵⁵
person two CL:FAMGP
人 二
'mother and child', literally 'people mother and child'
母子两个 / 母子两人
(KL-Elicitation)

(254) i³³ kɛi³³ i³³ sɛi⁴⁴ mo³³ kɛi³³ i³³tsʰɤ³³ ŋ³¹ ma⁵⁵ kʰua³¹la³¹ i³²³ wa³²³.
3SG CONJ 3SG family mother CONJ 3PL two CL:FAMGP Kunming go PFV
她 和 她 家 母亲 和 她们 二 昆明 去
'She and her mother, they two went to Kunming.'
她和她妈妈，她们母女两个去昆明了。
(KL-Elicitation)

6.2.2.6 Partitive Classifiers

Some classifiers are partitive in use — that is, they refer to a portion of a noun rather than to the complete whole. For example, *pa⁵⁵* means 'half' and can be used with a wide variety of nouns. The classifier *fɤ³⁵* is used with nouns that are often divided into portions, such as rice or land, to denote a 'part' or 'share'. Similarly, *tʰɛi³³* denotes short sections, such as pieces of firewood or sugarcane, while *tʰa³¹* refers to sections of longer items, such as roads and highways. The classifier *sau³³* is used for segments of time. The classifier *tʰi³¹* is also fairly restricted; it is used to denote 'one of a pair' when referring to nouns such as socks, shoes, earrings and chopsticks. And, as already noted in § 6.2.2.3, when the plural classifier *ko⁵⁵* is used with *tɛi³¹* 'one' its meaning is 'some, several'.

6.2.2.7 Temporal Classifiers

Time is generally conveyed through the use of classifiers in Khatso. These classifiers can be loosely grouped into basic units and units relating to dates and times. These constructions serve an adverbial function in discourse, and thus typically occur between A/S and verb, though their placement is somewhat flexible (see § 9.3).

Basic temporal units include *ŋ³³* and *ŋ³²³* 'day', *xa⁵³* 'night', *la³³* 'month' and *kʰo⁵³* 'year'. Three additional classifiers *tʰɤ⁵⁵*, *sau³³* and *tsɛi³⁵* are used to describe a 'period of time'. All of these words pattern as classifiers rather than nouns, which means that they follow numerals and demonstratives directly and cannot themselves be modified by other classifiers. Examples are shown in (255) and (256).

(255) **tɕi³¹** **xa³²³** **kʰo⁵³** ʐɿ³¹xɯ³⁵
one hundred CL:TMP after
一 百 年 以后
'after one hundred years'
一百年以后
(KL-Sewing)

(256) **ŋ³¹** **si³³** **ŋ³³** ka³²³ i³³ la²⁴ ŋ³³xa⁵³ tso³²³.
two three day walk go REL time EXIST
两 三 天 走 去 时候 有
'There were times (we) went for two or three days.'
有时候去两三天的也有。
(YJF-Dance Parties)

Note that there are two alternants for 'day', *ŋ³³* and *ŋ³²³*. Their meaning is identical, but their uses differ slightly. The form *ŋ³³* is used with numerals one and two and in the question *xa³³ni³³ŋ³³* 'how many days?'. The other form, *ŋ³²³*, combines with numerals three and greater and in the universal temporal construction *tɕi³¹ŋ²⁴ŋ³²³* 'every day' (with idiomatic tone sandhi). The classifiers *sau³³* and *tsɛi³⁵*, which are used for unspecified periods of time, usually only take the numeral one. They may refer to any amount of time, from minutes to years, and the exact meaning is determined by context. The construction may be modified by the diminutive suffix –*za³¹*, such as in *tɕi³¹sau³³za³¹* 'short while', to denote a briefer period.

The modern system of dates and times is borrowed from Chinese culture and so are the classifiers used to express it. Consequently, these constructions also require numerals from the system borrowed from Hanyu (see § 6.1). The basic units are *n̥ɛ³²³* 'year', *jɛ³³* 'month' and *xau³⁵* 'day', and they are presented in that order. They are preceded by numerals, which is the canonical pattern in both Khatso and Hanyu, as shown in (257) and (258). Note that calendar years are said as individual digits (e.g. one nine seven six) rather than a single complex numeral (e.g. one thousand nine hundred seventy-six).

(257) ŋa³³ **pa³²³** **jɛ³²³** **tsʰŋ³²³** xau³⁵ fv̩³³ ŋɛi³³.
1SG eight month seven number be.born ASRT
我 八 月 七 号 生
'I was born on August 7.'
我是八月七号出生的。
(KL-Elicitation)

(258) i³³ ɤ³⁵ li³²³ i³²³ li³²³ n̠ɛ³²³ li³²³ ŋɛi³³.
3SG two zero one zero year come ASRT
他 二 零 一 零 年 来
'He came in 2010.'
他是二零一零年来的。
(KL-Elicitation)

Again following Hanyu usage, months do not have distinct names, as in English, but are conveyed with numerals and a borrowed classifier, pronounced both *jeˀ³³* and *jeˀ³²³*, meaning 'month'. Thus, 'January' is *zɿ³³jeˀ³³* and 'March' is *sa³³jeˀ³²³*, literally 'one month' and 'three month' respectively; the ordinal construction is not used, however. A list of the month names can be found in Table 6.3. Note that several have alternate versions, mirroring the patterns found in the borrowed numeral system (see § 6.1). For simplicity, only one form of 'month' is included.

The basic construction for telling time involves the noun *tso³³* 'clock' which is modified by one of three classifiers, *miau³¹* 'second', *fɛi³³* 'minute' and *tiɛ³¹* 'hour'. A numeral must accompany the classifier, but both precede the noun in accordance with Hanyu syntax. This construction likewise requires numerals from the Hanyu-originated numeral system. Examples are shown in (259) and (260). To ask the time, two different constructions apply, as shown in (261) and (262). They both have the same meaning, but use different classifiers. The first contains *tiɛ³¹* 'hour'; the second idiomatically uses the more general classifier *tʰɤ⁵⁵* 'while'. Note that the verb *lo⁵³* 'to be enough' here carries the sense of 'to reach'.

(259) **sa³³** **tiɛ³¹** **tso³³**
three hour clock
三 点 钟
'three o'clock'
三点钟
(KL-Elicitation)

(260) **o³¹** **tiɛ³¹** **sɿ³²³o³¹** **fɛi³³**
five hour fifteen minute
五 点 十五 分
'five fifteen'
五点十五分钟
(KL-Elicitation)

(261) **xa³³ni³³**   tiɛ³¹   lo⁵³   ŋa³¹?
    how.many hour   reach CNT.Q
    多少   点   到
    'What time is it?'
    有几点了？
    (KL-Elicitation)

(262) **xa³³ni³³**   tʰɤ⁵⁵   lo⁵³   ŋa³¹?
    how.many CL:TMP reach CNT.Q
    多少   会   到
    'What time is it?'
    有几点了？
    (KL-Elicitation)

Table 6.3: Months in Khatso

Khatso	Morphology	English	Chinese
zๅ³²³jɛ³³ i³²³jɛ³³	zๅ³²³ ('one') or i³²³ ('one') + jɛ³³ (CL:TMP)	'January'	一月
ɤ³⁵jɛ³³ zๅ³⁵jɛ³³	ɤ³⁵ ('two') or zๅ³⁵ ('two') + jɛ³³ (CL:TMP)	'February'	二月
sa³³jɛ³³	sa³³ ('three') + jɛ³³ (CL:TMP)	'March'	三月
sๅ³⁵jɛ³³	sๅ³⁵ ('four') + jɛ³³ (CL:TMP)	'April'	四月
o³¹jɛ³³	o³¹ ('five') + jɛ³³ (CL:TMP)	'May'	五月
lɤ³²³jɛ³³	lɤ³²³ ('six') + jɛ³³ (CL:TMP)	'June'	六月
tsʰๅ³²³jɛ³³	tsʰๅ³²³ ('seven') + jɛ³³ (CL:TMP)	'July'	七月
pa³²³jɛ³³	pa³²³ ('eight') + jɛ³³ (CL:TMP)	'August'	八月
tɕo³¹jɛ³³	tɕo³¹ ('nine') + jɛ³³ (CL:TMP)	'September'	九月
tsʰi³³jɛ³³ sๅ³²³jɛ³³	tsʰi³³ ('ten'), sๅ³²³ ('ten') + jɛ³³ (CL:TMP)	'October'	十月
sๅ³²³zๅ³²³jɛ³³ sๅ³²³i³²³jɛ³³	sๅ³²³ ('ten') + zๅ³²³ ('one') or i³²³ ('one') + jɛ³³ (CL:TMP)	'November'	十一月
sๅ³²³ɤ³⁵jɛ³³ sๅ³²³zๅ³⁵jɛ³³	sๅ³²³ ('ten') + ɤ³⁵ ('two') or zๅ³⁵ ('two') + jɛ³³ (CL:TMP)	'December'	十二月

In discussing birthdates, the Khatso also use the traditional astrological system in which each year is associated with an animal in the Chinese zodiac. These terms are compounds consisting of the animal noun and the classifier *kʰo⁵³* 'year', such as *lo³¹kʰo⁵³* 'dragon year' and *ɲo⁵³kʰo⁵³* 'monkey year'. To ask for a birthdate in a general way, the question in (263) is used; to ask more specifically for the astrological year, the question in (264) is employed. Responses to the first question often include both the calendar year and the zodiac year. A list of the months in the astrological year is presented in Table 6.4. Note that in Chinese *yáng* 羊 can mean either 'sheep' or 'goat', but in Khatso these are separate words; either may be used in this construction.

(263) nɛi³³   **xa³³**   **kʰo⁵³**   fv̩³³   ŋa³¹?
      2SG   which   CL:TMP   be.born   CNT.Q
      你   几   年   出生
      'Which year were you born?'
      你是哪年出生的？
      (KL-Elicitation)

(264) nɛi³³   **xa³³ma⁴⁴**   **kʰo⁵³**   fv̩³³   ŋa³¹?
      2SG   what   CL:TMP   be.born   CNT.Q
      你   什么   年   出生
      'Which (astrological) year were you born?'
      你是什么年出生的？
      (KL-Elicitation)

Table 6.4: The zodiac year in Khatso

Khatso	Morphology	English	Chinese
xa⁵⁵kʰo⁵³	xa⁵⁵ ('rat') + kʰo⁵³ (CL:TMP)	'Year of the Rat'	鼠年
ŋ̍³¹kʰo⁵³	ŋ̍³¹ ('ox, cow') + kʰo⁵³ (CL:TMP)	'Year of the Ox'	牛年
la³¹kʰo⁵³	la³¹ ('tiger') + kʰo⁵³ (CL:TMP)	'Year of the Tiger'	虎年
tʰa⁵⁵la⁵⁵kʰo⁵³	tʰa⁵⁵la⁵⁵ ('rabbit') + kʰo⁵³ (CL:TMP)	'Year of the Rabbit'	兔年
lo³¹kʰo⁵³	lo³¹ ('dragon') + kʰo⁵³ (CL:TMP)	'Year of the Dragon'	龙年
zʅ²⁴kʰo⁵³	zʅ²⁴ ('snake') + kʰo⁵³ (CL:TMP)	'Year of the Snake'	蛇年
m̥³¹kʰo⁵³	m̥³¹ ('horse') + kʰo⁵³ (CL:TMP)	'Year of the Horse'	马年
jo³²³kʰo⁵³, tsʰʅ⁵³kʰo⁵³	jo³²³ ('sheep') or tsʰʅ⁵³ ('goat') + kʰo⁵³ (CL:TMP)	'Year of the Sheep/Goat'	羊年
n̻o⁵³kʰo⁵³	n̻o⁵³ ('monkey') + kʰo⁵³ (CL:TMP)	'Year of the Monkey'	猴年
ɣa⁵³kʰo⁵³	ɣa⁵³ ('chicken') + kʰo⁵³ (CL:TMP)	'Year of the Rooster'	鸡年
tsʰʅ³¹kʰo⁵³	tsʰʅ³¹ ('dog') + kʰo⁵³ (CL:TMP)	'Year of the Dog'	狗年
wa⁵³kʰo⁵³	wa⁵³ ('pig') + kʰo⁵³ (CL:TMP)	'Year of the Pig'	猪年

Unlike months and years, terms for days of the week do not involve classifiers. They are discussed in § 9.3.1.

6.2.2.8 Monetary Classifiers

Discussing money also often involves classifiers. There are two common nouns for 'money' in Khatso, $tsŋ^{31}xɤ^{35}$ and the borrowed $tɕʰɛ^{323}$. The construction for talking about specific amounts of money is borrowed from Hanyu and, like the time and date constructions, typically uses the borrowed numeral system (see § 6.1). The relevant classifiers are $fɛi^{33}$ 'cent', $tɕo^{323}$ and xau^{323} 'dime', and $kʰuai^{31}$ 'yuan', the basic monetary unit of China. Examples are presented in (265) through (268). Usually, the syntax follows the Chinese noun-final formulation, as in the first three examples, but if a Khatso numeral or noun is used, then the traditional noun-first order may also occur, as in (268). Note the borrowed numeral lia^{31} 'two' may accompany classifiers of all kinds.

(265) **lia³¹**   **fɛi³³**   **tɕʰɛ³²³**
 two   CL:MNY   money
 两   分   钱
 'two cents'
 两分钱
 (KL-Elicitation)

(266) **o³¹**   **tɕo³²³**   **tɕʰɛ³²³**
 five   CL:MNY   money
 五   角   钱
 'five dimes' / 'fifty cents'
 五角钱
 (KL-Elicitation)

(267) **lia³¹**   **kʰuai³¹**   **tɕʰɛ³²³**
 two   CL:MNY   money
 两   块   元
 'two *yuan*'
 两块元
 (KL-Elicitation)

(268) **tɕʰɛ³²³**   **ŋ³¹**   **kʰuai³¹**
 money   two   CL:MNY
 钱   二   块
 'two *yuan*'
 两块元
 (KL-Elicitation)

It is usual in discourse to omit the common noun when using k^huai^{31} since the latter specifies the basic unit, a pattern also found in Chinese. Thus, when asked the price of an item one may reply o^{31} k^huai^{31} 'five yuan'. This classifier also takes Khatso numerals, depending on speaker preference, so $ŋa^{31}$ k^huai^{31} 'five yuan' is also grammatical.

6.2.2.9 Adverbial Classifiers

While most classifier constructions may appear without an overt noun if it is understood from context, some are nounless. That is, there is no specific noun in the lexicon that they modify. In discourse, they usually indicate time or manner and thus serve an adverb-like function. One subset of these, the temporal classifiers, has already been discussed (see § 6.2.2.7). However, it is worth mentioning again the classifier $t^hɤ^{55}$, which is very frequent in discourse and has some special functions. When modified by the numeral $tɕi^{31}$ 'one' it means 'awhile', although the numeral is often omitted in natural speech. This construction is also used to soften imperative expressions and other requests (see § 12.2). For example, in the phrase in (269) the temporal meaning is clear, but in (270) it is used to soften a plea to strangers for help. In some phrases, both meanings hold. In (271), for example, $t^hɤ^{55}$ softens the command to demonstrate a sewing technique which will also take some time. In present and future phrases $t^hɤ^{55}$ immediately precedes the verb, as just shown, but in perfective clauses it follows the verb, as in (272). Thus, this classifier also helps mark verbal aspect. The aspectual system is described more fully in § 9.2.

(269) ŋa³³   **t^{h}ɤ^{55}**   ɕa³¹   ŋ²⁴ka³³   jo³³   wa³²³.
       1SG   CL:TMP   think   see   must   PFV
       我   下   想   看   应该
       'I must think a while.'
       我应该想一想了。
       (KL-Weeds)

(270) ŋa³³   **tɕi³¹**   **t^{h}ɤ^{55}**   to³⁵   pa³²³   liɛ³³.
       1SG   one   CL:TMP   cross   help   come
       我   一   下   渡   帮   来
       'Come help me cross [the river].'
       来帮我渡一下。
       (HPH-Weeds)

(271) a³³ ko⁵⁵ **tʰɤ⁵⁵** ŋ²⁴ka³³ kɯ³¹.
that CL:PL CL:TMP see INDR.CAUS
那 些 下 看
'Show (him how you make) those a while.'
给那些看一下。
(KL-Sewing)

(272) tʰau³⁵ **tʰɤ⁵⁵** wa³²³.
trap CL:TMP PFV
套 下
'(It) trapped (them) for a while.'
套着了。
(KXC-Fishing)

Although infrequent, it is possible to use numerals greater than one with *tʰɤ⁵⁵*, in which case it means 'time, instance, occasion', as shown in (273), making it synonymous with *xuɛi³²³*, another manner classifier shown in (274). The latter has an additional meaning of 'trip, circuit' which is used for completed journeys, as illustrated by the example in (275). The distinction is often made clear by context.

(273) tɛi³³ni³³ **ŋ³¹** **tʰɤ⁵⁵** ɤɤ³⁵ tso²⁴ ni³¹
this.way two CL:TMP move ITER TOP
这么 二 次 动
'when moving (it) like this twice'
这么摇两下呢
(GCS-Childhood)

(274) sa²⁴tʰa³¹ tɕi⁵⁵ tɛi³¹ jo³⁵ **tɛi³¹** **xuɛi³²³** vɤ³²³.
candy CL:TYPE one CL:HUM one time buy
糖 种 一 位 一 回 买
'One person (would) buy candy one time.'
糖呢一个买一回。
(YJF-Dance Parties)

(275) **tɛi³¹** **xuɛi³²³** kɯ³³ li⁴⁴ ni³¹
one trip enter come TOP
一 回 进 来
'after making one return trip'
回来一回呢
(ZRF-Grandfather)

Other manner classifier constructions are much more semantically restricted. These classifiers — including *piɛ³²³* 'step', *tɕo²⁴* 'foot', *pa³³tsa³¹* 'palm' and *tɕi⁵⁵* 'sound' — are paired with specific verbs to enumerate the action and provide emphasis. For example, in the phrase in (276), which literally means 'he/she kicked me one foot', *tɛi³¹ tɕo²⁴* describes the number of times a kick occurred. Likewise in (277), which literally means 'shouted a shout', *tɛi³¹ tɕi⁵⁵* describes the number of shouts. These classifiers are also common nouns, but in these constructions they directly follow numerals and are not themselves modified by a classifier. This suggests that in this usage they function as classifiers, which is how they are analyzed here. Other nouns serving as classifiers are discussed in § 6.2.2.2.

(276) i³³   ŋa³³   **tɛi³¹** **tɕo²⁴**   tɕʰɛ⁵⁵ wa³²³.
     3SG   1SG   one   CL:FOOT   kick   PFV
     他   我   一   脚   踢
     'He kicked me once.', literally 'He kicked me one foot.'
     他踢了我一脚了。
     (KL-Elicitation)

(277) za³¹ni²⁴za³¹   jo³⁵   **ŋ³¹**   **tɕi⁵⁵**   v²⁴   wa³²³.
     girl   CL:HUM   two   shout   call   PFV
     女孩子   位   二   声   叫
     '(He) shouted twice (at) the girl.', literally '(He) shouted two shouts (at) the girl.'
     叫了女孩子两声了。
     (KL-Elicitation)

The comparative classifier *pɛi³⁵* likewise has an adverb-like function, although it occurs with a much greater variety of verbs (see § 12.5.4).

6.2.2.10 The Classifier Inventory

The previous sections describe the various types of classifiers that are found in Khatso. This section aggregates all of the classifiers identified in the language to date, which so far number more than 130. They are presented in Table 6.5 below. This list is no doubt incomplete; there are likely others that occur too infrequently in discourse to identify easily.

The table provides glosses in both English and Chinese as well as examples of the types of nouns each classifier modifies. Not all classifiers correspond to words in English, and thus some are untranslatable, but it is hoped that the examples provide enough information to define the salient characteristic of each classifier, or at least describe its use. The noun types in parentheses refer to categories that are described in the various sections above.

The Khatso classifier system is similar to that of Chinese, and indeed many forms were borrowed from Hanyu, but the systems are not identical. There is often a many to one relationship. For example, *jiàn* 件 in Putonghua is used both with items of clothing as well as with accidents and events. In Khatso these two categories take different classifiers: tsa^{24} for clothing, $t^h\varepsilon i^{323}$ for events.

For these reasons, it is difficult to determine how to group items served by a single classifier. For example, jo^{53} is used with medicine, herbs, spices, languages and classes. With the first three noun types, the classifier corresponds to the English word 'dose', but this sense is unrelated to the others, raising the question of whether this is polysemy or two or more homophonous lexemes. Since there are no historical data to resolve the issue, all such cases are grouped together in the table by default.

Also note that classifiers that carry tones 55, 53 and 31 may induce tone change in the numerals si^{33} 'three', $x\gamma^{33}$ 'four' and $k\gamma^{33}$ 'nine' (see § 3.2.1).

Table 6.5: Classifier inventory in Khatso

Classifier	English	Chinese	Types of Nouns
$f\varepsilon i^{33}$	'cent', 'minute'	分	(time); (money)
$f\gamma^{24}$	'brother'	兄/弟	(family groups)
$f\gamma^{35}$	'piece, share'	份	part of shared items: land, food, money
fo^{33}	–	封	postal letter
$f\gamma^{55}$	'pair, set'	副	paired items: couplets, eyeglasses, dentures; items in sets: playing cards, mahjong tiles
$\gamma\mathrm{u\!\!\!l}^{53}$	'household'	户	organized groups of people: families, businesses, institutions
$j\varepsilon^{31}$	'page'	页	page in bound items
jo^{35}	'human'	位	humans
jo^{53}	'dose'	剂, 种	items consumed in measured increments: medicine, herbs, spices; languages; school classes
ka^{24}	'branch'	枝	tree branches separated from tree but still retaining smaller branches, leaves
ka^{31}	–	枝, 杆	long, rigid, smooth items: flagpoles, rifles, sticks
ka^{33}	–	股	items that flow: air, water, aromas, tides
ka^{35}	'branch'	枝	tree branches separated from tree with no smaller branches, leaves
$k\varepsilon i^{35}$	–	届	scheduled items: meetings, classmate groups
$k\gamma^{24}$	'head', 'strip'	头, 条	large animals: cattle, yaks, elephants; long, thin, flexible items: ropes, threads, cords, antennas, whips, fishing lines, rivers, roads
$k\gamma^{35}$	'room'	间, 所	inhabited structures: rooms, buildings

Classifier	English	Chinese	Types of Nouns
kʰɤ³²³	'quarter hour'	刻	(time)
kʰɤ³³	'pair'	对	paired items: earrings, bracelets
kʰɤ⁵³	'stick'	根	cigarettes
kʰɯ³¹	'lump'	块	mineral pieces: coal, dirt
kʰo⁵³	'year'	年, 岁	(time); (age)
kʰuai³¹	'yuan'	块	(money)
kʰuɛi³¹	'bundle'	捆	bundles of larger items: clothes, paper, etc.
ko³³li³¹	'kilometer'	公里	(distance)
ko²⁴sɛi³³	'pint'	小升	(volume)
ko³³tɕi³³	'gram'	公斤	(weight)
ko³³tsʰŋ²⁴	'meter'	公尺	(distance)
ko⁵⁵	'crowd, group', PL	些, 拨	people, animals in groups; any noun made plural
kɤ³¹	'tube', 'strand'	管, 缕	long, thin items: toothpaste, hair, smoke
la³³	'month'	月	(time)
la⁵³	'piece', 'face'	块, 面	pieces of larger items: cloth, land, rocks, glass, plastic, metal; flat items: mirrors, signs, cloth, framed pictures, drapes, carpets
lɛi³²³	'arm span'	庹	(distance)
lɤ²⁴	–	园	agricultural units: orchards, gardens
li³¹	'li'	里	(distance)
li³²³mi³¹	'centimeter'	厘米	(distance)
lo³¹	'ounce'	两	(weight)
m̩³¹	'6ᵗʰ of an acre'	亩	(space)
ma²⁴	'grain', 'item'	粒, 只, 个	small round items: rice, corn, beans, candy, seeds, fruit pits; some animals: dogs, cats, sheep, horses, pigs, birds, fish; otherwise unclassified items: songs, occupations, many other nouns including abstract nouns
ma⁵³	'pile'	堆	items often piled: grain, coal, clothes, etc.
ma⁵⁵	–	母女	(family groups)
mɛi³³	'mouthful'	口	consumable items: food, liquids
mɛi⁴⁴	–	个	(alternant of general classifier ma²⁴)
mi³¹	'meter'	米	(distance)
miau³¹	'second'	秒	(time)
mo³¹	'couple'	对	paired humans (husband & wife)
nɛi²⁴	'sister'	姐/妹	(family groups)
nɛi³¹	–	个	(alternant of general classifier ma²⁴)
ɲa³⁵	'handful'	把	items held/scooped by hand: rice, salt, flowers

Classifier	English	Chinese	Types of Nouns
ŋ^{33}, ŋ^{323}	'day'	天	(time)
o^{33}, o^{33}lo^{33}	'flock'	群	groups of non-human animates: animals, birds, fish, insects
pa^{31}	'roll'	卷	items in rolls: paper, cloth
pa^{35}	'bowl'	碗,	measure for item typically placed in bowls: food, beverages but also other items such as pins, coins
pa^{53}	'handle', 'pair'	把,对	items lifted in one hand, such as those with handles: teapots, pitchers, spoons; and those without: firewood, split wood; pair (of people) working together
pa^{55}	'half'	半	measure to denote a half portion: sortal items that can be divided
pa^{55}	–	父子	(family groups)
pau^{33}	'small bag'	袋	items sold in small packets: herbs, spices, medicine, candy
pɛi^{31}	'volume'	本	items with bound paper: books, magazines, notebooks, etc.
pɛi^{323}	–	泡	human waste: urine, feces
pɛi^{35}	'multiple'	倍	(stative verbs)
pɣ^{31}	'piece'	块	increments of land: farms, fields
pʰa^{31}	–	父子	(family groups)
pʰa^{323}	'plate'	盘	any item served or held on plates, platters, pans, trays
pʰa^{55}	'half'	半	(partitive)
pʰɛi^{323}	'row'	排	items grouped in rows: trees, houses, people
pʰi^{323}	'bottle (glass/plastic)'	瓶	liquids
pʰiɛ^{33}	'page'	页	print media: books, magazines, newspapers, articles
pi^{24}	–	笔	amount of money
piɛ^{323}	'step'	步	(verbs)
piɛ^{55}liɛ^{55}	–	子孙	(family groups)
po^{24}	–	支	long, thin, rigid items: pen, stick, cane, pole, fishing pole
po^{31}	'alms bowl'	钵	large quantity of food
po^{53}	'piece'	块	cloth items: towels, handkerchiefs, tablecloths
pɣ̥^{53}	'can, jar'	罐	liquids: beverages, pickled items
sau^{33}	'while'	下	(verbs)
sɛi^{33}	'liter'	升	(volume)

Classifier	English	Chinese	Types of Nouns
sɤ³³	'row'	串, 排	items in rows: beads in necklace, humans, animals
sɤ³⁵	'side'	扇	items with two panels: doors, windows, ribs
ta³²³	–	条	long, thin animals that wriggle: snakes, eels, worms, caterpillars, lizards, dragons, etc.
ta³⁵	'armful'	抱	items that can be held in the arms
tau³⁵	–	道	linear items: light rays
tɕa³⁵	–	台, 架	machines: televisions, computers, telephones, airplanes, musical instruments
tɕa⁵⁵	–	张	flat paper items: loose paper, newspapers, paintings, stamps
tɕɛ³¹	'roll'	卷	items in rolls: paper, cloth
tɕɛ³²³	'bottle, pitcher (ceramic)'	壶	liquids
tɕʰa³¹	'leaf', 'slice'	叶, 片	small, thin items: leaves, slices of larger items
tɕi⁵⁵	'type, sort', 'phrase', 'item'	种, 句, 件	any noun; audible items: language, speech, noises; incidents: events, accidents
tɕo³²³	'dime'	角	(money)
tɛi³¹	'ten liters'	斗	(volume)
tɛi³²³	'meal',	顿, 台	food; machines: televisions, tractors
tɛi³⁵	'mid-sized bag', 'generation'	袋, 捧, 代	any noun; items held in cupped hands: rice, beans, sand, etc.; humans
tɤ⁵³	'sack', 'womb'	袋, 胎	items traditionally carried in bags: rice, food, things; items in wombs: litter of animals
tʰa³¹	'block, section'	段	sections of larger items; roads, highways
tʰau³⁵	'set'	套	items in sets: clothes, tools, furniture, etc.
tʰɛi³²³	'item'	件	incidents: events, accidents, movies, plays
tʰɛi³³	–	段	sections of smaller items: firewood, sugarcane, thread
tʰɤ⁵⁵	'while'	下	(verbs)
tʰi³¹	'leg'	肘, 只	meat; one of a pair
tʰo³²³	'cylinder'	卷	cylinders; paper, batteries
tʰʏ³¹	'bucket'	桶	any noun
ti⁵³	'dot, piece, small amount'	点	small things or amounts: small items, food portions, portions of mass nouns, etc.
tiau³⁵	–	串	hanging items: lamps, drapes, ancient Chinese money
tiɛ²⁴	'drop'	滴	liquids
tiɛ³¹	'hour'	点钟	(time)

Classifier	English	Chinese	Types of Nouns
tiɛ⁵⁵	'pair'	双	paired items: gloves, couples (human), twins (human and animal)
to³¹	–	朵	flowers
to³⁵	–	栋	large buildings
tsa²⁴	'item'	件	clothing (pants, shirts, underwear, coats, robes, etc.), beds, mats
tsa³³	'few', 'handle'	把	humans; handheld items: knives, tools, oars
tsa³⁵	'3⅓ meters'	丈	(distance)
tsau³⁵	–	盏	lamps
tsɛi²⁴	'pair'	双, 座, 辆	paired items: socks, shoes, chopsticks, scissors; bridges; vehicles: cars, bicycles, motorcycles, trains
tsɛi³⁵	'while'	段	verbs
tsɤ³¹	'bundle'	捆	bundles of larger items: clothes, paper, etc.
tsɤ³²³	–	棵	flora: trees, plants, grass
tsɤ³⁵	'bundle'	捆	bundles of smaller items: herbs, pens, etc.
tsʰa³¹	'field, court'	场	staged events: contests, plays, operas, movies
tsʰa³⁵	'branch'	枝	parts of flora; trees, plants
tsʰau³³	–	捧	liquids cupped in hands, usually water
tsŋ⁵⁵miɛ⁵⁵	'brother's wife'	妯娌	(family groups)
tsʰɛi³²³	'floor, layer'	层	layered items: buildings, cloth, bricks
tsʰɤ³³	human, collective	们	group of people that share a common feature (relatives, friends, etc.)
tsʰŋ²⁴	'foot'	尺	(distance)
tsʰŋ³¹	'piece'	块	items that come in pieces: wood, bricks, tiles
tsʰua³⁵	'string'	串	items strung together: pearls, kabob meat
tsʰuɛi³⁵	'inch'	寸	(distance)
tso³⁵	'stump'	桩	tree stump
tsŋ²⁴	'half gram'	斤	(weight)
tsŋ³³	'branch'	枝	tree branches
tsŋ³⁵	–	节	plants with sections: bamboo, sugarcane, palms
tsŋ⁵⁵	'row'	行	items in rows: trees, corn, books, Chinese characters
tsɤ⁵⁵	'net'	网, 堵	fishing nets; walls
tʏ³¹	–	堵, 朵	walls; clouds
xa⁵³	'night'	夜	(time)
xau³²³	'dime'	角	(money)
xo²⁴	'box'	盒	any noun

Classifier	English	Chinese	Types of Nouns
xo³²³	'finger span'	–	cloth
xuɛi³²³	'time, trip'	次, 趟	(verbs)

6.3 Lexical Quantifiers

The quantitative nouns *tɛi³¹ko⁵⁵ma³³* 'many, a lot' and *tɛi³¹ti⁵³za³¹* 'few, a little' modify head nouns in discourse. Because they are derived from classifier constructions, they pattern slightly differently than common nouns. They follow the heads they modify, as shown in (278) and (279), and typically no other classifier is required in the phrase. They are also able to modify nouns of any sort, whether human, animate or inanimate. Note that in quick speech the final syllable of *tɛi³¹ti⁵³za³¹* is often omitted without a change in meaning or degree.

(278) ja⁵³ni³²³ nɛi³³ sɛi⁴⁴ m̥³²³ **tɛi³¹ko⁵⁵ma³³** vɤ³²³ ŋa³²³.
then   2SG   family field many   buy   able
然后   你   家   田   很多   买   能
'Then your family was able to buy a lot of fields.'
然后你家买得了很多田。
(KL-Grandfather)

(279) i²⁴pa³³ tsʰi³²³kʰua³⁵ ɣ³⁵ko³³   **tɛi³¹ti⁵³** kɯ³¹ tɤ³³ sa³⁵   ŋɛi³³.
usual   situation   compensation a.little   give   PROG perhaps.FOC ASRT
一般   情况   误工   一点   给   可能
'Usually (they will) perhaps give a little compensation.'
一般情况下可能会给一点误工。
(ZRF-Competition)

Head nouns are often omitted in discourse, either because they have already been mentioned or they are obvious from context, and in this case the quantitative nouns serve as pronouns just as classifier constructions do. For example, the phrase in (280) is spoken by a woman who lived many decades outside the village and thus knows few local people. The example in (281), which refers to the haircuts of the speaker's youth, features the shortened form. Note that even when they are the only nouns in the phrase, no additional classifiers are required.

(280) **tɕi³¹ko⁵⁵ma³³** ma³¹ sɿ⁵⁵.
 many come PFV
 很多 来
 '(I) don't know many.'
 很多不认识。
 (WYY-Sewing)

(281) to³³ **tɕi³¹ti⁵³** tsi⁵³, ŋ³³ ŋuo³¹?
 also a.little cut.with.scissors COP COP.Q
 也 一点 剪 是
 '(They) also cut off a little, right?'
 也剪了一点，是吧？
 (YJF-Childhood)

The unusual pattern in these constructions is that the quantitative nouns follow their heads. Typically, nouns modifying other nouns precede the head (see § 7.2.1). The post-nominal position, however, is the canonical place for classifiers. Morphologically, in fact, these nouns are derived from classifiers. The quantifier *tɕi³¹ko⁵⁵ma³³* 'many', consists of *tɕi³¹* 'one', the plural classifier *ko⁵⁵* and the general noun suffix *-ma³³*. The other, *tɕi³¹ti⁵³za³¹* 'few', contains the same numeral, but with the classifier *ti⁵³* denoting 'dot, piece, small amount' and the diminutive suffix *-za³¹* (see § 4.2.3.2 for a discussion of suffixes). Likely due to their classifier origins, they continue to occupy the classifier position vis-à-vis the head as well as obviate the need for an independent classifier in the phrase. In clauses without a head, such as those in (280) and (281) above, they serve as pronouns, a function that common nouns and numeral classifier constructions share, but not one possible for bare classifiers.

6.4 Universal Quantification Construction

Universal quantifiers invoke all members of a category, corresponding to the English pronouns 'everyone' and 'everything'. In Khatso, however, pronouns are typically not employed for this purpose. Instead, the most common expression involves a four-syllable construction

 tɕi³¹ ____ ma³¹ xɛi³⁵ VERB
 one CL NEG PART

in which the second syllable is the classifier or morpheme that is associated with the referent. Thus, 'everyone', *tɕi³¹ jo³⁵ ma³¹ xɛi³⁵*, includes the human classifier *jo³⁵*, and *tɕi³¹ na⁵³ ma³¹ xɛi³⁵* 'everywhere', contains the locative morpheme *na⁵³*. A list of these constructions is presented in Table 6.6. Note that the morpheme *tsy²⁴*, which is used for most common nouns, does not have an identifiable meaning outside this expression. *xuɛi²⁴*, which is used in the temporal expression, is likely the classifier *xuɛi³²³* that refers to the iteration of an event; its tone change suggests that the adverb *to³³* 'also' was once part of this construction (see § 3.2.4). The compositional meaning of the construction is likewise unclear. The word *xɛi³⁵* is identical to the adverb meaning 'still, yet', but in this phrase it follows the negative marker *ma³¹*, which in all other instances can only precede a verb. Perhaps the idiomatic word order evolved in order to separate *ma³¹* from the matrix verb and thus keep the positive polarity of the construction. If this is the case, the compositional meaning may be akin to '(even) one not remaining'.

Table 6.6: Universal indefinite constructions in Khatso

Khatso	Morphology	English	Chinese
tɛi³¹ jo³⁵ ma³¹ xɛi³⁵	*tɛi³¹* ('one') + *jo³⁵* (CL:HUM) + *ma³¹* (NEG) + *xɛi³⁵* [unknown]	'everyone'	谁都
tɛi³¹ tsɣ²⁴ ma³¹ xɛi³⁵	*tɛi³¹* ('one') + *tsɣ²⁴* (CL:UNK) + *ma³¹* (NEG) + *xɛi³⁵* [unknown]	'everything'	什么都
tɛi³¹ xuɛi²⁴ ma³¹ xɛi³⁵	*tɛi³¹* ('one') + *xuɛi²⁴* (CL:TMP) + *ma³¹* (NEG) + *xɛi³⁵* [unknown]	'every time'	每次都
tɛi³¹ n̻a⁵³ ma³¹ xɛi³⁵	*tɛi³¹* ('one') + *n̻a⁵³* (DEM 'place') + *ma³¹* (NEG) + *xɛi³⁵* [unknown]	'everywhere'	什么地方都

This construction may serve as a verbal argument without any additional marking. Examples are shown in (282), (283) and (284).

(282) **tɛi³¹ jo³⁵ ma³¹ xɛi³⁵** ko³²³ i³³ ti³³ ja³³.
everyone draw go PROG
每个人 抽 去
'Everyone was going to draw (water).'
每个人都去抽的。
(GCS-Childhood)

(283) **tɛi³¹ tsɣ²⁴ ma³¹ xɛi³⁵** tsʰau³³si³³ ja³³.
Everything be.concerned IPFV.EMP
什么 操心
'(We) are interested in everything.'
什么都要操心。
(KL-Sewing)

(284) **tɛi³¹ tsɣ²⁴ ma³¹ xɛi³⁵**　　kɣ³³　　li³²³　　　ja³³　　　　　a³³　　tsɛi³⁵.
　　　everything　　　　　　make　know.how　IPFV.EMP　that　CL:TMP
　　　什么　　　　　　　　　做　　会　　　　　　　　　那　　段
　　　'(I) knew how to make everything, at that time.'
　　　那个时候什么都会做。
　　　(WYY-Sewing)

In discourse, this construction may denote particular referents as well as the expected general referents. For example, the phrase in (285) may refer to the number of friends in a particular group who want to sing karaoke. Or, discussing the worldwide popularity of the Great Wall as a tourist destination, it may refer to all people everywhere.

(285) **tɛi³¹ jo³⁵ ma³¹ xɛi³⁵**　mo⁵⁵　i³²³.
　　　everyone　　　　　　　want　go
　　　谁　　　　　　　　　　要　　去
　　　'Everyone wants to go.'
　　　谁都想去。
　　　(KL-Elicitation)

Another construction can be used when 'everything' serves as P. In this construction, which seems to be borrowed from Hanyu, the interrogative pronoun *xa³³ma⁴⁴* 'what' is followed by the adverb *to³³* 'also', as shown in (286). However, it is not nearly as common as the expression described above. Moreover, this construction is not possible with any of the other interrogative pronouns. This seems to be related to the more productive use of interrogative pronouns in indefinite constructions (see § 7.3).

(286) **xa³³ma⁴⁴　to³³**　vɣ³²³　wa³²³.
　　　what　　　also　buy　　PFV
　　　什么　　　也　　买
　　　'(I) bought everything.'
　　　什么都买了。
　　　(KL-Elicitation)

7 Noun Phrases

Comprising one of the largest word classes in the language, nouns are naturally frequent in discourse. They rarely occur alone, however. At the very least, they are usually accompanied by a classifier, even in brief responses to questions. But they may also be modified by a number of other elements. In addition, they may combine with particles and other nouns in more complex constructions such as relative clauses and nominalizations. This chapter explores the various permutations possible within noun phrases. First, canonical word order is presented in § 7.1. Then the adjectival use of both nouns and stative verbs is described in § 7.2, followed by a discussion of indefinite constructions in § 7.3. Possessive constructions are discussed in § 7.4, while relative clauses are described in § 7.5. Nominalizing constructions are explained in § 7.6, followed by a discussion of noun coordination strategies in § 7.7. The quantification of nouns and the use of classifiers are discussed in Chapter 6.

7.1 Constituent Order

The ordering of constituents within a noun phrase is relatively fixed, in contrast with the more flexible order found in clauses (see § 10.3). The elements that modify nouns usually follow the noun, with the exception of relative clauses (see § 7.5). The order of these constituents is mapped as follows:

$$\text{NP} \rightarrow (\text{POSR}) + (\text{RELC}_1) + (\text{N}) + \text{N} + (\text{ADJSV}) + (\text{RELC}_2) + (\text{DEM}) + (\text{NUM}) + (\text{CL})$$

where POSR denotes possessors, RELC$_1$ indicates non-stative relative clauses, RELC$_2$ refers to stative relative clauses, and ADJSV denotes adjectival stative verbs; the other abbreviations are identical to those used elsewhere.

It is unusual, though, for a noun to carry the full array of modifiers in discourse. Shorter combinations of these elements are well attested in natural speech, as shown below in examples (287) through (294). The elicited example in (295) presents a phrase employing most of the modifiers. Although impossible in English, modifying a single noun with both a possessor and a demonstrative is perfectly grammatical Khatso.

(287) POSR + N

ɕo³²³ɕau³⁵ mɛi⁴⁴ pɣ³²³ wɛi³²³tɕʰa³²³ mɛi⁴⁴ ɣ³³ tɕa³³ i³³ ȵa³¹.
school CL:GEN POSS wall CL:GEN count cross go speak
学校 个 围墙 堵 数 过 去 说
'Count over from the wall of the school.'
从学校的围墙数过去。
(YAY-Erasers)

(288) N + N

tɕa⁵³ m̩³²³ a³³ tɕi⁵⁵
toothgrass field that CL:TYPE
牙齿草 田 那 种
'that type of toothgrass field'
那种牙齿草田
(HPH-Weeds)

(289) RELC₁ + N

nɛi³³ kɛi³³ sa³³ la²⁴ tʰo³³pɛi³³
2SG AGT sew REL upper.garment
你 缝 褂子
'the upper garment you sewed'
你缝的褂子
(WYY-Sewing)

(290) N + CL

ŋa³¹ ma²⁴ vɣ³²³ kɯ³³ li³³.
fish CL:GEN buy enter Come
鱼 个 买 进 来
'Buy a fish.'
买条鱼回来。
(KL-Hotpot)

(291) N + ADJSV + CL

o³¹ tsɛi²⁴ kɣ²⁴ o³¹ma³³ kʰɣ³³ ti⁵³za³¹ tso³⁵ mɛi⁴⁴.
vegetable be.sour CL:STRIP turnip CL:STRIP a.little EXIST DSC.EMP
菜 酸 根 萝卜 条 一点 有
'There are some turnips and sour vegetables.'
有点儿酸菜萝卜条吃。
(GCS-Childhood)

(292) N + RELC₂

tsʰo³³   sa⁵⁵   tʰɛi³²³   la²⁴   jo³⁵
person   be.poor   very   REL   CL:HUM
人   穷   很   位

'a person who is very poor'
很穷的人
(KL-Elicitation)

(293) N + DEM + CL

i³²³tɕa⁵³   tɛi³³   kɣ³¹
water   this   CL:STRIP
水   这   股

'this stream of water'
这股水
(HPH-Horse Dug Well)

(294) N + NUM + CL

suo³³ta³³ko³²³   tɛi³¹   ma²⁴   tso³²³.
tomato   one   CL:GEN   EXIST
番茄   一   个   有

'There was one (plate) of tomatoes.'
有一盘番茄。
(KL-Duanwu Festival)

(295) POSR + RELC₁ + N + ADJSV + DEM + NUM + CL

ŋa³³   pɣ³²³   nɛi³³   kɛi³³   xa³³   la²⁴   tsʰɿ³¹   na⁵³   a³³   ŋ³¹   ma²⁴.
1SG   POSS   2SG   AGT   send   REL   dog   black   that   two   CL:GEN
我   你   送   狗   黑   那   两   个

'(Those) two black dogs of mine that you sent.'
我的你送给我的那两只黑狗。
(KL-Elicitation)

Given nouns that are recoverable in discourse are often omitted, a feature known as zero anaphora. They may also be replaced by personal pronouns (see § 5.3.1) or collocations that may serve as pronouns, such as demonstrative-classifier constructions (see § 5.3.2), numeral-classifier constructions (see § 6.1.1) or relativized classifiers (see § 7.5).

7.2 Adjectival Function of Nouns and Stative Verbs

Khatso does not have a separate class of adjectives; stative verbs typically perform this function (see § 8.1.2 and the discussion in § 8.1.2.1). However, nouns and certain stative verbs may be used to directly modify a head noun with descriptive information. These constructions do not require additional marking on the modifying elements. As a result, they approximate attributive adjectival constructions, and their function is given its own section here.

7.2.1 Nouns Modifying Nouns

As just mentioned, nouns may modify other nouns in Khatso without additional marking. In this construction, the modifier precedes the head and creates a compound. Such compounds can be roughly divided into two groups. Some have become lexicalized — they are now the preferred terms for certain concepts — and are themselves common nouns. Others are produced in an ad hoc fashion in discourse, and can be considered noun phrases containing temporary syntactic compounds. In both cases, it is the head noun that controls classifier selection.

Several representative lexical compounds are presented in (296). In Khatso, compounds tend to maintain their compositional meaning, often providing additional detail as in these examples, rather than creating nouns with a completely idiosyncratic meaning. In fact, it is unusual for either $f\gamma^{33}$ 'egg' or $ts^h\eta^{31}$ 'feces' to be used without a noun modifier, perhaps to differentiate them from the related verbs $f\gamma^{33}$ 'to give birth, lay (eggs)' and $ts^h\eta^{31}$ 'to be smelly'. Although the compound forms have become the basic terms for these items in discourse, they are not bound morphemes since they may still be used independently. The morphology of lexical compounds is discussed in § 4.2.3.3.

(296) $s\gamma^{55}$ 'book' 书 + $pau^{33}pau^{33}$ 'bag' 书 → $s\gamma^{55}pau^{33}$ 'backpack' 书包
η^{31} 'cow' 牛 + $x\gamma^{33}$ 'house' 房 → $\eta^{31}x\gamma^{33}$ 'cow shed' 牛圈
γa^{53} 'chicken' 鸡 + $f\gamma^{33}$ 'egg' 蛋 → $\gamma a^{53}f\gamma^{33}$ 'chicken egg' 鸡蛋
$m̥^{31}$ 'horse' 马 + $ts^h\eta^{31}$ 'feces' 屎 → $m̥^{31}ts^h\eta^{31}$ 'horse manure' 马屎

More germane to this section are those compounds created on the fly in discourse. As the examples in (297) and (298) demonstrate, these are clearly created because of pragmatic need, rather than because they are common items. For example, in (297) $m̥^{323}$ 'field' is modified by a hardy type of weed called tca^{53} in Khatso and *yáchǐcǎo* 牙齿草 in Chinese. This detail is crucial to the story, but fields of this grass are not items commonly encountered in modern life. Likewise, the temporary compound in (298) describes one type of porridge, but there are many others.

(297) **tɕa⁵³**   **m̩³²³** a³³ tɕi⁵⁵ n̩a³¹ tɤ⁴⁴.
toothgrass field that CL:TYPE be.many STAT.EMP
牙齿草   田   那   种   多
'That type of toothgrass field is plentiful.'
那种牙齿草田多的。
(HPH-Weeds)

(298) **tsʰɛi³³n̩o³¹** **tsa³²³xo³¹** xa⁵⁵ tsa³¹ jo³⁵   wa³³.
glutinous.rice porridge boil eat must.FOC CRS
糯米   稀饭   煮   吃   应该
'(I) should make rice porridge to eat.'
煮糯米稀饭吃得了。
(KL-Plans)

7.2.2 Adjectival Stative Verbs

In Khatso, the attributive function is mainly performed by stative verbs. However, a subset of these verbs can directly modify a noun without a relativizing particle, thus serving an adjectival function. Unlike nominal modifiers, verbal modifiers immediately follow the head, mirroring clausal word order (see § 10.3). When present, numerals, classifiers and demonstratives follow the verb, demonstrating that these compounds are nouns. They can also serve as heads of possessive constructions and relative clauses, satisfying the nounhood tests. For a thorough discussion of these adjectival stative verbs, see § 8.1.2.1.

Like the nominal modifiers discussed in the previous section, these compounds can also be loosely divided into two groups: lexical compounds and syntactic compounds. The former have become the preferred terms for specific concepts. The latter occur in an ad hoc fashion, and are thus the result of a productive compounding process. A few examples of lexical compounds are shown in (299). Note that their meanings have changed somewhat from that of their component parts.

(299) o³¹ma³³ 'turnip' 萝卜 + ŋ²⁴ 'to be red' 红   →   o³¹ma³³ŋ²⁴ 'carrot' 胡萝卜
     tsʰɿ³¹ 'dog' 狗 + v³¹ 'to be crazy' 疯   →   tsʰɿ³¹v³¹ 'rabid dog' 疯狗
     m̩³²³ 'field' 田 + fɤ³³ 'to be dry' 干   →   m̩³²³fɤ³³ 'dry farmland' 干田
     ɣa⁵³fv³³ 'chicken egg' 鸡蛋 + sɤ²⁴ 'yellow' 黄 → ɣa⁵³fv³³sɤ²⁴ 'egg yolk' 蛋黄

In discourse, the productive compounding process may create new compounds on the fly. Examples are presented in (300) and (301). Attributes are often introduced in separate clauses, however, making this construction far less common than the other noun phrase constructions discussed in this section.

(300) **xua³²³kua³³ ɣɤ³⁵** tɛi³¹ ma²⁴ tso³²³.
cucumber be.salted one CL:GEN EXIST
黄瓜 腌 一 个 有
'There is one (plate) of salt-preserved cucumbers.'
有一个腌黄瓜。
(KL-Duanwu Festival)

(301) **tɤ²⁴ na⁵³** a³³ tɣ³¹ ɣɤ³¹ tʰɛi³²³ ja³³.
cloud be.black that CL:ITEM be.big very IPFV.EMP
云 黑 那 朵 大 很
'That black cloud is very big.'
那朵乌云很大呀。
(KL-Elicitation)

If an adjectival stative verb is modified, as in (302), then the resulting construction must be placed inside a relative clause to modify a noun, which is the construction required for stative verbs that cannot serve as adjectives as well as non-stative verbs. When a relative clause contains a stative verb, it may either precede or follow the head noun, as shown in (303). This flexibility is not possible with other types of relative clauses, which canonically precede the head (see § 7.5), but rather seems to be a unique property of stative verbs.

(302) **sa⁵⁵ tʰɛi³²³ la²⁴** tsʰo³³ jo³⁵
be.poor very REL person CL:HUM
穷 很 人 位
'a very poor person'
很穷的人
(KL-Elicitation)

(303) tsʰo³³ **sa⁵⁵ tʰɛi³²³ la²⁴** jo³⁵
person be.poor very REL CL:HUM
人 穷 很 位
'a very poor person', literally 'one who is (a) very poor person'
很穷的人
(KL-Elicitation)

Stative nominalizations, which involve the third person pronoun i^{33} rather than common nouns, are described in § 7.6.

7.3 Indefinite Constructions

There is no syntactic distinction between 'definite' and 'indefinite' nouns in Khatso. Of more importance is the difference between 'specific' and 'non-specific' reference, and this is typically determined by the use of classifiers. Classifiers mark both number and specificity, and nouns without a classifier are considered non-specific (see § 6.2.1). Beyond this, definiteness is largely determined through context. As a result, there are no indefinite pronouns that point to undetermined or unknown referents, like the terms 'someone' and 'nothing' in English. Instead, the language employs a variety of constructions to convey these concepts, depending on the specificity of the referents. Interrogative pronouns are often used for this purpose, but more complex constructions are also used.

Nine types of indefinite constructions have been identified cross-linguistically (Haspelmath 1997: 52). However, the Khatso constructions do not neatly correspond to these types. There are equivalents to seven of them, which can be grouped into specific, non-specific and negative indefinite constructions (see Table 7.1). Two of the cross-linguistic types — non-specific irrealis indefinites, which point to unknown referents in the future, and indirect negatives, which are employed in embedded clauses — do not exist in Khatso. Instead realis and direct negative constructions are employed for those purposes. In addition, Khatso has two general realis constructions that make use of non-specific noun phrases. These are seen as alternates to indefinite constructions and thus placed outside the typological framework (Haspelmath 1997: 52–57), but in Khatso they are functionally similar and thus included here. In some cases, Khatso constructions map to several cross-linguistic types, and some types may correspond to more than one Khatso expression — a degree of multifunctionality common in pragmatics-based languages like Khatso (see Bisang 2009). Each of the Khatso constructions is described in more detail below.

Table 7.1: Khatso indefinite constructions

	Khatso Constructions [1]	Cross-Linguistic Types
specific	N CL (VERB)	specific, known referent
		specific, unknown referent (also replaces non-specific irrealis)
		polar questions
non-specific	REL EXIST	(general realis) (also replaces non-specific irrealis)
	N (VERB)	(general realis)
	IPRO (N/CL) to^{33} (VERB)	free choice
	IPRO (VERB) ni^{31} (VERB)	conditional
		free choice
	IPRO la^{33} (VERB)	standard of comparison
negative	$t\varepsilon i^{31}$ (CL) to^{33} ma^{31} (VERB)	direct negative (also replaces indirect negative)

7.3.1 Specific Indefinite Construction

The specific indefinite construction points to a member of a category, corresponding to English pronouns such as 'someone' and 'somewhere'. Khatso does not have a direct equivalent of these words. Common nouns or classifier phrases, rather than an indefinite construction, are employed instead. The referent may or may not be known to the speaker, making this construction equivalent to two of the typologically common types of indefinite constructions (see Table 7.1 above). Context resolves any ambiguity in discourse. Thus, the dog mentioned in (304) may be a particular animal the speaker wants to buy, or the phrase may merely describe the general wish to have a pet. The classifier phrases in (305), which would typically point to specific singular referents, are more logically interpreted as indefinite here.

---

[1] Table abbreviations: CL classifier, EXIST existential verb, IPRO interrogative pronoun, N noun, REL relative clause.

(304) ŋa³³ **tsʰŋ³¹** ma²⁴ mo⁵⁵ vɤ³²³.
1SG dog CL:GEN want buy
我 狗 个 要 买
'I want to buy a dog.'
我想要买一只狗。
(KL-Elicitation)

(305) **tɛi³¹ jo³⁵** kɛi³³ n̪a³¹ sɛi⁴⁴ m̪³¹tso³³ma³³ jo³⁵ ŋ³⁵ tsɛi³¹,
one CL:HUM AGT speak TOP woman CL:HUM COP.FOC HSY
一 位 说 女人 位 是
'Some people say (that it) was a woman,'
有的人说是一个女的

tɛi³¹ jo³⁵ kɛi³³ n̪a³¹ sɛi⁴⁴ ni³¹ i²⁴tsɤ²⁴ jo³⁵ ŋ³³ n̪a³³ tsɛi³¹,
one CL:HUM AGT speak TOP TOP man CL:HUM COP COP.EMP HSY
一 位 说 男人 位 是
'Some people say (that it) was a man,'
有的人说是一个男的,

tɕi³³ ti³³ ja³³.
say PROG
说
'(They) say (that).'
这么说的。
(PYX-Dragon Pools)

Some general nouns however, tend to be interpreted as referring to unknown referents. This is often the case with *tsʰo³³* 'person' and *n̪o³¹* 'thing', as (306) and (307) illustrate. Thus, nouns with specific reference rather than interrogative pronouns are employed in Khatso for indefinite constructions. This is, in fact, one of the strategies for reformulating the cross-linguistic non-specific irrealis construction, which does not exist in Khatso.

(306) **tsʰo³³ jo³⁵** li³²³ wa³²³.
person CL:HUM come PFV
人 位 来
'Someone came.' / 'A person came.'
有人来了。
(KL-Elicitation)

(307) i³³   **ŋ̍o³¹**   **ko⁵⁵**   vʏ³²³.
     3SG   thing   CL:PL   buy
     他   东西   些   卖
     'She is buying some things.' / 'She is buying things.'
     他买一些东西。
     (KL-Elicitation)

Likewise, polar questions involving an indefinite construction also require a noun modified by a classifier, as the example in (308) demonstrates.

(308) **tsʰo³³**   **jo³⁵**   kɛi³³   nɛi³³   pa⁵³mo³³   ko⁵³   ko⁵³?
     person   CL:HUM   AGT   2SG   tell   EXP   EXP
     人   位   你   告诉   过   过
     'Did someone tell you (that)?' / 'Did a person tell you (that)?'
     有没有人告诉过你？
     (KL-Elicitation)

7.3.2 Non-Specific Indefinite Constructions

The non-specific indefinite constructions point to a member of a category in situations where the exact referent is unimportant or unknown. They often correspond to English pronouns such as 'whoever' and 'anything'. As listed in Table 7.1 above, there are five constructions that belong in this group. The first two, both general realis constructions, are described in § 7.3.2.1, followed by a discussion of the free choice construction in § 7.3.2.2. The indefinite conditional construction, which may also express free choice, is found in § 7.3.2.3, and the indefinite standard of comparison is explained in § 7.3.2.4.

7.3.2.1 Indefinite Realis Constructions

There are two constructions in Khatso that are considered alternates to the cross-linguistic types of indefinite constructions described above (see Table 7.1). These are noun phrases that have a general realis sense, but do not satisfy the particular requirements of other typologically common non-specific constructions. The first combines a headless relative clause with the existential verb *tso³²³*. Without a classifier, which would be the head of the relative clause, the referent is non-specific (see § 6.2.1). Thus, a phrase like that in (309), which describes the giving of wedding gifts, means 'there were (some people) who gave muslin'. Note that it is the context, rather than the construction itself, which indicates that the referent is plural here.

(309) **i³³n̪o²⁴ kɯ³¹ la²⁴ tso³²³.**
   muslin give REL EXIST
   细布   给   有
   'There were (some) who gave muslin.'
   也有的给蓝细布。
   (YJF-Weddings)

The second general realis construction consists of a bare noun serving as P of a verb. As just mentioned, the lack of a classifier denotes non-specific reference (see § 6.2.1), and thus the noun is consequently indefinite. In fact, Khatso has a number of routinized noun-verb compounds in which P, without a classifier, is so semantically bleached that it arguably has no reference. For example, in (310) $n̪o^{31}\ m^{33}$, literally 'do thing', means 'to work' — covering everything from farming the fields to working in an office — and information about the thing(s) done is extremely general. Thus the meaning of the noun is backgrounded with only non-specific reference, if there is any referent at all. Similar compounds include $tsa^{323}\ tsa^{31}$, 'eat' (literally 'eat rice') and $tʰo^{33}\ sa^{33}$ 'sew' (literally 'sew clothing').

(310) **n̪o³¹ m³³ m̰³³ ta³³   sa³¹?**
   thing do do IPFV.IRR still.Q
   事   做 做   还
   'Does (he) still work?'
   还有没有在工作？
   (KL-Erasers)

7.3.2.2 Indefinite Free Choice Construction

Indefinite constructions are often employed to express free choice, meaning that any member of a referent category suffices. In this construction, the interrogative pronouns introduced in § 5.3.3 function as indefinite pronouns. Table 7.2 relists the pronouns with their indefinite meanings. The differing English translations reflect the fact that the pronouns may refer both to known and unknown referents, as described below.

Table 7.2: Non-specific indefinite pronouns in Khatso

Khatso	Morphology	English	Chinese
xa³³jo³⁵	xa³³ (interrogative morpheme) + jo³⁵ (CL:HUM)	'anyone', 'whoever'	谁
xa³³ma⁴⁴	xa³³ (interrogative morpheme) + ma⁴⁴ (DEM form of CL:GEN ma²⁴)	'anything', 'whatever'	什么
xa³³tɕʰa⁵⁵kʰɣ³³ xa³³tsɛi³⁵ xa³³sau³³	xa³³ (interrogative morpheme) + tɕʰa⁵⁵kʰɣ³³ (part of temporal DEM) or tsɛi³⁵ (CL:TMP) or sau³³ (CL:TMP)	'any time', 'whenever'	什么时候
xa³³n̪a⁵³	xa³³ (interrogative morpheme) + n̪a⁵³ (DEM 'place')	'any place', 'wherever'	哪里
xa³³ni³³ko⁵⁵ xa³³ni³³ma⁴⁴ xa³³ni³³+CL	xa³³ (interrogative morpheme) + ni³³ (ADV morpheme) or ko⁵⁵ (CL:PL) or ma⁴⁴ (DEM form of CL:GEN ma²⁴)	'any amount', 'whatever amount'	多少
xa³³ma⁴⁴+N/CL	xa³³ (interrogative morpheme) + ma⁴⁴ (DEM form of CL:GEN ma²⁴)	'any N/CL', 'whichever'	哪个
xa³³ni³³	xa³³ (interrogative morpheme) + ni³³ (ADV morpheme)	'any way', 'however'	怎么

This contruction is formed by using an interrogative pronoun and the adverb *to³³* 'also', although *xa³³ma⁴⁴* 'what' is usually followed by a noun or classifier. As discussed in § 5.3.3.2, the presence of a noun or classifier changes the scope of the choice. For example, without a classifier the phrase in (311) is more general and suggests that there is a wide range of choices. In contrast, the classifier in (312) makes the phrase more specific; the choices are fewer and familiar to both speaker and interlocutor.

(311) **xa³³ma⁴⁴** sɣ⁵⁵ **to³³** ta³²³ ja³³.
    what book also be.acceptable IPFV.EMP
    什么 书 也 行
    'Any book will do.'
    什么书也可以。
    (KL-Elicitation)

(312) sɣ⁵⁵ **xa³³** pɛi²⁴ **to³³** ta³²³ ja³³.
    book what CL:VOL also be.acceptable IPFV.EMP
    书 哪 本 也 行
    'Whichever book will do.'
    哪本书都行。
    (KL-Elicitation)

When coupled with the conditional construction, as described in the next section, the interrogative pronouns may also have a free choice interpretation.

7.3.2.3 Indefinite Conditional Construction

The interrogative pronouns presented in Table 7.2 above may also take part in conditional constructions. The indefinite element is overt in the first clause, which contains the condition and is followed by the topic marker ni^{31}, marking the construction as conditional. Examples are shown in (313) and (314). Note that in addition to the conditional sense, this construction may also be understood as presenting free choice. Thus, the phrase in (313) may also mean 'whatever (you) want to watch, (you can) watch'.

(313) **xa³³ma⁴⁴** mo⁵⁵ ŋ²⁴ka⁴⁴ ni³¹ **xa³³ma⁴⁴** ŋ²⁴ka³³.
what want see TOP what see
什么 要 看 什么 看
'If (you) want to watch something, watch (it).' / 'If (you) want to watch anything, watch (it)' / 'Whatever (you) want to watch, (you can) watch.'
想看什么，看什么。
(HPH-Toys)

(314) **xa³³ma⁴⁴** mo⁵⁵ tsa²⁴ ni³¹ **xa³³ma⁴⁴** tɕi³³.
what want eat TOP what make
什么 要 吃 什么 做
'If (you) want to eat something, make (it).' / 'Whatever (you) want to eat, make (it).'
要吃什么，就做什么。
(KL-Hotpot)

Conditional constructions are described further in § 14.4.

7.3.2.4 Indefinite Comparison Construction

The interrogative pronouns listed in Table 7.2 above may also serve as standards of comparison. As always, they occur in situ; no special word order is required. An example is shown in (315). Comparative constructions are described more fully in § 12.5.

(315) kʰua³¹la³¹ **pɣ³²³** m̩³¹tsʰa³³ mɛi⁴⁴ tso³³kuo³²³ pɣ³²³ **xa³³n̩a⁵³** la⁴⁴ to³³ na²⁴.
Kunming POSS weather CL:GEN China POSS where CMP also be.good
昆明 天气 个 中国 哪里 比 也 好
'Kunming's weather is better than anywhere in China.'
昆明的天气比中国什么地方的都好。
(KL-Elicitation)

7.3.3 Negative Indefinite Constructions

Negative indefinite constructions are used to declare that there are no potential referents in a given category, corresponding to English pronouns such as 'no one' and 'nowhere'. There are three strategies for constructing such phrases in Khatso. The most common involves a set phrase that combines a singular classifier construction with the the adverb *to³³* 'also' and a verb modified by the negative marker:

tɛi³¹ ____ to³³ ma³¹ VERB
one CL also NEG

The second slot contains the classifier or morpheme that is associated with the referent, and the resulting phrase means 'even one [referent] does not [verb]'. The adverb *to³³*, which typically translates as 'also', has a meaning closer to that of 'even' in this construction. For example, *tɛi³¹ jo³⁵ to³³ ma³¹*, with the human classifier *jo³⁵*, conveys the literal meaning 'even one (person) does not', as shown in (316). A list of the possible negative indefinite constructions of this type is presented in Table 7.3 below. Semantically, the meaning of the expression is not as strong as its literal English translation; this is considered a neutral expression in discourse. Note that *to³³* may trigger tone change in the preceding syllable (see § 3.2.4.1).

(316) **tɛi³¹ jo³⁵ to³³ ma³¹** mo⁵⁵ i³²³.
one CL:HUM also NEG want go
一 位 也 不 要 去
'No one wants to go.', literally 'Not even one wants to go.'
谁都不想去。
(KL-Elicitation)

Table 7.3: One type of negative indefinite construction in Khatso

Khatso	Morphology	English	Chinese
tɛi³¹ jo³⁵ to³³ ma³¹	tɛi³¹ ('one') + jo³⁵ (CL:HUM) + to³³ ('also, even') + ma³¹ (NEG)	'no one'	谁都不
tɛi³¹ tsʏ²⁴ to³³ ma³¹	tɛi³¹ ('one') + tsʏ²⁴ (CL:UNK) + to³³ ('also, even') + ma³¹ (NEG)	'nothing'	什么都不
tɛi³¹ xuɛi²⁴ to³³ ma³¹	tɛi³¹ ('one') + xuɛi²⁴ (CL:TMP) + to³³ ('also, even') + ma³¹ (NEG)	'never'	什么时候都不
tɛi³¹ n̪a⁵³ to³³ ma³¹	tɛi³¹ ('one') + n̪a⁵³ (DEM 'place') + to³³ ('also, even') + ma³¹ (NEG)	'nowhere'	什么地方都不
tɛi³¹ N/CL to³³ ma³¹	tɛi³¹ ('one') + N/CL + to³³ ('also') + ma³¹ (NEG)	'no N/CL'	什么[名词/量词]都不

This construction serves as a verbal argument without additional marking, as shown in (317). Moreover, the construction may be altered in several ways. For example, in (318) a noun appears rather than just a classifier phrase, but because the bare classifier marks the noun as singular the meaning of the construction is unchanged (see § 6.2.1). And in (319) the agent marker is inserted and *to³³* is omitted. However, the sandhi evident in *kɛi³³*, changing its tone to 44, indicates that the meaning and function of the adverb remain (see § 3.2.4.1).

(317) **tɛi³¹ tsʏ²⁴ to³³ ma³¹** tso³²³.
one   CL:UNK also NEG   EXIST
一   也   不   有
'(They) had nothing.'
我什么也没有。
(GCS-Childhood)

(318) i³³   **sʏ⁵⁵**   **ma²⁴**   **to³³** **ma³¹** sɿ⁵⁵.
3SG   Chinese.character   CL:GEN   also   NEG   know
他   字   个   也   不   知道
'He doesn't know even one Chinese character.'
他一个字也不认识。
(YAY-Erasers)

(319) **tɛi³¹ jo³⁵ kɛi⁴⁴ ma³¹** ma⁵⁵.
one CL:HUM AGT NEG teach
一 位 不 教
'No one taught (me).'
一个人也没有教。
(WYY-Sewing)

The second negative construction involves negating the free choice construction described above (see §7.3.2.2), in which an interrogative pronoun replaces the numeral-classifier or numeral-morpheme collocation in the construction described above. Thus, the phrase in (320) is semantically the same as that in (316) above; both mean 'no one wants to go'. This construction is identical to its counterpart in Hanyu and is likely borrowed.

(320) **xa³³jo³⁵ to³³ ma³¹** mo⁵⁵ i³²³.
whoever also NEG want go
谁 也 不 要 去
'No one wants to go.', literally 'Even whoever does not want to go.'
谁也不想去。
(KL-Elicitation)

The adverbial indefinite constructions operate in the same way. The interrogative form appears without change, and the verb is modified by *to³³ ma³¹* 'even NEG', as shown in (321) and (322).

(321) **xa³³tsɛi³⁵ to³³ ma³¹** i³²³.
whenever also NEG go
什么时候 也 不 去
'(She) is not going at any time.', literally '(She) is not going even whenever.'
什么时候都不去。
(KL-Elicitation)

(322) nɛi³³ **xa³³ni³³ tɕi⁴⁴ to³³ ma³¹** ta³²³.
2SG however do also NEG be.acceptable
你 怎么 做 也 不 行
'However you do (it) is unacceptable.', literally 'Even however you do (it) is unacceptable.'
你怎么做都不行。
(KL-Elicitation)

The third negative indefinite construction in Khatso employs a headless relative clause as an argument of the existential verb *tso³²³* which is modified by the negative marker *ma³¹*. This is, in other words, the negative counterpart to one of the general realis constructions described in § 7.3.2.1 above. Thus, the phrase in (323), which is equivalent in meaning to the two phrases in (316) and (320) above, literally means 'those who go do not exist'. An example from discourse is shown in (324). Note that the absence of a classifier in this construction underscores that fact that the referent is non-specific (see § 6.2.1). This construction is often used as a replacement for the indirect negative construction found cross-linguistically which does not have an exact counterpart in Khatso.

(323) i³²³ la²⁴ ma³¹ tso³²³.
go REL NEG EXIST
去   不   有
'No one goes.', literally 'Those who go do not exist.'
去的没有。
(KL-Elicitation)

(324) zŋ³¹sŋ³⁵ la²⁴ to³³ ma³¹ tso³²³.
pay.attention REL also NEG EXIST
理会   也   不   有
'No one pays attention (to her).', literally '(People) who pay attention (to her) do not exist.'
也没有人会理。
(PYX-Dragon Pools)

7.3.4 Multiple Indefinite Constructions

Phrases may contain more than one indefinite expression. Just as in the constructions described above, the pronouns occur in situ. Examples are presented in (325) and (326). These phrases are not frequent in discourse, but are more likely to occur than questions with multiple interrogative pronouns (see § 5.3.3.7).

(325) tɛi³¹ jo³⁵ ma³¹ xɛi³⁵   tɛi³¹ tsy̩²⁴ ma³¹ xɛi³⁵   vɤ³²³   wa³²³.
everyone   everything   buy   PFV
谁   什么   买
'Everyone bought everything.'
每个人都什么都买了。
(KL-Elicitation)

(326) tɛi³¹ jo³⁵ ma³¹ xɛi³⁵   tɛi³¹ tsɤ²⁴   to³³   ma³¹   vɤ³²³   la³¹.
everyone   everything   also   NEG   buy   PFV.IRR
谁   什么   也   不   买
'No one bought anything.'
每个人都什么都没有买了。
(KL-Elicitation)

7.4 Possession

There are two constructions that are used to indicate possession. One employs the possessive marker *pɤ³²³* and the other the noun *sɛi⁴⁴* 'family'. Any type of noun may be a possessum, including proper names, pronouns, numerals and classifiers. There is no syntactic distinction in Khatso between inalienable possessums that are inborn or inherent, such as body parts or kin, and those that are alienable which may be acquired or divested, such as money or other tangible items.

pɤ³²³ is the general possessive marker and it is by far the more productive of the two. It follows the possessor, which can be any kind of noun phrase — from pronouns and classifier constructions to nouns with multiple modifiers — and can refer to animate or inanimate nouns. For example, in (327) the possessor is a common noun denoting a place; in (328) it is a pronoun referring to a human; and in (329) it is a common noun denoting an inanimate object.

(327) pɛi³²³ko⁵³   **pɤ³²³**   tuɛi³⁵tsa³¹
pɛi³²³ko⁵³   POSS   team leader
白阁   队长
'*pɛi³²³ko⁵³* village's team leader'
白阁的队长
(ZRF-Competition)

(328) ŋa³³tsʰɤ³¹   **pɤ³²³**   ɤ⁵⁵za³¹
3PL   POSS   grandson
我们   孙子
'our grandsons'
我们的孙子
(KL-Sewing)

(329) ɕo³²³ɕau³⁵ mɛi⁴⁴ pɣ³²³ wɛi³²³tɕʰa³²³ mɛi⁴⁴ ɣ³³ tɕa³³ i³³ n̠a³¹.
school   CL:GEN POSS wall   CL:GEN count cross go   speak
学校   个   围墙   堵   数   过   去   说
'Count over from the wall of the school.'
从学校的围墙数过去。
(YAY-Erasers)

As just mentioned, *pɣ³²³* may be used with possessums that are inherently and permanently owned, as in (330), or those that are temporary, as in (331). Moreover, the possessum may be modified as any other common noun. For example, in (330) and (331) the possessum is followed by a bare classifier, and in (332) by a demonstrative construction.

(330) ŋa³³ **pɣ³²³** ni³¹na²⁴ mɛi⁴⁴
      1SG   POSS   mouth   CL:GEN
      我   嘴   个
      'my mouth'
      我的嘴
      (YAY-Erasers)

(331) nɛi³³tsʰɛi³³ **pɣ³²³** si⁴⁴mo³¹   tsʅ³¹ɕa³¹ mɛi⁴⁴
      2PL   POSS   Xingmeng   luck   CL:GEN
      你们   兴蒙   吉祥   个
      'your Xingmeng luck'
      你们的兴蒙吉祥
      (ZRF-Competition)

(332) i³³   **pɣ³²³** sʅ³¹tsʅ³²³ a³³   tɕi⁵⁵
      3SG   POSS   thing   that CL:TYPE
      他   事   那   种
      'that matter of his'
      他的那种事
      (ZRF-Competition)

Possessive phrases may be stacked. That is, the possessor in one construction may also be the possessum of another, as shown in (333). It is quite common, however, to omit the marker after a pronoun in these cases, as shown in (334). The possessum may also be omitted altogether, as in (335).

(333) ŋa³³tsʰɤ³¹ **pɤ³²³** fɤ³¹pi³¹li³¹ **pɤ³²³** pi³³ma⁵³ ko⁵⁵
3PL POSS Kublai.Khan POSS military.forces CL:PL
我们 忽必烈 兵马 些
'our Kublai Khan's military forces'
我们的忽必烈的兵马
(HPH-Horse Dug Well)

(334) ŋa³³tsʰɤ³³ kʰa⁵⁵tso³¹kʰua⁵⁵ mɛi⁴⁴ **pɤ³²³** ka³²³tɕʰi³²³
1PL Xingmeng CL:GEN POSS door
我们 兴蒙 个 门
'our Xingmeng village's (type of) door'
我们兴蒙的门
(KL-Doors)

(335) i³³ **pɤ³²³** ma³¹ na²⁴.
3SG POSS NEG be.good
他 不 好
'His aren't good.'
他的不好。
(KL-Elicitation)

The noun *sɛi⁴⁴* 'family' may also be used to indicate possession, but its use is largely idiomatic. It follows a proper name, kin term or personal pronoun, and the possessum is most often a kin term, as the examples in (336) and (337) illustrate. These phrases literally mean 'my family's daughter' and 'my family's maternal grandmother' respectively.

(336) ŋa³³ **sɛi⁴⁴** za³¹m̩³¹ jo³⁵
1SG family daughter CL:HUM
我 家 女儿 位
'my daughter'
我家的女儿
(WYF-Stools)

(337) ŋa³³ **sɛi⁴⁴** po³²³ tsʰɤ³³ ni³⁵?
1SG family maternal.grandmother PL TOP.Q
我 家 外婆 们
'And my maternal grandmother and those (people)?'
我家外婆她们呢？
(KL-Sewing)

This construction can be used without a possessum, in which case it is alternately interpreted as '(X)'s family', as in (338), or as the locative expression '(X)'s house', as in (339).

(338) ja⁵³ni³²³ nɛi³³ **sɛi⁴⁴** m̩³²³ tɛi³¹ko⁵⁵ma³³ vɤ³²³ ŋa³²³.
then 2SG family field many buy able
然后 你 家 田 很多 买 能
'Then your family was able to buy a lot of fields.'
然后你家买得了很多田。
(KL-Grandfather)

(339) i³³ **sɛi⁴⁴** li⁴⁴ tso³²³ ŋɛi³³.
3SG family in EXIST ASRT
他 家 里 有
'(It) is at his house.'
在他家里。
(KL-Elicitation)

The use of *sɛi⁴⁴* with family members is not obligatory, however. The marker *pɤ³²³* may be used instead, as shown in (340), or the two may be used together, as in (341).

(340) fɤ³¹pi³¹li³¹ **pɤ³²³** ja²⁴n̩o³¹ ŋ³³ n̩a³³.
Kublai.Khan POSS older.brother COP COP.EMP
忽必烈 兄长 是
'(He was) Kublai Khan's older brother, (that) is (right).'
忽必烈的兄长。
(KLT-History)

(341) nɛi³³ **sɛi⁴⁴** **pɤ³²³** a³³ tɕi⁵⁵
2SG family POSS that CL:TYPE
你 家 那 种
'your family's type (of thing)'
你家的那种
(KL-Grandfather)

The possessum following *sɛi⁴⁴* may also be an inanimate common noun. Such a phrase often refers to an item that belongs to a family as a whole rather than an individual within it, as shown in (342), although the relationship may be one of association rather than ownership, as the phrase in (343) illustrates. The marker *pɤ³²³* may also be added to this construction, as in (344), without changing the meaning.

(342) nɛi³³ **sɛi⁴⁴** xɤ³³ tɕi⁵⁵ jo³⁵ ɳ̊ɛ²⁴.
2SG family house CL:TYPE even be.small
你 家 房 种 又 小
'Your family's type of house is even smaller.'
你家的房子又小。
(YJR-Grandfather)

(343) nɛi³³ **sɛi⁴⁴** kʰua⁵⁵ mɛi⁴⁴ xa³³ɳa⁵³ tso³²³?
2SG family village CL:GEN where EXIST
你 家 村 个 哪里 有
'Where is your family's village?'
你家的村子在哪里？
(KL-Childhood)

(344) ŋa³³ **sɛi⁴⁴** pɤ³²³ xɤ³³ kɤ³⁵
1SG family POSS house CL:BDG
我 家 房子 所
'our family's house'
我家的房子
(GCS-Childhood)

7.5 Relativization

Nouns are modified by clauses through use of the relative clause construction. Typically, the modified noun is co-referential with an element in the relative clause, though this is not obligatory. In many Sino-Tibetan languages, the morpheme that marks possessive constructions and nominalized clauses is often identical to the relative clause marker (e.g. Matisoff 1972; Zhan and Miao 2012). This is not the case in Khatso, where each function has its own marker. The relative clause marker in Khatso is *la²⁴*, which is distinct from the possessive marker *pɤ³²³* and the nominalizers *tsɿ³²³* and *kɤ³²³* (see § 7.4 and § 7.6 respectively).

In Khatso, the word order within relative clauses is identical to that of matrix clauses, with the exception of a gap where the equivalent of the head noun would be, as shown in (345). The syntax in relative clauses does show two regular patterns. First, verbs are not marked for aspect; the time frame is understood from context, although temporal adverbs and serial verb constructions may overtly convey temporal meaning. Second, the agent in a relative clause is almost always marked by the agent marker *kɛɿ³⁵* even though it is fairly rare in matrix clauses. This helps disambiguate arguments within the relative clause where gapping may otherwise cause confusion (see § 10.4). In addition, because relative clauses make their head nouns specific by definition, post-head classifiers are not obligatory.

(345) [i³³   kɛi³³   ____   vɤ³²³]   **la²⁴**   sʅ⁵⁵
      3SG   AGT   buy   REL   book
      他   买   书
      'the book he bought'
      他买的书
      (KL-Elicitation)

For the most part, relative clauses formed with *la²⁴* are restrictive, meaning that they are used to narrowly define the identity of a particular referent in discourse. For example, in (346) the clause meaning 'that the government gives' specifies that the money discussed is a government pension rather than funds received from other sources. Non-restrictive information is typically not introduced via relative clauses, but rather through supplementary independent clauses.

(346) [kuo³²³tɕa³³   sɛi⁴⁴   kɛi³³   kɯ³¹]   **la²⁴**   a³³   ti⁵³   zɛi³¹   lo⁵³   wa³²³.
      country   CL:COL   AGT   give   REL   that   CL:PCE use   be.enough PFV
      国家   个   给   那   块   用   够
      'The little bit that the government gives is enough.'
      国家给的那点够用了。
      (YJF-Childhood)

Because Khatso is a pragmatics-based language (see Bisang 2009), relativized nouns in Khatso may be any argument in the relative clause, whether S, A, P, R or possessor. None are differentiated through syntactic marking. For example, in (347) S is the head of the relative clause, in (348) the head is A, in (349) it is P, in (350) R and in (351) the head is the possessor.

(347) *Relativized S*
      [mo³¹]   **la²⁴**   ko⁵⁵
      be.old   REL   CL:PL
      老   些
      'those who are old'
      老的人
      (YAY-Erasers)

(348) *Relativized A*
[tɕi³³ li³²³]   **la²⁴** tsʰɤ³³ ni³¹   tɕo³⁵ mɤ³¹zɛi³²³   tɕi³³.
pack know.how REL   PL   TOP   then   for.oneself pack
装   会   们   就   自个   装
'Those who knew how to bundle (it), (each) would bundle (it) for (her) own use.'
会装的那些呢就自己装。
(YJF-Dance Parties)

(349) *Relativized P*
[nɛi³³ kɛi³³ sa³³] **la²⁴** tʰo³³pɛi³³
2SG   AGT   sew   REL   upper.garment
你   缝   褂子
'the upper garment you sewed'
你缝的褂子
(WYY-Sewing)

(350) *Relativized R*
[ŋa³³ kɛi³³ tɕʰɛ³²³ kɯ³¹] **la²⁴** tsʰo³³ jo³⁵
1SG AGT   money   give   REL   person CL:HUM
我   钱   给   人   位
'the person I gave money to'
我给钱的人
(KL-Elicitation)

(351) *Relativized possessor*
[ko³³ko³³   kʰua³¹la³¹ tso³²³] **la²⁴** tsʰo³¹pa³⁵ a³³ jo³⁵
older.brother Kunming   EXIST   REL   friend   that CL:HUM
哥哥   昆明   有   朋友   那   位
'that friend whose older brother lives in Kunming'
哥哥住在昆明的那个朋友
(KL-Elicitation)

Likewise, the head noun may be any semantic argument in the main clause, regardless of its role in the relative clause. For example, in (352) the P of the relative clause is the S of the matrix clause. And in (353) and (354), the relativized noun is the P and R respectively.

(352) *Relativized noun as S*
　　　[nɛi³³　kɛi³³　n̠a³¹]　**la²⁴**　tɕi⁵⁵　to³³　n̠ɛ²⁴　　ŋɛi³⁵.
　　　2SG　　AGT　　speak　REL　CL:PHR　also　be.small　ASRT.FOC
　　　你　　　　　　说　　　　　　句　　　也　　小
　　　'You spoke little.', literally 'The phrases you spoke are small.'
　　　你说的也是小的。
　　　(KL-Grandfather)

(353) *Relativized noun as P*
　　　ŋa³³　[nɛi³³　kɛi³³　tsʰo⁵⁵]　**la²⁴**　xɤ³³　kɤ³⁵　　vɤ³²³　wa³²³.
　　　1SG　　2SG　　AGT　　build　　REL　house　CL:BDG　buy　　PFV
　　　我　　你　　　　　　盖　　　　　　房子　所　　　买
　　　'I bought the house you built.'
　　　我买了你盖的房子。
　　　(KL-Elicitation)

(354) *Relativized noun as R*
　　　i³³　　kɛi³³　sɤ⁵⁵　ko⁵⁵　[kʰua³¹la³¹　i³²³]　**la²⁴**　jo³⁵　　kɯ³¹　　wa³²³.
　　　3SG　　AGT　　book　CL:PL　Kunming　　go　　REL　CL:HUM　give　　PFV
　　　他　　　　　　书　　些　　昆明　　　　去　　　　　位　　　　给
　　　'He gave books to the man who went to Kunming.'
　　　他把书给了去昆明的人了。
　　　(KL-Elicitation)

These examples all show common nouns as heads of relative clauses. But, any type of noun may be the head of a relative clause, including proper names, pronouns, numerals and classifiers. An example of each is shown below in (355) through (358). Note that some, like their English equivalents, require very particular pragmatic situations to make sense. In discourse, relative clauses most often modify common nouns and classifiers.

(355) [kʰua³¹la³¹　tso³²³]　**la²⁴**　kʰuɛi⁴⁴i³¹
　　　Kunming　　EXIST　　REL　　Kui Ying
　　　昆明　　　　有　　　　　　奎滢
　　　'the Kui Ying who lives in Kunming'
　　　住在昆明的奎滢
　　　(KL-Elicitation)

(356) [ŋ⁵⁵lo⁵³ tso³²³] **la²⁴** i³³tsʰɤ³³
     Tonghai EXIST REL 3PL
     通海 有 他们
     'they who live in Tonghai'
     住在通海的他们
     (KL-Elicitation)

(357) [i³³ n̠a³¹] **la²⁴** "xɤ³³" ma³¹ xo²⁴.
     3SG speak REL four NEG be.correct
     他 说 四 不 对
     'The "four" he said is not right.'
     他说的"四"不对。
     (KL-Elicitation)

(358) [ni³¹tsɤ̩³³pa³³pa³³ mɛi⁴⁴ xɛi⁵³] **la²⁴** jo³⁵
     millstone CL:GEN stand REL CL:HUM
     石碾团 个 站 位
     'the one (person) standing on the millstone'
     站在石碾团的人
     (PYX-Performing)

As already demonstrated, there are few constraints in the relationship between the relativized noun and its role in the dependent clause. In fact, not only may modified nouns not be core arguments, they need not even play a semantic role in the relative clause at all. Thus, Khatso falls into the category of languages with generalized noun-modifying clause constructions, such as Putonghua and Japanese (e.g. Comrie 1998; Matsumoto 1997). A number of examples similar to those cited in the literature will help illustrate the point. Relative clauses modifying locative expressions such as $a^{33}n̠a^{53}$ 'there' and the noun $n̠a^{53}$ 'place' can describe semantic goals, places or paths, as shown in (359), (360) and (361) respectively. Temporal nouns are also frequently relativized, as the phrase in (362) illustrates. Likewise, the manner classifier, $tɕi^{55}$ 'style, type' may be modified by a relative clause, as shown in (363).

(359) [n̠a³¹ fɤ³³] **la²⁴** a³³n̠a⁵³ tsʰɹ̩³³ ŋɛi³³.
     fish raise REL there arrive ASRT
     鱼 养 那里 到
     '(They) arrived (at) the place where (they) raise fish.'
     到了养鱼的那里。
     (WYF-Stools)

(360) [tɕo³¹lo³²³tsʰɿ³²³   tɕi³³]   **la²⁴**   n̥a⁵³
Nine.Dragon.Pond   say   REL   place
九龙池   说   地方
'the place that (they) call Nine Dragon Pond'
九龙池的那个地方
(PYX-Dragon Pools)

(361) [ŋa³³   kɛi³³   ka³²³   ko⁵³]   **la²⁴**   tɕa³²³
1SG   AGT   walk   cross   REL   street
我   走   过   路
'the street I walked across'
我走过的路
(KL-Elicitation)

(362) [kʰai³³sɿ³⁵   zɿ³²³n̥ɛ³²³tsɿ³¹   so²⁴]   **la²⁴**   tsɛi³⁵
start   one.grade   study   REL   CL:TMP
开始   一年级   读   段
'(the) time when I started studying first grade'
开始读一年级的时候
(YAY-Erasers)

(363) [tsʰo³¹ka³³   i³³]   **la²⁴**   tɕi⁵⁵
perform   go   REL   CL:TYPE
演   去   种
'the style (in) which (they) perform'
去演出玩的那种
(PYX-Performing)

Accompaniments and instruments are also easily relativized, as shown in (364) and (365). Even quasi-relational nouns – that is, those that are semantically one step removed from the action in the relative clause – may be relativized. For example, *tɕʰɛ³²³* 'money' in (366) is a typical outcome of a teaching job; similarly, *li³²³tɕʰɛ³²³* 'change' in (367) is a common result of shopping. Neither is a core argument of the verb in the relative clause.

(364) [ŋa³³   tɕa³³mɛi³³   n̥o³¹   ky³³]   **la²⁴**   jo³⁵
SG   together   thing   do   REL   CL:HUM
我   一起   事   做   位
'the one I work (with)'
和我一起做事的人
(KL-Elicitation)

(365) [ŋa³³ kei³³ si³⁵ vɤ⁵³] **la²⁴** piɛ³⁵ po²⁴
　　　1SG　AGT　letter　write　REL　pen　CL:ROD
　　　我　　　　　信　　写　　　　　笔　　支
　　　'the pen I wrote a letter (with)'
　　　我写信的笔
　　　(KL-Elicitation)

(366) [ŋa³³ kei³³ jɛ⁴⁴ʐɿ³³ ma⁵⁵] **la²⁴** tɕʰɛ³²³
　　　1SG　AGT　English　teach　REL　money
　　　我　　　　　英语　　教　　　　钱
　　　'the money I (earn from) teaching English'
　　　我教英语的钱
　　　(KL-Elicitation)

(367) [sv⁵⁵ vɤ³²³] **la²⁴** li³²³tɕʰɛ³²³
　　　book　buy　REL　change
　　　书　　买　　　　零钱
　　　'the change from buying books'
　　　买书的零钱
　　　(KL-Elicitation)

Typically, relative clauses modify a noun or classifier in discourse, but headless relative clauses are also possible, as (368) illustrates. Some of these constructions have become lexicalized and are the usual ways of expressing these concepts; a few are listed in (369). Although these are technically headless relative clauses, in many phrases a classifier follows in order to mark number and specific reference. In such cases, the classifier may be analyzed as the head. An example of this is shown in (370).

(368) [i³³n̻o²⁴ kɯ³¹] **la²⁴** tso³²³,
　　　muslin　give　REL　EXIST
　　　细布　　给　　　　有
　　　'there were (some) who gave muslin,'
　　　有给蓝细布的，

　　　[tsʰua³²³ la³²³ kɯ³¹] **la²⁴** tso³²³.
　　　green　blue　give　REL　EXIST
　　　翠　　　蓝　　给　　　　有
　　　'There were (some) who gave dark blue (muslin).'
　　　也有给翠蓝的。
　　　(YJF-Weddings)

(369) koˤ³tʰa³¹ ȵɛ²⁴   **la²⁴** → 'young people'
      age   be.small REL   年轻人
      年龄   小

      tso³¹mo³¹ m̥³³   **la²⁴** → 'government official'
      official   make   REL   大官
      官   当

      m̥³²³ tɤ²⁴   **la²⁴** → 'farmer'
      field plant REL   农民
      田   栽

      ȵo³¹   ŋ³¹   **la²⁴** → 'sales clerk'
      thing sell   REL   售货员
      东西   卖

(370) [koˤ³tʰa³¹ ȵɛ²⁴] **la²⁴** ko⁵⁵   to³³   kʰa⁵⁵tso³¹ma³³ tʰo³³   ma³¹ vi⁵³
      age   be.small REL   CL:PL also   Khatso.F   clothing NEG   wear
      年龄   小   些   也   喀卓女人   衣服   不   穿

      tɤ³³   wa³³.
      PROG   CRS

      'Those young (women) no longer wear (traditional) Khatso clothing.'
      年轻人也不穿喀卓衣服了。
      (WYY-Sewing)

In addition, headless relative clauses are employed in both non-specific indefinite and negative indefinite constructions (see § 7.3.2 and § 7.3.3 respectively).

7.6 Nominalization

Unlike many other Tibeto-Burman languages, Khatso does not have a nominalization process that is productive in all environments. However, there are several constructions that nominalize verbs in certain circumstances, and they are described in turn below.

In the first construction, the third person singular pronoun i^{33}, semantically bleached here, is combined with a stative verb to create a noun that points out a referent in terms of a salient feature, as the examples in (371) demonstrate. An example from discourse is presented in (372). Not all stative verbs may participate in this construction; it seems to mainly involve verbs that describe color, dimension and physical properties, and referents are typically inanimate. These compounds are nouns, and are, in fact, identical in structure to the combinations of common nouns and stative verbs described earlier (see § 7.2.2).

(371) i³³ 3SG 它 + ŋ²⁴ 'to be red' 红 → i³³ŋ²⁴ 'the red one' 红的
i³³ 3SG 它 + vɤ³³ 'to be round' 圆 → i³³vɤ³³ 'the round one' 圆的
i³³ 3SG 它 + sɤ²⁴ 'to be long' 长 → i³³sɤ²⁴ 'the long one' 长的
i³³ 3SG 它 + tsʅ²⁴ 'to be straight' 直 → i³³tsʅ²⁴ 'the straight one' 直的

(372) **i³³na⁵³**   ɕi³³   kɯ³¹   nɛi³⁵.
3SG.be.black be.accustomed give   ASRT.FOC
它黑   习惯   给
'(They) used to give black ones (instead).'
会给黑的。
(YJF-Weddings)

Second, the reduplicated stative construction has a nominal function in addition to its adjectival and adverbial functions (see § 8.1.2.2). In this use, it serves as a verbal argument, as shown in (373). Semantically, it is similar to the previous construction, in which a stative verb is used to identify a referent in terms of a salient feature. But the zero anaphora here means that the noun is omitted altogether rather than being replaced by a pronoun. There is no overt syntactic clue marking this construction as nominal. Instead, context determines the most relevant interpretation.

(373) suɛi³¹ʐʅ³¹ **lɤ⁵⁵**   **lɤ⁵⁵**   za³¹   ni³³,   li³³pɤ³³   kɤ²⁴   ka⁵³   nɛi³¹.
all   be.green   be.green   DIM   ADV   field.ridge CL:STRIP   on   grow
所有   绿   绿   田埂   条   上   长
'So all the really green ones, (they) grew on the ridges between fields.'
所有绿绿的, 长在田埂上的。
(YJF-Childhood)

In addition, headless relative clauses may also serve as nouns, as shown in (374). Many have become lexicalized and now are the common way to express certain concepts in Khatso (see § 7.5).

(374) [tsʰua³²³   la³²³   kɯ³¹]   **la²⁴**   tso³²³.
green   blue   give   REL   EXIST
翠   蓝   给   有
'There were (some) who gave dark blue (ones).'
也有给翠蓝的。
(YJF-Weddings)

Finally, there are two particles, $tsɿ^{323}$ and $kɤ^{323}$, that create nominal expressions from verbs, though they are only used in very particular environments. The first, $tsɿ^{323}$, has a meaning akin to 'thing', and when suffixed to a verb it creates an expression that means 'a thing for [VERB]ing'. While $tsɿ^{323}$ may modify any non-stative verb, the resulting nominalization typically only serves as P of the same verb or S of the existential verb tso^{323}. Examples are shown in (375) and (376). When the verbs are identical, the construction has an idiomatic universal sense, so that $kv̩^{33}\ tsɿ^{323}\ kv̩^{33}$ in (376) means 'whatever needs doing, (I'll) do'. With the existential verb, the meaning is more literal, as (375) illustrates.

(375) ɤ²⁴   tsɿ³²³   ma³¹   tso³²³.
       call   NMLZ   NEG   EXIST
       叫   不   有
       '(It) doesn't have a name', literally 'A call-thing doesn't exist.'
       没有什么叫的。
       (YLW-Qin)

(376) kv̩³³   tsɿ³²³   kv̩³³
       do   NMLZ   do
       做   做
       'do whatever needs doing', literally 'do do-things'
       有什么做什么
       (KL-Elicitation)

The second nominalizing particle, $kɤ^{323}$, carries a meaning of 'place', and when modifying a verb it creates an expression that means 'a place for [VERB]ing'. Like $tsɿ^{323}$, it may modify any non-stative verb, but its use is restricted to serving as S of the existential verb tso^{323}. An example is shown in (377). One such construction, $i^{323}\ kɤ^{323}\ ma^{31}\ tso^{323}$ which means 'no place to go', has developed an emphatic sense of 'no place to turn' or even 'to the ultimate degree', as the phrase in (378) illustrates.

(377) kʰo⁵³tʰa³¹   ȵɛ²⁴   sɿ³²³,
       age   be.small COP
       年龄   小   是

       la²⁴ka³³   kɤ³²³   ma³¹   tso³²³.
       play   NMLZ   NEG   EXIST
       玩   不   有
       'When (I) was young, there was no place to play.'
       年轻的时候，没有玩的地方。
       (YLW-Learning)

(378) ja⁵³   mi²⁴   to⁵³   tɤ⁴⁴   i³²³   kɤ³²³   ma³¹   tso³²³.
later name exit   CLNK go   place   NEG   EXIST
然后   名   出   去   地方   不   有
'Then (it) became extremely famous.' literally, 'Then (it) became famous with no place to go.'
然后出名的不得了。
(HPH-Horse Dug Well)

Complementation, which allows subordinate clauses to serve as arguments in matrix clauses, does not involve a nominalization process in Khatso. Rather, the temporal and topic marker *sɛi⁴⁴* is used to link clauses, as described in Chapter 15.

7.7 Coordination and Disjunction

Khatso employs several methods for coordinating nouns. Often juxtaposition is used, with no overt conjunction necessary. Nonetheless, conjunctions do exist in the language. In some cases a single conjunction is required, and in others one is required for every coordinand. Nouns are also coordinated in disjunctive constructions, which provide a choice between one or more options. These three strategies — juxtaposition, coordination with a conjunction, and coordination through disjunction — are discussed below.

7.7.1 Juxtaposition

Juxtaposition, in which nouns are placed next to one another without an overt conjunction, is a common strategy in Khatso. This construction may be used with common nouns, as in (379) and (380), or proper nouns, as shown in (381) and (382).

(379) nɛi³³ sɛi⁴⁴   pa³¹   nɛi³³ sɛi⁴⁴   mo³³   tsʰɤ³³ kʰua³¹ tsɤ²⁴.
       2SG   family father 2SG   family mother PL   speak   CONT.IMP
       你   家   爸爸   你   家   妈妈   们   说
       'Talk about your father's (and) your mother's people.'
       就说你爸爸家，你妈妈家。
       (KL-Grandfather)

(380) **wa⁵³sa³¹ ŋ³¹sa²⁴** to³³ mo⁵⁵ vɤ³²³.
pork beef also want buy
猪肉 牛肉 也 要 买
'(I) also want to buy pork (and) beef.'
猪肉牛肉也想要买。
(KL-Elicitation)

(381) **lo³²³m³¹tsʅ³³ ŋa³⁵tso⁵³ na⁵³pa³¹kʰua⁵⁵** tsɛi³⁵tsɛi³³za³¹ tsʰo³¹ tso²⁴ i³³
Luxi Tanjiaying Ngwi.village everywhere perform ITER go
碌溪村 谭家营 彝族村 到处 演出 去
ti³³ja³³.
PROG
'Luxi, Tanjiaying, Ngwi Village, (they) were performing everywhere.'
碌溪村，谭家营，彝族村，到处都去演出的呀。
(PYX-Performing)

(382) **lau³¹xua³⁵, lau³¹kʰuɛi⁴⁴, lau³¹tsʰʅ⁴⁴**, i³³tsʰɤ³³ tsʰo³¹pa³⁵ tsʰɤ³³ ŋ³³ ja³³.
lau³¹xua³⁵ lau³¹kʰuɛi⁴⁴ lau³¹tsʰʅ⁴⁴ 3PL friend PL COP IPFV.EMP
老华 老奎 老期 他们 朋友 们 是
'*lau³¹xua³⁵, lau³¹kʰuɛi⁴⁴* (and) *lau³¹tsʰʅ⁴⁴*, they are all friends.'
老华，老奎，老期，他们是朋友呀。
(KL-Elicitation)

As (381) and (382) above demonstrate, this method is also used for listing items in discourse. There is no limit to the number of nouns that may be juxtaposed in this way. The largest number attested in the corpus is five, shown in (383), which discusses ingredients in a recipe.

(383) **xa³⁵tɕʰɛ³²³, tɕɛ³⁵, ŋ²⁴tɕa³²³, no⁵³tsʅ³¹, wa⁵³sa³¹**, tɕɛi³¹ tiɛ⁵⁵ tiɛ⁵³ ni³³
celery mushroom other tofu pork, one slice slice ADV
芹菜 菌 别的 豆腐 猪肉 一 片 片
so³⁵ pa³¹.
chop be.thin
切 薄
'Celery, mushrooms, other (vegetables), tofu, pork, chop (them) into thin slices.'
芹菜，菌，别的，豆腐，猪肉，一片片地切成薄片。
(KL-Hotpot)

Disjunctive coordination may also be conveyed through juxtaposition; see § 7.7.3 below.

7.7.2 Coordination with Conjunctions

Coordination is also indicated through of the use of the nominal conjunction *kɛi³³* 'and', which is derived from the homophonous agent marker (see § 10.4). In this construction, the conjunction is typically placed after each noun, regardless of how many there are. For example, two nouns are coordinated in (384), and four in (385). However, in discourse the construction may be altered somewhat. For example, a conjunction may be omitted in quick speech, as in (386), or an entire coordinand may be absent due to zero anaphora, leaving only a single overt coordinand in the phrase, as in (387).

(384) pɛi³²³ko⁵³   pɣ³²³   tuɛi³⁵tsa³¹ma³³   jo³⁵   **kɛi³³**   i³³   **kɛi³³**   la³¹?
     pɛi³²³ko⁵³   POSS   team.leader.F   CL:HUM   CONJ   3SG   CONJ   PFV.IRR
     白阁   队长   位   和   她   和
     '*pɛi³²³ko⁵³*'s team leader and her?'
     白阁的队长和她吗？
     (ZRF-Competition)

(385) ɕa³³pa³¹ko⁵⁵   tsʰɣ³³   **kɛi³³**,   tsʰŋ⁴⁴mɛi²⁴   tsʰɣ³³   **kɛi³³**,   so³³xua²⁴   tsʰɣ³³   **kɛi³³**,
     ɕa³³pa³¹ko⁵⁵   PL   CONJ   tsʰŋ⁴⁴mɛi²⁴   PL   CONJ   so³³xua²⁴   PL   CONJ
     小八哥   们   和   期妹   们   和   锁华   们   和

     na³²³kua³³pɣ³³mɛi⁴⁴   tsʰɣ³³   **kɛi³³**,   a³³   ko⁵⁵   ŋɛi³⁵.
     na³²³kua³³pɣ³³mɛi⁴⁴   PL   CONJ   that   CL:PL   ASRT.FOC
     南瓜煎   们   和   那   些
     '*ɕa³³pa³¹ko⁵⁵* and (his) friends, and *tsʰŋ⁴⁴mɛi²⁴* and (his) friends, and *so³³xua²⁴* and (his) friends, and *na³²³kua³³pɣ³³mɛi⁴⁴* and (his) friends, those ones.'
     小八哥和期妹和锁华和煎南瓜和他们那些。
     (PYX-Performing)

(386) kua²⁴la³¹   **kɛi³³**   tsɛi³⁵tsɛi³³za³¹   tsʰo³¹   tso²⁴   i³³   tɣ³³   tsɛi³¹   mɛi⁴⁴.
     Qutuoguan   CONJ   places   perform   ITER   go   PROG   HSY   DSC.EMP
     曲陀关   和   到处   演   去
     '(They) say (they) performed in Qutuoguan and everywhere.'
     听说曲陀关啦，到处都去演出。
     (PYX-Performing)

(387) i⁵³tɕo³⁵   ŋa³¹   ko⁵⁵   tɕo³⁵   i³³kʰɤ³³   tɕi³³   ta³²³   wa³³.
then   fish   CL:PL   then   inside   put   be.acceptable CRS
然后   鱼   些   就   里面   放   可以
'Then, (you) can then put the fish inside.'
然后，就可以把鱼放在里面了。

ja⁵³ni³²³   tsʰo³¹   **kɛi³³**   kɛi³³   tɕi³³.
then   ginger   CONJ   AGT   put
然后   姜   和   放
'Then, and ginger can be put (in).'
然后，把姜放进去。
(KL-Hotpot)

Despite the fact that *kɛi³³* is derived from the agent marker, it may coordinate any type of argument, including P and R. In (388), for example, the coordinated nouns are P of the verb m̩³³ 'to make'. Since all arguments precede the verb, marking coordinands individually helps differentiate them from any other overt arguments in the clause.

(388) no⁵³   **kɛi³³**   tsa³²³   **kɛi³³**   m̩³³   ɕo⁵⁵   tɤ³⁵   ni³¹,
bean   CONJ   rice   CONJ   make   together   PROG.FOC   TOP
豆   和   饭   和   做   一起

tsa³²³   mei⁴⁴   to³³   ŋ²⁴lɤ³⁵ma³³   ta⁵⁵   la³⁵   wa³³.
rice   CL:GEN   also   very.red   be.type   FOC   CRS
饭   个   也   红红   样
'(When you) make rice and beans together, the rice becomes really red.'
蚕豆和饭参和着煮在一起呢，饭也煮成红红的了。
(YBF-Three Ladies)

The conjunction *kɛi³³* is also used in one of the constructions for equal comparison, as shown in (389). Here too it appears after every coordinand. Making this kind of comparison does not require the use of the conjunction, however. There are several ways to say the same thing without it.

(389) i³³   **kɛi³³**   lau³¹xua³⁵   **kɛi³³**   tɕi³¹tɕʰau³³   m̩²⁴   tso³²³.
3SG   CONJ   lau³¹xua³⁵   CONJ   same   be.tall   EXIST
他   和   老华   和   一样   高   有
'He and *lau³¹xua³⁵* are the same height.'
他和老华一样高。
(KL-Elicitation)

The conjunction *kɛi³³* cannot coordinate clauses; other strategies are used instead (see § 13.1). In addition, the conjunction-like particle *y̠³²³*, which also translates as 'and', is only found in reciprocal and related comparative constructions, and is thus not generally productive. Reciprocal constructions are discussed in § 12.3; comparative constructions in § 12.5.

7.7.3 Coordination through Disjunction

Disjunctive coordination presents a choice between referents, and is typically expressed in one of two ways: through juxtaposition or use of the disjunctive coordinator. It is also common to present the choice by juxtaposing entire clauses rather than just the noun phrases, as described below.

Juxtaposition can be used for both coordination and disjunction. If the coordinated nouns are in semantic opposition, and thus clearly present a choice, then they are interpreted as disjunctive, as (390) shows. Note that the phrase in (391) can be interpreted as either a literal choice between two numerals or the more figurative meaning of 'several'. Juxtaposition in coordination is discussed in § 7.7.1; approximate numerical constructions are described in § 6.1.

(390) **wa⁵³sa³¹   ŋ³¹sa³¹   vɤ²⁴   to³³   ta³²³.**
      pork   beef   buy   also   able
      猪肉   牛肉   买   也   可以
      '(You) can buy pork (or) beef.'
      猪肉牛肉也可以买。
      (KL-Elicitation)

(391) **ŋ³¹   si³⁵   jo⁵³   tso³²³.**
      two   three   CL:TYPE   EXIST
      二   三   种   有
      'There are two (or) three types.' / 'There are several types.'
      有两三种。
      (KL-Doors)

Alternately, the disjunctive coordinator *ŋ³³si⁴⁴* 'or' can be used to frame a choice in a more overt way. In this construction, the coordinator is placed between the noun phrases, as (392) and (393) illustrate. Unlike the coordinator *kɛi³³*, it does not follow the second coordinand.

(392) mɣ³²³tɕa³³ jo³⁵   **ŋ³³si⁴⁴**   jɛ³²³tɕa³³   jo³⁵
Mojiang   CL:HUM   or   Yuanjiang   CL:HUM
墨江   位   或   元江   位
'Mojiang (people) or Yuanjiang (people)'
是墨江的人还是元江的人
(KL-Elicitation)

(393) ŋa³⁵tso⁵³   **ŋ³³si⁴⁴**   a³³   ko⁵⁵   tsʰo³¹   tso²⁴ i³³   ti³³   sa²⁴   ja³³.
Tanjiaying   or   that   CL:PL perform   ITER   go   PROG   perhaps   IPFV.EMP
谭家营   或是   那   些   演出   去   可能
'They maybe went to Tanjiaying or those (places) to perform.'
可能是去谭家营或是那些地方表演。
(PYX-Performing)

In addition, it is common in Khatso to repeat the verb along with the noun phrase when presenting a choice. This is not obligatory, but rather depends on speaker preference. Mirroring the pattern for noun phrases, this construction can be done through juxtaposition, as in (394), or with the disjunctive coordinator, as in (395). The disjunctive coordinator may link clauses as well as noun phrases, as the examples demonstrate. Its use in clause combining is discussed in § 13.1.2.

(394) i³³   [wa⁵³sa³¹   vɣ³²³]   [ŋ³¹sa³¹   vɣ³²³].
3SG   pork   buy   beef   buy
他   猪肉   买   牛肉   买
'He is buying pork (or) buying beef.'
他买猪肉买牛肉。
(KL-Elicitation)

(395) [ɣa⁵³   mɛi⁴⁴   si⁵³]   **ŋ³³si⁴⁴**   [tsʰŋ³¹   mɛi⁴⁴   si⁵³]?
chicken CL:GEN   kill   or   dog   CL:GEN   kill
鸡   个   杀   或是   狗   个   杀
'(Shall I) kill a chicken or kill a dog?'
杀鸡或是杀狗?
(KL-Elicitation)

The disjunctive constructions just described are roughly the same in terms of semantics. It is largely a matter of speaker preference as to which phrasing is used in which context. Thus, the five disjunctive phrases presented in (396) through (399) are equally likely to occur and are equivalent in meaning.

(396) nɛi³³ [wa⁵³sa³¹ vɤ²⁴ to³³ ta³²³] [ŋ³¹sa³¹ vɤ²⁴ to³³ ta³²³].
2SG pork buy also able beef buy also able
你 猪肉 买 也 可以 牛肉 买 也 可以
'You can either buy pork or you can buy beef.'
你可以买猪肉也可以买牛肉。
(KL-Elicitation)

(397) wa⁵³sa³¹ ŋ³¹sa³¹ vɤ²⁴ to³³ ta³²³.
pork beef buy also able
猪肉 牛肉 买 也 可以
'(You) can buy pork or beef.'
买猪肉和牛肉也可以。
(KL-Elicitation)

(398) [wa⁵³sa³¹ vɤ³²³] ŋ³³si⁴⁴ [ŋ³¹sa³¹ vɤ³²³].
pork buy or beef buy
猪肉 买 或是 牛肉 买
'(You) buy pork or beef.'
买猪肉还是买牛肉。
(KL-Elicitation)

(399) wa⁵³sa³¹ ŋ³³si⁴⁴ ŋ³¹sa³¹ vɤ³²³.
pork or beef buy
猪肉 或是 牛肉 买
'(You) buy pork or beef.'
买猪肉或是牛肉。
(KL-Elicitation)

8 Verbs

Alongside nouns, the verb class is the other large category in the Khatso lexicon. Like nouns, verbs are unmarked — that is, there is nothing in their morphological structure that marks their membership in the class. In fact, most verbs are monosyllabic (see § 4.2), as are many nouns, adverbs and grammatical particles. And, aside from a few verbs such as $\eta^{24}ka^{33}$ 'to look, see' and $na^{24}\eta^{24}$ 'to ask', almost all of the disyllabic verbs are Hanyu loans. No trisyllabic verbs are attested, although serial verb constructions may combine two or more verbs to describe a unitary event, as described below (see § 8.8).

Khatso verbs comprise an open class, meaning that the category readily accepts new words as members. Today, this is largely done through borrowing from Hanyu, a process that the Khatso have apparently employed for centuries. Thus, as has already been mentioned, a great deal of the Khatso vocabulary, including verbs, consists of loans from Hanyu (see § 1.5). These include basic terms such as $s\eta^{31}xua^{33}$ 'to like', p^hiau^{33} 'to float' and $ma^{323}fa^{323}$ 'to be bothersome' as well as newer concepts such as $t\varcitau^{33}$ 'to pay (tuition)' and $k^h\varepsilon i^{33}$ 'to drive (vehicles)'. Because today the Khatso are all bilingual in Hanyu, if not Putonghua, it is often unclear in discourse whether newer verbs are truly Khatso lexemes or Hanyu words given Khatso pronunciation on an ad hoc basis.

Compounding is not a productive process for creating new verbs in the language. Multiple verbs may be combined in serial verb constructions, but these seem largely to be routine collocations rather than spontaneous inventions (see § 4.2.3). Verbs do create compounds with nouns in interesting ways. For example, a few adjective-like stative verbs may directly modify nouns (see § 8.1.2.1). The result is a compound noun, as in (400) and (401), and some of these have become lexicalized, such as the second example. And some nouns, serving as P, form compounds with certain verbs in which the nouns are almost completely bleached of meaning, as shown in (402) and (403).

(400) m̥^{323} fɤ^{33}
field   be.dry
田   干
'non-irrigated field'
干田
(KL-Elicitation)

(401) tsʰ121³¹ v³¹
dog   be.crazy
狗   疯
'rabid dog'
疯狗
(KL-Elicitation)

(402) tsa³²³ tsa³¹
rice   eat
饭   吃
'to eat', literally 'to eat rice'
吃饭
(KL-Elicitation)

(403) ɲo³¹   m̩³³
thing   do
事   做
'to work', literally 'to do things'
做事
(KL-Elicitation)

Verbs are morphologically invariant in discourse. They show no agreement with arguments, nor do they inflect for tense or aspect. As a result, the evidence for verbs as a class relies solely on syntactic patterns. First, verbs may be modified by the negative marker *ma³¹* as the examples in (404) and (405) show. The negative marker, in fact, cannot precede any other element in a clause. A possible exception is its collocation with the adverb *xɛi³⁵* in the universal quantifier construction (see § 6.4).

(404) **ma³¹** **tɕɛ³¹ta³³**   wa³³.
      NEG   be.simple   CRS
      不   简单
      '(It) wasn't easy.'
      不简单了。
      (HPH-Toys)

(405) m̩³²³   **ma³¹** ɲa³¹   **ma³¹** mɛi⁵⁵   tɛi³¹ ko⁵⁵   tso³²³ ni³¹
      field NEG   be.many NEG   be.few   one   CL:PL EXIST   TOP
      田   不   多   不   少   一   些   有
      'there were several fields, neither many nor few'
      田不多不少有一些呢
      (GCS-Childhood)

Second, verbs may be modified by aspectual particles. These are considered separate words rather than suffixes in Khatso (see § 4.2.1), though in discourse they pattern as phonological clitics. Because of the wide range of states and events represented by verbs, not every aspect marker is compatible with every verb. Generally, however, the perfective marker wa^{323} is grammatical with almost every verb. Examples are shown in (406) and (407).

(406) a³³   ma⁴⁴   ti³⁵kua³³pʰiɛ³⁵   to³³   **ka³²³**   **tsʰi³³**   **wa³²³**.
that   CL:GEN   sequin   also   walk   fall   PFV
那   个   电光片   也   走   掉
'That sequin also fell off.'
那个电光片也掉了。
(WYY-Sewing)

(407) i³³   kɛi³³   ŋa³³   **ma⁵⁵**   **wa³²³**.
3SG   AGT   1SG   teach   PFV
他   我   教
'He taught me.'
他教我了。
(KL-Doctor)

Overt verbal arguments are not obligatory in Khatso. Regardless of their role in a clause, arguments that are given or inferable by context may be completely omitted, a phenomenon known as zero anaphora. As a result, the following discussions on valency refer to the maximal number of core arguments semantically possible for a given verb, which is often greater than those found in natural speech. Consequently, elicited examples are more illustrative in many cases than excerpts from discourse.

The following sections explore the various kinds of verbs in Khatso. Intransitive verbs, including both the dynamic and stative subtypes, begin the discussion in § 8.1. Transitive verbs are described in § 8.2, followed by ditransitive verbs in § 8.3 and ambitransitive verbs in § 8.4. Two specialized verbs, the copula $ŋ^{33}$ and the existential verb tso^{323}, are analyzed in § 8.5 and § 8.6 respectively. Auxiliary verbs are examined in § 8.7, followed by a discussion of serial verb constructions in § 8.8.

8.1 Intransitive Verbs

Intransitive verbs are those that only take a single core argument S. In Khatso, this category can be divided into two groups. The first involves dynamic verbs that describe an event or process, which are discussed in § 8.1.1. The second group is comprised of stative verbs, which denote properties and are discussed in § 8.1.2.

8.1.1 Dynamic Intransitive Verbs

Dynamic intransitive verbs in Khatso include verbs of motion, such as i^{323} 'to go', ka^{323} 'to walk' and $kɤ^{31}$ 'to run', posture verbs such as $xɯ^{53}$ 'to stand' and $kγ^{55}$ 'to kneel', and physiological processes, such as $ŋ^{323}$ 'to cry', $ɕa^{24}$ 'to rest' and $sŋ^{33}$ 'to die'. S, like all verbal arguments, precedes the verb, as illustrated in (408) and (409). Intransitive verbs denoting motion also play an important role in directional serial verb constructions (see § 8.8.1.1).

(408) pʰi²⁴ŋ²⁴pʰa³¹ ko⁵⁵   ma³¹   li³²³   sɛi⁴⁴
   Han.M   CL:PL   NEG   come   TOP
   汉人   些   不   来
   'Chinese people didn't come'
   汉族不来呢
   (PRL-Education)

(409) tsŋ³¹   tɤ⁴⁴   xa³²³tsɛi³³   i³²³   wa³³.
   beat   CLNK   Hangzhou   go   CRS
   打   杭州   去
   '(They) went to attack Hangzhou.'
   打到杭州去了。
   (KLT-History)

When place names are used with the verbs i^{323} 'to go' and li^{323} 'to come', locative particles are dispreferred even though they are typically employed with common nouns (see § 10.6.2). Because this pattern occurs with all verbs and not just motion verbs, the exception seems to be triggered by the proper names rather than the verbs themselves. Thus, these two dynamic verbs are not considered ambitransitive in this analysis.

That said, many other verbs that may superficially seem intransitive, or even ambitransitive, are transitive in Khatso. For example, the verbs tsa^{31} 'to eat' and to^{323} 'to drink' are almost always accompanied by a P argument. In these cases, the collocation of noun and verb has become routinized to the point that the always-present P is semantically bleached and carries little meaning, even though it still functions syntactically as a noun. A case in point is tsa^{323} tsa^{31}, literally 'to eat rice', which may refer to the general act of eating even when rice is not involved.

8.1.2 Stative Verbs

Stative verbs comprise a subset of intransitive verbs. Instead of denoting dynamic events, however, they describe an unchanging state of being and typically denote properties which have an unbounded duration in time. As a result, they correspond to adjectives in other languages and cover a broad range of attributes, including the seven basic semantic types of adjectives found cross-linguistically (Dixon 2004: 3–5). These are age (mo^{31} 'to be old', $sŋ^{35}$ 'to be new'), color ($sγ^{24}$ 'to be yellow', $ŋ^{24}$ 'to be red'), dimension (to^{33} 'to be flat', $m̩^{24}$ 'to be tall'), human propensity ($si^{33}si^{33}$ 'to be happy', $γ^{31}$ 'to be crazy'), physical property ($k^hγ^{24}$ 'to be empty', $zεi^{24}$ 'to be sour'), speed ($tɕi^{31}$ 'to be fast', jo^{33} 'to be slow') and value (na^{24} 'to be good', $tso^{35}jau^{35}$ 'to be important'). In many Ngwi languages, special forms for verbs of dimensional extent have grammaticalized over time (Bradley 1995), but this has not occurred in Khatso. Dimension verbs pattern no differently than any other stative verb in the language.

In Khatso, it is very clear that statives are verbs. First, they may take any noun as S without the copula, as shown in (410) and (411). The copula is, in fact, ungrammatical in these phrases. Second, they may be directly negated, as shown in (412) and (413). And third, they may be directly modified by aspect markers, as shown in (414) and (415). These latter two patterns satisfy the test for verbhood discussed above.

(410) pɛi³⁵ tɕʰa³¹ **n̩a³¹**
grass leaf be.many
草　叶　多
'(there are) a lot of leaves'
草的叶多
(WYF-Stools)

(411) tʰγ⁵⁵sɛi⁴⁴ tɕo³⁵ sŋ³⁵tsʰŋ³⁵ ko⁵⁵ to³³ mɛi⁴⁴ **tɕʰa³²³**.
suddenly then energy CL:PL also very be.strong
突然　　就　　士气　　些　也　很　强
'Then (their) energy was very strong.'
士气一下子就很强。
(HPH-Horse Dug Well)

(412) i³²³tso³³ mɛi⁴⁴ **ma³¹** ɕo³³ tɕɛ⁴⁴ ni³²³.
well CL:GEN NEG be.clean say BKGD
水井　　个　　不　干净　说
'(They) say (the) well wasn't clean.'
说是水井不干净。
(PYX-Dragon Pools)

(413) **ma³¹ kʰɤ²⁴** ni³¹ mɤ³²³ ma³¹ li³²³ sa⁴⁴?
NEG be.empty TOP make.sound NEG know.how CRTN.Q
不 空 响 不 会
'If (it) isn't hollow, (it) won't make a sound?'
不空呢，不会响吗？
(KL-Qin)

(414) sɿ³²³xɯ³⁵ mɛi⁴⁴ ni³¹ **lɤ³³** wa³²³.
time CL:GEN TOP be.late PFV
时间 个 晚
'(The) time, (it) got late.'
时间呢，以经晚了。
(HPH-Weeds)

(415) tɕo³⁵ tɕɛi³¹ti⁵³za³¹ **xua²⁴tsa²⁴** wa³²³.
then a.little be.busy PFV
就 一点 忙
'Then (they) were a little busy.'
就忙一点了。
(WYF-Stools)

Because the agent marker *kɛi³³* is mainly used to disambiguate arguments in transitive and ditransitive clauses, it typically does not mark the S of stative verbs. However, this does occur in superlative phrases (see § 12.5.5.3), in pseudo-passive clauses (see § 10.5), and clauses in which *kɛi³³* marks contrastive focus rather than agentivity (see § 10.4).

As just described, stative verbs in Khatso pattern with other verbs in important ways. However, there are some syntactic differences. A subset of them may directly modify a noun in an attributive construction (see § 8.1.2.1), while nearly all of them may be reduplicated in a versatile construction that has adjectival, nominal and adverbial uses (see § 8.1.2.2). A separate and more limited subset may take part in a nominalization construction (see § 7.6). Stative verbs also appear in three types of serial verb constructions (see § 8.8.1.2, § 8.8.1.3 and § 8.8.1.4). In addition, they are the only type of verb that is modified by intensifiers (see § 9.3.5). Dynamic intransitive verbs, by contrast, cannot occur in these constructions.

8.1.2.1 Attributive Stative Verb Construction

Like every other kind of verb, stative verbs are typically placed in a relative clause when modifying a noun phrase (see § 7.5), as (416) illustrates. However, there is a subset that may directly modify nouns without the relativizer *la²⁴*, as shown in (417) and (418). This attributive use is not a productive process and only a small subset of stative verbs may pattern in this way; a list of the most common is presented in Table 8.1. It is also not obligatory, and placing them in relative clauses also occurs routinely, as shown by *mo³¹* in (419).

(416) **tʰa⁵⁵**   la²⁴   tɛi³³   tɛi³¹   jo³⁵.
      be.pointed REL   this   one   CL:HUM
      尖   这   一   位
      'That one with the bound (feet).'
      一位小脚的女人。
      (HPH-Weeds)

(417) **xua³²³kua³³** ɣɤ³⁵   tɛi³¹   ma²⁴   tso³²³.
      cucumber   be.salted   one   CL:GEN   EXIST
      黄瓜   腌   一   个   有
      'There was one (plate) of salt-preserved cucumbers.'
      有一个腌黄瓜。
      (KL-Duanwu Festival)

(418) i³³   tɕo³⁵   **sʅ³¹tsʅ³²³ na²⁴**   ma³¹   jɛ³⁵ȵ³⁵   m̩³³.
      3SG   then   thing   be.good   NEG   willing   do
      他   就   事   好   不   愿意   做
      'So, they were not willing to do good deeds.'
      他们就不愿意做好事。
      (HPH-Weeds)

(419) **mo³¹** la²⁴   ko⁵⁵   ni³¹   i²⁴fa³³   n̩a³¹   ma³¹   li³²³.
      old   REL   CL:PL   TOP   more   speak   NEG   know.how
      老   些   更   说   不   会
      'The old ones, (they) are even less able to speak (it).'
      那些老的呢，更不会说。
      (YAY-Erasers)

Table 8.1: Attributive stative verbs in Khatso

Type	Khatso	English	Chinese	Nouns Modified
age	mo³¹	'to be old'	老	all nouns
	sŋ³⁵	'to be new'	新	all nouns
color	la³²³	'to be blue'	蓝	all nouns
	lɣ⁵⁵	'to be green'	绿	all nouns
	na⁵³	'to be black'	黑	all nouns
	ŋ²⁴	'to be red'	红	all nouns
	sɤ²⁴	'to be yellow'	黄	all nouns
	tsʰŋ³³	'to be white'	白	all nouns
	xuɛi³³	'to be gray'	灰	all nouns
dimension	m̥²⁴	'to be tall'	高	humans
	nɤ²⁴	'to be short'	矮	humans
	ɲɛ²⁴	'to be small'	小	all nouns
	sɤ²⁴	'to be long'	长	clothing
	tsʰɛi²⁴	'to be short'	短	things
human/animal propensity	lɛi³⁵	'to be foolish'	傻	humans
	mɤ³³	'to be dizzy, drunk'	晕	humans, animals
	v³¹	'to be crazy'	疯	humans, animals
	sɛi³²³	'to be unusual'	特别	humans
	zŋ³¹	'to be wild'	野生	animals
physical property	ɕo³³	'to be clean'	干净	all nouns
	fɤ³³	'to be dry'	干	food, clothing
	i³⁵	'to be dirty'	脏	all nouns
	kʰɣ²⁴	'to be empty'	空	houses, containers
	na³⁵	'to be deep'	深	bodies of water
	ɲɛ³²³	'to be sweet'	甜	food
	pʰɤ³³	'to be hot & spicy'	辣	food
	pʰiɛ³¹	'to be plump'	饱满	beans, grain
	sa⁵⁵	'to be poor'	穷	humans
	tɕa³³	'to be skinny'	瘦	humans, animals
	tɕɛ³³	'to be full'	满	containers
	tsʰv³³	'to be fat'	胖	humans, animals
value	na²⁴	'to be good'	好	all nouns

As the table shows, these verbs instantiate six of the seven basic adjectival semantic types denoting age, color, dimension, human propensity, physical property and value (Dixon 2004: 3–5). Given the broad range of types, there is no unifying theme among these verbs and each type also contains verbs that cannot directly modify nouns. Instead, it appears that certain collocations of nouns and verbs have been routinized by frequent use.[1] For example, mo^{31} 'to be old' and $sŋ^{35}$ 'to be new' can be used this way with any type of noun, as can any of the basic monosyllabic color terms. Examples are shown in (420) and (421). But, na^{35} 'to be deep' may only modify nouns pertaining to bodies of water such as $tɕʰa^{31}$ 'river' and $fʮ^{33}ma^{33}$ 'lake'; the latter is shown in (422). When used with other nouns, such as to^{35} 'hole' for example, it must appear in a relative clause, as in (423). Similarly, $sɤ^{24}$ 'to be long' can be used attributively with the noun $tʰo^{33}$ 'clothing', shown in (424), but must occur in a relative clause with $o^{31}ma^{33}ŋ^{24}$ 'carrot', as in (425). Others are naturally constrained by their lexical meaning. For example, sa^{55} 'to be poor (i.e. without money)' can only modify human nouns, and $zŋ^{31}$ 'to be wild' only modifies plants and animals. Thus, frequency in association seems to be the most important factor in this construction rather than any semantic or syntactic categorization.

(420) **$tʰo^{33}$**   **$sŋ^{35}$** $tʰau^{35}$ $vɤ^{323}$ wa^{323}.
clothing   be.new   CL:SET   buy   PFV
衣服   新   套   买
'(I) bought a new set of clothes.'
买了一套新衣服了。
(KL-Elicitation)

(421) **$tsʰŋ^{31}$ $tsʰŋ^{33}$** $mɛi^{44}$ $tɕi^{31}$ $tʰɛi^{323}$ ja^{33}.
dog   white   CL:GEN   be.fast   very   IPFV.EMP
狗   白   个   快   很
'The white dog is very fast.'
白狗很快的。
(KL-Elicitation)

(422) **$fʮ^{33}ma^{33}$ na^{35}** a^{33} ma^{44}
lake   be.deep   that   CL:GEN
湖   深   那   个
'that deep lake'
那个深湖
(KL-Elicitation)

---

1 It is not clear why the basic verbs indicating speed, $tɕi^{31}$ 'to be fast' and jo^{33} 'to be slow', do not participate in this construction. It is likely a historical lack of routine collocations involving these two particular verbs rather than a categorial restriction.

(423) **na³⁵** **la²⁴** to³⁵ a³³ ma⁴⁴
be.deep REL hole that CL:GEN
深 洞 那 个
'that deep hole'
那个深的洞
(KL-Elicitation)

(424) **tʰo³³** **sɤ²⁴** ŋ³¹ tsa²⁴
clothing be.long two CL:ITEM
衣服 长 二 件
'two long garments'
两件长衣服
(KL-Elicitation)

(425) **sɤ²⁴** **la²⁴** o³¹ma³³ŋ²⁴ tɛi³¹ tsɤ³⁵
be.long REL carrot one CL:BNCH
长 红萝卜 一 捆
'one bunch of long carrots'
一捆长的红萝卜
(KL-Elicitation)

It appears that only monosyllabic stative verbs may occur in these collocations. Given that the vast majority of stative verbs are monosyllabic, it is unclear if this is a condition for the attributive use or merely a coincidence. In any case, this criterion is not sufficient to predict attributivity – there are many monosyllabic stative verbs that cannot take on this function.

If an attributive stative verb is modified, then the resulting construction must be placed inside a relative clause to modify a noun. Compare, for example, the two phrases in (426) and (427). This is, in fact, the canonical construction for verb phrases modifying nouns. However, when a relative clause contains a stative verb, it may either precede or follow the head noun, as shown in (428). This flexibility is not prototypical for relative clauses, which typically precede the head (see § 7.5), but rather seems to be a unique property of stative verbs.

(426) tsʰo³³ **sa⁵⁵** jo³⁵
person be.poor CL:HUM
人 穷 位
'a poor person'
一个穷人
(KL-Elicitation)

(427) **sa⁵⁵** tʰɛi³²³ la²⁴ tsʰo³³ jo³⁵
be.poor very REL person CL:HUM
穷 很 人 位
'a very poor person', literally 'a person who is very poor'
很穷的人
(KL-Elicitation)

(428) tsʰo³³ **sa⁵⁵** tʰɛi³²³ la²⁴ jo³⁵
person be.poor very REL CL:HUM
人 穷 很 位
'a very poor person', literally 'one who is very poor'
很穷的人
(KL-Elicitation)

It is also possible to modify a single noun with multiple stative verbs from the attributive subset. These also usually require a relative clause, as shown in (429) and (430). In some instances, the relative marker may be omitted, but there is no clear pattern — it seems to depend on a speaker's judgment about how common the collocations are. The patterns governing the order of the two verbs is likewise unclear; speakers have preferences for some verbs but not all.

(429) tʰo³³ **mo³¹** ɕo³³ la²⁴ tsa²⁴
clothing be.old be.clean REL CL:ITEM
衣服 旧 干净 件
'old and clean clothing'
旧的干净的衣服
(KL-Elicitation)

(430) tsʰo³³ **tsʰɣ³³** nɣ²⁴ la²⁴ jo³⁵
person be.fat be.short REL CL:HUM
人 胖 笨 位
'a short and fat person'
胖的笨的人
(KL-Elicitation)

The attributive verbs may also be linked by the *jo³⁵...jo³⁵* 'both...and' construction, which emphasizes the descriptors (see § 13.2.3.1). In this case, the descriptive phrase must be relativized. Again, the fact that these relative clauses may follow rather than precede the head seems to be a special property of stative verbs in this construction. Examples are shown in (431) and (432).

(431) tsʰo³³   jo³⁵   ɣɤ³¹   jo³⁵   tɕi³¹   la²⁴   a³³   jo³⁵
person both   be.big both   be.fast REL   that   CL:HUM
人   又   大   又   快   那   位
'that person both big and fast'
那位又大又快的人
(KL-Elicitation)

(432) o³¹   jo³⁵   tsɛi²⁴   jo³⁵   kʰa³¹   la²⁴   pa³⁵
vegetable both   be.sour both   be.bitter REL   bowl
菜   又   酸   又   苦   碗
'a bowl of vegetables both sour and bitter'
又酸又苦的那碗菜
(KL-Elicitation)

Superficially, attributive constructions look like compounds, such as *o³¹fɤ³³* 'dried vegetable', from *o³¹* 'vegetable' and *fɤ³³* 'to be dry', and *tsʰη³¹ɣ̍³¹* 'rabid dog', from *tsʰη³¹* 'dog' and *ɣ̍³¹* 'to be crazy' (see § 4.2.3.3). However, the attributive combinations of noun and verb, though driven by collocation frequency, are not lexicalized; speakers still have pragmatic freedom to pair them as they wish. Stative verbs also look adjective-like in this construction, and certain approaches would suggest that a separate adjective class be identified based on these data (Dixon 2004: 1–49). However, the members of this subset do not form a natural class, crosscutting as they do six of the seven adjectival semantic types. This subset also differs from the one that may be nominalized in combination with the third person pronoun *i³³* (see § 7.6), another construction unique to stative verbs. As a result, attempting to establish clear boundaries for an adjective class is problematic and, in the end, not especially informative.

8.1.2.2 Reduplicated Stative Verb Constructions

Another construction unique to stative verbs involves reduplication, and the resulting form has adjectival, nominal and adverbial uses. Syntactically, the reduplication is part of an adverbial construction along with the particles *za³¹ ni³³*, as shown in (433). *ni³³* is the adverbial marker (see § 9.3.4), and *za³¹* is likely the diminutive suffix (see § 4.2.3.2). The diminutive seems to be semantically bleached in this construction, although there are examples in discourse where the meaning is still present. In quick speech *ni³³* is often omitted leaving only *za³¹*, which may be reduced to *a³¹*, as show in (434). *ni³³* without *za³¹* is also attested in discourse, but mainly with adverbs that are not derived from stative verbs (see § 9.3.4). Note that in many cases this reduplication triggers tone sandhi (see § 3.2.3), which helps differentiate it from the verb reduplication found in polar questions (see § 12.4.1).

(433) **ja³²³**   **ja³²³**   **za³¹**   **ni³³**
       be.light   be.light   DIM   ADV
       轻   轻
       'lightly'
       轻轻地
       (YJF-Dance Parties)

(434) i³²³tɕa⁵³   ko⁵⁵   ɕo³⁵   ɕo³³   a³¹   o²⁴li⁴⁴   tso³²³   ja³²³   sɛi³¹.
       water   CL:PL   be.clean   be.clean   DIM   there   EXIST   PFV.EMP again
       水   些   干净   干净   那里   有   还
       'Really clean water is still there.'
       干干净净地水还在那里。
       (HPH-Horse Dug Well)

Reduplicating two-syllable stative verbs results in four-word constructions in which each syllable is reduplicated consecutively, as demonstrated by the example in (435). In some cases monosyllabic stative verbs also take part in three- and four-word expressions that have become lexicalized, as illustrated in (436). Often, the additional syllables do not have a function outside these collocations, suggesting they are either nonce syllables used to fill out the phrase or archaic words that have disappeared from the modern lexicon. Examples of four-syllable expressions from discourse are shown in (437) and (438). Note that *za³¹ ni³³* may be partially or completely omitted with these longer expressions.

(435) tsi³⁵sʅ²⁴   →   tsi³⁵ tsi³⁵ sʅ²⁴ sʅ²⁴
       'to be quiet'   'to be very quiet', 'quietly'
       安静   安安静静
       (KL-Elicitation)

(436) ɣ̩³¹   →   ɣ̩³¹ fo³³ ɣ̩³¹ tsʰɣ³¹
       'to be crazy'   'to be very crazy', 'in a crazy way'
       疯   疯疯癫癫
       (KL-Elicitation)

       mɣ³³→   →   mɣ³³ lo³³ tʰɛi⁵³ lɛi⁵³
       'to be dizzy'   'to be very dizzy', 'dizzily'
       晕   晕头晕脑
       (KL-Elicitation)

(437) tsʰo³³   jo³⁵   to³³   **tsi³³ tsi³³ lɤ³³ lɤ³³**   ta⁵⁵   sɛi⁴⁴   la³³   ŋ³³   ta³¹.
person   CL:HUM   also   be.sloppy.be.sloppy   be.type   TOP   CMP   COP   SFP
人   位   也   邋里邋遢   样   比   是
'(This) person's appearance was also very sloppy, (he) looked like (that).'
这个人的样子也像是邋里邋遢的。
(HPH-Weeds)

(438) **kʰɛi³³ kʰɛi³³ si³³ si³³**   ni³³,
be.happy.be.happy   ADV
开 开 心 心

xa³³ma⁴⁴   mo⁵⁵   ŋ²⁴ka³³   ni³¹   xa³³ma⁴⁴   ŋ²⁴ka³³
what   want   watch   TOP   what   watch
什么   要   看   什么   看
'Happily, whatever (they) want to watch, (they) watch.'
开开心心地，想看什么看什么。
(HPH-Toys)

As mentioned above, the reduplicative construction has adjectival, nominal and adverbial functions. The adjectival use allows it to directly modify a noun or pronominal expression with no additional marking. It may either precede or follow the noun with no change in meaning or function, a flexibility also found in relativized stative clauses (see § 7.2.2). Examples are shown in (439) and (440).

(439) **lɤ⁵⁵**   **lɤ⁵⁵**   za³¹   ni³³   a³³   tɕi⁵⁵   tɕo³⁵   kɤ³³   tɤ⁴⁴
be.green   be.green   DIM   ADV   that   CL:TYPE   then   make   CLNK
绿   绿   那   种   就   做
tsa³¹   li³³   tɤ³³ wa³³.
eat   come   INCP
吃   来
'The really green ones, (we) then began to prepare (them) to eat.'
绿绿的那种就弄来吃了。
(YJF-Childhood)

(440) i³²³tɕa⁵³   ko⁵⁵   **ɕo³⁵**   **ɕo³³**   a³¹   o²⁴li⁴⁴   tso³²³   ja³²³   sɛi³¹.
water   CL:PL   be.clean   be.clean   DIM   there   EXIST   PFV.EMP   again
水   些   干净   干净   那里   有   还
'Really clean water is still there.'
干干净净地水还在那里。
(HPH-Horse Dug Well)

The reduplicative construction also has a nominal use, in which it serves as a verbal argument, as shown in (441). In equational phrases the copula is optional, so a phrase in which the construction is accompanied only by another argument, such as in (442), is a complete clause in Khatso.

(441) suɛi³¹z̞ŋ³¹ **lγ̞⁵⁵** **lγ̞⁵⁵** za³¹ ni³³ li³³pγ̞³³ kɤ²⁴ ka⁵³ nɛi³¹.
all be.green be.green DIM ADV field.ridge CL:STRIP on grow
所有 绿 绿 田埂 条 上 长
'All the really green ones grew on the ridges between fields.'
所有绿绿的，长在田埂上的。
(YJF-Childhood)

(442) ŋa³³ pγ̞³²³ n̪ɛ³²³ jo³⁵ **m̪²⁴** **m̪²⁴** za³¹ ni³³
1SG POSS younger.brother CL:HUM be.tall be.tall DIM ADV
我 弟弟 位 高 高
'(my) younger brother (is a) really tall (guy)'
我的弟弟高高的
(KL-Elicitation)

The reduplicative construction frequently co-occurs with the verb *ta⁵⁵* 'be a type, sort, style', as shown in (443), or a demonstrative-classifier construction, as in (444). In fact, the reduplication cannot be modified by a classifier alone. This is because, despite its nominal use, the construction is not a true noun. It does not satisfy the tests for nounhood (see Chapter 5); it cannot serve alone as the head of either a possessive construction or a relative clause. Rather, it must be followed by noun, pronoun or demonstrative-classifier construction, which then acts as the head of the noun phrase. Examples are shown in (445) and (446). This raises the possibility of another analysis for the nominal function shown above. It may be a case of the adjectival use modifying a noun that is absent due to zero anaphora, in other words, a headless attributive construction. Or, it may be that the nominal function arose through the grammaticalization of such a pattern, and no absent noun is inferred in the modern construction.

(443) **xo³⁵** **xo³¹** **za³¹** ta⁵⁵ ni³²³ tʰɛi³²³tʰɛi³²³ la⁵³ la²⁴ a³³n̪a⁵³ ti⁴⁴
be.soft be.soft DIM be.type BKGD beginning wind REL there on
软 软 样 头头 卷 那里 上
tʰi³⁵.
place.under
垫
'The soft type, put (those) under the place where (you) first roll (it) up.'
软软那样的垫在开始卷的那里。
(WYF-Stools)

(444) **lɣ⁵⁵** **lɣ⁵⁵** **za³¹ ni³³** a³³ tɕi⁵⁵ tɕo³⁵ kɣ³³ tɣ⁴⁴
be.green be.green DIM ADV that CL:TYPE then make CLNK
绿 绿 那 种 就 做

tsa³¹ li³³ tɣ³³ wa³³.
eat come INCP
吃 来

'The really green ones, (we) then began to prepare (them) to eat.'
绿绿的那种就弄来吃了。
(YJF-Childhood)

(445) kʰua³¹la³¹ kɛi³³ li³²³ la²⁴ **tsʰŋ³⁵ tsʰŋ³³ za³¹ ni³³** a³³ jo³⁵
Kunming from come REL be.fat be.fat DIM ADV that CL:HUM
昆明 从 来 胖 胖 那 位

'that very fat one who comes from Kunming'
从昆明来的那个胖胖的
(KL-Elicitation)

(446) i³³ pɣ³²³ **tɕi³¹** **tɕi³²³ za³¹ ni³³** a³³ ma⁴⁴
3SG POSS be.quick be.quick DIM ADV that CL:GEN
他 快 快 那 个 那 个

'that very quick one of his'
他的快快地那个
(KL-Elicitation)

If the reduplication involves stative verbs that semantically describe manner, the construction may serve an adverbial function, as shown in (447) and (448).

(447) **ja³⁵** **ja³¹** **za³¹ ni³³** tɕi³²³ tsa²⁴ kɛi³³ kɛi³³ pʰɛi³¹.
be.good be.good DIM ADV rainwear CL:ITEM INS AGT cover
好 好 蓑衣 件 用 盖

'(They are) well covered by rainwear.'
用蓑衣好好盖着。
(WYF-Stools)

(448) "na²⁴ wa³³, nɛi³³ **jo³³** **jo³³ za³¹** o⁵³" tɕɛ⁵³, tɛi³³ xuɛi³²³.
be.good CRS 2SG be.slow be.slow DIM weed say.after this CL:TMP
好 你 慢 慢 薅 说 这 回

' "Good, you (just) weed slowly" (she) said, this time,'
"那么，你就慢慢地薅"说完，这次。
(HPH-Weeds)

Occasionally, the adverbial use creates ambiguity with the pronominal function, especially in phrases with zero anaphora. For example, in (449) the construction *tɕi³¹tɕi³²³ za³¹ ni³³* may be interpreted as adverbial, in which case the phrase means '(doing it) quickly is correct' (a more colloquial translation is 'it is better if done quickly'). Or, it may be analyzed as a noun phrase, meaning '(the) quick one is correct'. Context typically resolves the ambiguity.

(449) **tɕi³¹**   **tɕi³²³**   **za³¹**   **ni³³**   tɕo³⁵   xo²⁴   wa³²³.
 be.quick be.quick DIM ADV then be.correct PFV
 快   快   就   对
 '(Doing it) quickly is correct.' / '(The) quick one is correct.'
 快快地就对了。
 (KL-Elicitation)

8.2 Transitive Verbs

Transitive verbs take a maximum of two core arguments, A and P. This category includes a wide variety of words, including verbs of manipulation, such as *tɕʰɛ³¹* 'to throw away' and *ỿ³²³* 'to take, hold'; verbs of perception, such as *ŋ²⁴ka³³* 'to see' and *na²⁴* 'to hear'; verbs of mental activity, such as *sɿ⁵⁵* 'to know' and *m̩³³to³¹* 'to forget'; and verbs in which P undergoes a change, such as *tsa³¹* 'to eat' and *si⁵³* 'to kill'. Ambitransitive verbs – those that can be used intransitively as well as transitively – are relatively rare in Khatso (see § 8.4). Some transitive verbs also take complement clauses as core arguments (see Chapter 15).

Khatso does not have obligatory case marking. Typically, word order and verbal semantics are enough to clearly establish the roles of arguments in transitive clauses (see § 10.3). Examples of basic transitive clauses are shown in (450) and (451). Note, however, that arguments that are given or inferable from context may be absent due to zero anaphora. Thus, it is common to find transitive verbs with no overt arguments, as in (452).

(450) ja⁵³ni³²³ [nɛi³³ sɛi⁴⁴] [m̩³²³ tɛi³¹ko⁵⁵ma³³] **vɤ³²³** ŋa³²³.
 then   2SG   family   field   many   buy   be.able
 然后   你   家   田   很多   买   可以
 'Then your family was able to buy a lot of fields.'
 然后你家买得很多田。
 (KL-Grandfather)

(451) [fv̩³¹pi³¹li³¹]   ta²⁴to³³   tɕo³⁵
      Kublai.Khan   still   then
      忽必烈   还   就

      [tsi³⁵sa³²³li³⁵]   **za⁵³**   ja³²³.
      no.kill.order   descend   PFV.EMP
      禁杀令   下
      'Then Kublai Khan handed down a decree not to kill (him).'
      忽必烈还是就下了禁杀令。
      (KLT-History)

(452) **tsi⁵³**   ja³²³.
      cut.with.scissors   PFV.EMP
      剪
      '(We) cut (it off).'
      剪了。
      (YJF-Childhood)

However, the agent marker *kɛi³³* — the only case marker in Khatso — is employed in clauses where the identity of A is ambiguous. Typically, such ambiguity arises either from unexpected pragmatic patterns or zero anaphora. For example, in (453) it is the horse that digs the well, a decidedly human endeavor. As result of this unexpected activity, the horse must be clearly marked as A. In (454), one of the arguments is absent because of zero anaphora, leaving the role of the remaining argument unclear. In this case, the pronoun is A and thus must be marked by *kɛi³³*. Otherwise, it would be interpreted as P, and the phrase would mean 'hold you for a while'. The various discourse functions of the agent marker are discussed more fully in § 10.4.

(453) [m̩³¹   mɛi⁴⁴]   **kɛi³³**   pʰa³²³   to⁵³   li³³   ŋɛi³³.
      horse   CL:GEN   AGT   excavate   exit   come   ASRT
      马   个   刨   出   来
      'The horse dug out (the well).'
      马刨出来了。
      (HPH-Horse Dug Well)

(454) [nɛi³³]   **kɛi³³**   v³²³   tsɤ²⁴.
      2SG   AGT   hold   CONT.IMP
      你   拿
      'You hold (it) for a while.'
      你拿着吧。
      (YJR-Grandfather)

As mentioned in § 5.3.1, reflexive verbs — that is, verbs that must be morphologically marked to show that the A and P are the same entity — do not exist in Khatso. However, there are transitive verbs that carry a reflexive sense lexically. The most frequently-encountered expressions combine a non-specific noun with a verb of grooming, such as $i^{31}tsʰŋ^{33}$ $kʰɤ^{55}$ 'to comb (one's) hair' and $i^{31}tsʰŋ^{33}$ tsi^{53} 'to cut (one's) hair'. The basic meaning of both of these verbs is reflexive; adding another argument requires additional syntactic marking. Compare the two phrases in (455) and (456). In the latter, both the third person possessor and the applicative verb $kɯ^{31}$ 'to give' expand the valency of the construction (see § 11.1). Transitive verbs that are not inherently reflexive, such as $kuai^{35}$ 'to blame', may be made so through the use of the reflexive term $tsŋ^{31}tɕa^{24}$ 'self', as (457) illustrates (see § 5.3.1). This construction may also signal that the agent performed a non-reflexive action alone.

(455) [ŋa³³] [i³¹tsʰŋ³³] **kʰɤ⁵⁵** wa³²³.
   1SG   hair   comb   PFV
   我   头发   梳
   'I combed (my) hair.'
   我梳头发了。
   (KL-Elicitation)

(456) [ŋa³³] [i³³ pɤ³²³ i³¹tsʰŋ³³] **kʰɤ⁵⁵** kɯ³¹ wa³²³.
   1SG   3SG POSS hair   comb   give PFV
   我   她   头发   梳   给
   'I combed her hair.'
   我给她梳头发了。
   (KL-Elicitation)

(457) [i³³] [tsŋ³¹tɕa²⁴] **kuai³⁵** tɤ³³ ŋɛi³³.
   3SG   self   blame   PROG ASRT
   他   自己   怪
   'He blames himself.'
   他在怪自己。
   (KL-Elicitation)

8.3 Ditransitive Verbs

Ditransitive verbs take a maximum of three core arguments: A, P and R. A distinction is made here between those that can do so without additional syntax and those that cannot. The latter are discussed in the section on applicative constructions (see § 11.1). Verbs that may take a complement clause as a core argument are explored in Chapter 15.

This leaves simple ditransitive verbs, a relatively small group within the Khatso lexicon. The prototypical verb of this type is *kɯ³¹* 'to give', which involves a giver, a receiver, and an item given. Other verbs in this category include *xa³³* 'to send, deliver, give (gifts)', *kʰo⁵³* 'to return (something)', *ma⁵⁵* 'to teach', *tsʰŋ²⁴to³³* 'to promise' and *ɣ²⁴* 'to call, name'. In addition, the few lexical causatives in the language, such as *tsa⁵⁵* 'to feed', are also syntactically ditransitive; they are discussed in the section on causative constructions (see § 11.2.1).

All three arguments precede the verb in ditransitive clauses. The canonical word order among them is

A R P VERB

This order mirrors the pattern evident in transitive clauses in which A is the first argument in a clause, and P is that closest to the verb. R, then, is typically the middle argument. Because of zero anaphora, it is rare to find ditransitive clauses with all three arguments overtly stated in discourse. Elicited examples are shown in (458) and (459) to instantiate the complete pattern.

(458) [ŋa³³]   kɛi³³   [za³¹m̩³¹za³¹ jo³⁵]   [a³³ŋ³⁵ tɛi³¹ ma²⁴]   **kɯ³¹**   wa³²³.
      1SG   AGT   girl   CL:HUM   cat   one   CL:GEN   give   PFV
      我   女孩子   位   猫   一   个   给
      'I gave the girl a cat.'
      我给女孩子一只猫了。
      (KL-Elicitation)

(459) [m̩³²³tɤ²⁴la²⁴ jo³⁵]   kɛi³³   [ŋa³³]   [ɣa⁵³fɤ³³   ko⁵⁵]   **xa³³**   wa³²³.
      farmer   CL:HUM   AGT   1SG   chicken.egg   CL:PL   send   PFV
      农民   位   位   我   鸡蛋   些   送
      'The farmer sent me eggs.'
      那个农民送我鸡蛋了。
      (KL-Elicitation)

Just as in transitive clauses, the agent marker is typically not used in ditransitive clauses unless there is ambiguity. For the most part, verbal semantics and context are enough to differentiate arguments in a clause. However, zero anaphora itself may create ambiguity, since for most ditransitive verbs A and R are both human. If one is absent from a clause, then it may be difficult to identify the role of the remaining argument. In these cases, *kɛi³³* is employed to mark A, as in (460). If a human argument is unmarked, as in (461), it is assumed to be R. Because P is typically inanimate in discourse, these pose no parsing problems, as (462) demonstrates. The various functions of the agent marker in discourse are discussed more fully in § 10.4.

(460) [i³³]   **kɛi³³**   [ŋa³³]   ma⁵⁵   wa³²³.
  3SG   AGT   1SG   teach   PFV
  他   我   教
  'He taught me.'
  他教我了。
  (KL-Doctor)

(461) [**ŋa³³tsʰɤ³¹**]   tɛi³¹   ŋ³²³   [lia³¹   tɕo³²³   tɕʰɛ³²³]   kɯ³¹   tɤ³⁵   ŋ³³.
  1PL   one   CL:TMP   two   CL:MNY   money   give   PROG.FOC   ASRT
  我们   一   天   二   角   钱   给
  'One day (they) gave us two dimes.'
  一天给我们两角钱。
  (KXC-Fishing)

(462) jo³²³tsʰŋ³⁵   to³³   [**tɛi³¹   ko⁵⁵**]   kɯ³¹.
  music.instrument   also   one   CL:PL   give
  乐器   也   一   些   给
  'Musical instruments, (he) also gave (them) some.'
  乐器也给了一些。
  (KLT-History)

The order of arguments in a ditransitive clause is somewhat flexible. A is usually the first argument. Moving it to second position, where it must be marked by the agent marker *kɛi³³*, typically creates a passive sense (see § 10.5), though this reading may be canceled by context. The order of the remaining arguments is less fixed. For example, in (463) P precedes R, which is the reverse of the canonical order. Similarly, in (462) above R is a topic and thus begins the clause, a position usually reserved for A; an overt topic marker is not obligatory. These variations typically do not create confusion, since the presence or absence of *kɛi³³* along with the animacy of the arguments will differentiate the arguments even if word order does not. For the most part, departures from the prototypical order seem to depend largely on speaker preference. A more detailed description of argument word order can be found in § 10.3.

(463) [ŋa³³]   tɕo³⁵   [**ŋ³¹   xa³²³**   **kʰuai³¹**]   [i³³]   kɯ³¹.
  1SG   then   two   hundred   CL:MNY   3SG   give
  我   就   二   百   块   她   给
  'So I gave her 200 yuan.'
  我就给她两百块。
  (WYF-Stools)

8.4 Ambitransitive Verbs

Ambitransitive verbs, also called labile verbs, may be used both transitively and intransitively without any morphosyntactic change. These are rather rare in Khatso, though a few have been identified through elicitation. These verbs do, however, follow the two main ambitransitive patterns found cross-linguistically (Dixon and Aikhenvald 2000: 4–5). In the first, the S of the intransitive use, which can feature either a dynamic intransitive or a stative verb, corresponds to the A of the transitive use. The verb tʁ⁵⁵ 'to be boastful/to boast about' follows this pattern, along with the verbs tɕʰa³¹ 'to climb, crawl' and tγ³¹ 'to gamble', among others. For example, in (464) i³³ 'he' is the S of the intransitive tʁ⁵⁵. The presence of the intensifier tʰɛi³²³, which is only possible with stative verbs, underscores its intransitive function in this clause. By contrast, in (465) the verb has a transitive function, meaning 'to boast about', and takes two core arguments without additional marking; i³³ is A and the individual boasted about is P.

(464) [i³³]   tʁ⁵⁵   tʰɛi³²³   ja³³.
      3SG   be.boastful   very   IPFV.EMP
      他   吹牛   很
      'He is very boastful.'
      他太吹牛了。
      (KL-Elicitation)

(465) [i³³]   [za³¹   jo³⁵]   tʁ⁵⁵   tγ³³   ŋɛi³³.
      3SG   son   CL:HUM   boast   PROG   ASRT
      他   儿子   位   夸
      'He is boasting (about his) son.'
      他在夸他儿子。
      (KL-Elicitation)

In the second type of ambitransitivity, the S of the intransitive use — which again can be either a dynamic intransitive or a stative verb — corresponds to the P of the transitive use. Verbs such as yʁ⁵⁵ 'to roll' and tsʰŋ⁵⁵ 'to have a fever/to burn (paper money)' follow this pattern. For example, in (466) yʁ⁵⁵ is intransitive and the single argument pʰi³²³ko³¹ 'apple' is S, whereas in (467) it is P in the transitive clause involving the same verb.

(466) [pʰi³²³ko³¹ mɛi⁴⁴]　ɣɤ⁵⁵　ka³²³　i³³　wa³²³.
　　　apple　　　　　CL:GEN　roll　walk　go　PFV
　　　苹果　　　　　个　　　滚　　走　　去
　　　'The apple rolled away.'
　　　苹果滚掉了。
　　　(KL-Elicitation)

(467) [i³³]　kɛi³³　[pʰi³²³ko³¹ mɛi⁴⁴]　ɣɤ⁵⁵　ko⁵³　li³³　wa³²³.
　　　3SG　AGT　apple　　　　　CL:GEN　roll　pass　come　PFV
　　　他　　　　苹果　　　　　个　　　滚　　过　　来
　　　'He rolled the apple over this way.'
　　　他把苹果滚过来了。
　　　(KL-Elicitation)

Because of zero anaphora, it is often difficult to determine whether verbs are ambitransitive or their arguments are simply omitted. For example, at first glance the clause in (468) appears to be intransitive. However, the verb may also take a P, as in (469). This raises the question of whether the phrase in (468) is truly intransitive or if a general item, such as 'something', is understood but omitted. Testing speaker intuition about this has so far been inconclusive.

(468) [i³³]　lo⁵⁵　wa³²³.
　　　3SG　vomit　PFV
　　　他　　吐
　　　'He vomited.'
　　　他吐了。
　　　(KL-Elicitation)

(469) [i³³]　[wa⁵³sa³¹]　lo⁵⁵　wa³²³.
　　　3SG　pork　　　　vomit　PFV
　　　他　　猪肉　　　　吐
　　　'He vomited (up) pork.'
　　　他吐猪肉了。
　　　(KL-Elicitation)

8.5 Copula *ŋ³³*

The copula in Khatso is *ŋ³³*, which often carries an epenthetic vowel phrase-finally as *ŋɛi³³*, and it is mainly used to link two noun phrases in equational clauses, as shown in (470). Like all verbs in Khatso, the copula is negated by the negative adverb *ma³¹*;

as the example in (471) illustrates. The copula does not take part in existential clauses; the verb *tso³²³* is employed for that purpose (see § 8.6).

(470) [tʰo³³pɛi³³ tɕi³³ ko⁵⁵] to³³ [ŋ³¹ jo³⁵ pʏ³²³] **ŋ³³** ja³³.
shirt this CL:PL also two CL:HUM POSS COP IPFV.EMP
小褂 这 些 也 二 位 是
'These shirts also belong to two people', literally 'these shirts are also two people's'
这些小褂也是两个人的。
(WYY-Sewing)

(471) tʰo³³tso⁵³ma³³ tɕi⁵⁵ ni³¹ tʏ⁴⁴ [tsʰua³³sʏ³³ la²⁴ tɕi⁵⁵] to³³ **ma³¹ ŋ³³** mɛi⁴⁴.
button CL:TYPE TOP FILL penetrate REL CL:TYPE also NEG COP DSC.EMP
纽扣 种 贯串 种 也 不 是
'As for (those) buttons, um, (they) aren't the kind that are sewn through.'
纽扣呢，那也不是穿好的那种。
(WYY-Sewing)

The copula may be omitted in discourse since juxtaposition alone may convey an equational meaning. Examples are shown in (472) and (473); note that in the latter the copula is part of the tag question and not the equational clause. Because it is optional, the presence of the copula often signals a stronger assertion on the part of the speaker. In fact, there is a strong assertion marker that is derived from and identical to the copula, which may modify a clause that already has a matrix verb (see § 12.6.5). For example, in (474) *ŋɛi³³* has no predicative function, the matrix verb is *ŋ³¹* 'to sell'; it is there for emphasis only. However, in some phrases the status of *ŋɛi³³* is unclear. For example, in (475) it may be analyzed as either the matrix verb or the strong assertion particle in a verbless equational phrase — semantically, there is little difference between the two.

(472) [ka³²³tɕʰi³¹ tɕi³³ ma⁴⁴],
door this CL:GEN
门 这 个

[ŋa³³tsʰʏ³³ kʰa⁵⁵tso³¹kʰua⁵⁵ mɛi⁴⁴ pʏ³²³].
3PL Khatso.village CL:GEN POSS
我们 喀卓村 个
'This door, (is) a Xingmeng (door).', literally 'This door, (is) our Xingmeng's.'
这个门是我们兴蒙乡的。
(KL-Doors)

(473) [nɛi³³] tɕo³⁵ [pɛi³²³ko⁵³ma³³ wa³²³, **ŋ³³ ŋuo³¹**?
2SG then pɛi³²³ko⁵³.F PFV COP COP.Q
你 就 白阁女人 是
'you (are) from *pɛi³²³ko⁵³*, right?', literally 'you (are) a *pɛi³²³ko⁵³* woman, right?'
你就是白阁人，是吧？
(KL-Sewing)

(474) sɿ³⁵ sɿ³²³ o³¹ kʰuai³¹ kɛi³³ o³¹ sɿ³²³ kʰuai³¹ kɛi³³ tɕi³³ni³³ **ŋ³¹** tʏ³³ **nɛi³³**.
forty-five CL:MNY CONJ fifty CL:MNY CONJ this.way sell PROG ASRT
四十五 块 和 五十 块 和 这么 卖
'45 yuan and 50 yuan, (they) sell (them) this way.'
四十五块和五十块这么卖的。
(WYF-Stools)

(475) ŋa³³ pɛi³²³ko⁵³ma³³ jo³⁵ **nɛi³³**.
1SG pɛi³²³ko⁵³.F CL:HUM COP/ASRT
我 白阁女人 位
'I (am from) *pɛi³²³ko⁵³*.' literally 'I (am a) *pɛi³²³ko⁵³* woman.'
我是白阁人。
(WYY-Sewing)

Typically, polar questions are formed by reduplicating the verb (see § 12.4.1). This is also possible with the copula, but it is not often used. Instead, an alternate construction, *ŋ³³ ŋa³³*, which includes an epenthetic vowel, is more frequently heard. This construction may serve as the matrix verb or as a tag question, as (476) and (477) demonstrate respectively. In content questions, however, the copula is almost always omitted, as in (478). The copula is also found in other, more expressive tag questions (see § 12.4.4), but the question particle *ŋa³³* only occurs with the copula.

(476) [m̩³²³ tɕi⁵⁵] [nɛi³³tsʰʏ³¹ tsɿ³¹tɕa²⁴ pʏ³²³ tɕi⁵⁵] **ŋ³³ ŋa³³**?
field CL:TYPE 3PL self POSS CL:TYPE COP COP.Q
田 种 你们 自己 种 是
'Were (those) fields your own?'
这些田是你们自己的吗？
(KL-Childhood)

(477) kɣ³³ tɤ⁴⁴ tau³⁵kɛi³³ nɛi³³ pɣ³²³ mɛi⁴⁴ la³³ tɛi³³ni³³ kɣ³³ kɯ³²³
do STAT.EMP contrary 2SG POSS CL:GEN CMP this.way make CSC
做　　反而　　你　　个　　这么　做

na²⁴ ma³¹ tso³²³,
be.good NEG EXIST
好　　不　有

'(What they) do, (on the) contrary isn't as good as yours,'
做得反而没有你做的这么好，

ŋ³³ ŋa³³?
COP COP.Q
是

'Isn't (that right)?'
是不是？
(KL-Sewing)

(478) xa³³ma⁴⁴ tɕi⁵⁵ ŋa³¹?
what CL:TYPE CNT.Q
什么　　　种

'What (is it)?'
是什么？
(KL-Elicitation)

The Hanyu copula has been borrowed into Khatso as *sʅ⁴⁴*, but it cannot replace *ŋ³³* in equational clauses. Instead, it seems to mainly occur after adverbs and conjunctions that are also loanwords, though this collocation is not required in the original Chinese. Examples are shown in (479) and (480). Note that it is sometimes pronounced *sʅ³²³sʅ⁴⁴*, which is likely an idiomatic reduplication.

(479) pʰi³²³sʅ³²³ **sʅ⁴⁴** tsʰʅ³³ni³⁵ ma³¹ ɕi³³ tɛi⁵³.
usually COP shoe NEG be.accustomed wear
平常　　　　是　鞋子　不　习惯　　穿

'(We) usually didn't wear shoes.'
平常是不穿鞋子的。
(YJF-Weddings)

(480) zv̩³²³ko³¹ **sɿ³²³sɿ⁴⁴** kʰo³¹zɿ³¹ ja³³ tɕi⁴⁴ ni³¹ tɕo³⁵,
      if   COP   be.able   IPFV.EMP say TOP then
      如果   是   可以   说   就

nɛi³³ tɕo³⁵ jɛ³⁵zɿ³⁵   tɛi³³ tʰɤ⁵⁵ tɕi³³ jo³⁵   ŋɛi³³.
2SG   then be.willling this CL:TMP say   must.FOC ASRT
你   就   愿意   这   下   说   应该

'If (you) are willing, then you should say (so).'
如果说可以的，你就说一下愿意的。
(KL-Childhood)

8.6 Existential Verb *tso³²³*

In many languages, the existential verb has a number of functions, and this is true in Khatso as well. The verb in question, *tso³²³*, is used to signal possession, location and existence and these uses are differentiated by structure as well as context.

The first function is that of possession, where *tso³²³* means 'to have'. Maximally, this function allows for two arguments, a possessor and a possessum, as shown in (481). However, due to zero anaphora, both arguments are rarely overt in discourse, as (482) illustrates.

(481) [xa³³ sɛi⁴⁴] [o³¹   ɕa²⁴   xa³³ tɕi³³] **tso³²³** ŋɛi³³ tɕi³³ ni³¹
      what   family vegetable be.salty what CL:TYPE EXIST   ASRT say   TOP
      哪   家   菜   咸   哪   种   有   说

'whichever family had whatever kind of salted vegetables'
说谁家有什么咸菜呢
(YJF-Dance Parties)

(482) tɕo³⁵ [tɛi³¹ jo³⁵] **tso³²³** wa³²³ tsɛi³¹ na³¹ni²⁴za³¹.
      then   one   CL:HUM EXIST   PFV   HSY   child
      就   一   位   有   孩子

'Then (he only) had one, (a) child.'
就有一个小孩子了。
(ZRF-Grandfather)

When used with locations and related phrases, the verb takes on a locative sense and may mean either 'to be at' or 'to live at'; context helps clarify the meaning in discourse. Like the possessive function, this construction also maximally contains two arguments, the located individual and the location, though because of zero anaphora it is rare for both to be overt in discourse. Examples are shown in (483) and

(484). Note that neither common locations, such as *xɣ³³pɛi³³* 'home' and place names, nor the interrogative pronoun *xa³³ŋa⁵³* 'where' require an accompanying postposition.

(483) [nɛi³³ pv³²³ tsɛi³⁵tsʅ³⁵ tɕi⁵⁵]   [xa³³ŋa⁵³]   **tso³²³**   ŋa³¹?
     2SG POSS proof CL:TYPE where EXIST CNT.Q
     你   证据   种   哪里   在
     'Where is your proof?'
     你的证据在哪里?
     (PYX-Performing)

(484) [xɣ³³pɛi³³]   **tso³²³**   la²⁴   nɛi³³.
     home   EXIST REL ASRT
     家   在
     '(He) is at home.', literally '(He is one) who is at home.'
     是在家里。
     (YAY-Erasers)

In its third function, the verb *tso³²³* has an existential sense, corresponding to the English construction 'there is/are'. Here, only one argument is possible, though even it may be absent due to zero anaphora. Examples are presented in (485) and (486).

(485) a³³tɕʰa⁵⁵kʰv̩³³ tsʅ³³kɛi³⁵   ni³¹   ma³¹   **tso³²³**   ni³²³.
     that.time   machinery TOP NEG EXIST BKGD
     那时候   机械   不   有
     'At that time machines, there weren't (any).'
     那时候呢没有机器。
     (YJF-Childhood)

(486) tɛi³³   tsɛi³⁵   **tso³²³**   ja³³   sɛi³¹   a³³   jo³⁵.
     this   CL:TMP EXIST IPFV.EMP still that CL:HUM
     现在   在   还   那   位
     '(He) is still alive now, that one.'
     那个现在还在着。
     (YJR-Grandfather)

Semantically, these three functions are not as distinct as they appear on paper, and in discourse more than one analysis may apply. The possessive and locational constructions, for example, are structurally identical. Thus, the phrase in (487) may be analyzed either way. In this case, it is only the knowledge that *na³²³ka⁵³* is the name of a village, which cannot be owned by an individual, that clarifies the meaning. Moreover, the possibility of zero anaphora also complicates matters. The most obvious analysis of (488) is that it is metaphorically locative, describing a sister who is figuratively located above (i.e. before) the grandfather in birth order. However, it is also possible that the third-person pronoun is absent due to zero anaphora, in which case the phrase contains the possessive construction along with an oblique locational phrase. The two English translations illustrate the difference. Similarly, any phrase which contains the single-argument existential construction may also be interpreted as a possessive construction in which the possessor is absent because of zero anaphora. Thus, a phrase such as that in (489) may have two meanings, as the translations illustrate. The ambiguity here is not a problem, however, because for the most part the basic idea of the phrase is unchanged, which underscores the close and often overlapping senses of *tso^{323}*.

(487) [lau^{33}ti^{33} jo^{35}]   [ɲa^{323}ka^{53}]   **tso^{323}** la^{24} po^{53}.
     paternal.grandfather CL:HUM ɲa^{323}ka^{53} EXIST   REL EPIS.EMP
     老爹   位   中村   有
     '(His) grandfather lived in ɲa^{323}ka^{53}, see?', literally '(His) grandfather was one who lived in ɲa^{323}ka^{53}, see?'
     爷爷是在中村的呀。
     (ZRF-Grandfather)

(488) ŋa^{33} sɛi^{44} pa^{31} ka^{53}la^{31} xɛi^{35} [ta^{35}kv̩^{33}mo^{33}] tɛi^{31} jo^{35}] **tso^{323}**.
     1SG family father above still father's.married.sister one CL:HUM EXIST
     我   家   爸   上面 还   大姑妈   一   位   有
     'Above my father there is an older married sister.' / 'My father has above (him) an older married sister.'
     我爸爸上面还有一个大姑妈。
     (YJR-Grandfather)

(489) a^{33}tɕʰa^{55}kʰv̩^{33} tsɿ^{33}kɛi^{35} ni^{31} ma^{31} **tso^{323}** ni^{323}.
     that.time machinery TOP NEG EXIST BKGD
     那时侯   机械   不   有
     'At that time machines, there weren't (any).' / 'At that time machines, (we) didn't have (any).'
     那时候呢没有机器。
     (YJF-Childhood)

In addition, *tso^{323}* takes part in several other constructions. They include a negative indefinite construction (see § 7.3.3) and certain comparative constructions (see § 12.5).

8.7 Auxiliary Verbs

There is a small group of auxiliary verbs in Khatso. They are distinguished from lexical verbs by the fact that they cannot serve as stand-alone verbs, but rather must modify another verb in the clause — the lone exception is $\eta a^{323}ta^{323}$ which is discussed below. Despite this restriction, auxiliaries are clearly verbs because they are negated directly by ma^{31} and also take aspect marking. In fact, it is the auxiliary rather than the matrix verb that is negated in these constructions — a key difference in comparison with multi-verb applicative and causative constructions (see § 11.1 and § 11.2 respectively).

Syntactically, auxiliary constructions fall into the broad category of serial verb constructions (see § 8.8). They are asymmetrical — almost any verb may serve as the matrix, but the auxiliaries themselves form a small restricted class, as shown in Table 8.2. Semantically, auxiliaries express deontic modality — that is, they provide information about the participants' likelihood, ability or obligation to perform an action or their attitudes about the action.

Table 8.2: Auxiliary verbs in Khatso

Khatso	English	Chinese	Origin	Syntactic Position
jo³³	'to need, must'	yīnggāi 应该, bìxū 必须	native	post-VERB
li³²³	'to know how'	huì 会	native	post-VERB
ŋa³²³ta³²³	'to be able, to be allowed, can'	néng 能, kěyǐ 可以	native	post-VERB
pa³²³	'to help'	bāngzhù 帮助	native	post-VERB
ta³²³	'to be able', 'to be acceptable'	néng 能	native	post-VERB
tso³³	'to be accustomed'	xíguàn 习惯	native	post-VERB
tso³¹	'(one's) turn', 'must'	gāi 该, yīnggāi 应该	native	post-VERB
ɕi³³	'to be accustomed'	xíguàn 习惯	borrowed	pre-VERB
pi³²³sɿ³³jau³⁵	'to need'	bìyào 必要	borrowed	pre-VERB
pi³²³sɿ³³sɿ⁴⁴	'must'	bìxū 必须	borrowed	pre-VERB
wɛi³²³	'to allow'	yǔnxǔ 允许	borrowed	pre-VERB
jɛ³⁵kɛi³³	'to need, must'	yīnggāi 应该	borrowed	pre-VERB
jo³⁵ɿ³⁵	'to be willing'	yuànyi 愿意	borrowed	pre-VERB

The group can be divided into two syntactic types. The first type consists of native auxiliaries that always follow the matrix verb, such as li^{323} 'to know how' and jo^{33} 'to need, must'. Examples are shown in (490), (491) and (492). Note that *li³²³* 'to know how' is homophonous with *li³²³* 'to come'. When the latter occurs in serial verb constructions it changes tone to avoid confusion with the auxiliary, which never changes tone (see § 3.2.2). In addition, the auxiliary *li³²³* may also create a sense of future action (see § 9.2.9).

(490) pɤ⁵³   **li³²³**   ŋɛi⁴⁴   ni³²³   tɕʰɛ⁵⁵   ma³¹   **li³²³**   sɛi³¹   pa³¹.
      play   know.how   ASRT   BKGD   dance   NEG   know.how   still   IMP.SOL
      弹   会   跳   不   会   还
      '(I) knew how to play, but not yet how to dance, see?'
      会弹了还不会跳呀。
      (YLW-Learning)

(491) ŋa³³   tʰɤ⁵⁵   ɕa³¹   ŋ²⁴ka³³   **jo³³**   wa³²³,
      1SG   CL:TMP   think   see   must   PFV
      我   下   想   看   应该

      tɛi³³   tɕi⁵⁵   xa³³ni³³   fa³³ʐɿ³²³   **jo³³**.
      this   CL:TYPE how   translate   must
      这   种   怎么   翻译   应该
      '(I) must think (and) see how (I) should translate this.'
      我想想看这个怎么翻译。
      (KL-Weeds)

(492) sa²⁴tʰa³¹   kʰo⁵³   **tso³¹**   wa³²³,   ŋa³³tsʰɤ³¹   kɛi³³   vɤ³²³   **tso³¹**   wa³²³.
      candy   pay   turn   PFV   1PL   AGT   buy   turn   PFV
      糖   赔   该   我们   买   该
      '(When it was our) turn to pay for candy, we bought (it) in turn.'
      该买糖赔了，该我们买一场了。
      (YJF-Dance Parties)

The second type of auxiliary consists of those borrowed from Hanyu, such as *jɛ³⁵zɿ³⁵* 'to be willing' and *pi³²³sɿ³³sɿ⁴⁴* 'to need'. Following Hanyu syntax, these auxiliaries precede the matrix verb, as shown in (493).

(493) tɕo³⁵   sɿ³¹tsɿ³²³   na²⁴   ma³¹   **jɛ³⁵zɿ³⁵**   m̩³³.
      then   thing   be.good NEG   be.willing   do
      就   事   好   不   愿意   做
      '(They) weren't willing to do good deeds.'
      就不愿意做好事。
      (HPH-Weeds)

As already mentioned, auxiliaries may be directly negated. In fact, in these phrases negation almost always occurs on the auxiliary rather than on the matrix verb, as (494) demonstrates. Negating the matrix verb instead is ungrammatical. Note that because $ŋa^{323}ta^{323}$ 'to be able, to be allowed, can' is derived from a double verb construction containing $ŋa^{323}$ 'to get, obtain' and ta^{323} 'to be able, be acceptable', the negative marker is placed between the two syllables, as in (495). In addition, negation of an auxiliary may alter the pragmatics somewhat. For example, in (496) $ma^{31} jo^{33}$ 'do not need' functions as a mild imperative to discourage the action from being performed (see § 12.2.4).

(494) na²⁴wa³³　ɲa³²³ka⁵³pʰa³¹　tsʰɤ³³　tsɛi³³　tsɿ³⁵　**ma³¹ li³²³**　po⁵³.
　　　so　　　ɲa³²³ka⁵³.M　　PL　　seaweed　scoop　NEG　know.how　EPIS.EMP
　　　那么　　中村男人　　　们　　海草　　捞　　不　会
　　　'Now, those $ɲa^{323}ka^{53}$ men didn't know how to scoop up seaweed, (see?)'
　　　那么中村的男人不会捞海草呀。
　　　(PYX-Performing)

(495) kɤ³³　**ŋa³²³　ma³¹　ta²⁴**　ni³¹,　tɤ⁴⁴　tɕo³⁵　ta³¹　kɤ³³　wa³³.
　　　do　obtain　NEG　be.able　TOP　FILL　then　PROH　do　CRS
　　　做　得到　不　能　　　　　　　　就　别　做
　　　'If (you) can't do (it), um, then don't do (it).'
　　　不能做呢，那就别做了。
　　　(KL-Sewing)

(496) mi³⁵tsɿ³⁵　ɣ̥²⁴　**ma³¹　jo³³**.　sɿ³⁵sɿ³³pʰa³¹　tɕi⁴⁴　tɕo³⁵　tɕʰɛ⁵³　wa³²³.
　　　name　call　NEG　must　Hui.M　say　then　finish　PFV
　　　名字　叫　不　用　回族男人　说　就　完
　　　'No need to give a name. Just say a Hui man, that's enough.'
　　　不用叫名字。说是回族就可以了。
　　　(KL-Grandfather)

There is, however, one instance in which the matrix verb and the auxiliary are both negated. This is a special construction that combines a matrix verb with the auxiliary ta^{323} 'to be acceptable'. The resulting phrase means 'to not [VERB] is unacceptable', as the example in (497) illustrates.

(497) **ma³¹　i³²³　ma³¹　ta³²³**.
　　　NEG　go　NEG　be.acceptable
　　　不　去　不　行
　　　'Not going is unacceptable.'
　　　不去不行。
　　　(KL-Elicitation)

The two types of auxiliaries also differ in the way they pattern in reduplicative polar questions. In both cases, it is the final verb that is repeated. Thus, auxiliaries that occur after the matrix verb are reduplicated, as in (498). But with auxiliaries that occur before the matrix verb, it is the latter that is repeated, as in (499).

(498) nɛi³³   kʰa⁵⁵tso³¹tɕʰi³¹   n̪a³¹   **li³²³**   **li³²³**?
      2SG   Khatso.language   speak   know.how   know.how
      你   喀卓语   说   会   会
      'Do you know how to speak Khatso?'
      你会不会说喀卓语？
      (KL-Elicitation)

(499) nɛi³³   kʰua³¹la³¹   jɛ³⁵ȵ³⁵   **i³²³**   **i³²³**?
      2SG   Kunming   be.willing   go   go
      你   昆明   愿意   去   去
      'Are you willing to go to Kunming?'
      你愿不愿意去昆明？
      (KL-Elicitation)

There are a number of lexical verbs that may also function as modal auxiliaries in Khatso, such as *sɿ³³wa³⁵* 'to wish', *sɿ³¹xua³³* 'to like', *kʰai³³sɿ³⁵* 'to begin', *tsɿ³⁵sʮ³²³* 'to continue', *ŋ²⁴ka³³* and *sɿ³⁵ŋ²⁴ka³³* 'to try', *mo⁵⁵* 'to want' and *ai³⁵* 'to like, love'. As auxiliaries, they precede the matrix verb, as shown in (500) and (501). This is expected for most of them, since they are obvious Hanyu loans. But for the native verb *mo⁵⁵*, word order differentiates two key functions. Serving as the first verb in the clause indicates that *mo⁵⁵* is an auxiliary and thus the A/S arguments are identical; serving as the second verb indicates that *mo⁵⁵* is the matrix verb, and thus the arguments are different. It is the only native verb to pattern in this way, which likely evolved to avoid potential confusion when A/S is absent because of zero anaphora. A comparison of (501) and (502) illustrates the difference. The role of these verbs in complementation is detailed in § 15.2.

(500) i³³   tsa³²³   mɛi⁴⁴   **ai³⁵**   m̪³³   ja³³.
      3SG   rice   very   love   make   IPFV.EMP
      他   饭   很   爱   做
      'He really loves to cook.'
      他很爱做饭。
      (KL-Elicitation)

(501) **mo⁵⁵** pɤ⁵³ la²⁴ tsʰɤ³³ ni³¹ pɤ⁵³ so²⁴.
want play REL PL TOP play learn
要 弹 们 弹 学
'Those who want to play, learn to play.'
想弹的人呢，学弹。
(YLW-Learning)

(502) tɕi³¹tsʅ²⁴ na⁵³tɕʰɛ⁵⁵ mo³³ **mo⁵⁵** ja³³.
actually sing.dance show want IPFV.EMP
硬是 跳乐 给看 要
'Actually, (they) want (us) to sing and dance.'
要跳乐给他们看。
(PYX-Performing)

It is also possible to combine auxiliaries, depending on their individual meanings. Examples are shown in (503) and (504). Note that in the latter the borrowed auxiliary *pi³²³sʅ³³sʅ⁴⁴* may optionally co-occur with its native counterpart *jo³³*, without a change in meaning or degree.

(503) ŋa³³tsʰɤ³³ tsa³²³ tsa³¹ **ŋa³²³ta³²³ jo³³** ja³³!
3PL rice eat be.able must IPFV.EMP
我们 饭 吃 能 应该
'We must be able to eat!'
我们应该能吃饭的！
(KL-Elicitation)

(504) nɛi³³ **pi³²³sʅ³³sʅ⁴⁴** sɤ⁵⁵ vɤ⁵³ li³²³ **jo³³**.
2SG must Chinese.character write know.how must
你 必须 字 写 会 应该
'You must know how to write Chinese.' (i.e. 'you must learn how')
你必须会写字。
(KL-Elicitation)

Most languages use a variety of syntactic methods to convey modality (Palmer 1986: 33–50). In addition to the auxiliaries, in Khatso this information may be conveyed lexically — for example, through adverbs such as *sa²⁴* 'perhaps' and *ta³⁵kai³⁵* 'probably', and through verbs such as *ɕa³³ɕi³⁵* 'to believe', *ɕa³¹* 'to think, suppose' and *ni³²³tsɤ³¹* 'to doubt'. In addition, certain interrogative and emphatic particles also contain modal information (see § 12.4.7 and § 12.6 respectively).

8.8 Serial Verb Constructions

Like many languages in the Tibeto-Burman family, Khatso allows multiple verbs to occur adjacently in a single clause. These serial verbs work together to form a unitary predicate that expresses one, or sometimes two, events. Syntactically, these constructions, which may contain two or three verbs, share the same arguments and aspect markers, with no indication that one verb is subordinate to another. For example, in (505) the three verbs $t\gamma^{35}$ 'to ford', ko^{53} 'to cross', and li^{33} 'to come' describe the single event of crossing a river. And in (506), the verbs ja^{24} 'to send' and tsa^{55} 'to feed' describe two closely-related events, the sending of food to feed others. For the most part, the verbs in these constructions are contiguous, but in some cases the negative marker or an imperfective aspect marker may intervene as described below.

(505) tɕi³³sa³³tɕa³³ kɤ²⁴   **tɤ³⁵**   **ko⁵³**   **li³³**.
      Jinsha.River   CL:STRIP   ford   cross   come
      金沙江   条   渡   过   来
      '(They) forded the Jinsha River.'
      渡过金沙江。
      (HPH-Horse Dug Well)

(506) tɛi³¹ ɣɯ⁵³   ɣɯ⁵³   **ja²⁴** **tsa⁵⁵** tso²⁴ tɤ³³ wa³³.
      one   CL:BDG   CL:BDG   send   feed   ITER   INCP
      一   户   户   送   喂
      'House after house (she) started to send (food) to feed (them).'
      这么一家一家送给了。
      (HPH-Weeds)

Although serial verb constructions comprise single syntactic units, semantically they may describe either a single event or two closely-related events, as the two examples above illustrate. The difference is largely indicated by the composition of the serialization itself, which is often how these constructions are analyzed cross-linguistically (e.g. Aikhenvald and Dixon 2006: 3). Some are asymmetrical, meaning that they contain a "main" verb from the open class of lexical verbs followed by a "minor" verb from a more restricted class. In Khatso, these form single-event predicates, as described in more detail in § 8.8.1. Symmetrical serializations, on the other hand, combine verbs that all belong to the open class of lexical verbs without restriction. In Khatso, these tend to describe situations in which there are two events that are closely bound in some fashion, as explained in § 8.2.2.

There are a number of other constructions that combine two or more verbs in Khatso. Like serial verb constructions, they may be contiguous or share arguments and aspectual marking. However, typically one of the verbs is functionally subordinate to the other, and the constructions often pattern in slightly different ways than prototypical serial verb constructions. As a result, they are not included in this section, but detailed separately elsewhere. For example, the small subset of verbs that serve as auxiliaries is described in § 8.7. Applicative constructions, which use the verb *ku^{31}* 'to give' to add a core argument to a clause, are discussed in § 11.1. And causative constructions, which may involve the verbs *mo^{55}* 'to want', *ky^{33}* 'to make' or *ku^{31}* 'to give', are explained in § 11.2.

8.8.1 One-Event Constructions

There are several types of serial verb constructions in Khatso that describe a single event. As just mentioned, they are composed of an open-class verb combined with one or two verbs from a more restricted group. The details of their compositions and functions vary. Directional constructions are discussed in § 8.8.1.1, resultative constructions in § 8.8.1.2, manner constructions in § 8.8.1.3, and complex stative constructions in § 8.8.1.4.

8.8.1.1 Directional Constructions

Verb serialization in Khatso is frequently used to describe the motion associated with a state or event in relation to the deictic center. These constructions combine two and frequently three verbs. In all cases, the first verb, which is largely unrestricted, conveys the main idea. The following verb or verbs, which come from a small set of lexical motion verbs, describe the path that the action takes. This set contains only a dozen verbs; they are presented in Table 8.3.

Table 8.3: Directional verbs in serial constructions

Khatso	English		Chinese
	Lexical Meaning	Directional Meaning	
i³³ (i³²³)	'to go'	(away from speaker)	去
ka³²³	'to walk'	'away'	走
kɯ³³	'to enter' / 'to return'	'in' / 'back'	进 / 回
ko⁵³	'to cross, pass'	'over, across'	过
li³³ (li³²³)	'to come'	(towards speaker)	来
ta⁵³	'to ascend'	'up'	上
tɕa³³	'to cross'	'over, across'	过
tɕi³³	'to load, pack'	'into (container)'	进
to⁵³	'to exit'	'out'	出
tsʰi³³	'to fall'	'down'	下
tsʅ²⁴	'to rise'	'up'	起
za⁵³	'to descend'	'down'	下

Two-verb directional constructions typically contain an unrestricted verb and either *li³²³* 'to come' or *i³²³* 'to go', which describe the path of the motion in terms of the speaker's location. Examples are presented in (507) and (508); note that these two motion verbs must take tone 33 in this construction (see § 3.2.2). When *kɯ³³*, which can mean either 'to enter' or 'to return', combines with *li³³* 'to come' as in (507), it means 'to return' or even 'to come home' — both indicating motion towards the speaker. In (508), *kɯ³³* is followed by *i³³* 'to go', indicating motion away from the speaker.

(507) ŋa³²³tv̩³³ **kɯ³³ li⁴⁴** ni³²³, na²⁴ŋ²⁴ la³⁵ wa³³ mɛi⁴⁴.
afterwards enter come BKGD ask FOC CRS DSC.EMP
后面 回 来 问
'After (I) came home, (I) asked (them).'
回来以后问了呀。
(YAY-Erasers)

(508) **kɯ³³** i³³ la²⁴ ŋ³³xa⁵³ tso³²³, ma³¹ **kɯ³³** i³³ la²⁴ ŋ³³xa⁵³ tso³²³.
enter go REL time EXIST NEG enter go REL time EXIST
回 去 时候 有 不 回 去 时候 有
'There were times (we) went back, there were times (we) didn't go back.'
有时候回去，有时候不回去。
(YJF-Dance Parties)

Three-verb directional constructions contain an unrestricted lexical verb and two directional verbs which describe the motion and the arc of the movement respectively. Specifically, the middle verb describes motion in terms of its association with the environment in which it takes place. This verb may be any of those listed in Table 8.3 except for *li³³* and *i³³*. The final verb conveys the path of the action in terms of the speaker's deictic center — again using *li³³* for motion towards the speaker and *i³³* for motion away from the speaker along with the appropriate tone change (see § 3.2.2). Together the verbs describe a single motion, so that the construction in (509) — combining *mau³⁵* 'to gush', *to⁵³* 'to exit' and *li³³* 'to come' — means 'to gush out (towards speaker)'. Additional examples from discourse are presented in (510) and (511). Note that in (510) the English translation does not capture the unitary motion conveyed in Khatso; *vɤ³²³ kɯ³³ li³³* describes the single act of buying and bringing home an item.

(509) i³²³tɕa⁵³ **mau³⁵ to⁵³ li³³** tɤ³³ wa³³.
water gush exit come INCP
水 冒 出 来
'Water began to gush out.'
水冒出来了．
(HPH-Horse Dug Well)

(510) ŋa³¹ ma²⁴ **vɤ³²³ kɯ³³ li³³**.
fish CL:GEN buy enter come
鱼 个 买 回 来
'Buy (and bring) home a fish.'
买条鱼回来。
(KL-Hotpot)

(511) tsa⁵³tsʰŋ³²³ tsa⁵³, **tsa⁵³ ko⁵³ i³³**.
chess push push cross go
象棋 推 推 过 去
'To play chess, (you) push (the pieces) across.'
下推棋，推过去。
(HPH-Toys)

Almost any type of verb, excluding the copula and the existential *tso³²³*, may appear in a directional construction of this type. The examples above include both transitive and dynamic intransitive verbs. Certain stative verbs may also occur in serializations with *tsɿ²⁴* 'to rise', as shown in (512) and (513). Though not grammatical in English, a more literal translation of these serializations would be 'fat up' and 'red up' respectively.

(512) i³³   tɛi³¹   ŋ²⁴   ŋ³²³   sa²⁴tʰa³¹ tsa²⁴ ta³¹ ni³²³ tɕo³⁵ **tsʰɣ³³** **tsɿ²⁴**
      3SG   one   CL:TMP CL:TMP candy   eat   after   then   be.fat   rise
      他   一   天   天   糖   吃   以后   就   胖   起
      li³³   wa³³.
      come   CRS
      来
      'After eating candy every day, (he) has become fat.'
      他天天吃糖，就胖起来了。
      (KL-Elicitation)

(513) i³³   tsɿ³²³   to³²³   ŋɛi³³, tsʰo³³n̩a⁵³ kʰɯ⁴⁴ to³³ ŋ²⁴   **tsɿ²⁴ li³³**   wa³³.
      3SG   liquor   drink   ASRT   face   CL:ITEM also be.red rise come   CRS
      他   酒   喝   脸   个   也   红   起   来
      '(When) he drinks, (his) faces becomes red.'
      他喝酒呢，脸都红起来了。
      (KL-Elicitation)

The meaning of directional serial verb constructions may be figurative rather than literal. For example in (514) the motion indicated in *tɕa³¹ tsʰi³³ li⁴⁴*, literally 'speak down come', refers to the passage of a folk story down through the centuries. In (515), where no real motion is meant, the second verb *i³³* 'to go' conveys an adverbial sense of 'continuously' or 'always'. And the serialization in (516), *tɕʰɛ³³ ka³²³ i³³*, literally 'invite walk go (away from speaker)', is an idiom that means 'to die'. Note that in (514) and (516), the final syllable of the serialization undergoes tone sandhi from tone 33 to 44 because of the following particle; in the latter the triggering particle, *to³³* 'also', is omitted (see § 3.2.2).

(514) tɕi³¹ tɕi³⁵ tɕi³⁵ ni³³,
one CL:TMP CL:TMP ADV
一 代 代

tɕa³¹ tshi³³ li⁴⁴ ta³¹ tshŋ³²³ pɣ³²³ to³³ n̪ɛ³²³ sɛi⁴⁴.
speak descend come after seven hundred more CL:TMP TMP
讲 下 来 后 七 百 多 年

'Generation after generation, (it has been) told for more than seven hundred years.'
七百多年了一代代地讲下来了。
(HPH-Horse Dug Well)

(515) jɛ⁵³ tɕo³⁵ tɕi³³ ta⁵⁵ **ka³²³ i³³ wa³²³.**
later then this be.type walk go PFV
然后 就 这 样 走 去

'So, it was always like this.'
然后就一直这样了。
(HPH-Weeds)

(516) ŋa⁴⁴ to³³ **tɕhɛ³³ ka³²³ i⁴⁴** ma³¹ sŋ⁵⁵ ta⁵⁵ la²⁴ tɕha⁵⁵khv̩³³
1SG also invite walk go NEG know be.type REL time
我 也 请 走 去 不 知道 样 时候

'the time that I (will) also die, (I) don't know when'
不知道那个时候我可能也死了
(KL-Sewing)

The directional constructions are negated in two ways, and the position of the negative marker *ma³¹* determines its scope. Specifically, only the verb(s) following the marker are negated. Thus, when placed before the entire serialization, as in (517), *ma³¹* indicates that none of the actions denoted by the verbs occur. When placed between the two verbs, or between the first and second verbs in a three-verb serialization, it indicates that only the directional verbs are negated. In other words, the event denoted by the first verb occurs but the flow of the action is then halted, signaling that it is not possible to complete the action in the manner described – a pattern also found in resultative constructions (see § 8.8.1.2). For example, in (518) *sɣ³³ ma³¹ tɕi³³*, literally 'pierce not enter' describes a situation in which a needle is stuck into cloth but cannot pass through, so another method must be employed.

(517) tɛi³³ni³³ tɛi³³ti⁵³ **ma³¹** **tsʰɛi³³** **to⁵³** **i⁴⁴** ni³¹ tɕo³⁵
this.way a.little NEG stretch exit go TOP then
这么 一点 不 伸 出 去   就
'(if it) doesn't stretch out a little like that then'
不这么伸出去一点呢
(WYF-Stools)

(518) **sɤ³³** **ma³¹** **tɕi³³** la²⁴ tɕi⁵⁵ tɕɛ⁵⁵ jo³³ ja³³.
pierce NEG enter REL CL:TYPE tack must IPFV.EMP
穿 不 进   种 钉 应该
'The ones that can't be pierced, (you) must tack (them) on.'
穿不进去的那种，要钉的。
(WYY-Sewing)

Typically, polar questions are formed by reduplicating the last syllable of a verb (see § 12.4.1). This strategy also applies to directional serializations, as shown in (519). In two-verb combinations, the first verb may also be reduplicated instead. Thus the phrase in (520) is also grammatical, and it has the same meaning as that in (519). With three-verb serializations, reduplicating the second verb is the preferred method, as in (521).

(519) to⁵³ **li³³** **li³³**?
exit come come
出 来 来
'Are (you) coming out?'
出不出来？
(KL-Elicitation)

(520) **to⁵³** **to⁵³** li³³?
exit exit come
出 出 来
'Are (you) coming out?'
出不出来？
(KL-Elicitation)

(521) kɤ³¹ **ka³²³** **ka³²³** i³³?
run walk walk go
跑 走 走 去
'Are (you) running away?'
要不要跑走？
(KL-Elicitation)

The directional verbs listed in Table 8.3 have a number of syntactic idiosyncrasies. Many of them — i^{323}, ka^{323}, $tɕi^{33}$, ko^{53}, li^{323}, to^{53}, ta^{53}, $tsʰi^{33}$ and za^{53} — can be used alone as matrix verbs. Most are dynamic intransitive verbs, but $tɕi^{33}$, to^{53}, ta^{53} and za^{53} have transitive functions as well, as shown in (522). The others, however — $kɯ^{33}$, $tɕa^{33}$, $tsɿ^{24}$ — must always be accompanied by another directional verb. Often, this is either li^{33} or i^{33}, as in $kɯ^{33}$ i^{33} 'to enter (away from speaker)' and $kɯ^{33}$ li^{33} 'to enter, return (towards speaker)'. But $tsɿ^{24}$ does not co-occur with these two verbs when the main idea is 'rise'; it follows ka^{323} 'to walk' instead, as in ka^{323} $tsɿ^{24}$ 'to rise, get up'. There are also several verbs among this group which overlap in meaning and function. For example, ko^{53} and $tɕa^{33}$ both mean 'over, across', but the latter only appears in three-verb serializations. $kɯ^{33}$ and $tɕi^{33}$ both mean 'in' but the latter, which as a lexical verb means 'to pack, load', is only used for placing items in containers or other enclosed spaces. za^{53} and $tsʰi^{33}$ both convey a downward path, though the former is the default in serializations. As lexical verbs, these two words have different functions. za^{53} is transitive and describes getting out of vehicles, while $tsʰi^{33}$ is a dynamic intransitive verb and denotes weather events, as in (523). Unlike the other pairs, za^{53} and $tsʰi^{33}$ may also be combined, as (524) shows.

(522) $kʰɯ^{55}$ to^{53}
sweat exit
汗 出
'to sweat', literally 'to emit sweat'
出汗
(KL-Elicitation)

$tsʰɤ^{33}$ ta^{53}
car ascend
车 上
'to get in/on vehicle'
上车

(523) $tsʰɤ^{33}$ za^{53}
car descend
车 下
'to get out of/off vehicle'
下车
(KL-Elicitation)

xua^{55} $tsʰi^{33}$
snow fall
雪 下
'to snow'
下雪

(524) za^{53} $tsʰi^{33}$ i^{33}
descend descend go
下 下 去
'to go down'
下去
(KL-Elicitation)

za^{53} $tsʰi^{33}$ li^{33}
descend descend come
下 下 来
'to come down'
下来

In addition to its directional meaning of 'across, over', shown in (511) above, the verb ko^{53} 'to cross, pass' also has an aspectual use. It indicates whether an action or state has ever been experienced (see § 9.2.10). As a result, it may also be appended to directional constructions. The two functions are syntactically different, however. When *ko⁵³* is followed by *i³³* or *li³³*, it has a directional meaning, as in (525). When it is the final verb in a construction, it is the aspect marker, as in (526).

(525) i³³   kɛi³³   sɣ⁵⁵   tɛi³³   pɛi³¹   **ɣ³²³**   **ko⁵³**   **li³³**.
      3SG   AGT   book   this   CL:VOL   take   pass   come
      她   书   这   本   拿   过   来
      'She brings this book over.'
      她把这本书拿过来。
      (KL-Elicitation)

(526) i³³   kɛi³³   sɣ⁵⁵   tɛi³³   pɛi³¹   **ɣ³²³**   **li³³**   **ko⁵³**.
      3SG   AGT   book   this   CL:VOL   take   come   EXP
      她   书   这   本   拿   来   过
      'She has brought this book (before).'
      她来拿过这本书。
      (KL-Elicitation)

8.8.1.2 Resultative Constructions

Resultative constructions, also called cause-effect constructions, involve two verbs. The first verb conveys the event, and may be a transitive or dynamic intransitive verb, but not a stative verb. The second verb, which is often but not always stative, describes the result of the event. For example, in (527) *tɛi⁵³ kʰuo⁵³*, literally 'put be.wet', describes puting an item in water until it is wet, and *o⁵³ ɕo³³* in (528), literally 'weed be.clean', denotes weeding an area until it is clean, that is, until it is empty of weeds.

(527) i⁴⁴ni³¹   ta³⁵,   i³²³tɕa⁵³   kɛi³³   **tɛi⁵³**   **kʰuo⁵³**.
      then   still   water   INS   put   be.wet
      然后   还   水   用   弄   湿
      'Then, with water get (it) wet.'
      然后呢，用水弄湿。
      (WYF-Stools)

(528) tɛi³¹   tɛi³⁵   to³³   **o⁵³**   **ɕo³³**   ma³¹   li³²³.
      one   CL:TMP   also   weed   be.clean   NEG   know.how
      一   代   也   薅   干净   不   会
      'Even in one generation (they) couldn't weed (it) clean.'
      一代也薅不干净。
      (HPH-Weeds)

The resultative construction is very productive in Khatso; there are countless possible combinations. The first verb in the serialization is largely unrestricted, although the semantics of the second verb may limit likely candidates. For example, po^{53} 'to be full' can only be used with verbs of consumption, such as tsa^{31} 'to eat' and to^{323} 'to drink'. Candidates for the second verb are typically stative, though this is still a rather large group of possibilities. Most of these are stand-alone verbs, but there are a few — such as $ɕɛ^{35}$, no^{53}, po^{53} and $tsɣ^{35}$ — that cannot be used outside of serial constructions. Table 8.4 presents some frequently encountered result verbs (VERB₂) and the types of matrix verbs (VERB₁) they typically modify.

Table 8.4: Verbs in serial resultative constructions

Khatso	VERB₂ English	Chinese	Meaning	Possible VERB₁
$ɕɛ^{35}$	'to miss'	失手	'to fumble, fail'	all non-stative verbs
$ɕo^{33}$	'to be clean'	干净	'to complete thoroughly, with nothing left'	verbs of cleaning, consumption, buying, selling
$kɣ^{53}$	'to break'	破	'to break'	verbs of striking, breaking
lo^{53}	'to be enough'	够	'to be enough'	all verbs
$mɛi^{55}$	'to be few'	少	'little, less'	all non-stative verbs
$mɣ^{33}$	'to achieve'	到, 着	'to achieve, complete'	verbs of achievement
mo^{323}	'to perceive'	见	'to (see) and understand'	$ŋ^{24}ka^{33}$ 'to see, look'
na^{24}	'to be good'	好	'to complete well'	all non-stative verbs
no^{53}	'to fall'	掉	'to complete, dispense with'	all transitive verbs
$n̥a^{31}$	'to be many'	多	'much, more'	all non-stative verbs
$ŋ^{24}ka^{33}$	'to see, look'	看	'to try and see'	verbs of cognition, evaluation, use
po^{53}	'to be full'	满	'to be full'	verbs of consumption
si^{53}	'to kill'	杀	'to result in death'	verbs of assault, killing, misfortune
$sŋ^{323}$	'to be sure'	确定	'to be sure'	verbs of cognition
$tɕa^{31}$	'to perceive'	凡	'to (hear) and understand'	na^{24} 'to hear, listen'
$tɕɛ^{33}$	'to be full'	满	'to be full'	verbs of placement (inanimate items)
$tɕʰɛ^{53}$	'to finish'	完	'to complete'	all non-stative verbs

	VERB₂		Meaning	Possible VERB₁
Khatso	English	Chinese		
tsʏ³⁵	'to grasp'	住	'(to hold) fast'	verbs of holding
vɤ³³	'to be round'	圆	'to complete well'	verbs of doing, performing
xo²⁴	'to be correct'	对	'to complete in a proper manner'	all non-stative verbs
ɕɛ³⁵	'to miss'	失手	'to fumble, fail'	all non-stative verbs

Semantically, the construction describes the end of a process, but context determines the actual time frame of the event. It may, for example, describe the desired result of current and future action. For example, in (529) the speaker uses *tso⁵⁵ tɕɛ²⁴* 'pull be.tight' to describe the action she is simultaneously performing. But in the instructions provided in (530), the result verb *na²⁴* 'to be good' describes potential future events. Regardless of the time frame, however, this construction applies only to particular instances of an event. It does not refer to a generalized state of affairs, which requires the complex stative particle *kɯ³²³* (see § 8.8.1.4).

(529) ti⁵³   **tso⁵⁵ tɕɛ²⁴**   ni³¹   tɕo³⁵ tɤ⁴⁴   kɯ²⁴ta³³ tɕi³³   ma⁴⁴   ma³¹   tso³²³
CL:PCE pull be.tight   TOP   then   all   knot   this   CL:GEN NEG   EXIST
点   拉   紧   就   都   结   这   个   不   有
wa³³.
CRS
'(I) pull (it) a bit tight, so there won't be a knot.'
拉紧一点呢，这个结那就没有了。
(WYY-Sewing)

(530) ŋa³¹   ma²⁴   vɤ³²³ kɯ³³   li³³.
fish   CL:GEN   buy   enter   come
鱼   个   买   回   来
'Buy a fish.
买条鱼回来。

ja⁵³   si⁵³   na²⁴   kɤ³³   na²⁴.
then   kill   be.good   do   be.good
然后   杀   好   做   好
'Then, kill (it) well (and) clean (it) well.'
然后杀好弄好。
(KL-Hotpot)

Like directional serial constructions, resultative serializations may be negated in two ways and the position of the negative marker determines its scope. To communicate that neither the action nor the result occur, the negative marker ma^{31} precedes the entire serialization, as shown in (531). Placing ma^{31} between the verbs negates only the result verb, indicating that the action is attempted but the result does not occur or is not possible, as in (532).

(531) pɛi³⁵ tɕʰa³¹ ko⁵⁵ **ma³¹** tɛi³¹ no⁵³
grass leaf CL:PL NEG shake complete
草 叶 些 不 抖 掉
'(if) the leaves don't shake off'
草叶不抖掉
(WYF-Stools)

(532) ŋa³³ sɛi⁴⁴ nei³³ ni³¹ i³²³tsʰa³¹ tsɛi²⁴ **kʰa³²³**
1SG family paternal.grandmother TOP waterwheel CL:MACH raise
我 家 奶奶 水车 台 抬
ma³¹ ɣɯ³⁵.
NEG move
不 动
'My grandmother wasn't able to move the waterwheel.'
我奶奶呢，抬不动水车。
(YJF-Childhood)

Polar questions formed with the resultative construction pattern just like two-syllable serializations — it is the second verb that is reduplicated, as shown in (533) and (534).

(533) nɛi³³ sʅ⁵⁵ **sʅ³²³** **sʅ³²³**?
2SG know be.sure be.sure
你 知道 确定 确定
'Are you sure?'
你确不确定？
(KL-Elicitation)

(534) vɤ³²³ **lo⁵³** **lo⁵³** wa³¹?
buy be.enough be.enough PFV.Q
买 够 够
'Did (you) buy enough?'
买够了吗？
(KL-Elicitation)

In addition to resultative constructions, clause combining constructions may also be used to describe situations that involve causes and their effects. These formulations are detailed in § 14.2.

8.8.1.3 Manner Constructions

Some stative verbs have meanings that may convey manner. When occurring as the second verb in a resultative construction, they describe the way in which the action of the first verb is performed rather than its result. There are only a handful that regularly appear in serializations, including lx^{33} 'to be late', na^{53} 'to be early', sa^{33} 'to be rich' but here meaning 'to be good, easy', and sa^{55} 'to be bitter, poor' which here means 'to be difficult'. An example is shown in (535); note that the continuous and iterative aspect markers typically occur between the verbs in these kinds of serializations.

(535) tɛi³³ tɕi⁵⁵   tʏ³⁵ ni³²³   **kv̩³³** tsʏ³¹ **na⁵³**   wa³³ mɛi⁴⁴.
      this CL:TYPE FOC   BKGD   make   CONT   be.early   CRS   DSC.EMP
      这   种   做   早
      'This type, (I) was making early on.'
      这种呢，做得早了。
      (WYY-Sewing)

Superficially, these may appear to be a stative verb preceded by a verbal complement. However, the first verb cannot take the complementizer-like particle $sɛi^{44}$, and the preverbal intensifier $mɛi^{44}$ occurs before the entire serialization rather than only before the stative verb, as shown in (536), indicating that this is a unitary predicate. These specialized manner verbs also readily occur in complex stative constructions (see § 8.8.1.4). Complementation, which patterns differently, is described more fully in Chapter 15.

(536) **mɛi⁴⁴** **so²⁴** **sa⁵⁵**   sa²⁴   ja³³.
      very   learn   be.difficult   perhaps   IPFV.EMP
      很   学   难   可能
      'Perhaps (it) was very hard to learn.'
      可能很难学。
      (KL-Learning)

It is also possible to describe manner by combining clauses in a more complex construction; this is detailed in § 14.5.

8.8.1.4 Complex Stative Constructions

As previously described, resultative serial verb constructions combine an action and its result (see § 8.8.1.2). For example, the serialization *tsa³¹ po⁵³*, shown in (537), refers to the action of eating one's fill at a meal. There is a similar construction that casts a resultative serialization as a general state of affairs rather than a particular event. In this construction, the particle *kɯ³²³*, which has no lexical meaning and only appears in this environment, is placed between the two verbs. Thus the event in (537) becomes (538), which describes the general state of having enough food to eat one's fill. This is the only serial verb construction that involves a particle.

(537) *tsa³¹* + *po⁵³*   →   *tsa³¹ po⁵³*
       eat   'be full'   'to eat one's fill'

(538) *tsa³¹* + *kɯ³²³* + *po⁵³*   →   *tsa³¹ kɯ³²³ po⁵³*
       eat   CSC   'be full'   'to have enough to eat one's fill'

Like in the other serializations, the second verb in this construction may describe either the result or the manner associated with the action expressed by the first verb. For example, in (539) *na²⁴* 'be good' describes the way sewing should be done. The second verb in (540) is *sa³³*, which means 'to be rich' as a stative verb but in this construction means either 'to be good' or 'to be easy'. Here it modifies *na²⁴* 'to hear' and the resulting sense is 'to sound good'.

(539) **kɣ³³   kɯ³²³   na²⁴**   ja³³   pa³¹,   tɤ⁴⁴   tɕɛi³³ni³³   ni³¹.
       do   CSC   be.good   IPFV.EMP   IMP.SOL   FILL   this.way   TOP
       做   好   这么
       '(It) can be done well, um, like this.'
       这样的话，做得好呀。
       (KL-Sewing)

(540) "**na²⁴   kɯ³²³   sa³³**   tʰɛi³²³   ja³³!   xai³⁵   xuɛi³²³   tsʰo³¹!"
       hear   CSC   be.good   very   IPFV.EMP   again   CL:TMP   perform
       听   好   很   还   回   演
       ' "(It) sounds very good! Perform (it) again!" '
       "很好听！再唱一次！"
       (PYX-Performing)

The negative marker *ma³¹* is inserted immediately before the second verb to cast the state of affairs in a negative light. Thus, *tsa³¹ kɯ³²³ ma³¹ po⁵³* 'to not have enough to eat one's fill' may be used to describe a dinner hosted by friends who are always too stingy to serve much food. Examples from discourse are presented in (541) and (542). The first verb is never negated in this construction.

(541) "la²⁴ kɯ³²³ ma³¹ sa³³."
 play CSC NEG be.good
 玩   不 好
 ' "(It) isn't fun." '
 "不好玩。"
 (PYX-Performing)

(542) tsʰy³³ la²⁴ tɕi⁵⁵ kɣ³³ kɯ³²³ ma³¹ sa³³.
 be.thick REL CL:TYPE do CSC NEG be.good
 粗   种   做   不 好
 'The thick ones are not easy to do.'
 粗的那种不好做。
 (WYY-Sewing)

Polar questions based on this construction are formed by reduplicating the second verb, as shown in (543).

(543) pɣ⁵³ kɯ³²³ sa³³ sa³³?
 play CSC be.good be.good
 弹   好   好
 'Is (it) easy to play?'
 好不好弹？
 (KL-Elicitation)

This construction is very productive in Khatso and there are a great many combinations possible. A few of them have become lexicalized. For example, *ŋ²⁴kɯ³²³sa³³* 'to be good-looking, pretty', *na²⁴kɯ³²³sa³³* 'to sound good' and *la²⁴kɯ³²³sa³³* 'to be fun' have become basic terms for these concepts.

8.8.2 Two-Event Constructions

Some serial verb constructions, though syntactically single predicates, semantically convey two separate but closely-related events. This is underscored by the fact that they are symmetrical, meaning that both of the component verbs belong to the open class of lexical verbs, with none of the semantic restrictions found in single-event serializations. Thus, each event is of equal importance. Syntactically, however, they are closely bound together, sharing arguments and aspect particles with no marking that indicates subordination. As a result, the events are understood to be pragmatically related, and in general the relationship involves a sequential order in time. In many cases, it also links an event to a purpose. Situations that involve three or more events must be packaged in separate clauses.

When the link between the verbs is based on time alone, it is understood that they occur in the order in which they are spoken. Thus, in (544) waiting happens before eating, and in (545) grabbing occurs before eating.

(544) "tʰɤ⁵⁵   xo³³   tsa³¹   tɕo³⁵,   ŋ³³   wa³²³   po⁵³."
      CL:TMP   wait   eat   then   COP   PFV   EPIS.EMP
      下   等   吃   就   是
      ' "Wait a while to eat, (that's) right!" '
      "等着吃，就是啦！"
      (PYX-Performing)

(545) tɛi³³ni³³   tɕʰa⁵⁵   tsa³¹   ŋɛi³³.
      this.way   grab   eat   ASRT
      这么   抓   吃
      'Grab and eat (it) this way.'
      这么抓着吃。
      (YJF-Dance Parties)

There is an exception to this logical order, and it involves the verbs li^{323} 'to come' and i^{323} 'to go'. These two motion verbs always appear in second position, regardless of when the travel occurs in relation to the other verb. For example, in (546) the travel must occur before the work can be done, and in (547) going to Hexi must occur before shopping can happen there. Again, note that when adjacent to another verb, li^{323} and i^{323} must change to tone 33 (see § 3.2.2). The position of these two verbs is identical to their placement in directional constructions, and it may be that the directional pattern influenced the formulation of two-event serializations over time. The resulting ambiguity is typically not a problem; context and the semantics of the individual verbs themselves resolve the meaning.

(546) tɛi³³ni³³   a³³   tɕi⁵⁵   kɤ̥³³   li³³   ŋɛi³³.
      this.way   that   CL:TYPE   do   come   ASRT
      这样   那   种   做   来
      '(He) came to do that kind (of work).'
      是这么来做那种的。
      (YJF-Childhood)

(547) kʰai³³tsɿ³²³ vɤ³²³ i³³ sɛi⁴⁴ nv̩³²³kʰɤ³³ **vɤ³²³ i³³** ŋɛi³³.
eraser buy go TOP Hexi buy go ASRT
橡皮擦 买 去 河西 买 去
'To buy erasers, (you) go buy (them in) Hexi.'
买橡皮擦是去河西买去的。
(YAY-Erasers)

The same construction may indicate that the relationship between the two events is one of purpose as well as time. Specifically, the second verb describes the goal or the reason for the event denoted by the first verb. Thus, in (548) liquor is made to be sold, and in (549) turnip soup is boiled to be eaten. Again, the order is iconic; these combinations are seen as two-phase processes that must by definition occur in a particular order.

(548) tsɿ³²³ tsʰɿ³³ **kɤ³³ ŋ³¹**.
liquor be.white make sell
酒 白 弄 卖
'(They) make white liquor to sell.'
做白酒卖。
(HPH-Horse Dug Well)

(549) tɛi³³ni⁴⁴ ta³¹ tɕo³⁵ o³¹ma³³tsa³⁵ tɛi³¹ ko⁵⁵ **xa⁵⁵ tsa³¹**.
this.way after then turnip.soup one CL:COL boil eat
这样 以后 就 萝卜汤 一 些 煮 吃
'Because of that, (we would) boil a batch of turnip soup to eat.'
这样呢就煮一些萝卜汤吃。
(YJF-Childhood)

The relationship between an event and its purpose may also be conveyed through clause combining; this construction is detailed in § 14.6.

9 Verb Modifiers

As noted in Chapter 8, verbs comprise one of the largest word classes in the language. And given widespread zero anaphora, many intonation units in discourse contain only verbs and their modifiers. The latter are not obligatory; even aspect need not be marked if the time frame is clear from context. However, there are a number of clausal elements that directly modify verbs and they are described in this chapter. They include negation, which is explained in §9.1, aspect, described in §9.2, and adverbs, which are discussed in §9.3.

Other constructions involving verbs are detailed elsewhere. The nominalizing constructions that derive nouns from verbs are discussed in §7.6. And, core arguments and other verbal complements are explained in the chapter on clause structure (see Chapter 10).

9.1 Negation

Negation is a fairly simple process in Khatso, and there are only two negative markers: *ma³¹* and *ta³¹*. The first is the general negator of verbs, and the second is used in prohibitive constructions.

9.1.1 General Negator *ma³¹*

The negator *ma³¹* is placed immediately before the verb it modifies, no other material may intervene. Examples are shown in (550), (551) and (552). The marker *ma³¹* cannot modify nouns, adverbs or particles in Khatso, nor does it ever occur without the verb it modifies, which makes the potential for its use one of the tests for verbhood (see Chapter 8). In addition, using a negated stative verb rather than its antonym is quite common in Khatso. In fact, in elicitation an attribute like 'dirty' is as likely to be translated as *ma³¹ ɕo³³* 'not clean' as *i³⁵* 'to be dirty'.

(550) pɣ̩³²³xai³¹   sɿ³⁵   mɛi⁴⁴   pɣ̩³²³   i³²³tso³²³   mɛi⁴⁴   **ma³¹** ɕo³²³   tɕɛ⁴⁴ ni³²³.
north.sea temple CL:GEN POSS well   CL:GEN NEG be.clean say   BKGD
北海   寺   个   水井   个   不 干净   说
'(They) say North Sea Temple's well wasn't clean.'
说是北海寺的水井不干净。
(PYX-Dragon Pools)

(551) **ma³¹** tʰo³²³ẓɿ³⁵ tɕi⁴⁴ tɕo³⁵, **ma³¹** tʰo³²³ẓɿ³⁵ tɕi³³.
NEG   agree   say   then   NEG   agree   say
不   同意   说   就   不   同意   说
'(If you) don't agree, then say (you) don't agree.'
不同意呢，就说不同意。
(KL-Childhood)

(552) tsɿ³⁵no²⁴ to³³ **ma³¹** tso³²³ a³³tɕʰa⁵⁵kʰɤ³³.
toy   also   NEG   EXIST   that.time
玩具   也   不   有   那时候
'There weren't any toys at that time.'
那时候什么玩具没有。
(HPH-Toys)

In phrases with more than one verb, the placement of the negative marker varies. In causative constructions, for example, *ma³¹* always precedes the matrix verb, as shown in (553), while in auxiliary constructions, it always precedes the auxiliary, as in (554). By contrast, in serial verb constructions *ma³¹* may occur in two places. When it precedes the entire serialization, it indicates that the event does not occur at all, as (555) demonstrates. When it precedes the second verb, it signals that the event expressed by the first verb occurs or is at least attempted, but that the rest of the event is halted or impossible to complete. For example, in (556) the phrase *kʰa³²³ ma³¹ ɣɤ³⁵*, literally 'raise not move', means 'tried to raise but could not move'. Serial verb constructions, and their negation, are discussed in § 8.8.

(553) "**ma³¹** tsʰo³¹ mo³³ **ma³¹** tɕʰɛ⁵⁵ mo⁴⁴ ni³¹ **ma³¹** ka³²³ kɯ³¹."
NEG sing show NEG dance show TOP NEG walk INDR.CAUS
不   演   给见 不   跳   给见   不   走
' " (If you) don't sing or dance (for us), (we) won't let (you) go." '
"不唱不跳不让你们走。"
(PYX-Performing)

(554) pʰi²⁴ŋ²⁴tɕʰi³¹ na³¹ **ma³¹** li³²³.
Hanyu   speak NEG   know.how
汉语   说   不   会
'(We) didn't know how to speak Hanyu.'
不会说汉语。
(YAY-Erasers)

(555) a³³   ta²⁴   to³³   **ma³¹** sa³³ tɕi³³   kɯ³¹   la³¹.
      that   CL:ITEM also   NEG   sew   enter   INDR.CAUS PFV.IRR
      那   条   也   不   缝   进
      'That one didn't get sewn in either.'
      那条也没给缝进去。
      (WYY-Sewing)

(556) ŋa³³ sɛi⁴⁴   nɛi³³   ni³¹ i³²³tsʰa³¹   tsɛi²⁴   kʰa³²³
      1SG   family paternal.grandmother TOP   waterwheel   CL:MACH   raise
      我   家   奶奶   水车   台   抬
      ma³¹ ɣɤ³⁵.
      NEG   move
      不   动
      'My grandmother wasn't able to move the waterwheel.'
      我奶奶呢抬不动水车。
      (YJF-Childhood)

As just mentioned, the negative marker does not modify anything other than verbs. However, there is a reduplicative construction derived from stative verbs that may function as an adjective, adverb or noun (see § 8.1.2.2). Because of its verbal origin, it may be negated by *ma³¹*, as shown in (557).

(557) pɛi³⁵   tɕi⁵⁵   **ma³¹** na²⁴   na²⁴   za³¹   a³³   tɕi⁵⁵   ni³¹   ŋ²⁴tɕa³³
      straw   CL:TYPE   NEG   be.good   be.good   DIM   that   CL:TYPE   TOP   other
      草   种   不   好   好   那   种   别的
      tʰi³⁵.
      place.under
      垫
      'The type of straw (that) is not so good, (we) put it under the other (straw).'
      不太好的那种草呢别处垫。
      (WYF-Stools)

There is no single word corresponding to 'no' in Khatso. Instead, negative responses to polar questions are typically formed by negating the verb in the interrogative clause, as shown in the exchange in (558). It is also possible to reply with a negated copula, but this tends to be reserved for questions that either feature the copula or have an equational sense, as in (559). *ma³¹* is never used without a verb to reply to questions.

(558) A: n̻o³¹   m̻³³   m̻³³   ta³³   sa³¹?
         thing   do   do   IPFV.IRR   still.Q
         东西   做   做   还
         'Does (he) still work?'
         还在干活吗？

    B: **ma³¹**   m̻³³   tɤ³³ wa³³.
        NEG   do   INCP
        不   干
        '(He) doesn't work anymore.'
        没干了。
    (KL, YAY-Erasers)

(559) A: xɯ³⁵lɣ³⁵ ni³¹,   na⁵³pʰa³¹kʰua⁵⁵   ŋ³³   sa⁴⁴?
         Houlu   TOP   mountain.village   COP   CRTN.Q
         后路   山村   是
         'Houlu, is (it) a mountain village?'
         后路是不是山村里？

    B: **ma³¹**   ŋ³³   pa³¹.
        NEG   COP   IMP.SOL
        不   是
        'No.'
        不是的。
    (KL, YJR-Grandfather)

9.1.2 Prohibitive Marker *ta³¹*

The second negative particle is *ta³¹*, which marks prohibitive constructions. Unlike positive imperative particles, which must follow the verb, *ta³¹* is like *ma³¹* in that it must immediately precede the verb. It can modify verbs of any valency, including stative verbs that denote changeable attributes, such as human propensities and certain physical properties. Examples are shown in (560) through (563). No additional syntax is required, although the particles that are employed to soften imperatives may also occur in *ta³¹* clauses (see § 12.2). It may be used with first and second person, but not with third person. And like *ma³¹*, *ta³¹* is never used without a verb.

(560) tsʰɤ³³ kʰɛi³³ tsɤ²⁴ ni³¹, **ta³¹** tsŋ³¹ wa³³.
car drive CONT TOP PROH call CRS
车 开 别 打
'If (you) are driving, don't use the phone.'
开着车呢，别打了。
(ZRF-Grandfather)

(561) tɛi³³ sɤ³³ **ta³¹** tsʰuo³³
this CL:ROW PROH string
这 串 别 穿
'don't string this row'
别穿这串
(WYY-Sewing)

(562) kɤ³³ ŋa³²³ ma³¹ ta²⁴ ni³¹, tɤ⁴⁴ tɕo³⁵ **ta³¹** kɤ³³ wa³³.
do obtain NEG able TOP FILL then PROH do CRS
做 得到 不 能 就 别 做
'If (you) can't do (it), um, then don't do (it).'
不能做呢，那就别做了。
(KL-Sewing)

(563) **ta³¹** sa⁵⁵to²⁴!
PROH be.shy
别 害羞
'Don't be shy!'
别害羞！
(KL-Elicitation)

The prohibitive marker generally replaces the other imperative markers, and in fact, cannot co-occur with the general imperative *jɛ²⁴*. However, the imperative *pa³¹*, which also solicits agreement, may be used with *ta³¹*. For example, the phrase in (564) is uttered as a joking retort to being teased by a friend.

(564) **ta³¹** xɯ³³ pa³¹!
PROH scold IMP.SOL
别 骂
'Don't scold (me), okay?'
别骂呀！
(KL-Sewing)

The prohibitive *ta³¹* may co-occur with several aspect markers. When used with the currently relative state marker *wa³³*, the phrase indicates that an activity in progress should be halted, as (565) illustrates. When either the continuous or iterative aspect markers are also present, the meaning is that one should no longer keep doing an activity, as in (566).

(565) **ta³¹** tsɿ³¹ wa³³.
PROH call CRS
别 打
'Don't use the phone (anymore).'
别打了。
(ZRF-Grandfather)

(566) **ta³¹** to³²³ tsɤ³¹ wa³³!
PROH drink CONT CRS
别 喝
'Don't keep drinking!'
别喝了！
(KL-Elicitation)

Note that the prohibitive is homophonous with the rhetorical particle *ta³¹* (see § 12.4.7.6). Word order differentiates the two. The prohibitive must precede the verb it modifies, like the negative marker *ma³¹*, while the rhetorical particle always occurs at the end of a phrase.

Double negatives are avoided in Khatso; such phrases are typically recast with positive polarity. Thus a phrase such as 'he doesn't want me not to go', would be phrased 'he wants me to go'. Likewise, the two negative markers *ma³¹* and *ta³¹* cannot be used to modify the same verb. Instead, another verb, such as the quotative *tɕi³³* 'to speak, say', is inserted, as in (567). The only other double negation construction found in discourse is the combination of a negated matrix verb with the negated auxiliary *ta³²³* 'to be acceptable' (see § 8.7), which carries the meaning of 'to not [VERB] is unacceptable', as (568) illustrates. This is the only auxiliary which patterns in this way.

(567) **ma³¹** i³²³ **ta³¹** tɕi³³.
NEG go PROH speak
不 去 别 说
'Don't say (you) won't go.'
别说不去。
(KL-Elicitation)

(568) tsa³²³ **ma³¹** tsa³¹ **ma³¹** ta³²³.
rice NEG eat NEG be.acceptable
饭 不 吃 不 行
'Not eating is unacceptable.'
不得不吃饭。
(KL-Elicitation)

Negation also plays a role in the universal quantification construction and in negative indefinite constructions (see § 6.4 and § 7.3.3 respectively).

9.2 Aspect

Like most Tibeto-Burman languages, Khatso has a verbal aspectual system. That is to say, instead of correlating the time of an event to the moment that the speaker describes it, as happens in tense systems, in Khatso the aspect denotes the inherent temporal structure of the event itself. For example, the perfective marker wa^{323} indicates that an event is complete and bounded in time while the future marker wa^{35} indicates that an event has yet to occur. Some are irrealis, like la^{31} and ta^{33}, and thus mark unrealized events. Aspect markers in Khatso are grammatical particles — they have a function but no true lexical meaning. The one exception is the experiential marker ko^{53}, which is a borrowed lexical verb that also occurs in directional serial verb constructions (see § 8.8.1.1). Table 9.1 below lists the aspect markers and their functions.

The aspect markers may be augmented by emphatic and question particles that also provide aspectual information. Often, these particles replace the aspect marker in question. For example, the emphatic particle $\eta\varepsilon i^{35}$ replaces wa^{35} in emphatic phrases to convey a future interpretation, and la^{31} is used in certain perfective questions in place of wa^{323}. Question formation is described in more detail in § 12.4.

Table 9.1: Aspect markers in Khatso

Aspect Marker	Function
wa³²³	perfective
wa³³	currently relevant state
tɤ³³ ti³³ja³³	progressive
tsɤ³¹	continuous
tso²⁴	iterative
la³¹	perfective irrealis
ta³³	imperfective irrealis
tɤ³³ wa³³ tsɤ³¹ wa³²³	inceptive
wa³⁵	future
ko⁵³	experiential

In actual discourse, the aspect categories are not as discrete as they appear on paper. There is overlap, for example, between the perfective and the currently relevant state, and in some phrases either can be used with no appreciable difference in meaning. Likewise, the progressive, continuous and iterative aspects — which are all imperfective in nature — are functionally similar and also overlap to some extent. The analysis provided here is based on the prototypical use of each marker, with the caveat that there are additional nuances in discourse not captured here.

Aspect markers occur immediately after the verb complex. And because Khatso is a verb-final language, this means that aspect markers are frequently the last elements in a phrase, as shown in (569). However, the imperfective markers — *tɤ³³*, *tsɤ³¹* and *tso²⁴* — are dispreferred in final position and usually require an additional particle of some sort to sound complete, as in (570) where an emphatic particle is included. Because they are semantically incompatible with the modal auxiliary verbs, the imperfective markers precede them, as in (571). Similarly, in serial verb constructions that end with *li³²³* 'to come' or *i³²³* 'to go', they also precede the final verb, as in (572). This does not alter the meaning in any way, but seems to be an idiomatic pattern imposed by the two motion verbs.

(569) na³²³tshɭ³¹　vɤ³²³　tsa³¹　jo³³　**wa³²³**.
　　　medicine　buy　eat　must　PFV
　　　药　　　　买　　吃　　应该
　　　'(I) had to buy medicine to take.'
　　　应该买药吃了。
　　　(WYY-Sewing)

(570) xa³³ma⁴⁴ xa³³ma⁴⁴ ɣ²⁴ **tɤ³³** ŋɛi³³ tɕi³³n̪ɛ³³?
what what call PROG ASRT this.way
什么 什么 叫 这么
'What in this world is (this) called?'
这里是叫什么？
(KL-Qin)

(571) i³³kʰɤ³³ kʰɤ²⁴ **tsɤ³¹** jo³³.
inside be.empty CONT must
里面 空 应该
'Inside (it) must always be empty.'
里面应该是空的
(YLW-Qin)

(572) pɤ⁵³ sɿ⁵⁵ tɕo³⁵ na⁵³pɤ³¹ **tso²⁴** i³³ wa³³.
play know then sing.dance ITER go CRS
弹 知道 就 跳乐 去
'(After) I knew how to play, I went dancing often.'
会弹就去跳乐去了。
(YLW-Learning)

As these examples show, some of the aspect markers may be combined. When this happens, the imperfective markers — *tɤ³³*, *tsɤ³¹* and *tso²⁴* — precede the others, as the example in (573) illustrates. Table 9.2 presents the combinations that are attested in Khatso. For the most part, the meaning of each combination is logical and compositional. For example, because the experiential aspect marker *ko⁵³* marks events that have been experienced before, thereby defining them as bounded in time, it may only combine with the perfective marker *wa³²³*. By contrast, the continuous marker *tsɤ³¹* and iterative marker *tso²⁴* point to the frequency of an event without reference to boundaries in time, and thus may freely co-occur with the perfective *wa³²³*, currently relevant state *wa³³* and future *wa³⁵* markers. There are two other combinations worth noting, both of which denote a type of inceptive aspect — *tɤ³³ wa³³* marks events that have just begun and *tsɤ³¹ wa³²³* marks events that are already underway (see § 9.2.8).

(573) ŋa³³ nɛi³³ pʰa³²³piɛ³³ ta³⁵ **tsɤ³¹ wa³⁵**.
1SG 2SG side hold CONT FUT
我 你 旁边 抱
'(I) will hold it continuously beside you.'
我在你旁边抱着了。
(KL-Grandfather)

Aspect is not the only way to convey the temporal structure of events. The lexical meaning of verbs may also inherently provide this kind of information, a phenomenon known as Aktionsart (e.g. Comrie 1976: 41–51; Vendler 1957). For example, a verb like $ŋ^{24}$ 'to be red' conveys a state that has duration but no internal change, which is contrasted with a verb like $kɤ^{31}$ 'to run' which expresses dynamic activity and duration without an obvious end. Verbs like $sŋ^{33}$ 'to die', on other hand, describe events that include a final endpoint. In addition, some verbs describe actions that are extremely brief. For example, verbs like tsa^{24} 'to find' are considered to occur instantaneously, while others occur so briefly as to have almost no duration at all, such as $tsʔ^{55}$ 'to cough'. All of these event types exist in Khatso.

Table 9.2: Aspect combinations in Khatso

ITER tso^{24}	CONT $tsɤ^{31}$	PROG $tɤ^{33}$	PFV.IRR la^{31}	IPFV.IRR ta^{33}	EXP ko^{53}	PFV wa^{323}	CRS wa^{33}	FUT wa^{35}	Combinations
		•					•		$tɤ^{33}$ wa^{33}
•		•							tso^{24} $tɤ^{33}$
•		•					•		tso^{24} $tɤ^{33}$ wa^{33}
•						•			tso^{24} wa^{323}
•								•	tso^{24} wa^{35}
•			•						tso^{24} la^{31}
•				•					tso^{24} ta^{33}
•					•	•			tso^{24} ko^{53} wa^{323}
	•					•			$tsɤ^{31}$ wa^{323}
	•						•		$tsɤ^{31}$ wa^{33}
	•							•	$tsɤ^{31}$ wa^{35}
	•		•						$tsɤ^{31}$ la^{31}
			•			•			la^{31} wa^{323}
					•	•			ko^{53} wa^{323}

In addition, phrasal elements other than verbs may help define temporal structure. Adverbs and certain noun phrases often establish the time frame of an event (see § 9.3.1), as do topic phrases (see § 10.1) and phrases marked by the temporal particle $sɛi^{44}$ (see § 13.2.1). Resultative serial verb constructions describe the end result of an event, and some refer to the internal structure as well (see § 8.8.1.2). Moreover, pragmatic inference alone is often enough to convey the temporal nature of an event in discourse. For these reasons, aspect markers are not obligatory in every clause in Khatso.

9.2.1 Perfective

Perfective aspect indicates that an event is complete and viewed in its entirety, without any reference to its internal temporal structure. For example, in (574) the speaker is discussing learning to play the *qin*, a banjo-like stringed instrument. This is obviously a process that takes time, likely with many ups and downs, but here the learning process is described as a simple event and so marked with the perfective particle *wa^{323}*. Additional examples are shown in (575) and (576).

(574) so^{24} sʅ^{55} **wa^{323}** tɕo^{35}.
learn know PFV then
学 知 就
'Then (I) learned (it).'
就学会了。
(YLW-Learning)

(575) mɛi^{53} ni^{31} mɛi^{44} mi^{53} **wa^{323}**, lui^{35} ni^{31} mɛi^{44} lui^{35} **wa^{323}**.
be.hungry TOP very be.hungry PFV be.tired TOP very be.tired PFV
饿 很 饿 累 很 累
'As for hunger, (they) were very hungry. As for fatigue, (they) were very tired.'
饿也很饿了，累也很累了。
(PYX-Performing)

(576) ŋa^{33} ta^{35} xɛi^{35} tɛi^{31} ma^{24} tsau^{35} ta^{55} **wa^{323}**.
1SG still still one CL:GEN take put PFV
我 还 还 一 个 照 放
'I still took one (photo).'
我还照了一张放着了。
(GCS-Childhood)

When the verb is modified by the negative marker, it takes a different particle — the perfective irrealis marker *la^{31}*. *wa^{323}* may also follow *la^{31}* or it may be omitted altogether without any change in meaning; *la^{31}* alone carries a perfective meaning. Examples are shown in (577) and (578).

(577) tɕo^{35} ma^{31} to^{35} pa^{323} **la^{31}** tsɛi^{31}.
then NEG ford help PFV.IRR HSY
就 不 渡 帮
'(It's) said (they) didn't help (her) cross at all.'
听说就是没有帮渡。
(HPH-Weeds)

(578) ma³¹ tɕau³³ **la³¹** **wa³²³**.
　　　NEG　pay　PFV.IRR　PFV
　　　不　　交
　　　'(I) didn't pay.'
　　　没有交了。
　　　(KL-Tuition)

In emphatic phrases *wa³²³* is replaced by either *ja³²³* or *ŋɛi³³*. The former is only used with bounded events and is thus a reliable indicator of perfectivity. The latter is a more general marker of strong assertion and may be used with imperfective as well as perfective aspect. Context usually clarifies any ambiguity in discourse. Examples are shown in (579) and (580). For a comparison of these two emphatic particles see § 12.6.5.

(579) n̩a⁵³　kʰʏ⁴⁴　to³³　xɛi³⁵　tɛi³¹　to³⁵　tʏ³²³　**ja³²³**　sɛi³¹.
　　　place　in　also　still　one　hole　penetrate　PFV.EMP　still
　　　这里　里　也　还　一　洞　通　　　还
　　　'There was a hole drilled here too.'
　　　这里也还通了一个洞。
　　　(YLW-Qin)

(580) za³¹tsʅ³²³　sɛi⁴⁴　kɛi³³　ʏ³²³　ka³²³　i³³　**ŋɛi³³**.
　　　brother's.son　family　AGT　take　walk　go　ASRT
　　　侄子　　　家　　　　拿　走　去
　　　'(It) was (my) nephew's family (who) took (it) away.'
　　　是侄儿家拿走了。
　　　(WYF-Stools)

The particle *wa³²³* does not occur in questions. Instead, it is replaced by the interrogative particles *la³¹*, *ŋa³¹* or *wa³¹*. These particles are not equivalent, however. The perfective irrealis *la³¹* occurs in polar questions formed through verb reduplication, as shown in (581). The emphatic *ŋa³¹* only occurs in questions containing an interrogative pronoun, as in (582). *wa³¹* is used in both types of questions, as shown in (583) and (584). It is also used in questions involving the currently relevant state (see § 9.2.2) and inceptive aspect (see § 9.2.8). Question formation is described in more detail in § 12.4.

(581) o⁵³tsɿ³³   tɛi³³   ma⁴⁴   kʰɣ³³   tɕi³³   tɕi³³   **la³¹**?
under   this   CL:GEN   in   put   put   IRR.Q
下面   这   个   里   放   放
'(Did you) put (it) under this?'
有没有放在下面这个里？
(KL-Sewing)

(582) tɛi³¹   la³³   xa³³ni³³   ma⁴⁴   tso³²³   **ŋa³¹**?
one   CL:TMP how.many CL:GEN EXIST   CNT.Q
一   月   多少   个   有
'How much is there a month?'
一个月有多少？
(KL-Childhood)

(583) sɿ⁵⁵   sɿ⁵⁵   **wa³¹**?
know   know   PFV.Q
知道   知道
'Did (you) know (that)?'
知道了吗？
(YJR-Grandfather)

(584) xa³³ɳa⁵³   i³²³   **wa³¹**?
where   go   PFV.Q
哪里   去
'Where did (it) go?'
去哪里了？
(WYY-Sewing)

As Li and Thompson (1981: 185–186) point out, other elements may contribute to the perfective nature of a phrase. For example, quantified events and unique events both typically take perfective aspect in Khatso. A quantified event is one in which additional information in the phrase semantically limits the activity, whether temporally, spatially or conceptually. For example, in (585) the phrase $ɣ^{35}\ sa^{33}\ sɿ^{323}\ nɛ^{323}$ '20 or 30 years' delineates the time frame thereby highlighting its boundaries. In (586), it is the classifier $mɛi^{33}$ 'mouthful' which provides spatial limits to the action, again making it a bounded event.

(585) ɣ³⁵   sa³³   sɿ³²³   n̥ɛ³²³   tsʰɣ³¹na³¹ **wa³²³**   sɛi³¹   mɛi⁴⁴
     two   three ten   CL:TMP   stop   PFV   also   DSC.EMP
     二   三   十   年   停   还
     '(I) also stopped (sewing) for 20 or 30 years'
     又停止了二三十年了
     (WYY-Sewing)

(586) i³²³tɕa⁵³   mɛi³³   to³²³   ta³⁵   **wa³²³**.
     water   CL:MSR drink   hold   PFV
     水   口   喝   上
     '(They) drank a mouthful of water.'
     喝上一口水了。
     (HPH-Horse Dug Well)

Events in which P has specific reference may also be interpreted as bounded in Khatso. For example, in (587) a particular sequin has fallen off a garment, a unique event in time that may only occur once. Similarly, in (588) giving birth to a particular child also occurs only once. This kind of construction contrasts with phrases such as i²⁴tɕʰɛ³²³ pɣ⁵³, literally 'qin play', in which the noun is non-specific and the event therefore refers to the generic notion of playing the instrument rather than a singular instance of it.

(587) a³³   ma⁴⁴   ti³⁵kua³³piɛ³⁵   to³³   ka³²³   tsʰi³³   **wa³²³**.
     that CL:GEN sequin   also   walk   fall   PFV
     那   个   电光片   也   走   掉
     'That sequin fell off too.'
     那个电光片也掉了。
     (WYY-Sewing)

(588) tɕo³⁵   tɛi³¹   jo³⁵   tso³²³   **wa³²³**   tsɛi³¹   na³¹ni²⁴za³¹.
     then   one   CL:HUM EXIST   PFV   HSY   child
     就   一   位   有   孩子
     'Then (they say that they) had one, (a) child.'
     就有一个小孩子了。
     (ZRF-Grandfather)

The perfective marker co-occurs with the continuous marker *tsɣ³¹* to indicate that an action is already underway. This construction is discussed in the section on inceptive aspect below (see § 9.2.8). The perfective is also used in superlative constructions involving stative verbs (see § 12.5.5.3).

9.2.2 Currently Relevant State

The particle *wa³³* indicates that a situation has undergone a change and that new conditions prevail — creating what is often termed a currently relevant state (Li and Thompson 1981: 240). For example, after some trimming, a piece of fabric becomes pointed in (589), a newly created state. And in (590), farmers were able to cut down a pernicious weed after many hundreds of years of losing the fight — a new state of affairs. Note that the currently relevant state may exist in any time frame. In (589) it applies to the moment the phrase was spoken, while in (590) it pertains to a moment in the mythical past of a folk story. Negative phrases, of course, indicate that an event or situation no longer exists, which may itself be considered a new state of affairs. For example, the phrase in (591) describes no longer knowing songs to sing, while (592) observes that younger Khatso women no longer wear traditional clothing.

(589) nɣ̥³⁵   pa²⁴   ni³¹   tɛi³¹   tʰɣ⁵⁵   tsi⁵³   tɕʰɛ²⁴   tɕo³⁵   tʰa⁵⁵
     pinch   flat   TOP   one   CL:TMP   cut.with.scissors   open.IMP then   be.sharp
     捏   扁   一   下   剪   开   就   尖

     i³⁵   wa³³.
     go.FOC CRS
     去

     'Holding it flat, cut (it) a bit (and it) becomes pointed.'
     捏扁呢，剪一下就尖了。
     (WYY-Sewing)

(590) tsɿ³¹   pɣ³²³   n̥ɛ³²³   tsɿ³¹   kɯ²⁴   tsʰau³²³tɛi³⁵   kɣ³³   ma³¹   tsuɛi²⁴
     several   hundred   CL:TMP   several   CL:GEN   dynasty   do   NEG   sever
     几   百   年   几   个   朝代   弄   不   绝

     tɕa⁵³   tɕi⁵⁵   tɛi³³tɕʰa⁵⁵kʰɣ³³   kɣ³³   tsuɛi²⁴   wa³³.
     toothgrass   CL:TYPE   this.time   do   sever   CRS
     牙齿草   种   这时候   弄   绝

     'Several hundred years, several dynasties, the toothgrass that (they) couldn't cut, now (they were able to) cut (it).'
     几百年几个朝代弄不绝牙齿草，现在弄绝了。
     (HPH-Weeds)

(591) tɛi³¹ tsɣ̥²⁴   to³³   ma³¹   sɿ⁵⁵   wa³³   mɛi⁴⁴,   tɛi³³tɕʰa⁵⁵kʰɣ³³   ni⁵³.
     everything   also   NEG   know   CRS   DSC.EMP   this.time   TOP.EPIS.EMP
     什么   也   不   知道   这时候

     '(I) don't know (any), now.'
     现在什么也不知道了。
     (YJF-Dance Parties)

(592) kʰa⁵⁵tso³¹ma³³ tʰo³³ tɕi⁵⁵ ma³¹ vi⁵³ **wa³³** sɛi⁴⁴ tɛi³³ tsɛi³⁵.
Khatso.F clothes CL:TYPE NEG wear CRS people this CL:TMP
喀卓女人 衣服 种 不 穿 人家 这 段
'People don't wear (traditional) Khatso women's clothes anymore now.'
现在呢都不穿喀卓服装了。
(WYY-Sewing)

There are several other contexts in which *wa³³* is employed. It is often found in imperative phrases — both positive and negative — since such directives are likely to bring about a new state of affairs. Examples are shown in (593) as well as in (589) above.

(593) kɣ³³ ŋa³²³ ma³¹ ta²⁴ ni³¹, tɤ⁴⁴ tɕo³⁵ ta³¹ kɣ³³ **wa³³**.
do obtain NEG able TOP FILL then PROH do CRS
做 得到 不 能 就 别 做
'If (you) can't do (it), um, then don't do (it).'
不能做呢，那就别做了。
(KL-Sewing)

The *wa³³* marker also plays a role in a number of discourse interjections such as *no³³ wa³³* 'okay', *ta³²³ wa³³* 'that's fine' and *na²⁴ wa³³* 'good'. These interjections signal approval, agreement or acceptance — presumably a new state of affairs in a discussion. Examples from discourse are shown in (594) and (595).

(594) no³³ **wa³³**. no³³ **wa³³**. ŋa⁴⁴ ni³³ v̩³²³ tsɤ³¹ wa³⁵.
be.good CRS be.good CRS 1SG way hold CONT FUT
好 好 我 这么 拿
'Okay, okay. I'll hold (it) like that.'
好的，好的。我来拿着。
(ZRF-Grandfather)

(595) tɛi³³ni⁴⁴ ni³¹ ta³²³ **wa³³** mɛi⁴⁴.
this.way TOP be.acceptable CRS DSC.EMP
这样 行
'Like this, (it) is fine.'
这样呢，那就好了。
(WYY-Sewing)

Like the perfective marker *wa³²³*, in questions *wa³³* is replaced by either *wa³¹*, *la³¹* or *ŋa³¹*. Both *wa³¹* and *la³¹* occur in polar questions formed by verb reduplication, as shown in (596) and (597). *wa³¹* may also occur in questions containing interrogative pronouns, but typically *ŋa³¹* is used instead, as in (598). Question formation is explained in § 12.4.

(596) mi³³   mi³³   **wa³¹?**
      be.ripe be.ripe PFV.Q
      成熟   成熟
      'Are (they) ripe?'
      熟了吗?
      (KL-Elicitation)

(597) mi³³   mi³³   **la³¹?**
      be.ripe be.ripe IRR.Q
      成熟   成熟
      'Are (they) ripe?'
      熟了没有?
      (KL-Elicitation)

(598) xa³³ni³³ mi³³   **ŋa³¹?**
      how   be.ripe CNT.Q
      怎么   成熟
      'How did (they) ripen?'
      怎么熟了?
      (KL-Elicitation)

Because *wa³³* indicates that a change is complete, pragmatically it shares similarities with the perfective aspect. Indeed, in some phrases the two are interchangeable without any clear difference in meaning. For example, the verb in (599) carries the perfective marker, yet *wa³³* is equally acceptable here, as shown in (600). Comparing the two, we see that semantically the difference is small; the same is true of the English translation. Similarly, learning to play an instrument at dances is presented as a bounded event in (601), yet *wa³³* is likewise grammatical in the phrase, as in (602). In both of these cases, the events described bring about results that continue on after the event is complete — in other words, they are currently relevant states. But these speakers apparently chose to focus on the completeness of the events rather than the continuing nature of the results. This highlights the freedom speakers have to manipulate aspect to shape narratives as well the flexible nature of the aspectual system itself.

(599) tɕi³¹   ta²⁴   ni³³   lio³²³tsʰua³²³   tɤ⁴⁴   tɕi³³tɕʰa⁵⁵kʰv̩³³   tsʰŋ̍³³   **wa³²³**.
      one   CL:ITEM   ADV   spread   CLNK   this.time   arrive   PFV
      一   直   流传   这时候   到
      '(It) was handed down to the present.'
      一直流传到现在了。
      (HPH-Horse Dug Well)

(600) tɕi³¹   ta²⁴   ni³³   lio³²³tsʰua³²³   tɤ⁴⁴   tɕi³³tɕʰa⁵⁵kʰv̩³³   tsʰŋ̍³³   **wa³³**.
      one   CL:ITEM   ADV   spread   CLNK   this.time   arrive   CRS
      一   直   流传   这时候   到
      '(It) is now handed down to the present.'
      一直流传到现在了。
      (KL-Elicitation)

(601) na⁵³tɕʰɛ⁵⁵   ni³¹   tɕo³⁵   a³³tɕʰa⁵⁵kʰv̩³³   so²⁴   sŋ̍⁵⁵   **wa³²³**.
      evening.dance   TOP   then   that.time   learn   know   PFV
      跳乐   就   那时候   学   知道
      'At dances, (that's) when (I) learned.'
      跳乐呢，那个时候就学会了。
      (YLW-Learning)

(602) na⁵³tɕʰɛ⁵⁵   ni³¹   tɕo³⁵   a³³tɕʰa⁵⁵kʰv̩³³   so²⁴   sŋ̍⁵⁵   **wa³³**.
      evening.dance   TOP   then   that.time   learn   know   CRS
      跳乐   就   那时候   学   知道
      'At dances, (that's) when (I) learned.'
      跳乐呢，那个时候就学会了。
      (KL-Elicitation)

Given its function of pointing to a new and ongoing state, the particle *wa³³* often co-occurs with the imperfective markers, such as the continuous *tsɤ³¹*, the iterative *tso²⁴* and the progressive *tɤ³³*. With the latter, *wa³³* also creates an inceptive meaning (see § 9.2.8).

9.2.3 Progressive

Progressive aspect indicates that an event is underway, and the start and end points are vague. In Khatso, progressive aspect is conveyed by the particle *tɤ³³*. There seems to be a dispreference for ending a phrase with this marker, so another particle is often appended. Typically, this is an emphatic marker, such as *ja³³* or *ŋɛi³³*, as shown in (603) and (604). Question markers or, in narratives the hearsay particle *tsɛi³¹*, may also attach to the aspect marker, as in (605). Note that, depending on context, the progressive may also imply habitual action, as illustrated in (604).

(603) kʰa⁵⁵tso³¹tɕʰi³¹   tsʰo³¹ **tɤ³³ ja³³**.
Khatso.language   sing   PROG IPFV.EMP
喀卓语   唱
'(They) were singing (in the) Khatso language.'
是用喀卓语唱的
(PYX-Performing)

(604) pʰa³¹xɛi³³kʰo³¹   mɛi⁴⁴   ɣ²⁴   **tɤ³³**   **ŋɛi³³**.
crab.shell   CL:GEN call   PROG   ASRT
螃海壳   个   叫
'(They) call (it) a crab shell.' literally '(They) are calling (it) a crab shell.'
是叫螃海壳。
(YLW-Qin)

(605) xa³³ni³³   xa³³ni³³   tɕi³³   **tɤ³³**   ŋa³¹?
how   how   do   PROG   CNT.Q
怎么   怎么   弄
'How do (you) work it?'
怎么弄的？
(KL-Qin)

There is another progressive construction, *ti³³ ja³³*, which is shown in (606). In some contexts, such as answering questions, it appears to be more immediate and emphatic than *tɤ³³ ja³³*, though speakers generally feel that *tɤ³³ ja³³*, *ti³³ ja³³*, *tɤ³³ ŋɛi³³* and *ti³³ ŋɛi³³* are all essentially equivalent. However, the morpheme *ti³³* does not occur outside of this particular construction and occurs much less frequently than *tɤ³³*. It does take part, though, in an idiomatic construction with *pa⁵³* 'to speak, set a betrothal' which means 'to plan', as shown in (607).

(606) ja⁵³   o³⁵sɛi⁴⁴   tɕo³⁵   tɛi³³n̩a⁵³   li⁴⁴   kɛi³³   ta⁵³   li³³   **ti³³ ja³³**.
later sound   then   here   in   from   rise   come   PROG
然后   韵   就   这里   里   从   上   来
'Then the sound is coming up from here.'
那么，声韵就是从这里出来的。
(YLW-Qin)

(607) xɛi³⁵   i²⁴tɕʰɛ³²³   pɤ⁵³   la²⁴   to³³   kɤ³³   tso²⁴   i³³   pa⁵³   **ti³³ ja³³**   sɛi³¹.
       still   qin   play   REL   also   do   ITER   go   speak   PROG   still
       还   琴   弹   也   做   去   说
       '(I) still plan to go (record) a *qin* player.'
       还打算要去弄弹琴的。
       (KL-Sewing)

Generally, the progressive aspect would be considered redundant with stative verbs since they already describe an unchanging property or state. However, this kind of collocation is possible with a few stative verbs in Khatso. In many cases, it changes the verb from a state to a process. For example, in (608) the stative verb *pʰi³²³* 'to be slow' carries the meaning of 'becoming slow'. However, in (609), which may answer the question 'are you hungry?', the more emphatic progressive marker *ti³³ ja³³* merely serves to emphasize the immediate state of hunger.

(608) pʰi³²³   **tɤ³³**   **ja³³**.
       be.slow   PROG   IPFV.EMP
       慢
       '(She) is slowing down.'
       正在慢了。
       (KL-Elicitation)

(609) mi⁵³   **ti³³ ja³³**!
       be.hungry   PROG
       饿
       '(I) am hungry!'
       俄的!
       (KL-Elicitation)

Negation restricts the use of the progressive marker. A negated verb may be followed by *tɤ³³* and the currently relevant state marker *wa³³* to indicate an event is no longer happening, as shown in (610). In this construction, the cessation of the event is considered currently relevant. In contrast, when an event simply does not occur and thus has no internal temporal structure, *tɤ³³* is replaced by the imperfective irrealis marker *ta³³* (see § 9.2.7), as shown in (611).

(610) ma³¹   m̩³³   **tɤ³³**   **wa³³**.
       NEG   do   PROG   CRS
       不   干
       '(He) doesn't work anymore.'
       不干了。
       (YAY-Eraser)

(611) a³³   tsɛi³⁵   i³³   kɛi⁴⁴   to³³   ma³¹   ma⁵⁵   tɤ³³.
      that   CL:TMP   3SG   AGT   also   NEG   teach   IPFV.IRR
      那   段   他   也   不   教
      'At that time, he didn't teach (me) either.'
      那时候他也没教。
      (YLW-Learning)

There are no restrictions on the use of the progressive marker in questions. In these constructions, a question marker replaces the emphatic marker that usually follows *tɤ³³*. In reduplicative polar questions either the verb or *tɤ³³* may be doubled, as shown in (612), although in discourse it is usually the verb that is repeated. In questions containing interrogative pronouns either of the question markers, *wa³¹* or *ŋa³¹*, may follow *tɤ³³*, as in (613) and (614). *la³¹*, which is associated with a perfective reading in reduplicative constructions, cannot co-occur with the progressive marker here.

(612) ka³²³ ka³²³ **tɤ³³** **wa³¹?**   ka³²³ **tɤ³³** **tɤ³³** **wa³¹?**
      walk   walk   PROG   PFV.Q   walk   PROG   PROG   PFV.Q
      走   走   走
      'Are you walking?'   'Are you walking?'
      有没有开始走路了？   正在走路吗？
      (KL-Elicitation)

(613) i²⁴la³¹   sɿ³²³xɯ³⁵ pɤ³²³   tsa³²³   tɕi⁵⁵   xa³³ni³³   m̥³³   tsa³¹   **tɤ³³**   **ŋa³¹?**
      before   time   POSS   rice   CL:TYPE   how   make   eat   PROG   CNT.Q
      以前   时候   饭   种   怎么   做   吃
      'Before, how were you cooking food to eat?'
      以前的饭是怎么做的？
      (KL-Childhood)

(614) i²⁴la³¹   sɿ³²³xɯ³⁵ pɤ³²³   tsa³²³   tɕi⁵⁵   xa³³ni³³   m̥³³   tsa³¹   **tɤ³³**   **wa³¹?**
      before   time   POSS   rice   CL:TYPE   how   make   eat   PROG   PFV.Q
      以前   时候   饭   种   怎么   做   吃
      'Before, how were you cooking food to eat?'
      以前的饭是怎么做的？
      (KL-Elicitation)

Because the progressive marker *tɤ³³* provides an imperfective view of an event, it cannot co-occur with the perfective marker *wa³²³* or the future marker *wa³⁵*. When combined with *wa³³*, the marker of currently relevant states, it creates an inceptive meaning (see § 9.2.8). *tɤ³³* may also co-occur with the iterative aspect marker *tso²⁴*, but not with the continuous marker *tsɤ³¹*. In addition, *tɤ³³* is the only aspect marker that may change tone to focus a clause (see § 3.2.5).

9.2.4 Continuous

Continuous aspect in Khatso is marked by *tsɤ³¹*, which is sometimes also pronounced *tsʅ³¹*. Like Putonghua (Li and Thompson 1981: 217), Khatso differentiates continuous and progressive aspect. The latter indicates that an event is in progress, and it may be the sole occurrence of that activity or point to a relatively brief event. Continuous aspect, by contrast, indicates that an event is not only underway but occurring in an uninterrupted fashion over a potentially longer period of time. Examples are shown in (615) and (616); in the latter the aspect marker changes tone due to the following topic marker (see § 3.2.4.1). Depending on context, phrases with continuous aspect may also convey a habitual sense, as the example in (615) demonstrates.

(615) tɛi³¹ti⁵³ piɛ³³ pa³³ **tsɤ³¹** sa⁵⁵ ŋɛi³³.
a.little weave hold CONT be.difficult ASRT
一点 编 把 难
'Holding it to weave is always a little difficult.'
把着来编有一点难。
(WYF-Stools)

(616) lau³¹sʅ³³ jo³⁵ kɛi³³ ma⁵⁵ **tsʅ²⁴** ni³¹,
teacher CL:HUM AGT teach CONT TOP
老师 位 教
'The teacher was always teaching (us),'
老师教着呢,

pʰi⁴⁴i⁴⁴ tsɤ²⁴ xa²⁴tsʅ²⁴ ni³¹ tsɤ²⁴ li³²³.
pinyin read Chinese.characters TOP read know.how
拼音 读 汉字 读 会
'(So) reading pinyin (and writing) Chinese characters, (I) know how (to do both).'
读拼音写汉字呢, 会写。
(YAY-Erasers)

Like the progressive and iterative markers, *tsɤ³¹* rarely occurs at the end of a phrase. It is often followed by another aspect marker or an emphatic particle, though these may be replaced by a grammatical particle such as the topic marker *ni³¹* or the background marker *ni³²³*. The examples above illustrate the pattern.

Continuous aspect also has restricted use in negated clauses. *tsɤ³¹* may co-occur with the perfective irrealis marker *la³¹*, as shown in (617), to indicate that an action has not yet begun. But otherwise, it is replaced by the imperfective irrealis marker *ta³³* to indicate that an event is not occurring, as shown in (618).

(617) tsa³²³ ma³¹ tsa³¹ **tsɤ³¹ la³¹**.
rice NEG eat CONT PFV.IRR
饭   不   吃
'(I) haven't eaten.'
还没有吃着饭。
(KL-Elicitation)

(618) tsa³²³ ma³¹ tsa³¹ **ta³³**.
rice NEG eat IPFV.IRR
饭   不   吃
'(I) am not eating.'
不吃饭。
(KL-Elicitation)

Unlike in negative constructions, there are no restrictions for the use of the continuous marker in questions. In polar questions it is *tsɤ³¹* that is reduplicated rather than the verb, as shown in (619). The imperfective irrealis marker *ta³³* is often included, but seems to be optional in many cases. In questions containing interrogative pronouns, either of the question markers *wa³¹* or *ŋa³¹* may be used, as in (620) and (621).

(619) nɛi³³ vɤ⁵³ **tsɤ³¹ tsɤ³¹** ta³³?
2SG   write CONT CONT IPFV.IRR
你   写
'Are you writing?'
你有没有在写着？
(KL-Elicitation)

(620) xa³³ma⁴⁴ tsa³¹ **tsɤ³¹ wa³¹**?
what   eat CONT PFV.Q
什么   吃
'What are (you) eating?'
在吃什么？
(KL-Elicitation)

(621) xa³³ma⁴⁴ tsa³¹ **tsɤ³¹ ŋa³¹**?
what   eat CONT CNT.Q
什么   吃
'What are (you) eating?'
在吃什么？
(KL-Elicitation)

The continuous marker co-occurs with the perfective wa^{323} to indicate that an event is already underway, and is one way to convey inceptive aspect (see § 9.2.8). It may also change tone to convey an imperative sense (see § 3.2.4.2).

9.2.5 Iterative

The aspect marker tso^{24} marks iterative action. It is used for events that occur more than once over a span of time, as shown in (622). These events need not be regular; they may occur in a haphazard fashion. However, often the implication is that the event is frequent and repeated, and thus tso^{24} may also be interpreted as conveying habitual action, as in (623).

(622) pɤ⁵³   sɿ⁵⁵   tɕo³⁵   na⁵³pɤ³¹   **tso²⁴**   i³³   wa³³.
play   know   then   sing.dance   ITER   go   CRS
弹   知道   就   跳乐   去
'(After) I knew how to play, I went dancing often.'
会弹就去跳乐去了。
(YLW-Learning)

(623) pɤ⁵³   **tso²⁴**   **tso²⁴**   ta³³   sa³¹?
play   ITER   ITER   IPFV.IRR   still.Q
弹   还
'Does (he) still play regularly?'
还有没有在弹？
(KL-Erasers)

In discourse, the use of tso^{24} may overlap with that of the continuous marker $tsɤ^{31}$. In prototypical use, the two can be differentiated by timing. Continuous aspect marks events that occur unceasingly while iterative aspect marks discrete events that occur more than once but perhaps separated by periods of inactivity. The example in (624) illustrates the difference — carrying a basket of eels on one's back is contrasted with selling the eels individually. The basket in question has leather straps that allow it to be shouldered continuously, while the transactions occur repeatedly yet randomly within the same time period. However, in some cases one marker may be replaced by the other without an appreciable change in meaning. For example, the phrase in (625) may be said with either continuous or iterative aspect. The basic sense of going many times to a work site is not altered much whether the individuals go 'continuously' (continuous aspect) or 'repeatedly' (iterative aspect).

(624) "xa³³ni³⁵   ŋa³¹tsʅ³²³   tɕi⁵⁵   ni³¹   nɛi³³   kɛi³   pỵ³¹   tsʅ³¹   tɤ⁴⁴
       how.FOC   eel   CL:TYPE   TOP   2SG   AGT   carry.on.back   CONT   CLNK
       怎么   鳝鱼   种   你   背
       ŋ³¹   **tso²⁴**   ŋa³²³ta³²³?"
       sell   ITER   be.able
       卖   可以
       ' "How can you carry eels on (your) back and sell (them)?" '
       "是鳝鱼你怎么可以背着卖呢？"
       (PYX-Dragon Pools)

(625) a³³   ko⁵⁵   li⁴⁴   n̠o³¹   m̠³³   **tso²⁴**   i⁴⁴   ni³²³
       that   CL:PL   to   thing   do   CONT   go   BKGD
       那   些   里   事   做   去
       'because (they) were going to those (places) to work'
       去那些地方干活呢
       (YJR-Grandfather)

Like the progressive and continuous markers, *tso²⁴* rarely occurs at the end of a phrase. It is often followed by another aspect marker or an emphatic particle, though these may be replaced by other grammatical particles when appropriate. Examples are shown in (626) and (627).

(626) ta³⁵si³³   tʰiau³⁵   **tso²⁴**   tɤ³³   ŋ³³   sa⁴⁴?
       always   dance   ITER   PROG   COP   CRTN.Q
       随时   跳   是
       '(They) were always dancing, is (that it)?'
       随时跳着的，是吗？
       (KY-Grandfather)

(627) ja⁵³ni³²³   tsʰo³³   ŋ³¹   jo³⁵   kɤ³³   **tso²⁴**   **ja³³**   po⁵³
       then   person   two   CL:HUM   make   ITER   IPFV.EMP   EPIS.EMP
       那么   人   二   位   做
       'So, (it) takes two people to make (them), (you know).'
       那么，有两个人在做着的。
       (WYF-Stools)

Unlike the way the progressive and continuous aspects pattern, there is no restriction on the iterative in negative clauses. An irrealis marker is required, but *tso²⁴* need not be omitted, as (628) illustrates. Together, their presence often implies a negative habitual sense, as shown in (629).

(628) ŋa³³   tsa³²³ **ma³¹** tsa³¹ **tso²⁴** **la³¹**   sɛi³¹.
     1SG   rice   NEG   eat   ITER   PFV.IRR   still
     我   饭   不   吃   还
     'I haven't eaten yet.'
     我还没有吃饭呢。
     (KL-Elicitation)

(629) **ma³¹** to³³   **tso²⁴** **ta³³**   tɛi³¹ti⁵³   to³³.
      NEG   compare   ITER   IPFV.IRR   a.little   also
      不   比较   一点   也
      '(I) usually don't compare (them), even a little.'
      平常不比较的。
      (WYY-Sewing)

The imperfective irrealis *ta³³* is also required in polar questions featuring *tso²⁴*. In this construction, *tso²⁴* is repeated instead of the verb or *ta³³*, as demonstrated by the example in (630). Questions containing interrogative pronouns, however, feature question markers *wa³¹* or *ŋa³¹* instead of *ta³³*, as in (631). Note that the phrase *n̠o³¹ m̠³³*, literally 'thing do', means 'to work' — an interpretation bolstered by the notion of regular activity conveyed by iterative aspect. Question formation is explained in greater detail in § 12.4.

(630) pɤ⁵³   **tso²⁴** **tso²⁴** **ta³³**   sa³¹?
      play   ITER   ITER   IPFV.IRR   still.Q
      弹   还
      'Does (he) still play regularly?'
      还有没有在弹？
      (KL-Erasers)

(631) xa³³ni³³   kʰo⁵³   za³¹   lo⁵³   ni³²³   n̠o³¹   ma³¹   m̠³³   **tso²⁴**   ŋa³¹?
      how.many   CL:TMP   DIM   reach   BKGD   thing   NEG   do   ITER   CNT.Q
      多少   年   到   事   不   做
      'At what age did (you) stop working?', literally 'Reaching what age are (you) not working?'
      到了多少岁没有干活了？
      (KL-Childhood)

Unlike the continuous marker, *tso²⁴* may freely co-occur with the progressive marker *tɤ³³* as well as the emphatic progressive construction *ti³³ ja³³*.

9.2.6 Perfective Irrealis

The particle la^{31} is a perfective irrealis marker that only appears in negative statements or polar questions that describe temporally bounded events.[1] In negative statements, it replaces the perfective marker, as shown in (632). Given its meaning, it often co-occurs with the adverb $sɛi^{31}$ 'still, again', as in (633), one of the few adverbs to occur phrase-finally.

(632) tɛi³¹   jo³⁵   kɛi⁴⁴   **ma³¹**   ma⁵⁵   **la³¹**.
     one   CL:HUM   AGT   NEG   teach   PFV.IRR
     一   位   不   教
     'not one person taught (me)'
     也没有谁人教。
     (WYY-Sewing)

(633) i³³   sɛi⁴⁴   ȵɛ³²³   jo³⁵   **ma³¹** tsʰ₁³³   **la³¹**   sɛi³¹.
     3SG   family younger.brother CL:HUM NEG   take.wife PFV.IRR   still
     他   家   弟弟   位   不   娶   还
     'His younger brother hasn't taken a wife yet.'
     他的弟弟还没娶亲。
     (YJR-Grandfather)

This particle is undoubtedly related to the basic question marker la^{31}, which is used to create questions from declarative statements (see § 12.4.7.4). Their functions are distinct, however. The perfective irrealis marker only occurs in reduplicative polar questions, as in (634), and in negative statements such as those above. In both it provides a clear perfective sense, and these constructions are the only way to refer to single unrealized events in the past. In questions without reduplication, however, the particle marks events occurring currently or in the future, but not the past. It may also indicate a moderate degree of certainty about the response, as in (635), which is not conveyed by the perfective constructions. As such, it is only one of several ways to frame questions.

---

[1] The term *irrealis* is often seen as something of a vague catchall, obscuring more than it explains (e.g. Bybee 1998). It is retained here because it best describes the function shared by la^{31} and ta^{33} (described in the next section), even though their use is rather narrow and not part of a larger reality system (cf. Michael 2014). Indeed, other constructions that deal with unrealized events — such as conditional, counterfactual and future events — do not require them. Irrealis coding for negative and interrogative constructions is not uncommon cross-linguistically (Cristofaro 2012).

(634) o⁵³tsɿ³³   tɛi³³   ma⁴⁴   kʰy̩³³   tɕi³³   tɕi³³   **la³¹**?
under   this   CL:GEN   in   put   put   IRR.Q
下面   这   个   里   放   放
'(Did you) put (it) under this?'
有没有放在下面这个里？
(KL-Sewing)

(635) kʰa⁵⁵tso³¹tɕʰi³¹   n̩a³¹   **la³¹**?
Khatso.language   speak   IRR.Q
喀卓语   说
'Do (you) speak Khatso?'
讲喀卓语吗？
(KL-Competition)

9.2.7 Imperfective Irrealis

The imperfective irrealis marker *ta³³* marks unrealized events without clear temporal boundaries in negative statements or polar questions. In negative statements, it replaces the progressive marker *tɤ³³* and the continuous marker *tsɤ³¹*, but may co-occur with the iterative *tso²⁴*. For comparison, elicited examples are provided in (636) and (637). An example with *tso²⁴* from discourse is shown in (638). Note that like the progressive, continuous and iterative markers, *ta³³* may convey a sense of habitual action.

(636) ŋa³³   vɤ⁵³   tɤ³³   ŋɛi³³   ŋa³³   **ma³¹**   vɤ⁵³   **ta³³**
1SG   write   PROG   ASRT   1SG   NEG   write   IPFV.IRR
我   写   我   不   写
'I'm writing'   'I'm not writing'
我在写   我没有在写
(KL-Elicitation)

(637) ŋa³³   vɤ⁵³   tsɤ³¹   ŋɛi³³   ŋa³³   **ma³¹**   vɤ⁵³   **ta³³**
1SG   write   CONT   ASRT   1SG   NEG   write   IPFV.IRR
我   写   我   不   写
'I'm writing (continuously)'   'I'm not writing (continuously)'
我在写着   我没有在写
(KL-Elicitation)

(638) **ma³¹** to³³ **tso²⁴ ta³³** tɛi³¹ti⁵³ to³³.
NEG compare ITER IPFV.IRR a.little also
不 比较 一点 也
'(I) usually don't compare (them), even a little.'
平常不比较的。
(WYY-Sewing)

In reduplicative polar questions, *ta³³* either replaces or co-occurs with the other imperfective markers. Examples are shown in (639) and (640) respectively. Note that if another aspect marker occurs in the phrase, it may be reduplicated instead of the verb — compare (640) and (641) — but *ta³³* is never reduplicated.

(639) pɤ⁵³ pɤ⁵³ **ta³³** sa³¹ tɛi³³tɕʰa⁵⁵kʰɤ³³?
play play IPFV.IRR still.Q this.time
弹 弹 还 这时候
'Does (he) still play these days?'
现在还在弹吗?
(KL-Erasers)

(640) tsa³²³ m̩³³ m̩³³ **tso²⁴ ta³³**?
rice make make ITER IPFV.IRR
饭 做 做
'Do (you) usually cook?'
平常做不做饭?
(KL-Elicitation)

(641) tsa³²³ m̩³³ **tso²⁴ tso²⁴ ta³³**?
rice make ITER ITER IPFV.IRR
饭 做
'Do (you) usually cook?'
平常做不做饭?
(KL-Elicitation)

Unlike its perfective counterpart *la³¹*, which can only describe events in the past, *ta³³* can be used with ongoing events that occur in any timeframe. For example, in (642) the speaker asks an elderly man about the smoking habits of his deceased father and grandfather, events that can only have happened in the past. The identical question can also be posed to a young interlocutor whose relatives are alive, in which case the smoking would occur now and presumably into the future.

(642) nɛi³³ sɛi⁴⁴ lau³³ti³³ tsʰɤ³³ nɛi³³ sɛi⁴⁴ pa³¹ tsʰɤ³³ a³³ ko⁵⁵,
2SG family grandfather PL 2SG family father PL that CL:PL
你 家 老爹 们 你 家 爸 们 那 些
'Your grandfather and those, your father and those, those (people),'
你爷爷你爸爸他们那些,

jɛ³³ to³²³ to³²³ **ta³³?**
tobacco smoke smoke IPFV.IRR
烟 抽 抽
'Did (they) smoke?'
抽不抽烟?
(KL-Doctor)

9.2.8 Inceptive

There is no single particle in Khatso that marks inceptive aspect in all cases. However, several of the other aspect markers may combine to convey that a particular state or event has begun or is underway. For example, the progressive *tɤ³³* followed by the currently relevant state marker *wa³³* indicates that an event has already begun, as shown in (643). The combination of the continuous marker *tsɤ³¹* with the perfective marker *wa³²³* indicates that an event is already in progress, as in (644). In addition, when *tɤ³³ wa³³* accompanies a resultative construction formed with *tɕʰɛ⁵³* 'to finish', as in (645), it indicates that the final portion of an event has begun or, in other words, that the event will soon be complete. Note that the habitual sense expressed in the latter two examples comes from pragmatic inference, rather than the aspectual constructions themselves.

(643) i³²³tɕa⁵³ mau³⁵ to⁵³ li³³ **tɤ³³ wa³³**.
water gush exit come INCP
水 冒 出 来
'Water began to gush out.'
水冒出来了。
(HPH-Horse Dug Well)

(644) za³¹m̩³¹za³¹ a³³ tsɛi³⁵ kɛi³³ kɤ̣³³ **tsɤ³¹ wa³²³** po⁵³.
girl that CL:TMP from do INCP EPIS.EMP
女孩 那 段 从 做
'(I) have been doing (it) since (I) was a girl, (didn't you know?)'
从姑娘那个时候就开始做着了。
(WYY-Sewing)

(645) ma³¹ kv̩³³ wa³³ kv̩³³ **tɕʰɛ⁵³ tɤ³³ wa³³**.
　　　 NEG   do   CRS   do   finish INCP
　　　 不   做   做   完
　　　 '(I) won't be doing (it) any longer, (I) am almost finished.'
　　　 不做了快做完了
　　　 (WYY-Sewing)

The actual duration implied by these constructions is vague, and in many cases *tɤ³³ wa³³* and *tsɤ³¹ wa³²³* are interchangeable in discourse. However, as an approximate rule of thumb *tɤ³³ wa³³* may be understood to refer to the beginning portion of an event, *tsɤ³¹ wa³²³* the middle portion and *tɕʰɛ⁵³ tɤ³³ wa³³* the final portion.

9.2.9 Future

There are a number of ways to mark a future event in Khatso. The most basic method employs the particle *wa³⁵*, which may refer both to immediate action and events in the distant future. For example, the phrase in (646) is uttered as a digital recorder is moved nearer the narrator of a story. By contrast, the phrase in (647) discusses helping people in future generations. Moreover, the use of *wa³⁵* in (646), where it is said simultaneously with the action expressed, demonstrates that it is not an irrealis marker. In fact, *wa³⁵* is typically not used in negative statements, underscoring its incompatibility with the irrealis aspect.

(646) ŋa³³　nɛi³³　pʰa³²³piɛ³³　ta³⁵　tsɤ³¹　**wa³⁵**.
　　　 1SG   2SG   side   hold   CONT   FUT
　　　 我   你   旁边   抱
　　　 'I'll hold (it) beside you.'
　　　 我在你旁边抱着了。
　　　 (ZRF-Grandfather)

(647) ŋa³³tsʰɤ³¹　pv̩³²³　ɤ⁵⁵za³¹　ɤ⁵⁵za³¹　ɤ⁵⁵za³¹　ɤ⁵⁵za³¹　ɤ⁵⁵ma³³
　　　 3PL   POSS   grandson grandson grandson grandson granddaughter
　　　 我们   孙子   孙子   孙子   孙子   孙女
　　　 ko⁵⁵　ŋa³³tsʰɤ³¹　ŋ²⁴ka³³　 kɯ³¹　 **wa³⁵** po⁵³.
　　　 CL:PL 3PL   see   INDR.CAUS FUT   EPIS.EMP
　　　 些   我们   看
　　　 'Our grandsons (and) granddaughters, we'll show (them our work, don't you see?)'
　　　 给我们的子子孙孙们看嘛。
　　　 (KL-Sewing)

The auxiliary verb *li³²³* 'to know how' may also serve as a future marker, though this seems to be a secondary use. The future sense is most apparent in phrases where the auxiliary meaning is incompatible, such as those in which A/S is an inanimate object. For example, (648) refers to a *qin*, a banjo-like instrument, and (649) refers to the fasteners sewn on traditional Khatso clothing. When the argument is human, it is often ambiguous whether the auxiliary or future sense applies. *li³²³* may co-occur with *wa³⁵* in such phrases, but it is not obligatory.

(648) ma³¹ kʰɣ̩²⁴ ni³¹ mɣ³²³ ma³¹ **li³²³** sa⁴⁴?
NEG be.empty TOP make.sound NEG know.how CRTN.Q
不 空 响 不 会
'If (it) isn't hollow, (it) won't make a sound?'
不空呢, 不会响吗?
(KL-Qin)

(649) i³³tsʰɣ³¹ pɣ³²³ tɕi⁵⁵ sɛi⁴⁴ li⁵⁵ tso²⁴ **li³²³** ŋɛi³³
3PL POSS CL:TYPE TOP move ITER know.how ASRT
他们 种 摇 会
'their type will move around a lot'
他们的那种是会摇的
(KL-Sewing)

In addition, there is a future form of the strong assertion particle *ŋɛi³³*, which is *ŋɛi³⁵*. It may refer to events at any future point, as in (650). However, if there is another future marker in the phrase, the basic form *ŋɛi³³* is used instead, as shown in (649) above. The emphatic particle *ja³³* may also convey a future sense, as shown in (651). However, this seems to arise from pragmatic inference; its basic function is to augment verbs modified by an imperfective aspect. That said, the future interpretation is a common one and thus worth mentioning here.

(650) ŋa³³ na³¹tɕi³³ŋ³³ ta³³ma⁴⁴tʰi³²³ kʰa⁵⁵tso³¹tɕʰi³¹ n̪a³¹ **ŋɛi³⁵**.
1SG tomorrow only Khatso.language speak FUT.ASRT
我 明天 只 喀卓语 说
'Tomorrow I will only speak Khatso.'
我明天只说喀卓语。
(KL-Elicitation)

(651) ŋa³³ kʰua³¹la³¹ i³²³ **ja³³**.
1SG Kunming go IPFV.EMP
我 昆明 去
'I'm going to Kunming.'
我要去昆明。
(KL-Elicitation)

The future marker is generally not used in reduplicative polar questions. Often the semantics of the verb itself makes a future interpretation clear, as shown in (652). In questions containing an interrogative pronoun, *pa⁵³* is placed between the verb and the question marker *ŋa³¹* to signal a future event, since by itself *ŋa³¹* implies a perfective interpretation (see § 12.4.2). An example is shown in (653). This *pa⁵³* is likely the lexical verb that means 'to speak, plan, set a betrothal'. But it does not occur in reported speech constructions (see § 15.3), and speakers do not translate it as lexical verb in this construction, so it seems to have partially grammaticalized into a future particle here.

(652) nɛi³³ kʰua³¹la³¹ **i³²³ i³²³**?
2SG Kunming go go
你 昆明 去 去
'Are you going to Kunming?'
你去不去昆明？
(KL-Elicitation)

(653) na³¹tɕi³³ m̩³¹tsʰ̩⁵³ xa³³ma³⁵ti⁴⁴li³³ tsʰa³⁵ko³³ tsʰa³⁵ **pa⁵³ ŋa³¹** lɛi³¹?
tomorrow evening why song sing FUT CNT.Q IRR.EMP
明天 晚上 为什么 歌 唱
'Why will (you) sing tomorrow evening?'
明天晚上为什么要歌唱呢？
(KL-Plans)

The future marker often modifies verbs alone, but it may also co-occur with both the continuous marker *tsɤ³¹* and the iterative marker *tso²⁴*. The former indicates that the future action will be uninterrupted, as in (654), and the latter that the event will occur a number of times, as in (655).

(654) ŋa³³ nɛi³³ pʰa³²³piɛ³³ ta³⁵ **tsɤ³¹ wa³⁵**.
1SG 2SG side hold CONT FUT
我 你 旁边 抱
'I'll hold (it) beside you continuously.'
我在你旁边抱着了。
(ZRF-Grandfather)

(655) kỵ³³   tɤ⁴⁴   tɕi³³   ta⁵⁵   ni³¹   tɕo³⁵   li⁵⁵   **tso²⁴**   **wa³⁵**   po⁵³.
make   CLNK   this   be.type   TOP   then   move   ITER   FUT   EPIS.EMP
做   这   样   就   摇

'(If) you do (it) that way, (they) will move around a lot, (see?)'
做才这样呢，就会摇了呀。
(WYY-Sewing)

9.2.10 Experiential

Experiential aspect indicates that an activity has been experienced at least once. As such, it presents the event as complete and bounded in time like the perfective marker wa^{323}. In Khatso this is done with the marker ko^{53}. An example from discourse is shown in (656).

(656) i²⁴la³¹,   tɕo³⁵   a³³   ko⁵⁵   tʰɤ⁵⁵   kʰua³¹   mo³³   **ko⁵³**   mɛi⁴⁴.
before   then   that   CL:PL   CL:TMP   speak   show   EXP   DSC.EMP
以前   就   那   些   下   讲   给见

'(I) have told those (stories) before.'
以前，就讲过一下那些。
(YJR-Grandfather)

This morpheme is an obvious loan from Chinese and, like in both Hanyu and Putonghua, it serves as a lexical verb as well as an aspect marker. As a verb it means 'to cross' and can be used to convey physical motion as well the act of passing or enduring a period of time. Thus, the experiential construction has a superficial similarity to a directional serial verb construction (see § 8.8.1.1). However, the two are distinct. Syntactically, ko^{53} is never the final verb in a directional serialization, while as an aspect marker it must be the last element in the verb complex, as shown in (656) above. Semantically, ko^{53} compositionally adds to the sense of motion in a directional construction, but there is no indication that motion is involved in the experiential use.

In negation the marker ma^{31} occurs between the matrix verb and ko^{53}, as shown in (657) and (658). Again, this is similar to the pattern found in serial verb constructions, which probably influenced it, and is unlike that of any other aspect marker. Despite its unusual placement, however, ma^{31} has scope over the entire verb complex, again differentiating the experiential function from serial verb constructions.

(657) ŋ²⁴tɕa³³ kʰua³¹ mo³³ **ma³¹ ko⁵³** mɛi⁴⁴.
other speak show NEG EXP DSC.EMP
别的 讲 给见 不
'(I) haven't told any other (stories).'
别的没有讲过。
(YJR-Grandfather)

(658) la⁵⁵ tsa²⁴ sa³³ **ma³¹ ko⁵³** la³⁵ ŋɛi³³.
trousers CL:ITEM sew NEG EXP FOC ASRT
裤子 件 逢 不
'(I) have never sewn a pair of trousers.'
就是没有缝过裤子。
(WYY-Sewing)

In polar questions, it is the aspect marker that is reduplicated rather than the verb, as illustrated in (659). Question formation is discussed further in § 12.4.

(659) kʰua³¹la³¹ i³²³ **ko⁵³ ko⁵³**?
Kunming go EXP EXP
昆明 去
'Have (you) ever gone to Kunming?'
去过昆明吗?
(KL-Elicitation)

9.3 Adverbs

Adverbs are considered a separate lexical class in Khatso. Their main function is to modify verbs, which they do in a variety of ways. Adverbs fail the tests for nounhood and verbhood. That is, they can neither serve as heads of possessive constructions or relative clauses like nouns, nor occur in simple noun phrases. In addition, adverbs can neither be negated nor modified by an aspectual particle, tests which all verbs satisfy. Moreover, adverbs cannot themselves be modified by any other element. But unlike particles, which also fail these tests, adverbs have definable lexical meanings and thus form a class distinct from the other categories.

In addition to prototypical adverbs, there are also a number of nouns and noun phrases that may also serve an adverbial function. For example, units of time are generally expressed by classifier phrases, which share the defining features of nouns (see § 6.2.2.7). Likewise, demonstrative pronouns may stand in for locations (see § 5.3.2). And as described in § 8.1.2.2, the reduplicated stative verb construction has adjectival and nominal functions in addition to its adverbial use. Because these nouns and noun phrases function as adverbs, they are included in the relevant subsections below.

As just mentioned, adverbs modify verbs in a number of ways. Temporal and locative adverbs specify time and place. Manner adverbs describe the way in which an action is performed, while degree adverbs describe the extent of a state or event. And some adverbs, such as *tsʰŋ³²³sŋ³²³* 'actually' and *ta³⁵kai³⁵* 'probably', have scope over the entire clause and not just the verb. In addition, a few adverbs have more than one meaning or function and may belong to more than one type. For example, as a time adverb *sa²⁴kɛi³³* may mean either 'just now' or 'until', and *ta³³ma⁴⁴tʰi³²³tʰi³²³* may be a manner adverb meaning 'alone' or a sentential adverb meaning 'only'. Many adverbs in Khatso are borrowed from Hanyu.

Adverbs generally carry no marking that sets them apart from other word classes. The one exception is certain manner adverbs, which may include the adverbial particle *ni³³*. This particle does not occur with all adverbs, however; even with manner adverbs it may be omitted, as described below. Moreover, there is considerable flexibility in the placement of adverbs in a phrase, although they tend to appear early in a clause. This issue is described in more detail in § 10.3.

The following sections provide details on the various types of adverbs identified in Khatso, including time adverbs in § 9.3.1, frequency adverbs in § 9.3.2, locative adverbs in § 9.3.3, manner adverbs in § 9.3.4, degree adverbs in § 9.3.5, and sentential adverbs in § 9.3.6.

9.3.1 Time Adverbs

Time adverbs provide temporal information that helps clarify and define an event in discourse. They may anchor the event to a particular point in time or describe its duration. In Khatso, there are a number of ways to communicate this information, not all of which involve true adverbs.

As briefly mentioned above, most units of time are classifiers in Khatso (see § 6.2.2.7), and thus classifier phrases often serve an adverbial function in the language. For example, *tɛi³³ tsɛi³⁵* 'now' literally means 'this time', and *tɛi³¹ tʰɛi³²³* 'at the same time, together' literally means 'one occurrence'. There are also a number of prototypical adverbs that relate to time, such as *i²⁴la³¹* 'in the past', *pi³²³ma³¹ŋ³³* 'afterwards, in the future', *sa²⁴kɛi³³* 'just now', *ŋa³²³tv³³* 'later' and *ta³⁵si³³* 'anytime'. Examples of both types are shown in (660) and (661) respectively. Note that in the latter both types are used together, a frequent occurrence in discourse though not obligatory.

(660) sa⁵⁵   ja³³,   **a³³tɕʰa⁵⁵kʰy̥³³** m̩³²³ tɤ²⁴ to³³.
be.difficult IPFV.EMP that.time   field plant also
苦   那时侯   田   栽   也
'(It) was difficult, planting the fields at that time.'
很苦的，那时候栽田。
(YJF-Childhood)

(661) **i²⁴la³¹** **a³³tɕʰa⁵⁵kʰy̥³³** ni³¹ tɕo³⁵ xɤ³³pɛi³³ sŋ³⁵   tʰɛi³¹.
in.past   that.time   TOP   then   home   firewood carry
以前   那时侯   就   家   柴   挑
'Before, at that time, (we) then carried firewood home.'
以前那个时候呢就在家里挑柴。
(GCS-Dance Parties)

Although borrowed from Hanyu like all time measurements, days of the week do not involve classifiers like the terms for months and years (see § 6.2.2.7). Instead, the common noun *si⁴⁴tsʰŋ⁴⁴* 'week' suffixes a numeral from the borrowed system corresponding to its order in the week. Thus, *si⁴⁴tsʰŋ³³zŋ³¹*, literally 'week one', is 'Monday' and *si⁴⁴tsʰŋ³³v̥³¹*, 'week five', is 'Friday'. Like in Chinese, the seventh day does not include a numeral but rather words that mean 'day'; *ŋ³²³* is the traditional Khatso form and *tʰiɛ³³* is a Hanyu loan. Note that in some cases the tone of the borrowed numeral in these words is different than that of plain numerals, suggesting that the borrowing occurred at different times. A list of the days of the week is presented in Table 9.3.

Table 9.3: Days of the week in Khatso

Khatso	Morphology	English	Chinese
si⁴⁴tsʰŋ⁴⁴zŋ³¹	si⁴⁴tsʰŋ⁴⁴ ('week') + zŋ³¹ ('one')	'Monday'	星期一
si⁴⁴tsʰŋ⁴⁴ɤ³⁵	si⁴⁴tsʰŋ⁴⁴ ('week') + ɤ³⁵ ('two')	'Tuesday'	星期二
si⁴⁴tsʰŋ⁴⁴sa³³	si⁴⁴tsʰŋ⁴⁴ ('week') + sa³³ ('three')	'Wednesday'	星期三
si⁴⁴tsʰŋ⁴⁴sŋ²⁴	si⁴⁴tsʰŋ⁴⁴ ('week') + sŋ²⁴ ('four')	'Thursday'	星期四
si⁴⁴tsʰŋ⁴⁴v̥³¹ si⁴⁴tsʰŋ⁴⁴o³¹	si⁴⁴tsʰŋ⁴⁴ ('week') + v̥³¹ ('five'), o³¹ ('five')	'Friday'	星期五
si⁴⁴tsʰŋ⁴⁴lv̥³¹	si⁴⁴tsʰŋ⁴⁴ ('week') + lv̥³¹ ('six')	'Saturday'	星期六
si⁴⁴tsʰŋ⁴⁴tʰiɛ⁴⁴ si⁴⁴tsʰŋ⁴⁴ŋ³²³ si⁴⁴tsʰŋ⁴⁴tʰiɛ⁴⁴ŋ³²³	si⁴⁴tsʰŋ⁴⁴ ('week') + tʰiɛ⁴⁴ ('day'), ŋ³²³ ('day')	'Sunday'	星期日

Regardless of form, temporal adverbs are typically placed either at the beginning of a phrase, as in (662) or directly following A/S, as in (663). It is also not uncommon to find them topicalized in a separate intonation unit, as in (664). Occasionally, they are placed after the entire clause as an afterthought, as in (665).

(662) **a³³tɕʰa⁵⁵kʰɣ³³**   tsʰɿ³²³sɿ³²³   lo⁵³   la²⁴   tsʰɤ³³   kɛi³³   tɕo³⁵   mo³¹   tʰɛi³²³   wa³²³.
that.time   seven.ten   reach   REL   PL   AGT   then   be.old   very   PFV
那时候   七十   到   　 们   　 就   老   很   　
'At that time, people who reached seventy were (considered) very old.'
那时候有七十岁的就很老了。
(YJF-Childhood)

(663) nɛi³³tsɤ³³   **a³³tɕʰa⁵⁵kʰɣ³³**   tso³²³   tso³²³   sa³¹?
2PL   that.time   EXIST   EXIST   still.Q
你们   那时侯   有   有   还
'Did you still have (them) at that time?'
你们那时候还有吗？
(KL-Childhood)

(664) **tɛi³³tɕʰa⁵⁵kʰɣ³³**,
this.time
这时候

kʰo⁵³tʰa³¹   ti⁵³   kɛi⁴⁴   ni³¹   sa²⁴   wa³³.
age   CL:PCE   INS   TOP   perhaps   CRS
年龄   点   用   　 可能   　
'These days, perhaps it's (because of a) little age.'
现在，可能是跟年纪大有关系吧。
(YAY-Erasers)

(665) tɛi³³ni³³   kɣ³³   kɯ³²³   na²⁴   tso³²³   ja³³,   **tɛi³³tɕʰa⁵⁵kʰɣ³³**.
this.way   make   CSC   be.good   EXIST   IPFV.EMP   this.time
这么   弄   　 好   有   　 这时候
'(They) are as good as this, now.'
做得这么好，现在。
(HPH-Toys)

Like many languages in the Ngwi family (Bradley 2013), Khatso has an idiosyncratic set of lexicalized forms for day and year ordinals. They are shown in Table 9.4. Although they are nouns — they may be modified by the general classifier *mɛi⁴⁴* and serve as a possessum — they are typically used alone in a clause, setting the time frame for an event. Also, note that the paradigms are not symmetrical. The day series has more future forms than past forms, while the year series has more past than future forms.

Table 9.4: Day and year ordinals in Khatso

Khatso	English	Chinese
sɿ³³o³¹ŋ³³	'three days ago'	大前天
sɿ³³ŋ³³	'day before yesterday'	前天
a³¹ŋ³²³	'yesterday'	昨天
i³¹ŋ³²³	'today'	今天
na³¹tɕi³³ŋ³³	'tomorrow'	明天
pʰa⁵³ŋ³³	'day after tomorrow'	后天
tʰi³²³lo³¹ŋ³³	'three days from now'	大后天
tʰi³²³ko³⁵ŋ³³	'four days from now'	大大后天
tʰi³²³po³⁵ŋ³³	'five days from now'	大大大后天
po³⁵lo³¹ŋ³³	'six days from now'	大大大大后天
sɿ³⁵o³¹ŋ³⁵tʰa³³	'three years ago'	大前年
sɿ³⁵ŋ³⁵tʰa³³	'year before last'	前年
a³¹ŋ³⁵tʰa³³	'last year'	去年
tsɿ³¹ŋ³⁵	'this year'	今年
na³²³xa⁵³	'next year'	明年
nau³⁵ŋ³⁵	'year after next'	后年

Time frames not specified in the table require periphrastic constructions, and there are several that may be used. Traditional constructions make use of the locative terms *o³¹tso³³* 'in front of' and *ŋa³²³tɿ³³* 'behind' to mean 'last' and 'next' respectively, as shown in (666) and (667). Future constructions may also use *na³¹tɕi³³*, as in (668), which is a component found in both *na³¹tɕi³³ŋ³³* 'tomorrow' and *na³¹tɕi³³tʰa³³* 'in the future'.

(666) **o³¹tso³³**   a³³   si⁴⁴tsʰɿ³³
in.front   that   week
前面   那   星期
'last week'
上个星期
(KL-Elicitation)

(667) **ŋa³²³tɤ³³**   a³³   la³³
behind   that   month
后面   那   月
'next month'
下个月
(KL-Elicitation)

(668) **na³¹tɕi³³**   a³³   la³³
future   that   month
未来   那   月
'next month'
下个月
(KL-Elicitation)

Adverbial and nominal expressions related to time may also communicate the duration of a state or event. For example, in (669), it is the classifier construction *tɤ³¹ xa⁵³* 'one evening' that describes the span of action, while in (670) it is the expression *tsɿ³¹ pɤ³²³ ȵɛ³²³* 'several hundred years' that does so. In addition, the frequently-used classifier *tʰɤ⁵⁵* marks activity that occurs for only a short time, though the actual duration is vague. Examples are shown in (671) and (672). It may co-occur with the numeral *tɕi³¹* 'one', but often the numeral is omitted in natural speech. Pragmatically, it is also often used to soften suggestions and requests (see § 12.2).

(669) jɛ⁵³   **tɤ³¹**   **xa⁵³**   tɤ⁴⁴   i³³tsʰɛi³³   xɤ³³   tɤ³⁵   ŋ³³.
then   one   evening   all   3PL   scold   PROG.FOC   ASRT
然后   一   晚   都   他们   骂
'Then (they) scolded them for an entire evening.'
然后一整晚都是在骂他们。
(PYX-Performing)

(670) i²⁴tsɿ³²³   tɤ⁴⁴   **tsɿ³¹**   **pɤ³²³**   **ȵɛ³²³**   tɤ⁴⁴   tsɿ³²³   tsʰɿ³³
continuously   all   several   hundred   CL:TMP   all   liquor   be.white
一直   都   几   百   年   都   酒   白
pɤ̩⁵⁵   ŋ³¹.
ferment   sell
酿   卖
'For several hundred years (they) have been continuously fermenting white liquor to sell.'
一直都几百年来都酿白酒卖。
(HPH-Horse Dug Well)

(671) ɕɛ³⁵tsʰa³¹ mɛi⁴⁴ ti³²³ **tʰɤ⁵⁵** ŋ²⁴ka³³ i³³ sɛi⁴⁴
scene CL:GEN at CL:TMP look go TMP
现场 个 里 下 看 去
'when (they) went to look at the scene for a while'
到现场里去看一下的时候
(HPH-Horse Dug Well)

(672) ŋa³³ **tʰɤ⁵⁵** ɕa³¹ ŋ²⁴ka³³ jo³³ wa³²³.
1SG CL:TMP think see must PFV
我 下 想 看 应该
'I must think about that for a while.'
我应该想一想看一看。
(KL-Weeds)

More complex temporal constructions, such as those found in oblique phrases, are discussed in § 10.6.3. Many clause-combining strategies also convey a temporal relationship (see § 13.2).

9.3.2 Frequency Adverbs

Another group of adverbs specifies the frequency of a state or event. The true adverbs of this type include *lɤ²⁴sɿ³³* 'often' and *ta³⁵sɿ³³* 'anytime, always'. Frequency may also be described by classifier phrases which denote units of time (see § 6.2.2.7). Regardless of form, adverbial expressions of frequency occur either at the beginning of the phrase or immediately following A/S. However, because of zero anaphora it is often difficult to distinguish the two positions. Examples are shown in (673) and (674). Note that the adverbial particle *ni³³* may be used with these adverbs, but it is not required.

(673) **tɛi³¹ ta²⁴ ni³³** pɤ³¹ tɤ⁴⁴ o³⁵o⁵³tsɿ³³ tɛi³³ tsʰɿ³³ i³³ wa³³.
one CL:ITEM ADV carry.on.back CLNK below area arrive go CRS
一 背 下面 边 到 去
'(She) continuously carried (them) on her back to the bottom.'
一直背到最下边了。
(PYX-Dragon Pools)

(674) **ta³⁵si³³**　tʰiau³⁵　tso²⁴　tɤ³³　ŋ³³　sa⁴⁴?
　　　always　dance　ITER　PROG　ASRT　CRTN.Q
　　　随时　　跳
　　　'(They) were always dancing, is (that it)?'
　　　随时跳着的吗？
　　　(KY-Grandfather)

9.3.3 Locative Adverbs

Locative adverbs establish the place in which a state or action occurs. In Khatso, this small group mainly consists of deictic pronouns, which relate the place mentioned in discourse to the actual location of the speaker. There are two sets of these pronouns in the language. One set, *tɕi³³ɳa⁵³* 'here' and *a³³ɳa⁵³* 'there', contains the demonstratives *tɕi³³* 'this' and *a³³* 'that' combined with the locative morpheme *ɳa⁵³* 'place'. The other set — *ɳa⁵³li⁴⁴* 'here', *o²⁴li⁴⁴* 'there (in sight)', *o³⁵li⁴⁴* 'away over there (out of sight)' — features a three-way distinction not found in any of the other deictic constructions in Khatso.

Like the other adverbs, locatives are typically placed either at the start of a phrase, as in (675), or immediately behind A/S, as in (676). They do not require additional marking, such as the postpositions found in oblique locative phrases. Because they may serve as heads of relative clauses, they satisfy the test for nounhood — though speakers rarely use them this way. Given their adverbial function in natural discourse, they are given their own section here. Examples of the second set are shown in (677) through (679).

(675) **tɕi³³ɳa⁵³**　tɕo³⁵　nɤ²⁴　tsʰi³³　o³³　tsʰi³³　tɤ³³　ŋɛi³³.
　　　here　　then　be.low　descend　be.concave　descend　PROG　ASRT
　　　这里　　就　　低　　下　　　凹　　　　下
　　　'Then here (it) lowers (and) becomes concave.'
　　　这里就是会落下去，凹下去了的。
　　　(WYF-Stools)

(676) ŋa³³tsʰɤ³¹ **tɛi³³n̪a⁵³** li⁴⁴ tɕo³⁵,
1PL here in then
我们 这里 里 就

ta³³sɹ̩³²³ xa³⁵tsʰɤ³²³ ma³¹ tso³²³.
that.time Han.ethnic.group NEG EXIST
当时 汉族 不 有
'We didn't have Chinese (people) here then.'
我们这里当时没有汉族。
(KLT-History)

(677) **n̪a⁵³li⁴⁴** ti⁵³za³¹ lo³¹ li³³ pa³¹.
here a.little approach come IMP
这里 点 拢 来
'Come here a little closer.'
过来这里一点。
(ZRF-Grandfather)

(678) i⁵³ni³²³ **o²⁴li⁴⁴** lo³¹sɹ̩²⁴ tʰɛi³¹ zɛi³¹ i³³ la²⁴ ma³¹ tso³²³.
later there not.many pick use go REL NEG EXIST
然后 那里 不多 挑 用 去 不 有
'So, not many people went there to gather (firewood) to use.'
然后去那里挑来用的人不是很多。
(PYX-Dragon Pools)

(679) i⁵³ni³²³ **o³⁵li⁴⁴** tɕa³²³ zɹ̩³¹ kɤ³²³, xɯ³⁵lɤ³⁵ tɕi⁴⁴ ni³¹ ma³¹ sɹ̩⁵⁵.
later there.far road be.far area Houlu say TOP NEG know
然后 那里 路 远 处 后路 说 不 知道
'Far away over there, (they) say Houlu, (I) don't know.'
然后路很远的地方，说是后路，不知道。
(YJR-Grandfather)

Location and direction may also be conveyed through oblique arguments. These require a more complex construction involving the use of postpositional particles (see § 10.6.2). Direction that is an integral part of the verbal action is expressed through serial verb constructions (see § 8.8). In addition, there are universal locative expressions, such as 'everywhere' (see § 6.4), and indefinite constructions, corresponding to 'nowhere' and 'anywhere' (see § 7.3.3 and § 7.3.2.2 respectively), that also convey locative concepts.

9.3.4 Manner Adverbs

Adverbs of manner describe the way in which an action is performed. In Khatso, there are two types of manner adverbs, lexical and derivational. The lexical group includes true adverbs such as *tʰɣ³²³za³²³* 'suddenly', *ta³³ma⁴⁴tʰi³²³tʰi³²³* 'alone', *tsŋ³¹tɕa²⁴* 'by oneself', *ni³³ɕɛ⁵⁵* 'hastily, immediately', *tɕa³³mɛi³³* 'together' and *tsuo³³zŋ³²³mɛi³²³* 'exclusively'. Examples from discourse are shown in (680) and (681). Like all adverbs, they may occur either phrase-initially or immediately after A/S.

(680) **tʰɣ³²³za³²³**   m̩³¹   mɛi⁴⁴   kɛi³³,
     suddenly   horse   CL:GEN   AGT
     突然   马   个

     i³²³tɕa⁵³   tɛi³¹   ko⁵⁵   pʰa³²³   to⁵³   li⁴⁴   ta³¹
     water   one   CL:PL   excavate exit   come   after
     水   一   些   刨   出   来   后
     'suddenly, after the horse dug out some water'
     突然，马刨出一些水来
     (HPH-Horse Dug Well)

(681) **ni³³ɕɛ⁵⁵**   n̠a⁵³li⁴⁴   ti⁵³za³¹   lo³¹   li³³   pa³¹.
     immediately   here   a.little   approach   come   IMP
     赶快   这里   点   拢   来
     'Hurry! Come here a little closer.'
     快点。过来这里一点。
     (ZRF-Grandfather)

The second group of manner adverbs is derived from stative verbs, which express attributes in Khatso. As described in § 8.1.2.2, stative verbs may be reduplicated for emphasis, with the diminutive suffix -*za³¹* and the adverbial marker *ni³³*, to create a construction with several uses. If the stative verb conveys an attribute that may be construed as manner, then the construction functions as an adverb, as (682) and (683) demonstrate. In rapid speech the construction is often reduced; *za³¹* or *ni³³* may be elided, and even one of the stative verbs may be omitted.

(682) "na²⁴   wa³³,   nɛi³³   **jo³³**   **jo³³**   **za³¹**   o⁵³"   tɕɛ⁵³,   tɛi³³   xuɛi³²³.
     be.good   CRS   2SG   be.slow   be.slow   DIM   weed   say.after   this   CL:TMP
     好   你   慢   慢   薅   说   这   回
     ' "Good, you (just) weed slowly" (she) said, this time.'
     "那么，你就慢慢地薅"说完，这次。"
     (HPH-Weeds)

(683) ta³⁵ n̠o³⁵ ko⁵⁵ **ja³⁵** **za³¹** tʰʏ⁵⁵ tsi⁵³ no⁵³ jo³³.
still hair CL:PL be.good DIM CL:TMP cut.with.scissors complete must
又 毛 些 好 下 剪 掉 应该
'(If there are) still threads, (you) must cut (them) off well.'
又要把毛好好地剪掉一下。
(WYF-Stools)

The adverbial particle *ni³³* also combines with the demonstrative morphemes in the deictic adverbs *tɛi³³ni³³* 'this way' and *a³³ni³³* 'that way' which also refer to manner. The former is greatly preferred in discourse, and it often co-occurs with *ta⁵⁵* 'be a manner, style, type'. Examples are shown in (684) and (685).

(684) **tɛi³³ni³³** li⁵⁵ tso²⁴ tʏ³³ ŋɛi³³.
this.way move ITER PROG ASRT
这么 摇
'(It) moves around this way.'
这么摇着的。
(KL-Sewing)

(685) "tsʅ³⁵za³¹ tsʰo³³ tɛi³³ ko⁵⁵ **tɛi³³ni³³** ta⁵⁵ ni³¹."
be.natural people this CL:PL this.way be.type TOP
自然 人 这 些 这么 样
' "Mortal people are like that." '
"自然这些人这样呢。"
(HPH-Weeds)

This particle *ni³³* also makes adverbial expressions out of classifier constructions. When different classifiers are involved there is often a distributive sense, as in (686). When a single classifier is reduplicated, it carries a consecutive interpretation, as in (687).

(686) na⁵³ tɛi³¹ tsɛi³⁵ tsʰo³¹, **tɛi³¹** **jo³⁵** **tɛi³¹** **jo³⁵** **tɛi³¹** **tɕi⁵⁵** **ni³³**.
sing one CL:TMP sing one CL:HUM one CL:HUM one CL:TYPE ADV
唱 一 段 唱 一 个 一 个 一 句
'(We would) sing for a while, one (person) one (phrase).'
唱一会儿歌,一个一句一个一句地。
(YJF-Dance Parties)

(687) **tɕi³¹ tɕi³⁵ tɕi³⁵ ni³³**,
one CL:TMP CL:TMP ADV
一 代 代

tɕa³¹ tsʰi³³ li⁴⁴ ta³¹ tsʰɿ³²³pɣ³²³ to³³ ȵɛ³²³ sɛi⁴⁴.
speak descend come after seven.hundred more CL:TMP TMP
讲 下 来 后 七百 多 年
'Generation after generation, (it has been) told for more than seven hundred years.'
七百多年了一代代地讲下来了。
(HPH-Horse Dug Well)

In addition, some lexical adverbs may also co-occur with *ni³³*, as shown in (688) and (689). This is not required, however, and in discourse the particle occurs most often with manner adverbs.

(688) **mau³³li⁴⁴ma³³tsau³⁵ ni³³** pʰɣ³¹sa³⁵ ko⁵⁵ la³³ ŋ³³ la³⁵ ŋɛi³³.
be.careless ADV caterpillar CL:PL CMP COP FOC ASRT
毛毛糙糙 毛毛虫 些 是
'Carelessly (made), (they) look like caterpillars.'
毛毛糙糙地像一些毛毛虫。
(KL-Sewing)

(689) ŋ⁴⁴li³³ **pʰi³³pʰi³³ ni³³** tsʰo³³ tsʰɣ³³ sɿ⁴⁴ tsɿ³⁵sɿ³³tsɿ³⁵li³⁵
but contrary ADV person PL COP be.selfish
但是 偏偏 人 们 是 自私自利
'but to the contrary people were very selfish'
就偏偏是自私自利的
(HPH-Weeds)

In addition, a few serial verb constructions and certain clause-combining constructions also express manner (see § 8.8.1.3 and § 14.5 respectively).

9.3.5 Degree Adverbs

Adverbs of degree specify the extent or intensity of an event or state. They are true adverbs; they fail the tests for nounhood. The most common of these are the intensifiers *tʰɛi³²³* and *mɛi⁴⁴*, both of which mean 'very'. Identical in meaning, they differ in syntax — *tʰɛi³²³* follows verbs and *mɛi⁴⁴* precedes them. They primarily modify stative verbs and constructions that contain them, such as resultative serial verb constructions and complex stative constructions. Examples are shown in (690), (691) and

(692). But, any verb modified by the auxiliary *li³²³* 'to know how' may also take an intensifier, as in (693).

(690) mo³¹   **tʰɛi³²³**   la²⁴   a³³   tɕi⁵⁵   tso³²³   tso³²³?
      be.old   very   REL   that   CL:TYPE   EXIST   EXIST
      老   很   那   种   有   有
      'Do really old ones exist?'
      有没有很老的那种？
      (KL-Childhood)

(691) **mɛi⁴⁴**   so²⁴   sa⁵⁵   sa²⁴   ja³³.
      very   learn   be.difficult   perhaps   IPFV.EMP
      很   学   难   可能
      'Perhaps (it) was very hard to learn.'
      可能很难学的。
      (KL-Learning)

(692) ja⁵³   tɕo³⁵   tɕɛ³⁵tsɿ³⁵   tɕɛ³⁵tsɿ³⁵   tɕo³⁵   **mɛi⁴⁴**   ko⁵³   kɯ³²³   sa³³
      later   then   be.gradual   be.gradual   then   very   cross   CSC   be.good
      然后   就   逐渐   逐渐   就   很   过   好
      tɤ³³ wa³³.
      INCP
      'Then later gradually (life) became much easier.'
      然后就逐渐逐渐就好过了。
      (YJF-Childhood)

(693) pʰi⁴⁴i⁴⁴   tsʅ²⁴   ni³¹   ta³⁵   **mɛi⁴⁴**   tsʅ²⁴   li³²³   ja³³.
      pinyin   write   TOP   still   very   write   know.how   IPFV.EMP
      拼音   注   还   很   注   会
      'As for reading and writing pinyin, (he) really knows how.'
      拼音注汉字很会注呀。
      (YAY-Erasers)

The complex stative construction is used in two idiomatic expressions of intensity. In one, the stative verb *o²⁴* 'to be fierce' is employed as the second verb, as in (694), and in the other the verb *tɤ²⁴* 'to be cruel' is similarly employed, as (695) shows. In both, these verbs function as extreme intensifiers, even if the first verb has a positive meaning, such as *na²⁴* 'to be good' or *si³³si³³* 'to be happy'. Complex stative constructions are discussed further in § 8.8.1.4.

(694) tɕi³¹tsʅ²⁴ na³²³tɤ³⁵   mei⁴⁴ ɤɤ³¹ kɯ³²³ **o²⁴**   ja³³.
      simply   difficulty.degree   very   be.big CSC   be.fierce IPFV.EMP
      简直   难度   很   大   凶
      'The degree of difficulty was really huge.'
      难度简直很大的。
      (KLT-History)

(695) tɕi³³ ɤ̩³¹   kɯ³²³ **tɤ²⁴**.
      this   be.crazy CSC   be.cruel
      这   疯   毒
      '(It) was really crazy.'
      有这么疯。
      (YJF-Weddings)

In addition, there is an idiomatic construction that also serves as an emphatic intensifier. In (696) the stative verb ȵɛ³²³ 'to be sweet' is reduplicated in the phrase ȵɛ³²³ tɤ²⁴ ȵɛ³²³ xɛi³⁵ to mean 'to be very, very sweet'. This expression is highly productive, and can be used with any stative verb. The exact meanings of tɤ²⁴ and xɛi³⁵ are unclear, although the former may be the verb 'to be cruel', which is used as an intensifier in (695) above; xɛi³⁵ may be the same morpheme that appears in the universal quantification construction (see § 6.4).

(696) ȵɛ³²³   **tɤ²⁴** ȵɛ³²³   **xɛi³⁵**
      be.sweet   UNK   be.sweet   UNK
      甜   甜
      'very, very sweet'
      很甜很甜的
      (HPH-Horse Dug Well)

The comparative adverb i²⁴fa³³ 'more, even more' is also used to describe degree, with both stative verbs and auxiliary constructions that feature li³²³ 'to know how'. An example is shown in (697). Note that the verb may be negated, which does not affect the use of i²⁴fa³³, even though the English translation requires a separate word. This adverb also features in certain comparative constructions as well as a clause-combining construction (see § 12.5.5 and § 14.4.4 respectively).

(697) mo³¹   la²⁴ ko⁵⁵   ni³¹ **i²⁴fa³³** ȵa³¹   ma³¹ li³²³.
      be.old REL   CL:PL TOP   more   speak NEG know.how
      老   些   更   说   不   会
      'The older (people), (they) know how to speak (it) even less.'
      那些老的呢更不会说
      (YAY-Erasers)

9.3.6 Sentential Adverbs

Some adverbs have scope over the entire clause. For example, *pɛi³²³ti³⁵* 'otherwise' in (698) applies to the potential result described in both of the phrases. Likewise, *tsʅ³³pɛi³¹sa³⁵* 'basically' modifies the entire clause in (699), not just the verb. Note that borrowed adverbs like these are often followed by the borrowed copula *sʅ⁴⁴* (see § 8.5). In Khatso, these words are true adverbs; they do not satisfy the tests for nounhood.

(698) **pɛi³²³ti³⁵**   ni³¹   xa³⁵   i³⁵   ɤ³⁵   sʅ³²³   n̻ɛ³²³   zʅ³¹xɯ³⁵   ni³¹   tɕo³⁵,
otherwise TOP   still   one   two   ten   CL:TMP   after   TOP   then
要不然 　　 还 　 一 　 二 　 十 　 年 　　 以后 　　 就

tɛi³³   ko⁵⁵   ma³¹   tso³²³   wa³⁵.
this   CL:PL   NEG   EXIST   FUT
这 　　 些 　　 不 　　 有
'Otherwise, after ten (or) twenty years these won't exist.'
要不然再过一二十年以后，这些就没有了。
(KL-Sewing)

(699) ja⁵³   tɛi³³tɕʰa⁵⁵kʰɤ³¹   tɕa⁵³   ma³¹   tso³²³.
later   this.time   toothgrass   NEG   EXIST
然后 　 这时候 　　　　 牙齿草 　 不 　 有
'Now there is no toothgrass.'
那么，现在没有牙齿草。

tsʅ³³pɛi³¹sa³⁵   sʅ⁴⁴   tɕa⁵³   ko⁵⁵   kɤ³³   tsuɛi²⁴   wa³³.
basically   COP   toothgrass   CL:PL   do   sever   CRS
基本上 　　　　 是 　 牙齿草 　 些 　 弄 　 绝
'Basically (they) cut down the toothgrass.'
基本上是牙齿草些弄绝了。
(HPH-Weeds)

Another frequently encountered sentential adverb is *sa²⁴*. When placed between the verb and the emphatic particles *nɛi³³* or *ja³³* or the aspect marker *wa³³*, it means 'perhaps' and modifies the entire clause, as shown in (700) and (701).

(700) nɛi³³   sʅ⁵⁵   **sa²⁴**   ja³³   pɛi³³?
2SG   know   perhaps   IPFV.EMP   CFRM.Q
你 　　 知道 　 可能
'Perhaps you know (her)?'
你知道吧？
(YJR-Grandfather)

(701) mɛi⁴⁴ so²⁴ sa⁵⁵ **sa²⁴** ja³³.
very learn be.difficult perhaps IPFV.EMP
很 学 难 可能
'Perhaps (it) was very hard to learn.'
可能很难学。
(KL-Learning)

The sentential adverbs frequently found in discourse are listed in Table 9.5. All but a few — *sa²⁴*, *sɛi³¹*, *xɛi³⁵*, *tsʰo³²³li³⁵* and *to³³* — are borrowed from Chinese. Borrowed adverbs also feature in certain clause-combining constructions (see Table 17.1).

Table 9.5: Sentential adverbs in Khatso

Khatso	English	Chinese
i²⁴ pa³³	'generally'	yībān 一般
i³²³ti³⁵, zɿ³²³tɿ³⁵	'certainly'	yídìng 一定
pɛi³¹lɛi³²³	'originally'	běnlái 本来
pɛi³²³ti³⁵	'otherwise'	yàoburán 要不然
sa²⁴	'perhaps'	kěnéng 可能
sɛi³¹, xɛi³⁵, tsʰo³²³li³⁵	'again'	yòu 又
ta³³za³²³	'of course'	dāngrán 当然
ta³⁵, ŋ⁴⁴li³³, ŋ³³ɳa⁴⁴li³³	'but'	dànshì 但是
ta³⁵kai³⁵	'probably'	dàgài 大概
tau³⁵kɛi³³, fa³¹ɣɤ³²³	'instead, on contrary'	fǎnér 反而
tɕʰo³²³sɿ³²³	'really'	quèshí 确实
to³³	'also'	yě 也
tsɛi³⁵sɿ³⁵ / tau³⁵ti³¹	'after all'	dàodǐ 到底
tsʰɿ³²³sɿ³²³	'actually'	qíshí 其实
tsʰɣ³³fɛi⁴⁴	'unless'	chúfēi 除非
tsɿ³³fɤ³³, mau³⁵sɿ²⁴	'almost'	jīhū 几乎
tsɿ³³pɛi³¹sa³⁵	'basically'	jīběnshang 基本上

10 Argument Structure

This chapter explores the argument structure of simple clauses. As mentioned previously, Khatso is a verb-final language and almost all arguments, whether core or oblique, occur before the verb. The constituent order of core arguments generally follows an A R P V pattern, but this is flexible. Moreover, because Khatso is a pragmatics-based language, verbal semantics and discourse context are often more important than syntax in determining meaning at the clause level (see Bisang 2009). This fact influences almost every aspect of clause structure, as the analysis in this chapter illustrates. Thus, the chapter begins with a discussion of the topic-comment information structure in Khatso in § 10.1. Grammatical relations are explored in § 10.2, and word order in § 10.3. Next, the disambiguating function of the pragmatic agentivity marker is examined in § 10.4, and its role in the pseudo-passive is described in § 10.5. Finally, the introduction of oblique arguments is described in § 10.6. For a discussion of the valency of different verb types, see Chapter 9. Valency-changing constructions are outlined in Chapter 11.

10.1 Topic-Comment Information Structure

Like many other languages in the Sino-Tibetan family, Khatso organizes information according to a topic-comment pattern. Topics are discourse themes that provide a pragmatic framework for one or more clauses that follow, which then make predications about the topic (e.g. LaPolla 2009; Li and Thompson 1976). One way to investigate this structure is to contrast topics with subjects, if possible, and to examine the correlation between the two. The topic often coincides with the A or S of a clause, but this is not obligatory. The former is a pragmatic notion and the latter a semantic-syntactic one, and the two may co-exist in the same phrase. For example, Khatso, like Putonghua, allows for the so called *double subject phrase*, illustrated by the examples in (702), (703) and (704). At first glance, these phrases appear to have two S. But closer examination shows that the two noun phrases have different functions. The first are topics which establish the theme for the rest of the clauses. The second noun phrases are the A or S of their respective verbs. Moreover, some topics are not core arguments of the verb. For example, in (702) the stative verb na^{53} 'to be many' is intransitive and thus can only take a single S argument, which is $ts^ho^{31}pa^{35}$ 'friend' here — the topic $k^hu\varepsilon i^{44}\ i^{31}$ is thus outside the core argument structure. Similarly, in (703), the verb ja^{35} 'to fertilize' is transitive, but the P is $i^{35}miau^{323}$ 'seedlings' rather than sa^{24} 'wheat', which is instead the topic of the entire clause. Furthermore, note that although Khatso has two topic markers, ni^{31} and $s\varepsilon i^{44}$, which are routinely used, overt marking is not obligatory for topics, as these examples demonstrate. Verbal semantics, along with context, is often enough to resolve meaning.

(702) **kʰuɛi⁴⁴ i³¹**   tsʰo³¹pa³⁵   n̪a⁵³   tʰɛi³²³   ja³³.
Kui Ying   friend   be.many   very   IPFV.EMP
奎滢   朋友   多   很
'Kui Ying, (her) friends are many.'
奎滢朋友多。
(KL-Elicitation)

(703) **sa²⁴**,   i³⁵miau³²³   ja³⁵   i³³   tsɛi³¹   lɛi³¹.
wheat   seedling   fertilize   go   HSY   IRR.EMP
小麦   幼苗   施肥   去
'As for the wheat, (they) say (he) went to fertilize (the) seedlings.'
小麦，说是去施幼苗肥去。
(YJF-Childhood)

(704) **i²⁴tɕʰɛ³²³**   **tɛi³³**   **tɕa³⁵**,
qin   this   CL:MACH
琴   这   台
'This *qin* [a banjo-like instrument],'
这把琴，

tɛi³³   ko⁵⁵   xa³³ma⁴⁴   xa³³ma⁴⁴   v̩²⁴?
this   CL:PL   what   what   be.called
这   些   什么   什么   叫
'What are these called (on it)?'
这些叫什么？
(KL-Qin)

Of the two topic markers *ni³¹* and *sɛi⁴⁴*, the former is the more productive of the two, and thus exemplified throughout this chapter. *sɛi⁴⁴*, on the other hand, is both a topic marker and a temporal marker, and also has a complementation function — and these uses overlap somewhat (see § 16.6). There are instances, however, where *sɛi⁴⁴* is translated as either a topic marker or a copula. In both interpretations, it serves to make the modified element more prominent and mark it as a theme for the following clause. For example, in (705) it highlights a noun phrase and in (706) an adverb, constituents that cannot be modified in either the temporal or complementation functions. In some clauses, the two topic markers are interchangeable, but not in every instance. The differentiating factors are not fully understood, and are likely due to the nuances of the particular clauses themselves.

(705) i³³tsʰɤ³³ pɤ³²³ tɕi⁵⁵ **sɛi⁴⁴** li⁵⁵ tso²⁴ li³²³ ŋɛi³³,
　　　3PL　　POSS　CL:TYPE　TOP　move.around　ITER　know.how　ASRT
　　　他们　　　　种　　　摇　　　　　　　　　会
　　　'Those ones of theirs, (they) will move around,'
　　　他们的那种呢会摇的，

　　　ŋ³³　n̪a³³.
　　　COP　COP.EMP
　　　是
　　　'That's right.'
　　　是的。
　　　(KL-Sewing)

(706) zɛi³¹za³²³ **sɛi⁴⁴** o²⁴li³²³ tso³²³ ja³²³ sɛi³¹.
　　　still　　　COP　　there　EXIST　PFV.EMP　still
　　　仍然　　　是　　那里　在　　　　　　还
　　　'As for (now) still, (it) is still there.'
　　　仍然是还在那里。
　　　(HPH-Horse Dug Well)

By contrast, almost any clausal element may be topicalized by *ni³¹*. These include verbal arguments, both core and oblique, as well as adverbial expressions. Even activities expressed as separate clauses may be topics. Further examples are presented in (707) through (711); the topics are placed within square brackets. Note that *ni³¹* may trigger tone change in the preceding syllable (see § 3.2.4.1).

(707) *A as topic*
　　　[ma³¹ mo⁵⁵ pɤ⁵³ so²⁴ la²⁴ tsʰɤ³³] **ni³¹** ma³¹ pɤ⁵³ so²⁴ ta⁵⁵
　　　NEG　want　play　learn　REL　PL　　　TOP　NEG　play　learn　type
　　　不　　要　　弹　　学　　　　　们　　　　　不　　弹　　学　　样
　　　la³⁵ ŋɛi³³.
　　　FOC　ASRT
　　　'As for those who don't want to learn, (they) don't learn.'
　　　不想学弹琴的人呢，不学这样的。
　　　(YLW-Learning)

(708) *P as topic*
[pɛi³⁵ tɕi⁵⁵ ma³¹ na²⁴ na²⁴ za³¹ a³³ tɕi⁵⁵] **ni³¹** ŋ²⁴tɕa³³
grass CL:TYPE NEG be.good be.good DIM that CL:TYPE TOP other
草　　种　　不　　好　　好　　　　那　　种　　　　别
tʰi³⁵.
place.under
垫
'As for the type of straw (that) is not so good, (we) put it under the other (straw).'
不太好的那种草呢，别处垫。
(WYF-Stools)

(709) *Adverb as topic*
[tɕi³³ni⁴⁴] **ni³¹** tɕo³⁵ tsɿ³¹tɕa²⁴ pɣ⁵³ so²⁴.
this.way TOP then self play learn
这么　　　　　就　　自己　　弹　　学
'In this way, (you) then learn to play (it) by yourself.'
这样呢就自己学着弹。
(KL-Learning)

(710) *Temporal expression as topic*
[nɛi³³tsʰɣ³³ ȵɛ²⁴ ȵɛ²⁴ za³¹ sɿ³²³xɣ³⁵],
2PL be.small be.small DIM time
你们　　　　小　　　小　　　　　时侯
'The time (when) you were small,'
你们小时候，

xa³³ma⁴⁴ tɕi³¹ ko⁵⁵ kv̩³³ tɣ³³ ŋa³¹?
what one CL:COL make PROG CNT.Q
什么　　一　　些　　做
'What (kinds of) things did you do?'
在做一些什么呢？
(KL-Childhood)

(711) *Clause as topic*
[tsi⁵³ ma³¹ lo⁵³] **ni³¹** ta³⁵ tɕi³¹ tsɛi³⁵ tsɛi³⁵ tsi⁵³.
chop NEG be.enough TOP still one CL:SEC CL:SEC chop
砍　　不　　够　　　　　又　　一　　段　　段　　砍
'(If you) don't chop enough, (you) chop awhile (more).'
砍不够呢，又砍一会儿。
(GCS-Dance Parties)

As these examples illustrate, topics are often marked with ni^{31}, but this is not always necessary. For example, in (710) above, setting off the temporal expression in its own intonation unit is sufficient to mark it as the topic, neither ni^{31} nor sei^{44} is necessary. In discourse, a topic marker often highlights the topicalized element for either additional prominence or for clarity. Topicalized clauses marked by ni^{31}, however, may take on a conditional meaning, as in (711) above — a reading that may not be obvious without the marker. With ni^{31}, however, the relationship between the two clauses is unmistakable; in this case, framing the condition under which the situation described in the second clause takes place. Given the different functions of sei^{44}, its interpretation is less obvious, though it never marks conditional clauses; these issues are discussed further in § 16.6.

These examples illustrate the topic-comment structure that forms the basis of much of Khatso discourse. Because of its importance, Khatso can be described as a pragmatics-based language — one in which verbal semantics and discourse context often play a greater role than syntax in understanding linguistic structures (see Bisang 2009). Indeed, grammatical relations (§ 10.2) and word order (§ 10.3), as well as pragmatic agentivity (§ 10.4) and the pseudo-passive (§ 10.5), cannot be analyzed without recognizing the primacy of topic in the language.

10.2 Grammatical Relations

Because of the pragmatics-based nature of the language, semantics and context are crucial in clarifying syntactic constructions in discourse (see Bisang 2009). And this is the case with grammatical relations as well. All arguments — whether A, S, P or R — occur before the verb and typically carry no case marking to define their roles; the one exception being the pragmatic agent marker, which is only used in certain circumstances (see § 10.4). Verbs show no agreement with any of the core arguments, likewise providing no overt cues for differentiating between them. Word order helps clarify matters, and the unmarked order of core arguments is

A/S   R   P   VERB

But, word order is somewhat flexible, and is often manipulated for discourse purposes (see § 10.3 below). Moreover, because zero anaphora is frequent in discourse, it is impossible, appealing only to syntax, to determine the correct interpretation of a transitive or ditransitive clause with only one overt argument. For example, the monkey in (712) may be interpreted as A, P or R. Context is needed to resolve this kind of ambiguity.

(712) a²⁴n̩o⁵³   mɛi⁴⁴   kɯ³¹   wa³²³.
monkey CL:GEN give   PFV
猴子   个   给
'The monkey gave (me a tangerine).' / '(I) gave (him) the monkey.' / '(I) gave the monkey (a tangerine).'
猴子给(我桔子)了。/(我)给(他)猴子了。/(我)给猴子(桔子)了。
(KL-Elicitation)

As a result, there is a great deal of flexibility in the way that core arguments are used and interpreted in discourse. For example, there are no syntactic restrictions on the co-reference of shared arguments in combined clauses, unlike languages like English; co-reference is determined by semantics instead. Four examples from discourse are shown in (713) through (716); to help illustrate co-reference, arguments absent due to zero anaphora are inserted and labeled. In the first example, the A and P of both clauses are respectively co-referential. In (714), A and S refer to the same argument. But in (715), the shared argument, the third person plural pronoun, is S in the first clause and P in the second. Similarly, in (716), the co-referential argument *tsɿ⁵⁵kʰɣ³¹* 'cloth' is P in the first clause and S in the second. In none of these sentences is syntactic marking required to accommodate one co-referential pattern over another. The meaning alone is sufficient to interpret the sentences correctly.

(713) A=A, P=P

  A   P   A
(i³³tsʰɣ³³) (m̩³²³ ko⁵⁵) sɿ²⁴   tɕʰɛ²⁴ ta³⁵   (i³³tsʰɣ³³) tɕi³¹ xuɛi³²³
3PL   field CL:PL divide open   again   3PL   one   CL:TMP
他们）   田   些   分   开   又   他们   一   回

  P
(m̩³²³ ko⁵⁵) pi³¹lo³¹.
field CL:PL merge
田   些   并合
'(They) divided (and) merged (the fields) once.'
分开了又合并一次。
(YJF-Childhood)

(714) A=S

         A   S

($ŋa^{33}tsʰɤ^{33}$) s$ɿ^{35}$ tʰɛi^{31} tɤ^{44} o^{24} tsʰɿ^{33} wa^{24} xɛi^{35} ($ŋa^{33}tsʰɤ^{33}$)
1PL   wood carry CLNK there arrive PFV still   1PL
我们   柴   挑   那   到   还   我们
mi^{53} tsɤ^{31} ŋɛi^{33}.
be.hungry CONT   ASRT
饿

'(We) carried firewood there while (we) were hungry.'
柴挑到那还饿着。
(GCS-Dance Parties)

(715) S=P

                                                                                                          P
        S

($ŋa^{33}tsʰɤ^{33}$) kɯ^{33} li^{44} ni^{31} xɛi^{35} tsʰo^{33}ɣɤ^{24}ma^{33} tsʰɤ^{33} kɛi^{33} ($ŋa^{33}tsʰɤ^{33}$)
1PL   enter go TOP still adult   PL   AGT 1PL
我们   回   来   还   大人   们   我们
xɤ^{33}.
scold
骂

'(When we) returned, the adults still scolded (us).'
回来后呢大人们还骂。
(GCS-Dance Parties)

(716) P=S

         A   P   S

(nɛi^{33}) tɛi^{31} tʰɤ^{55} (tsɿ^{55}kʰɤ^{31}) tsi^{53} tɕʰɛ^{24} (tsɿ^{55}kʰɤ^{31}) tɕo^{35}
2SG   one CL:TMP cloth   cut.with.scissors open.IMP   cloth   then
你   一下   布   剪   开   布   就
tʰa^{55} ka^{323} i^{35} wa^{33}.
be.pointy walk   go.FOC CRS
尖   走   去

'(You) cut (the cloth) away a bit (and) then (the cloth) becomes pointy.'
剪一下就尖了。
(WYY-Sewing)

    Another example of this flexibility involves relativization. As discussed in § 7.5, Khatso falls into the category of languages with generalized noun-modifying clause constructions (e.g. Comrie 1998; Matsumoto 1997) — there are no syntactic restrictions on which clausal element may be relativized. For example, in addition to core arguments, oblique elements such as locative expressions are routinely relativized, and the latter may describe semantic goals, places or paths. Accompaniments and instruments are also easily relativized. And even quasi-relational nouns — that is, those that are semantically one step removed from the action in the relative clause — may be relativized, as (717) illustrates. The relationship between teaching and receiving money that is implied here is only understood through pragmatics rather than syntactic structure.

(717) ŋa³³ kɛi³³ jɛ⁴⁴ẓ̩³³ ma⁵⁵ la²⁴ **tɕʰɛ³²³** tɕi⁵⁵
 1SG AGT English teach REL money CL:TYPE
 我 英语 教 钱 种
 'the money I (earn from) teaching English'
 我教英语的钱
 (KL-Elicitation)

Thus, syntax is not always sufficient in defining the role of arguments in a clause. Word order and the animacy of arguments may help clarify the situation (see § 10.3 below), but they too are not necessarily enough for the job in every instance. There is one case marker in Khatso, *kɛi³³*, but it is mainly used in cases where the identity of the agent is potentially ambiguous (see § 10.4). Moreover, the topic-comment information structure makes the topic, a pragmatic relation, as important as A or S in discourse (see § 10.1). Indeed, the syntactic ambiguity of many constructions underscores the importance of semantics and pragmatics in interpreting meaning on a clausal level. This is also true of many clause-combining constructions (see Chapter 16).

10.3 Word Order

Khatso is a verb-final language, so most elements precede the verb in a clause — the exceptions being a few idiosyncratic adverbs, all aspect markers and most discourse markers. A template of possible elements in a clause is

TOP	ADV	A/S	ADV	R/B	P	ADV	VERB	ASP	DSC

where the topic establishes the discourse theme for the clause, A canonically precedes R/B and P, aspect directly follows the verb, and discourse particles occur in phrase-final position. The adverb slots may be filled by adverbs or nominal constructions that convey adverbial information, such as temporal or locative expressions, and there is a great deal of flexibility in their placement (see § 10.3). Note also that the verb slot may contain more than one verb, since serial verb constructions are frequent in discourse (see § 8.8). Despite the tidy view presented in the template, the ordering of constituents before the verb is flexible and largely shaped by pragmatics. In addition, given elements, especially core arguments, are often absent. As a result, in natural speech it is rare to find a clause as full as the template above. In fact, a single verb alone may form a grammatical clause or sentence.

Within the template of verbal arguments, S precedes the verb in intransitive or stative clauses. In a maximal ditransitive clause, overt verbal arguments typically follow this basic order:

$$A \quad \begin{matrix} R \\ B \end{matrix} \quad P \quad \text{VERB}$$

in which A is the first argument, and P is that closest to the verb. R and B, which cannot co-occur, occupy the identical position between the other two arguments. The general reliability of this order helps to identify semantic roles in a clause, especially since there is no obligatory case marking in the language. Zero anaphora, however, complicates matters, since all core arguments precede the verb and any or all of them may be absent. Because this is often the case in natural speech, the elicited phrase in (718) is offered to demonstrate basic word order in a ditransitive clause.

(718) A R P
i³³ ŋa³³ jɛ⁴⁴z̩³³ ma⁵⁵ wa³²³.
3SG 1SG English teach PFV
他 我 英语 教
'He taught me English.'
他教我英语了。
(KL-Elicitation)

Because of the topic-comment pattern of information flow in Khatso, changing the basic word order tends to alter the pragmatic prominence of an argument. Fronted arguments are generally interpreted as topics, even if they are not marked as such (see § 10.1). By contrast, arguments that follow the verb have low prominence, and are often afterthoughts uttered to remind interlocutors of a known argument or clarify a potentially unclear utterance. Examples are presented in (719) and (720).

(719) s̩²⁴tɕʰɛ²⁴ ŋ³³ sa⁴⁴? m³²³ ko⁵⁵.
divide COP CRTN.Q field CL:PL
分开 是 田 些
'(They were) divided, right? The fields.'
就分开了吗？那些田。
(KL-Childhood)

(720) kɯ²⁴ta³³   ma³¹   so⁵³   ta³³   **ŋa³³**.
 knot   NEG   tie   IPFV.IRR   1SG
 结   不   打   我
 '(I) usually don't tie knots, me.'
 平常不打结，我。
 (WYY-Sewing)

One consequence of this variable word order is that it is not possible to classify a verb phrase — defined as a verb and its objects (or P and R) — as a privileged constituent in Khatso. As just described, P may occur before other core arguments for pragmatic purposes. Other verb phrase tests also fail. For example, substitution — which allows for an entire verb phrase to be replaced by a pro-form, such as the verb 'to do' — is not possible in Khatso. In the English sentence 'she studies Khatso in Xingmeng and I do too', the verb 'do' replaces the entire phrase 'studies Khatso in Xingmeng'. But in Khatso, it is ungrammatical to substitute a general verb, such as $m̩³³$ or $kv̩³³$, both of which mean 'to make, do', for any other verb. Instead, the same verb is used in both clauses.

Beyond core arguments, the word order of other elements in a clause is considerably more flexible. The canonical position for many of these items is between A and the next core argument or between A/S and the verb if there are no other arguments. For example, in (721) the adverbial construction $jo³³\ jo³³\ za³¹$ 'slowly' occurs between A and the verb. And in (722), a complex locative expression, involving a noun and three adverbs, likewise sits between S and the existential predicate.

(721) "nɛi³³   **jo³³**   **jo³³**   **za³¹**   o⁵³"   tɕɛ⁵³,   tɛi³³   xuɛi³²³.
 2SG   be.slow   be.slow   DIM   weed   say.after   this   CL:TMP
 你   慢   慢   薅   说   这   回
 '"You (just) weed slowly" (she) said, this time.'
 "你就慢慢地薅吧"说完，这回。
 (HPH-Weeds)

(722) nɛi³³   sɛi⁴⁴   ɕo³²³ɕau³⁵   mɛi⁴⁴   **o⁵³tsʅ³³**   **pi³¹tɕa³³**   **a³³n̩a⁵³**   tso³²³   tso³²³   la³¹
 2SG   family   school   CL:GEN   under   beside   there   EXIST   EXIST   IRR.Q
 你   家   学校   个   下边   旁边   那里   有   有
 sa³¹?
 still.Q
 还
 'Is your home still just down there beside the school?'
 你家还在不在学校旁边下面那里？
 (KL-Erasers)

However, in discourse locative and temporal expressions, which are often nominal constructions that set the stage for the following predication, are equally likely to precede A or S, as shown in (723) and (724). In some cases, they may also be topicalized.

(723) **nɣ³²³kʰɣ³³** ŋa³³ tɛi³¹ ŋ³²³ ŋ³³ i³²³ ti³³ja³³.
Hexi 1SG one CL:TMP CL:TMP go PROG
河西 我 一 天 天 去
'I go to Hexi every day.'
我每天去河西。
(KL-Elicitation)

(724) **a³³tɕʰa⁵⁵kʰɣ³³** nɛi³³tsʰɣ³³ xa³³ni³³ kʰo⁵³ za³¹ lo⁵³ ŋa³¹?
that.time 2PL how.many CL:TMP DIM reach CNT.Q
那时候 你们 多少 年 到
'At that time about how old were you?'
那时候你们大概有多少岁了？
(KL-Childhood)

Adverbs show the most flexibility of all. They may occur before or after A/S, or even immediately before the verb. Examples are shown in (725) and (726). They may also occur after the verb, as in (727), but this is rather rare in discourse — except for *sɛi³¹* 'still, again' which only occurs in the post-verbal position, as shown in (728).

(725) ŋa³³ **ta³⁵ xɛi³⁵** tɛi³¹ ma²⁴ tsau³⁵ ta⁵⁵ wa³²³.
1SG still still one CL:GEN take put PFV
我 还 还 一 个 照 放
'I still took one (photo).'
我还照了一张了。
(GCS-Childhood)

(726) nɛi³³ ɣ³⁵sɻ³²³sa³³ xau³⁵ tɕo³⁵ **jo³³ jo³³** za³¹ ni³³ i³²³
2SG two.ten.three CL:TMP then be.slow be.slow DIM ADV go
你 二十三 号 就 慢 慢 去
ŋa³²³ta³²³ wa³³.
be.able CRS
能
'You can then slowly go (there) on the 23rd.'
你二十三号就能慢慢地去了。
(KY-Plans)

(727) tɛi³³ni³³ kv̩³³   kɯ³²³ na²⁴   tso³²³ ja³³, **tɛi³³tɕʰa⁵⁵kʰv̩³³**.
      this.way make   CSC   be.good EXIST IPFV.EMP this.time
      这么   弄   好   有   这时候
      '(They) are as good as this, now.'
      做得这么好，现在。
      (HPH-Toys)

(728) i³²³tɕa⁵³ ko⁵⁵ ɕo³⁵   ɕo³³   a³¹ o²⁴li⁴⁴ tso³²³ ja³²³ **sɛi³¹**.
      water   CL:PL be.clean be.clean DIM there   EXIST PFV.EMP still
      水   些   干净   干净   那里   在   还
      'Really clean water is still there.'
      干干净净地水还在那里。
      (HPH-Horse Dug Well)

Aspect and phrasal discourse markers, however, always follow the verb, as the examples in (729) and (730) illustrate. Imperative and question markers also occur at the end of a clause (see § 12.2 and § 12.4 respectively). The presence of these postverbal markers is often the only cue for recognizing that a phrase serves as a matrix clause or sentence.

(729) na⁵³tɕʰɛ⁵⁵ ni³¹ tɕo³⁵ a³³tɕʰa⁵⁵kʰv̩³³ so²⁴   sɿ⁵⁵ **wa³²³**.
      dance   TOP then that.time   learn know PFV
      黑跳   就   那时候   学   知
      'Dancing, so (you) learned (it) at that time.'
      跳乐呢，那个时候就学会了。
      (KL-Learning)

(730) tsʰɿ³²³sɿ³²³sɿ⁴⁴ lo³¹   tɕi⁵⁵   ŋ³³ **ja³³**   **tsɛi³¹**.
      actually   dragon CL:TYPE COP IPFV.EMP   HSY
      其实   龙   种   是
      '(They) say actually (they) were dragons.'
      其实说是龙的。
      (PYX-Dragon Pools)

10.4 Pragmatic Agentivity

Khatso has one case marker, *kɛi³³*, which is used to mark agents. The marker is not obligatory; rather, it is used to disambiguate potential agents when other factors are not sufficient. This phenomenon is often called optional ergativity (McGregor 2010), since the A of transitive verbs receives marking that does not occur on either the S of intransitive verbs or the P of transitive verbs. However, because its use in Khatso is determined by context rather than syntax, the term pragmatic agentivity is more precise. It is a feature found in many other Tibeto-Burman languages (LaPolla 1995).

In discourse, speakers rely on a number of factors — such as valency, animacy, word order and context — to determine the semantic role of any given argument. And for the most part, these factors are sufficient to clarify any potential uncertainty among arguments. However, ambiguity may still arise in certain circumstances. For example, a clause may contain an unexpected agent or there may be two similar arguments whose roles cannot be easily differentiated. In addition, structural ambiguity may come about when zero anaphora omits one argument and thereby makes it difficult to judge the role of the remaining argument(s). When ambiguity cannot be resolved by the factors just mentioned, $k\varepsilon i^{33}$ is inserted to mark the agent. Before the function of $k\varepsilon i^{33}$ is discussed, a closer look at the factors that frequently obviate its use will be helpful.

The first of these factors is the valency of the verb. Valency not only indicates how many arguments are involved in a given activity, but also what kind of entities they are likely to be. Thus, while a verb like tsa^{31} 'to eat' seems fairly general, in Khatso discourse it has, more often than not, a human A consuming an inanimate P. Secondarily, it may be an animal A likewise eating an inanimate P or even another animate P lower on the food chain. Clauses that follow these patterns are semantically expected, and do not require agent marking. But, if such a clause contains two animate arguments, then the roles may not be so clear. To allow for easy comparison, elicited clauses with overt arguments, which are rare in discourse due to zero anaphora, are presented below. The examples in (731) and (732) show tsa^{31} with a human and an animal A respectively; no marking is required. In (733) and (734), however, either animal has the potential to be A, and therefore the insertion of $k\varepsilon i^{33}$ is preferred to clarify the roles. In an example from discourse, shown in (735), the ambiguity hinges on the argument $a^{33}\,ma^{44}$ 'that CL:GEN', which may either denote an inanimate object or an animal, but not a human. Without $k\varepsilon i^{33}$ it is possible to interpret the two arguments as co-referential inanimate Ps, meaning that an unknown A 'ate up that, that little bit'. The presence of $k\varepsilon i^{33}$, however, marks the first argument as A, differentiating it from the role of the second argument which remains P. Moreover, in context it is clear that $a^{33}\,ma^{44}$ refers to a pig and $a^{33}ti^{53}za^{31}$ refers to its food. Note that even when $k\varepsilon i^{33}$ is present in these clauses, the canonical A R P word order is usually maintained.

(731) i^{33} tsa^{323} tsa^{31} wa^{323}.
     3SG   rice   eat   PFV
     他   饭   吃
     'He ate rice.'
     他吃饭了。
     (KL-Elicitation)

(732) ŋ³¹   kɤ²⁴   z̩³¹   tsa³¹ wa³²³.
      cow   CL:ANM   grass eat   PFV
      牛   头   草   吃
      'The cow ate grass.'
      牛吃草了。
      (KL-Elicitation)

(733) ŋ⁵⁵ŋau³²³ mɛi⁴⁴   **kɛi³³** tsʰʅ³¹ mɛi⁴⁴   tsa³¹ wa³²³.
      wolf   CL:GEN AGT   dog   CL:GEN eat   PFV
      狼   个   狗   个   吃
      'The wolf ate the dog.'
      狼吃狗了。
      (KL-Elicitation)

(734) tsʰʅ³¹ mɛi⁴⁴   **kɛi³³** ŋ⁵⁵ŋau³²³ mɛi⁴⁴   tsa³¹ wa³²³.
      dog   CL:GEN AGT   wolf   CL:GEN eat   PFV
      狗   个   狼   个   吃
      'The dog ate the wolf.'
      狗吃狼了。
      (KL-Elicitation)

(735) a³³   ma⁴⁴   **kɛi³³** a³³   ti⁵³za³¹   tsa³¹ tɕi³³   sɛi⁴⁴
      that   CL:GEN   AGT   that   CL:PCE DIM   eat   enter   TMP
      那   个   那   点   吃   进
      'after that one ate up that little bit'
      那个吃掉那点后
      (PYX-Weeds)

Clearly, the selectional restrictions imposed by verbal semantics are also closely tied to the notion of animacy. Many languages have constructions that vary according to the differences between human, animal and inanimate referents. These differences no doubt arise from real world observations, in which humans impact other entities and are typically the center of our attention and discussion. This concept is often called the animacy or agency hierarchy (Silverstein 1976; see also Dixon 1979: 85-86; Du Bois 1987: 840–843). In Khatso, prototypical ideas about animacy help differentiate the semantic roles of arguments in a clause. Generally, agents are assumed to be human. If there is no human in a clause, then the next likely candidate is a non-human animate; the least expected A is an inanimate object. For P, the hierarchy is less clear cut, but since most verbs take inanimate objects as P, the latter are considered prototypical. Thus, clauses that fit this pattern do not require the disambiguating help of *kɛi³³*, as shown in (736). Clauses that deviate, however, usually require it. For example, in (737) it is a horse that digs a well, normally a human activity, and so it takes the agent marker. Similarly, in (738) an inanimate rock kills the human, and so it too must be marked as A, even though it has no volition of its own. These types of clauses do not occur frequently in discourse, but when they do the basic function of *kɛi³³* seems to be to disambiguate arguments rather than point to the most prototypical of agents.

(736) ŋa³³ a²⁴ȵo⁵³ mɛi⁴⁴ sɛi³¹ kɯ³¹ wa³²³.
　　　 1SG monkey CL:GEN peach give PFV
　　　 我 猴子 个 桃子 给
　　　 'I gave the monkey (a) peach.'
　　　 我给猴子桃子了。
　　　 (KL-Elicitation)

(737) m̩³¹ mɛi⁴⁴ **kɛi³³** pʰa³²³ to⁵³ li³³ ŋɛi³³ tɕɛ⁵³, ma³³pʰau³¹tɕi³³
　　　 horse CL:GEN AGT excavate exit come ASRT say.after horse.dig.well
　　　 马 个 刨 出 来 说 马刨井
　　　 ɣ̍²⁴ wa³²³.
　　　 call PFV
　　　 叫
　　　 '(They say) the horse dug (it) out, so (it's) called Horse Dug Well.'
　　　 说是马刨出来的，叫马刨井了。
　　　 (HPH-Horse Dug Well)

(738) no⁵³ma³³ ɣɤ²⁴ma³³ mɛi⁴⁴ **kɛi³³** i³³ ʐ̩⁵³ si⁵³ wa³²³.
　　　 rock big.one CL:GEN AGT 3SG press kill PFV
　　　 石头 大的 个 他 压 杀
　　　 'A big rock crushed him to death.'
　　　 大石头压死他了。
　　　 (KL-Elicitation)

Word order may also help disambiguate arguments, as discussed in the previous section (§ 10.3). The general pattern is A R P and if all of the expected arguments are present, it may be enough to define their roles. An example is shown in (739). Without marking or context to the contrary, the arguments are understood to follow canonical word order.

(739) m̩³²³ tɤ²⁴ la²⁴ jo³⁵ ŋa³³ tsʰɛi³³ xa³³ wa³²³.
　　　 field plant REL CL:HUM 1SG rice send PFV
　　　 田 种 位 我 稻谷 送
　　　 'The farmer sent me rice.'
　　　 农民送我稻谷了。
　　　 (KL-Elicitation)

Context, of course, also helps resolve ambiguity. For example, the clause in (740) has non-canonical word order; P precedes R. However, in the anecdote cited it follows a phrase explaining that a merchant is asking for two hundred yuan, and so it is clear semantically that $ŋa^{33}$ is A and i^{33} is R in this particular phrase. Context may also include real world facts or cultural knowledge. For example, in (741), where both A and R are again human and $kɛi^{33}$ might otherwise be required to mark A, it is unnecessary. In Khatso culture, it is the bride's mother who provides bedclothes to the newlyweds, and this information is enough to resolve ambiguity. Word order helps here too, but, as just shown, it may not always be sufficient to disambiguate every clause.

(740) ŋa³³ tɕo³⁵ ŋ³¹xa³²³ kʰuai³¹ i³³ kɯ³¹.
 1SG then two.hundred CL:MNY 3SG give
 我 就 二百 块 她 给
 'So I gave her 200 *yuan*.'
 我就给她两百块。
 (WYF-Stools)

(741) i²⁴ma³³ tsʰɤ³³ pɣ³²³ tɕi⁵⁵ tɕo³⁵ za³¹m̥³¹ tsʰɤ³³ kɯ³¹,
 3SG.mother PL POSS CL:TYPE then daughter PL give
 母亲 们 种 就 女儿 们 给
 'The mother's side gave (them) to the daughters,'
 母亲们的给女儿们，

 tɛi³³ni³³ ɕi³³ kɯ³⁵ po⁵³.
 this.way be.accustomed give.FOC EPIS.EMP
 这么 习惯 给
 '(We) would give like that (see?)'
 就这么给的。
 (YJF-Weddings)

Working together, these factors — valency, animacy, word order and context — are typically enough to resolve ambiguity in discourse. As a result, semantic ambiguity — in which it is impossible to distinguish between two potential A in a clause, as shown in (733) and (734) above — is rare in discourse, which has been noted in other languages with pragmatic agentivity (McGregor 2010). Much more common in Khatso is ambiguity that arises for structural reasons, and this is often related to zero anaphora. As already mentioned, any argument may be omitted in discourse. This increases the difficulty of analyzing the semantic roles of any remaining arguments. For example, if a verb such as na^{31} 'to speak, talk about' — which may take two human arguments — heads a clause with only one argument, the phrase becomes ambiguous. If the overt argument were not marked as A, as in (742), it could be understood as P, and the phrase would mean 'when (someone) spoke (about) her'. The same analysis holds for (743), where the sole argument of $xɤ^{33}$ 'to scold' would be interpreted as P without the clarifying presence of the agent marker. Similarly, in (744) the lexically ditransitive verb ma^{55} 'to teach' typically takes a human R. When R is omitted, as is the case here, the agent marker is required to define the remaining argument as the teacher rather than the student. Contrast these examples with the phrase in (745), in which the agent marker is unnecessary because the lexical semantics of the verb $sɤ^{55}$ 'to watch, mind, carry (children)' alone disambiguates the two human arguments.

(742)   i³³   **kɛi³³**   n̠a³¹   sɛi⁴⁴
        3SG   AGT   speak   TMP
        他   说
        'when she spoke'
        他这么一说呢
        (YJR-Grandfather)

(743)   kɯ³³   li⁴⁴   ni³¹   xɛi³⁵   tsʰo³³ɤɤ²⁴ma³³   tsʰɤ³³   **kɛi³³**   xɤ³³.
        return   come   TOP   still   adult   PL   AGT   scold
        回   来   还   大人   们   骂
        '(When we) came home, (the) adults scolded (us).'
        回来后呢还被大人们骂。
        (GCS-Dance Parties)

(744)   ta³⁵tɕo³⁵   **kɛi³³**   ma⁵⁵.
        mother's.oldest.brother   AGT   teach
        大舅   教
        '(Your) uncle taught (you).'
        大舅教的。
        (KL-Learning)

(745)   i³³   na³¹ni²⁴za³¹   ko⁵⁵   **sɤ⁵⁵**   tsɤ³¹   sɛi⁴⁴
        3SG   child   CL:P   watch   CONT   TMP
        她   小孩   些   带
        'when she was watching (the) children'
        带着一那些小孩的时候
        (ZRF-Grandfather)

Structural ambiguity also arises in relative clauses and clause-combining constructions. In Khatso any element may be relativized, and a gap is left in the dependent clause where the head noun would be in a matrix clause (see § 7.5). This gapping strategy poses the same problem as zero anaphora. As a result, an A argument that remains in the relative clause is usually marked with $kɛi^{33}$ in order to clarify its role vis-à-vis the head noun. Examples are shown in (746) and (747). Gapping may also occur in certain clause-combining constructions where A and P may appear in separate though linked clauses. This is the case in (748), where the complement clause occurs outside the matrix clause, which is topicalized here, making the role of the first person pronoun unclear without kei^{33}. Complementation has its own inherent ambiguity, which is discussed in Chapter 15.

(746) [nɛi³³ **kɛi³³** n̠a³¹] la²⁴ tɕi⁵⁵ to³³ n̠ɛ³⁵ ŋɛi³³.
   2SG   AGT   speak   REL   CL:TYPE   also   be.few.FOC   ASRT
   你   说   种   也   小
   'You too have said little.' literally 'The words you spoke are few.'
   你说的也是小的。
   (KL-Grandfather)

(747) [ɤ⁵⁵za³¹ a³³ ko⁵⁵ **kɛi³³** la²⁴ka³³] la²⁴ wa³²³tsɿ³⁵ a³³ ko⁵⁵
   grandson that CL:PL AGT play REL toy that CL:PL
   孙子   那   些   玩   玩具   那   些
   'those toys that the grandchildren play (with)'
   那些孙子玩的那些玩具
   (HPH-Toys)

(748) [ŋa³³ **kɛi³³** sɿ⁵⁵ sɛi⁴⁴] mɛi⁴⁴ so²⁴ sa⁵⁵ sa²⁴ ja³³
   1SG   AGT   know   TOP   very   learn   be.difficult   perhaps   IPFV.EMP
   我   知道   很   学   难   可能
   ŋ³³ lɛi³¹.
   COP IRR.EMP
   是
   'I know (it) was probably very difficult to learn.'
   我觉得很难学的样子。
   (KL-Learning)

Given the pragmatic underpinnings of the agent marker, there is naturally a great deal of speaker variation in its use. In general, kei^{33} may be inserted after any A and the result is acceptable to native speakers, even though in discourse it only appears in those situations where clarity cannot be achieved in any other way. However, depending on context, using the marker where it is not necessary for disambiguation increases its prominence, and may assign a sense of contrastive focus. For example, in (749) it is used to highlight the fact that it was the Khatso rather than another ethnic group who traveled to perform. And in (750), a pair of clauses, both containing kei^{33}, contrast different A performing the same task; the absent P in both clauses is prototypically inanimate and thus expected. Moreover, these functions are not mutually exclusive — *kɛi³³* may simultaneously disambiguate and provide contrastive focus in a clause. Context usually determines the appropriate interpretation.

(749) kʰa⁵⁵tso³¹pʰa³¹ ko⁵⁵ **kɛi³³** ni³¹ka³³tsʰo³¹ i³³ sɛi⁴⁴
Khatso.M   CL:PL AGT   perform   go   TMP
喀卓男人   些   演戏   去
'when (it was) the Khatso men (who) went to perform'
是喀卓男人去演戏的时候
(PYX-Performing)

(750) za³¹m̥³¹za³¹ ko⁵⁵ **kɛi³³** tɛi³¹ xuɛi³²³ vɤ³²³ li⁴⁴ ni³¹,
girl   CL:PL AGT   one   CL:TMP buy   come TOP
女孩   些   一   回   买   来
'The girls (would) buy (and) bring (food) one time,'
女孩子们买来一回呢,

i²⁴tsɤ²⁴ ko⁵⁵ **kɛi³³** tɛi³¹ xuɛi³²³ vɤ³²³ tsa⁵⁵.
man   CL:PL AGT   one   CL:TMP buy   feed
男孩   些   一   回   买   喂
'(And) the men (would) buy (some to) feed (everyone) one time.'
男孩子们买一回来吃。
(PYX-Performing)

The pragmatic agent marker *kɛi³³* also plays a crucial role in the pseudo-passive. In this construction, the P is fronted and the A is marked by *kɛi³³* because, as the second argument, it is in a non-canonical position. This is not a true passive, but rather a specialized use of *kɛi³³* and word order to downgrade the prominence of A, thereby creating a discourse effect very much like that of a syntactic passive. This construction is described separately in § 10.5.

In addition, *kɛi³³* appears to be related to a number of other functions in the language. It is isomorphic with the instrumental marker (see § 10.6.1) as well as the directional particle 'from' (see § 10.6.2), and may have grammaticalized from one of these uses — a pattern found in other Tibeto-Burman languages (LaPolla 1995). In addition, there is a nominal conjunction *kɛi³³*, which may be used with both A and S as well as P and R (see § 7.7.2). And, as just described, the contrastive focus *kɛi³³*, which highlights one participant over another in discourse, may mark any argument regardless of its semantic role. It is likely that these latter two constructions evolved from the agent marker, since they both serve to highlight one or more arguments over the others. As a result of these multiple functions, two or more *kɛi³³* may be found in a single phrase, as shown in (751). This situation superficially undermines the role of *kɛi³³* as a disambiguator, since the competing functions also need to be differentiated in discourse, thus highlighting the importance of pragmatics for parsing constructions in the language.

(751) tɕi³²³ tsa²⁴ **kɛi³³** kɛi³³ pʰɛi³¹.
rainwear CL:ITEM INS AGT cover
蓑衣 张 用 盖
'(It) gets covered with rainwear.'
然后用蓑衣好好盖着。
(WYF-Stools)

10.5 Pseudo-Passives

Khatso does not have a true passive construction. There is, however, a construction that promotes P and downplays A, creating a discourse effect that is functionally similar to more prototypical passive constructions. This is done by reversing the word order of A and P before the verb, effectively making P the topic, and overtly marking A with the agent marker *kɛi³³* because of its non-canonical position in the phrase. Compare the declarative clause in (752) with the pseudo-passive in (753); an example from discourse is presented in (754). This construction is consistently translated using the passive *bèi* 被 particle in Putonghua. However, like the Chinese construction (LaPolla 1993: 21–24), the Khatso formulation does not undergo the changes expected of a prototypical syntactic passive. The verb is not transformed to differentiate passive from active voice, nor does the agent cease being a core argument. Rather, this is a specialized use of pragmatic agent marking. It is different enough, however, to warrant its own section, and in order to convey its discourse function, the construction is called a pseudo-passive in this analysis. Topic-comment structure is described in § 10.1, and pragmatic agentivity is discussed in § 10.4.

(752) i³³ ŋ³¹ kɤ²⁴ kʰy̠³¹ wa³²³.
3SG cow CL:ANM steal PFV
他 牛 头 偷
'He stole a cow.'
他偷了牛了。
(KL-Elicitation)

(753) ŋ³¹ kɤ²⁴ i³³ **kɛi³³** kʰy̠³¹ wa³²³.
cow CL:ANM 3SG AGT steal PFV
牛 头 他 偷
'The cow was stolen by him.'
牛被他偷了。
(KL-Elicitation)

(754) sa²⁴tʰa³¹ tɕi⁵⁵   xa³³   tsʰɤ³³   **kɛi³³**   vɤ³²³   tɤ³³   ŋa³¹?
      candy CL:TYPE who   PL   AGT   buy   PROG   CNT.Q
      糖   种   谁   们   买
      'The candy was bought by whom?'
      糖是哪些买的？
      (KL-Dance Parties)

If A is absent due to zero anaphora, as in (755), the agent marker remains to differentiate the clause from a simple declarative. Without *kɛi³³*, the phrase would be a neutral statement meaning '(you) pile up the tile pieces', and P would have little prominence. This formulation is avoided if the P is animate, since the lone argument can then easily be mistaken for A.

(755) wa³³   kʰɤ⁵³   ko⁵⁵   **kɛi³³**   ma⁵³   ni³¹
      tile   piece   CL:PL AGT   pile   TOP
      瓦   片   些   堆
      'the tile pieces were piled up'
      瓦片被堆的
      (HPH-Toys)

Because given arguments are typically omitted in Khatso, the pseudo-passive construction is never obligatory in tracking referents in discourse, and it is not frequently attested in the corpus. When it is employed, it serves to highlight P rather than A, usually because P is a newly-introduced argument that is crucial in the current context. For example, the passage in (756) is an excerpt from a longer description of how to make stools from straw. The continuing topic of stools is understood, as is the fact that A may be any person who wants to follow the procedure. Because P, *tsa³⁵fʋ³³* 'rope', is significant in the step described here, it is made prominent by pseudo-passivization.

(756) i⁴⁴ni³¹ ta³⁵, tɕi³¹ tsɛi³⁵   za³¹   tsʰɤ³¹na²⁴ ni³¹   ta³⁵   tɕo³⁵,
      then   still one   CL:TMP   DIM   stop   TOP   still then
      然后   还   一   段   停   还   就
      'Then, stop for a short while, then,'
      然后，停一会呢，就又，

      tsa³⁵fʋ³³   ko⁵⁵   **kɛi³³**   ta⁵³.
      rope   CL:PL   AGT   put.on
      绳子   些   上
      'the ropes are put on.'
      上绳子。

i⁵³	ni³²³,	tsa³⁵fv̩³³	ko⁵⁵	**kɛi³³**	ta⁵³	ni³¹	ta³⁵,
then	BKGD	rope	CL:PL	AGT	put.on	TOP	still
然后		绳子	些		上		还

'Then, (after) the ropes are put on,'
然后，上绳子呢又，

tsa³⁵fv̩³³	ko⁵⁵	ta⁵³	tɕʰɛ⁵³	ni³¹	tɕo³⁵,
rope	CL:PL	put.on	finish	TOP	then
绳子	些	上	完		就

'(after) the ropes are (all) on,'
上完绳子呢就，

tɕo³⁵	tʐ³¹	tʰɤ⁵⁵	kv̩³³	to³³	jo³³.
then	one	CL:TMP	make	flat	must
就	一	下	弄	平	应该

'Then (you) must make (them) flat.'
就要弄平一下。
(WYF-Stools)

10.6 Oblique Arguments

Khatso verbs all have a basic argument structure, but these structures may be expanded by adding extra elements to a clause. Instrumental, locative and temporal elements are usually introduced through the use of postpositions, and typically sit between A/S and the verb. For the most part, they are oblique arguments. That is, the information conveyed is not crucial to understanding the basic activity described by the verb. These constructions are discussed in § 10.6.1, § 10.6.2 and § 10.6.3 respectively. Constructions that add core arguments — such as the applicative and causatives — are described separately in Chapter 11.

10.6.1 Instrumental Arguments

In some cases, the additional argument in a clause is an instrument. That is, it highlights the tool or method a participant uses to carry out the activity described by the verb. In Khatso, the instrument is followed by the particle $kɛi^{33}$, as shown in (757) and (758). Note that unlike in Putonghua, the matrix verb zei^{31} 'to use' is never employed as an instrumental marker.

(757) lo³²³tsʴ³³tau³³ pa⁵³   **kɛi³³** tɕi³¹   tʰɤ⁵⁵   to²⁴
      screwdriver   CL:HNDL INS   one   CL:TMP poke
      螺丝刀   把   用   一   下   捅
      'poke (it) in with a screwdriver'
      用螺丝刀捅一下
      (WYF-Stools)

(758) ja⁵³   tɕo³⁵   ŋ³⁵ma³³ mɛi⁴⁴   **kɛi³³** tsʴ³⁵   tsɤ³¹.
      later then   heart   CL:GEN INS   remember   CONT
      然后   就   心   个   用   记
      'Afterwards (he) always remembered (it) by heart.'
      然后就用心记着。
      (KL-Learning)

This particle is identical to the pragmatic agentivity marker (see § 10.4), the directional particle 'from' (see § 9.3.3) and the nominal conjunction (see § 7.7.2). Nonetheless, since in this function it almost always follows a common noun, its function is usually distinct from the agent and directional markers. And since the conjunction usually occurs in pairs, its use is likewise distinguishable from the instrumental particle.

In addition, some verbs in Khatso include instrumental information lexically, so that an oblique phrase is unnecessary. As just one example, there is a group of verbs related to carrying, as shown in Table 10.1, and each lexically specifies a different way in which an item is handled.

Table 10.1: Verbs of carrying in Khatso

Khatso	English	Chinese
sɤ⁵⁵	'to carry children in one's arm(s)'	带
sʴ³³	'to carry in one's hand'	拿
tɛi³⁵	'to carry in cupped hands'	捧
ta³⁵	'to carry in one's arm(s)'	抱
pv³¹	'to carry on one's back'	背
kʰa³²³	'to carry on one's shoulder(s)'	扛
tʰɛi³¹	'to carry with a shoulder pole'	担
tɕi³⁵	'to carry a load (on back of animal or vehicle)'	驮

10.6.2 Locative Arguments

Locative adverbs and nouns that denote location describe the place in which an event occurs, and they do not require an adposition (see § 9.3.3). However, to specify the location of an argument within its environment or to describe the source or goal of an action, an oblique locative phrase is required. Locations may also occur in the complex purpose construction with the clause linker *tɤ⁴⁴* (see § 14.6). Note that movement associated with performing the action itself is expressed through a serial verb construction (see § 8.8).

The most frequently-used postpositions in Khatso that describe spatial and directional situations are shown in Table 10.2. Phrases containing them typically occur directly behind A/S and before the other elements of a clause, as shown in (759). Additional examples from discourse are shown in (760) through (763).

Table 10.2: Locative and directional particles in Khatso

Khatso	English	Chinese
ka⁵³(la³¹)	'on'	上面
ka⁵³la³¹ a³³ɳa⁵³ li⁴⁴	'above'	上方
kʰɤ³³, i³³kʰɤ³³, li⁴⁴, ti⁴⁴	'in', 'at', 'to'	里
o⁵³tsɿ³³	'under'	下面
o³¹tso³³	'in front of'	前面
ɳa³²³tɤ³³	'behind'	后面
pʰa³²³piɛ³³	'beside'	旁边
ɳa³⁵tso³³	'outside'	外面
tɕa⁵⁵la³¹, tsɛi³⁵tsɛi³⁵ko²⁴la³¹	'between', 'in the middle of'	之间，中间
la³³tsʰo³³	'towards'	往
kɛi³³	'from'	从
ta⁵⁵, ta⁵⁵ta⁵⁵	'at'	在

(759) i³³ [la³²³la³³ mɛi⁴⁴ kʰɤ³³] **kɛi³³** pʰi³²³kuo³¹ ɤ̯³²³ wa³²³.
　　　3SG　basket　CL:GEN　in　from　apple　hold　PFV
　　　她　　篮子　　个　　里　从　苹果　　拿
　　'She picked (up) an apple from inside the basket.'
　　她从篮子里拿了苹果。
　　(KL-Elicitation)

(760) tɛi³³ jo³⁵ [wai³⁵kuo³²³ li⁴⁴] **kɛi³³** li³²³ ŋɛi³³, [mɛi³¹kuo³²³ li⁴⁴] **kɛi³³**.
this CL:HUM foreign.country in from come ASRT USA in from
这 位 外国 里 从 来 美国 里 从
'This person is from overseas, from the United States.'
这个是外国来的，从美国那里。
(KL-Childhood)

(761) [piɛ³⁵ po²⁴] **ka⁵³la³¹** tɛi³⁵ la²⁴ a³³ ti⁵³
pen CL:ROD on carry REL that CL:PCE
笔 支 上 带 那 块
'that piece on (the end of) pencils'
笔上带的那块
(YAY-Erasers)

(762) [tɛi³³n̪a⁵³] **kɛi³³** kɯ³³ i³³ xa³⁵ [tɛi³³ ko⁵⁵] **kɛi³³** to⁵³ li³³ kɯ³¹
here from enter go still this CL:PL from exit come INDR.CAUS
这里 从 进 去 还 这 些 从 出 来
tɤ³³ ŋ³³ sa⁴⁴?
PROG ASRT CRTN.Q
'(It) goes in from here, (then) is let out through these, right?'
从这里进去又从这些这里出来的，是吗？
(KL-Qin)

(763) [tsʰau³¹to³³ mɛi⁴⁴ pɤ³²³ a³³n̪a⁵³ li⁴⁴] **ŋa³⁵tso³³** tʰi³¹ la²⁴
stool CL:GEN POSS there in outside weave REL
草墩 个 那里 里 外面 编
'those woven on the stool's outside there'
编在草墩外面的那里的
(KL-Stools)

These particles are typically omitted with place names, as shown in (764), and with the noun *xɤ³³pɛi³³* 'home', as (765) illustrates. Often they are omitted with the deictic adverbs as well, though including them is grammatical, as in (766).

(764) kʰai³³tsʅ³²³ vɤ³²³ i³³ sɛi⁴⁴ **nɤ³²³kʰɤ³³** vɤ³²³ i³³ ŋɛi³³.
eraser buy go TOP Hexi buy go ASRT
橡皮擦 买 去 河西 买 去
'To buy erasers, (you) go (to) Hexi to buy (them).'
买橡皮擦是去河西买去的。
(YAY-Erasers)

(765) tɛi³¹ ŋ²⁴ ŋ³²³ **xɤ³³pɛi³³** tso³²³ la³⁵ wa³³ sa⁴⁴?
one CL:TMP CL:TMP home EXIST FOC CRS CRTN.Q
一 天 天 家 有
'(He) is at home every day?'
天天都在家了吗？
(KL-Erasers)

(766) ŋa³³tsʰɤ³¹ jɛ³²³na³²³sɛi³¹ mei⁴⁴ tɛi³³n̩a⁵³ **li⁴⁴**
1PL Yunnan.Province CL:GEN here in
我们 云南省 个 这里 里
'here in our Yunnan Province'
我们云南省这里
(HPH-Horse Dug Well)

Because *kɛi³³* 'from' is homophonous with the pragmatic agent marker (see § 10.4), it does not modify human arguments in directional constructions. The particle *li⁴⁴* is used instead, as shown in (767). This may be augmented with a directional phrase involving a locative adverb, as shown in (768), but it is not obligatory.

(767) ŋa³³ nei³³ **li⁴⁴** tsɿ³¹xɯ³⁵ tsɿ⁵⁵ wa³²³.
1SG 2SG from money borrow PFV
我 你 从 钱 借
'I borrowed money from you.'
我跟你借钱了。
(KL-Elicitation)

(768) ŋa³³ i³³ **li⁴⁴** a³³n̩a⁵³ kɛi³³ ŋa³²³ nei³³.
1SG 3SG from there from obtain ASRT
我 他 里 那里 从 得到
'I got (it) from him there.'
我从他那里得到的。
(KL-Elicitation)

10.6.3 Temporal Arguments

Temporal adverbs and nominal constructions that denote time, which require no postpositions, set the time frame or duration of an event in a clause (see § 9.3.1). Oblique postpositional constructions are used, however, to express complex temporal relationships, such as *i³¹ŋ³²³ o³¹tso³³* 'before today' or *tɛi³³tɕʰa⁵⁵kʰɤ³³ tsʰɿ³³* 'up to now'. Like locative expressions, these constructions may either precede or directly follow A/S. The postpositions are drawn from vocabulary involving locations (see

§ 10.6.2). For example, *o³¹tso³³* 'before' and *ŋa³²³tɣ³³* 'after' are also the locative adverbs for 'behind' and 'in front of'. Moreover, *li⁴⁴ kɛi³³ tsɛi³³* 'from [TIME] on' contains the directional particle *kɛi³³* 'from', and *tsʰɿ³³* is the lexical verb 'to arrive'. Examples are shown in (769) and (770).

(769) **i³¹ŋ³²³   o³¹tso³³**   i³³   li³²³   ŋa³²³   ma³¹   ta³²³.
      today   before   3SG   come   obtain   NEG   be.able
      今天   以前   他   来   得到   不   能
      'He couldn't come before today.'
      今天以前他不能来。
      (KL-Elicitation)

(770) ja⁵³   **ŋa³²³tɣ³³**   tɕo³⁵   sɿ²⁴tɕʰɛ²⁴   tɕo³⁵   **tʰɛi³³tɕʰa⁵⁵kʰɣ³³   tsʰɿ³³**.
      later   afterwards   then   divide   then   this.time   arrive
      然后   后面   就   分开   就   这时候   到
      'So, afterwards (they) have been divided up to now.'
      然后，后来就分开就到现在了。
      (KL-Childhood)

Describing time frames that occur at a set point in time typically requires a periphrastic phrase that combines a temporal noun and the verb serialization *ko⁵³ no⁵³*, which means 'completely passed', as in (771). *ŋa³²³tɣ³³* is now mainly used independently to mean 'later, afterwards', as (770) above illustrates. The expression *ta³¹ ni³²³* 'after', which involves the background marker, is only used with clauses and cannot modify noun phrases; it is discussed in § 13.2.4.3. In addition, phrases corresponding to 'when' and 'while' typically require relative clause constructions (see § 7.5) or the general temporal marker *sɛi⁴⁴* (see § 13.2.1).

(771) **i³¹ŋ³²³   ko⁵³   no⁵³**   ni³²³,   sɣ⁵⁵   ma³¹   vɣ³²³.
      today   pass   complete   BKGD   book   NEG   buy
      今天   过   掉   书   不   买
      'After today, (he) won't buy books.'
      今天以后不买书。
      (KL-Elicitation)

In discourse, one of the most frequently encountered temporal expressions is *tɛi³¹tʰɣ⁵⁵*, which denotes duration and means 'awhile'. Compositionally, it is a classifier construction containing the numeral *tɛi³¹* 'one' and the temporal classifier *tʰɣ⁵⁵*, though often it is abbreviated to the classifier alone. Examples from discourse are shown in (772), (773) and (774). Note that in (774) the diminutive suffix *-za³¹* is added to the classifier to indicate a relatively brief period of time. When *tʰɣ⁵⁵* is combined with *sɛi⁴⁴*, as in (775), the construction means 'all at once, suddenly', which describes an even briefer duration. See § 6.2.2.7 and § 6.2.2.9 for the other functions of this classifier.

(772) ɕɛ³⁵tsʰa³¹ mɛi⁴⁴ ti³²³ **tʰɤ⁵⁵** ŋ²⁴ka³³ i³³ sɛi⁴⁴
scene CL:GEN at CL:TMP look go TMP
现场 个 里 下 看 去
'when (they) went to look at the scene for a while'
现场里去看一下
(HPH-Horse Dug Well)

(773) ŋa³³ **tʰɤ⁵⁵** ɕa³¹ ŋ²⁴ka³³ jo³³ wa³²³.
1SG CL:TMP think see must PFV
我 下 想 看 应该
'I must think about that for a while.'
我应该想想看。
(KL-Weeds)

(774) kv̩³³ ŋa³²³ta²⁴ ni³¹, **tʰɤ⁵⁵** za³¹ kv̩³³
do be.able TOP CL:TMP DIM do
做 能 下 做
'if (you) can do (it), do (it) for a little while'
能作呢，做一下
(KL-Sewing)

(775) **tʰɤ⁵⁵sɛi⁴⁴** tɕo³⁵ sɹ̩³⁵tsʰɹ̩³⁵ ko⁵⁵ to³³ mɛi⁴⁴ tɕʰa³²³.
suddenly then energy CL:PL also very be.strong
一下子 就 士气 些 也 很 强
'Suddenly, their energy was strong.'
一下子士气就很强了。
(HPH-Horse Dug Well)

Pragmatically, delimiting an activity with *tʰɤ⁵⁵* serves to downplay the potential difficulty of the activity. For this reason, the construction is often used to soften imperatives, as shown in (776) and (777). Note that the temporal sense may also be present, since the desired event may take time to carry out. See § 12.2 for a discussion of imperatives.

(776) "ŋa³³ tɛi³¹ tʰɤ⁵⁵ to³⁵ pa³²³ liɛ³³."
1SG one CL:TMP ford help come
我 一 下 渡 帮 来
' "Come help me cross." '
"来帮我渡一下。"
(HPH-Weeds)

(777) a³³ ko⁵⁵ tʰɤ⁵⁵ ŋ²⁴ka³³ kɯ³¹
that CL:PL CL:TMP see INDR.CAUS
那 些 下 看
'show (him how to make) those awhile'
给那些看一下
(KL-Sewing)

11 Valency-Changing Constructions

The previous chapter outlines the basic argument structure of verbs. It is possible to change this structure by inserting an additional core argument in a clause. This may be done through two separate strategies, the applicative construction and the causative constructions. The applicative, which adds a third argument that may be interpreted as a recipient, beneficiary or a causee, is described in § 11.1. The three causative constructions, in which agents cause an activity to occur involving other arguments, are discussed in § 11.2. Unlike the prototypical passive found in other languages, the pseudo-passive construction in Khatso does not alter the valency of verbs and so is not included here (see § 10.5.)

11.1 Applicative Construction

As mentioned in § 8.3, there are a handful of verbs in Khatso that are inherently ditransitive — they may take three core arguments without additional marking of any sort. Transitive verbs outside of this small group require an applicative construction to add a third argument. This construction places the verb $kɯ^{31}$ 'to give' after the matrix verb in a specialized serial verb construction; the new argument is placed between A and P:

$$\text{A} \quad \text{3RD.ARGUMENT} \quad \text{P} \quad \text{VERB} \quad kɯ^{31}$$

This is the same word order found in clauses headed by lexically ditransitive verbs. But in this case, the construction is semantically ambiguous. The new argument may be interpreted as a recipient, a beneficiary or a causee. Given this flexibility, the construction is more properly defined as applicative. In discourse, the ambiguity is resolved through the semantics of individual verbs as well as discourse context and real-world knowledge, but routinized use also seems to play a role.

Verbal semantics often differentiates recipients from beneficiaries. For example, with the verb $ŋ^{31}$ 'to sell' the third argument is usually interpreted as a recipient, as (778) shows. But in (779) with $vɤ^{323}$ 'to buy', it is a typically seen as a beneficiary, though it may mean either 'for my benefit' or 'in my place' — a difference clarified in context. Semantically, these senses are not far apart — buying clothes for me, whether in my stead or not, implies that I receive the clothing purchased; I am simultaneously recipient and beneficiary.

(778) i³³ **ŋa³³** sɣ⁵⁵ ko⁵⁵ ŋ³¹ kɯ³¹
 3SG 1SG book CL:PL sell give
 她 我 书 些 卖 给
 'She sold books to me.'
 她卖书给我了。
 (KL-Elicitation)

(779) i³³ **ŋa³³** tʰo³³ vɣ³²³ kɯ³¹ wa³²³.
 3SG 1SG clothes buy give PFV
 她 我 衣服 买 给
 'She bought clothes for me.'
 她买给我衣服了。
 (KL-Elicitation)

The same pattern may also be interpreted as an indirect causative construction, as (780) illustrates. That is, instead of recipient or beneficiary, the third argument is the causee who is allowed to perform the action by the agent. In fact, the phrase in (778) above may also be understood as the causative phrase 'she lets me sell books', but without context this reading is dispreferred for the phrase in (779). Applicative constructions modifying intransitive and stative verbs also tend to be analyzed as causatives, as demonstrated by (781) and (782) below. Such differences among individual verbs suggest that routinized use plays a role in using this construction. Speakers may turn to an alternate but more complex construction to specify that the third argument is not a causee; it is discussed in § 14.6. The causative constructions that feature *kɯ³¹* are described further in § 11.2.2.2 and § 11.2.2.3.

(780) i³³ ŋa³³ tsa³²³ m̩³³ **kɯ³¹**.
 3SG 1SG rice make INDR.CAUS
 她 我 饭 做
 'She lets me cook.'
 她让我做饭。
 (KL-Elicitation)

(781) ŋa³³ i³³ kɣ³¹ **kɯ³¹**.
 1SG 3SG run INDR.CAUS
 我 他 跑
 'I let him run.'
 我让他跑。
 (KL-Elicitation)

(782) i³³   ŋa³³   tɕi³¹   **kɯ³¹**.
     3SG   1SG   be.fast   INDR.CAUS
     他   我   快
     'He lets me (go) fast.'
     他让我快。
     (KL-Elicitation)

Another way to highlight the benefactive nature of an activity is to use *pa³²³* 'to help' instead of the *kɯ³¹* construction, as in (783). However, this verb presents a different sort of ambiguity, since it may imply that one does something *with* someone else as well as *for* that person. As a result, the phrase in (783) may mean either that the speaker sold books in place of a friend or that she worked alongside the friend selling books. Again, context largely resolves the ambiguity. In addition, there is a clause-combining construction that also creates a benefactive sense (see § 14.6).

(783) ŋa³³   i³³   sa²⁴kɛi³³   sɤ⁵⁵   ŋ³¹   **pa³²³**.
     1SG   3SG   just   book   sell   help
     我   他   刚   书   卖   帮
     'I sell books for him (in his stead).' / 'I help him sell books (alongside him).'
     我帮他买书。
     (KL-Elicitation)

The applicative construction is negated by modifying the matrix verb rather than *kɯ³¹*, as shown in (784) and (785). Polar questions are formed by reduplicating *kɯ³¹* and not the matrix verb, as (786) illustrates.

(784) i³³   kɛi³³   ŋa³³   tʰo³³   **ma³¹**   **vɤ³²³**   **kɯ³¹**.
     3SG   AGT   1SG   clothing   NEG   buy   give
     她   我   衣服   不   买   给
     'She is not buying clothes for me.'
     她不买给我衣服。
     (KL-Elicitation)

(785) ŋa³³   nɛi³³   sɤ⁵⁵   tɕi³³   pɛi³¹   **ma³¹**   **ŋ³¹**   **kɯ³¹**.
     1SG   2SG   book   this   CL:VOL   NEG   sell   give
     我   你   书   这   本   不   卖   给
     'I am not selling you this book.'
     我不卖给你这本书。
     (KL-Elicitation)

(786) nɛi³³ i³³ tsa³²³ m̩³³ **kɯ³¹** **kɯ³¹**?
      2SG   3SG rice   make INDR.CAUS INDR.CAUS
      你   他   饭   做
      'You let him cook?'
      你让不让他做饭？
      (KL-Elicitation)

The exact syntactic nature of this construction is difficult to assess. The verb *kɯ³¹* 'to give' retains its general meaning here — though it may convey the figurative transmittal of assistance or permission instead of the literal movement of goods — so it cannot be viewed as a grammatical particle. Nor is it an auxiliary (see § 8.7); *kɯ³¹* is a stand-alone verb that is not deontic, nor is it ever negated in this construction. Syntactically, the *kɯ³¹* construction most closely resembles two-event verb serializations (see § 8.8.2). Both negation and the formation of polar questions pattern like those involving two-event constructions. And, when functioning ditransitively and benefactively, the two events can be seen as separate but closely linked by both time and purpose. For example, if one cooks for someone else, the making not only precedes the giving but it is done expressly for that purpose. But, this temporal logic does not extend to the causative reading, where the permission (instantiated by *kɯ³¹*) occurs after the verb describing the allowed activity. And although the two verbs share aspect markers, they do not share the same arguments. The cook is separate from the person who receives the food, and the authority is not the causee. Thus, the construction does not neatly fit the two-event verb serialization pattern, suggesting that it evolved separately, perhaps as a metaphoric extension of the ditransitive *kɯ³¹* clause, without regard to the other multi-verb structures in the language.

11.2 Causative Constructions

Causative constructions add an argument to clauses by introducing a causer who controls the state or action specified. Typically the causer is human, but animal or inanimate causers are also possible in Khatso, depending on the semantics of the verb. There are two basic types of causative construction formation in Khatso. The first involves a handful of lexical causatives, described in § 11.2.1. The second, and by far the most productive type, involves periphrastic constructions, of which there are three. They are examined in § 11.2.2.

11.2.1 Lexical Causatives

As both Dai, Liu and Fu (1987: 155–56) and Mu (2002: 86) note, there are only a few verbs in Khatso that intrinsically carry a causative meaning. Those identified to date are listed in Table 12.1. Each differs from its non-causative counterpart in lexical tone; examples of their use are shown in (787) and (788). Note that, unlike the other verbs, mo^{33} can only be used in compounds with other verbs. The earlier sources include another pair, k^ho^{53} 'to be bent' and ko^{53} 'to bend', but the latter is an intransitive verb and cannot form a causative phrase without ky^{33} 'to make, do', one of the periphrastic constructions discussed below (see § 11.2.2.2).

Table 11.1: Lexical causatives in Khatso

	Non-Causative		Causative		
Khatso	English	Chinese	Khatso	English	Chinese
mo^{323}	'to see'	见	mo^{33}	'to show'	给见
tsa^{31}	'to eat'	吃	tsa^{55}	'to feed'	喂
to^{323}	'to drink'	喝	to^{33}	'to give to drink'	使喝
$tɕo^{53}$	'to be afraid'	害怕	$tɕo^{35}$	'to scare'	吓唬

(787) $i^{24}tsɤ^{24}$ ko^{55} $kɛi^{33}$ $tɛi^{31}$ $xuɛi^{323}$ $vɤ^{323}$ **tsa^{55}**.
      man   CL:PL AGT   one   CL:TMP   buy   feed
      男   些   一   回   买   喂
      '(And) the men (would) buy (some to) feed (everyone) one time.'
      男孩子们买一回来吃。
      (PYX-Performing)

(788) $t^ho^{33}tso^{53}ma^{33}$ $tɛi^{31}$ ma^{24} la^{53} **mo^{33}** i^{33} ta^{323} ta^{323}?
      button   one   CL:GEN   wrap   show   go   be.acceptable   be.acceptable
      纽扣   一   个   绕   给看   去   行   行
      'Wrap a button knot to show (him), okay?'
      去绕一个纽扣看看，行不行？
      (KL-Sewing)

These verbs do not differentiate between force and permission, a distinction found in the periphrastic constructions. Thus, a phrase such as (787) above may be interpreted as either 'give to eat' or 'force-feed'; context makes the intended meaning clear. In addition, they are incompatible with all but the $la^{33}ta^{55}...mo^{55}$ periphrastic causative construction.

These kinds of pairs are a typological feature of the Tibeto-Burman language family (e.g. Bradley 1979: 238–239; Gerner 2007; Matisoff 1976: 414–419), although the process is more productive in some languages than others. In Khatso it is not productive at all; it is not possible to use tone change to create more pairs beyond these four clearly lexicalized forms.

11.2.2 Periphrastic Causative Constructions

In modern Khatso, causatives are primarily created through periphrastic constructions. There are three such patterns and each differs from the other, although their uses overlap in some cases. The $la^{33}ta^{55}...\ mo^{55}$ construction indicates inescapable force or compulsion, the $k\gamma^{33}$ construction refers to "hands on" force, and kw^{31} denotes permission and accidental results. In addition, there is an auxiliary verb $w\varepsilon i^{323}$ 'to allow' that expresses causation, but it is rare in the corpus. Other verbs, such as $tc^h\varepsilon^{35}$ 'to urge' and p^hai^{35} 'to send, dispatch', may also convey a causative meaning, but they require complementation (see § 15.1).

11.2.2.1 Causative Construction with $la^{33}ta^{55}...mo^{55}$

The causative construction that entails the causee being forced or compelled to action is formed with the nominal postposition $la^{33}ta^{55}$ and the verb mo^{55}, which means both 'to want' and 'to require'. As the matrix verb in this construction, mo^{55} sits in the phrase-final position, which indicates that the causer and the causee are different individuals. As mentioned in § 8.7, mo^{55} functions as an auxiliary only if it precedes another verb. The postposition $la^{33}ta^{55}$ marks the causee, and the clausal caused event occurs between it and mo^{55}. A schematic is shown below; examples are provided in (789) and (790).

CAUSER CAUSEE $la^{33}ta^{55}$ CAUSED.EVENT mo^{55}

(789) ŋa³³ i³³ **la³³ta⁵⁵** [ka³²³] **mo⁵⁵** wa³²³.
1SG 3SG CAUS walk require PFV
我 他   走 要
'I made him leave.'
我让他走了。
(KL-Elicitation)

(790) i³³tsʰɣ³³ **la³³ta⁵⁵** [tɕʰɛ⁵⁵] **mo⁵⁵** ni³¹
3PL CAUS dance require TOP
他们   跳 要
'(when they) made them dance'
要让他们跳呢
(PYX-Performing)

Because of the polysemy inherent in *mo⁵⁵*, this construction has two meanings, one causative and one desiderative. As a causative, it indicates that the causer acts deliberately and the causee has little or no control over the matter. The implied force is not necessarily physical; it may refer to a threat of force, parental or governmental authority, rules and customs, or even a request that cannot easily be refused. As a desiderative construction, it signals that the ultimate agent wants the causee to perform an action, but there is no force or compulsion involved. The causee has complete control over the action in this case and, in fact, may not even be aware of the desire of the agent. Context primarily resolves the ambiguity in discourse. Since the focus here is on causative constructions, possible desiderative interpretations are not discussed beyond this point; desiderative clauses are discussed in § 8.7 and § 15.2.

The causative construction may be used with verbs of any valency, and in each case an additional nominal argument is introduced. Already shown in the examples above are phrases involving intransitive verbs. Stative verbs may also be made causative, as (791) and (792) illustrate, in which case the meaning is that the causee is deliberately compelled to achieve a new state. Transitive and ditransitive verbs may also take part in this construction, as (793) and (794) respectively demonstrate.

(791) ŋa³³ i³³   **la³³ta⁵⁵** [tɕi³¹]   **mo⁵⁵**.
      1SG   3SG   CAUS   be.quick   require
      我   他   快   要
      'I make him go faster.'
      我让他快。
      (KL-Elicitation)

(792) ŋa³³ i³³   **la³³ta⁵⁵** [si³³si³³] **mo⁵⁵**.
      1SG   3SG   CAUS   be.happy   require
      我   他   高兴   要
      'I make him put up a happy front.', literally 'I make him be happy.'
      我勉强他高兴。
      (KL-Elicitation)

(793) ŋa³³ sɛi⁴⁴   pa³¹   ŋa³³ **la³³ta⁵⁵** [m³²³ tɤ²⁴]   **mo⁵⁵**.
      1SG   family father 1SG   CAUS   field plant   require
      我   家   爸爸   我   田   种   要
      'My father makes me plant (the) fields.'
      我的爸爸让我种田。
      (KL-Elicitation)

(794) ŋa³³ sɛi⁴⁴ mo³³ ŋa³³ **la³³ta⁵⁵** [n̠ɛ³²³ jo³⁵ tɕʰɛ³²³ kɯ³¹]
     1SG family mother 1SG CAUS younger.brother CL:HUM money give
     我 家 妈妈 我 弟弟 位 钱 给
mo⁵⁵.
require
要
'My mother makes me give (my) younger brother money.'
我妈妈让我给弟弟钱。
(KL-Elicitation)

Because the *la³³ta⁵⁵* construction indicates that the causer deliberately controls the causee, often against the will of the latter, the causer must be human. Situations in which a non-human causer forces a human to act tend to be expressed through other means, such as the *kɯ³¹* construction described below (see § 11.2.2.3) or with a reason construction, as in (795). This sentence is the semantic equivalent of the English phrase 'the changing weather made me run home', although causation is only implied through pragmatics.

(795) m̩³¹ma²⁴ mɛi⁴⁴ piɛ⁵³ ta³¹ ni³²³, ŋa³³ kɤ³¹ kɯ³³ i³³ wa³²³.
     weather CL:GEN change after BKGD 1SG run enter go PFV
     天气 个 变 以后 我 跑 回 去
'Because the weather changed, I ran home.' / 'The changing weather made me run home.'
天气变了呢,我跑回家了。
(KL-Elicitation)

Negation in these clauses occurs on the matrix verb *mo⁵⁵*, just as in non-causative clauses featuring this verb, as (796) illustrates. This occurs regardless of whether one describes a lack of causation or a lack of desire to prevent the caused event. In other words, because of the polysemy of *mo⁵⁵*, the phrase in (796) may be interpreted two ways depending on the context. It may mean 'I don't make him cry' or 'I make him (stop) crying', literally 'I make him not cry'. Context generally resolves the ambiguity.

(796) ŋa³³ i³³ **la³³ta⁵⁵** [ŋ³²³] **ma³¹ mo⁵⁵**.
     1SG 3SG CAUS cry NEG require
     我 他 哭 不 要
'I don't make him cry' / 'I make him (stop) crying'.
我不让他哭。/ 我让他不哭。
(KL-Elicitation)

Polar questions are formed by reduplicating the verb mo^{55}, as shown in (797). The basic nature of reduplication tends to emphasize the verb here, heightening the ambiguity created by its polysemy.

(797) nɛi³³   i³³   la³³ta⁵⁵   [ka³²³]   **mo⁵⁵**   **mo⁵⁵**?
      2SG   3SG   CAUS   walk   require require
      你   他   走   要   要
      'Are you making him go?' / 'Do you want him to go?'
      你让不让他走？/ 你要不要他走？
      (KL-Elicitation)

The categorial status of $la^{33}ta^{55}$ is unclear. It is not a verb; it cannot be negated nor can it support aspectual particles. Morphologically it may be a combination of the comparative postposition la^{33} and ta^{55} 'be a type, manner, style', which suggests it might carry an adverbial meaning such as 'in this manner'. However, it cannot be used productively in clauses headed by verbs other than mo^{55}; the demonstrative adverbs $tɕi^{33}ni^{33}$ 'this way' and $a^{33}ni^{33}$ 'that way' are used for that purpose. Because it has a clear-cut function but its status is not obvious, it is considered a grammatical postposition in this analysis.

The nature of the postposition also has a bearing on the syntactic analysis of this construction. In some languages, caused event phrases are considered subordinate clauses, but this does not seem to be the case in Khatso. Instead, the causee is an additional argument in the mo^{55} clause, marked by $la^{33}ta^{55}$ — which is unlike any other clause-combining mechanism in the language. It occurs in no other embedding process, not even with semantically similar verbs like $tɕʰɛ^{35}$ 'to urge' and $sη^{33}wa^{35}$ 'to wish, hope'. Its only function is to mark the causee, thereby disambiguating it from the other arguments in this particular construction, just as $kɛi^{33}$ highlights A wherever it may not be clear (see § 10.4).

11.2.2.2 Causative Construction with $kγ^{33}$

The verb $kγ^{33}$ 'to do, make' is found in a separate causative construction. Because the verb conveys purposeful action, this construction is mainly used to describe situations in which the causer directly impacts the causee, often with a "hands on" sense, although the impact need not literally be physical in nature. To form the construction, $kγ^{33}$ is placed before the verb expressing the caused event, and the causer and causee precede it. Usually, the construction also includes $kɯ^{31}$ 'to give' at the end of the phrase, mirroring the indirect causative (see § 11.2.2.3), but this is not obligatory. A schematic of the construction is shown below; an example is provided in (798).

                CAUSER   CAUSEE $kγ^{33}$ CAUSED.EVENT   ($kɯ^{31}$)

(798) i³³   ŋa³³ **kɣ³³** [ŋ³²³] **kɯ³¹**.
    3SG 1SG make cry   INDR.CAUS
    他   我   弄   哭
    'He makes me cry.'
    他把我弄哭。
    (KL-Elicitation)

This construction is frequently used with stative verbs, and it is thus similar to a resultative serial verb construction (§ 8.8.1.2). The second verb describes the new state that arises as a result of the causer's action. For example, the phrase in (799) describes the preparation of straw so that it may be woven into a stool. Note that the "hands on" connotation is often literal in these cases.

(799) tɤ³¹   tʰɤ⁵⁵   **kɣ³³**   to³³.
    one   CL:TMP make   be.flat
    一   下   弄   平
    'Make (it) flat.'
    弄平一下。
    (WYF-Stools)

With the presence of *kɯ³¹*, these phrases mirror the syntax of the applicative construction (see § 11.1) and thus they often have multiple meanings. For example, the phrase in (800) may be interpreted as a causative construction referring to force-feeding, or as a benefactive construction describing aiding someone who is too ill to eat without assistance. Likewise, the phrase in (801) may be translated as 'she forces me to wear (it)' or 'she makes (it) for me to wear'. Again, context helps point to the most relevant meaning.

(800) i³³   kɛi³³ ŋa³³ tsa³²³ **kɣ³³** [tsa³¹] **kɯ³¹**.
    3SG AGT   1SG   rice   make   eat   INDR.CAUS
    他   我   饭   让   吃
    'He forces me to eat.' / 'He helps me eat.'
    他做饭给我吃。/ 他给我做饭吃。
    (KL-Elicitation)

(801) i³³   kɛi³³ ŋa³³ **kɣ³³** [vi⁵³] **kɯ³¹**.
    3SG AGT   1SG   make   wear   INDR.CAUS
    她   我   让   穿
    'She forces me to wear (it) .' / 'She makes (it) for me to wear.'
    她给我穿衣服。/ 她做衣服给我穿。
    (KL-Elicitation)

If the caused event is represented by a verb other than a stative verb, then only kv^{33} is modified by the negative marker ma^{31}, as (802) shows. But if the caused event is stative, then the construction may be negated in two ways, mirroring negation in resultative serializations (see § 8.8.1.2). Thus, when ma^{31} modifies kv^{33}, it means that neither the action nor the result occurs, as shown in (803). Placing ma^{31} between the verbs negates only the result, as in (804), indicating that the action is attempted but the result does not occur or is not possible.

(802) i³³   ŋa³³   **ma³¹** **kv̩³³** [ŋ³²³] **kɯ³¹**.
     3SG   1SG   NEG   make   cry   INDR.CAUS
     他   我   不   让   哭
     'He didn't make me cry.'
     他没有把我弄哭。
     (KL-Elicitation)

(803) i³³   tɛi³³   ma⁴⁴   **ma³¹**   **kv̩³³**   [to³³].
     3SG   that   CL:GEN   NEG   make   be.flat
     她   这   个   不   弄   平
     'She does not make that one flat.'
     她不把这个弄平。
     (KL-Elicitation)

(804) i³³   tɛi³³   ma⁴⁴   **kv̩³³**   **ma³¹**   [to³³]   ŋɛi³³.
     3SG   that   CL:GEN   make   NEG   be.flat   ASRT
     她   这   个   弄   不   平
     'She is not able to make that one flat.'
     她弄不平这个。
     (KL-Elicitation)

Polar questions are formed by either reduplicating the second verb or, if present, the verb $kɯ^{31}$, as shown in (805) and (806) respectively.

(805) **kv̩³³**   [**to³³**   **to³³**]?
     make   be.flat   be.flat
     弄   平   平
     'Are (you) making (it) flat?'
     弄不弄平？
     (KL-Elicitation)

(806) i³³   nɛi³³   ky³³   ŋ³²³   **kɯ³¹**   **kɯ³¹**   la³¹?
      3SG   2SG   make   cry   INDR.CAUS   INDR.CAUS   IRR.Q
      他   你   弄   哭
      'Did he make you cry?'
      他有没有把你弄哭？
      (KL-Elicitation)

Because of the variable nature of this construction, it straddles several syntactic categories. Technically, it is a serial verb construction since it combines two or more verbs together in a single clause. Without *kɯ³¹*, and when the second verb is stative, it patterns much like a resultative serialization, especially with regard to negation (see § 8.8.1.2). When the second verb is not stative, it more closely resembles a two-event serialization (see § 8.8.2). And although the verbs share the same aspect markers, the arguments of the verbs are not identical, as they must be in serial verb constructions. When *kɯ³¹* is present, the formulation also resembles the applicative construction which, as described in § 11.1, similarly evades neat categorization. Here again the arguments are not fully shared. And, in addition, the imperfect aspect markers *tsɤ³¹* and *tso²⁴* may modify the caused-event verb as well as *kɯ³¹*, which is not possible in a verb serialization.

11.2.2.3 Causative Construction Formed Only with *kɯ³¹*

In contrast to the two constructions described above, causative phrases formed only with the verb *kɯ³¹* 'to give' describe situations of indirect causation, in which the causer does not exert deliberate force on the causee. This encompasses scenarios in which the causer grants permission or inadvertently triggers an action or state to come about. In this construction, *kɯ³¹* is placed behind the verb expressing the caused event, and the causer and causee precede it. A schematic is shown below, and an example in (807). Syntactically, this is the general construction employed to add a third core argument, and it is thus identical in structure to the applicative construction, which may convey recipient and benefactive interpretations in addition to the causative sense (see § 11.1).

                      CAUSER   CAUSEE   CAUSED.EVENT   kɯ³¹

(807) ŋa³³   i³³   [ka³²³]   **kɯ³¹**   wa³²³.
      1SG   3SG   walk   INDR.CAUS   PFV
      我   他   走
      'I let him leave.'
      我同意他走了。
      (KL-Elicitation)

The causative $kɯ^{31}$ may be used with all types of verbs, except for the lexical causatives. In (807) above it co-occurs with an intransitive verb, in (808) it is used with a stative verb, and (809) it modifies a transitive verb. In the latter, the phrase $ŋ^{24}ka^{33}$ $kɯ^{31}$, which literally means 'let see', has become a lexicalized way to express the concept 'to show'. $kɯ^{31}$ also features a tone change to mark an imperative use (see § 12.2.5).

(808) tsa²⁴ to³³ ma³¹ tsa⁵⁵, [mi⁵³ tsʁ³¹] **kɯ³¹** nɛi³³.
rice also NEG feed be.hungry CONT INDR.CAUS ASRT
饭 也 不 吃 饿
'(They) didn't feed (us) either, making (us) hungry.'
饭也不给吃，给饿着。
(GCS-Dance Parties)

(809) nɛi³³ tʰʁ⁵⁵ la⁵³ tʁ⁴⁴ i³³ tʰʁ⁵⁵ [ŋ²⁴ka³³] **kɯ²⁴**.
2SG CL:TMP wrap CLNK 3SG CL:TMP see INDR.CAUS.IMP
你 下 绕 他 下 看
'Wrap (some) for a while (to) show him.'
你绕一下给他看一下。
(KL-Sewing)

This construction also describes an event indirectly or inadvertently triggered by the causer, as in (810) below. If the causee is inanimate, there is no permission implied but rather the idea that it may be left unattended — the 'let boil' sense in (811). Because deliberate control is not implied, animals or inanimate objects may be causers in this construction. Monkeys, of course, have a will of their own, but the human causee in (812) still retains some control over her own actions. And because the causers are inanimate in (813) and (814), and thus the least prototypical of agents, they are marked by $kɛi^{33}$ — which may be interpreted as either the agent or instrument marker in these examples, blurring the line between the two (see § 10.4 and § 10.6.1 respectively). Note that in (811) and (813) $kɯ^{31}$ changes tone due to the following particle wa^{33} (see § 3.2.4.3). Given these varied uses, it is clear that the $kɯ^{31}$ construction allows for greater semantic latitude in describing caused events than the other two causative constructions described above.

(810) ŋa³³ kɛi³³ tsʰŋ³¹ mɛi⁴⁴ [mi⁵³ si⁵³] **kɯ³¹** wa³²³.
1SG AGT dog CL:GEN be.hungry die INDR.CAUS PFV
我 狗 个 饿 死
'I let the dog die of hunger (by accident).'
我把一只狗给饿死了。
(KL-Elicitation)

(811) kv³³ tɤ⁴⁴, [a³³n̠a⁵³ ti⁴⁴ xa⁵⁵] **kɯ²⁴** wa³³ tsɛi³¹.
make STAT.EMP there in boil INDR.CAUS CRS HSY
做 那里 里 煮
'Making (it), they say (you) let (it) boil there.'
说是放在那里给煮了。
(ZRF-Grandfather)

(812) a²⁴n̠o⁵³ mɛi⁴⁴ kɛi³³ ŋa³³ [i³²³sa³³] **kɯ³¹**.
monkey CL:GEN AGT 1SG smile INDR.CAUS
猴子 个 我 笑
'The monkey makes me smile.'
猴子让我笑。
(KL-Elicitation)

(813) no⁵³ma³³ mɛi⁴⁴ kɛi³³ ŋa³³ [pʰa³⁵ to³¹ lɤ³³] **kɯ²⁴** wa³³.
rock CL:GEN AGT 1SG mix fall fall INDR.CAUS CRS
石头 个 我 拌 摔 倒
'The rock made me trip.'
石头让我摔倒了。
(KL-Elicitation)

(814) na³²³ta³²³mo³²³ mɛi⁴⁴ kɛi³³ ŋa³³ [si³³si³³] **kɯ³¹** wa³²³.
Naadam CL:GEN AGT 1SG be.happy INDR.CAUS PFV
那达慕 个 我 高兴
'(The) Naadam (Festival) made me happy.'
那达慕节让我高兴了。
(KL-Elicitation)

In this construction, negation occurs on the verb expressing the caused event rather than on the causative *kɯ³¹*, as (815) shows.

(815) "ma³¹ tsʰo³¹ mo³³ ma³¹ tɕʰɛ⁵⁵ mo⁴⁴ ni³¹ **ma³¹** [ka³²³] **kɯ³¹**."
NEG sing perceive NEG dance perceive TOP NEG walk INDR.CAUS
不 演 见 不 跳 见 不 走
' " (If you) don't sing or dance (for us), (we) won't let (you) go." '
"不唱不跳不让你们走。"
(PYX-Performing)

Reduplicative polar questions are formed by repeating the causative marker *kɯ³¹*, as shown in (816).

(816) na³²³ta³²³mo³²³tɕɛ³²³ mɛi⁴⁴ kɛi³³ nɛi³³ [si³³si³³] **kɯ³¹** **kɯ³¹** wa³¹?
Naadam.Festival CL:GEN AGT 2SG be.happy INDR.CAUS INDR.CAUS PFV.Q
那达慕节 个 你 高兴
'Did (the) Naadam Festival make you happy?'
那达慕节让你高兴了吗？
(KL-Elicitation)

As already mentioned, this construction also has recipient and benefactive interpretations, as (817) illustrates. The phrase may refer to permission to eat soup, being given soup to eat or being fed soup. Context generally clarifies the meaning. Syntactically, this construction does not neatly fit any other category in the language. As discussed in § 11.1, it resembles a two-event verb serialization (see § 8.8.2), but does not fully follow the pattern. Instead, the construction seems to have evolved separately, perhaps modeled on the ditransitive clause.

(817) i³³ ŋa³³ o³¹tsa²⁴i³²³ [to³²³] **kɯ³¹**.
3SG 1SG soup drink give/INDR.CAUS
他 我 汤 喝 给
'He lets me eat soup.' / 'He gives me soup to eat.' / 'He feeds me soup.'
他让我喝汤。 / 他给我汤喝。
(KL-Elicitation)

There is a lexical verb *wɛi³²³* 'to allow' that can be used in place of the permissive sense of the *kɯ³¹* construction. The verb appears before the matrix verb, patterning like a borrowed auxiliary, as shown in (818). There are no examples of this verb in the corpus, suggesting that the *kɯ³¹* construction is preferred by most speakers.

(818) [ŋa³³ sɛi⁴⁴ pa³¹] [ŋa³³] [sɤ⁵⁵ ko⁵⁵] wɛi³²³ vɤ³²³ wa³²³.
1SG family father 1SG book CL:PL allow buy PFV
我 家 爸爸 我 书 些 允许 买
'My father allowed me to buy books.'
我爸爸允许了我买书。
(KL-Elicitation)

11.2.2.4 Multiple Causation

The causative constructions do not lend themselves to endless recursion. The *la³³ta⁵⁵* postposition may only appear once in a clause, and reduplicating *kɯ³¹* creates a polar question (§ 12.4.1). As a result, if there are two semantic causers in a clause, the *la³³ta⁵⁵* and *kɯ³¹* constructions are combined, as shown in (819). Such a clause may also include *kɤ³³*, as in (820). The differences in meaning between the various causative constructions, however, create ambiguity about the wishes of the ultimate causee. For example, the phrase in (819) may mean either 'he makes you make me go' or 'he makes you let me go'. Situations involving more than two causers — semantically possible but a rarity in natural speech — are typically described using separate clauses in discourse.

(819) i³³   nɛi³³   **la³³ta⁵⁵**   [ŋa³³   ka³²³]   **kɯ³¹**   **mo⁵⁵**.
      3SG   2SG   CAUS   1SG   walk   INDR.CAUS   require
      他   你   我   走   要
      'He makes you make me go.' / 'He makes you let me go.'
      他让你让我走。
      (KL-Elicitation)

(820) i³³   ŋa³³   **la³³ta⁵⁵**   [tɕi³³   ma⁴⁴   **kɣ³³**   to³³]   **kɯ³¹**   **mo⁵⁵**.
      3SG   1SG   CAUS   this   CL:GEN   make   be.flat INDR.CAUS   require
      他   我   这   个   弄   平   要
      'He makes me make this one flat.' / 'He lets me make this one flat.'
      他让我把这个弄平。
      (KL-Elicitation)

12 Basic Clause Types

In this chapter, important clause and sentence types are explored. There is, in fact, no clear syntactic distinction between a clause and a sentence in Khatso. Verbs do not inflect, nor is aspect marking obligatory, and any and all arguments may be absent due to zero anaphora. As a result, a well-formed clause, even one containing only a verb or verb complex, as in (821), may serve as a fully grammatical sentence. And even though certain subordinate clauses have restrictions against aspect marking, the fact that aspect may be unnecessary in simple clauses renders this difference moot. In discourse, matrix clauses are primarily identifiable by the presence of a sentence-final particle of some sort, be it an aspect marker, an imperative marker, an interrogative marker or an emphatic marker. But absent these particles, none of which are required in any clause, pragmatics alone is sufficient to clarify the relationship between a single clause and those surrounding it. Because of these factors, the simple clause structure described in this chapter is the same as basic sentence structure. Constructions that combine clauses are described in Chapters 13 through 16.

(821) tʰɛi³¹ i³³.
pick go
挑　去
挑去。
'(We would) go gather (firewood).'
(GCS-Dance Parties)

Despite the frequent omission of arguments, there are a number of identifiable clause and sentence types in the language. Declarative clauses are described in § 12.1, followed by a discussion of imperatives in § 12.2. The reciprocal construction is analyzed in § 12.3, question formation in § 12.4 and comparative constructions in § 12.5. Finally, emphatic particles are described in § 12.6. Formulations that add core arguments, such as the applicative and causative constructions, are detailed in Chapter 11.

12.1 Declarative Clauses

Declarative clauses contain information that a speaker generally believes is true, and as such they make up the largest category of phrases in natural speech. They are unmarked in Khatso discourse; there is no particle or construction that labels them as declarative. Instead, imperative and interrogative clauses are marked to differentiate them from the unmarked declaratives (see § 12.2 and § 12.4 respectively).

In declaratives, arguments typically follow the basic word order of A R P, as discussed in § 10.3. However, because of zero anaphora — which allows for the omission of arguments that are given or easily inferrable from context — verbs are frequently accompanied by fewer arguments than their valency requires. As a result, grammatically complete clauses and sentences may contain nothing but a single verb or a verb with a few modifiers. Examples of simple declaratives are presented in (822), (823) and (824).

(822) i³²³tɕa⁵³   mɛi³³   to³²³   ta³⁵   wa³²³.
   water   CL:MSR   drink   ascend   PFV
   水   口   喝   上
   '(They) drank a mouthful of water.'
   喝上一口水了。
   (HPH-Horse Dug Well)

(823) ŋa³³   kʰa³¹kʰy̩³³   mɛi⁴⁴   sa³³   tɕi⁵³   li³²³.
   1SG   hat   CL:GEN   sew   wear   know.how
   我   帽子   个   逢   戴   会
   'I know how to make hats to wear.'
   我会做帽子戴。
   (WYY-Sewing)

(824) tso³²³   ja³³.
   EXIST   IPFV.EMP
   有
   '(I) have (brothers and sisters).'
   有的。
   (YJF-Childhood)

In discourse, declaratives may be modified by a variety of phrase-final particles, especially emphatic markers. The most common of these are presented in § 12.6.

12.2 Imperatives

Imperative clauses include commands, requests, invitations, instructions and suggestions. Propositive and optative constructions are included in this section as well. In Khatso, imperative constructions typically end with an imperative marker. *jɛ²⁴* is the general marker, but *pa³¹* may be used interchangeably with *jɛ²⁴* in many cases; it also has a separate function of soliciting agreement. The optative marker is *pa³²³jɛ²⁴*, which may mark verbs in any person. Unlike the imperative markers, the general prohibitive ta^{31} precedes the verb, patterning identically to the negative marker ma^{31}; as a result it is described in § 9.1. The negative auxiliary construction ma^{31} jo^{33}, which has a mild prohibitive sense, patterns more like the imperative markers, and is thus included here. In addition, it is possible for any verb, as well as a few grammatical particles, to signal the imperative function through tone change alone (see § 3.2.4.2). However, just four such expressions are regularly attested in discourse; each of which is discussed below.

Overtly marking imperatives is not obligatory. An unmarked declarative may be interpreted as an imperative based on pragmatics. Or, in the case of a harsh command, voice quality alone may be sufficient. However, imperative markers are used more often than not in discourse. They not only clarify the intent of the speaker, but also tend to soften the effect. The classifier construction $tɛi^{31}$ $t^hɤ^{55}$ 'awhile' is also used to further soften directives (see § 6.2.2.9), and its presence alone may be enough to turn a declarative phrase into an imperative.

12.2.1 Imperative Marker *jɛ²⁴*

The particle *jɛ²⁴* is the basic marker of imperative clauses in Khatso. It may mark any type of imperative, from commands to requests and suggestions, but it can only be used in the second person. Second person pronouns are grammatical in imperatives, but they are typically omitted. Examples are shown in (825) and (826).

(825) tɛi³¹tsɤ²⁴ma³¹xɛi³⁵ t^hɤ⁵⁵   k^hua³¹ pa⁵³mo³³ **jɛ²⁴**.
everything   CL:TMP say   tell   IMP
什么   下   讲   告诉
'Talk about everything.'
什么都讲一下。
(KL-Dance Parties)

(826) "xa³⁵ xuɛi³²³ ts^ho³¹   **jɛ²⁴**."
still CL:TMP perform   IMP
再   回   演
' "Perform (it) once more." '
"再演一回。"
(PYX-Performing)

12.2.2 Imperative Marker *pa³¹*

When used as a general imperative marker, *pa³¹* is largely interchangeable with *jɛ²⁴*. Examples are shown below in (827) and (828). This marker is an obvious loan from Chinese; it is identical to the imperative marker *ba* 吧 in Putonghua.

(827) n̠a⁵³li⁴⁴ ti⁵³za³¹ lo³¹ li³³ **pa³¹**.
here a.little approach come IMP
这里 点 拢 来
'Come a little closer here.'
过来这里一点。
(ZRF-Grandfather)

(828) nɛi³³ tɛi³¹ ma²⁴ vʏ³²³ tʏ⁴⁴ ŋa³³ kɯ³¹ li³³ **pa³¹**.
2SG one CL:GEN buy CLNK 1SG give come IMP
你 一 个 买 我 给 来
'Buy one for me.'
你买一个来给我吧。
(ZRF-Grandfather)

In Chinese, *ba* often functions to solicit agreement or sympathy with the speaker, akin to the English tag question 'wouldn't you agree?' (Li and Thompson 1981: 307–311), and this use is also found in Khatso discourse, though the nature of the appeal may vary according to context. Consider the examples in (829) and (830). In both, the speakers are talking about themselves, so these are not prototypical directives. Instead, the speaker in (829) uses the particle to mark the unusual situation of being able to play the *qin* (a banjo-like instrument) before learning to dance; typically both are done together. And in (830), after describing the remedies that have failed, the speaker solicits sympathy about her insomnia. In this function, *pa³¹* may co-occur with an A or S of any person or number. For example, in (831) the S denotes a button that has been sewn incorrectly, although the solicitation is directed at the listener.

(829) pʏ⁵³ li³²³ ŋɛi⁴⁴ ni³²³ tɕʰɛ⁵⁵ ma³¹ li³²³ sɛi³¹ **pa³¹**.
play know.how ASRT BKGD dance NEG know.how still IMP.SOL
弹 会 跳 不 会 还
'(I) knew how to play (the *qin*), but still didn't know how to dance (do you see?).'
会弹了但还不会跳。
(YLW-Learning)

(830) na²⁴   na²⁴   za³¹   ta⁵⁵   la³⁵ ŋ⁴⁴   to³³ ʐ̩⁵³ ma³¹ sa³³   **pa³¹**.
      be.good be.good DIM   be.type FOC COP also sleep NEG be.good IMP.SOL
      好   好   样   是   也   睡   不   好
      '(That) kind (of) really good (sleep), (I) don't sleep well (don't you know?).'
      好好的也睡不着呀。
      (KL-Sewing)

(831) tɛi³³   ma³⁵   ma³¹   xo²⁴   **pa³¹**.
      this   CL:GEN   NEG   be.correct   IMP.SOL
      这   个   不   对
      'This one isn't right (don't you agree?).'
      这个不对吧.
      (WYY-Sewing)

12.2.3 Optative Marker *pa³²³jɛ²⁴*

The optative particle *pa³²³jɛ²⁴* marks declarative statements that express wishes or hopes, which may or may not be realizable. As such, they may mark clauses that feature A or S in first and third person as well as second person. Examples are shown in (832) and (833).

(832) ŋa³³tsʰɤ³³   tɕʰɛ³²³   tso³²³   **pa³²³jɛ²⁴**.
      1PL   money   EXIST   OPT
      我们   钱   有
      '(I hope) we get rich.'
      我希望我们会有钱。
      (KL-Elicitation)

(833) na²⁴   kɯ³²³   sa³³   **pa³²³jɛ²⁴**.
      play   CSC   be.good   OPT
      完   好
      '(I hope it) is fun.'
      我希望会好玩。
      (KL-Elicitation)

The marker is considered noncompositional in Khatso. But, it may be a compound formed by the verb *pa³²³* 'to help' and the imperative *jɛ²⁴* (see § 12.2.1), semantically beseeching the world to help bring about one's wish.

12.2.4 Prohibitive Auxiliary Construction *ma³¹ jo³³*

Khatso has a small group of auxiliary verbs that express deontic modality (see § 8.7). When negated, one such auxiliary, *jo³³* 'need, must', is functionally similar to a prohibitive construction. However, unlike the prohibitive marker *ta³¹*, which precedes the verb, the negated auxiliary follows the matrix verb, thus patterning like an imperative. It provides a mild prohibitive sense of 'no need to', as shown in (834) and (835), and may thus be employed for polite discouragement. It may only modify a positive verb, and no other imperative marker is required, although *pa³¹* may be added to solicit agreement, as (835) demonstrates. This construction is not a true imperative, but rather implies prohibition depending on context. Because it is based on an auxiliary verb, the construction is not restricted to second person.

(834) ta³¹ **ma³¹ jo³³**.
 connect NEG must
 接 不 应该
 'No need to connect (them).' / 'Don't connect (them).'
 不用接。
 (WYY-Sewing)

(835) tɕʰɛ⁵³ **ma³¹ jo³³** pa³¹.
 finish NEG must IMP.SOL
 完 不 应该
 'No need to stop, okay?'
 不用完。
 (ZRF-Grandfather)

Making imperatives of clauses containing the other auxiliary verbs requires either *jɛ²⁴* or *pa³¹*; *ma³¹ jo³³* is the only auxiliary to have developed an imperative sense of its own.

12.2.5 Imperatives Formed through Tone Change

Imperative clauses may also be marked through a simple tone change pattern (see § 3.2.4.2). Any verb, and a few grammatical particles, may be made imperative in this way, and no marker is required. The tone change occurs only on the final syllable of the clause. Syllables with tone 33 change to tone 44, while those with tone 31 and 323 change to tone 24. Although this process is productive in elicitation, in discourse it mainly occurs with four specific morphemes in which the resulting tone is 24 — mirroring the tone of the basic imperative *jɛ²⁴*. Verbs with tone 33 typically append an imperative marker in discourse, thus eliminating the need for tone change.

In the first example of imperative tone change, the verb *pa³²³* 'to help' becomes *pa²⁴*, as shown in (836). It can only be used in the second person.

(836) tsa³²³ tɕi³¹ tʰɤ⁵⁵ m̩³³ **pa²⁴**.
rice one CL:TMP make help.IMP
饭 一 下 做 帮
'(Go) help cook.'
帮做一下饭吧。
(KL-Elicitation)

In the second example, the causative verb *kɯ³¹* 'to give' changes to *kɯ²⁴*, which permits or urges another person to perform an action. Examples are shown in (837) and (838). Note that *pa³¹* may be added to solicit agreement. The indirect causative construction, which features *kɯ³¹*, is discussed in § 11.2.2.3.

(837) nɛi³³ tʰɤ⁵⁵ la⁵³ tɤ⁴⁴ i³³ tʰɤ⁵⁵ ŋ²⁴ka³³ **kɯ²⁴**.
2SG CL:TMP wrap CLNK 3SG CL:TMP see INDR.CAUS.IMP
你 下 绕 他 下 看
'Wrap (some) for a while (to) show him.'
你绕一下给他看一下。
(KL-Sewing)

(838) a³³ jo³⁵ li⁴⁴ tɕʰɛ⁵³ **kɯ²⁴** **pa³¹**.
that CL:HUM in finish INDR.CAUS.IMP IMP.SOL
那 个 里 完
'Let's stop there, okay?', literally 'Let (it) finish (with) that one, okay?'
到那个那里完吧。
(YJR-Grandfather)

In the third example of imperative tone change, the verb *tɕʰɛ³¹* 'to open' follows the matrix verb to form a resultative serialization (see § 8.8.1.2) and changes to tone 24. Examples are shown in (839) and (840). This construction often provides a sense of trial and error, as (840) illustrates, and is restricted to second person only. The classifier construction *tɕi³¹ tʰɤ⁵⁵*, which means 'awhile', frequently accompanies *tɕʰɛ²⁴*, underscoring the fact that the repetitive nature of the action may require a longer duration.

(839) tɛi³¹ tʰɤ⁵⁵ tsʰɛi²⁴ **tɕʰɛ²⁴**.
one CL:TMP guess open.IMP
一 下 猜 开
'Try and guess (a few times)!'
猜一猜！
(KL-Elicitation)

(840) nɛi⁴⁴ to³³ tɛi³¹ tʰɤ⁵⁵ n̩a³¹ **tɕʰɛ²⁴**.
2SG also one CL:TMP speak open.IMP
你 也 一 下 说 开
'You try talking for a while too.'
你也说一下吧。
(KL-Childhood)

In the fourth example, the continuous aspect marker *tsɤ³¹* changes to *tsɤ²⁴* to urge the addressee to either begin or continue performing an ongoing action. Examples are presented in (841) and (842). Unlike the other imperatives formed through tone change, *tsɤ²⁴* is not restricted to second person, as the example in (843) illustrates.

(841) tɛi³¹ xuɛi³²³ ɣ̩³²³ **tsɤ²⁴**.
one CL:TMP hold CONT.IMP
一 回 拿
'Hold (it) for a while.'
拿着一次吧。
(ZRF-Grandfather)

(842) tɤ⁴⁴ nɛi³³ tʰɤ⁵⁵ ɕa³¹ **tsɤ²⁴**.
FILL 2SG CL:TMP think CONT.IMP
你 下 想
'Well, you think (about it) for a while.'
那你想一想吧。
(WYY-Sewing)

(843) ŋa³³tsʰɤ³³ kɤ̩³³ **tsɤ²⁴**.
1PL make CONT.IMP
我们 做
'Let's keep working.'
我们做着吧。
(KL-Elicitation)

Forming imperatives through tone change is never obligatory; imperative markers may be used instead. However, the four types of imperative tone change just presented are regularly found in discourse.

12.3 Reciprocal Constructions

An activity that is performed by two agents on each other is considered reciprocal. In Khatso, verbs may be made reciprocal by the use of the i^{33} γ^{323} i^{33} construction, which is usually placed between the A and the verb. An example is shown in (844).

(844) no³²³mi³²³ a³³   ŋ³¹   jo³⁵   **i³³ ɣ³²³ i³³**   kɣ³³   pa³²³.
      farmer   that two   CL:HUM   RECP   do   help
      农民   那   两   位   互相   做   帮
      'Those two farmers help each other.'
      那两位农民互相帮忙。
      (KL-Elicitation)

This construction appears to contain two third-person singular pronouns connected by a special conjunction γ^{323}, which only occurs in reciprocal constructions. But, here the pronouns are invariant and do not necessarily show agreement with the actual referents. This is seen in (845), where the individuals are not third person yet the construction does not change, and in (846), where there are potentially three arguments. As a result, overt arguments may co-occur with the construction without creating redundancy. If there are two independent overt agents, they take the nominal conjunction $k\varepsilon i^{33}$ to identify them as co-agents in the action. The pronouns in the reciprocal construction, by contrast, never take such marking. Interestingly, the reciprocal conjunction is homophonous with the verb γ^{323} 'to hold, pick up, bring' and may have evolved from it.

(845) ŋa³³ kɛi³³ nɛi³³ kɛi³³ **i³³ ɣ³²³ i³³** tsɿ³²³   tsɿ³¹   wa³²³.
      1SG   CONJ   2SG   CONJ   RECP   quarrel   fight   PFV
      我   和   你   和   互相   架   打
      'You and I fought each other.'
      我和你彼此打架了。
      (KL-Elicitation)

(846) tsʰo³¹pa³⁵ za³¹ ŋ³¹ si³⁵   jo³⁵   tso²⁴   ni³¹,
      friend   DIM   two three   CL:HUM   EXIST   TOP
      伙伴   二   三   位   有
      '(If) there are two or three friends,'
      有两三个伙伴呢,

i³³ ɣ³²³ i³³   kɣ³¹tiɛ³¹   tʰɣ⁵⁵   tʰɣ⁵⁵   za³¹   tɕa³¹   ka³³.
RECP   story   CL:TMP CL:TMP DIM   speak   play
互相   故事   下   下   讲   玩
'(They) tell each other stories for a little while.'
有时候彼此讲讲故事玩。
(HPH-Toys)

Most overt nouns must be accompanied by the full three-word reciprocal construction. However, a few short nouns, such as *tsʰo³³* 'person' and *tsʰo³³pa³⁵* 'friend' may be used with *ɣ³²³* alone, as (847) demonstrates. The nouns must be identical for this to be grammatical, which allows them to serve simultaneously as A and P. The reciprocal construction also appears in certain comparisons of equality that retain a sense of reciprocity (see § 12.5.1).

(847) **tsʰo³¹pa³⁵**   **ɣ³²³**   **tsʰo³¹pa³⁵**   to³³   tɕo³⁵   tɛi³³   xɣ³³   ja³³.
       friend   RECP   friend   also   then   this   scold IPFV.EMP
       伙伴   互相   伙伴   也   就   这   骂
       'Friends (would) then scold each other this way.'
       伙伴之间也就这么骂的。
       (YJF-Weddings)

In addition, some verbs lexically encompass the idea of mutual action, such as *ta³⁵* 'to hug', *la⁵³ sɣ³³* 'to shake hands', *pa³⁵* 'to help each other', *tsʅ³²³ tsʅ³¹* 'to fight' and *tsʅ³²³ xɣ³³* 'to argue'. Because *tsʅ³²³* appears in several of these expressions, it has been previously identified as a reciprocal marker (Dai, Liu and Fu 1987: 156). However, it is a noun meaning 'quarrel', and even though it seems to only occur with these few verbs, it may be counted or pluralized like any common noun. The reciprocal *i³³ ɣ³²³ i³³* construction may be used with these lexically reciprocal verbs, but it is typically omitted as unnecessary. Verbs which denote actions that one performs on oneself are reflexive; they are discussed in § 5.3.1 and § 8.2.

12.4 Questions

Khatso employs a variety of strategies to formulate questions, depending on the type of question, the aspect, and the speaker's ideas about the likelihood of an answer. Verb reduplication, interrogative pronouns, clause-final markers and even tone change are all used to frame different types of questions. This section explores these constructions. Polar questions are explored in § 12.4.1, followed by a discussion of content questions in § 12.4.2. Choice questions are analyzed in § 12.4.3, and tag questions in § 12.4.4. Next, interrogative interjections are described in § 12.4.5, followed by echo questions in § 12.4.6. Finally, more specialized question markers are

12.4.1 Polar Questions

The function of polar questions is to elicit a simple positive or negative response. In Khatso, the most straightforward way of forming such a construction is through the reduplication of the verb in situ; the rest of the clause remains unchanged. An elicited example is shown in (848), which compares a declarative statement and its polar counterpart. If the verb has two syllables, only the final syllable is doubled, as shown in (849). Additional examples from discourse are shown in (850) and (851). This construction is functionally equivalent to the A-not-A pattern in Putonghua, but in Khatso the negative marker is never used.

(848) i^{33} tsa^{323} tsa^{31} 　　　　　　　i^{33} tsa^{323} **tsa^{31}**   **tsa^{31}**?
　　　3SG　rice　eat　　　　　　　　　　3SG　rice　eat　eat
　　　他　　饭　　吃　　　　　　　　　　他　　饭　　吃　　吃
　　　'he is eating'　　　　　　　　　　　'is he eating?'
　　　他吃饭　　　　　　　　　　　　　　他吃不吃饭
　　　(KL-Elicitation)

(849) za^{31}ni^{24}za^{31}　ko^{55}　**la^{24}ka^{33}**　**ka^{33}**?
　　　child　　　　　　CL:PL　play　play
　　　小孩　　　　　　些　　　玩　　玩
　　　'Are the children playing?'
　　　小孩子们玩不玩？
　　　(KL-Elicitation)

(850) so^{24}　**sa^{55}**　**sa^{55}**?
　　　learn　be.difficult　be.difficult
　　　学　　难　　　　　　难
　　　'Was (it) difficult to learn?'
　　　难不难学？
　　　(KL-Learning)

(851) ȵɛ³²³za³¹   ȵɛ³²³   ȵɛ³²³za³¹   ȵɛ³²³ma³³   **tso³²³**   **tso³²³?**
      younger.brother be.small   younger.brother younger.sister   EXIST   EXIST
      弟弟   小   弟弟   妹妹   有   有
      'Younger brothers, did (you) have younger brothers and sisters?'
      小弟弟，有没有小弟弟、小妹妹？
      (KL-Childhood)

Simple reduplication is possible with the copula, yielding η³³ η³³, but it is not often employed. A slightly modified second verb is typically employed instead, yielding η³³ ηa³³. An example is shown in (852). This phrase, and other phrases formed with the copula, is also frequently used as a tag question (see § 12.4.4).

(852) m̥³²³   tɕi⁵⁵   nɛi³³tsʰɤ³¹   tsɿ³¹tɕa²⁴   pɤ³²³   tɕi⁵⁵   **ŋ³³**   **ŋa³³?**
      field   CL:TYPE 2PL   self   POSS   CL:TYPE   COP   COP.Q
      田   些   你们   自己   些   是
      'Those fields, were (they) your own?'
      这些田是你们自己的吗？
      (KL-Childhood)

The basic polar construction implies a current or future interpretation, with no additional aspect marking necessary. If the event has past time reference, then an aspect marker is required, but neither the perfective *wa³²³* nor the currently relative state marker *wa³³* may occur in questions. Instead, one of three other markers usually replaces them. The first is the particle *wa³¹*, which is the basic interrogative substitute for both *wa³²³* and *wa³³*. Thus, questions formed with *wa³¹* may indicate that the action is either perfective or in a currently relevant state, as shown in (853) and (854).

(853) **sɿ⁵⁵**   **sɿ⁵⁵**   **wa³¹?**
      know   know   PFV.Q
      知道   知道
      'Did (you) know (her)?'
      认识了没有？
      (YJR-Weeds)

(854) tɕi³¹   kʰua⁵⁵   kʰua⁵⁵   ni³³   **fɛi³³**   **fɛi³³**   **wa³¹?**
      one   village   village   ADV   divide   divide   PFV.Q
      一   村   村   分开   分开
      'Did (they) divide (them) village by village?'
      一个村一个村地分了没有？
      (KL-Childhood)

The other two aspect markers permissible in polar questions are the irrealis *la³¹* and the imperfective irrealis *ta³³*. As irrealis markers, their presence signals a degree of uncertainty about the premise of the question in addition to their basic aspectual meanings. Examples are shown in (855) and (856). Their functions as aspect markers are discussed in § 9.2.6 and § 9.2.7 respectively.

(855) o⁵³tsŋ³³ tɛi³³ ma⁴⁴ kʰy̩³³ tɕi³³ tɕi³³ la³¹?
under this CL:GEN in pack pack IRR.Q
下面 这 个 里 放 装
'(Did you) put (it) under this?'
有没有放在下面这里？
(KL-Sewing)

(856) **pɤ⁵³ pɤ⁵³ ta³³** sa³¹ tɛi³³tɕʰa⁵⁵kʰy̩³³?
play play IPFV.IRR still.Q this.time
弹 弹 还 这时候
'Is (he) still playing these days?'
现在还在弹吗？
(KL-Erasers)

There are a number of constructions that combine verbs in Khatso, and their interrogative reduplication patterns vary. For example, in auxiliary verb constructions (see § 8.7), it is always the second verb that doubles, as shown in (857) and (858), even though this may be either the auxiliary or the matrix verb. In serial verb constructions, which may contain two or three verbs (see § 8.8), the reduplication differs according to the number of verbs involved. In two-verb serializations, either the first or the second verb may be reduplicated, as shown in (859) and (860). In three-verb serializations, the medial verb is reduplicated, as in (861). These differences appear to be idiosyncratic and do not affect the meaning in any appreciable way. Note that the verbs *i³²³* 'to go' and *li³²³* 'to come' must change to tone 33 in serial verb constructions, but never change tone as matrix verbs (see § 3.2.2).

(857) tʰo³³tso⁵³ma³³ tɛi³¹ ma²⁴ la⁵³ mo³³ i³³ **ta³²³ ta³²³**?
button one CL:GEN wrap show go be.able be.able
纽扣 一 个 绕 给看 去 能 能
'Can (you) go show (him how to) wrap a button?'
绕一个纽扣看看，行不行？
(KL-Sewing)

(858) nɛi³³ kʰua³¹la³¹ jɛ³⁵zɿ³⁵ i³²³ i³²³?
2SG Kunming be.willing go go
你 昆明 愿意 去 去
'Are you willing to go to Kunming?'
你愿不愿意去昆明？
(KL-Elicitation)

(859) to⁵³ li³³ li³³?
exit come come
出 来 来
'Are (you) coming out?'
出来不出来？
(KL-Elicitation)

(860) to⁵³ to⁵³ li³³?
exit exit come
出 出 来
'Are (you) coming out?'
出来不出来？
(KL-Elicitation)

(861) kɤ³¹ ka³²³ ka³²³ i³³?
run walk walk go
跑 走 走 去
'Are (you) running away?'
要不要跑走？
(KL-Elicitation)

There are no independent words that correspond to 'yes' and 'no' in Khatso, so other strategies are employed for responding to polar questions. Repeating the verb, and including an aspect marker if appropriate, provides a positive response. If the reply is negative, the negative marker *ma³¹* is added; an irrealis marker may also be used depending on the aspect being conveyed. Thus, the question in (862) may be answered by the reponses presented in (863).

(862) kʰua³¹la³¹ i³²³ i³²³ wa³¹?
Kunming go go PFV.Q
昆明 去 去
'(Did you) go to Kunming?'
你去了昆明没有？
(KL-Elicitation)

(863) i³²³   wa³²³.   ma³¹ i³²³   la³¹.
      go   PFV   NEG   go   PFV.IRR
      去   不   去
      '(I) went.'   '(I did) not go.'
      去了。   没有去。
      (KL-Elicitation)

12.4.2 Content Questions

Content questions ask for specific information about an event, such as who, when or how. In Khatso, the interrogative pronouns are used for this purpose. They are listed in Table 12.1 (which repeats the data in Table 5.2), and are discussed further in § 5.3.3

The pronouns are placed in situ, meaning that they occupy the slot of the element they query. No change in word order is necessary, nor is reduplication possible. Usually the question particle ŋa³¹ ends the question, though occasionally it may be omitted. Examples from discourse are shown in (864), (865) and (866). ŋa³¹ may also be used optionally in choice questions (§ 12.4.3); it is replaced by ta³¹ in rhetorical questions (see § 12.4.7.6).

(864) **xa³³ni³³**   nεi²⁴   **xa³³ni³³**   fɤ²⁴   tso³²³   **ŋa³¹**?
      how.many   CL:ITEM   how.many   CL:ITEM   EXIST   CNT.Q
      几个   姐妹   几个   兄弟   有
      'How many brothers and sisters were there?'
      有几个姐妹几个兄弟。
      (KL-Grandfather)

(865) a³³tɕha⁵⁵kʰɤ³³   **xa³³jo³⁵**   kεi³³   nεi³³   ma⁵⁵   **ŋa³¹**?
      that.time   who   AGT   2SG   teach   CNT.Q
      那时   谁   你   教
      'At that time who taught you?'
      那个时候谁教你的？
      (KL-Sewing)

(866) **xa³³n̪a⁵³**   lεi⁵³   tɤ³³   **ŋa³¹**?
      where   drill   PROG   CNT.Q
      哪里   钻
      'Where are (you) drilling?'
      钻哪里？
      (KL-Sewing)

Table 12.1: Interrogative pronouns in Khatso

Khatso	Morphology	English	Chinese
xa^{33}jo^{35}	xa^{33} (interrogative morpheme) + jo^{35} (CL:HUM)	'who'	谁
xa^{33}ma^{44}	xa^{33} (interrogative morpheme) + ma^{44} (DEM form of CL:GEN ma^{24})	'what', 'which'	什么, 哪个
xa^{33}tɕʰa^{55}kʰγ^{33} xa^{33}tsɛi^{35} xa^{33}sau^{33}	xa^{33} (interrogative morpheme) + tɕʰa^{55}kʰγ^{33} (part of temporal DEM), tsɛi^{35} (CL:TMP), sau^{33} (CL:TMP)	'when'	什么时候
xa^{33}ma^{35}li^{33}li^{323} xa^{33}ma^{35}li^{44}li^{323} xa^{33}ma^{35}li^{44}li^{33} xa^{33}ma^{35}ta^{55}li^{44}li^{33}li^{323} xa^{33}ma^{35}ta^{55}tγ^{44}li^{323} xa^{33}ma^{35}ta^{55}tγ^{44}li^{33} xa^{33}ma^{35}ti^{33}li^{323} xa^{33}ma^{35}ti^{33}li^{33} xa^{33}ma^{35}ti^{44}li^{323} xa^{33}ma^{35}ti^{44}li^{33} xa^{33}ma^{44}ta^{35}ti^{33} xa^{33}ma^{44}ta^{55}ta^{31}ni^{323}li^{323} xa^{33}ma^{44}ta^{55}tγ^{44}li^{323} xa^{33}ma^{44}ta^{55}ti^{33} xa^{33}ma^{44}ti^{35}ti^{33}	xa^{33} (interrogative morpheme) + ma^{44} (DEM form of CL:GEN ma^{24}); the remaining syllables are unanalyzable	'why'	为什么
xa^{33}ŋa^{53}	xa^{33} (interrogative morpheme) + ŋa^{53} (DEM 'place')	'where'	哪里
xa^{33}ni^{33} xa^{33}ni^{33}ko^{55}	xa^{33} (interrogative morpheme) + ni^{33} (ADV morpheme), ko^{55} (CL:PL)	'how', 'how many'	怎么, 几, 多少

Questions of extent follow the same pattern. Here the interrogative pronoun *xa^{33}ni^{33}* 'how' is used to query a comparison of extent, which consists of a stative verb followed by the existential *tso^{323}* (see § 12.5.2). Because an interrogative pronoun is present, the question ends with *ŋa^{31}*, as the examples in (867) and (868) illustrate. This type of question may query locative or temporal information, as the examples in (869) and (870) demonstrate.

(867) **xa³³ni³³**   m̩²⁴   tso³²³   **ŋa³¹**?
how   be.tall   EXIST   CNT.Q
怎么   高   有
'How tall is (he)?'
有多高？
(KL-Elicitation)

(868) tsʰo³¹to³³   tɕi³¹   ma²⁴   ti²⁴   ni³¹,   **xa³³ni³³**   sɤ²⁴   tso³²³   jo³³   **ŋa³¹**?
straw.stool one   CL:GEN weave TOP   how   be.long EXIST   must   CNT.Q
草墩   一   个   编   多么   长   有   应该
'To weave one straw stool, how long must (the straw) be?'
编一个草墩要多长？
(KL-Stools)

(869) **xa³³ni³³**   z̩³¹   tso³²³   **ŋa³¹**?
how   be.far EXIST   CNT.Q
怎么   远   有
'How far is (it)?'
有多远？
(KL-Elicitation)

(870) **xa³³ni³³**   sau³³   mo⁵⁵   jo³³   **ŋa³¹**?
how.much   CL:TMP   want   must   CNT.Q
要多   时   要   应该
'How much time does (it) take?'
要多少时间？
(KL-Elicitation)

When stative verbs denoting dimension are involved, the positive verb in a dimensional pair is queried rather than its negative counterpart. Thus, when the size of an item is unknown, the general question is *xa³³ni³³ ɣɤ³¹ tso³²³ ŋa³¹?* 'how big is it?' rather than *xa³³ni³³ nɛ²⁴ tso³²³ ŋa³¹?* 'how small is it?', though the latter is acceptable if the topic of smallness is already in play. This is a common semantic pattern found in a great many languages (Lyons 1977). A number of Ngwi languages have special interrogative forms for these dimensional pairs (Bradley 1995), but this is not the case in Khatso. Any stative verb may participate in this construction, and it follows the basic periphrastic pattern regardless of the attribute it denotes.

The content question construction has an intrinsic perfective or progressive sense, depending on context, as in the examples above. To query future events, the verb *pa⁵³* 'to want, tell' immediately precedes *ŋa³¹*, as shown in (871). Aspect is discussed in more detail in § 9.2.

(871) nɛi³³ **xa³³ni³³** tɕi³³ **pa⁵³** **ŋa³¹**.
2SG how make FUT CNT.Q
你 什么 做
'What will you do?'
你要干什么？
(YJR-Grandfather)

The copula is often omitted in equational clauses, and the same is true in content questions as well. For example, the question in (872) has no verb; the interrogative pronoun, classifier and question particle are sufficient to form a grammatical question. Occasionally, speakers translate *ŋa³¹* with the Chinese copula, especially in equational phrases, raising the possibility that it evolved from the copula *ŋ³³* or its polar question form *ŋa³³*.

(872) **xa³³ma⁴⁴** tɕi⁵⁵ **ŋa³¹**?
what CL:TYPE CNT.Q
什么 种
'What type (is it)?'
是什么？
(KL-Elicitation)

Because content questions typically ask for a specific argument to be identified, a noun phrase is often a sufficient response, as the exchange in (873) illustrates. However, when the interrogative pronoun is reduplicated, the question becomes more specific and a more detailed response is expected. Thus, the answer to the question in (874) should provide a detailed itinerary, a list of tourist attractions perhaps, rather than the name of a city only. Likewise, the response to the query in (875) is likely to contain step-by-step instructions rather than a general description.

(873) A: tɕi³³ tsɤ³²³ **xa³³ma⁴⁴** tsɤ³²³ **ŋa³¹** tɕi³³ tsɤ³²³?
this CL:PLNT what CL:PLNT CNT.Q this CL:PLNT
这 棵 什么 棵 这 棵
'What (type of) tree (is) this, this tree?'
这棵是什么树，这棵。

B: tɕi³³tsɤ²⁴ tɛi³¹ tsɤ³²³.
golden.bamboo one CL:PLNT
金竹 一 棵
'A golden bamboo tree.'
一棵金竹。
(KL, YLW-Qin)

(874) **xa³³n̪a⁵³ xa³³n̪a⁵³ i³²³ ŋa³¹?**
where where go CNT.Q
哪里 哪里 去
'Where all are (you) going?'
去了哪些地方？
(KL-Elicitation)

(875) **xa³³ni³³ xa³³ni³³ kɣ³³ pa⁵³ ŋa³¹?**
how how do FUT CNT.Q
怎么 怎么 做
'How (exactly) do (you) do (it)?'
要怎么怎么做？
(KL-Elicitation)

12.4.3 Choice Questions

In choice questions, the speaker already has potential answers in mind and incorporates them into the question itself. To form a choice question, two declarative clauses are conjoined by a disjunctive coordinator. There are two in Khatso; *ŋ³³si⁴⁴* 'or' may be used with statements or questions, *mɛi⁴⁴sɿ⁴⁴* is only used in questions. No other marking is required, though the particle *ŋa³¹*, which also appears in content questions (see § 12.4.2), may be included phrase-finally. Examples are shown in (876), (877) and (878). Clausal disjunction is described further in § 13.1.2.

(876) **i³²³ mɣ²⁴ ŋ³³si⁴⁴ i³²³ ma³¹ mɣ²⁴?**
go have.time or go NEG have.time
去 忙 或 去 不 忙
'Do (you) have time to go?', literally 'Do (you) have time to go or not have time to go?'
有没有空去？
(YJF-Dance Parties)

(877) **tsʰɿ³¹ma³³sɿ³⁵ kʰɣ⁵⁵ tɣ³³ ŋ³³si⁴⁴ za³¹m³¹za³¹ kʰɣ⁵⁵ tɣ³³ ŋa³¹?**
bride comb PROG or girl comb PROG CNT.Q
新娘 梳 或 女孩 梳
'Were (you) combing a bride's (hair style) or were (you) combing a girl's (style)?'
是梳新娘头呢，还是梳女孩头？
(KL-Weddings)

(878) tɤ⁴⁴ tɕʰɛ⁵⁵ li³²³ sa²⁴kɛi³³ pɤ⁵³ li³²³ sa³⁵ pei³³,
FILL kick know.how until play know.how perhaps.FOC CFRM.Q
跳 会 才 弹 会 可能
'So, (you) probably knew how to dance before knowing how to play,'
那，会跳才会弹的吧，

mɛi⁴⁴sɿ⁴⁴ pɤ⁵³ li³²³ sa²⁴kɛi³³ tɕʰɛ⁵⁵ liɛ³²³?
or play know.how until kick know.how
还是 弹 会 才 跳 会
'Or, (did you) know how to play before knowing how to dance?'
还是会弹才会跳？
(KL-Learning)

If the same verb appears in both clauses, then the focus is on the noun phrases, as (879) illustrates. Repeating the verb is not obligatory — it rather depends on speaker preference — but it is not an uncommon way to offer choices involving nouns. Noun phrase coordination is described in § 7.7; parallel clause-linking is discussed in § 13.1.1.

(879) pa⁵³ kʰo⁵³ ko⁵³ no⁵³ ŋ³³si⁴⁴,
half CL:TMP pass complete or
半 年 过 掉 或
'Half a year passed or,'
过了半年，

tɛi³¹ kʰo⁵³ ko⁵³ no⁵³ to³³ ma³¹ sɿ⁵⁵.
one CL:TMP pass complete also NEG know
一 年 过 掉 也 不 知道
'A year passed, (I) don't know.'
还是过了一年也不知道。
(YAY-Erasers)

Responses to choice questions will include one of the choices presented. This may be a clause, in which case the focus is the entire activity, or just a noun phrase in cases where only the identity of the noun is queried.

12.4.4 Tag Questions

Tag questions are declarative statements made interrogative by the placement of a brief and separate question at the end. Typically, they seek agreement or confirmation of the information in the main clause. In Khatso, tags are formed by combining the copula η^{33} with one of several question markers. There are nuanced differences between them which do not translate well on the page; English uses intonation for this purpose. The most neutral tag is the polar question η^{33} ηa^{33}, which leaves considerable room for the listener to disagree. An example is shown in (880). The tags η^{33} sa^{44} and η^{44} ηuo^{31} (with idiosyncratic tone sandhi) both indicate that the speaker expects agreement, as in (881) and (882), but the former conveys more doubt than the latter. The tag η^{33} wa^{31} 'right?' adds a slightly reproachful sense to the inquiry, as shown in the exchange in (883).

(880) kɣ³³   tɤ⁴⁴   tau³⁵kɛi³³ nɛi³³ pɣ³²³ mɛi⁴⁴ la³³   tɕi³³ni³³ kɣ³³   kɯ³²³
      do   STAT.EMP   contrary   2SG   POSS CL:GEN CMP   this.way   make   CSC
      做   反而   你   个   这么   做
      na²⁴   ma³¹   tso³²³.
      be.good   NEG   EXIST
      好   不   有
      '(What they) do, (on the) contrary isn't as good as yours.'
      做得还是没有你做得这么好。

      ŋ³³ ŋa³³?
      COP COP.Q
      是
      'Is it?'
      是不是？
      (KL-Sewing)

(881) sɿ²⁴tɕʰɛ²⁴ ŋ³³   sa⁴⁴   m̩³²³   ko⁵⁵?
      divide   COP   CRTN.Q field   CL:PL
      分开   是   田   些
      '(They were) divided, right? The fields.'
      田分开了吗？
      (KL-Childhood)

(882) tsʰa⁵³ŋa³⁵ ko⁵⁵   ŋ³³   n̩a³³,   ŋ⁴⁴   ŋuo³¹?
      magpie   CL:PL COP   COP.EMP   COP   COP.Q
      喜鹊   些   是   是
      '(They) are magpies, right?'
      这些是喜鹊，是吧？
      (KL-Qin)

(883) A: kʰa⁵⁵tsɿ³³   sɿ³⁵   tuɛi³⁵   tɕi³³   pa³¹.
         kʰa⁵⁵tsɿ³³   four   district say   IMP.SOL
         下村   四   组   说
         '(You should) say kʰa⁵⁵tsɿ³³ District Four, okay?'
         说下村四组。

   B: ŋ²⁴   kʰa⁵⁵tsɿ³³   li³²³.
       INTJ kʰa⁵⁵tsɿ³³   come
             下村   来
       'Um, (I) came to kʰa⁵⁵tsɿ³³.'
       嗯，来下村。

   C: sɿ³⁵   tuɛi³⁵,   ŋ³³   wa³¹?!
       four   district COP   PFV.Q
       四   组   是
       'District Four, right?!'
       四组，是吧？！
   (YJF, GCS, KL-Childhood)

Since tag questions contain the copula, they may be used to directly query noun phrases, though the phrase may then be considered a single copular clause, as in (884). In discourse, tag questions nearly always co-occur with clauses that have their own matrix verbs.

(884) tɕi³³tsʏ²⁴   tsʏ³²³   ŋ³³   sa⁴⁴?
      golden.bamboo   CL:PLNT COP   CRTN.Q
      金竹   树   是
      'Golden bamboo, right?' / '(It) is golden bamboo, right?'
      金竹树，是吗？
      (KL-Qin)

As previously mentioned, there are no independent words that correspond to 'yes' and 'no' in Khatso. Thus, responses to tag questions often involve a copular phrase, such as the emphatic ŋ³³ n̩a³³ '(it) is', as shown in (885). An interjection of assent, such as ŋ³¹, ŋ⁵³, ŋɣ³¹, m̩³¹ or m̩⁵³, may also be used; they are similar in meaning to 'uh-huh' and 'yeah' in English. An example is shown in (886). Negative responses generally consist of the copula, in its phrase-final form, modified by the negative marker, ma³¹ ŋɛi³³, as in (887).

(885) A: so²⁴ kɯ³²³ sa³³ tʰɛi³²³ la³⁵ sa⁴⁴?
learn CSC be.good very FOC CRTN.Q
学 好 很
'So (it was) really so easy to learn?'
很好学吗？

B: ŋ³³ n̠a³³.
COP COP.EMP
是
'Yes.', literally 'Is.'
是的
(KL, YLW-Learning)

(886) A: i²⁴la³¹ sɿ³²³xɤ³⁵ pɤ³²³ tsa³²³ tɕi⁵⁵ xa³³ni³³ m̠³³ tsa³¹ ŋa³¹?
past time POSS rice CL:TYPE how make eat CONT.Q
以前 时候 饭 些 怎么 做 吃
'How were meals in the past cooked?'
以前的饭是怎么做着吃的？

B: tsa³²³ m̠³³ sɛi⁴⁴ la³¹?
rice make TMP IRR.Q
饭 做
'When (we) cooked?'
做饭吗？

A: ŋɤ³¹.
INTJ
'Yeah.'
嗯。
(KL, YJF-Childhood)

(887) A: i³³sɿ³⁵ tɕi⁵⁵ sa²⁴ ja³³ pɛi³³?
PRO.be.new CL:TYPE perhaps IPFV.EMP CFRM.Q
新的 种 可能
'Was it perhaps a new one?'
是新的吗？

B: **ma³¹ ŋɛi³³.**
    NEG   COP
    不   是
    'No.', literally 'Isn't.'
    不是。
(KL, YJF-Weddings)

12.4.5 Interrogative Interjections

The simplest question heard in Khatso discourse is an interjection used to indicate that one has not heard the previous utterance and it should be repeated, much like 'huh?' in English. A number of syllables are used for this — a^{35} is the most common, but $ʏ^{35}$, $æ^{35}$ and $m̩^{35}$ are also attested in natural speech. Exchanges from discourse are shown in (888) and (889). It is also possible to use the interrogative pronoun $xa^{33}ma^{44}$ 'what' in this context, but the interjection is much more frequent in discourse. The high rising tone of the interjection may be the source of the tone fusion involved in echo questions (see § 12.4.6 below).

(888) A: nɛi³³tsʰʏ³³ na⁵³tsʰo³¹ li³²³   li³²³?
           2PL   sing   know.how   know.how
           你们   唱   会   会
           'Do you know how to sing?'
           你们会不会唱歌？

       B: **a³⁵?**
           INTJ.Q
           'Huh?'
           啊？

       A: na⁵³tsʰo³¹ li³²³   li³²³?
           sing   know.how   know.how
           唱歌   会   会
           '(Do you) know how to sing?'
           会不会唱歌？
(KL, YJF-Dance Parties)

(889) A: ja⁵³   ŋa³³ sɛi⁴⁴ pʰo³²³   tsʰɤ³³ ni³⁵?
          FILL   1SG   family maternal.grandmother PL   TOP.Q
          我   家   外婆   们
          'So, what about my grandmother's people?'
          那，我外婆她们呢？

   B: m̩³⁵?
       INTJ.Q
       'Huh?'
       啊？

   A: ŋa³³ sɛi⁴⁴ pʰo³²³   tsʰɤ³³ ni³⁵?
       1SG   family maternal.grandmother PL   TOP.Q
       我   家   外婆   们
       'And my grandmother's people?'
       我外婆她们呢？
   (KL, WYY-Sewing)

12.4.6 Echo Questions

Echo questions are those that repeat part or all of a previous utterance. In discourse, these occur either because the listener was not paying close attention or because the content surprises or raises doubts. Thus, it has a slightly different function than the interrogative interjection, which signals that nothing was heard at all.

In Khatso, echo questions are formed by a tone fusion pattern involving a high rising tone similar to tone 35. This tone, which is likely related to that in the interrogative interjection a^{35} (see § 12.4.5), is fused to the tone of the final syllable in the utterance. Examples are shown in (890) and (891). Note that it is not necessary to repeat elements from the phrase in question; an interrogative pronoun with the tone change may be used instead. The tone fusion pattern is discussed further in § 3.2.6.2.

(890) A: ja⁵³   a³³tɕʰa⁵⁵kʰɤ³³ nɛi³³tsʰɤ³³ xa³³ni³³   kʰo⁵³   za³¹ lo⁵³   ŋa³¹?
          FILL   that.time   2PL   how.many   CL:TMP DIM   reach CNT.Q
          那时侯   你们   多少   到
          'So, at that time how old were you?'
          那么那时候你们有多少岁了？

B: a³³tɕʰa⁵⁵kʰɤ³³⁵?
   that.time.ECHO
   那时后
   'At that time?'
   那时候?
(KL, YJF-Childhood)

(891) A: i³³   sɛi⁴⁴   mo³³   sa²⁴kɛi³³   sl̩³³   ja³²³   sɛi³¹.
        3SG   family   mother   just   die   PFV.EMP   still
        她   家   母亲   刚才   死   还
        'Her mother just died.'
        她的母亲刚死了。

   B: xa³³ma³⁵?!
      what.ECHO
      什么
      'What?!'
      什么？！
   (KL-Elicitation)

Echo questions may trigger different kinds of responses. If a specific word or phrase is queried, as in (890) above, then a simple affirmative is sufficient. If an interrogative pronoun is involved, then typically most or all of the previous utterance is repeated.

12.4.7 Question Markers

As the previous sections illustrate, most questions involve an interrogative marker of some sort. Many of them co-occur with other question-forming constructions, such as reduplication or interrogative pronouns. In addition to these, there are six other specialized interrogative markers in Khatso. They may roughly be divided into two groups. The first contains two portmanteau particles, *sa³¹* and *ni³⁵*, which are the interrogative forms of other morphemes. The second group — consisting of *sa⁴⁴*, *la³¹*, *pɛi³³* and *ta³¹* — is epistemic in nature. Its members convey information about either the speaker's certainty in the underlying premise or in the listener's ability to reply. All but *sa³¹* may form questions with their presence alone. Each is discussed below.

12.4.7.1 'Still' Question Marker *sa³¹*
The particle *sa³¹* is the question form of the adverb *sɛi³¹* 'again, still', which is one of the only adverbs to occur canonically after the verb. It occurs with questions formed

through reduplication or interrogative pronouns, and cannot follow a declarative statement alone. As a result, it often co-occurs with other question markers, such as *la³¹*, *wa³¹* and *ŋa³¹*. Examples are shown in (892), (893) and (894). Responses mirror those for polar or content questions. And given its lexical meaning, the marker is not permissible in queries of noun phrases.

(892) n̩o³¹ **m̩³³** **m̩³³** ta³³ **sa³¹**?
thing do do IPFV.IRR still.Q
东西 做 做 还
'Does (he) still work?'
还在干活吗?
(KL-Erasers)

(893) a³³tɕʰa⁵⁵kʰv³³ pv³²³ ɕa³⁵pʰiɛ³⁵ **tso³²³ tso³²³ sa³¹**?
that.time POSS photo EXIST EXIST still.Q
那时候 相片 有 有 还
'Do you still have photos from that time?'
还有没有那时候的照片?
(KL-Childhood)

(894) **xa³³n̩a⁵³** kɛi³³ tsʰa³¹lia³⁵ tso³²³ **sa³¹** **pa⁵³ ŋa³¹**?
where from yield EXIST still.Q FUT CNT.Q
哪里 从 产量 有 还
'Where would there still be (such a) yield?'
哪里还有什么产量?
(HPH-Weeds)

12.4.7.2 Topic Question Marker *ni³⁵*

The particle *ni³⁵* is the question form of the topic marker *ni³¹*. The tone 35 on the particle likely evolved from the tone fusion found in echo questions (§ 3.2.6.2), but today *ni³⁵* seems to be an independent marker. Its exact meaning depends on context, but it may generally be translated as 'and [X]?' or 'what about [X]?'. It modifies nouns of all types, as shown in (895), and may also occur with question markers such as *ŋa³¹*, as in (896). The exchange in (897) illustrates the relationship between *ni³⁵* and *ni³¹*; the former occurs in the two questions while the latter occurs in the declarative response. Note that unlike the topic marker *ni³¹*, *ni³⁵* does not trigger tone change.

(895) o³¹ tsɿ³²³ pa³²³ nɛ³²³ a³³tɕʰa⁵⁵kʰv̩³³ **ni³⁵**?
five seven eight CL:TMP that.time TOP.Q
五 七 八 年 那时候
'And '57, '58 that period?'
五七八年那时候呢？
(KL-Childhood)

(896) xa³³ma⁴⁴ tɕi⁵⁵ kɛi³³ ŋa³¹ **ni³⁵**?
what CL:TYPE INS CNT.Q TOP.Q
什么 种 用
'And with what type (of thing)?'
是用什么东西呢？
(HPH-Weeds)

(897) A: ja⁵³ tsau²⁴li³¹ **ni³⁵**?
FILL tsau²⁴li³¹ TOP.Q
赵力
'And *tsau²⁴ li³¹*?'
那，赵力呢？

tsau²⁴li³¹ sɛi⁴⁴ **ni³⁵**?
tsau²⁴li³¹ family TOP.Q
赵力 家
'What about *tsau²⁴ li³¹*'s family?'
赵力家呢？

B: tsau²⁴li³¹ sɛi⁴⁴ **ni³¹**,
tsau²⁴li³¹ family TOP
赵力 家
'As for *tsau²⁴ li³¹*'s family,'
赵力家呢，

tsʰi³³ tsʰi³³ ni³³ zɿ³⁵tɕo³⁵ sɛi⁴⁴ ma³¹ ŋ³³ wa³³ sɛi³¹.
close close ADV mother's.second.brother family NEG COP CRS still
亲 亲 二 舅 家 不 是 还
'(They) are not closely (related to my) second uncle's family.'
也不是亲亲的二舅家了。
(KL, WYY-Sewing)

ni³⁵ may also modify clauses, as shown in (898) and (899). In some cases, both topic markers are used together, as in (899). Nouns may also co-occur with both markers, but typically *ni³¹* is omitted in these constructions.

(898) xa³³ma⁴⁴ n̪a³¹ **ni³⁵**?
what speak TOP.Q
什么 说
'And say what?'
什么说呢？
(YJR-Grandfather)

(899) i³³ kɛi³³ ŋ³¹ no⁵³ **ni³¹ ni³⁵**?
3SG AGT sell complete TOP TOP.Q
她 卖 掉
'And does she sell out (of them)?'
她卖掉呢？
(KL-Stools)

In discourse, questions formed with *ni³⁵* may be rhetorical. For example, the phrase in (900) is excerpted from a monologue in which the speaker asks a question in order to answer it himself.

(900) tɕo³⁵ ma³¹ŋ²⁴ ɣɤ³¹ wa²⁴ to³³ tɕo³⁵, xa³³ma⁴⁴ la²⁴ka³³ tɤ³³ **ŋa³¹ ni³⁵**?
then a.little be.big CRS also then what play PROG CNT.Q TOP.Q
就 点 大 也 就 什么 玩
'Then when (we were) a bit bigger, what were we playing?'
就，有点大了就玩什么呢？

vɤ³³lɤ³³tshl̩³²³ ɣɤ³⁵.
marble move
弹子 动
'(We) played marbles.'
动团棋。
(HPH-Toys)

Regardles of how *ni³⁵* is used, responses typically contain further explanation of the topic at hand.

12.4.7.3 Certainty Question Marker *sa⁴⁴*

The marker *sa⁴⁴* is added to a declarative statement to form a question. It indicates that the speaker has a high degree of certainty about the premise of the question and an affirmative response is expected. In discourse, *sa⁴⁴* questions often query a statement that has just been said, typically repeating the same material. This may register some doubt about the previous utterance. For example in (901), a skilled musician is downplaying the talent required to play an instrument, which triggers a doubtful response. But in (902), the question serves as a confirmatory backchannel comment. The speaker being recorded has already given her assent non-verbally, but the interviewer wants her to repeat it aloud for the recording. The sa^{44} clause at the end of the exchange is, thus, not a real question but rather a summary statement confirming the exchange. No further response is expected.

(901) A: so²⁴ sa⁵⁵ sa⁵⁵?
learn be.difficult be.difficult
学 难 难
'Is (it) difficult to learn?'
难不难学？

B: ma³¹ so²⁴ sa⁵⁵.
NEG learn be.difficult
不 学 难
'(It) is not difficult to learn.'
不难学。

A: ma³¹ so²⁴ sa⁵⁵ **sa⁴⁴?**
NEG learn be.difficult CRTN.Q
不 学 难
'(It) isn't difficult to learn?'
不难学吗？
(KL, YLW-Learning)

(902) A: nɛi³³tsʰɤ³³ jɛ³⁵ʐ̩³⁵ n̠a³¹ ja³³. tɕi⁴⁴ ni³¹, tɕo³⁵ n̠a³¹ n̠a³¹?
2PL agree speak IPFV.EMP speak TOP then speak speak
你们 愿意 说 说 就 说 说
'You agree to speak (with us). That said, (will you) say it (aloud)?'
你们愿意说呢就说不说？

B: ŋ³¹.
INTJ
'Uh-huh.'
嗯。

A: ŋ³³ n̠a³³. jɛ³⁵ʐ̩³⁵ n̠a³¹ n̠a³¹?
COP COP.EMP agree speak speak
是 愿意 说 说
'Okay. (Do you) agree to speak?'
是的。愿不愿意说？

B: jɛ³⁵ʐ̩³⁵   ja³³   pa³¹.
   agree   IPFV.EMP   IMP.SOL
   愿意
   '(I) agree, okay?'
   愿意呀！

A: jɛ³⁵ʐ̩³⁵   ja³³   **sa⁴⁴**?
   agree   IPFV.EMP   CRTN.Q
   愿意
   '(So, you) agree?'
   愿意啦？
(KL,GCS-Childhood)

This particle is not used with noun phrases unless it appears in a tag question with the copula. See § 12.4.4 for a discussion of tag questions.

12.4.7.4 Irrealis Question Marker *la³¹*

When used in reduplicative polar questions, the irrealis particle *la³¹* contributes a perfective sense (see § 12.4.1). When modifying a declarative clause without reduplication, it merely conveys an irrealis sense, marking activities occurring currently or in the future — context clarifies the time frame. An example is shown in (903). *la³¹* may also form irrealis questions with noun phrases and postpositional phrases, as in (904).

(903) kʰa⁵⁵tso³¹tɕʰi³¹   n̪a³¹   **la³¹**?
      Khatso.language   speak   IRR.Q
      喀卓语   说
      'Do (you) speak Khatso?'
      讲喀卓语吗？
      (KL-Competition)

(904) pɣ³²³xai³¹s̩³⁵   mɛi⁴⁴   kʰv̩³³   a³³   ma⁴⁴   **la³¹**?
      north.sea.temple   CL:GEN inside   that CL:GEN IRR.Q
      北海寺   个   里   那   个
      'In North Sea Temple, that one?'
      北海寺里边那个吗？
      (KL-Dragon Pools)

In this construction, there is also a degree of certainty about the response, but not to the extent of the question marker *sa⁴⁴*. For example, if one were to see at the bus stop someone who regularly travels to Yuxi, one would ask a question with this particle to determine whether she is going there again as presumed. Short affirmative or negative responses are the typical replies to this sort of question.

12.4.7.5 Confirmation Question Marker *pɛi³³*

The particle *pɛi³³* is used to form confirmatory questions in which the speaker is not sure of the answer. As such, it often co-occurs with the post-verbal adverb *sa²⁴* 'perhaps', which highlights the uncertainty of the question. Syntactically, *pɛi³³* is always the last element in the phrase, placed behind any and all aspect and emphatic markers. Examples are shown in (905) and (906). The particle marks only clauses; it cannot query a noun phrase directly.

(905) tɛi³¹　ma²⁴　kɛi³³　kɛi³³　ta³¹　　jo³³　　**sa²⁴**　　ja³³　　**pɛi³³**?
　　　one　CL:GEN　INS　AGT　connect　must　perhaps　IPFV.EMP　CFRM.Q
　　　一　　个　　　用　　　　　　接　　　应该　可能
　　　'One (of these) must be used to connect (the pieces) perhaps?'
　　　要用一个来接着的是吧？
　　　(KL-Sewing)

(906) pɛi³⁵　tɕʰa³¹　ko⁵⁵　ɕo³¹　no⁵³　　　ti³³　　**sa²⁴**　　ja³³　　**pɛi³³**?
　　　grass　leaf　　CL:PL　pare　complete　PROG　perhaps　IPFV.EMP　CFRM.Q
　　　草　　　叶　　　些　　　削　　掉　　　　　　可能
　　　'(And so you) are cutting off the leaves?'
　　　要把草叶给削掉的吧？
　　　(KL-Stools)

Responses to such questions may be simple affirmative or negative phrases, or further explanation of the topic at hand.

12.4.7.6 Rhetorical Question Marker *ta³¹*

Like *ŋa³¹*, *ta³¹* only occurs in questions formed with interrogative pronouns. However, its purpose is to mark rhetorical questions or questions for which the listener is not expected to have an authoritative answer, though it does not preclude the listener from responding. A frequently heard question of this type is shown in (907), which may either invite suggested solutions to a problem or serve as a general lament at an unfortunate situation.

(907) **xa³³ni³³**   tɕi³³   **ta³¹?**
how   do   RHET.Q
怎么   做
'What should (I) do?' / 'What (can one) do?'
怎么办?
(KL-Elicitation)

This construction may also carry a sense of criticism. For example, in (908) a seamstress is querying a suggestion that she finds unsuitable. In addition, when the construction contains only a noun phrase, it questions the credentials or competence of the referent with a sarcastic or mocking flavor. The phrase in (909), for example, might be followed with a comment such as 'she never went to high school!' or 'his students hate him!'.

(908) i³²³xo³²³   mɛi⁴⁴   mo⁵⁵   tɤ⁴⁴   **xa³³ma⁴⁴**   m̩³³   **ta³¹?**
flat.button CL:GEN want   CLNK   what   do   RHET.Q
纽扣   个   要   什么   做
'(You) want a flat button (here) to do what?'
要扁纽扣做什么嘛?
(KL-Sewing)

(909) **xa³³ma⁴⁴**   lau³²³sɿ³³   **ta³¹?**
what   teacher   RHET.Q
什么   老师
'What (do you mean) teacher?'
什么老师呀?
(KL-Elicitation)

Note that the rhetorical particle is homophonous with the prohibitive *ta³¹* (see § 9.1.2). Word order differentiates the two. The prohibitive must precede the verb it modifies, while the rhetorical particle always occurs at the end of the phrase.

12.5 Comparative Constructions

In comparative constructions, two items are compared in terms of a property or quality. There are a number of strategies for creating such constructions in Khatso, depending on the relationship described. Comparisons of equality are described in § 12.5.1, and those of extent in § 12.5.2. Comparisons of superiority are explored in § 12.5.3, and quantitative comparisons are discussed in § 12.5.4. In addition, there are several constructions that implicitly contain a comparison even though only one item is mentioned; they are described in § 12.5.5. There are no dedicated constructions that express inequality or inferiority; simply negating an equal or superior comparison is sufficient — negation is discussed in each subsection.

12.5.1 Comparisons of Equality

In comparisons of equality, two or more items are considered to be the same. There are several ways to express this notion in Khatso, which are described below. Comparisons of inequality are formed by negating these same constructions.

To convey that noun phrases are exactly the same, the classifier construction $t\varepsilon i^{31} t\varsigma^h a u^{33}$ is used. This is likely a translation from Hanyu, which has a similar construction, since the Khatso word is now idiomatic and not compositional. The first syllable is the numeral $t\varepsilon i^{31}$ 'one'; $t\varsigma^h a u^{33}$ is a classifier that has no other use but this one. If two separate nouns are compared, the arguments precede $t\varepsilon i^{31} t\varsigma^h a u^{33}$ and are both marked by the conjunction $k\varepsilon i^{33}$, as shown in (910). Or, the comparative postposition la^{33} is used to mark the standard of comparison, always the second comparand, which obviates the need for conjunctions, as in (911). If a plural noun comprises both arguments, then neither conjunctions nor la^{33} are necessary, as in (912). All of these constructions may include the copula, as in (913), but it is not necessary — equational phrases often omit it (see § 8.5). In addition, the example in (914) shows that clauses may also be compared in the same way.

(910) [ŋa³³]   kɛi³³   [nɛi³³]   kɛi³³   tɛi³¹tɕʰau³³.
   1SG   CONJ   2SG   CONJ   same
   我   和   你   和   一样
   'You and I (are) the same.'
   我和你一样。
   (KL-Elicitation)

(911) [ŋa³³]   [nɛi³³]   la³³   tɛi³¹tɕʰau³³.
   1SG   2SG   CMP   same
   我   你   一样
   'You and I (are) the same'.
   我和你一样。
   (KL-Elicitation)

(912) [tsʰo³³   a³³   ŋ³¹   jo³⁵]   tɛi³¹tɕʰau³³.
   people   that   two   CL:HUM   same
   人   那   二   位   一样
   'Those two people (are) the same.'
   那两个人一样。
   (KL-Elicitation)

(913) [tsʰo³³ a³³ ŋ³¹ jo³⁵] **tɕɛi³¹tɕʰau³³ ŋ³³**.
people that two CL:HUM same COP
人　　那　　二　　位　　　　　一样　　　　是
'Those two people are the same.'
那两个人是一样的。
(KL-Elicitation)

(914) A: [za³¹ fv³³] **kɛi³³** [za³¹m̩³¹ fv³³] **kɛi³³** tɕɛi³¹ –
son give.birth CONJ daughter give.birth CONJ one
儿子 生　　　和　　女儿　　生　　　　和　　一
'Having a son or having a daughter –'
生儿子和生女儿–

B: **tɕɛi³¹tɕʰau³³ ŋɛi³⁵**.
same COP.FOC
一样　　　　是
'Is the same.'
是一样。
(KL, YJF-Having Children)

Another expression of equal comparison involves the comparative postposition *la³³* and the copula, without *tɕɛi³¹tɕʰau³³*. In this construction, the arguments precede *la³³* and no conjunction is necessary. Examples are shown in (915) and (916). Even though *la³³* is a particle and has no lexical meaning, it is regularly translated into Putonghua as *xiàng* 'to resemble' 像. Thus, semantically *la³³ ŋ³³* seems to carry a less exact notion of equivalence than *tɕɛi³¹tɕʰau³³* — much like the way that 'to be like' and 'to be the same' differ in English. In discourse, however, the two largely function interchangeably. Clauses, however, cannot be compared with *la³³* without the complementizer-like topic marker *sɛi⁴⁴*, as in (917). Complementation is discussed in Chapter 15.

(915) [nɛi³³] [tsʰo³³ v³¹ jo³⁵] **la³³ ŋ³³** la³⁵ ŋɛi³³.
2SG person be.crazy CL:HUM CMP COP FOC ASRT
你　　　人　　疯　　位　　　　　　是
'You're like a crazy person.'
你就像疯子一样。
(PYX-Dragon Pools)

(916) [tɛi³³ tɕi⁵⁵]   wa³²³tɕʰɛ³²³ [fɣ³³ma³³ ko⁵⁵] **la³³** **ŋ³³** tsɛi³¹.
      this CL:TYPE complete   lake   CL:PL CMP COP   HSY
      这   些   完全   湖   些   是
      '(They) say those (places) were completely like lakes.'
      说是这些地方象海一样。
      (PYX-Dragon Pools)

(917) [kʰua³¹la³¹ i³²³] **sɛi⁴⁴** [ŋ⁵⁵lo⁵³ i³²³] **sɛi⁴⁴** **la³³** ti⁵³ na²⁴ kɯ³²³ sa³³.
      Kunming go   TOP   Tonghai go   TOP   CMP   CL:PCE play CSC be.good
      昆明   去   通海   去   点   玩   好
      'Going to Kunming is a bit more fun than going to Tonghai.'
      去昆明比去通海好玩。
      (KL-Elicitation)

In comparisons of equality involving verbs other than the copula, *la³³* combines with the adverbial marker *ni³³*, as shown in (918) and (919). The addition of *ni³³* differentiates this construction from a comparison of superiority (see § 12.5.3).

(918) [a³³ tsɛi³⁵] **la³³** **ni³³** ȵa³¹.
      that CL:TMP CMP   ADV   speak
      那   段   说
      'Talk like before.'
      和刚才一样说。
      (KL-Grandfather)

(919) [i²⁴tɕʰɛ³²³ tɕi⁵⁵] tɕo³⁵ tsuo³³ʐ̩³²³mɛi³²³ [po³¹po³¹ mɛi⁴⁴] **la³³** **ni³³**
      qin   CL:TYPE then   especially   drum   CL:GEN CMP   ADV
      琴   种   就   专门   鼓   个
      i³³kʰɣ³³ kʰɣ²⁴   tsɤ³¹ jo³³.
      inside   be.empty CONT must
      里面   空   应该
      'The *qin* [a stringed instrument] is just like a drum (in that it) must always be hollow inside.'
      琴就像鼓一样，里面是要空着的。
      (YLW-Qin)

la³³ participates in two other comparative constructions. With the existential verb *tso³²³*, it forms comparisons of extent (see § 12.5.2). With stative verbs, it forms the basic construction for comparisons of superiority (see § 12.5.3).

In addition, the reciprocal construction *i³³ ɣ³²³ i³³* may also be used in comparisons of equality, but it retains a sense of reciprocity which limits the types of verbs it may accompany. For example, it is used with *tɛi³¹tɕʰau³³* and *tɛi³¹tɕʰau³³ ŋ³³* to denote equality, as shown in (920). This kind of phrase can be viewed as reciprocal, since each noun is identically related to the other. In many cases, often in phrases featuring demonstratives or classifer constructions, the reciprocity is interpreted as cyclical, as in (921) and (922), in which a series of identical items are compared one by one. Like its use in reciprocal clauses, the third-person pronoun in the construction may stand for any type of noun regardless of animacy or number (see § 12.3).

(920) i³³ ɣ³²³ i³³ tɛi³¹tɕʰau³³ (ŋ³³).
       RECP   same   COP
       互相   一样   是
       '(They) are the same.', literally 'He and he are the same.'
       互相一样。
       (KL-Elicitation)

(921) [tɛi³¹ ma²⁴] ɣ³²³ [tɛi³¹ ma²⁴] la³³ tɛi³¹tɕʰau³³ ma³¹ ŋ³³.
       one CL:GEN RECP one CL:GEN CMP same NEG COP
       一 个 互相 一 个 比 一样 不 是
       'Each one is different than the next', literally 'one and one are not the same.'
       一个和一个不一样。
       (KL-Doors)

(922) [tɛi³¹ kʰo⁵³] ɣ³²³ [tɛi³¹ kʰo⁵³] ko⁵³ kɯ³²³ sa³³ tɤ³³wa³³ po⁵³.
       one CL:TMP RECP one CL:TMP pass CSC be.good INCP EPIS.EMP
       一 年 互相 一 年 过 好
       'Each year is becoming easier to live through than the next.', literally 'One year and one year are becoming easy to live through.'
       一年比一年好过了。
       (YJF-Childhood)

Negation in comparative constructions is performed by placing the negative marker ma^{31} before the verb. Examples are shown in (923) through (926). Note that the copula is required in negated $tɕi^{31}tɕʰau^{33}$ clauses, as (923) demonstrates, since the latter is not a verb and thus cannot be directly modified by ma^{31}.

(923) [wa⁵³sa³¹] kɛi³³ [ŋ³¹sa³¹] kɛi³³ tɛi³¹tɕʰau³³ ma³¹ ŋ³³.
       pork CONJ beef CONJ same NEG COP
       猪肉 和 牛肉 和 一样 不 是
       'Pork and beef are not the same.'
       猪肉和牛肉不一样。
       (KL-Elicitation)

(924) [i³³] [i³³ sɛi⁴⁴ pa³¹] **la³³ ma³¹ ŋ³³**.
3SG 3SG family father CMP NEG COP
他 他 家 爸 不 是
'He and his father are not the same.' / 'He does not resemble his father.'
他和他的爸爸不一样。 / 他不像他的爸爸。
(KL-Elicitation)

(925) [a³³tɕʰa⁵⁵kʰv̩³³], ɕa³⁵pʰiɛ³⁵, [tɕi³³tɕʰa⁵⁵kʰv̩³³] **la³³ ni³³ tɕi³³ ma³¹**
that.time photos this.time CMP ADV this NEG
那时候 相片 这时候 这 不
ɕi³³ tsau³⁵.
be. accustomed take
习惯 照
'At that time, photos, (we were) not accustomed to taking (them) like today.'
那时候的照片不会像现在照这么多。
(YJF-Childhood)

(926) [tɕi³¹n̩a⁵³] v̩³²³ [tɕi³¹n̩a⁵³] **la³³ tɕi³¹tɕʰau³³ ma³¹ ŋ³³**.
one.place RECP one.place CMP same NEG COP
一处 互相 一处 一样 不 是
'Each place is different than the next.'
一个地方和一个地方不一样。
(KL-Doors)

Another way of expressing equivalence between two noun phrases is by comparing them in terms of a specific attribute. This construction is discussed in the following section on comparisons of extent.

12.5.2 Comparisons of Extent

Describing the extent of an attribute or comparing two arguments with regard to that attribute is done by combining a stative verb or a complex stative construction with the existential verb *tso³²³* and marking the standard of comparison with the comparative postposition *la³³*. And although expressions denoting dimension often appear in this construction, any stative or complex stative construction may be compared this way. Examples are shown in (927), (928) and (929). Note that the classifer construction *tɕi³¹tɕʰau³³*, which is used in comparisons of equality (see § 12.5.1), may emphasize the equivalence, as in (928), but is not obligatory. These comparisons are a type of serial verb construction (see § 8.8) — the only one to involve *tso³²³* — since the verbs share the same arguments and form a unitary predicate describing a single state. Many Ngwi languages have special forms for verbs of dimensional extent (Bradley

1995), but this is not the case for Khatso. Dimension verbs pattern no differently than any other stative verb in the language.

(927) [ŋa³³]   [nɛi³³]   **la³³**   m̩²⁴   **tso³²³**.
1SG   2SG   CMP   be.tall   EXIST
我   你   高   有
'I am as tall as you.'
我和你一样高。
(KL-Elicitation)

(928) [i³³]   **la³³**   tɛi³¹tɕʰau³³   ɣɤ³¹   **tso³²³**   la²⁴   [ko⁵⁵]
3SG   CMP   same   be.big   EXIST   REL   CL:PL
他   一样   大   有   些
'those who (are) as old as he is'
和他一样大的那些
(YAY-Erasers)

(929) [ɕi³³ɕi³³]   [kʰua³¹la³¹]   **la³³**   na²⁴   kɯ³²³   sa³³   **tso³²³**.
Yuxi   Kunming   CMP   play   CSC   be.good   EXIST
玉溪   昆明   玩   好   有
'Yuxi is as fun as Kunming.'
玉溪和昆明一样好玩。
(KL-Elicitation)

It is also possible to include a quantitative measurement in the comparison, as (930) illustrates. Other types of quantifiable comparisons are described in § 12.5.4.

(930) [tɛi³³ni³³]   [o³¹sɹ̩³²³]   m̩²⁴   **tso³²³**   wa³²³.
this.way   five.ten   be.tall   EXIST   PFV
这么   五十   高   有
'(It) was as tall as fifty (centimeters).'
有五十这么高了。
(WYF-Stools)

In comparisons of extent the negative marker modifies *tso³²³* rather than the attribute, as the examples in (931) and (932) demonstrate. This structure is syntatically identical to that of negated complex stative constructions, but semantically the two are different. The comparative construction only has one option for negation, and the fact that *ma³¹* occurs between the verbs does not mean that the action was begun but not completed (see § 8.8.1.4 for more on complex stative constructions). Rather, negation has scope over both verbs in this construction.

(931) tɛi³³ni³³ jɛ⁵³   **ma³¹** **tso³²³** ŋɛi³³.
      this.way be.smooth NEG   EXIST   ASRT
      这么   滑   不   有
      '(It) is not as smooth as this.'
      没有这么滑的。
      (WYF-Stools)

(932) [tɛi³³tɕʰa⁵⁵kʰɣ³³ pɣ³²³ ko⁵⁵] **la³³** tɛi³³ni³³ fo³³lio³²³   **ma³¹** **tso³²³**.
      this.time   POSS   CL:PL CMP   this.way   be.sophisticated NEG   EXIST
      这时候   些   这么   风流   不   有
      '(They) were not as sophisticated as those of today.'
      没有现在的这些这么风流。
      (YJF-Weddings)

When heading a clause, complex stative constructions may be negated. But a negated complex stative construction typically cannot serve as the standard of comparison. Thus, the phrase in (933), which is equivalent to 'not as fun as' is much preferred over that in (934), which means 'as not fun as'.

(933) na²⁴   kɯ³²³ sa³³   **ma³¹** **tso³²³**
      play   CSC   be.good   NEG   EXIST
      玩   好   不   有
      'not as fun as'
      没有那么好玩
      (KL-Elicitation)

(934) na²⁴   kɯ³²³ **ma³¹** sa³³   **tso³²³**
      play   CSC   NEG   be.good   EXIST
      玩   不   好   有
      'as not fun as'
      没有那么不好玩
      (KL-Elicitation)

12.5.3 Comparisons of Superiority/Inferiority

Often, the purpose of comparison is to describe the superiority of one noun phrase over another in terms of some feature or attribute. In Khatso, this construction combines the comparative postposition *la³³* and a stative verb or a complex stative construction. The arguments precede *la³³* and no conjunction is necessary; the verb follows the postposition. Examples are shown in (935) and (936).

(935) [ŋa³³] [nɛi³³] **la³³** m̥²⁴ ja³³.
    1SG   2SG   CMP be.tall IPFV.EMP
    我   你   像   高
    'I'm taller than you.'
    我比你高。
    (KL-Elicitation)

(936) [tɛi³³ ma⁴⁴] [a³³ ma⁴⁴] **la³³** na²⁴ kɯ³³ sa³³ ja³³.
    this CL:GEN that CL:GEN CMP hear CSC be.good IPFV.EMP
    这   个   那   个   听   好
    'This one sounds better than that one.'
    这个比那个好听。
    (KL-Elicitation)

The degree of difference may be specified by inserting the relevant modifier between *la³³* and the verb. For example, the classifier construction *tɛi³¹ti⁵³ za³¹* 'a little' in (937) diminishes the difference, while *tɛi³¹ko⁵⁵ma³³* 'a lot' augments it in (938).

(937) [ŋa³³] [nɛi³³] **la³³** tɛi³¹ti⁵³za³¹ m̥²⁴   ja³³.
    1SG   2SG   CMP   a.little   be.tall IPFV.EMP
    我   你   一点   高
    'I'm a little taller than you.'
    我比你高一点。
    (KL-Elicitation)

(938) [ŋa³³] [nɛi³³] **la³³** tɛi³¹ko⁵⁵ma³³ m̥²⁴   ja³³.
    1SG   2SG   CMP   a.lot   be.tall IPFV.EMP
    我   你   很多   高
    'I'm a lot taller than you.'
    我比你高很多。
    (KL-Elicitation)

There is no separate construction for comparisons of inferiority in Khatso as there is in Chinese. Instead, a comparison of superiority may be negated, as shown in (939). In discourse, however, a negative comparison of extent, as in (940), may provide a more natural response. When the matrix verb is *tsʰŋ³³* 'to arrive, reach', as in (941), it provides a general sense of inferiority.

(939) [ɣa⁵³sa³¹ tɕi⁵⁵] [wa⁵³sa³¹ tɕi⁵⁵] **la³³** tsa³¹n̠a²⁴ **ma³¹** n̠a²⁴.
chicken CL:TYPE pork CL:TYPE CMP be.tasty NEG be.good
鸡肉 种 猪肉 种 吃 不 好
'Chicken is not tastier than pork.'
鸡肉没有猪肉好吃。
(KL-Elicitation)

(940) [ɣa⁵³sa³¹ tɕi⁵⁵] [wa⁵³sa³¹ tɕi⁵⁵] **la³³** tsa³¹n̠a²⁴ **ma³¹** **tso³²³**.
chicken CL:TYPE pork CL:TYPE CMP be.tasty NEG EXIST
鸡肉 种 猪肉 种 吃 不 有
'Chicken is not as tasty as pork.'
鸡肉没有猪肉好吃。
(KL-Elicitation)

(941) [nɛi³³] [i³³] **la³³** **ma³¹** tsʰɤ³³.
2SG 3SG CMP NEG reach
你 他 不 到
'You aren't his equal.', literally 'You don't reach him.'
你不如他。
(KL-Elicitation)

la³³ participates in two other comparative constructions. When used with non-stative verbs, it forms comparisons of equality (see § 12.5.1). With the existential verb *tso³²³*, it forms comparisons of extent (see § 12.5.2). Contrastive comparisons, which focus on the superiority of a single argument and do not involve *la³³*, are described in § 12.5.5.

12.5.4 Quantitative Comparisons

Comparisons of inequality may also involve enumerated quantities. If the difference is measured in multiples, then a classifier borrowed from Hanyu, *pɛi³⁵* 'times' 倍, is used with a numeral, and this element is placed between the comparative particle *la³³* and the verb. An example is shown in (942).

(942) [i³³] [ŋa³³] **la³³** [ŋ³¹ **pɛi³⁵**] ɣɣ³¹ ja³³.
3SG 1SG CMP two CL:MLT be.big IPFV.EMP
他 我 二 倍 大
'He is twice as big as I.'
他比我大两倍。
(KL-Elicitation)

If the comparison involves another type of measure, then a mensural classifier is employed. For example, the phrase in (943) describes a difference in weight while that in (944) discusses a difference in height. Mensural classifiers are described in § 6.2.2.2.

(943) [i³³]   [nɛi³³] **la³³** [ŋa³¹ **tsɿ²⁴**] tsɿ³¹   ja³³.
      3SG   2SG   CMP   five   CL:MSR   be.heavy   IPFV.EMP
      他   你   五   斤   重
      'He's heavier than you by 5 *jin*.'
      他比你重五斤。
      (KL-Elicitation)

(944) [ŋa³³] [nɛi³³] **la³³** [ŋa³¹ **li³²³mi³¹**] m̩²⁴   ja³³.
      1SG   2SG   CMP   five   CL:MSR   be.tall   IPFV.EMP
      我   你   五   厘米   高
      'I'm taller than you by 5 centimeters.'
      我比你高五厘米。
      (KL-Elicitation)

Like comparisons of superiority, negation in this construction occurs by placing the negative marker *ma³¹* before the stative verb; see § 12.5.3 for examples. Comparisons of extent may also involve enumerated quantities, see § 12.5.2.

12.5.5 Implicit Comparative Constructions

Not all comparative clauses are transitive — some, in fact, are intransitive and only focus on a single comparand. Typically, the standard of comparison is already mentioned and is thus given information at that point in discourse. These comparisons may simply contrast, such as those described in § 12.5.5.1, or compare the status of an single item over time, as in § 12.5.5.2. Extreme constructions, which often have a superlative sense, are also a type of comparison; they are described in § 12.5.5.3.

12.5.5.1 Contrastive Comparisons

Contrastive comparisons focus exclusively on the attributes of a single comparand. They are formed by combining one of several words in Khatso that mean 'more, even more' with a stative verb or complex stative construction. Three of these words are the adverbs *i³¹kɯ³⁵*, *to³³i³¹* and *i²⁴fa³³*, which are identical in meaning and use. Examples are shown in (945), (946) and (947) respectively. Note that a few gradable non-stative verbs may be modified in this way, such as *sɿ⁵⁵* 'to know' in (948).

(945) kʰua³¹la³¹ **i³¹kɯ³⁵** na²⁴ kɯ³²³ sa³³ ja³³ sɛi³¹.
Kunming more play CSC be.good IPFV.EMP still
昆明 更 玩 好 还
'Kunming is even more fun still.'
昆明更好玩呀。
(KL-Elicitation)

(946) ŋ̩³¹sa³¹ tɕi⁵⁵ **to³³i³¹** pʰɣ³¹kʰa⁵⁵.
beef CL:TYPE more be.expensive
牛肉 种 更 贵
'Beef is (even) more expensive.'
牛肉更贵。
(KL-Elicitation)

(947) ŋa³²³tv̩³³ kʰo⁵³ ni³⁵? **i²⁴fa³³** sa⁵⁵.
behind CL:TMP TOP.Q more be.difficult
后面 年 更 苦
'And the year after? (It) was even more difficult.'
第二年呢？更苦。
(YJF-Childhood)

(948) ŋa³³ sɛi⁴⁴ ni³¹ **i²⁴fa³³** ma³¹ s̩ɹ⁵⁵.
1SG family TOP more NEG know
我 家 更 不 知道
'As for my family, (I) know even less about (them).'
我家呢，更不知道。
(ZRF-Grandfather)

In addition, the classifier-based modifiers *tɕi³¹ti⁵³* and *tɕi³¹ti⁵³za³¹* 'a little' may be used in place of these words, in which case the comparative notion is implied. Often, the numeral *tɕi³¹* 'one' is omitted without a change in meaning, as the example in (949) illustrates. The serial verb construction *m̩³³ tsa³¹* in the example, which literally means 'do, make (in order) to eat', is an idiom that translates as 'making a living' or 'livelihood'.

(949) ko³¹zɛi³²³   m̥³³   tsa³¹ tɕo³⁵   **ti⁵³za³¹**   ko⁵³   kɯ³²³ sa³³   wa³²³.
each.person make eat then a.little pass CSC be.good PFV
各人   做   吃   就   点   过   好
'Each person's livelihood then went a little better.', literally 'Each person making a living then went a little better.'
自己干活吃饭就好过一点了。
(YJF-Childhood)

Contrastive comparisons often co-occur with stative verbs or complex stative constructions, as the examples above demonstrate. But the modifiers may accompany verbs of any valency. The example in (950), for example, contains a stative verb in the first clause and a ditransitive verb in the second. Note also that in this construction, $to^{33}i^{31}$ modifies the verb and not the omitted P.

(950) tɛi³¹ti⁵³za³¹ xɯ³²³   la²⁴ tsʰɤ³³ ni³¹ tɤ⁴⁴ **to³³i³¹** ti⁵³za³¹ kɯ³¹.
a.little   be.strong REL PL   TOP all more   a.little Give
点   厉害   们   都   更   点   给
'So, the stronger ones, (they) gave (them) all a little more.'
那，厉害一点儿的呢，多给一点儿。
(YJF-Work Brigades)

To convey a negative contrast, the verb is modified by the negative marker ma^{31} and the same modifiers — $i^{31}kɯ^{35}$, $to^{33}i^{31}$, $i^{24}fa^{33}$ and $tɛi^{31}ti^{53}$ — are used. An example is shown in (951).

(951) mo³¹   la²⁴   ko⁵⁵   ni³¹   **i²⁴fa³³**   n̥a³¹   **ma³¹**   li³²³.
be.old REL CL:PL TOP more speak NEG know.how
老   些   更   说   不   会
'The old ones, (they) know how to speak (it) even less.'
那些老的呢，更不会说。
(YAY-Erasers)

The words that mark contrastive comparisons also occur in temporal comparisons (see § 12.5.5.2) and comparative conditional constructions (see § 14.4.4).

12.5.5.2 Temporal Comparisons

In temporal comparisons, an attribute of an single entity is compared over time. This is done by reduplicating the adverb $i^{24}fa^{33}$ 'more' before the stative verb, providing a reading of 'more and more'. Examples are shown in (952) and (953). Note that the implied time frame is vague and depends on context. The change may occur in minutes, as in (952), or over many years, as in (953). The other contrastive adverbs, *i³¹kuɯ³⁵* and *to³³i³¹*, cannot participate in this construction.

(952)　**i²⁴fa³³**　**i²⁴fa³³**　**mɤ³³**
　　　more　　more　　be.dizzy
　　　更　　　更　　　晕
　　　'more and more confused'
　　　(KL-Elicitation)

(953)　**i²⁴fa³³**　**i²⁴fa³³**　fa³²³tsa³¹　tɤ⁴⁴
　　　more　　more　　develop　STAT.EMP
　　　更　　　更　　　发展
　　　'more and more developed'
　　　越来越发展的
　　　(HPH-Toys)

Like contrastive comparisons, this construction is negated by modifying the verb; the reduplication of *i²⁴fa³³* does not change. An example is shown in (954).

(954)　i³³　pɤ³²³　na³²³　mɛi⁴⁴　**i²⁴fa³³**　**i²⁴fa³³**　ma³¹　na²⁴　tɤ³³ wa³³.
　　　3SG　POSS　illness　CL:GEN　more　more　NEG　be.good　INCP
　　　他　　　　　病　　　个　　　更　　　更　　　不　　好
　　　'His illness is getting worse and worse.'
　　　他的病越来越不好了。
　　　(KL-Elicitation)

When used singly, *i²⁴fa³³* has a simple contrastive meaning, as discussed in § 12.5.5.1. It may also be used to combine clauses, a structure that is described in § 14.4.4.

12.5.5.3 Superlative Construction

Khatso has no dedicated particle for marking superlatives. Instead, several particles with other uses are combined to convey an extreme sense, which may have a superlative meaning depending on context. The basis for this construction is the agent marker *kɛi³³*, here serving as a contrastive focus marker (see § 10.4), which is accompanied by a gradable stative verb or complex stative construction modified by the intensifier *tʰɛi³²³*. Examples are shown in (955), (956) and (957). Often, the perfective marker *wa³⁷³* accompanies the construction, though the strong assertion marker *ŋɛi³³* may appear instead. The alternative intensifier *mɛi⁴⁴*, however, is never used in this construction.

(955) wa³¹ sau²⁴tsa⁴⁴ **kɛi³³** tɤ²⁴li²⁴ **tʰɛi³²³ wa³²³**.
wa³¹ sau²⁴tsa⁴⁴ AGT be.fierce very PFV
王绍章 厉害 很
'wa³¹ sau²⁴tsa⁴⁴ is the most capable.'
王绍章最厉害了。
(KXC-Fishing)

(956) ŋa³³tsʰɤ³¹ kʰa⁵⁵tso³¹ ko⁵⁵ sɿ⁴⁴ tɕi³³ jo³⁵ **kɛi³³** to²⁴ kɯ³²³ na²⁴
1PL Khatso CL:PL TOP this CL:HUM AGT spear CSC be.good
我们 喀卓 些 这 个 叉 好
tʰɛi³²³ wa³²³.
very PFV
很
'(Among) us Khatso, that one is the best at spear(fishing).'
我们喀卓人里，这个是叉得最好的了。
(KXC-Fishing)

(957) tɕi³³ ma⁴⁴ **kɛi³³** tsa³¹na²⁴ **tʰɛi³²³** ŋɛi³³.
this CL:GEN AGT be.tasty very ASRT
这 个 好吃 很
'This (is) the tastiest.'
这个是最好吃的。
(KL-Elicitation)

In contrast to the examples above, the phrase in (958) does not have a superlative meaning. It states that people who were older than age seventy were considered very old, not that anyone at that age was literally the oldest person in the village.

(958) a³³tɕʰa⁵⁵kʰɤ³³ tsʰɿ³²³sɿ³²³ lo⁵³ la²⁴ tsʰɤ³³ **kɛi³³** tɕo³⁵ mo³¹ **tʰɛi³²³ wa³²³**.
that.time seven.ten reach REL PL AGT then be.old very PFV
那时候 七十 到 们 就 老 很
'At that time, people who reached seventy were (considered) very old.'
那时候有七十岁的就很老了。
(YJF-Childhood)

The construction is even more ambiguous in relative clauses, such as (959), where aspect markers are typically omitted. Moreover, in cases where A is absent because it is the head noun, only the presence of the intensifier signals a potential superlative reading, as shown in (960) and (961). In these examples, in fact, both the extreme sense and the superlative sense fit the context.

(959) [ɣɤ³¹ **tʰɛi³²³** la²⁴ tʏ³⁵kʰɯ³¹ tɛi³³ ma⁴⁴] xa³³ ma⁴⁴ ɣ²⁴ ŋa³¹?
be.big very REL ford this CL:GEN what call CNT.Q
大 很 渡口 这 个 什么 叫
'What is the biggest ford called?'
这个最大的渡口叫什么？
(KLT-History)

(960) [tʰiau³⁵ **tʰɛi³²³** la²⁴ tsʰɣ³³] ŋ³³ n̪a³³ mɛi⁴⁴ tɤ⁴⁴.
be.naughty very REL PL COP COP.EMP DSC.EMP STAT.EMP
调 很 们 是
'(They) were the naughtiest ones.' / '(They) were very naughty ones.'
是很调皮的人呀。
(PYX-Performing)

(961) tsɿ³²³ tsɿ³¹ sɛi⁴⁴ [o²⁴ **tʰɛi³²³** la²⁴ tɛi³¹ jo³⁵] **wa³²³**.
war fight TMP be.fierce very REL one CL:HUM PFV
战 打 厉害 很 一 位
'When waging war, (he) was the fiercest one.' / 'When waging war, (he) was a very fierce one.'
打战最厉害的一个了。
(KLT-History)

This construction is negated by placing the negative marker *ma³¹* before the stative verb. The perfective marker *wa³²³* is then replaced by the perfective irrealis *la³¹* (see § 9.2.6). An example is shown in (962).

(962) i³³ **kɛi³³** ma³¹ m̪²⁴ **tʰɛi³²³** la³¹.
3SG AGT NEG be.tall very IRR.PFV
他 不 高 很
'He is not the tallest.'
他不是最高的。
(KL-Elicitation)

Without the contrastive *kɛi³³*, matrix clauses with *tʰɛi³²³* alone are considered intensified, but not to an extreme or superlative degree. This is further clarified by the presence of the imperfective emphatic particle *ja³³*, which never occurs in the extreme construction. An example is shown in (963).

(963) "na²⁴ kɯ³²³ sa³³   **tʰɛi³²³ ja³³!**   xai³⁵ xuɛi³²³ tsʰo²⁴!"
      hear CSC be.good very IPFV.EMP   still CL:TMP perform.IMP
      听   好   很   还   次   演
      ' "(That) sounded great! Perform (it) again!" '
      "很好听的！再演一回。"
      (PYX-Performing)

12.6 Emphasis

Khatso has a number of emphatic particles, each with a slightly different degree and function, and they are almost always the final element in a phrase. In fact, their presence indicates that the clause in question is a gramatically complete sentence. Almost all of them operate at the clausal level, where their use is conditioned by certain syntactic features, such as aspect or question formation. For example, *ja³³* and *ja³²³* are both general emphatic markers, the first is imperfective and the second perfective (§ 12.6.1 and § 12.6.2 respectively). *ɲa³³* is similar in function, but it only modifies the copula (§ 12.6.3). *lɛi³¹* is likewise restricted; it appears only in irrealis constructions (§ 12.6.4). Other particles are motivated more by pragmatics and the interactional flow of discourse information. For example, *ŋɛi³³* marks strong assertions, and is often used in a contrastive way (§ 12.6.5). *po⁵³* and *na³¹* both mark clauses that the speaker believes the interlocutor either needs to know or ought to know (§ 12.6.6 and § 12.6.7 respectively). *tɤ⁴⁴* presents an event as a state or habitual situation (§ 12.6.8), and *mɛi⁴⁴* is used to mark key points in discourse (§ 12.6.9). None of these particles are obligatory, and there is a great deal of speaker variation in the manner and frequency of their use. They also modify the clause-combining constructions discussed in Chapters 13 through 16.

12.6.1 Imperfective Emphatic Marker *ja³³*

The particle *ja³³* is frequently used to mark emphasis in Khatso. It imparts a sense of immediacy, and thus often occurs in imperfective clauses — such as those containing stative verbs or non-statives modified by progressive, continuous and iterative markers — where it may replace the current relative state marker *wa³³*. As a result, it is difficult to translate into English, which has no equivalent. Examples are shown in (964) through (967). Its aspectual use is discussed in § 9.2.3.

(964) kɣ³⁵sɿ³⁵ tɛi³³ ko⁵⁵ i³³kʰy³³ tso³²³ **ja³³**.
story   this   CL:PL inside   EXIST   IPFV.EMP
故事   这   些   里面   有
'There are these stories in (it.)'
里面有这些故事的。
(HPH-Horse Dug Well)

(965) kʰa⁵⁵tso³¹tɕʰi³¹   tsʰo³¹ tɤ³³ **ja³³**.
Khatso.language   sing   PROG IPFV.EMP
喀卓语   唱
'(They) were singing (in) Khatso.'
是用喀卓语唱的。
(PYX-Performing)

(966) mɛi⁴⁴ ŋ²⁴ kɯ³²³ sa³³   ta³²³   **ja³³**.
very   look CSC   be.good be.able IPFV.EMP
很   看   好   能
'(It) must have been really pretty!'
会很好看的。
(KL-Childhood)

(967) ŋɛi³³ n̪a³³.   ŋa³³ sɿ⁵⁵ **ja³³**.
COP   COP.EMP 1SG   know IPFV.EMP
是   我   知道
'Yes. I know.'
是的。我知道呀。
(ZRF-Grandfather)

ja³³ differs from *ja³²³* only in aspect; the latter marks perfective rather than imperfective clauses. *ja³³* is also milder in emphasis than the strong assertion particle *ŋɛi³³*, and tends to mark declarative statements and corroborative information rather than the contrast often associated with the latter particle. Aspect is discussed further in § 9.2.

12.6.2 Perfective Emphatic Marker *ja³²³*

The particle *ja³²³* is similar in function to that of *ja³³*. However, instead of providing emphasis to imperfective clauses, it is used to mark perfective clauses, as shown in (968). As such, it replaces the perfective marker *wa³²³* in discourse. Like its counterpart *ja³³*, *ja³²³* is milder in emphasis than *ŋɛi³³*. Its aspectual use is described in § 9.2.1.

(968) ʐɿ²⁴   i³¹tsɿ³³kɯ³⁵   mɛi⁴⁴   ka⁵³   xɯ⁵³   **ja³²³**.
boat head   CL:GEN   on   stand   PFV.EMP
船   头   个   上   站
'(I) stood on the bow of the boat.'
站在船头上面的。
(ZMF-Fishing)

12.6.3 Copular Emphatic Marker *n̩a³³*

The emphatic marker *n̩a³³* occurs only with the copula. Semantically, its function is identical to the general emphatic force of *ja³³*, which cannot co-occur with the copula. In discourse, it frequently appears in affirmative answers or in short exclamations, as shown in (969) and (970) respectively. It may also modify a copula clause, as in (971).

(969) A: tsɿ³¹tɕa²⁴   pv̩³²³   tɕi⁵⁵   ni³¹   tsɿ³¹tɕa²⁴   pv̩³²³   tɕi⁵⁵   kɤ³³   tɤ³³   ŋ³³
self   POSS   CL:TYPE TOP   self   POSS   CL:TYPE do   PROG   COP
自己   种   自己   种   弄   是
sa⁴⁴?
CRTN.Q
'As for your own, (you) were making (your) own, right?'
是自己的自己弄，是吗？

B: ŋ³³   **n̩a³³**.
COP   COP.EMP
是
'That's right.'
是的。
(KL, YJF-Weddings)

(970) A: ŋa³³   sɛi⁴⁴   pa³¹,   ŋa³³   sɛi⁴⁴   mo³³.
1SG   family father   1SG   family mother
我   家   爸爸   我   家   妈妈
'My father, my mother.'
我爸爸，我妈妈。

B: ŋ³³ **n̩a³³**.   nɛi³³ sɛi⁴⁴ ba³¹,   nɛi³³ sɛi⁴⁴ mo³³   tsʰɤ³³ kʰua³¹
   COP COP.EMP   2SG family father   2SG family mother   PL speak
   是 是   你   家   爸爸   你   家   妈妈   们 讲
   tsɤ²⁴.
   CONT.IMP
   'Yes. Talk about your father's people (and) your mother's people.'
   是的。就说你爸爸家，你妈妈家。
   (ZRF, KL-Grandfather)

(971) xɤ³³pɛi³³   mɛi⁴⁴   pɤ³²³   tsʰo³³   tsʰɤ³³ ŋ³³   **n̩a³³**   po⁵³.
      family   CL:GEN POSS   person   PL   COP COP.EMP   EPIS.EMP
      家   个   人   们   是
      '(He) is a relation (don't you know?).', literally '(He) is a person of (our) house (don't you know?)'
      是一个家门的人嘛。
      (KL-Sewing)

12.6.4 Irrealis Emphatic Marker *lɛi³¹*

The particle *lɛi³¹* serves to lend emphasis to irrealis constructions, which the other emphatic particles cannot do. In declarative clauses, it usually co-occurs with some other element that either marks the clause as irrealis or at least casts doubt on the content. For example, in (972), the clause contains a negated verb and the imperfective irrealis marker *ta³³*. In (973), the clause is marked with the hearsay particle *tsɛi³¹*, and in (974) the adverb *sa²⁴* 'perhaps' marks the content as uncertain and thus potentially untrue.

(972) ma³¹ kɤ̩³³ ta³³   **lɛi³¹**.
      NEG   do   IPFV.IRR   IRR.EMP
      不   做
      '(I) wasn't doing (it).'
      没有做呀。
      (KL-Elicitation)

(973) m̩³²³ ja³⁵   i³³   tsɛi³¹   **lɛi³¹**.
      field fertilize go   HSY   IRR.EMP
      田   施肥   去
      '(They) say (he) went to fertilize the fields.'
      说是去田里施肥去。
      (YJF-Childhood)

(974) mɛi⁴⁴ so²⁴ sa⁵⁵ sa²⁴ ja³³ ta⁵⁵ ŋ³³ **lɛi³¹**.
very learn be.difficult perhaps EMP be.type COP IRR.EMP
很 学 难 可能 样 是
'Perhaps (it) was very difficult to learn, (it) was that type.'
可能很难学的样子。
(KL-Learning)

Because they involve unknown information, questions, too, are irrealis constructions, and *lɛi³¹* may occur in any type of interrogative construction. For example, in (975) it modifies a polar question, which also contains the imperfective irrealis marker *ta³³*, and in (976) it occurs in a content question.

(975) sɛi⁴⁴i⁴⁴ tɕi⁵⁵ tsʰo³³ ko⁵³ ko⁵³ i³³ ta³³ **lɛi³¹**?
sound CL:TYPE rush pass pass go IPFV.IRR IRR.EMP
声音 种 冲 过 过 去
'Is the sound (level) going past (the limit)?'
声音冲过去了没有？
(KL-Tuition)

(976) xa³³ni³³ tɕi³³ pa⁵³ ŋa³¹ **lɛi³¹**?
how do FUT CNT.Q IRR.EMP
怎么 做
'What will (you) do?'
要做什么？
(WYY-Sewing)

See § 9.2.6 and § 9.2.7 for information on the irrealis aspect markers, and § 15.3 for a description of the hearsay particle *tsɛi³¹*.

12.6.5 Strong Assertion Marker *ŋɛi³³*

The strong assertion marker is derived from the copula. They are, in fact, homophonous — in phrase-final position they take the form *ŋɛi³³*, and in other instances the form *ŋ³³*. Their functions are distinct, however. The copula only occurs in equational clauses, and even then is optional. The strong assertion marker modifies clauses containing other verbs, where it has no predicative function. For example, in (977) *γ²⁴* 'to be called' is the matrix verb rather than *ŋɛi³³*. That said, there are ambiguous cases. For example, in (978) *ŋɛi³³* may be analyzed as either the matrix verb or as the emphatic particle in a non-copular equational phrase. Since the copula is routinely omitted from equational clauses, the emphatic use is more likely. Typically the marker is the last element in a clause, and so the *ŋɛi³³* form is frequent. An example showing the non-final ŋ³³ form is presented in (979). The copula is described further in § 8.5.

(977) ɕa²⁴pʰi³¹ ɣ²⁴ tɤ³³ **ŋɛi³³**.
eraser call PROG ASRT
橡皮擦 叫
'(It) is called (an) eraser.'
是叫橡皮擦。
(YAY-Erasers)

(978) ta³⁵tɕa³⁵ a³³ jo³⁵ pv̩³²³ za³¹ a³³ jo³⁵ **ŋɛi³³**.
commander that CL:HUM POSS son that CL:HUM COP/ASRT
大将 那 个 儿子 那 个
'(He) was the commander's son.' / '(It) was the commander's son.'
是那个大将的那个儿子。
(KLT-History)

(979) m̩³²³ ja³⁵ i³³ tɕi³³ tɤ³³ **ŋ³³** po⁵³.
field fertilize go say PROG ASRT EPIS.EMP
田 施肥 去 说
'(He) was going to fertilize the field, (see?)'
说是去田里施肥。
(KL-Childhood)

The emphatic *ŋɛi³³* differs in several ways from the imperfective emphatic *ja³³*, which is also employed widely. When used as a general emphatic, it marks a strong assertion and is thus more forceful than *ja³³*. Depending on context, it may also have a contrastive meaning, emphasizing a phrase that confirms or rejects a supposition arising in discourse. As a result, it often co-occurs with the focus marker *la³⁵* and may itself change tone to convey focus (see § 3.2.5), though these elements need not be present to express contrast. Examples are shown in (980), (981) and (982). *ŋɛi³³* co-occurs with imperfective aspect markers, but replaces perfective and future markers; context often determines the aspect of a *ŋɛi³³* clause.

(980) tɕi³³ni³³ jɛ⁵³ ma³¹ tso³²³ **ŋɛi³³**.
this.way be.smooth NEG EXIST ASRT
这么 光滑 不 有
'(They) weren't as smooth as this.'
没有这么光滑的。
(WYF-Stools)

(981) tsɿ³¹tɕɛ²⁴ vɤ³²³ la²⁴ ŋ³³xa⁵³ n̠a³⁵   **ŋɛi³³**.
      self   buy   REL   time   be.many.FOC ASRT
      自己   买   时候   多
      '(There) were more times when (we) bought (them) ourselves.'
      是自己买的时候多。
      (YJF-Having Children)

(982) i²⁴la³¹ ni³⁵? tsa³³   tʰɛi³²³ la³⁵ **ŋɛi³³**, i²⁴la³¹.
      past   TOP.Q be.dirty very   FOC   ASRT   past
      以前   脏   很   以前
      'In the past? (It) was really dirty, in the past.'
      以前呢，很脏的啦，以前。
      (PYX-Dragon Pools)

The pragmatic agent marker *kɛi³³* often co-occurs with *ŋɛi³³* to contrastively highlight A or S in a clause. Semantically, this construction is similar to the cleft constructions in English and Putonghua, even though *ŋɛi³³* is not always required and, if present, always sits at the end of the clause rather than close to the focal argument. In discourse, this contrastive construction occurs mainly with transitive verbs, as (983) and (984) show, but it is also possible to apply it to intransitive and even stative verbs, as (985) and (986) illustrate.

(983) za³¹tsɿ³²³   sɛi⁴⁴   **kɛi³³** ɣ³²³   ka³²³ i³³   **ŋɛi³³**.
      brother's.son   family AGT   take   walk   go   ASRT
      侄子   家   拿   走   去
      '(It) was (my) nephew's family (who) took (it) away.'
      是侄儿家拿走了。
      (WYF-Stools)

(984) tsʰo³³ ŋ³¹ jo³⁵   **kɛi³³** ɣɤ³⁵   tɤ³³ **ŋɛi³³**.
      people two CL:HUM   AGT   move   PROG ASRT
      人   二   位   动
      '(It) is played (by) two people.'
      是两个人动的。
      (HPH-Toys)

(985) i³³   **kɛi³³** kɤ³¹ **ŋɛi³³**.
      3SG   AGT   run   ASRT
      他   跑
      'It's he who ran.'
      是他跑的。
      (KL-Elicitation)

(986) ȵɛ³²³   jo³⁵   **kɛi³³** tɕa³³   **ŋɛi³³**.
younger.brother CL:HUM AGT   be.skinny   ASRT
弟弟   位   瘦
'It's (the) younger brother (who) is skinny.'
弟弟是瘦的。
(KL-Elicitation)

12.6.6 Epistemic Emphatic Particle *po⁵³*

The emphatic particle *po⁵³* expresses a speaker's opinion about the interlocutor's knowledge. It marks clauses that contain information that either a listener probably does not know or information that the listener ought to know, either because it has been previously explained, is inferrable from discourse or is part of the community's culture or history. In both cases, it highlights explanatory information, but in the latter use it may also impart a chiding flavor. It may co-occur with the emphatic markers *ja³³*, *ja³²³* and *ŋɛi³³*, but unlike them *po⁵³* does not interfere with aspectual marking. Examples are presented in (987) and (988).

(987) tɛi³¹ tsʏ̩²⁴   to³³   la²⁴ka³³ tsʅ³²³ ma³¹ tso³²³ **po⁵³**,   a³³   tsɛi³⁵   ni³¹.
everything also   play   NMLZ   NEG   EXIST   EPIS.EMP   that CL:TMP TOP
什么   也   玩   不   有   那   段
'There was nothing to play with (as you can imagine), in those days.'
没有什么可玩的嘛，那个时候呢。
(YLW-Learning)

(988) tɛi³¹   xa³²³   tsʅ²⁴   ni³¹   tsʰi³³   ko²⁴   tso³²³   ŋ³³   **po⁵³**.
one   hundred CL:MSR   TOP   ten   liter EXIST   ASRT   EPIS.EMP
一   百   斤   十   升   有
'One hundred *jin*, (that) equals ten liters, (don't you know?)'
十升有一百斤呀。
(YJF-Weddings)

Given its explanatory function, *po⁵³* often co-occurs with the focus marker *la³⁵* (see § 13.1.3.3) and words that take on contrastive tone change (see § 3.2.5). A nearly identical marker, *na³¹*, is described in the following section.

12.6.7 Epistemic Emphatic Particle *na³¹*

Like *po⁵³*, *na³¹* marks clauses containining information that a listener ought to know. Thus, the two are very similar in function. However, *na³¹* phrases are considered more direct than phrases ending in *po⁵³* and thus slightly less polite, although context and voice quality can mitigate these nuances in discourse. And, unlike *po⁵³*, it rarely co-occurs with other emphatic markers. Examples are shown in (989) and (990).

(989) sa²⁴tʰa³¹ tɕi⁵⁵   tɕi³¹ jo³⁵   tɕi³¹   xuɛi³²³   vɤ³²³.
      candy   CL:TYPE one CL:HUM one   CL:TMP   buy
      糖   种   一   位   一   回   买
      'As for candy, one person (would) buy (it) one time.'
      糖呢一个买一次。

      tɕi³¹   tsʰɤ³³   tɕi³¹   xuɛi³²³   vɤ³²³   **na³¹**.
      one   CL:PL   one   CL:TMP   buy   EPIS.EMP
      一   们   一   回   买
      'Some people (would) buy (some) another time, (it was like that).'
      一些买一次呀。
      (YJF-Dance Parties)

(990) ɤ²⁴   tso³²³ tsʅ²⁴ ma³¹ ta³²³ ŋ³¹ fɤ³³ tsʅ²⁴ ma³¹ ta³²³,
      boat   EXIST afford NEG be.able cow raise afford NEG be.able
      船   有   起   不   能   牛   养   起   不   能
      '(If you are) unable to afford a boat, unable to afford a cow,'
      有不起船，养不起牛。

      ja⁵³   tɕo³⁵   kʰa³³   jo³³   **na³¹**.
      then   then   rent   must   EPIS.EMP
      那么   就   租   要
      'Then, (you) must rent, (see?).'
      那么就要租了。
      (YJF-Childhood)

12.6.8 Stative Emphatic Particle *tɤ⁴⁴*

The emphasis created by the particle *tɤ⁴⁴* serves to present an event as an ongoing state or habitual situation. As a result, it is incompatible with aspect marking, which provides temporal information about a particular activity. For example, in (991) the first speaker mentions that her friend's mobile phone fell on the floor — a particular event that has its own aspect marking. The owner of the phone repeats the phrase with *tɤ⁴⁴*, which recasts the mishap as a state without temporal boundaries, meaning 'the situation is that (it) fell (and) broke' or '(it is a) falling-(and)-breaking situation', and then suggests a solution. Similarly, in (992), where the speaker recalls life before indoor plumbing, the use of tɤ⁴⁴ frames the act of drawing water from a well as a habitual situation.

(991) A: tɕʰɛ³¹ kɤ⁵³   jɛ²⁴   ta³²³   wa³³.
         fall   break go   be.able   CRS
         摔   破   去   能
         '(It) fell (and) broke.'
         摔破得了。

B: tɕʰɛ³¹ kɤ⁵³   **tɤ⁴⁴**,
    fall   break STAT.EMP
    摔   破
    '(If) the situation is that (it) fell (and) broke,'
    摔破的呢，

nɛi³³   tɛi³¹ ma²⁴   vɤ³²³ tɤ⁴⁴   ŋa³³ kɯ³¹   li³³   pa³¹.
2SG   one   CL:GEN buy   CLNK   1SG   give   come   IMP
你   一   个   卖   我   给   来
'Buy (another) one for me.'
你买一个来给我吧。
(KL, ZRF-Grandfather)

(992) i³³   sɛi³³   ko³²³ wa³⁵   tɕi⁴⁴ ni³¹   tɕo³⁵   ŋ³³xa⁵³   mɛi⁴⁴   ti³⁵   ta⁵⁵
      3SG   family draw   FUT   say   TOP   then   time   CL:GEN fix   be.type
      他   家   抽   说   就   日子   个   订   样
      ni³¹   tɕo³⁵,
      TOP   then
             就
      'If (a) family (plans) to draw (water), then if (the) time is fixed, then,'
      说他家抽了就，订下日子呢就，

tɛi³³ni³³   ko³²³   **tɤ⁴⁴**.
this.way   draw   STAT.EMP
这么   抽
'(It is) drawn (out) this way.'
这么抽的。
(GCS-Childhood)

This particle seems to be borrowed from the nominalizer *de* 的 [tɤ] in the Chinese *shì...de* 是...的 construction, which likewise functions to convey a situation rather than a single event (Li and Thompson 1981: 587–593). But, there are several differences. The copula *shì* is optional in the Chinese formulation, but in Khatso the copula is never involved. Moreover, the Khatso construction is not a nominalization; it fails all of the tests for nounhood. Instead, tɤ⁴⁴ functions as a phrase-final emphatic particle.

The particle is identical to the clause linker tɤ⁴⁴, which also follows the verb in a clause, but there is a key syntactic difference. The clause linker is usually immediately followed by a second clause, as in the final clause of (991) above, which may describe the purpose, goal or effect brought about by the event described in the first clause (see § 14.6). The emphatic tɤ⁴⁴, on the other hand, marks its clause as a syntactically independent statement. Occasionally, clauses conjoined by the linker tɤ⁴⁴ are uttered in separate intonation units, making the first clause syntactically indistinguishable from the stative emphatic use. In these cases, pragmatics serves to clarify the situation.

12.6.9 Discourse Emphatic Particle mɛi⁴⁴

The emphatic particle *mɛi⁴⁴* has a discourse rather than clausal function. It marks phrases that a speaker feels are especially important to the topic at hand, explaining key facts and highlighting them as a specific state of affairs. As a result, its use is motivated purely by pragmatics and not by any syntactic condition, differentiating it from most of the other particles just described. In (993), for example, the speaker is describing the way farming was done in her childhood when manual labor was the norm, a theme that runs through a number of her comments. *mɛi⁴⁴* is also employed to highlight crucial or even climactic points in a particular exchange, such as emphasizing the result of an anecdote or an overarching conclusion. For example, in (994), the speakers are discussing the traditional clothing fasteners that are wrapped in colored thread. The first speaker complains that many are shoddily made these days. The second speaker, who is known for her own expert sewing skills, explains that this is a state of affairs that is hard to avoid.

(993) m̩³²³ tɤ²⁴ la²⁴ tʰa³³,
 field plant REL CL:TMP
 田 栽 段
 'Planting time,'
 栽田的时候，

 na²⁴wa³³ i³²³tɕa⁵³ tsʰɛi³³ la²⁴ ma³¹ tso²⁴ ta³¹ ni³²³,
 FILL water draw REL NEG EXIST after BKGD
 水 抽 不 有 后
 'Well, because there was no water drawing (machine),'
 那么，没有抽水的，

tsʰo³³   tsʰʏ³³   kɛi³³   ko³²³   tʏ³⁵   **mɛi⁴⁴**.
people   PL   AGT   draw   PROG.FOC   DSC.EMP
人   们   抽
'People were drawing (it themselves by hand).'
用人工抽的。
(GCS-Childhood)

(994) A: kʏ³³   kɯ³²³   ma³¹   na²⁴.
           make   CSC   NEG   be.good
           做   不   好
           '(They) are badly made.'
           做得不好。

   mau³³li⁴⁴mau³³tsau³⁵   ni³³   pʏ³¹sa³⁵   ko⁵⁵   la³³   ŋ³³   la³⁵   ŋɛi³³.
   careless   ADV   caterpillar CL:PL   CMP   COP   FOC   ASRT
   毛毛糙糙   毛毛虫   些   是
   'Carelessly (they) look like caterpillars.'
   毛毛糙糙地像一些毛毛虫。

B: tʏ⁴⁴   xa³³jo³⁵   kɛi³³   kʏ³³   la²⁴   tɕi⁵⁵   tɕo³⁵   tɛi³³   ta⁵⁵   la³⁵
     FILL   who   AGT   make   REL   CL:TYPE then   this   be.type FOC
             谁   做   种   就   这   样
     ŋ³³   **mɛi⁴⁴**.
     ASRT   DSC.EMP
     'Well, no matter who makes them, (they) will be like that.'
     那谁做的都是这样的。
     (KL, WYY-Sewing)

Clauses highlighted by *mɛi⁴⁴* do not necessarily contain new information. Often, they repeat a point that the speaker wants to make sure is understood, as in (995). Likewise, responses to questions may also be emphasized with *mɛi⁴⁴*, as in (996).

(995) A: na⁵³tɕʰɛ⁵⁵   ni³¹   tɕo³⁵   a³³tɕʰa⁵⁵kʰʏ³³   so²⁴   sʅ⁵⁵   wa³²³.
           dance   TOP   then   that.time   learn   know   PFV
           黑跳   就   那时候   学   知
           'As for dancing, (you) learned (to do it) then.'
           跳乐呢，那个时候就学会了。

B: ŋ⁵³.   a³³   tsɛi³⁵ kɛi³³ tɕo³⁵   so²⁴   sʅ⁵⁵   wa³²³   **mɛi⁴⁴**.
    INTJ that   CL:TMP from   then   learn   know   PFV   DSC.EMP
          那   段   从   就   学   知道
    'Yeah, (I) learned (it) then.'
    是的，那个时候就学会了。
(KL, YLW-Learning)

(996) A: ja⁵³   tɕo³⁵   pɛi³²³ko⁵³ kɛi³³ tsʰʅ³¹ma³³ m̩³³   tʏ⁴⁴   n̩a⁵³   li³²³   wa³³.
         later then   pɛi³²³ko⁵³ from   wife   make CLNK   here   come   CRS
         然后   就   白阁   妻子   做   这里   来
         'Then I married (and) came here from pɛi³²³ko⁵³.'
         然后就从白阁结婚到这里了。

    B: tɕi³³n̩a⁵³   xa³³n̩a⁵³   ŋa³¹?
        here   where   CNT.Q
        这里   哪里
        'Where is here?'
        这里是哪里？

    A: tɕi³³n̩a⁵³   tʏ⁵³   sʅ³⁵   tʰɛi³⁵   wa³²³   **mɛi⁴⁴**,   tɕi³³n̩a⁵³.
        here   STAT.EMP   four   CL:ITEM   PFV   DSC.EMP   here
        这里   四   组   这里
        'The fourth district, here.'
        这里是四组了呀，这里。
(GCS, KL-Childhood)

This particle is identical to the general classifier *mɛi⁴⁴*, which never takes a numeral and indicates that the modified noun has a specific referent in the world (see § 6.2.1). This suggests that clauses ending with *mɛi⁴⁴* may be some kind of nominalized construction. Non-embedded clausal nominalizations are found in many Tibeto-Burman languages (Matisoff 1972: 250), and are often used to highlight individual facts or provide exclamatory force, a function similar to that of the emphatic *mɛi⁴⁴*. However, in the other languages the clausal nominalizer is identical to the possessive and relative clause markers, making explicit the link between them. But in Khatso, each of these functions has a separate particle. Moreover, clauses ending with *mɛi⁴⁴* are always independent; they can never be embedded in other clauses or modified as functional nouns. As a result, there is no way to test their status and the question must remain unresolved.

Dai (2008: 81) notes that many words that carry lexical tone 44 are loanwords (see § 3.1.2). This is true of very recent borrowings as well as a few grammatical particles, such as *tʏ⁴⁴* and *sɛi⁴⁴* (see § 16.5 and § 16.6 respectively). However, there is no obvious Chinese counterpart for *mɛi⁴⁴*, and so its origin remains unclear.

13 Basic Clause-Linking

The previous chapters explore the various elements that may occur in a single clause. This chapter discusses the various ways that two or more clauses may be combined in Khatso. Traditionally, linguists consider multi-clause constructions to contain coordinate clauses or matrix and dependent clauses, and the latter are often grouped into relative, adverbial and complement categories (e.g. Cristofaro 2003; Dixon 2010; Payne 1997; Shopen 2007). However, because of the pragmatics-based nature of Khatso, this approach would leave out many frequently-used constructions. Clauses are combined largely through the use of grammatical particles, a few conjunctions and some adverbs, which typically occur at the end of the first clause, though a few occur in the second. And although the particles signal a syntactic link between clauses, their exact meaning usually depends on verbal semantics and discourse context. In fact, few of these constructions are obligatory; juxtaposition alone is often enough to establish a particular link. For this reason, this chapter and the next include common pragmatic linking strategies along with the syntactic ones.

The analysis of the Khatso constructions also presents several challenges. In discourse, dependent clauses and matrix clauses are usually structured identically. Since verbal inflection does not exist in Khatso, there is no morphosyntactic difference between verbs in different types of clauses. And because aspect marking is not obligatory, the two verbs may be equally bare, doing away with another possible clue. In addition, because arguments are routinely absent due to zero anaphora, even the identification of argument sharing is problematic. Zero anaphora, in fact, extends to entire clauses, so even complement-taking verbs may occur without arguments in discourse. As a result, often the only overt marker of clause combining is the linking particle itself, and it may mark a clause as pragmatically as well as syntactically incomplete.

These issues make it difficult to divide clause-combining strategies neatly into discrete syntactic categories. It is more helpful, in fact, to compare and contrast them according to their degree of syntactic integration (e.g. Lehmann 1988; Ohori 1992). In Khatso, the features most relevant to integration are aspect marking, argument sharing and center embedding — none are obligatory, but their presence helps differentiate different types of structures. Generally, the loosest integration is marked by the free marking of aspect in both clauses, the lack of argument sharing, and the inability to embed one clause within another. The tightest integration, at the other extreme, is indicated by aspect marking occurring in the matrix clause and having scope over both clauses, the possibility of not only argument sharing but also subject raising, and the potential for the dependent clause to be center-embedded in the matrix clause itself. Mapping the most common clause-combining constructions along a continuum, as in Figure 13.1, shows that juxtaposition and parallel clause linking have no integration at all, while complementation strategies rank highly. The territory in between contains a great deal of overlap, since various functions of a particle may place it in different positions on the continuum. For ease of description, the terms dependent and matrix are retained in this discussion where helpful, but they should be understood as prototypes rather than distinct categories.

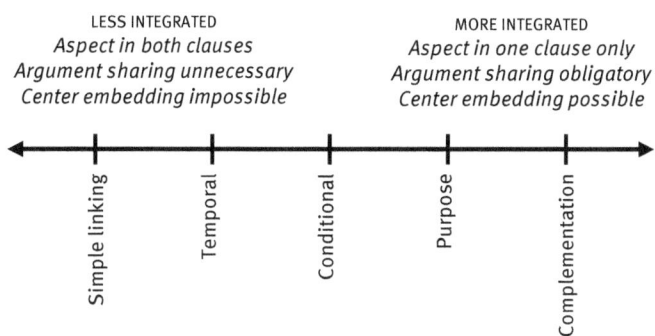

Fig. 13.1: Degree of integration across clause-combining strategies

There is general similarity in the placement of clause-linking morphemes with regard to combined clauses. In most constructions, the dependent clause occurs before the matrix clause. As a result, most of the linking particles occur at the end of the first clause, indicating that more information is to come. These include the clausal conjunction to^{33}, the conditional ni^{31} and the backgrounding ni^{323}. The clause linker $t\gamma^{44}$ likewise occurs at the end of the first clause, but it is the matrix clause, not a dependent clause. By contrast, there are two particles that always occur at the end of the second clause; they are the focus marker la^{35} and the hearsay marker $ts\varepsilon i^{31}$. The topic and temporal marker $s\varepsilon i^{44}$ typically occurs at the end of the dependent clause, but when involved in complementation it may occur at the end of either clause, an unusual development explored further in Chapter 15. Conjunctions, which link clauses in parallel structures, usually occur at the beginning of the second clause, though some speakers may prefer to end the first clause with them, again signaling that there is another clause to follow. Borrowed conjunctions, on the other hand, tend to begin dependent clauses, in accordance with Chinese syntax. Separate from the above are the adverbs that pragmatically link clauses but do not integrate them. They occur in their original pre-verbal positions, since there is no need to form a syntactic link to another clause.

There are a number of other multi-verb constructions in Khatso that cannot be analyzed as combined clauses. Auxiliary verbs, for example, modify matrix verbs (see § 8.7). But they form a small class of verbs that cannot themselves serve as stand-alone verbs, and thus they function more like grammatical particles then fully-fledged verbs. There are some verbs that can serve as both auxiliaries and matrix verbs; they are discussed in § 15.2. Serial verb constructions may combine two or three verbs in a single clause. In many of these, such as directional or resultative serializations, the verbs work together to describe a single coherent event and thus do not link clauses describing separate events. Two-event serializations blur the line, however, and they are discussed in § 14.6. The causative constructions pattern more like the applicative or serial verb constructions than clause combining, which are discussed in § 11.1 and § 8.8 respectively. Relative clauses, by contrast, are clearly dependent clauses, but their heads are noun phrases rather than other clauses, and so they are described in the chapter on noun modifiers (see § 7.5).

Some clause-combining particles have only a single well-defined purpose, but many have multiple functions. Moreover, each function may be carried out by a variety of particles and constructions. Thus, at first glance there seems to be a large number of overlapping methods for combining clauses. In actual practice, however, few are completely synonymous — their use is largely determined by verbal semantics and discourse context. Nonetheless, this complexity makes it difficult to present a holistic view of clause combining in the language. This chapter, along with Chapters 14 and 15, is organized by function, since that is likely to be more helpful to most readers. The subsections essentially move from the least to the most integrated, with the various strategies therein roughly ordered in terms of frequency of use and specificity of function. Moreover, the focus is limited mainly to combining two clauses, since that is the typical use of these constructions. The syntactic linking of three or more clauses occurs rarely in discourse.

The most basic forms of clause combining are explored in this chapter. Simple clause linking is described in § 13.1, which includes parallel linking, disjunction and adversative linking. And temporal linking strategies are discussed in § 13.2, from the general temporal marker $sɛi^{44}$ to the use of adverbs, followed by the various ways of conveying simultaneous and sequential relationships. More specialized strategies — such as reason, cause and effect, concession, condition, manner and purpose constructions — are detailed in Chapter 14. Complementation strategies are described in Chapter 15. Chapter 16 provides an overview of clause-linking in terms of form rather than function, focusing especially on multi-functional particles. Table 16.1, which lists all of the clause-linking particles and their functions, is found there as well.

13.1 Simple Clause-Linking

In simple clause linking, two or more clauses are linked but retain equal syntactic status. That is, neither is subordinate to the other. In fact, in some cases, there is no syntactic integration at all. There are three main types of linking clauses in this way. The first is parallel linking, described in § 13.1.1, in which the sense is additive, much like using 'and' in English. The second type is disjunctive, discussed in § 13.1.2, in which the clauses are presented as mutually exclusive choices. The third type, explained in § 13.1.3, conveys an adversative relationship, in which one clause provides information that limits or contrasts with the other.

13.1.1 Parallel Clause-Linking

Parallel clause linking is similar to coordination in that two clauses are considered linked, but there is no syntactic integration. There are two strategies for linking clauses in this way, and they mirror those for coordinating noun phrases, though the markers employed differ (see § 3.5.7). By far the most common strategy is juxtaposition, which is described in § 13.1.1.1. The adverb *to^{33}* 'also' links clauses as well, and this construction is discussed in § 13.1.1.2.

13.1.1.1 Parallel Clause-Linking through Juxtaposition

In Khatso, the semantics and pragmatics of an utterance are enough to establish a parallel link between clauses. For example, in (997) the speaker presents a list of her retired father's daily activities. The activities are linked pragmatically, but no conjunction is required. And in (998) two options are presented, but again an overt marker is unnecessary.

(997) [tɕo^{35} tsa^{323} tʰɣ^{55} m̩^{33} tsa^{31}].
   then   rice   CL:TMP   make   eat
   就   饭   下   做   吃
   '(He) makes food to eat.'
   就做一下饭吃。

   [za^{31}ni^{24}za^{24} tsʰɣ^{33} kai^{33} kua^{55} tʰɣ^{55} kua^{55}]   [wɛi^{35}sɛi^{44} tʰɣ^{55}
   child   PL   must   manage   CL:TMP   manage   hygiene   CL:TMP
   孩子   们   该   管   下   管   卫生   下
   ta^{53}sau^{31}].
   clean
   打扫
   '(And he) watches the children (he) must watch (and) cleans up.'
   小孩子该管的管一下打扫打扫卫生。
   (YAY-Erasers)

(998)   [kɯ³³   i³³   la²⁴   ŋ³³xa⁵³ tso³²³]   [ma³¹   kɯ³³   i³³   la²⁴   ŋ³³xa⁵³ tso³²³].
        enter go   REL   time   EXIST   NEG   enter   go   REL   time   EXIST
        回   去   时候   有   不   回   去   时候   有
        'There were times (we) went home (and) times (we) didn't go home.'
        有时候回去，有时候不回去。
        (YJF-Dance Parties)

Certain types of words may highlight the relationship between clauses without linking them syntactically. For example, in (999) the temporal noun *tɛi³³tɕʰa⁵⁵kʰv̩³³* 'now' contrasts the situation in the first phrase with an earlier time, in which toothgrass overran the fields. In the following phrase, the adverb *tsi³³pɛi³¹sa³⁵* 'basically' provides an explanation for the change. The most common adverb of this type is *to³³* 'also', which links a clause pragmatically to a similar situation already mentioned. For example, in (1000) the traditional marriage age of men mentioned in the second clause is compared to that of women in the first clause. Likewise, in (1001) the speaker compares the skills of comprehension and speaking in separate clauses; *to³³* is the only overt link between the two. Note that *to³³* often triggers tone change in the preceding syllable (see § 3.2.4.1).

(999)   [ja⁵³   **tɛi³³tɕʰa⁵⁵kʰv̩³³**   tɕa⁵³   ma³¹   tso³²³].
        later   this.time   toothgrass   NEG   EXIST
        然后   这时候   牙齿草   不   有
        'Now there is no toothgrass.'
        那么，现在没有牙齿草。

        [**tsi³³pɛi³¹sa³⁵**   s̩⁴⁴   tɕa⁵³   ko⁵⁵   kv̩³³   tsuɛi²⁴].
        basically   COP   toothgrass   CL:PL do   sever
        基本上   是   牙齿草   些   弄   绝
        'Basically (they) cut down the toothgrass.'
        牙齿草基本上些弄绝了。
        (HPH-Weeds)

(1000)[a³³tɕʰa⁵⁵kʰv̩³³   tsʰn̩³¹ma³³   m̩³³   kɯ³²³   ɲɛ²⁴   ta³¹].
        that.time   daughter-in-law   make   CSC   be.small   later
        那时候   太太   做   小   后
        '(At) that time, women became wives (when) young.'
        那时候出嫁的年龄小。

[i²⁴tsɤ²⁴za³¹	tsʰɤ⁴⁴	**to³³**	tsʰɿ³¹ma³³		tsʰɿ³³	kɯ³²³	n̠ɛ²⁴].
young.man	PL	also	daughter-in-law		take	CSC	be.small
男孩子	们	也	太太		娶		小

'Young men also took wives (when) young.'
男孩子结婚年龄也小。
(YJF-Childhood)

(1001) [kʰai³³sɿ³⁵ ʐɿ³²³n̠ɛ³²³tsɿ³¹ so²⁴ la²⁴ tsɛi³⁵, [pʰi²⁴ŋ²⁴tɕʰi³¹ n̠a³¹ ma³¹
begin   first.grade   study REL CL:TMP   Hanyu   speak NEG
开始   一年级   读   段   汉语   说   不
li³²³].
know.how
会

'When (I) started first grade, (I) couldn't speak Hanyu.'
开始读一年级的时候，不会说汉语。

sɤ⁵⁵   so²⁴ sɛi⁴⁴, [pʰi²⁴ŋ²⁴tɕʰi³¹ tɕi⁵⁵   **to³³** lo³¹sɿ²⁴ na²⁴ ma³¹
book study TMP   Hanyu   CL:TYPE also   much   hear NEG
书   读   时   汉语   种   也   很多   听   不
li³²³].
know.how
会

'When (I was) studying, I also couldn't understand much Hanyu.'
上学的时候，也听不懂很多汉语。
(YAY-Erasers)

Juxtaposition involves no syntactic integration; each clause is syntactically separate from the others. Aspect marking is unrestricted and center embedding is impossible. The same arguments may occur in more than one clause, but this is not obligatory. Rather, the link is a natural result of the overarching discourse theme. Narratives, for example, typically contain a series of events performed by a single protagonist. Prosody likewise provides no cues to integration. Juxtaposed clauses may be uttered in a single intonation unit, especially if they are short, but again this is not obligatory. They are just as likely to be uttered separately.

13.1.1.2 Parallel Clause-Linking with *to³³*

Given its role in linking juxtaposed clauses pragmatically, as described in the previous section, it is not surprising to find that *to³³* has evolved into a syntactic marker of clause linking. In this function, it occurs at the end of one clause to link it to the next one, rather than the preverbal position of the typical adverbial use. Semantically, it is much closer to 'and' here rather than the adverbial 'also'. Examples are shown in

(1002) and (1003). Note that wherever it is used, *to³³* may trigger tone change in the preceding syllable (see § 3.2.4.1).

(1002) [i³²³tɕa⁵³   ma³¹   tso²⁴]   **to³³**,
water   NEG   EXIST   and
水   不   有   也

[ta²⁴to³³   tsʰo³³   tso³²³   ŋa³²³   ma³¹   ta³²³].
still   people   EXIST   be.able   NEG   be.able
还   人   有   能   不   能

'There was no water, and people weren't able to live (there).'
没有水，也就不能居住人。
(PYX-Dragon Pools)

(1003) [ŋa³³tsʰɤ³¹   ka³²³   tɤ⁴⁴   xa³³ɳa⁵³   tsɿ⁴⁴]   **to³³**,
1PL   walk   CLNK   where   arrive   and
我们   走   哪里   到   也

[tɕʰi⁵³   ti⁴⁴   ti³³ni³³   mi³²³   tso³²³   la²⁴   tɕi⁵⁵,
play   CLNK   this.way   be.accurate   EXIST   REL   CL:TYPE
咬   这么   明确   有   种

na²⁴   ma³¹   mɤ³³   wa³³   piɛ⁴⁴liɛ³³].
hear   NEG   achieve   CRS   EMP
听   不   着

'We go all over, and this type of expert playing (we) never hear.'
我们走到哪里也听不到弹得这么准确的啦。
(YAY-Erasers)

Since speakers are able to infer a pragmatic link between clauses based on context, linking with *to³³* is never obligatory. Often, its use seems to be a strategy for signaling that a speaking turn is not complete. The tone change pattern it triggers is identical to that caused by the topic marker *ni³¹* and the backgrounding clause marker *ni³²³*, which link clauses in more specific ways. This tone change creates a pattern in which these three markers are preceded by a tone contour higher than the ones they themselves carry, which serves to highlight non-final phrases phonologically in discourse (see § 3.2.4.1).

Although *to³³* overtly links the two clauses, they remain syntactically unintegrated. Each clause retains its independent status, and arguments and aspect marking may be completely different. Moreover, structural elements in the second clause — such as aspect, imperative or interrogative markers — never have scope over the first. Likewise, center embedding, in which the dependent clause occurs between

A/S and verb of the matrix clause, is not possible. Often the clauses occur in separate intonation units, though this is not obligatory.

13.1.2 Disjunctive Clause-Linking

In some cases, linked clauses have a disjunctive relationship — that is, they present a choice between alternatives. In Khatso, these types of clauses are combined primarily with *ŋ³³si⁴⁴* 'or'. Depending on context, this construction may be declarative, as in (1004), or interrogative, as in (1005).

(1004) [i³²³   mɤ²⁴]   **ŋ³³si⁴⁴**   [i³²³   ma³¹   mɤ²⁴]   ni³¹
      go   have.time   or   go   NEG   have.time   TOP
      去   有空   或是   去   不   有空
      'if (we) have time to go or don't have time to go'
      有没有空去呢
      (YJF-Dance Parties)

(1005) [nɛi³³   sɛi⁴⁴   mo³³   tsʰɤ³³   kɛi³³   kɤ³³   tɤ³³]   **ŋ³³si⁴⁴**
      2SG   family mother   PL   AGT   make   PROG   or
      你   家   妈妈   们   做   还是

      [i³³   sɛi³³   kɛi³³   ɣ³²³   tɕa³³   li³³   tɤ³³   ŋa³¹]?
      3SG   family AGT   bring   cross   come   PROG   CNT.Q
      他   家   拿   过   来
      'Did your mother make (them) or did his family bring (them) over?'
      是你妈妈家做的，还是从她家拿来的？
      (KL-Weddings)

    The disjunctive conjunction *ŋ³³si⁴⁴* is typically interpreted as exhaustive, meaning that the options mentioned are the only ones in contention. To refer to multiple choices, one may either add additional clauses, as in (1006), or use a question word as one of the two choices, as in (1007).

(1006) [pʰai³²³   tsɿ³¹]   **ŋ³³si⁴⁴**   [tiɛ³⁵sɿ³⁵   ŋ²⁴ka³³]   **ŋ³³si⁴⁴**   [kʰɛi⁴⁴tʰi⁴⁴vi⁴⁴   tsʰa³⁵   i³³].
      card   play   or   movie   see   or   karaoke   sing   go
      牌   打   或   电视   看   或   KTV   唱   去
      '(We can) play cards or see a movie or sing karaoke.'
      打牌或是看电视或是去唱 KTV。
      (KL-Elicitation)

(1007) [tsʰi³²³ tɕi³³ pa⁵³ tɕi³³ tʏ³³] **ŋ³³si⁴⁴** [xa³³ni³³ tɕi³³ tʏ³³ ŋa³¹ lɛi³¹]?
qin   this CL:HNDL say   PROG   or   how   say PROG CNT.Q IRR.EMP
琴   这   把   说   　 或是   怎么   说
'(Is) this called a *qin* or what is (it) called?'
这把琴是叫琴呢或是怎么说的？
(KL-Qin)

As described in § 7.7.3, *ŋ³³si⁴⁴* may also be used to coordinate noun phrases. In many cases, a choice between nouns is presented through clauses with identical verbs. Thus, in (1008) the serial verb construction *ko⁵³no⁵³* 'to pass (of time)' is found in both clauses, and the choice actually centers on the length of time expressed by the noun phrase. The verbs could be omitted here without an appreciable change in meaning.

(1008) [pa⁵³   kʰo⁵³   ko⁵³   no⁵³]   **ŋ³³si⁴⁴**,
       half   CL:TMP pass   complete   or
       半   年   过   掉   或是
       'Half a year passed or,'
       过了半年，

       [tɛi³¹   kʰo⁵³   ko⁵³   no⁵³]   to³³   ma³¹   sl̩⁵⁵.
       one   CL:TMP pass   complete also NEG   know
       一   年   过   掉   也   不   知道
       'A year passed, (I) don't know.'
       还是过了一年也不知道。
       (YAY-Erasers)

There is another disjunctive conjunction, *mɛi⁴⁴sl̩⁴⁴*, which is only used when the choices presented are meant as a question. It is relatively rare in the corpus compared to *ŋ³³si⁴⁴*; an example is shown in (1009). Note that although each clause has its own interrogative marker in this example, this structure is not obligatory. A single marker after the second clause can have scope over the entire construction.

(1009) tʏ⁴⁴   [tɕʰɛ⁵⁵   li³²³   sa²⁴kɛi³³   pʏ⁵³   li³²³   sa³⁵   pɛi³³]?
       FILL   kick   know.how   until   play   know.how   perhaps.FOC   CFRM.Q
              跳   会   才   弹   会   可能
       'So, (you) probably knew how to dance before knowing how to play?'
       那会跳才会弹的吧？

mɛi⁴⁴sɿ⁴⁴ [pɤ⁵³   li³²³   sa²⁴kɛi³³   tɕʰɛ⁵⁵   liɛ³²³]?
or   play   know.how   until   kick   know.how
还是   弹   会   才   跳   会
'Or, (did you) know how to play before knowing how to dance?'
还是会弹了才会跳？
(KL-Learning)

Also possible but rare are two complex constructions that correspond to the English choice construction 'either... or'. In the first, a topic phrase containing the verb *mo⁵⁵* 'to want' prefaces each clause, as in (1010). In the second, the negated copula is topicalized in each clause, as in (1011), but note that the negation has no scope over the options presented. If A or S is present in the second clause, then the agent marker is usually included to contrast the arguments (see § 10.4).

(1010) **mo⁵⁵**   **ni³¹**   [ŋa³³   kɛi³³   i³²³],   **mo⁵⁵**   **ni³¹**   [nɛi³³   kɛi³³   i³²³].
       want   TOP   1SG   AGT   go   want   TOP   2SG   AGT   go
       要   我   去   要   你   去
       'Either you go or I go.'
       要么我去要么你去。
       (KL-Elicitation)

(1011) **ma³¹**   **ŋ⁴⁴**   **ni³¹**   [tɕo³⁵   tsʰɛi³³   vɤ³¹   kɯ³¹],
       NEG   COP   TOP   then   grain   sift   INDR.CAUS
       不   是   就   稻谷   筛

       ma³¹   **ŋ⁴⁴**   **ni³¹**   [tɕo³⁵   no⁵³   vɤ³¹   kɯ³¹].
       NEG   COP   TOP   then   broad.bean   sift   INDR.CAUS
       不   是   就   豆   筛
       'Either (they) make (you) sift grain or (they) make (you) sift broad beans.'
       不是让筛稻谷就是让筛蚕豆。
       (YJF-Childhood)

Unlike clauses linked by *to³³* 'also, and', those linked by *ŋ³³si⁴⁴* and *mɛi⁴⁴sɿ⁴⁴* are integrated to a certain degree. Arguments need not be shared and center embedding is not possible, but phrase-final interrogative markers do have scope over both clauses, as demonstrated by (1007) above. The two 'either... or' constructions just described, however, cannot be said to be integrated. The initial clauses marked by *ni³¹* are fixed phrases, allowing no other material. So even though they may not take separate aspect marking, their frozen syntax suggests they are more akin to particles than fully-fledged clauses. The two matrix clauses are likewise not integrated; the link between them is pragmatic rather than syntactic.

13.1.3 Adversative Clause-Linking

Some linked clauses have an adversative relationship. In this construction, the second clause provides information that may limit or contrast with that of the first clause. There are four strategies for creating such a construction in Khatso. The first and most frequent in discourse involves the conjunctions $\eta^{44}li^{33}$ and $\eta^{33}na^{44}li^{33}$ 'but' (see § 13.1.3.1), but the adverb to^{33} 'also' is also employed often for this purpose (see § 13.1.3.2). Using the focus particle la^{35}, and its related tone change pattern, differs from $\eta^{44}li^{33}$ or to^{33} by making the contrastive information much more prominent pragmatically (see § 13.1.3.3). In addition, a conjunction borrowed from Hanyu is often used by speakers who are accustomed to speaking Chinese (see § 13.1.3.4).

13.1.3.1 Adversative Clause-Linking with $\eta^{44}li^{33}$ and $\eta^{33}na^{44}li^{33}$ 'but'

There are two adversative clause linkers in Khatso. The first is $\eta^{44}li^{33}$, sometimes pronounced $\eta\varepsilon i^{44}li^{33}$, and $\eta^{33}na^{44}li^{33}$; both translate into English as 'but'. The former is the more general of the two; it may introduce any kind of adversative information. For example, in (1012) the second clause presents a situation contrary to the expectation established in the first clause. And in (1013), the second clause provides an exception to the first. $\eta^{44}li^{33}$ may occur at either the beginning or the end of clauses, as the examples illustrate, which seems mainly to be a function of speaker preference. It is also employed to coordinate nouns and noun phrases (see § 7.7.3).

(1012) [ŋ³¹   jo³⁵   tɤ⁴⁴   tɛi³¹   tʰa³³   tsɤ⁵³   tso²⁴   wa³²³]   **ŋɛi⁴⁴li³³**,
two   CL:HUM all   one   CL:TMP weave ITER   PFV   but
两   个   都   一   段   打   但是
'Two (people) wove (them) for a while, but,'
两个打了一段时间了，但是，

[tɛi³³   tsɛi³⁵   pai³⁵   ma³¹   tso²⁴   ni³²³   ta³⁵   ma³¹   tsɤ⁵³   tso²⁴   tɤ³³
this   CL:TMP straw   NEG   EXIST   BKGD again   NEG   weave ITER   PROG
这   段   草   不   有   又   不   打
wa³³   sɛi³¹].
CRS   still
          还
'Now because there is no straw (they) aren't weaving any more.'
现在没有草，不打了。
(WYF-Stools)

(1013) [tsʰo³³ xa³³ni³³ li⁴⁴ tso³²³ tsɤ³¹ tsɤ³⁵ ta³²³ ja³³],
people how in EXIST CONT hold be.able IPFV.EMP
人 什么 里 有 住 可以
'Many people were able to live here,'
在这里可以居住很多的人，

ŋ⁴⁴li³³ [kʰo³¹zŋ³⁵].
but be.pitiful
但是 可惜
'But it was (a) pitiful (place).'
但是可惜。
(PYX-Dragon Pools)

The second linker, *ŋ³³n̩a⁴⁴li³³*, is far less frequent in discourse, and seems to have a more limited function. It confirms the information in the first clause and introduces a restriction, as the example in (1014) illustrates. This linker appears only phrase-finally in the few examples attested in discourse.

(1014) [tʰo³³pɛi³³ tɛi³³ tɕi⁵⁵ nɛi³³ kɛi³³ sa³³ la²⁴ tʰo³³pɛi³³ tɕi⁵⁵]
upper.garment this CL:TYPE 2SG AGT sew REL upper.garment CL:TYPE
褂子 这 种 你 缝 褂子 种
ŋ³³n̩a⁴⁴li³³,
but
但是
'This garment is (indeed) a garment sewn by you but,'
是的，这个褂子是你缝的褂子但是，

[xa³³ni³³ ŋ³³xa⁵³ li⁴⁴ lo⁵³ sa²⁴ wa³³].
how.much time in reach perhaps CRS
多少 时间 里 到 可能
'Maybe (it) was a long time ago.'
可能有好长时间了。
(WYY-Sewing)

Like the disjunctive *ŋ³³si⁴⁴* and *mɛi⁴⁴sŋ⁴⁴*, the adversative clause linkers do integrate clauses syntactically to a small degree. An imperative marker at the end of the second clause has scope over both clauses, though this is not true of similarly-placed aspect or interrogative markers. Arguments are often shared between the clauses, but this is not obligatory; center embedding, in which the dependent clause occurs between the A/S and verb of the matrix clause, however, is impossible.

Compositionally, these conjunctions appear to be derived from the copula *ŋ³³* and the verb *li³²³/li³³* 'to come' — the longer form apparently also includes the copular emphatic na^{33}. The tone change in the syllable preceding li^{33} suggests that the adverb to^{33} was once part of the construction (see § 3.2.4.1), an omission that is now obligatory in the modern formulation. to^{33} itself may be used in an adversative fashion, as described in the following section.

13.1.3.2 Adversative Clause-Linking with to^{33} 'also'

Although the adverb to^{33} 'also' is mainly considered a simple clause linker corresponding to 'and' (see § 13.1.1.2), context may color its meaning. If the second clause presents a situation contrary to the first, then to^{33} is interpreted as an adversative conjunction meaning 'but'. Examples of the latter function are presented in (1015) and (1016). Again, to^{33} may trigger tone change in the preceding syllable (see § 3.2.4.1).

(1015) ai²⁴ [tsʰo³¹ li²⁴ ja⁴⁴] **to³³** [m̩³³to³¹ kɤ³²³ kɤ²⁴ wa³³ mɛi⁴⁴].
INTJ sing know.how IPFV.EMP also forget finish finish CRS DSC.EMP
哎 会 　　　　　　　　　也 忘记 完 完
'Oh, (I used to) know how to sing, but (I) completely forgot how.'
哎，会唱的，但也全部都忘记了。
(YJF-Dance Parties)

(1016) [pɤ³¹ wa²⁴] **to³³** [xɛi³⁵ tsa³²³ ma³¹ tsa⁵⁵].
dance PFV also still rice NEG feed
娱乐 　　 也 还 饭 不 喂
'(We) danced, but still (they) didn't feed (us).'
跳了也还不给饭吃。
(GCS-Dance Parties)

Like its simple counterpart described in § 13.1.1.2, the adversative function does not create syntactic integration. The two clauses remain independent, and each may carry its own aspect marking, as (1015) above illustrates.

13.1.3.3 Contrastive Focus with la^{35} and Related Tone Change

Contrasting one clause with another is often accomplished through the use of the focus particle la^{35}. In its basic function, la^{35} serves primarily to link a contrastive clause pragmatically to an earlier comment in discourse, though the relationship may also be interpreted as emphatic agreement or cause and effect. The particle sits in the clause providing contrastive information, placed between the verb and one of a few phrase-final morphemes. It frequently co-occurs with the strong assertion particle $\eta\varepsilon i^{33}$; other possible choices include the currently relevant state marker wu^{77}, the epistemic emphatic po^{53}, the discourse emphatic $m\varepsilon i^{44}$ and the affirmative interrogative particle sa^{44}. The contrastive phrase may point to one's own comment, as in (1017) and (1018), or to something said by another, as in (1019). Because the meaning depends heavily on context, and its corresponding function in English is mainly conveyed through prosody, there is no simple translation for *la³⁵*. In its contrastive use, it may be interpreted as 'thus', 'just', 'only', 'like that' or 'instead'. Note that in some cases a tone change may replace *la³⁵* altogether, though this does not change its underlying discourse functions (see § 3.2.5).

(1017) [i³²³tso³³ a³³ ma⁴⁴ ɕo³³ tʰɛi³²³ ja³³ tɛi³³ tsɛi³⁵].
well that CL:GEN be.clean very IPFV.EMP this CL:TMP
井 那 个 干净 很 这 段
'That well is very clean, now.'
现在那口井很干净。

i²⁴la³¹ ni³⁵? [tsa³³ tʰɛi³²³ **la³⁵** ŋɛi³³, i²⁴la³¹].
past TOP.Q be.dirty very FOC ASRT past
以前 脏 很 以前
'And (in) the past? (It) was really dirty, (in) the past.'
以前呢，很脏的啦。
(PYX-Dragon Pools)

(1018) [pʰi³²³sʴ³²³ sʴ⁴⁴ tsʰʴ³³ni³⁵ ma³¹ ɕi³³ tɛi⁵³,
usually COP shoe NEG be.accustomed wear
平常 是 鞋子 不 习惯 穿
'(We) usually didn't wear shoes,'
平常是不穿鞋子的，

a³³tɕʰa⁵⁵kʰv̩³³].
that.time
那时候
'(In) those days.'
那时候。

[kɛi³¹fa³⁵ no⁵³ sa²⁴kɛi³³ tɛi³³ni³³ ɕi³³ tɛi⁵³ **la³⁵** ŋɛi³³].
liberate complete until this.way be.accustomed wear FOC ASRT
解放 完 才 这么 习惯 穿
'(It wasn't) until after Liberation (that we were) used to wearing (them) like this.'
解放以后才这么穿的。
(YJF-Weddings)

(1019) A: [zɛi³⁵   mɤ³³   la²⁴   kɛi³³   ma³¹   zɛi³¹   mɤ³³   la²⁴   kɛi³³
recognize achieve REL   CONJ   NEG   recognize achieve REL   CONJ
认   到   和   不   认   到   和
ta⁵⁵   ŋɛi³³].
be.type   ASRT
样
'There were some who swore (an oath) some who didn't.'
有的结拜到，有的没有结拜到，这样的。

B: ei³²³ja³¹,   [i³²³   sɛi⁴⁴   sl̩³²³   to³³   kɤ⁵⁵   i³²³   ja³²³].
INTJ   go   TMP   ten   more   CL:PL   go   PFV.EMP
去   十   多   个   去
'Oh, when (they) went, more than ten went.'
唉呀，去的时候去了十多个。

[tɕo³⁵   a³³   ŋ³¹   jo³⁵   kɛi³³   m̩³³   **la³⁵**   ŋɛi³³].
then   that   two   CL:HUM   AGT   do   FOC   ASRT
就   那   两   个   做
'But only two (actually) did (swear an oath).'
就只有那两个做了。

(YBF, KYF-Three Ladies)

Syntactically, there is no integration between the *la³⁵* clause and its pragmatic antecedent. Each is independent and may have its own arguments. Center embedding within the *la³⁵* clause is not possible. Aspect marking in the *la³⁵* clause is restricted, but this is part of the construction itself rather than a sign of integration. In fact, a *la³⁵* clause need not link back to only one clause. It may refer to the discourse theme of several clauses or even an entire passage. The tone change that replaces *la³⁵* likewise creates no integration with the pragmatic antecedent.

As already mentioned, *la³⁵* and its related tone change pattern have several functions. Their use in introducing a reason is described in § 14.1.3, and their use in linking a cause and effect is discussed in § 14.2.3. An overview of the particle is presented in § 16.4.

13.1.3.4 Borrowed Adversative Conjunction

The traditional adversative constructions just described are still frequently used in Khatso discourse. However, a conjunction borrowed from Hanyu, *ta³⁵sɿ³⁵* or *ta³⁵sɿ²⁴* 'but', is also increasingly common. Following Chinese syntax, it tends to occur mainly at the beginning of clauses, unlike *ŋ⁴⁴li³³* and *ŋ³³na⁴⁴li³³* which often occupy phrase-final position (see § 13.1.3.1). An example is shown in (1020).

(1020) [pa³²³sʅ³²³tɕo³¹ n̪ɛ³²³   jɛ³²³tsʰau³²³   tso³³guo³²³ li³²³sʅ³¹ sa³⁵].
eight.ten.nine CL:TMP Yuan.Dynasty China   history on
八十九   年   元朝   中国   历史   上
'(For) 89 years the Yuan Dynasty (was) in China's history.'
那么，元朝在中国历史上八十九年。

ta³⁵sʅ³⁵ [tsɛi³⁵ jɛ³²³na³²³sɛi³¹   mɛi⁴⁴ ti³²³ xa³³ni³³ kʰo⁵³ tʰo³¹tsʅ³⁵
but   at   Yunnan.Province CL:GEN in   how.many CL:TMP rule
但是   在   元南省   个   里   多少   年   统治
ŋa³¹]?
CNT.Q
'But, how long did (they) rule in Yunnan?'
但是在云南省统治了多少年？
(KLT-History)

13.2 Temporal Constructions

In discourse, events are generally understood to occur in the same temporal order in which they are uttered, and no special marking is required. Rather, the exceptions to the rule typically require marking instead. However, at times speakers may wish to emphasize a particular temporal relationship between two clauses. There are a number of strategies in Khatso for doing so, and they may be grouped into four temporal types. In the first, *sɛi⁴⁴* marks clauses that convey the general temporal time frame of the following clause (§ 13.2.1). The second type involves adverbs that describe particular temporal relationships between clauses, such as 'before' and 'after' (§ 13.2.2). The third and fourth types concern constructions that present events occurring simultaneously (§ 13.2.3) and sequentially (§ 13.2.4). Cause and effect constructions and conditional constructions also often entail a temporal relationship between clauses; they are described separately in § 14.2 and § 14.4 respectively.

13.2.1 Temporal Construction with *sɛi⁴⁴*

The particle *sɛi⁴⁴* has a number of uses, but its most basic function appears to be to mark the time of an event. When combining clauses, it follows the first clause, which provides the time frame for the second clause. Examples are shown in (1021) and (1022). Although it often translates into Chinese as a relativized noun 'the time that' and into English as the temporal conjunction 'when', in Khatso *sɛi⁴⁴* is a grammatical particle and not a noun.

(1021) [sɿ³⁵   tɕi³³]   **sɛi⁴⁴**   [nɛi³³tsʰɤ³³ kɛi³³ tɕi³³   tɕi³³   ta³³]?
       firewood   pack   TMP   2PL   AGT   pack   pack   IPFV.IRR
       柴   装   你们   装   装
       'When the firewood was packed up, was it you (who) packed (it)?'
       装柴是不是你们装的？
       (KL-Dance Parties)

(1022) [i²⁴tɕʰɛ³²³   tɕa³⁵   so²⁴   sɿ⁵⁵]   **sɛi⁴⁴**,
       qin   CL:MACH   learn   know   TMP
       琴   台   学   知道
       'When (I) learned the *qin*,'
       学会了琴的时候，

       [na⁵³tɕʰɛ⁵⁵   la²⁴   ko⁵⁵   tɕo³⁵   na⁵³pɤ³¹   la²⁴   ko⁵⁵,
       dance   REL   CL:PL   then   dance.party   REL   CL:PL
       跳舞   些   就   跳乐   些
       'Those who dance (that is) those from dance parties,'
       跳舞的就是娱乐的那些，

       tɕo³⁵   tsʰɤ²⁴to³⁵   tɤ³³   wa³³   a³³   tsɛi³⁵].
       then   begin   INCP   CRS   that   CL:TMP
       就   出动   那   段
       '(I) started (at) that time.'
       那时候就出动了。
       (YLW-Learning)

The temporal marker also serves as a topic marker (see § 10.1). In many cases, either reading of *sɛi⁴⁴* is possible. For example, the first intonation unit (IU) in (1022) above may mean either 'when (I) learned the *qin*,' or 'as for (me) learning the *qin*'; the semantic difference is slight. The marker also plays a role in complementation, as described in Chapter 15.

This construction does integrate clauses to a certain degree. Arguments need not be shared, but aspect marking is possible in the second clause only. The aspect marker may optionally have scope over both clauses, but typically the matrix clause is viewed as a separate event happening within the larger background of the temporal clause. As a result, the exact time frame of the *sɛi⁴⁴* clause is often vague. For example, in (1022) above, the currently relevant marker in the third IU may also be analyzed as applying to the first IU; both describe situations that began many decades before and continue into the present. But in (1023) below, the *sɛi⁴⁴* clause describes a potentially long and undefined span of time, while the second clause contains an event that occurs in a brief moment of time. Additional syntactic properties of *sɛi⁴⁴* are discussed in more detail in § 16.6.

(1023) [ŋa³²³tʏ³³ tsʰɿ³³] **sɛi⁴⁴**, pʰiɛ³⁵ ka³²³ i³³ wa³³ sɿ³¹ tsɛi³¹.
afterwards arrive TMP   cheat walk   go   CRS   again HSY
后来   到   骗   走   去   又
'Afterwards, (they) say that (they) cheated (him) again.', literally 'When afterwards arrived, (they) say that (they) cheated (him) again.'
到后来，说是被骗走了。
(YJR-Grandfather)

Depending on context, *sɛi⁴⁴* may also be interpreted as linking separate but simultaneous events (see § 13.2.3.3), but this is not its primary purpose. It is also involved in manner constructions (see § 14.5).

13.2.2 Constructions with Borrowed Temporal Adverbs

There is a subset of adverbs that specifically relate to time. They are often employed in simple clauses to detail the time frame of an event (see § 9.3.1). Two of the adverbs borrowed from Chinese — *zɿ³¹tɕʰɛ³²³* or *i³¹tɕʰɛ³²³* 'before' and *zɿ³¹xɯ³⁵* 'after' — may also combine clauses in a way that specifies the temporal relationship between them. In this construction, the adverb occurs at the end of the first clause, following Chinese syntax. Examples are presented in (1024) and (1025).

(1024) [jɛ³²³tsʰau³²³   ma³¹ tɕɛ³⁵li³²³] **zɿ³¹tɕʰɛ³²³** [sɿ⁴⁴ fɛi³³li³³ la³⁵ ŋɛi³³
Yuan.dynasty   NEG establish   before   COP   divide   FOC   ASRT
元朝   不   建立   以前   是   分裂
tso³³kuo³²³].
China
中国
'Before the Yuan Dynasty was established, (it was) divided, China.'
没有建立元朝以前中国是分裂的。
(KLT-History)

(1025) [tʰo³¹zɿ²⁴] **zɿ³¹xɯ³⁵** sa²⁴kɛi³³ [na³²³so³⁵   ɕau³³miɛ³²³ no⁵³
unify   after   until   Southern.Song eliminate   complete
统一   以后   才   南宋   消灭   掉
ta³⁵   ŋɛi³³].
be.able.FOC   ASRT
能
'The Southern Song (dynasty) was (not) eliminated until after (China) was unified.'
统一以后才能够消灭南宋。
(KLT-History)

The temporal adverb provides a certain degree of integration between the clauses. The temporal clause cannot stand alone, although it need not share arguments with the second clause, as (1026) illustrates. Aspect marking, however, occurs only in the second clause — in other words, at the end of the matrix clause. And such marking has scope over both clauses, as the translation demonstrates. Moreover, the first clause is considered incomplete; a second clause is expected to follow.

(1026) [i^{33} kʰua^{31}la^{31} i^{323}]   **zɿ^{31}tɕʰɛ^{323}**   [ŋa^{33} tsa^{323} m̩^{33} wa^{323}].
   3SG   Kunming   go   before   1SG   rice   make   PFV
   他   昆明   去   以前   我   饭   做
   'I cooked before he went to Kunming.'
   他去昆明以前，我做饭了。
   (KL-Elicitation)

Though the borrowed adverbs are increasingly common in discourse, many speakers still employ traditional Khatso constructions. For example, the topic marker *ni^{31}* may be used instead of either marker, though this makes the exact temporal relationship vague and dependent on context for the correct interpretation (see § 13.2.4.4). The construction *ta^{31} ni^{323}* is still the preferred method of conveying the notion of 'after' (see § 13.2.4.3).

13.2.3 Simultaneous Events

There are four strategies for indicating that the events described in two clauses occur simultaneously. Employing *wa^{24} xɛi^{35}* or its borrowed counterpart *jo^{35}* is the most frequent in discourse (§ 13.2.3.1), but the adverb *ni^{31}nɛ^{323}* is also employed for this purpose (§ 13.2.3.2). Although typically interpreted as a general temporal marker, *sɛi^{44}* may also link clauses that are specifically understood as concurrent (§ 13.2.3.3). Much rarer is the use of the clause linker *tʏ^{44}* for this purpose, but this is possible in certain circumstances (§ 13.2.3.4).

13.2.3.1 Simultaneous Constructions with *wa^{24} xɛi^{35}* and *jo^{35}*

One way of denoting concurrent events is through the clause-linking phrase *wa^{24} xɛi^{35}*. This expression is a reduction of three particles, *wa^{24} to^{33} xɛi^{35}*, which are respectively the perfective aspect marker *wa^{323}*, the adverb *to^{33}* 'also' and the adverb *xɛi^{35}* 'still'. *to^{33}* is obligatorily absent in the modern phrase, but the tone change it induces in the perfective marker signals its participation, a common pattern in the language (see § 3.2.4.1). Today, the reduced expression functions only to mark concurrence between clauses, as the examples in (1027) and (1028) demonstrate. Note that the perfective marker seems to be semantically bleached here. Both examples describe ongoing states without obvious temporal boundaries.

(1027) [na²⁴]   **wa²⁴**   xɛi³⁵   [pʰɤ³¹lo³²³]
      be.good PFV   still   be.inexpensive
      好   还   便宜
      'both good and cheap'
      又好又便宜
      (KL-Elicitation)

(1028) [n̥o⁵³   tɕi³³]   **wa²⁴**   xɛi³⁵   [tsʰɤ³³   kʰɛi⁴⁴]   ni³¹,
      drink   enter   PFV   still   car   drive   TOP
      喝   进   还   车   开
      '(If you're) drinking and driving,'
      喝了酒后还开车呢，

      na²⁴po²⁴tɕʰa³¹   tsɿ³⁵   ŋa³²³ta³²³   sa³⁵   wa³³.
      ear   pull   be.able   perhaps.FOC   CRS
      耳朵   揪   可以   可能
      'Perhaps (I'll) have to pinch (your) ears.'
      得揪耳朵了。
      (ZRF-Grandfather)

Semantically, this construction is identical to one in Chinese involving the adverb *yòu* 又 'both'. And, in fact, the latter has been borrowed into Khatso as *jo³⁵*. It may be used in place of *wa²⁴ xɛi³⁵*, as in (1029), or the two constructions may be combined, as in (1030). Unlike *wa²⁴ xɛi³⁵*, which may be used with any type of verb, *jo³⁵* tends to mainly be used with stative verbs, much like its Chinese counterpart. The only attested exception is *jo³⁵ tsa³¹ jo³⁵ to³²³* 'to both eat and drink', which has become a routinized expression.

(1029) **jo³⁵**   [na²⁴]   **jo³⁵**   [pʰɤ³¹lo³²³]
      both   be.good   both   be.inexpensive
      又   好   又   便宜
      'both good and cheap'
      又好又便宜
      (KL-Elicitation)

(1030) **jo³⁵** [na²⁴] **wa²⁴ xɛi³⁵ jo³⁵** [pʰɤ³¹lo³²³]
both be.good PFV still both be.inexpensive
又 好 还 又 便宜
'both good and cheap'
又好还又便宜
(KL-Elicitation)

Both of these constructions integrate clauses syntactically to a certain degree. Aspect is restricted in both; wa²⁴ xɛi³⁵ already incorporates aspect into the construction, even if it is semantically bleached. And since jo³⁵ mainly links verbs that describe states, additional aspect marking is unnecessary. Although arguments tend to be omitted, both clauses must share the same A/S. Center embedding, though, is not possible here.

It is possible to coordinate more than two clauses with these constructions, but this is rarely done in natural speech. In addition, both constructions usually combine only bare verbs or verbs accompanied by unmodified nominal Ps. More complex clauses are combined using the particle tɤ⁴⁴, which is discussed in § 14.6.

13.2.3.2 Simultaneous Construction with *nĩ³¹nɛ³²³*

There is a construction involving the adverb nĩ³¹nɛ³²³ that specifically indicates that two events occur at the same time, but it is only used with non-stative verbs. Here the adverb is placed at the beginning of each clause, as the examples in (1031) and (1032) illustrate. Note that the temporal boundaries are not specified in this construction, although in discourse they are often interpreted as being roughly the same. In any case, there must be a certain amount of temporal overlap for this construction to be used. The adverb employed here means 'first (in sequence)' when used alone, and is typically found in descriptions of procedures. Marking both clauses as 'first' creates the simultaneous sense. It is possible to coordinate more than two clauses with nĩ³¹nɛ³²³, but this is rarely done in natural speech.

(1031) tɕɛ³³tɕɛ³³ ko⁵⁵ ni³¹ **nĩ³¹nɛ³²³** [tʰi³¹ tsɤ³¹] **nĩ³¹nɛ³²³** [tɕʰɛ³¹xa³³ tsɤ³¹].
straw.tip CL:PL TOP first weave CONT first drop CONT
草尖 些 一 编 一 丢掉
'As for the straw tips, (you) weave and push (them in) at the same time.'
草尖呢，一边编着一边丢掉。
(KL-Stools)

(1032) xa⁵⁵tsʅ²⁴ ni³¹ tɕo³⁵ **ni³¹n̪ɛ³²³** [kɣ³³ tɕi³³] **ni³¹n̪ɛ³²³** [tsa³¹ tsɤ³¹ ŋa³²³ta³²³
      boil   TOP then   first   make enter first   eat   CONT be.able
      煮沸   就   一   做   放   一   吃   可以
      wa³³].
      CRS
      '(When it's) boiling, (you) can put (food) in and eat (some) at the same time.'
      煮沸呢，就可以一边放进去一边吃了。
      (KL-Hotpot)

Like the *wa²⁴ xɛi³⁵* and *jo³⁵* constructions, the *ni³¹n̪ɛ³²³* construction shows a certain degree of syntactic integration. Aspect is restricted — typically neither clause is marked, although the continuous aspect marker *tsɤ³¹* may be used to underscore the sense of concurrence, as the examples above illustrate. Again, the two clauses must share the same A/S. Center embedding is not possible here.

13.2.3.3 Simultaneous Construction with *sɛi⁴⁴*

Clauses marked by the temporal marker *sɛi⁴⁴* typically present a general time frame against which the matrix event occurs. However, they may also be interpreted as simultaneous events, as (1033) demonstrates, though this is not the primary function of *sɛi⁴⁴*. Typically, this construction lacks aspect marking, giving it the sense of a habitual state of affairs. For its other syntactic properties, see the description of the basic temporal use of *sɛi⁴⁴* (§ 13.2.1).

(1033) [i³³ tɕa³²³ ka³²³] **sɛi⁴⁴** [jɛ³³ to³²³].
      3SG road   walk   TMP   tobacco smoke
      他   路   走   烟   吸
      'He walks and smokes.', literally 'When he walks, (he) smokes.'
      他走路吸烟。
      (KL-Elicitation)

13.2.3.4 Simultaneous Construction with *tɤ⁴⁴*

The particle *tɤ⁴⁴* is used to combine clauses, and it may point to a variety of relationships between the two, such as an event and its purpose or the manner with which it is carried out. With certain verbs, it may also link simultaneous events, as the examples in (1034) and (1035) illustrate. Although not obligatory, the continuous aspect marker *tsɤ³¹* may be used in the first clause to underscore the sense of simultaneity, as (1036) shows.

(1034) [ɕi³³   la²⁴ka³³]   **tɤ⁴⁴** [ɕi³³   tsa³¹] nɛi³³.
      be.accustomed play   CLNK   be.accustomed eat   ASRT
      习惯   玩   习惯   吃
      '(We) would play and eat (there).'
      会在那儿玩在那儿吃。
      (YJF-Dance Parties)

(1035) [so²⁴] **tɤ⁴⁴** [kv³³ tso²⁴], ŋ³³ ŋa³¹?
      learn   CLNK   do   ITER   COP CNT.Q
      学   做   是
      '(You) learned while doing (it) repeatedly, is that right?'
      学着做，是吗？
      (KL-Sewing)

(1036) [ɣ³²³ tsɤ³¹] **tɤ⁴⁴** [n̻a³¹ ta³²³] wa³³.
      hold   CONT   CLNK   speak   be.able CRS
      拿   说   可以
      '(You) can hold (it) and talk.'
      拿着说吧。
      (ZRF-Grandfather)

The simultaneous function of this construction is not productive with all verbs. In most cases, speakers much prefer to use either the *wa²⁴ xɛi³⁵* or *ni³¹nɛ³²³* constructions to describe concurrent events (see § 13.2.3.1 and § 13.2.3.2 respectively). There is no apparent pattern that explains these limitations. It seems that verbs that may be linked with *tɤ⁴⁴* are the exceptions, likely resulting from historically frequent collocations in discourse.

Nonetheless, all *tɤ⁴⁴* constructions are fairly tightly integrated (see § 14.6). The two clauses must share A/S arguments. Aspect is restricted to the second clause and has scope over the entire construction. The single exception involves the continuous marker *tsɤ³¹*, which may optionally mark the first clause to underscore the notion of temporal concurrence. Although semantically it does not matter which of the simultaneous events comes first, each event must be described in a separate clause; center embedding is not possible.

As already mentioned, *tɤ⁴⁴* has a number of functions. The purpose construction is described in § 14.6, the cause and effect construction is discussed in § 14.2.2, and the manner construction is detailed in § 14.5. An overview of all the functions is presented in § 16.5.

13.2.4 Sequential Events

To mark two clauses overtly as occurring sequentially in time, Khatso offers a number of different strategies. The simplest and most common strategy provides a general sense of sequentiality, employing either the adverb $tɕo^{35}$ 'then' or a more complex phrase $ja^{53}\,ni^{323}$ 'later', as discussed in § 13.2.4.1 and § 13.2.4.2 respectively. Other strategies convey a more particular sequential link. The phrase $ta^{31}\,ni^{323}$, for example, means 'after' and suggests that the two events occur fairly closely together, as described in § 13.2.4.3. The topic marker ni^{31} provides a temporal meaning when employed in tail-head linkages, which suggests an even briefer break between events, as explained in § 13.2.4.4. And finally, the conjunction $sa^{24}kɛi^{33}$ 'until' denotes a situation in which one event ends just as another begins, as detailed in § 13.2.4.5. Borrowed temporal adverbs may also link clauses in this way; they are discussed in § 13.2.2.

13.2.4.1 Sequential Linking with $tɕo^{35}$

Clauses that are related because of a sequential order in time may be linked with the adverb $tɕo^{35}$ 'then'. In discourse, the placement of $tɕo^{35}$ in a clause is quite flexible. Typically, adverbs occur immediately after A/S and before the other pre-verbal elements, and $tɕo^{35}$ often occurs in this position, as shown in (1037). But, because of zero anaphora, $tɕo^{35}$ may link verbs directly, as in (1038).

(1037) tɛi³³   jo³⁵   **tɕo³⁵**   tʰau³²³   tɤ⁴⁴   jau³²³ɣa³³.
      this   CL:HUM   then   escape   CLNK   Yao'an
      这   个   就   逃   　　　姚安
      'This one then escaped to Yao'an.'
      这个就逃到姚安。
      (KLT-History)

(1038) [pɤ⁵³   sɻ⁵⁵]   **tɕo³⁵**   [na⁵³pɤ³¹   tso²⁴   i³³]   wa³³.
      play   know   then   dance   ITER   go   CRS
      弹   知道   就   跳乐   　　　去
      '(After) I knew how to play, I then went to dances many times.'
      会弹就去跳乐了。
      (YLW-Learning)

In addition, $tɕo^{35}$ may also be found at the beginning or the end of intonation units, as (1039) and (1040) illustrate. The latter use suggests that in addition to linking clauses, $tɕo^{35}$ may also serve to signal that the speaker has not finished the turn and plans to continue speaking. Unlike to^{33} 'also' (see § 3.2.4.1), however, in this use $tɕo^{35}$ never triggers tone change. Occasionally, it also occurs in its own intonation unit, as in (1041), a use more consistent with a discourse filler — that is, a word or phrase uttered while the speaker decides what to say next.

(1039) A: xa³³ni³³   kʰua³¹?
          how   speak
          怎么   讲
          'What (should I) say?'
          怎么讲？

      B: **tɕo³⁵**   kɣ³¹tiɛ³¹   kʰua³¹   ta³²³   wa³³.
          then   story   speak   be.able   CRS
          就   故事   讲   好
          '(You) can tell stories then.'
          就讲故事吧。
     (PYX, KL-Performing)

(1040) sɤ²⁴   la²⁴   mɛi⁴⁴   ni³¹   **tɕo³⁵**,
        be.long   REL   CL:GEN   TOP   then
        长   个   就
        'As for the long ones then,'
        长的呢就，

        [tɛi³³ni³³   tɕi⁴⁴]   ni³¹   **tɕo³⁵**,
        this.way   do   TOP   then
        这么   做   就
        'Done this way then,'
        这么弄呢就，

        [tɛi³³   kɤ²⁴   **tɕo³⁵**   mau³⁵   tso²⁴   tɤ³³ wa³³].
        this   CL:STRIP   then   protrude   ITER   INCP
        这   条   就   冒
        'This thread (will) then begin to stick out.'
        这条就冒出来了。
     (KL-Sewing)

(1041) ɕi³³   ja²⁴   ja³³.
        be.accustomed   feed   IPFV.EMP
        习惯   喂
        '(They) would feed (us).'
        会喂呀。

tɕo³⁵,
then
就

ŋ³¹,
FILL

ɕi³³	ja²⁴	nɛi³³	**tɕo³⁵**	nɛi³³	tɛi³¹	mɛi³³	ŋa³³	tɛi³¹	mɛi³³
be.accustomed	feed	ASRT	then	2SG	one	CL:MSR	1SG	one	CL:MSR
习惯	喂		就	你	一	口	我	一	口

ni³³.
ADV

'(They) would then feed (us), a mouthful (for) you, a mouthful (for) me.'
就, 嗯, 就是会喂给吃的, 你一口我一口的。
(YJF-Dance Parties)

The adverb *tɕo³⁵* appears to be borrowed from Chinese, cf. *jiù* 就 in Putonghua, but given its frequency and lack of synonyms, it is probably a very early loan. Like its counterpart in Chinese, *tɕo³⁵* may also indicate a cause and effect relationship between clauses (see § 14.2.1).

13.2.4.2 Sequential Linking with *ja⁵³ ni³²³*

Similar in function to the adverb *tɕo³⁵*, the expression *ja⁵³ ni³²³* also frequently marks sequential order among clauses. This phrase combines a morpheme *ja⁵³*, which roughly means 'later', with the backgrounding particle *ni³²³*. Its general meaning is akin to 'and then, later, after that', and it introduces a clause that describes an event or state that occurs at some unspecified time after that in the first clause. Typically, it appears at the beginning of the second clause, but does not syntactically combine the clauses; they remain separate, with their own arguments and aspect marking. Often, it is reduced to *ja⁵³* in rapid speech. Examples are shown in (1042) and (1043). Although they are synonymous, the adverb *tɕo³⁵* often follows *ja⁵³ ni³²³* in discourse; this is not considered redundant in Khatso.

(1042) [tɕɛ³³tɕɛ³³ ko⁵⁵   ni³¹n̠ɛ³²³ ni³¹n̠ɛ³²³ ni³³ kɛi²⁴   xa³³   tsɤ³¹],
       straw.tip CL:PL side   side   ADV   separate send   CONT
       草尖   些   边   边   隔开   送

'(You) slowly separate (and) cut off the straw ends.'
草尖呢慢慢的隔开了,

ja⁵³ni³²³   tɕo³⁵   [la⁵³   fv̩³⁵   wa³⁵   pa³¹].
later   then   roll   bury   FUT   IMP
然后   就   卷   埋

'Then (you) will roll (them) up inside.'
然后就卷了埋起来了吧。
(WYF-Stools)

(1043) [tɛi³³ni³³ tɛi³¹ kʰo⁵³   ma³¹pa³¹   za³¹ sa⁵⁵   tʰɤ⁵⁵   ŋɛi³³].
       this.way   one   CL:TMP approximately DIM   be.bitter CL:TMP ASRT
       这么   一   年   左右   苦   下

'For about a year (it) was really awful like that.'
这么苦了一年左右。

ja⁵³   tɕo³⁵   [tɕɛ³⁵tsɿ³⁵   tɕɛ³⁵tsɿ³⁵   tɕo³⁵   mɛi⁴⁴   ko⁵³   kɯ³²³   sa³³
later   then   be.gradual   be.gradual   then   very   pass   CSC   be.good
然后   就   逐渐   逐渐   就   很   过   好

tɤ³³ wa³³].
INCP

'Then gradually (it) became easier to endure.'
然后就逐渐逐渐就好过了。
(YJF-Childhood)

ja⁵³ ni³²³ is also frequently employed as a discourse filler. That is, a speaker may utter it to fill time while considering the next phrase. Often, in this use the temporal sense is absent. An example is shown in (1044), where *ja⁵³ ni³²³* introduces a clause providing background information rather than the next sequential action. Likely because of this semantic bleaching, there is a great deal of variation in how it is pronounced as a filler. *ja⁵³ni³²³* is the most common form, but also attested are *i⁵³ni³²³* and *jɛ⁵³ni³²³*, along with similar expressions that seemingly involve the topic marker, such as *ja⁵³ni³¹* and *i⁴⁴ni³¹*.

(1044) piɛ³⁵   po²⁴   ka⁵³la³¹ tɛi³⁵ la²⁴   a³³   ti⁵³   kʰai³³ ɕo⁴⁴   wa³³.
       pencil   CL:ROD on   carry REL   that CL:PCE   rub   be.clean   CRS
       笔   支   上面   带   那   块   擦   干净

'That piece on the end of a pencil was rubbed off.'
笔上带的那块擦完了。

i⁵³ni³²³,
FILL

kʰai³³tsɿ³²³   vɤ³²³   i³³   sɛi⁴⁴   nɤ³²³kʰɤ³³   vɤ³²³   i³³   ŋɛi³³.
eraser   buy   go   TMP   Hexi   buy   go   ASRT
橡皮擦   买   去   河西   买   去
'When (you) buy erasers, (you must) go to Hexi to buy (them).'
买橡皮擦是去河西买去的。
(YAY-Erasers)

13.2.4.3 Sequential Linking with *ta³¹ ni³²³*

The backgrounding particle *ni³²³* often marks locative and temporal information in simple clauses (see § 16.2). When combined with the particle *ta³¹*, it conveys the temporal meaning of 'after'. Examples are presented in (1045) and (1046). The temporal sense has logical implications — since the reason for an event exists before the event is realized. Thus, this same construction is employed to provide a reason for a following matrix clause (see § 14.1.1). Semantically, either meaning is appropriate in the examples, but because of context they are interpreted as sequential constructions here. Also, like *ni³²³*, *ta³¹ ni³²³* may trigger tone change in the preceding syllable, though *ta³¹* is never affected by its adjacency to *ni³²³* (see § 3.2.4.1).

(1045) [kʰo³³ɕo³²³   mɛi⁴⁴   fa³²³ta²⁴]   **ta³¹ ni³²³**,
       science   CL:GEN develop   after
       科学   个   发达   以后
       'After science developed,' / 'Because science developed,'
       因为科学发达,

[xua³⁵fɛi³²³   no³²³jo³²³   a³³   ko⁵⁵   kɛi³³   ŋ³³   n̩a³³].
fertilizer   pesticide   that CL:PL INS   COP   COP.EMP
化肥   农药   那   些   用   是
'(We used) those fertilizers and pesticides, that's right.'
用那些化肥农药,是吧.
(PYX-Weeds)

(1046) [i³²³tɕa⁵³   ko⁵⁵   to³²³   tɕi⁴⁴]   **ta³¹ ni³²³**,
       water   CL:PL   drink   enter   After
       水   些   喝   进   以后
       'After drinking water,' / 'Because (they) drank water,'
       喝了水以后呢,

[tʰɤ⁵⁵sɛi⁴⁴ tɕo³⁵ sɿ³⁵tsʰɿ³⁵ ko⁵⁵ to³³ mɛi⁴⁴ tɕʰa³²³].
suddenly then energy CL:PL also very be.strong
一下子 就 士气 些 也 很 强
'(Their) energy suddenly got strong.'
士气一下子就很强了。
(HPH-Horse Dug Well)

There is a certain degree of integration between clauses in the *ta³¹ ni³²³* construction. Although the arguments need not be identical in the two clauses, the verb preceding *ta³¹ ni³²³* never takes aspectual marking, even though it is understood as having a perfective sense. If the second clause is marked for aspect, which is not obligatory, it may have scope over both clauses, but this depends on context. The *ta³¹ ni³²³* clause may occur after the matrix clause as an afterthought, as (1047) shows, but it cannot be center embedded within the matrix clause itself. Semantically, the *ta³¹ ni³²³* clause is incomplete; a second clause is expected. Moreover, the tone change pattern triggered by *ta³¹ ni³²³* is shared by the topic marker *ni³¹* and the clause linker *to³³* to mark non-final clauses in discourse (see § 3.2.4.1).

(1047) [na³¹ni²⁴za³¹ tsʰɤ³³ ni³¹ ma³¹ sɿ⁵⁵],
child PL TOP NEG know
小孩 们 不 知道

[ɕɛ²⁴ ɕɛ²⁴ za³¹ sɿ³²³xɤ³⁵ kɛi³³ pa⁵³ tɕi⁴⁴] **ta³¹ ni³²³**.
be.small be.small DIM time from betroth say because
小 小 时候 从 订亲 说 因为
'As for (the) children, (they) didn't know, because (they) were betrothed from when very young.'
小孩子呢不知道，小的时候就订得亲了。
(YJF-Childhood)

13.2.4.4 Sequential Linking with *ni³¹*

The topic marker *ni³¹* may modify any element in a clause (see § 10.1). Typically, it establishes a discourse theme about which the following clause makes a comment, and in some cases the topic is a conditional clause (see § 14.4.1). These uses may imply a sequential temporal relationship, and in certain contexts the simple sequential reading is the most relevant one. This is most apparent in procedural instructions, where tail-head linkages are common — that is, the previous step is repeated in a clause ending in *ni³¹*, followed by the matrix clause detailing the next step. The examples in (1048) and (1049), which are excerpted from a monologue on how to weave stools from straw, illustrate the pattern.

(1048) i⁴⁴ni³¹   ta³⁵   i³²³tɕa⁵³   kɛi³³   tɛi⁵³   kʰuo⁵³.
later   again   water   INS   take   be.wet
然后   又   水   用   带   湿
'Later, use water to make (it) wet.'
然后又用水弄湿，

[tɛi⁵³   kʰuo⁵³] **ni³¹**   [kv̩³³   tɤ⁴⁴   kɛi³³   tsɿ³⁵].
take   be.wet   TOP   make   CLNK   AGT   soak
带   湿   做   泡
'Having made (it) wet, let (it) soak.'
弄湿了泡着
(WYF-Stools)

(1049) i⁵³   tɕo³⁵   tɛi³³ni³³   tʰi³¹   la⁵³.
later   then   this.way   weave   bind
然后   就   这么   编   裹
'Later, then bind (it) tight like this.'
然后就这么编.

[la⁵³   tsɿ²⁴]   **ni³¹**   ta³⁵   tɕo³⁵,
bind   rise   TOP   again   then
裹   起   又   就
'Having bound (it) up, then,'
裹起来呢就又,

ŋ³¹,   [tɤ³¹   tʰɤ⁵⁵   kv̩³³   to³³].
FILL   one   CL:TMP   make   be.flat
         一   下   做   平
'Um, make (it) flat.'
嗯，弄平一下。
(WYF-Stools)

There is another construction based on the sequential sense of *ni³¹* which corresponds to the English adverbial expression 'as soon as'. Here the numeral *tɛi³¹* 'one' is placed before the verb in the dependent *ni³¹* clause, where it has a meaning akin to 'first'. The main event is described in the second clause. The adverb *tɕo³⁵* 'then' often follows *ni³¹*, either as the final word in the first clause or early in the second clause. An example is shown in (1050). Note that *ni³¹* may trigger tone change in the preceding syllable (see § 3.2.4.1), and in rapid speech it may be omitted altogether, as in (1051), without changing the meaning of the construction.

(1050) [tsʰo³³ɣɤ²⁴ma³³ tsʰɤ³³ kɛi³³ **tɛi³¹** ɣ²⁴ li⁴⁴] **ni³¹** tɕo³⁵,
adult   PL   AGT   one   call come TOP then
大人   们   一   叫   来   就

'As soon as the adults came (and) called (us),'
大人一来叫呢就，

[kɯ³³ i³³ tɤ⁴⁴ kuɛi³³ tɕa³³ ka³²³ i³³ wa³³].
enter go CLNK return home walk go CRS
进   去   归   家   走   去

'Then (we) went home.'
回去归家去了。
(HPH-Toys)

(1051) [tsʰɻ̩³¹ma³³ **tɛi³¹** m̩³³ no⁵³ tɕɛ³²³xuɛi³³ no⁵³],
wife   one   make complete marry   complete
太太   一   做   掉   结婚   掉

'As soon as (we) became wives, got married,'
一结婚以后，结婚后，

[tɕo³⁵ n̩o³¹ m̩³³ ka³²³ i³³ wa³³ mɛi⁴⁴].
then thing do   walk go CRS DSC.EMP
就   东西   做   走   去

'Then (we) went to work.'
就去干活了。
(WYX-Three Ladies)

Regardless of meaning, *ni³¹* clauses are not independent. Although the arguments need not be identical, the first clause typically does not carry aspect marking. If present, aspect marking occurs in the second clause instead. And although the *ni³¹* clause may occur either before or after the matrix clause, embedding it within the matrix clause itself is not possible. Moreover, a clause ending in *ni³¹* is considered a semantically incomplete idea, and a follow-up clause is expected.

As previously mentioned, *ni³¹* is multi-functional. Its use as a topic marker is described in §10.1, the conditional construction is discussed in §14.4.1, and its role in marking a reason clause is detailed in §14.1.2. An overview of the particle is provided in §16.3.

13.2.4.5 Sequential Linking with *sa²⁴kɛi³³* 'until'

The conjunction *sa²⁴kɛi³³* 'until, before', occasionally also pronounced as *tsʰɤ²⁴kɛi³³* and *sɛi⁴⁴kɛi³³*, is often used with temporal noun phrases in simple clauses. But, it may also combine clauses in the same temporal way. In this construction, the conjunction follows the dependent clause and precedes the matrix clause. Semantically, it not only indicates a sequential order in time, it may also mean that the event described in the first clause is a condition for that in the second clause. Examples are shown in (1052), (1053) and (1054). Note that, unlike the English translation, the construction does not require negation in either clause.

(1052) [tɛi³¹ tsɛi³⁵ tɕʰɛ⁵⁵] **sa²⁴kɛi³³** [kɛi³³ li³³].
      one CL:TMP kick   until   enter come
      一   段   跳   才   进   来
      '(We didn't) come home until (we had) danced a while.'
      跳一会儿才回来。
      (YJF-Dance Parties)

(1053) [tʰo³¹ʐ̩²⁴ ʐ̩³¹xɯ³⁵] **sa²⁴kɛi³³** [na³²³so³⁵   ɕau³³miɛ³²³ no⁵³
      unify   after   until   Southern.Song eliminate complete
      统一   以后   才   南宋   消灭   掉
      ta³⁵   ŋɛi³³].
      be.able.FOC ASRT
      能
      'The Southern Song (dynasty) was (not) eliminated until after (China) was unified.'
      统一以后才能够消灭南宋。
      (KLT-History)

(1054) [ŋa³³ ŋ²⁴ka³³ jo³³ ja³³ sɛi³¹] **sa²⁴kɛi³³** [sɿ⁵⁵ ŋɛi³⁵].
      1SG see must IPFV.EMP still until know ASRT.FOC
      我   看   应该   还   才   知道
      'I (won't) know until (I) see (it).'
      我看了才知道。
      (KL-Three Ladies)

The clauses in this construction are not tightly integrated. They need not share arguments, since the condition in the first clause may be unrelated to the actors in the second. Aspect marking may also occur on both clauses. However, because the construction has an inherent contrastive sense, the second clause often contains the focus particle *la³⁵* or its related tone change pattern, as in (1053) and (1054) above, which restricts the choice of aspect markers (see § 13.1.3.3). It is also possible to leave the construction unmarked, as in (1052) above, which may have either a habitual interpretation or derive its temporal setting from context. Perfective aspect is rarely applied to the construction; if it is required then the expression *ta³¹ ni³²³* 'after' replaces *sa²⁴kɛi³³*. Likewise, polar question formation is not possible here, but the confirmatory question maker *sa⁴⁴* may be used with *la³⁵* or its related tone change pattern.

14 Specialized Clause-Linking Constructions

Chapter 13 presents the most basic of clause-linking constructions. This chapter focuses on more specialized constructions, many of which functionally correspond to adverbial clause combining in other languages. In Khatso, however, grammatical particles are just as likely as adverbs to link clauses. As described in the previous chapter, the exact nature of the link typically depends on verbal semantics and discourse context. In some cases, juxtaposition alone is enough to establish a link, and so common pragmatic linking strategies are described here along with the syntactic ones.

Strategies that link an event with the reason for its realization are explained in § 14.1, followed by cause and effect strategies in § 14.2. Concessive strategies are described in § 14.3, and conditional constructions in § 14.4. Manner constructions are explained in § 14.5, and the purpose construction is detailed in § 14.6. Complementation strategies are described in Chapter 15, and a summary of all clause-linking particles is presented in Chapter 16.

14.1 Reason Strategies

Clause combining may be employed to link an event with the reason motivating that event. There are several ways to do this in Khatso. The backgrounding particle ni^{323}, and its temporal counterpart $ta^{31}\ ni^{323}$, is the most common formulation, as discussed in § 14.1.1. The phrase $tɕi^{44}\ ni^{31}$, which includes the quotative verb $tɕi^{33}$ 'to say', tends to be less frequent in discourse, as § 14.1.2 explains. The particle la^{35} or its related tone change pattern marks focal clauses, which may include the reason for a given event. It is a much more prominent way of presenting this kind of information, as described in § 14.1.3. Finally, the borrowed conjunction $jɛ^{33}wi^{35}$ 'because' often replaces the traditional expressions, as discussed in § 14.1.4.

14.1.1 Reason Strategy with ni^{323} and $ta^{31}\ ni^{323}$

The backgrounding particle ni^{323} often marks locative and temporal information in simple clauses, but it may also combine clauses. In the latter construction, the first clause ends with ni^{323} and presents the reason for the event in the second clause, as shown in (1055). The construction $ta^{31}\ ni^{323}$, which contains a temporal morpheme meaning 'after' in addition to the backgrounding particle, is also employed for this purpose. Presumably, this is an extension of the temporal function, since an event occurs later in time than the reason for its realization. As a result, *ta³¹ ni³²³* is often interchangeable with *ni³²³*, as the example in (1056) illustrates. Although they canonically precede the matrix clause, in discourse the dependent reason clauses may occur afterwards as an afterthought, as (1057) illustrates. Note that both *ni³²³* and *ta³¹ ni³²³* may trigger tone change in the preceding syllable (see §3.2.4.1). *ta³¹*, however, never changes tone before *ni³²³*; it is unaffected by this tone change pattern.

(1055) tsɛi³⁵tsŋ³⁵ ma³¹   tso³²³   wa³³.
      evidence   NEG   EXIST   CRS
      证据   不   有
      'There's no evidence.'
      没有证据了。

      tɤ⁴⁴   [lɤ²⁴   xɛi³¹   no⁵³]   **ni³²³**   [xa³³n̪a⁵³   tsa²⁴tso²⁴   i³³]?
      FILL   land   burn   complete   BKGD   where   find   Go
              坡   烧   完   哪里   找   去
      'Because (the) land was burned, where (can you) go to find (proof)?'
      被烧了，去哪里找？
      (PYX-Dragon Pools)

(1056) [kʰo³³ɕo³²³   mɛi⁴⁴   fa³²³ta²⁴]   **ta³¹ ni³²³**,
      science   CL:GEN   develop   after
      科学   个   发达   以后
      'Because science developed,'
      因为科学发达，

      [xua³⁵fɛi³²³   no³²³jo³²³   a³³   ko⁵⁵   kɛi³³   ŋ³³   n̪a³³].
      fertilizer   pesticide   that   CL:PL INS   COP   COP.EMP
      化肥   农药   那   些   用   是
      '(We used) those fertilizers and pesticides, that's right.'
      用那些化肥农药，是吧。
      (PYX-Weeds)

(1057) [i⁴⁴ni³¹   ta³⁵   tsʰɛi³³   ta³⁵   kɯ³¹   tɤ⁴⁴   tɛi³³ni³³   ko³²³   ti³³ ja³³],
      later   again raise   on   INDR.CAUS CLNK this.way   draw   PROG
      然后   又   抬   上   这么   抽
      'Later, (it was) still being lifted up this way to draw (water),'
      然后又抬给起来这么抽的。

[a³³tɕʰa⁵⁵kʰɣ³³   tsɿ³³tsʰɿ³⁵   ma³¹   tso²⁴]   **ni³²³**.
that.time   machine   NEG   EXIST   BKGD
那时侯   机器   不   有
'Because (at) that time there were no machines.'
那时候没有机器的。
(YJF-Childhood)

There is very little integration in these constructions. The reason clause need not share arguments with the matrix clause. Aspect marking is not possible in the *ni³²³* clause; it occurs only at the end of the second clause. It may have scope over both clauses, but this may depend on context. Generally, it is understood that the reason precedes the event in time, so if the second clause is marked as perfective, then both clauses are perfective. However, if the second clause is marked with future aspect, the timing of the reason clause is vague; it may occur in any time frame. Center embedding is impossible in this construction, the *ni³²³* clause may only occur before or after the matrix clause.

The temporal function of *ta³¹ ni³²³* is described in § 13.2.4.3.

14.1.2 Reason Strategy with *tɕi⁴⁴ ni³¹*

When the topic marker *ni³¹* modifies clauses, the resulting formulation may be interpreted as a conditional construction (see § 14.4.1). But when the quotative verb *tɕi³³* 'to say' occurs in the *ni³¹* clause with a complement, the construction may also be understood as a reason clause. Context plays a crucial role here, because the realis status of the first clause determines the best interpretation. For example, if the interlocutor in (1058) has already agreed, then the first clause is realis and thus a reason clause. If she has not yet agreed, then the first clause is irrealis and the construction is conditional. The two translations illustrate the difference in English. Also, note that the topic marker typically triggers tone change in the preceding syllable (see § 3.2.4.1), which is why the quotative verb always takes tone 44 in this expression.

(1058) [tʰo³²³zɿ³⁵   ja³³]   **tɕi⁴⁴ ni³¹**   [tɕo³⁵ tʰo³²³zɿ³⁵ ja³³]   tɛi³¹ tʰɣ⁵⁵ tɕi³³].
       agree   IPFV.EMP   say TOP   then   agree   IPFV.EMP   one CL:TMP say
       同意   说   就   同意   一   下   说
'Since (you) agree, then say "(I) agree".' / 'If (you) agree, then say "(I) agree".'
同意呢就说一下 "同意"。
(KL-Childhood)

To help avoid this potential ambiguity, the complement of *tɕi³³* may be modified by the strong assertion particle *ŋɛi³³*, which cancels the conditional interpretation. An example is presented in (1059).

(1059) [tɕi³¹   jo³⁵   tɕi³¹   jo³⁵   tsʰŋ̍³³ kɯ³³   li³³   ŋɛi³³] **tɕi⁴⁴ ni³¹** tɕo³⁵,
       one   CL:HUM one   CL:HUM marry enter come   ASRT   say   TOP   then
       一   位   一   位   娶   进   来   说   　 就
       'Since one after another (they) married in(to the family), then,'
       一个一个娶进来呢就，

[ŋ³¹   jo³⁵   tsʰŋ̍³³ kɯ³³   li⁴⁴   ni³¹   tɕo³⁵ ŋ³¹   tsŋ̍⁵⁵miɛ⁵⁵].
two   CL:HUM marry enter come   TOP   then   two   CL:FAMGP
二   位   娶   回   来   　 就   二
'Since two married in, then (they became my) two sisters-in-law.'
娶两个回来呢就是妯娌俩。
(HPH-Family)

A more detailed discussion of the quotative verb *tɕi³³* is found in § 15.3.

14.1.3 Reason Strategy with *la³⁵* or Related Tone Change

The focus particle *la³⁵* links a clause to an earlier comment in discourse, and may have a number of interpretations — such as emphatic agreement or contrast. In some cases, it highlights a clause that describes the reason for a previous situation. Like all constructions involving *la³⁵*, the particle sits between the verb and one of a few sentence-final morphemes, such as the currently relevant state marker *wa³³* and the strong assertion particle *ŋɛi³³*. For example, the second clause in (1060), containing *la³⁵*, provides the reason for the speaker's forgetfulness, which is described in the first clause. Likewise, the second clause in (1061) describes the busy job of the speaker's uncle, which is the reason why he was not able to teach his nephew to play the *qin*, a banjo-like instrument popular among the Khatso.

(1060) [tɕi³¹ tsv̩²⁴   to³³   ma³¹   sŋ̍⁵⁵   wa³³   mɛi⁴⁴,   tɕi³³tɕʰa⁵⁵kʰv̩³³ ni⁵³].
       everything also   NEG   know   CRS   DSC.EMP this.time   TOP
       什么   也   不   知道   这时侯
       '(I) don't know anything anymore, these days.'
       现在什么也不知道了。

[ky̩³¹ tʰiɛ³³ ky̩³¹ ti³⁵ ta⁵⁵ **la³⁵** wa³³].
old heaven old land be.type FOC CRS
古 天 古 地 样
'Because (I'm) old now.'
成老古人了。
(YJF-Dance Parties)

(1061) [a³³ tsɛi³⁵ i³³ kɛi⁴⁴ to³³ ma³¹ ma⁵⁵ ta³³].
that CL:TMP 3SG AGT also NEG teach IPFV.IRR
那 段 他 也 不 教
'He didn't teach (me) either then.'
那时候也不是他教的。

[i⁴⁴ to³³ ɕa³³tsɛi³⁵fv̩³¹ mɛi⁴⁴ tso³²³ **la³⁵** ŋa³³].
3SG also village.government CL:GEN EXIST FOC ASRT
他 也 乡政府 个 有
'Because he was also in the village government.'
他是在乡政府的。
(YLW-Learning)

The *la³⁵* construction creates no syntactic integration between the relevant clauses. It may also be replaced by a tone change pattern. These properties are described further in § 13.1.3.3.

14.1.4 Borrowed Reason Conjunction

In addition to the more traditional reason expressions, the Chinese conjunction *yīnwèi* 因为 'because' has also been borrowed into Khatso. As with many newer loans, there are several pronunciations in use: *jɛ³³wi³⁵*, *jɛ³³wi⁴⁴* and *i³³wi³⁵*. The conjunction seems to be used largely by those who speak Chinese regularly; it has not yet superseded the traditional constructions for most speakers.

In Chinese, *yīnwèi* canonically begins the reason clause, which precedes the matrix clause. In conversation, however, the order is much more flexible. This flexibility is apparent in Khatso as well. In (1062), for example, the reason clause is the first of the two. By contrast, in (1063), it occurs after the matrix clause. Note that the borrowed conjunction begins the reason clause, following Chinese syntax, rather than the more traditional clause-final position in Khatso. Also, these clauses are often uttered as separate intonation units, which is less likely with the more traditional reason constructions.

(1062) **i³³wi³⁵**   [mo³²³kɣ³¹pʰa³¹   ko⁵⁵   tɕʰa³²³ta³⁵   ja³³],
because Mongol.M   CL:PL   be.powerful   IPFV.EMP
因为   蒙古人   些   强大
'Because (the) Mongols were powerful,'
因为蒙古人很强大，

[i³³   tɣ³¹   tsɤ³¹   ma³¹   tsɣ³⁵].
3SG   resist   CONT   NEG   hold
他   抵   不   住
'He (could) not resist (them).'
他抵不住。
(KLT-History)

(1063) [ŋ³¹   si³⁵   tsɿ⁵⁵miɛ⁵⁵   tɣ⁴⁴   kua³³sɿ³⁵   a³³   ma⁴⁴   kau³¹   kɯ³²³
two   three CL:ITEM   all   relationship that CL:GEN manage CSC
两   三   都   关系   那   个   摘

na²⁴   tʰɛi³²³   ja³³],
be.good very   IPFV.EMP
好   很
'(My) two or three sisters-in-law all got along very well.'
妯娌两个都把关系处理得很好。

jɛ³³wi⁴⁴   [mɛi⁴⁴   zɛi³¹   ta³²³   ja³³   i³³ ɣ³²³ i³³].
because   very   be.patient be.able IPFV.EMP RECP
因为   很   耐心   能   互相
'Because (they) were able to be very patient, one to another.'
因为相互之间很有耐心。
(HPH-Family)

Although a reason clause does not present a complete semantic idea, clauses linked by this borrowed conjunction in Khatso have no real syntactic integration. Arguments need not be shared between clauses. And, the clauses may be marked separately by both aspect and sentence-final particles, which only have scope over the particular clause they modify. Likewise, negation may occur in either clause or both clauses, and its scope is local.

14.2 Cause and Effect Strategies

In cause and effect constructions, clauses are combined to join an event with the situation that brought it about. There are a number of ways to communicate this type of relationship in Khatso. Aside from the borrowed conjunction, these formulations all have several different functions depending on context. For example, the adverb *tɕo³⁵* 'then' and the expression *ja⁵³ ni³²³* 'then, later', both of which typically mark sequentiality, are routinely employed to describe cause and effect relationships, as explained in § 14.2.1. The clause linker *tɤ⁴⁴* may also be so interpreted in certain circumstances, as outlined in § 14.2.2. The focus particle *la³⁵* often links a result or effect with a previous idea in discourse, but the information presented is much more prominent as a result, as discussed in § 14.2.3. There are also several adverbs meaning 'more, even more' that create comparative conditional constructions, which likewise point to causes and effects, as described in § 14.2.4. And finally, the borrowed conjunction *so³¹ʐŋ³¹* 'so, therefore' is likewise employed by some speakers, as discussed in § 14.2.5. Conditional constructions, which inherently contain a causal though irrealis relationship, are detailed separately in § 14.4.

14.2.1 Cause and Effect Strategy with *tɕo³⁵* and *ja⁵³ ni³²³*

As previously described, the adverb *tɕo³⁵* 'then, so then' and the semantically similar expression *ja⁵³ ni³²³* 'later, then' mark sequential order between clauses (see § 13.2.4.1 and § 13.2.4.2 respectively). Depending on context, these constructions may also indicate a cause and effect relationship. Syntactically, these clauses are independent; there is no integration beyond the pragmatics. Examples are shown in (1064) and (1065).

(1064) [kʰo⁵³tʰa³¹   n̠ɛ²⁴   sl³²³,
        age   be.small   TMP
        年龄   小
        'When (I) was young,'
        年轻的时候,

        la²⁴ka³³ kɤ³²³   ma³¹   tso³²³].
        play   place   NEG   EXIST
        玩   地方   不   有
        'There was no place to play.'
        没有玩的地方。

        tɕo³⁵ [tsʰo³³ɣɤ²⁴ma³³ ko⁵⁵   kɯ³³   tsɤ³¹   tɤ⁴⁴],
        then   adult   CL:PL enter   CONT   STAT.EMP
        就   人大   些   进
        'So, (I) was always with the adults'
        就跟着大人们,

[pɤ⁵³ so²⁴].
play learn
弹   学
'(And) learned to play (the *qin*).'
学弹。
(YLW-Learning)

(1065) [ŋa³³tsʰɤ³¹ ta³⁵ o³¹ tsʰɿ³²³ pa³²³ n̪ɛ³²³ a³³tɕʰa⁵⁵kʰv̩³³ tɕi³³ni³³ lo³¹sɿ²⁴
       1PL   still five seven eight CL:TMP that.time   this.way much
       我们   又 五 七   八 年   那时候   这么   很多
m̩³³ ma³¹ li³²³ sɛi³¹].
do NEG know.how still
做   不   会   还
'We, (in) '57 and '58 that time, didn't yet know how to work.'
我们呢，五七八年那个时候还不太会干活。

ja⁵³ ni³²³, [tɕi³³ni³³ kv̩³³ tso²⁴ ma³¹ ko⁵³].
later   this.way do   ITER NEG EXP
然后   这么   做   不   过
'So, (we) didn't do (it) a lot.'
所以没有这么做过。
(YBF-Three Ladies)

14.2.2 Cause and Effect Strategy with *tɤ⁴⁴*

While *tɤ⁴⁴* is associated primarily with the purpose construction (see § 14.6), one variation denotes a cause and effect relationship. In this construction, the second clause contains a stative verb which describes a state brought about by the activity in the first clause. The resultant state is usually not planned, but rather inadvertent or uncontrolled, which is why it is considered an effect rather than a purpose. For example, the phrase in (1066) describes a situation in which one becomes angry because of walking, perhaps because of becoming lost or having missed a bus. Likewise, the examples in (1067) and (1068) describe the unforeseen results of common activities. In addition to simple statives, the second clause may also include a resultative serial verb construction or a complex stative construction — essentially any formulation that conveys an ongoing state.

(1066) [ka³²³]   tɤ⁴⁴   [ɕɛ⁵⁵fɤ³⁵]
       walk   CLNK   be.furious
       走   愤怒
       'walk until furious' / 'become furious from walking'
       走得愤怒
       (KL-Elicitation)

(1067) nɛi³³   ŋ³¹   pɛi³²³ti³⁵   ni³¹   [ŋ³³]   tɤ⁴⁴   [ma³¹ sɤ³³fɤ²⁴]   ni³¹.
       2SG   FILL otherwise   TOP   sit   CLNK   NEG be.comfortable TOP
       你   要不然   坐   不 舒服
       'You, uh, otherwise, (you) will be uncomfortable from sitting.'
       要不然你坐得不舒服了。
       (KL-Doctor)

(1068) [tɕa³³tʰi³²³ a³³   ko⁵⁵   sɿ⁴⁴   kɤ³³]   tɤ⁴⁴   [tʰua³²³tɕɛ³²³   tʰɛi³²³   ja³²³].
       family   that CL:PL COP   do   CLNK   be.united   very   PFV.EMP
       家庭   那   些   是   做   团结   很
       '(They) made (it so) those families were harmonious.'
       那些家庭弄的很和睦。
       (HPH-Family)

Like all *tɤ⁴⁴* constructions, this variation is syntactically integrated. The arguments need not be identical, but aspect marking may occur only in the second clause. Semantically, the construction is similar to resultative serial verb constructions, in which verbs conveying an event and its result are adjacent with no marking. The key syntactic difference is that the arguments may be different in the *tɤ⁴⁴* construction, which is not possible in a verb serialization. Resultative serial verb constructions are described further in § 8.8.1.2.

The *tɤ⁴⁴* construction may also denote the manner in which an event is performed, but in the latter the stative verb occurs in the first clause rather than the second (see § 14.5). Like the manner counterpart, the cause and effect construction may be a loan from Chinese. In Putonghua, the particle *de* 得, pronounced [tɤ] with neutral tone and homophonous with the adverbial *de* 地, is used in just this way; it links a cause in the first clause to a state in the second.

14.2.3 Cause and Effect Strategy with *la³⁵* or Related Tone Change

As described earlier, the focus particle *la³⁵* links a clause pragmatically to an earlier comment in discourse. This link may be interpreted in a number of ways — from contrastive emphasis to explanation. It is also employed to link an effect to a previously mentioned cause. For example, in (1069) the second clause highlights a result related to the scenario described in the first clause. Tone change may replace the use of *la³⁵* in some functions; this process is described further in § 13.2.5. A more detailed description of the properties of *la³⁵* is provided in § 13.1.3.3.

(1069) ma³¹   mo⁵⁵   pʏ⁵³   so²⁴   la²⁴   tsʰʏ³³   ni³¹,
      NEG   want   play   learn REL   PL   TOP
      不   要   弹   学   们
      'As for those who don't want to learn to play,'
      不想学弹的人呢,

      [ma³¹   pʏ⁵³   so²⁴   ta⁵⁵   **la³⁵**   ŋɛi³³].
      NEG   play   learn be.type FOC   ASRT
      不   弹   学   样
      '(They) just don't learn to play.'
      不学这样的。
      (YLW-Learning)

14.2.4 Borrowed Cause and Effect Conjunction

Many traditional Khatso clause-combining expressions have counterparts borrowed from Chinese, and this is the case with cause and effect constructions as well. The conjunction *so³¹ʐŋ³¹* 'so, therefore' tends to be used by Khatso speakers who also frequently speak Hanyu, but it has not yet superseded the traditional expressions. Following Chinese syntax, *so³¹ʐŋ³¹* often begins the second clause, i.e. the effect clause, but in discourse the order is flexible. An example is shown in (1070).

(1070) jɛ³³wi³⁵   [i³³   kʰa⁵⁵tso³¹tɕʰi³¹   n̪a³¹   ma³¹   li³²³],
      because   3SG   Khatso.language   speak   NEG   know.how
      因为   他   喀卓语   说   不   会

      so³¹ʐŋ³¹   [kʏ³³   ma³¹   ta³²³].
      so   do   NEG   be.able
      所以   做   不   能
      'Because he doesn't know how to speak Khatso, (he) can't do (the work).'
      因为他不会讲喀卓语,所以他不能做。
      (KL-Elicitation)

14.3 Concessive Strategies

Concessive constructions link two clauses, one of which describes a situation that may be expected to prevent the event described in the other, but in the end does not. The primary strategy for syntactically linking clauses in this manner involves the adverb *to³³* 'also' (§ 14.3.1). The borrowed conjunction *suɛi³¹za³²³* 'although' is also employed in discourse, however (§ 14.3.2).

14.3.1 Concessive Strategy with *to³³*

The adverb *to³³* 'also' is often employed to link clauses, and context may assign it a coordinative or adversative meaning (see § 13.1.1.2 and § 13.1.3.2 respectively). This second function, which often introduces contrastive or contrary information, is the basis of the concessive construction. There are several variations, but in all cases the first clause is the concession and the second is the unaffected event. Often, the first clause contains the strong assertion particle *ŋɛi³³* and is presented as a complement of the quotative verb *tɕi³³* 'to say', which is then linked to the primary event by *to³³*. Examples are presented in (1071), (1072) and (1073). The first shows the canonical construction; the second omits the strong assertion particle. In the third example, *to³³* is replaced by the adversative conjunction *ŋ⁴⁴li³³* 'but' (see § 13.1.3.1). The adverb is also repeated in the final clause, which is not unusual — often the clause containing the unaffected event will contain a pragmatically-linking adverb such as *to³³* 'also, but', *xɛi³⁵* 'still' or *sɛi³¹* 'again, still'. Also, note that *to³³* may trigger tone change in the preceding syllable (see § 3.2.4.1).

(1071) [xɤ³³   ŋɛi³³]   **tɕi⁴⁴**   **to³³**   [i³³   tɕo³⁵   ma³¹   ɣɤ³⁵   tso²⁴].
scold   ASRT   say   also   3SG   then   NEG   move   ITER
骂   说   也   他   就   不   动
'(Although you) scold (him), he doesn't move.'
骂他，他就是不动。
(PRL-Education)

(1072) ma³¹   tɕɛ⁵⁵   pa³²³   wa³³   **tɕi⁴⁴**   **to³³**,
NEG   sew   help   CRS   say   also
不   钉   帮   说   也
'(Although I) say (I) can't help sew anymore,'
也说不帮钉了,

fɤ³⁵   ma³¹   tso³²³   pa³¹.
way   NEG   EXIST   IMP.SOL
办法   不   有

'There's nothing (I) can do.' [i.e. people still bring clothes to be sewn]
没有办法。
(WYY-Sewing)

(1073) [tɕi³³   tsɛi³⁵   ni³¹   tɛi³³ni³³   ɕi³³   nɛi³³]   **tɕi³³**   **ŋ⁴⁴li³³,**
       this   CL:TMP   TOP   this.way   be.accustomed ASRT   say   but
       这   段   这么   习惯   说   但是

'Nowadays, although (we Khatso) are used to doing (it) like this, but,'
现在呢虽然会这么做，

tɤ⁴⁴   [a³³   tɕi⁵⁵   ni³¹,
FILL   that   CL:TYPE TOP
        那   种

'Uh, that type,'
那么，那种呢，

pʰi²⁴ŋ²⁴   ko⁵⁵   to³³   ɕi³³],   ŋ⁴⁴   ŋuo³¹?
Han   CL:PL   also   be.accustomed   COP   COP.Q
汉   些   也   习惯   是

'Han people are accustomed (to it) too, isn't that right?'
汉人也会，是吧？
(YBF-Three Ladies)

The presence of *tɕi³³* is dependent on the aspect of the concessive clause. It is usually associated with future events, general states and events that did not happen. With perfective events, *tɕi³³* is ungrammatical; *to³³* is typically used alone in these cases, as (1074) illustrates.

(1074) [pɤ³¹   wa²⁴]   **to³³**   [xɛi³⁵   tsa³²³   ma³¹   tsa⁵⁵].
       dance   PFV   also   still   rice   NEG   feed
       娱乐   也   还   饭   不   喂

'(Although we) danced, still (they) wouldn't feed (us).'
跳了也还不给饭吃。
(GCS-Dance Parties)

Thus, in the right context, the presence of *to³³* alone is enough to signal a concessive relationship. For example, in (1075) *to³³* may be analyzed as a simple clausal conjunction — its primary clause-combining function — as the first translation demonstrates. However, because there is a pragmatic contrast between the first and third clauses, *to³³* may just as easily be translated as a concessive particle.

(1075) [ŋa³³tsʰʏ³¹   ka³²³   tʏ⁴⁴   xa³³n̯a⁵³   tsʰŋ⁴⁴]   **to³³**,
       1PL   walk   CLNK   where   arrive   and
       我们   走   哪里   到   也

   [tɕʰi⁵³   ti⁴⁴   ti³³ni³³   mi³²³   tso³²³   la²⁴   tɕi⁵⁵,
    play   CLNK   this.way   be.accurate   EXIST   REL   CL:TYPE
    咬   这么   明确   有   种

   na²⁴   ma³¹   mʏ³³   wa³³   piɛ⁴⁴liɛ⁴⁴].
   hear   NEG   achieve   CRS   EMP
   听   不   着

   'We go all over, and never hear anyone who plays this well.' / 'Although we go all over, (we) never hear anyone who plays this well.'
   我们走到哪里也听不着弹的这么准确的啦。
   (YAY-Erasers)

Since the concessive construction, regardless of the exact formulation, is based on the conjunction *to³³*, its two clauses are not syntactically integrated. Each clause may contain a different argument, different aspect marking and even different emphatic particles. Neither clause is subordinate to the other; both may serve as a matrix clause.

14.3.2 Borrowed Concessive Conjunction

Consistent with the other clause-linking strategies, a Chinese loan may replace the more traditional concessive construction. This loan, *suɛi³¹za³²³* or *suɛi³³za³²³* 'although', is typically placed after the A/S of the first clause, which contains the concession; the second clause details the primary event, and often includes an adverb such as *to³³* 'also' or *xɛi³⁵* 'still'. The syntax is likewise borrowed from Chinese. An example is shown in (1076).

(1076) [i³³   **suɛi³³za³²³**   mɛi³¹kuo³²³pʰa³¹   jo³⁵]   [to³³   kʰa⁵⁵tso³¹tɕʰi³¹   n̯a³¹
       3SG   although   American.M   CL:HUM   also   Khatso.language   speak
       他   虽然   美国男人   位   也   喀卓语   说

   li³²³   ja³³].
   know.how   IPFV.EMP
   会

   'Although he (is) American, (he) can also speak Khatso.'
   他虽然是美国人，也会说喀卓语。
   (KL-Elicitation)

As with its more traditional counterpart above, there is no syntactic integration in this construction. The two clauses may contain different arguments as well as different aspect or emphatic particles. The concession clause, however, is semantically incomplete. The presence of $suɛi^{31}za^{323}$ signals to the interlocutor that another clause will follow.

14.4 Conditional Constructions

Conditional constructions express unrealized propositions that depend on a condition that has not yet occurred or is hypothetical. In many languages, conditions and topics are treated identically, since both provide a frame of reference against which the main clause is understood (Haiman 1978). This is the case in Khatso as well. The basic conditional construction contains the topic marker ni^{31}, which appears in both positive and negative constructions, as discussed in § 14.4.1. Universal conditionals, however, rely on the expression $tɕi^{44}$ to^{33}, as outlined in § 14.4.2. The concessive conditional, described in § 14.4.3, is now rare in modern Khatso. In addition, a conditional conjunction borrowed from Chinese may also be employed, as discussed in § 14.4.4. Despite the presence of unrealized events, the irrealis aspect markers are unnecessary in these constructions.

Other clause-combining constructions may also indicate a conditional relationship. Those involving $sa^{24}kɛi^{33}$ 'until' are discussed in § 13.2.4.5, while those relating to causes and effects are described in § 14.2. Concessive constructions (see § 14.3), which relate a result clause to a factual event or state, are likewise similar to conditional constructions. In some cases, the constructions just mentioned may be employed in place of the conditionals described in this section.

14.4.1 Conditional Construction with ni^{31}

The particle ni^{31} is employed to mark topics in discourse, which may include words or phrases of any syntactic form, from single nouns to clauses (see § 10.1). When discourse context indicates that a clause modified by ni^{31} is irrealis, it may be interpreted as a condition which, if realized, would result in the event presented in the following clause. Examples are presented in (1077) and (1078). The adverb $tɕo^{35}$ 'then' often appears in the second clause, further highlighting the logical link between the two clauses. While the canonical position for the ni^{31} clause is before the matrix clause, it may follow instead as an afterthought, as in (1079). Also note that ni^{31} may trigger tone change in the preceding syllable (see § 3.2.4.1).

(1077) [tsɤ⁵³ mɤ²⁴]   **ni³¹**   [tɕo³⁵ tʰɤ⁵⁵   tʰɤ⁵⁵   tsɤ⁵³].
beat have.time TOP then CL:TMP CL:TMP beat
打 有空 就 下 下 打
'If (I) have time to do (it), then (I'll) do (it) for a while.'
有空打呢就打一下。
(WYF-Stools)

(1078) [ti⁵³   tso⁵⁵ tɕɛ²⁴]   **ni³¹**   [tɕo³⁵ tɤ⁴⁴ kɯ²⁴ta³³ tɕi³³ ma⁴⁴ ma³¹ tso³²³
CL:PCE pull be.tight TOP then all knot this CL:GEN NEG EXIST
点 拉 紧 就 都 结 这 个 不 有
wa³³].
CRS
'If (you) pull (it) tighter, then there won't be this knot.'
拉紧一点呢，这个结就没有了。
(WYY-Sewing)

(1079) [tsʰo³¹to³³   mɛi⁴⁴   tɕʰɛ⁵³   wa³²³],
straw.stool CL:GEN finish PFV
草墩 个 完
'(You) finish the straw stool,'
成草墩了，

[tsa³⁵fʏ³³ ko⁵⁵ ta⁵³   tɕʰɛ⁵³]   **ni³¹**.
rope CL:PL put.on finish TOP
绳子 些 上 完
'Having put on the rope.'
上完绳子呢。
(WYF-Stools)

There are many similarities between discourse topics and conditionals (Haiman 1978), which explains why *ni³¹* is used to mark both in Khatso. Semantically, the *ni³¹* clause may be interpreted as a topic, a condition or a temporal expression — there is often little difference between the three. Consider the first clause in (1080). It may be understood as the topic 'doing (it) that way', the condition 'if (you) do (it) that way' or the temporal clause 'when (you) do (it) that way'. In Khatso, these various interpretations are equally possible because each establishes a pre-condition for the following clause.

(1080) [kɤ³³ tɤ⁴⁴ tɛi³³ ta⁵⁵]   **ni³¹**   [tɕo³⁵ li⁵⁵   tso²⁴ wa³⁵ po⁵³].
       do   CLNK this be.type   TOP   then move ITER FUT EPIS.EMP
       做   这   样   就   摇
       'Doing (it) that way,
       'If (you) do (it) that way,   ⎫
       'When (you) do (it) that way,   ⎬ (it) will move (around).'
                                        ⎭
       做得这样呢，就会摇了。
       (WYY-Sewing)

The use of the topic and temporal marker *sɛi⁴⁴* at times overlaps with that of *ni³¹*. However, *sɛi⁴⁴* can only co-occur with factual and not hypothetical information, and so it is not used in conditional constructions, which is one of the main differences between the two particles. For an overview of these particles and their functions, see § 16.3 and § 6.6 respectively.

Some languages, such as English and Putonghua, have lexemes or constructions dedicated to negative conditionals which convey notions like *chúfēi* 除非 'unless' or *yàobushì* 要不是 'if not for'. Khatso has none of these; negating a condition clause marked by *ni³¹* is enough to express this type of relationship. For example, the phrase in (1081) may be translated with these more specialized constructions, but the Khatso construction itself is a simple conditional.

(1081) [**ma³¹** kʰv²⁴]   **ni³¹**   [mɤ³²³   ma³¹   li³²³   sa⁴⁴]?
       NEG   be.empty   TOP   make.noise NEG   know.how   CRTN.Q
       不   空   响   不   会
       'Not being empty,
       'Unless (it) is empty,   ⎫
                                       ⎬ (it) won't make noise?'
       'If not for being empty,   ⎭
       不空呢，不会响吗？
       (KL-Qin)

The conditional may also be employed to introduce exceptions or additions, either of which may be noun phrases or clauses. In this construction, the topicalized condition clause ends with the verb serialization *to⁵³ no⁵³*, which is composed of *to⁵³* 'exit' and the resultative *no⁵³* 'complete', which together mean 'excluded' but more colloquially correspond to 'except for, besides' in English. When the exception or addition is a clause, it requires the clause linker *tɤ⁴⁴* to join it with *to⁵³ no⁵³*. Examples of both types are shown in (1082) and (1083). This construction may be replaced with the Hanyu loan *zŋ³¹wɛi³⁵* 'outside, besides', as shown in (1084).

(1082) [i³³] **to⁵³ no⁵³ ni³¹** [ŋa³³tsʰɤ³³ tɛi³¹ ko⁵⁵ tɤ⁴⁴ kʰa⁵⁵tso³¹tɕʰi³¹ n̠a³¹
       3SG   excluded TOP   1PL   one   CL:PL all   Khatso.language speak
       他   出好   我们   一   些   都   喀卓语   说
       li³²³   ja³³].
       know.how   IPFV.EMP
       会
       'Except for him, we all know how to speak Khatso.'
       除了他以外，我们都会说喀卓语。
       (KL-Elicitation)

(1083) [mo³²³kɤ³¹ i³²³] **tɤ⁴⁴ to⁵³ no⁵³ ni³¹** [pɤ²⁴tɕi⁴⁴ to³³ i³²³ wa³²³].
       Mongolia go   CLNK excluded TOP   Beijing   also go   PFV
       蒙古   去   出好   北京   也   去
       'Aside from going to Mongolia, (we) also went to Beijing.'
       除了去蒙古以外也去了北京。
       (KL-Elicitation)

(1084) [mo³²³kɤ³¹ i³²³] **zɿ³¹wɛi³⁵ ni³¹** [pɤ²⁴tɕi⁴⁴ to³³ i³²³ wa³²³].
       Mongolia go   besides   TOP   Beijing   also go   PFV
       蒙古   去   以外   北京   也   去
       'Besides going to Mongolia, (we) also went to Beijing.'
       除了去蒙古以外也去了北京。
       (KL-Elicitation)

Aspect is restricted in the condition clause. Typically, only the progressive aspect markers may appear, though they are not obligatory. However, serial verb constructions containing verbs that lexically convey aspectual information are possible, such as the resultative *tɕʰɛ⁵³* 'finish' in (1079) above. There are no limitations to aspect marking in the second clause. The adverb *tɕo³⁵* 'then' often occurs in this clause, marking both sequential action and result, but it is not necessary. Consequently, there is no syntactic difference between past or future events, or between real, hypothetical or counterfactual events. Thus, pragmatics plays an important role in parsing the meaning of any given instance of *ni³¹*.

Given the restriction on aspect in the condition clause, it can be considered dependent on the result clause. If the latter is marked for aspect, it may have scope over the entire construction, though this varies according to the condition presented. If it is an ongoing situation or state, then the aspect may not logically apply. Arguments need not be shared across the clauses. And negation, too, works independently in the two clauses. Semantically, a *ni³¹* clause is not considered a complete idea, but rather the set-up for the result clause. The latter, by contrast, may serve as a stand-alone matrix clause.

14.4.2 Universal Conditional Construction

When the condition is universal — that is, when it encompasses all possible options — the topic marker ni^{31} is not used to link the clauses. Instead, a concessive construction involving to^{33} 'also' is employed (see § 14.3.1). If there are only two choices, then typically the verb in the condition clause will be presented in both positive and negative forms, as shown in (1085). Note that the insertion of ma^{31} prevents this type of reduplication from being interpreted as a polar question (see § 12.4.1). If there are multiple options, then an interrogative pronoun is used instead, lending an indefinite reading to the construction, as (1086) illustrates. One such formulation, $xa^{33}ni^{33}\ ji^{44}\ to^{33}$, literally 'whatever (one) says', has become a routinized expression that means 'in any case, no matter what', as shown in (1087).

(1085) [i³³   li³²³   **ma³¹**   li³²³   ŋɛi³³]   tɕi⁴⁴   **to³³**   [ŋa³³tsʰɤ³³   ka³²³   wa³⁵].
      3SG   come   NEG   come   ASRT   say   also   1PL   walk   FUT
      他   来   不   来   说   也   我们   走
      'Whether he comes or not, we will go.'
      无论他来不来，我们都要走了。
      (KL-Elicitation)

(1086) [i³³   kɛi³³   **xa³³ni³³**   tɕi³³   ŋɛi³³]   tɕi⁴⁴   **to³³**   [ŋa³³   kʰua³¹la³¹   i³²³   wa³⁵].
      3SG   AGT   how   say   ASRT   say   also   1SG   Kunming   go   FUT
      他   怎么   说   说   也   我   昆明   去
      'Whatever he says, I'll go to Kunming.'
      无论他说什么，我都要去昆明。
      (KL-Elicitation)

(1087) **xa³³ni³³**   tɕi⁴⁴   **to³³**   [ŋa³³   kʰua³¹la³¹   i³²³   wa³⁵].
      how   say   also   1SG   Kunming   go   FUT
      怎么   说   也   我   昆明   去
      'No matter what, I'll go to Kunming.', literally 'Whatever (one) says, I'll go to Kunming.'
      无论如何，我都要去昆明了。
      (KL-Elicitation)

14.4.3 Concessive Conditional Construction

In the concessive conditional construction, the first clause presents a condition that may be expected to, but in the end does not, prevent the event described in the second clause. In this construction, $nɛi^{33}tɕo^{35}$ 'even, even if, even though' precedes the first clause, and *to*^{33} 'also' links the second clause to the first. An example is presented in (1088); recall that *to*^{33} may trigger tone change in the preceding syllable (see § 3.2.4.1).

(1088) **nɛi³³tɕo³⁵** [i³³tsʰɣ³³ kɛi³³ tɕʰɛ³²³ kɯ²⁴] **to³³** [ŋa³³ ma³¹ i³²³].
even 3PL AGT money give also 1SG NEG go
即使 他们 钱 给 也 我 不 去
'Even (if) they give money, I still won't go.', literally 'Even (if) they give money, I also won't go.'
即使是他们给钱，我也不去。
(KL-Elicitation)

This seems to be an older construction that has fallen out of favor with modern speakers — the only examples available come from elicitation rather than the corpus. Today, the more basic concessive construction is employed instead; it may be interpreted as conditional depending on context (see § 14.3.1).

14.4.4 Comparative Conditional Construction with *i²⁴fa³³*, *i³¹kɯ³⁵*, *to³³i³¹*

There are a number of adverbs that mean 'more, even more' in Khatso — *i²⁴fa³³*, *i³¹kɯ³⁵* and *to³³i³¹* — and they are essentially identical in function and meaning. In addition to modifying verbs in implicit single clause comparisons (see § 12.5.5.1), they also combine clauses in a comparative conditional relationship. Whichever adverb is employed, it occurs before the verb in each clause, and the first clause is marked by the topic marker *ni³¹*, consistent with its use in simple conditional clauses (see § 14.4.1). The resulting construction indicates that the increase in activity described in the first clause creates a condition which may lead to an increase in the activity described in the second. An example with *i²⁴fa³³* is shown in (1089). The other two adverbs may operate in the same way, but in discourse *i²⁴fa³³* is preferred in this construction. Note that the topic marker may trigger tone change in the preceding syllable (see § 3.2.4.1).

(1089) [i²⁴fa³³ n̠a²⁴] **ni³¹** [i²⁴fa³³ n̠ɛ²⁴ ka³²³ i³³ tɣ³⁵ mɛi⁴⁴].
more speak TOP more be.small walk go PROG.FOC DSC.EMP
越 说 越 小 走 去
'The more (you) talk the quieter (your voice) gets.'
越说声音越发小。
(KL-Grandfather)

This construction shows a degree of integration similar to that of the other uses of *ni³¹*, which may be considered a simultaneous temporal marker here. The clauses need not share the same arguments, as (1090) shows, but aspect is restricted to the second clause if present, which has scope over both clauses.

(1090) [i³³   i²⁴fa³³   to³²³   mɣ⁴⁴]   **ni³¹**   [ŋa³³   i²⁴fa³³   tɕo⁵³]   ja³³·
       3SG   more   drink   be.dizzy TOP   1SG   more   fear   IPFV.EMP
       他   越   喝   晕   我   越   害怕
       'The more he drinks the more afraid I (become).'
       他越喝醉我越害怕。
       (KL-Elicitation)

As previously mentioned, *ni³¹* has a number of functions. Its use as a topic marker is described in § 10.1. Its role in linking sequential clauses is discussed in § 13.2.4.4, which is related to its use in reason expressions, explained in § 14.1.2. An overview of the multiple functions of *ni³¹* is provided in § 16.3.

14.4.5 Borrowed Conditional Conjunction

A construction based on the Chinese loanword *zɣ³²³ko³¹* 'if' may replace the traditional conditional expressions. It begins the first clause, which describes the condition; the second clause contains the result. An example from discourse is shown in (1091). Like many borrowed conjunctions, *zɣ³²³ko³¹* is often followed by *sɿ³²³sɿ⁴⁴* or just *sɿ⁴⁴*, which appear to be related to the Hanyu copula; but this collocation is not obligatory. Likewise, the traditional Khatso topic marker may occur at the end of the condition clause, thus combining the traditional and borrowed formulations, but this too is optional.

(1091) **zɣ³²³ko³¹**   sɿ³²³sɿ⁴⁴   [kʰo³¹zɿ³¹   ja³³]   tɕi⁴⁴]   ni³¹   tɕo³⁵,
       if   COP   be.able   IPFV.EMP   say   TOP   then
       如果   是   可以   说   就

[nɛi³³   tɕo³⁵   jɛ³⁵zɿ³⁵   tɕi³³   tʰɣ⁵⁵   tɕi³³   jo³⁵   ŋɛi³³].
 2SG   then   be.willling   this   CL:TMP   say   must.FOC   ASRT
 你   就   愿意   这   下   说   应该
'If (you) can, then you should say you're willing.'
如果说是可以的，你就说一下愿意的。
(KL-Childhood)

As in the traditional construction, the condition here is a dependent clause. Aspect is restricted in this clause, which is not the case in the matrix clause. Moreover, the condition clause is not considered a complete semantic idea; a follow-on clause is expected.

14.5 Manner Constructions with *tɤ⁴⁴* and *sɛi⁴⁴*

Because attributes are conveyed by stative verbs in Khatso (see § 8.1.2), describing the manner in which an activity is performed may require clause combining. Both the clause linker *tɤ⁴⁴* and the complementation-related topic marker *sɛi⁴⁴* may be used for this purpose. Stative verbs also take part in an adverbial construction that obviates the need to combine clauses (see § 8.1.2.2).

As already noted, the clause linker *tɤ⁴⁴* may combine clauses for several different purposes (see § 16.5 for an overview). One such is to link clauses that occur simultaneously, and this may be the origin of the manner construction involving *tɤ⁴⁴*. In this construction, the linker occurs at the end of the stative verb clause and is followed by the clause describing the primary event. Examples are shown in (1092) and (1093). Intensifiers may modify the stative verb, but aspect or other phrase-final markers are excluded from the first clause, as they are in all *tɤ⁴⁴* constructions. See § 14.6 for a discussion on the degree of integration in these constructions.

(1092) [kɤ³¹tsɤ³¹] **tɤ⁴⁴** [ka³²³] la²⁴ tsʰɤ³³
     be.stubborn CLNK walk REL PL
     固执   走   们
     'the ones who walk stubbornly'
     那些固执地走的
     (YJF-Dance Parties)

(1093) [xo³¹] **tɤ⁴⁴** [z̩⁵³] m̩²⁴ tsɛi³⁵ tsɛi³⁵ kɤ⁵⁵] tɤ³⁵ wa³³ po⁵³.
     be.soft CLNK sleep nap CL:TMP CL:TMP doze INCP.FOC EPIS.EMP
     软   睡   瞌   段   段   打
     'So, (I) now weakly doze off from time to time, (see?)'
     弱地一阵一阵地打瞌睡了呀。
     (WYY-Sewing)

However, stative verbs relating to speed, such as *tɕi³¹* 'to be fast' and *jo³³* and *pʰi³²³* 'to be slow', require a reverse formulation. That is, the stative verb occurs in the clause following *tɤ⁴⁴*, and the primary event precedes it, as (1094) and (1095) illustrate. It is unclear why these verbs require this difference; semantically there is no difference between this construction and the one just described. In fact, the stative clause is never construed as an effect here, even though this is possible with other stative verbs that occur in the second clause (see § 14.2.2). Moreover, not all potential matrix verbs may be combined with the speed verbs in this construction, a limitation that seems to depend on individual verbs rather than a definable pattern. This is not the only construction in which speed verbs deviate from the established pattern, however; they likewise cannot serve as adjective-like modifiers (see § 8.1.2.1).

(1094) [jo⁵³]   tɤ⁴⁴   [tɕi³¹]   wa³²³.
grow   CLNK   be.fast   PFV
长   快
'(It) grew quickly.'
长得快了。
(KL-Elicitation)

(1095) [fa³²³tsa³¹]   tɤ⁴⁴   [pʰi³²³   tʰɛi³²³]   ja³³.
develop   CLNK   be.slow   very   IPFV.EMP
发展   慢   很
'(It) is developing very slowly.'
发展得很慢。
(KL-Elicitation)

Although there is a logical link between this construction and the other tɤ⁴⁴ constructions (see § 16.5), this one also mirrors the Chinese adverbial construction, suggesting that it may be a loan. In Putonghua, the particle de 地, pronounced [tɤ] with neutral tone, follows a stative verb to make it adverbial, exactly like the Khatso construction. Often the Chinese verb is reduplicated, but the analogous reduplicative adverbial construction in Khatso requires a different particle, the adverbial marker ni³³ (see § 9.3.4). There is no appreciable difference in meaning between the ni³³ construction and the tɤ⁴⁴ manner construction just described.

Constructions involving the particle sɛi⁴⁴, which has temporal, topic and complementation functions, may also be interpreted as manner expressions. In this use, the primary event clause is marked by sɛi⁴⁴, and it may precede or follow the stative matrix clause. This syntax is, in fact, identical to that of the temporal and topicalizing sɛi⁴⁴ constructions; the difference here is pragmatic. When the matrix verb is a stative verb that may be construed to describe manner, then the phrase is interpreted as a manner construction, conveying the same meaning as the tɤ⁴⁴ construction described above. For example, more literal translations of the phrase in (1096) would be the temporal expression '(it) is very slow, when (we) do (it)' or the topic construction '(it) is very slow, our doing (it)', but speakers are just as likely to render it into Putonghua as '(we) do (it) very slowly.' The same holds for the example shown in (1097), where sa⁵⁵ 'to be bitter' has the colloquial sense of 'to be difficult'. An overview of the multiple functions of sɛi⁴⁴ is presented in § 16.6.

(1096) [mɛi⁴⁴ pʰi³²³   ja³³]   [ŋa³³tsʰɤ³¹ kɛi³³ kɤ³³] **sɛi⁴⁴**.
very   be.slow IPFV.EMP   1PL   AGT   do   TMP
很   慢   我们   做
'(We) do (it) very slowly.', literally '(It) is very slow, when (we) do (it).' or '(It) is very slow, our doing (it).'
我们做得很慢的。
(WYY-Sewing)

(1097) o³¹   tsɿ³²³   pa³²³   n̪ɛ³²³   ni³¹   [tɕo³⁵ n̪o³¹   m̪³³   **sɛi⁴⁴**] [sa⁵⁵].
five seven   eight   CL:TMP   TOP   then   thing   do   TMP   be.bitter
五   七   八   年   就   东西   做   苦
'(In) '57 and '58, (we) worked (with) difficulty.', literally '(In) '57 and '58, when (we) worked, (it) was difficult.' or '(In) '57 and '58, our working, (it) was difficult.'
五七八年呢就干活，干得苦。
(YJF-Childhood)

The *tɤ⁴⁴* construction shows a certain degree of integration. The A/S arguments must be identical, and aspect may only be marked on the second clause, which may have scope over both. Even considering the speed verb exceptions, clause order is fixed, and so center embedding is not possible. For more details on the syntactic properties of *tɤ⁴⁴* constructions, see § 14.6. The *sɛi⁴⁴* construction is slightly less integrated, since the two clauses need not share arguments. Aspect marking is likewise restricted to the second clause. See § 15.1 for a more detailed discussion of the syntactic properties of *sɛi⁴⁴*.

These manner constructions overlap somewhat with the complex stative construction involving *kɯ³²³*, which also expresses manner (see § 8.8.1.4). However, the latter typically describes an ongoing situation or state which has no obvious temporal boundaries. The *tɤ⁴⁴* and *sɛi⁴⁴* manner constructions, by contrast, are often employed to describe events that occur at a particular moment in time, as in (1093) above, and which may therefore take any type of aspect marking.

14.6 Purpose Construction with *tɤ⁴⁴*

As previously discussed in § 8.8.2, certain two-event serial verb constructions link an event to a purpose, as shown in (1098). In these serializations, the two actions are so closely bound together that they are syntactically presented as a single predication. Moreover, the verbs share the same arguments and time frame, and neither is subordinate to the other.

(1098) tsɿ³²³ tsʰɿ³³ **kɤ³³ ŋ³¹**.
 liquor be.white make sell
 酒 白 弄 卖
 '(They) make white liquor to sell.'
 做白酒卖。
 (HPH-Horse Dug Well)

However, this is not the only way to combine an event with its purpose. The clause linker *tɤ⁴⁴* may more loosely link two clauses to express such a relationship. As already noted, the function of this particle is quite broad; it often introduces clauses that convey a purpose or effect or conjoins clauses that describe simultaneous events. Context clarifies which use is most relevant to the flow of information. In the purpose construction, *tɤ⁴⁴* occurs immediately after the verb conveying the main event and before the purpose clause. Examples are shown in (1099) and (1100).

(1099) [sɿ³⁵ tʰɛi³¹] **tɤ⁴⁴** [tsɤ³³].
 firewood pick CLNK burn
 柴 挑 烧
 '(We) gathered firewood to burn.'
 挑柴烧。
 (YJF-Childhood)

(1100) [ja³⁵ kɯ³³ tsɿ²⁴] **tɤ⁴⁴** [xa³³ma⁴⁴ m³³]?
 be.good gather rise CLNK what do
 好 收 起 什么 做
 '(You) are diligently gathering (them) up to do what?'
 好好地收起来做什么？
 (WYY-Sewing)

There are a number of verbs that routinely occur in purpose clauses. For example, the motion verbs *i³²³* 'to go', *li³²³* 'to come' and *tsʰŋ³³* 'to arrive, reach' are used with destinations, as shown in (1101). The latter verb, along with *lo⁵³* 'to be enough, to reach' is also employed in temporal clauses, as in (1102). Note that although locative and temporal purposes are often translated as prepositional phrases in English, in Khatso they always contain a verb in this construction.

(1101) [ja⁵³ tɛi³¹ ma²⁴ tsɤ⁵³] **tɤ⁴⁴** [lɛi³²³ tʰa⁵³ ta⁵⁵ i³⁵] wa³³.
 later one CL:GEN beat CLNK story top put go.FOC CRS
 然 一 个 打 楼 上 放 去
 'Later, (I) made one to put upstairs.'
 然后打一个放到楼上了。
 (WYF-Stools)

(1102) tɛi³¹ ta²⁴ ni³³ [lio³²³tsʰua³²³] tɤ⁴⁴ [tɛi³³tɕʰa⁵⁵kʰy³³ tsʰɻ³³] wa³²³.
one CL:ITEM ADV spread CLNK this.time arrive PFV
一 直 流传 这时候 到
'(It) has continuously spread (down) to modern times.'
一直流传到现在了。
(HPH-Horse Dug Well)

The verb kɯ³¹ 'to give' also frequently occurs in purpose clauses, where it is used with recipients and beneficiaries. Thus, the tɤ⁴⁴ expression provides an alternative to the applicative construction which also involves kɯ³¹ (see § 11.1). Like the applicative, the tɤ⁴⁴ construction does not syntactically differentiate between the two semantic roles; this is done through context. Examples (1103) and (1104) contain recipients, but note that the item given may be tangible or intangible. In the former it is a stool made of straw, but in the latter it is the Khatso language itself. An example containing a beneficiary is provided in (1105).

(1103) [tɛi³³ tɕi⁵⁵ tsɤ⁵³] tɤ⁴⁴ [za³¹m³¹ jo³⁵ kɯ³¹ i³³] sɛi⁴⁴ ni³¹ tɕo³⁵,
this CL:TYPE beat CLNK daughter CL:HUM give go TMP TOP then
这 种 打 女儿 位 给 去 就
'When making this type to give to my daughter,'
这种打给女儿呢就，

sɻ³²³pa³²³ kʰuai³¹ kɛi³³ sɻ³²³lɤ³²³ kʰuai³¹ kɛi³³ tɛi³³ni³³ mo⁵⁵ tɤ³⁵ ŋɛi³³.
ten.eight CL:MNY INS ten.six CL:MNY INS this.way require PROG.FOC ASRT
十八 块 用 十六 块 用 这么 要
'(It) takes 16 or 18 yuan.'
十八块和十六块这么要的。
(WYF-Stools)

(1104) [ja⁵³ ŋa³³ kʰa⁵⁵tso³¹tɕʰi³¹ n̥a³¹] tɤ⁴⁴ [nɛi³³tsʰɤ³³ kɯ³¹].
later 1SG Khatso.language speak CLNK 2PL give
那 我 喀卓语 说 你们 给
'So, I (will) speak Khatso to you.'
那我用喀卓语说给你们。
(KL-Childhood)

(1105) [nɛi³³ tɛi³¹ ma²⁴ vɤ³²³] tɤ⁴⁴ [ɲa³³ kɯ³¹ li³³] pa³¹.
2SG one CL:GEN buy CLNK 1SG give come IMP
你 一 个 买 找 给 米
'Buy one to give me.'
你买一个来给我吧。
(ZRF-Grandfather)

Regardless of meaning, $tɤ^{44}$ constructions show a high degree of integration. The two clauses often share arguments, though this is not obligatory with every matrix verb. However, subject raising is preferred wherever possible. That is, if the A/S of the second clause is different than that of the first clause, then it is placed in the first clause as P. Leaving it in the second clause is ungrammatical, as is having identical overt arguments in both clauses. An example is shown in (1106). With some matrix verbs, such as $tɕʰɛ^{35}$ 'to urge', a human argument is expected as P, undermining an analysis of raising. But with others, such as $a^{33}pʰai^{323}$ 'to arrange' in (1106), an inanimate P is the norm. Thus, there may be a situation in which the semantic argument of the second clause becomes a syntactic argument in the first clause — the prototypical pattern associated with subject raising (Noonan 2007: 79–83). Aspect marking also points to integration, since it is only possible at the end of the second clause, where it has scope over both clauses, as (1106) also demonstrates. Center embedding is not possible, however. That is, the purpose clause cannot be inserted into the matrix clause; the two are always separated by $tɤ^{44}$. Reduplicated polar questions and negation provide further evidence for integration. Only the verb in the second clause — the final verb in the sentence — may be reduplicated to form polar questions, as shown in (1107) and (1108). The resulting question applies to the entire premise of the sentence and not just to that clause. Negation, too, only occurs in the second clause, with scope over the entire construction, as (1109) and (1110) illustrate.

(1106) [ŋa³³ i³³ a³³pʰai³²³] **tɤ⁴⁴** [kʰua³¹la³¹ i³²³] wa³²³.
1SG 3SG arrange CLNK Kunming go PFV
我 他 安排 昆明 去
'I arranged (for) him to go to Kunming.'
我安排他去昆明了。
(KL-Elicitation)

(1107) [ʐɻ³¹mo³¹ tʰɛi³¹] **tɤ⁴⁴** [tsɤ³³ tsɤ³³]?
straw pick CLNK burn burn
茅草 挑 烧 烧
'(Did you) gather straw to burn?'
挑不挑茅草烧?
(KL-Elicitation)

(1108) [i³³ i³²³] **tɤ⁴⁴** [kʰua³¹la³¹ tsʰɻ³³ tsʰɻ³³]?
3SG go CLNK Kunming arrive arrive
她 去 昆明 到 到
'(Did) she go to Kunming?' / '(Did) she arrive in Kunming?'
她去不去到昆明? / 她到不到昆明?
(KL-Elicitation)

(1109) [ẓ³¹mo³¹ tʰɛi³¹] **tɤ⁴⁴** [ma³¹ tsɤ³³ la³¹].
straw   pick   CLNK   NEG burn PFV.IRR
茅草   挑   不   烧
'(We) didn't gather straw to burn.'
不挑茅草烧。
(KL-Elicitation)

(1110) [vɤ³²³] **tɤ⁴⁴** [ma³¹ tsɳ³⁵] ni³¹ tɕo³⁵,
buy   CLNK   NEG weave   TOP then
买   不   打   就
'If (you) don't buy (rope) to weave (with), then,'
不买来打呢就,

tɛi³¹ ŋ³²³ tɛi³¹ tsɛi³³ ni³¹ tɕo³⁵ tɛi³¹ti⁵³za³¹ xua²⁴tsa²⁴.
one CL:TMP one CL:ITEM TOP then a.little   be.busy
一   天   一   俩   就   一点   忙
'(You will) be stretched (to make even) a pair in a day.'
一天打一两个呢就忙一点了。
(WYF-Stools)

As noted above, the function of the purpose construction overlaps with that of two-event serial verb constructions. And, indeed, in some cases they are semantically interchangeable. The key syntactic difference is that the verb serialization must share every argument, which presents the serialization as a single seamless event. And although the A/S of both clauses in the *tɤ⁴⁴* construction may be identical, this is not obligatory since the A/S of the purpose clause may correspond to the P of the first clause instead. This pattern highlights the fact that *tɤ⁴⁴* may link clauses describing relatively distinct events. Two-event serial verb constructions are described in more detail in § 8.8.2.

The fact that the purpose clause occurs after the main clause in the *tɤ⁴⁴* construction is unusual in Khatso syntax. Almost all of the other clause-linking constructions described in this chapter place the dependent clause before the matrix clause. However, the syntax of this construction is identical to a particular motion construction in Chinese, in which the matrix verb likewise comes first, followed by *dào* 到 'to arrive' and a destination. Moreover, the Chinese construction is typically interpreted as perfective even if there is no aspectual marking (Li and Thompson 1981: 206), and this seems to be the case in Khatso as well. Absent information to the contrary, the basic construction in (1111) is considered perfective, and this is one difference between the *tɤ⁴⁴* construction and the simpler locative construction in (1112), which is temporally vague without aspect marking. The perfective sense of the *tɤ⁴⁴* construction may be canceled, however, if it is specifically marked otherwise, as (1113) illustrates. The similarities between these two constructions suggest that the Khatso version was borrowed, and then expanded to include purposes of all types. The phonological rules for borrowing are not clear, but it has been noted that tone 44 occurs most often in loanwords, further pointing to a possible foreign source for *tɤ⁴⁴* (see § 3.1.2). A more detailed discussion of this particle is presented in § 16.5.

(1111) [i³³ i³²³] **tɤ⁴⁴** [kʰua³¹la³¹ tsʰŋ³³].
      3SG go CLNK Kunming arrive
      他 去 昆明 到
      'He went to Kunming.'
      他去到昆明。
      (KL-Elicitation)

(1112) i³³ kʰua³¹la³¹ i³²³.
      3SG Kunming go
      他 昆明 去
      'He goes/is going/went/will go to Kunming.'
      他去昆明。
      (KL-Elicitation)

(1113) [i³³ i³²³] **tɤ⁴⁴** [kʰua³¹la³¹ tsʰŋ³³] wa³⁵.
      3SG go CLNK Kunming arrive FUT
      他 去 昆明 到
      'He will go to Kunming.'
      他要去到昆明。
      (KL-Elicitation)

As already mentioned, the *tɤ⁴⁴* construction is also used to link a cause and its effect, or to conjoin two simultaneous events. These functions are described in § 14.2.2 and § 13.2.3.4 respectively. There are several other morphemes pronounced *tɤ⁴⁴*, which are not related to the clause linker and are almost certainly historically independent of one another (see § 16.5). One is a sentence-final particle, which brings emphasis to a single clause rather than combine two clauses (see § 12.6.8). There also is a borrowed adverb meaning 'all' which occurs before verbs, and a discourse particle, roughly translated as 'then, in that case, so', which often begins utterances.

15 Complementation

Complementation is a construction in which one clause serves as an argument of another, creating a single integrated unit (Dixon 2006: 4-7; Noonan 2007: 52-53). The argument clause is typically subordinate, and its verb is often syntactically restricted. The matrix clause usually has no restrictions, and carries tense or aspect and other sentence-level marking. While every language has verbs that may take propositions as arguments — such as 'to see', 'to forget' and 'to urge', among many others — not all languages have fully-integrated complement constructions. Instead, they may use other types of clause-combining strategies that involve a lesser degree of integration (Dixon 2006: 33-40). This is the case in Khatso, where the most widespread strategy involves the particle sɛi⁴⁴, which otherwise has temporal and topicalizing functions (see § 13.2.1 and § 10.1 respectively). Its use is detailed in § 15.1. Verbs that do not allow sɛi⁴⁴ and those for which it is optional are described in § 15.2. And the special case of reported speech, which has a number of strategies, is discussed in § 15.3.

15.1 Complementation Strategies with sɛi⁴⁴

Only a small subset of verbs may take clausal propositions as arguments, including the perception verbs ŋ²⁴ka³³ 'to see' and na²⁴tɕa³¹ 'to hear', the knowledge verbs tɕɛ³²³ti³⁵ 'to decide' and m̩³³to³¹ 'to forget', the utterance verbs n̪a³¹ 'to speak, say' and tsʰŋ²⁴to³³ 'to answer, promise', the manipulation verbs a³³pʰai³²³ 'to arrange' and tɕʰɛ³⁵ 'to urge', and the propositional attitude verbs ni³²³tsɤ³¹ 'to doubt' and ma³²³fa³²³ 'be troublesome', among others. Frequent complement-taking verbs are presented in Table 15.1. Most of these verbs are transitive, although a few are ditransitive, such as pa⁵³mo³³ 'to tell' and ma⁵⁵ 'to teach'. Certain stative verbs and complex stative constructions, which are intransitive, may also take propositions as arguments; only a few illustrative examples are included in the table, such as tsʰŋ³¹kuɛi³⁵ 'be strange' and na²⁴ kɯ³²³ sa³³ 'be fun'. Many of these verbs are loans from Chinese.

Table 15.1: Complement-taking verbs in Khatso

Khatso	English	Chinese	Origin
a³³pʰai³²³	'to arrange'	安排	borrowed
ɕa³¹(tsɤ³¹)	'to think, suppose'	想	borrowed
ɕa³³ɕi³⁵	'to believe'	相信	borrowed
ɕɛ³¹	'to choose'	选	borrowed

Khatso	English	Chinese	Origin
fa²⁴ɕɛ³⁵	'to discover'	发现	borrowed
m̥³¹tsɤ³¹	'to estimate, think'	想	native
m̥³³to³¹	'to forget'	忘记	native
ma³²³fa³²³	'to be troublesome'	麻烦	borrowed
ma⁵⁵	'to teach'	教	native
mi³⁵li³⁵	'to order'	命令	borrowed
na²⁴	'to hear'	听见	native
na²⁴ kɯ³²³ sa³³	'to be fun'	好玩	native
na²⁴ŋ²⁴	'to ask'	问	native
na²⁴tɕa³¹	'to heard'	听见	native
na⁵³tsɤ³¹	'to watch, look'	看	native
ni³²³tsɤ³¹	'to doubt'	怀疑	native
ŋ̊a³¹	'to speak, say'	说	native
ŋ²⁴ka³³	'to see'	看	native
ŋ²⁴mo³²³	'to saw'	看见	native
pa⁵³mo³³	'to tell'	告诉	native
pʰɛi³⁵	'to send (someone)'	派	borrowed
so²⁴	'to learn'	学	native
sɿ⁵⁵	'to know, realize'	知道	native
tɕɛ³²³ti³⁵	'to decide'	决定	borrowed
tɕʰɛ³³	'to invite'	请	borrowed
tɕʰɛ³⁵	'to urge'	劝	borrowed
tɕi³¹kau³⁵	'to warn'	警告	borrowed
tɕi³³	'to say'	说	native
tɕo³⁵	'to threaten'	恐吓	native
tɕo⁵³	'to scare'	吓唬	native
tʰo³²³zɿ³⁵	'to agree'	同意	borrowed
tsɛi³⁵mi³²³	'to prove'	证明	borrowed
tsʰɛi²⁴	'to guess'	猜	borrowed
tsʰɛi³²³ta³³	'to undertake'	承担	borrowed
tsʰɛi³²³zɛi³⁵	'to admit'	承认	borrowed
tsʰɿ²⁴to³³	'to answer, agree'	答应	native
tsʰɿ³²³kuɛi³⁵	'to be strange'	奇怪	borrowed
tsɿ³⁵tsɤ³¹	'to remember'	记住	borrowed
xɛi³⁵xuɛi³¹	'to regret'	后悔	borrowed

The basic complementation strategy in Khatso involves the particle *sɛi⁴⁴*, which has temporal (see § 13.2.1) and topicalizing functions (see § 10.1). In this strategy, *sɛi⁴⁴* follows the putative complement clause, making it the topic about which the second clause, which contains the complement-taking verb, provides information. The simple elicited example in (1114) illustrates the pattern. Thus, even though the Chinese and English translations use complement constructions, the Khatso phrase contains a topic-comment structure, more properly translated as 'as for going to Kunming, (it) is a lot of trouble'. The temporal sense is present as well, and so it may also be interpreted as 'when (you) go to Kunming, (it) is a lot of trouble'. Context and verbal semantics determine which meaning is most relevant. But, only if the matrix clause contains a complement-taking verb is the complementation interpretation a possibility.

(1114) [kʰua³¹la³¹ i³²³] **sɛi⁴⁴** [ma³²³fa³²³ tʰɛi³²³ ja³³].
Kunming go TOP be.troublesome very IPFV.EMP
昆明 去 麻烦 很

Complement translation
'Going to Kunming is a lot of trouble.'
去昆明很麻烦。

Topic translation
'As for going to Kunming, (it) is a lot of trouble.'
去昆明呢，很麻烦。

Temporal translation
'When (you) go to Kunming, (it) is a lot of trouble.'
去昆明的时候，很麻烦。
(KL-Elicitation)

Regardless of whether the *sɛi⁴⁴* clause is considered a topic or an adverbial temporal clause, it is not a core argument of the matrix clause, and thus this strategy cannot be considered true complementation. Instead, the S of *ma³²³fa³²³* in the example above is understood as a pronoun that refers to the topic, such as 'it' or 'that', which is absent due to zero anaphora. Moreover, *sɛi⁴⁴* clauses are not nominalizations; they cannot be relativized or modified by a classifier, and therefore fail the tests for nounhood (see Chapter 5). Note that the other topic marker in Khatso, *ni³¹*, may not take part in the complementation strategy.

Topics typically precede matrix clauses in Khatso, unless they are added as an afterthought (see § 10.1). However, clause order is more flexible with the complementation strategy. When the matrix clause contains an intransitive verb, the *sɛi⁴⁴* clause usually precedes it, as shown in (1114) above. The same is true for complex stative constructions as well, as (1115) illustrates. When the matrix clause contains a transitive verb, the *sɛi⁴⁴* clause may either precede or follow the matrix clause, as shown in (1116) and (1117). The order does not affect the basic meaning, and a postposed topic does not necessarily indicate that it is an afterthought in this use. It is also possible to insert the *sɛi⁴⁴* clause into the matrix clause itself, where it sits between A and the matrix verb, as (1118) illustrates. This is the canonical position for P in a simple clause (see § 10.3), making this center-embedding formulation look much more like prototypical complementation. But all examples of this type come from elicitation, and so it is unclear whether this formulation is widely used in discourse. Speakers say its meaning is the same as the preposed and postposed orders, but even in elicitation it seems to be the least preferred of the three. While most of the transitive complement-taking verbs allow all of these variations in clause order, postposing and center embedding are not possible with all of them. There is no clear-cut pattern to these restrictions; rather, it is likely that verbal semantics, and perhaps also frequency effects, plays a role here. Table 15.2 provides an overview of the complement-taking verbs in Khatso organized according to the patterns they allow.

(1115) [na⁵³pɤ³¹ i³²³] **sɛi⁴⁴** [na²⁴ kɯ³²³ sa³³ tʰɛi³²³ ja³³].
night.dance go TOP play CSC be.good very IPFV.EMP
跳乐 去 玩 好 很
'Going dancing is a lot of fun.', literally 'As for going dancing, (it) is a lot of fun.'
去跳乐很好玩。
(KL-Elicitation)

(1116) [i³³ kʰa⁵⁵tso³¹tɕʰi³¹ n̪a³¹ li³²³] **sɛi⁴⁴** [ŋa³³ m̩³³to²⁴ wa³³].
3SG Khatso.language speak know.how TOP 1SG forget CRS
她 喀卓语 说 会 我 忘记
'I forgot she can speak Khatso.', literally '(That) she can speak Khatso, I forgot (about it).'
我忘了她会说喀卓语。
(KL-Elicitation)

(1117) [ŋa³³ m̩³³to²⁴ wa³³] [i³³ kʰa⁵⁵tso³¹tɕʰi³¹ n̪a³¹ li³²³] **sɛi⁴⁴**.
1SG forget CRS 3SG Khatso.language speak know.how TOP
我 忘记 她 喀卓语 说 会
'I forgot she can speak Khatso.', literally 'I forgot (it), she can speak Khatso.'
我忘了她会说喀卓语。
(KL-Elicitation)

(1118) ŋa³³ [i³³ kʰa⁵⁵tso³¹tɕʰi³¹ n̪a³¹ li³²³] **sɛi⁴⁴** [m̪³³to²⁴ wa³³].
1SG 3SG Khatso.language speak know.how TOP forget CRS
我 她 喀卓语 说 会 忘记
'I forgot she can speak Khatso.', literally 'I, as for her speaking Khatso, forgot (about that).'
我忘了她会说喀卓语。
(KL-Elicitation)

Table 15.2: Patterning of *sɛi⁴⁴* with complement-taking verbs

Khatso	English	Chinese	*sɛi⁴⁴* required	*sɛi⁴⁴* follows topic	*sɛi⁴⁴* follows C-taking verb	Center embedding possible
ɕa³³ɕi³⁵	'to believe'	相信	yes	yes	yes	yes
fa²⁴ɕɛ³⁵	'to discover'	发现	yes	yes	yes	yes
na²⁴tɕa³¹	'to hear'	听见	yes	yes	yes	yes
pa⁵³mo³³	'to tell'	告诉	yes	yes	yes	yes
tɕɛ³²³ti³⁵	'to decide'	决定	yes	yes	yes	yes
tʰo³²³z̩³⁵	'to agree'	同意	yes	yes	yes	yes
tsɛi³⁵mi³²³	'to prove'	证明	yes	yes	yes	yes
tsʰɛi³²³zɛi³⁵	'to admit'	承认	yes	yes	yes	yes
tsɿ³⁵tsʁ³¹	'to remember'	记住	yes	yes	yes	yes
a³³pʰai³²³	'to arrange'	安排	yes	yes	yes	no
mi³⁵li³⁵	'to order'	命令	yes	yes	yes	no
n̪a³¹	'to speak, say'	说	yes	yes	yes	no
ŋ²⁴mo³²³	'to saw'	看见	yes	yes	yes	no
tɕʰɛ³⁵	'to urge'	劝	yes	yes	yes	no
tɕi³¹kau³⁵	'to warn'	警告	yes	yes	yes	no
tɕo⁵³	'to scare'	吓唬	yes	yes	yes	no
tsʰɛi²⁴ta³³	'to undertake'	承担	yes	yes	yes	no
tsʰŋ²⁴to³³	'to answer, agree'	答应	yes	yes	yes	no
m̪³³to³¹	'to forget'	忘记	yes	yes	no	yes
ŋ²⁴ka³³	'to see'	看	yes	yes	no	yes
xɛi³⁵xuɛi³¹	'to regret'	后悔	yes	yes	no	yes
ɕɛ³¹	'to choose'	选	yes	yes	no	no

Khatso	English	Chinese	sɛi⁴⁴ required	sɛi⁴⁴ follows topic	sɛi⁴⁴ follows C-taking verb	Center embedding possible
ma³²³fa³²³	'to be troublesome'	麻烦	yes	yes	no	no
na²⁴	'to hear'	听见	yes	yes	no	no
na²⁴ kɯ³²³ sa³³	'to be fun'	好玩	yes	yes	no	no
tɕʰɛ³³	'to invite'	请	yes	yes	no	no
tsʰŋ³¹kuɛi³⁵	'to be strange'	奇怪	yes	yes	no	no
ɕa³¹(tsɤ³¹)	'to think, suppose'	想	yes	no	yes	no
m̩³¹tsɤ³¹	'to estimate, think'	想	yes	no	yes	no
na²⁴ŋ²⁴	'to ask'	问	yes	no	yes	no
na⁵³tsɤ³¹	'to watch, look'	看	yes	no	yes	no
ni³²³tsɤ³¹	'to doubt'	怀疑	yes	no	yes	no
pʰɛi³⁵	'to send (someone)'	派	yes	no	yes	no
tɕo³⁵	'to threaten'	恐吓	yes	no	yes	no
tsʰɛi²⁴	'to guess'	猜	yes	no	yes	no
sŋ⁵⁵	'to know, realize'	知道	no	yes	yes	yes
ma⁵⁵	'to teach'	教	no	yes	no	yes
so²⁴	'to learn'	学	no	yes	no	no
tɕi³³	'to say'	说	no	no	yes	no

In addition, many complement-taking verbs allow sɛi⁴⁴ to follow the matrix clause instead of the topic clause. These include $a^{33}pʰai^{323}$ 'to arrange', $tɕi^{31}kau^{35}$ 'to warn', $tɕʰɛ^{35}$ 'to urge', $sŋ^{55}$ 'to know' and $ɕa^{33}ɕi^{35}$ 'to believe' among others. Examples are presented in (1119), (1120) and (1121); these verbs are also labeled in Table 16.2. This flip-flopping of clausal function is impossible in true complementation, but poses no problems for topic-comment structures. Either clause may be topicalized depending on what information is already given in discourse and the degree of prominence a speaker wishes to assign to it. In addition, there is a handful of verbs — $ɕa^{31}tsɤ^{31}$ 'to think, assume, suppose', $m̩^{31}tsɤ^{31}$ 'to estimate, reckon, think', $ni^{323}tsɤ^{31}$ 'to doubt', na^{31} 'to speak, say', and $tsʰɛi^{24}$ 'to guess' — which are almost always followed by sɛi⁴⁴ rather than the second clause. In this case, the sɛi⁴⁴ clause almost always comes first, as in (1122). Again, the clauses may be interpreted in a number of ways. Some of the translations are not smooth in English, but are perfectly acceptable in Khatso and Hanyu. Why these few complement-taking verbs are almost always topicalized is unclear.

(1119) [jɛ⁴⁴ẓ̍³³   so²⁴]   **sɛi⁴⁴**   [ŋa³³   tɕɛ³²³ti³⁵   wa³²³].
English learn   TOP   1SG   decide   PFV
英文   学   我   决定
'As for learning English, I decided (to do it).'
我决定学英文了。
(KL-Elicitation)

(1120) [ŋa³³   tɕɛ³²³ti³⁵]   **sɛi⁴⁴**   [jɛ⁴⁴ẓ̍³³   so²⁴   wa³⁵].
1SG   decide   TOP   English   learn   FUT
我   决定   英文   学
'As for my deciding, (I) will learn English.'
我决定学英文了。
(KL-Elicitation)

(1121) [ŋa³³   kɛi³³   sɹ̍⁵⁵]   **sɛi⁴⁴**   [mɛi⁴⁴   so²⁴   sa⁵⁵   sa²⁴   ja³³
1SG   AGT   know   TOP   very   learn   be.difficult   perhaps   IPFV.EMP
我   知道   很   学   难   可能
ta⁵⁵   ŋ³³   lɛi³¹].
type   COP   IRR.EMP
样   是
'I know (that it) was probably very difficult to learn.', literally, 'I know (it), (it) was probably very difficult to learn.'
我觉得很难学的样子。
(KL-Learning)

(1122) [ŋa³³   kɛi³³   tsʰɛi²⁴]   **sɛi⁴⁴**   [i³³   ŋ⁵⁵lo⁵³   i³²³].
1SG   AGT   guess   TOP   3SG   Tonghai   go
我   猜   他   通海   去

Complement translation
'I guess he went to Tonghai.'
我猜他去通海了。

Topic translation
'As for me guessing, (I guess) he went to Tonghai.'
我猜呢，去通海了。

Temporal translation
'When I guess, (I guess) he went to Tonghai.'
我猜的时候，去通海了。
(KL-Elicitation)

The various functions of *sɛi⁴⁴* impact the way that negation and reduplicative polar questions may pattern in the complementation strategy. Its temporal and topicalizing origins indicate that *sɛi⁴⁴* is largely associated with propositions that are certain. As a result, there is a tendency to avoid negating verbs in a *sɛi⁴⁴* clause regardless of its position or content, though there is no such restriction in the second clause. With complement-taking verbs that may optionally be followed by *sɛi⁴⁴*, the construction is simply formulated so that negation occurs ouside the *sɛi⁴⁴* clause; compare (1123) and (1124), for example. This also occurs with complement-taking verbs that usually take *sɛi⁴⁴*, demonstrating that the latter pattern is not absolute. The negated complement-taking verb sits in its own clause, and *sɛi⁴⁴* occurs in the second clause, as (1125) illustrates. The exception to this pattern involves stative verbs. Since they are never followed by *sɛi⁴⁴*, the topic clauses accompanying them may include the negative marker without restriction, as (1126) demonstrates.

(1123) [ŋa³³ kɛi³³ tsʰɛi²⁴] **sɛi⁴⁴** [i³³ kʰua³¹la³¹ ma³¹ i³²³].
      1SG   AGT   guess   TOP   3SG Kunming NEG go
      我   猜   他   昆明   不   去
'I guess he didn't go to Kunming.', literally 'As for me guessing, he didn't go to Kunming.'
我猜他不去昆明。
(KL-Elicitation)

(1124) [i³³ kʰua³¹la³¹ i³²³] **sɛi⁴⁴** [ŋa³³ kɛi³³ ma³¹ tsʰɛi²⁴ la³¹].
      3SG Kunming go   TOP 1SG AGT NEG guess PFV.IRR
      他   昆明   去   我   不   猜
'I didn't guess he went to Kunming.', literally 'He went to Kunming, I didn't guess (it).'
我没猜过他去昆明。
(KL-Elicitation)

(1125) [ŋa³³ ni³²³tsɤ³¹ ma³¹ ko⁵³], [i³³ kʰa⁵⁵tso³¹tɕʰi³¹ n̻a³¹ li³²³]
      1SG doubt NEG EXP 3SG Khatso.language speak know.how
      我   怀疑   不   过   他   喀卓语   说   会
sɛi⁴⁴.
TOP
'I never doubted he could speak Khatso', literally 'I never doubted (it), he can speak Khatso.'
我没怀疑过他会说喀卓语。
(KL-Elicitation)

(1126) [i³³ pʰi²⁴ŋ²⁴tɕʰi³¹ n̪a³¹ ma³¹ li³²³] sɛi⁴⁴ [tsʰŋ³¹kuai³⁵ tʰɛi³²³ ja³³].
      3SG   Hanyu   speak NEG know.how TOP be.strange very IPFV.EMP
      他   汉语   说   不   会   奇怪   很
'As for his not knowing how to speak Hanyu, (it) is very strange.'
他不会说汉语很奇怪。
(KL-Elicitation)

Likewise, *sɛi⁴⁴* clauses may not contain questions, which is true of any topic clause. Moreover, interrogative constructions, like negation, query the reality of the event described and are thus incompatible with the certainty associated with *sɛi⁴⁴*. For complement-taking verbs that may optionally be followed by *sɛi⁴⁴*, the construction is easily formulated so that the interrogative construction occurs outside the *sɛi⁴⁴* clause. Compare the declarative phrase in (1127) with the polar question in (1128) and the content question in (1129). For verbs that are almost always followed by *sɛi⁴⁴*, the interrogative formulation likewise occurs outside the *sɛi⁴⁴* clause, as (1130) demonstrates. Logically, in this example thinking is a certain event which occurs regardless of the Khatso speaking abilities of the person discussed. Tag questions may be appended to matrix clauses with no problem, as (1131) shows, since they function to confirm rather than query the information conveyed.

(1127) [nɛi³³ kɛi³³ tsɛi³⁵mi³²³] **sɛi⁴⁴** [i³³ n̪o³¹ kʰy³¹].
      2SG   AGT   prove   TOP   3SG   thing steal
      你   证明   他   东西 偷
'You proved that he steals things', literally 'As for you proving (it), he steals things.'
你证明他偷东西。
(KL-Elicitation)

(1128) [i³³   n̠o³¹   kʰɣ³¹]   **sɛi⁴⁴**   [nɛi³³   kɛi³³   tsɛi³⁵mi³²³   mi³²³   wa³¹]?
      3SG   thing   steal   TOP   2SG   AGT   prove   prove   PFV.Q
      他   东西   偷   你   证明   明
      'Did you prove that he steals things?', literally 'As for his stealing things, did you prove (it)?'
      他偷东西，你证明了没有？
      (KL-Elicitation)

(1129) [nɛi³³   xa³³ni³³   tsɛi³⁵mi³²³   ŋa³¹]   [i³³   n̠o³¹   kʰɣ³¹]   **sɛi⁴⁴**?
      2SG   how   prove   CNT.Q   3SG   thing   steal   TOP
      你   怎么   证明   他   东西   偷
      'How did you prove that he stole things?', literally 'How did you prove (it), his stealing things?'
      你怎么证明他偷东西了？
      (KL-Elicitation)

(1130) [nɛi³³   kɛi³³   ɕa³¹tsɣ³¹]   **sɛi⁴⁴**   i³³   [kʰa⁵⁵tso³¹tɕʰi³¹   n̠a³¹   li³²³]?
      2SG   AGT   think   TOP   3SG   Khatso.language   speak   know.how
      你   想   她   喀卓语   说   会
      li³²³]?
      know.how
      会
      'Do you think she knows how to speak Khatso?', literally, 'As for your thinking, does she know or (not) know how to speak Khatso?'
      你想她会不会说喀卓语？
      (KL-Elicitation)

(1131) [nɛi³³   kɛi³³   tsɛi³⁵mi³²³]   **sɛi⁴⁴**   [i³³   n̠o³¹   kʰɣ³¹   ŋ³³   sa⁴⁴]?
      2SG   AGT   prove   TOP   3SG   thing   steal   COP   CRTN.Q
      你   证明   他   东西   偷   是
      'You proved that he stole things, right?', literally 'As for your proving (it), he steals things, right?'
      你证明他偷东西了，是吗？
      (KL-Elicitation)

Due to several factors, this complementation strategy is rather rare in the corpus. First, many of the complement-taking verbs require rather particular semantic contexts in which to occur, and so they do not frequently appear. Second, these verbs may occur without a complement. Often, the information that would appear in a topic clause is mentioned separately, as in (1132). Once it becomes given information, it need not be repeated in subsequent clauses, since zero anaphora applies to clauses as well as simple nouns. Third, even if both clauses are present, their relationship need not be overtly structured as topic and comment. Thus, in (1133) the verb ɕa³¹ 'to think' occurs in a stand-alone clause, so indicated by the fact that it has its own aspect marker. The topic to be thought about, which otherwise might occur in a sɛi⁴⁴ clause, occurs in a second clause which is likewise syntactically complete. Pragmatics alone is enough to link the two clauses in the interlocutor's mind.

(1132) A: tɛi³¹   xa⁵³   sɛi⁴⁴   tɛi³¹   ma²⁴   la⁵³   na²⁴   tɛi³¹   ma²⁴   tɕɛ⁵⁵
           one   CL:TMP   TMP   one   CL:GEN   wrap   be.good one   CL:GEN sew
           一   晚   一   个   绕   好   一   个   钉
           ti³³ ja³³   tsɛi³¹,
           PROG   HSY
           '(They say) in one evening (they) can completely wrap (and) sew one,'
           听说一晚上绕好一个钉一个地，

           ta³³ma⁴⁴tʰi³²³   tɛi³¹   jo³⁵   to³³.
           alone   one   CL:HUM   also
           单独   一   位   也
           '(They say) in one evening (they) can completely wrap (and) sew one, by themselves.'
           自己。

       B: ai²⁴²,   ma³¹   sɿ⁵⁵.
           INTJ   NEG   know
                    不   知道
           'Oh, I didn't know (that).'
           唉，不知道。
           (KL, WYY-Sewing)

(1133) ŋa³³   tʰɤ⁵⁵   ɕa³¹   ŋ²⁴ka³³   jo³³   wa³²³.
       1SG   CL:TMP   think   see   must   PFV
       我   下   想   看   应该
       'I must try and think (about it).'
       我应该想想看。

       tɛi³³   tɕi⁵⁵   xa³³ni³³   fa³³ʐɿ³²³.
       this   CL:TYPE how   translate
       这   种   怎么   翻译
       'How (I should) translate this phrase.'
       这个怎么翻译。
       (KL-Weeds)

Because *sɛi⁴⁴* clauses are not core arguments, they are not tightly integrated into the matrix clause. Argument sharing does not provide strong evidence for integration, but there are two features that point to a certain degree of integration, aspect and center embedding. Aspect is restricted in the *sɛi⁴⁴* clause, regardless of whether or not it contains the complement-taking verb. The clause without *sɛi⁴⁴* may take any aspect marking, which may optionally have scope over the *sɛi⁴⁴* clause, though the latter is often seen as an ongoing event with vague temporal boundaries. Thus, in (1134), the act of seeing is perfective; the cooking, however, may be complete or ongoing. Similarly, in (1135), the seeing has not yet occurred, but whether the cooking has begun or not is unclear. In any case, the fact that the *sɛi⁴⁴* clause may not freely take its own aspect marking indicates that it is dependent on the matrix clause, and this is true of the particle's other functions as well. Note that some verbs — such as *m̩³¹tsɤ³¹* 'to estimate, reckon', *ni³²³tsɤ³¹* 'to suspect, doubt' and *tsŋ³⁵tsɤ³¹* 'to remember' — include the continuous aspect marker, but the morpheme here is a bound and obligatory part of the lexical form, and cannot be replaced by any other marker.

(1134) ŋa³³ [i³³ tsa³²³ m̩³³] **sɛi⁴⁴** [ŋ²⁴ka³³ wa³²³].
     1SG 3SG rice make TOP   see   PFV
     我   她   饭   做   看
     'I saw her cook.' / 'I saw her cooking.', literally 'I, as for her cooking, saw (it).'
     我看了她做饭。
     (KL-Elicitation)

(1135) ŋa³³ [i³³ tsa³²³ m̩³³] **sɛi⁴⁴** [ŋ²⁴ka³³ wa³⁵].
     1SG 3SG rice make TOP   see   FUT
     我   她   饭   做   看
     'I will see her cook.' / 'I will see her cooking.', literally 'I, as for her cooking, will see (it).'
     我要看她做饭。
     (KL-Elicitation)

The second feature pointing to integration is center embedding. As Table 16.2 shows, a good number of transitive verbs allow for the *sɛi⁴⁴* clause to be inserted into the matrix clause. That is, it may appear between the A of the matrix clause and the matrix verb itself, as (1136) and (1137) illustrate. This position, which is the canonical slot for P, suggests that it is indeed a core argument and thus highly integrated in the matrix clause. Moreover, this clause order is not possible for the temporal and topicalizing functions of *sɛi⁴⁴*, nor for the other topic marker *ni³¹*. However, because this pattern is found in elicitation but not in the corpus, and even then seems to be preferred less than preposing or postposing, its value as evidence should not be overstated. It does suggest, though, that the complementation strategy diverges somewhat from the other functions of *sɛi⁴⁴*. It may be in the early stages of grammaticalizing into a more prototypical complementation construction.

(1136) i³³   kɛi³³   [kʰua³¹la³¹   i³²³]   **sɛi⁴⁴**   [ŋa³³   pa⁵³mo³³].
        3SG   AGT   Kunming   go   TOP   1SG   tell
        她   昆明   去   我   告诉
        'She told me (she) is going to Kunming', literally 'She, as for her going to Kunming, told me.'
        她告诉我（她）去昆明。
        (KL-Elicitation)

(1137) ŋa³³   [i³³   tsa³²³   m³³]   **sɛi⁴⁴**   [ŋ²⁴ka³³   wa³²³].
        1SG   3SG   rice   make   TOP   see   PFV
        我   他   饭   做   看
        'I saw him cook.', literally 'I, as for his cooking, saw (it).'
        我看了他做饭。
        (KL-Elicitation)

As just mentioned, argument sharing does not provide strong evidence for integration. While some complement-taking verbs require that the A/S of both clauses be the same, which allows for it to be omitted from one of the clauses, this seems to follow the basic patterning of zero anaphora rather than clausal integration. In fact, in many cases is it possible for the same argument to overtly appear in both clauses, suggesting that the clauses are syntactically independent. Moreover, some complement-taking verbs lexically require that the arguments be different. For example, the verbs *tɕʰɛ³⁵* 'to urge' and *mi³⁵li³⁵* 'to order' describe one person addressing another about an activity, and thus the A of these verbs are necessarily different from those in the second clauses.

At first glance, *sɛi⁴⁴* and the clause linker *tɤ⁴⁴* have clearly separate functions. *sɛi⁴⁴* occurs in a topic-comment structure that serves as a complementation strategy, and *tɤ⁴⁴* links clauses with particular semantic relationships such as cause and effect or event and purpose. However, there are instances in which the two particles are interchangeable. For example, the two phrases in (1138) and (1139) both carry the same meaning and are both grammatical, though *tɤ⁴⁴* may be preferred. At times, the semantics of individual verbs help differentiate the two. For example, the phrase in (1140), which features *sɛi⁴⁴*, is vague on whether the person urged to travel will agree or not. But that in (1141) may be interpreted as a cause and effect *tɤ⁴⁴* construction, implying that the person urged to travel is either already at the destination or at least has agreed to go. When the verb *na³¹* 'to speak' is used with *tɤ⁴⁴*, as in (1142), the second clause is also considered a result, so that the construction takes on the meaning of 'persuade', a sense it does not have with $sɛi^{44}$. The inherent perfective sense of $tɤ^{44}$ plays a role here as well.

(1138) [ŋa³³ kɛi³³ i³³ a³³pʰai³²³] **sɛi⁴⁴** [kʰua³¹la³¹ i³²³].
　　　 1SG　 AGT　 3SG　 arrange　 TOP　 Kunming　 go
　　　 我　　　　　 他　 安排　　　　　 昆明　　 去
　　　 'I arranged (for) him to go to Kunming.', literally 'As for me arranging (things) for him, (I arranged for him to) go to Kunming.'
　　　 我安排他去昆明。
　　　 (KL-Elicitation)

(1139) [ŋa³³ kɛi³³ i³³ a³³pʰai³²³] **tɤ⁴⁴** [kʰua³¹la³¹ i³²³].
　　　 1SG　 AGT　 3SG　 arrange　 CLNK　 Kunming　 go
　　　 我　　　　　 他　 安排　　　　　 昆明　　 去
　　　 'I arranged (for) him to go to Kunming.'
　　　 我安排他去昆明。
　　　 (KL-Elicitation)

(1140) [ŋa³³ i³³ tɕʰɛ³⁵] **sɛi⁴⁴** [kʰua³¹la³¹ i³²³].
　　　 1SG　 3SG　 urge　 TOP　 Kunming　 go
　　　 我　 他　 劝　　　　 昆明　　 去
　　　 'I urge him to go to Kunming.', literally 'As for me urging him, (I urge him to) go to Kunming.'
　　　 我劝他去昆明。
　　　 (KL-Elicitation)

(1141) [ŋa³³ i³³ tɕʰɛ³⁵] **tɤ⁴⁴** [kʰua³¹la³¹ i³²³].
　　　 1SG　 3SG　 urge　 CLNK　 Kunming　 go
　　　 我　 他　 劝　　　　 昆明　　 去
　　　 'I urged him to go to Kunming (and he's on his way).'
　　　 我劝他去昆明。
　　　 (KL-Elicitation)

(1142) [i³³ kɛi³³ ŋa³³ n̪a³¹] **tɤ⁴⁴** [kʰua³¹la³¹ i³²³].
　　　 3SG　 AGT　 1SG　 speak　 CLNK　 Kunming　 go
　　　 他　　　　　 我　 说　　　　 昆明　　 去
　　　 'He persuaded me to go to Kunming.'
　　　 他说服我去昆明。
　　　 (KL-Elicitation)

As mentioned earlier, in addition to its role in the complementation strategy, $sɛi^{44}$ has a number of other functions. It may serve as a temporal marker and a topic marker, both of which may co-occur with noun phrases as well as clauses (see § 13.2.1 and § 10.1 respectively). An overview of the particle is presented in § 16.6.

15.2 Complementation Strategies without *sɛi⁴⁴*

There is a small group of verbs that may take propositions as arguments without additional marking. They may be roughly sorted into two groups: those that never employ the *sɛi⁴⁴* complementation strategy and those for which the *sɛi⁴⁴* strategy is optional. The first group consists of verbs that appear in constructions in which the use of *sɛi⁴⁴* is ungrammatical. Most of these verbs function as auxiliaries when co-occurring with another verb, such as *sɿ³³wa³⁵* 'to wish', *sɿ³¹xua³³* 'to like', *kʰai³³sɿ³⁵* 'to begin', *tsɿ³⁵sɤ³²³* 'to continue', *sɿ³⁵ŋ²⁴ka³³* and *ŋ²⁴ka³³* 'to try', and *mo⁵⁵* 'to want'. The exception is the quotative verb *tɕi³³* 'to say', which is explained in § 15.3. Among the auxiliary-like verbs, all but the last three are Hanyu loans and thus pattern like the other borrowed auxiliaries. That is, they precede the matrix verb, as (1143) and (1144) illustrate. These verbs are not true auxiliaries, however, since they also readily function as matrix verbs in simple clauses and may take noun phrases as complements. For a more detailed discussion of native and borrowed auxiliary verbs and their different syntactic patterns, see § 8.7.

(1143) **kʰai³³sɿ³⁵**   zɿ³²³n̠ɛ³²³tsɿ³¹   so²⁴   la²⁴   tsɛi³⁵,
begin   grade.one   study   REL   CL:TMP
开始   一年级   读   段
'When (we) began to study (in) first grade,'
开始读一年级的时候，

pʰi²⁴ŋ²⁴tɕʰi³¹   n̠a³¹   ma³¹   li³²³.
Hanyu.language   speak   NEG   know.how
汉语   说   不   会
'(We) didn't know how to speak Hanyu.'
不会说汉语。
(YAY-Erasers)

(1144) **tsɿ³⁵sɤ³²³**   na³²³so³⁵   ɕau³³mi³²³   i³⁵   wa³³.
continue   Southern.Song   eliminate   go.FOC   CRS
继续   南宋   消灭   去
'So (they) continued to eliminate the Southern Song (kingdom).'
继续去消灭南宋。
(KLT-History)

The remaining three verbs pattern somewhat differently. As a matrix verb, $ŋ^{24}ka^{33}$ means 'to see' and it requires $sɛi^{44}$ if its P is a clause. But as an auxiliary it does not; here its meaning is 'to try' much like the English construction 'VERB and see'. The longer form includes $sɿ^{35}$, which may be derived from the Chinese verb *shì* 试 'to try'. Either form may serve as an auxiliary — there is no difference in meaning — but they must follow the matrix verb, following the canonical pattern for native Khatso auxiliaries (see § 8.7). In addition, $sɿ^{35}ŋ^{24}ka^{33}$ has an alternate form $ŋ^{24}sɿ^{35}ka^{33}$, in which the borrowed morpheme is interposed between the two syllables of the native verb. The former tends to be used more often as a matrix verb, while the latter is preferred in the auxiliary construction. The phrases in (1145), (1146) and (1147) exemplify these patterns.

(1145) ŋa³³   tʰɤ⁵⁵   ɕa³¹   **ŋ²⁴ka³³**   jo³³   wa³²³.
     1SG   CL:TMP think   see   must PFV
     我   下   想   看   应该
     'I must try and think for a while.', literally 'I must think and see for a while.'
     我应该想想看。
     (KL-Weeds)

(1146) tʰɤ⁴⁴   **sɿ³⁵ŋ²⁴ka³³**   jɛ²⁴.
     while   try.see   IMP
     下   试
     'Try (it and) see.'
     试一试吧。
     (KL-Elicitation)

(1147) ŋa³³   kʰa⁵⁵tso³¹tɕʰi³¹   n̪a³¹   **ŋ²⁴sɿ³⁵ka³³**   wa³⁵.
     1SG   Khatso.language speak try.see   FUT
     我   喀卓语   说   试看
     'I'll try to speak Khatso.'
     我要试试说喀卓语。
     (KL-Elicitation)

The final verb in this group, mo^{55} 'to want', is unique in that it has a causative-desiderative function in addition to its role as an auxiliary. The difference centers on whether or not the A in both clauses is identical. If they are the same, then mo^{55} serves as an auxiliary. But unlike the other native auxiliaries, it precedes rather than follows the matrix verb in this case, as shown in (1148). When mo^{55} is the final verb in a clause, it serves as the matrix verb and its A must be different from that of the preceding verb. The postposition $la^{33}ta^{55}$ also marks the causee, as in (1149). Depending on context, this construction may be interpreted as causative, which is the case in the example, or desiderative, in which case the phrase would mean '(when they) wanted them to dance'. The different syntax in these two constructions likely evolved to avoid potential confusion caused by zero anaphora. The causative construction is described further in § 12.5.2.1.

(1148) ŋ⁴⁴li³³   ma³¹   **mo⁵⁵**   n̪a³¹.
but   NEG   want   speak
但是   不   要   说
'But (he) didn't want to speak.'
但是不想说。
(YBF-Three Ladies)

(1149) i³³tsʰɤ³³   la³³ta⁵⁵   tɕʰɛ⁵⁵   **mo⁵⁵**   ni³¹
3PL   CAUS   dance   want   TOP
他们   跳   要
'(when they) made them dance'
让他们跳的时候呢
(PYX-Performing)

The second group of verbs that do not require the *sɛi⁴⁴* complementation strategy is small. It consists of a few basic verbs — *sɿ⁵⁵* 'to know', *so²⁴* 'to learn' and *ma⁵⁵* 'to teach' — for which *sɛi⁴⁴* is optional. As matrix verbs, they typically occur as the final verbs in the combined clause. Examples are shown in (1150), (1151) and (1152). Without the particle, these constructions seem to be prototypical complementation constructions. But, the use of *sɛi⁴⁴* with these verbs is always grammatical, and it may be employed without a change in meaning. This suggests that, given the frequency of these verbs in discourse and the frequent possibility that P will be a clause, the organizing function of *sɛi⁴⁴* is considered unnecessary and thus the particle is omitted. Using *sɛi⁴⁴* here largely seems to be matter of speaker preference, although more complex formulations may be made clearer by its use.

(1150) [xa³³ni³³   ta⁵⁵   ŋa²⁴]   [ma³¹   **sɿ⁵⁵**].
how   be.type   CNT.Q   NEG   know
怎么   样   不   知道
'What (it really) was, (I) don't know (either).'
怎么样也不知道。
(PYX-Dragon Pools)

(1151) [pʰi²⁴ŋ²⁴tɕʰi³¹ n̪a³¹] [so²⁴].
Hanyu speak learn
汉语 说 学
'(We) learned to speak Hanyu.'
学说汉语。
(YAY-Erasers)

(1152) [i³³ kɛi³³ ŋa³³ [tsa³²³ m̪³³] **ma⁵⁵**].
3SG AGT 1SG rice make teach
她 我 饭 做 教
'She teaches me to cook.'
她教我做饭
(KL-Elicitation)

15.3 Complementation Strategies for Reported Speech

There are several verbs in Khatso that denote the act of speaking, such as *n̪a³¹* 'speak, talk, say', *kʰua³¹* 'speak, talk', *pa⁵³* 'to speak, set a betrothal' and *tɕi³³* 'say'. However, in reporting the speech of others *tɕi³³* is employed most often. In simple clauses, *tɕi³³* occurs with A of any person, as one would expect of all verbs. But in reporting speech, *tɕi³³* tends to only be employed for utterances made by a third person. Examples are shown in (1153) and (1154). The one exception is when it is used in an imperative construction, as shown in (1155).

(1153) ["ŋa³³ mi⁵³ tɤ⁴⁴ i³²³ kɤ³²³ ma³¹ tso³²³ wa³³"] **tɕi⁴⁴** to³³.
1SG be.hungry CLNK go NMLZ NEG EXIST CRS say also
我 饿 去 不 有 说 也
' "I'm extremely hungry" (she) also said.'
"我饿的没办法了"这么说了也。
(HPH-Weeds)

(1154) ta³⁵pɤ³⁵fɛi³⁵ tɕo³⁵ [tɛi³³ ɕi³³] **tɕi³³** ja³³.
large.part then this be.accustomed say IPFV.EMP
大部分 就 这 习惯 说
'Almost everyone says (it) this way.'
大部分人都会这么说。
(YAY-Erasers)

(1155) ["kʰa⁵⁵tsɿ⁴⁴ sɿ³⁵   tuɛi³⁵"] **tɕi³³** pa³¹.
       kʰa⁵⁵tsɿ⁴⁴   four   CL:ITEM   say   IMP.SOL
       下村   四   组   说
       'Say "kʰa⁵⁵tsɿ⁴⁴ Fourth District", okay?'
       说 "下村四组" 吧。
       (KL-Childhood)

The A of *tɕi³³* is almost always absent — zero anaphora is frequent in Khatso discourse — and this seems to be a routinized feature of this construction. In discourse, protagonists are typically introduced before they begin to interact, and so labeling speakers seems to be unnecessary. Moreover, utterances introduced with *tɕi³³* never take *sɛi⁴⁴*, and *tɕi³³* itself rarely does. As a result, center embedding is not possible with this construction, pointing to a lack of tight integration between the two clauses. Indeed, reported speech constructions are only loosely bound, as the following paragraphs outline. The verb *tɕi³³* also takes part in several other types of clause combining, such as a reason construction (see § 14.1.2), a concessive construction (see § 14.3.1) and the universal conditional construction (see § 14.4.2).

If the A of *tɕi³³* is not third person, then the verb *n̠a³¹* is preferred, and A is usually present in the clause. In this construction the *sɛi⁴⁴* complementation strategy is obligatory, as (1156) illustrates. It is possible to use *n̠a³¹* with a third person A, as in (1157), but this is not frequently found in discourse. Although *sɛi⁴⁴* may follow either the *n̠a³¹* clause or the reported speech clause, pairing the particle with *n̠a³¹* is preferred in discourse, and this clause typically precedes the utterance clause. This may be related to syntactic heaviness, since the utterance may be long and even span more than one intonation unit. As a result, center embedding is not possible in this construction either, but negation and questions readily occur in the utterance clause since the latter never includes *sɛi⁴⁴*. The verbs *kʰua³¹* 'to speak, talk' and *pa⁵³* 'to speak, betroth' are almost never used to report speech. The latter, in fact, is usually interpreted as a future marker when combined with another verb (see § 9.2.9). The complementation strategy involving *sɛi⁴⁴* is discussed further in § 15.1.

(1156) [ŋa³³ kɛi³³ n̠a³¹] **sɛi⁴⁴** ["nɛi³³ kʰua³¹la³¹ i³²³   jo³³   ŋɛi³³"].
       1SG   AGT   say   TOP   2SG   Kunming   go   must   ASRT
       我   说   你   昆明   去   应该
       'I said "You should go to Kunming".', literally 'As for (what) I said, (I said) "You should go to Kunming".'
       我说 "你应该去昆明"。
       (KL-Elicitation)

(1157) [vɛi³²³xua³⁵tɕo³²³   mɛi⁴⁴   pʏ³²³ ko⁵⁵   kɛi³³ n̪a³¹]   **sɛi⁴⁴**   ["wɛi²⁴², lau³¹ta³⁵tiɛ⁵³,
Culture.Bureau   CL:GEN POSS CL:PL AGT   say   TOP   INTJ   old.father
文化局   个   些   说   老大爹
'The people from the Culture Bureau said "Wow, Father,
文化局的那些人说"哇，老大爷，

"nɛi³³   pʏ³²³   i³³   tɕi⁵⁵   tɕʰi⁵³   kɯ³²³   mi³²³   o²⁴   ja³³   lɛi³¹"].
2SG   POSS   sound CL:TYPE bite   CSC   be.exact be.fierce IPFV.EMP IRR.EMP
你   音   种   咬   明确   凶
"Your music is really amazing".'
"您的音键弹的很准确"。
(YAY-Erasers)

As these examples demonstrate, the same construction is used for both direct and indirect speech; there is no syntactic difference between the two. Compare the *tɕi³³* examples in (1153) and (1154) above, and the *n̪a³¹* examples in (1156) and (1157) above. Moreover, because arguments are often absent in discourse, it may be difficult to differentiate the two without context. For example, the phrase in (1158) may be analyzed as either indirect or direct speech, as the two English translations indicate. The omission of the copula in equational constructions is commonplace and occurs in both simple and combined clauses (see § 8.5).

(1158) [n̪a³²³ka⁵³pʰa³¹ ko⁵⁵]   **tɕi³³**   tʏ³³   ŋ³³   po⁵³,   ŋ⁴⁴   ŋuo³¹?
n̪a³²³ka⁵³.M   CL:PL   say   PROG   ASRT   EPIS.EMP   COP   COP.Q
n̪a³²³ka⁵³男人   些   说   是
'(They) say (they were) *n̪a³²³ka⁵³* people, isn't that right?' / '(They) say "(They) were) *n̪a³²³ka⁵³* people", isn't that right?'
说的是中村的男的，是吗？/ 说"是中村的男的"，是吗？
(KL-Performing)

However, in some cases the utterance clause may contain elements that signal a change in the deictic center, such as first or second person pronouns or emphatic particles. For example, in (1159) the first person pronoun *ŋa³³* and the term of address *ta³⁵sʏ²⁴²*, which carries a vocative tone change (see § 3.2.7), both mark a shift in deixis, thus making it direct speech. Likewise, the fact that the utterance clause in (1160) ends with the imperfective emphatic marker *ja³³*, which normally occupies phrase-final position, indicates that it originates from a character in the story rather than the narrator.

(1159) ["ta³⁵sʏ²⁴²,   ŋa³³   xa³³n̪a⁵³   xɛi⁵³?"]   **tɕi³³**   tʏ³³   wa³³   tsɛi³¹.
big.uncle   1SG   where   stand   say   PROG   CRS   HSY
大叔   我   哪里   站   说
' "Uncle, where (should) I stand?", (they) were asking.'
"大叔，我站在哪里"，这么问。
(PYX-Performing)

(1160) ["mɛi⁴⁴   na²⁴   kɯ³²³   sa³³   ja³³!"]   **tɕi³³**   tʏ³³   ŋ³³   tsɛi³¹.
very   hear   CSC   be.good   IPFV.EMP   say   PROG   ASRT   HSY
很   听   好   说
' "(It) sounds great!" (they) said.'
说是"很好听！"
(PYX-Performing)

As the example in (1159) above illustrates, the utterance clause may contain a question. If it is direct speech, then usually only *tɕi³³* is used in the matrix clause. It is possible for the verb *na²⁴ŋ²⁴* 'to ask' to introduce direct speech, but in discourse it is typically used to repeat a question and so the utterance is almost always indirect speech. Without context, the phrase may be interpreted either way, as (1161) illustrates. Note that even if the quoted material in (1161) is indirect, it must still pattern as a question. Other verbs related to speech — such as *pa⁵³mo³³* 'to tell', *tsʰɛi³²³zɛi³⁵* 'to admit' and *tsʰŋ²⁴to³³* 'to promise' — seem to mainly co-occur with indirect speech. An illustrative example is shown in (1162).

(1161) [ŋa³³   kɛi³³   na²⁴ŋ²⁴]   **sɛi⁴⁴**   [i³³   kʰua³¹la³¹   i³²³   i³²³   la³¹].
1SG   AGT   ask   TOP   3SG   Kunming   go   go   IRR.Q
我   问   他   昆明   去   去
'I asked (if) he went to Kunming.' / 'I asked, "Did he go to Kunming?".'
我问了他去了昆明没有。/ 我问了"他去了昆明没有？"
(KL-Elicitation)

(1162) [i³³   kɛi³³   tsʰɛi³²³zɛi³⁵]   **sɛi⁴⁴**   [i³³   n̪o³¹   kʰʏ³¹   wa³²³].
1SG   AGT   admit   TOP   3SG   thing   steal   PFV
他   承认   他   东西   偷
'He admitted that he stole things.'
他承认他偷东西了。
(KL-Elicitation)

There are two verbs that are homophonous with *tɕi³³* — one means 'to do' and the other 'to pack, load'. Context largely differentiates them in discourse, but aspectual patterns are also employed for this purpose. Progressive aspect, especially *tʏ³³* and *ti³³ ja³³*, is primarily used with the quotative verb, even if the speech act is completed and thus eligible for perfective marking. Examples are shown in (1163) and (1164). Emphasis may be shown by the strong assertion marker $ŋɛi^{33}$ or a construction involving contrastive tone 35, as shown in (1165) and (1166) respectively. The construction may also be modified by the hearsay particle $tsɛi^{31}$, which is described further below.

(1163) [mɛi⁴⁴ ɕo³³   wa³²³]   **tɕi³³** **tɤ³³** wa³³   po⁵³.
       very   be.clean   PFV   say   PROG   CRS   EPIS.EMP
       很   干净   说
       '(They) say (it) became very clean, (don't you know?).'
       说的是很干净了。
       (PYX-Dragon Pools)

(1164) ["ŋ³¹   ta³²³   za³¹   ŋ³¹   kɤ³¹   li³³"]   **tɕi³³** **ti³³ ja³³**   tsɛi³¹.
       two   CL:ANM   DIM   sell   cross   come   say   PROG   HSY
       二   条   卖   过   来   说
       ' "Sell (us) two small (ones)," (they) said.'
       "卖两条来吧" 这么说的。
       (PYX-Dragon Pools)

(1165) [xua²⁴   ma³¹   tʰɤ⁵⁵]   **tɕi³³** ŋɛi³³.
       be.worthwhile NEG   achieve   say   ASRT
       划   不   着   说
       '(It) is not worth the expense, (they) say.'
       说是不划算。
       (WYF-Stools)

(1166) [m³³tso³³ma³³   jo³⁵   ŋɛi³³]   **tɕi³³** **tɤ³⁵**   po⁵³!
       woman   CL:HUM   ASRT   say   PROG.FOC   EPIS.EMP
       女人   位   说
       '(They) say (it) was (a) woman, that's right!'
       好像说的是女人嘛！
       (KL-Dragon Pools)

Unlike other dependent clauses, utterances are completely unrestricted in their syntactic composition. They routinely contain arguments, aspect marking and even phrase-final particles that differ from those in the matrix clause. For example, in (1167) the S in the utterance is first person, but the A of $tɕi^{33}$ is third person. In (1168), the utterance clause has the perfective aspect marker while that modifying $tɕi^{33}$ is the currently relevant state marker. And in (1169), the utterance contains the imperfective emphatic ja^{33}, while $tɕi^{33}$ has no emphatic marker. An even more dramatic difference occurs when the utterance is a question, and the $tɕi^{33}$ clause remains declarative, as in (1170). As a result, syntactic elements in the matrix clause have no scope over the utterance complement, pointing to a much looser degree of integration than that found in *sɛi*⁴⁴ clauses. This is a necessary exception to the basic complementation strategy — grammatical particles provide crucial information to any clause and must be repeated when reporting speech, whether directly or indirectly. The fact that the utterance may be replaced by a simple noun phrase, such as a^{33} ma^{44} 'that CL:GEN' or a^{33} $tɕi^{55}$ 'that phrase', indicates that it remains an argument of the verb despite a lack of tight syntactic integration.

(1167) ["ŋa³³ mi⁵³   tʏ⁴⁴   i³²³ kʏ³²³ ma³¹ tso³²³ wa³³"] **tɕi⁴⁴** to³³.
         1SG be.hungry CLNK   go   NMLZ   NEG   EXIST   CRS   say   also
         我   饿   去   不   有   说   也
       ' "I'm extremely hungry," (they) said.'
       "我饿的没办法了" 这么说了也。
       (PYX-Weeds)

(1168) [mɛi⁴⁴ ɕo³³   wa³²³] **tɕi⁵³** tʏ³³ wa³³ po⁵³.
         very   be.clean PFV   say   INCP   EPIS.EMP
         很   干净   说
       '(They) say (it) became very clean, (don't you know?)'
       说的是很干净了。
       (PYX-Dragon Pools)

(1169) ["nɛi³³ kʰai³³tsɿ³²³ ti⁵³   mo⁵⁵   ja³³!"] **tɕi³³** tɕo³⁵.
         2SG   eraser   CL:PCE want   IPFV.EMP say   then
         你   橡皮擦   块   要   说   就
       'Then (he) said "You want an eraser!".'
       就说"你要橡皮"。
       (YAY-Erasers)

(1170) sɛi³⁵xo³⁵jɛ³²³ jo³⁵   kɛi³³,
         sales.clerk   CL:HUM AGT
         售货员   位
       'the sales clerk,'
       售货员

         ["na³³   xa³³ma⁴⁴ mo⁵⁵   pa⁵³ ŋa³¹?"] **tɕi⁴⁴** sɛi⁴⁴
         2SG   what   want   FUT   CNT.Q   say   TMP
         你   什么   要
       'when (he) said "What do you want?" '
       说"你要什么？"的时候
       (YAY-Erasers)

Although *tɕi*³³ is routinely employed to mark direct speech, it is not obligatory. Quoted material may be presented without any marking at all; context often makes its source clear. For example, in the passage in (1171) the use of *tɕi*³³ in the first clause establishes that characters in the story are being quoted, and so succeeding utterances do not need to be marked again. And in (1172), the fact that the protagonist approaches a group of people suggests that she will address them, and so her utterance is introduced only by the sequential construction *ja*⁵³*ni*³²³ 'and then'. The use of the first person pronoun also signals that this phrase is reported speech and not part of the narration.

(1171) "tɤ⁴⁴   xa³³ma⁴⁴   tsʰo³¹   xa³³ma⁴⁴ tsʰo³¹?"   **tɕi³³**   tɤ³³ wa³³   sɿ³¹   tsɛi³¹.
FILL   what   perform   what   perform   say   INCP   again   HSY
什么   演   什么   演   说   　 又

' "So, what (should we) perform? What (should we) perform?" (they) began to ask again.'
"那，演什么？演什么？"又在问。

"xa³³ma³³ mo³²³ ni³¹,   xa³³ma³³   tsʰo³¹.   xuɛi²⁴ma³¹kua⁴⁴   tsʰo³¹   ŋa³²³ta³²³
what   see   TOP   what   perform   be.careless   perform   be.able
什么   看   　 什么   演   胡乱   演   能
wa³⁵."
FUT

' "Perform whatever you see. (You) can perform anything (at all)." '
"看见什么，演什么，只能胡乱演了"。
(PYX-Performing)

(1172) o²⁴ti³²³   tsʰɿ³³   li³³   wa³³   tsɛi³¹   ja⁵³ni³²³,
there   arrive   come   CRS   HSY   later
那里   到   来   　 　 然后

'(They say she) came (over) there, then,'
来到了那里（听说），然后，

"ta³⁵tsi³¹tsi²⁴,   ŋa³³   tɛi³¹   tʰɤ⁵⁵   to³⁵   pa³²³   liɛ³³."
big.older.sister   1SG   one   CL:TMP   cross   help   come
大姐姐   我   一   下   渡   帮   来

' "Sister, come help me cross (the river)." '
"大姐姐，来帮我渡一下。"
(HPH-Weeds)

When *tɕi*³³ is employed, it is often followed by the hearsay particle *tsɛi*³¹, which almost always ends the clause, as (1173) demonstrates. The meanings of the two lexemes overlap a great deal, but their functions differ slightly. *tɕi*³³ is the verb used to mark reported speech, which may be a direct quote or an indirect summary of another's utterance. Because it is a verb, it may be modifed by aspect, focus and emphatic markers, allowing a speaker to provide details about when and how an utterance was made, as in (1174). *tsɛi³¹* is a particle that likewise marks speech. But when it occurs without *tɕi³³*, the clause is considered indirect speech, as in (1175). This information may be heard first-hand or learned through a chain of many intermediaries, but it is generally assumed to paraphrase an utterance made at some point by another person. Note that the presence of the particle does not necessarily indicate that the content of the modified clause is uncertain, though at times this may be inferred through context. Because *tsɛi³¹* is a particle and not a verb, it cannot be modified by any other marker, and thus does not provide ancillary information like *tɕi³³*. Moreover, its status as a particle means that no complementation is involved — it is included here because of its close functional association with *tɕi³³*.

(1173) ta²⁴to³³   tsʰo³³   tso³²³   ŋa³²³   ma³¹   ta³²³   **tɕi³³**   ŋ³³   **tsɛi³¹**.
        still   people   EXIST   be.able   NEG   be.able   say   ASRT   HSY
        还   人   有   能   不   能   说
        'People couldn't live there, (they) say.'
        说也不可能居住人类。
        (PYX-Dragon Pools)

(1174) i²⁴la³¹   sɿ³²³xɯ³⁵   pɤ³²³   tsʰo³³   tsʰɤ³³   tɕi³³   tɕi⁵⁵   kɤ³³   ti³³ ja³³   **tɕi³³**
        past   time   POSS   person   PL   this   CL:TYPE   do   PROG   say
        过去   时候   　 人   们   这   种   做   　 说
        wa³⁵   **po⁵³**.
        FUT   EPIS.EMP
        'People (in) the past did (things) this way, (they) will say, (see?)'
        以前的人是做这种的，要这样说了。
        (KL-Sewing)

(1175) tɛi³¹   xa⁵³   tɛi³¹   sɤ³³   la⁵³   tɛi³¹   sɤ³³   tɕɛ⁵⁵   mɤ²⁴   ja³³
        one   CL:TMP   one   CL:ROW   wrap   one   CL:ROW   sew   have.time   IPFV.EMP
        一   晚   一   串   绕   一   串   钉   有空
        tsɛi³¹   mɛi⁴⁴.
        HSY   DSC.EMP
        '(They) have time to wrap (and) finish one bunch in an evening, (they say).'
        说是可以一个晚上绕一串钉一串的。
        (KL-Sewing)

16 Summary of Clause-Linking Particles

As mentioned in Chapter 13, the many-to-many relationship between clause-linking particles and their functions makes it difficult to present a holistic view of clause-combining in Khatso. And because Chapters 13 through 15 are organized according to function, particles that take part in more than one clause-combining strategy appear in multiple sections and often overlap with single-function particles and constructions. This chapter provides an alternate view of clause-combining by looking at form rather than function, focusing particularly on those particles that have multiple uses. The fact that Khatso is a pragmatics-based language, meaning that verbal semantics and context are often more important than syntax in understanding the function of any given lexeme or construction in discourse, means that multifunctionality is readily accepted in the language (see Bisang 2009). And despite the appearance of overlap, few particles are completely synonymous with those that have similar functions. There are typically semantic nuances, or even collocations routinized over time, that determine which is used in any given discourse context.

The clause-combining particles and constructions discussed in Chapters 13 through 15 are listed in Table 16.1, along with their functions and the sections in which they are described. Most support a single function, but there are six particles that warrant additional discussion. These six — to^{33}, ni^{323}, ni^{31}, la^{35}, $tɤ^{44}$ and $sɛi^{44}$ — have multiple clause-linking functions and thus are especially frequent in discourse. Most of them may be analyzed as flexible particles that allow for multiple interpretations depending on verbal semantics and context, an expected feature of a pragmatics-based language like Khatso. However, in some cases the functions and their syntax differ enough to suggest that new uses have grammaticalized over time. Moreover, $tɤ^{44}$ and $sɛi^{44}$ may be borrowed from Hanyu, adding another layer of complexity to the analysis. Without dependable historical data for the language, it is not always obvious which explanation is most likely. These issues are explore further in the following sections.

Table 16.1: Clause-combining particles and their functions

Construction	Function	Section
$i^{24}fa^{33}$, $i^{31}kɯ^{35}$, $to^{33}i^{31}$ 'more'	comparative conditional	§ 14.4.4
ja^{53} ni^{323} 'then, and then'	cause/effect	§ 14.2.1
	sequential	§ 13.2.4.2
jo^{35}	simultaneous	§ 13.2.3.1

Construction	Function	Section
juxtaposition	complementation	§ 15.1
	parallel clause linking	§ 13.1.1.1
	reported speech	§ 15.3
la³⁵ & related tone change	adversative/contrast	§ 13.1.3.3
	cause/effect	§ 14.2.3
	focus	§ 13.1.3.3
	reason	§ 14.1.3
loanwords	adversative coordination	§ 13.1.3.4
	cause/effect	§ 14.2.4
	concessive	§ 14.3.2
	conditional	§ 14.4.5
	reason	§ 14.1.4
	temporal linking	§ 13.2.2
mɛi⁴⁴sŋ⁴⁴ 'or'	interrogative disjunction	§ 13.1.2
mo⁵⁵ ni³¹... mo⁵⁵ ni³¹ 'either... or'	disjunction	§ 13.1.2
nɛi³³tɕo³⁵	concessive conditional	§ 14.4.3
ni³¹	conditional	§ 14.4.1
	reason	§ 14.1.2
	sequential	§ 13.2.4.4
	topic	§ 10.1
ni³¹n̠ɛ³²³	simultaneous	§ 13.2.3.2
ni³²³	backgrounding	§ 16.2
	reason	§ 14.1.1
ŋ³³n̠a⁴⁴li³³ 'but'	adversative linking	§ 13.1.3.1
ŋ³³si⁴⁴ 'or'	disjunction	§ 13.1.2
ŋ⁴⁴li³³ 'but'	adversative linking	§ 13.1.3.1
sa²⁴kɛi³³ 'until'	sequential	§ 13.2.4.5
sɛi⁴⁴	complementation	§ 15.1
	manner	§ 14.5
	general temporal linking	§ 13.2.1
	topic	§ 10.1
	simultaneous	§ 13.2.3.3
ta³¹ ni³²³	reason	§ 14.1.1
	sequential	§ 13.2.4.3
tɛi³¹... ni³¹ tɕo³⁵ 'as soon as'	sequential	§ 13.2.4.4

Construction	Function	Section
tɕo³⁵ 'then'	cause/effect	§ 14.2.1
	sequential	§ 13.2.4.1
tɤ⁴⁴	cause and effect	§ 14.2.2
	manner	§ 14.5
	purpose	§ 14.6
	simultaneous	§ 13.2.3.4
to³³ 'also, and'	adversative linking	§ 13.1.3.2
	concessive	§ 14.3.1
	concessive conditional	§ 14.4.3
	parallel clause linking	§ 13.1.1.2
	universal conditional	§ 14.4.2
tsɛi³¹	hearsay	§ 15.3
wa²⁴ xɛi³⁵	simultaneous	§ 13.2.3.1

16.1 *to³³*

The adverb *to³³* figures in a number of clause-linking strategies. Its primary function is as a simple adverb, but it also appears in simple clause linking, adversative linking, the concessive construction and the universal conditional construction. These formulations all share the basic function of linking a proposition to a clause providing additional information, which may either support it, contrast with it or negate it altogether.

As an adverb, *to³³* means 'also'. When placed immediately before a verb, it links a clause pragmatically to a related situation already mentioned (see § 13.1.1.1). Its meaning is thus additive, often signaling that either a single actor performs a second activity or that a second actor performs the same activity as another already mentioned. The examples in (1176) and (1177) illustrate both situations respectively. Note that in all of its uses, *to³³* may trigger tone change in the immediately preceding syllable (see § 3.2.4.1).

(1076) kʰai³³sɿ³⁵   zɿ³²³n̻ɛ³²³tsɿ³¹   so²⁴   la²⁴ tsɛi³⁵,   [pʰi²⁴ŋ²⁴tɕʰi³¹ n̻a³¹   ma³¹
      begin   first.grade   study   REL   CL:TMP   Hanyu   speak   NEG
      开始   一年级   读   段   汉语   说   不
      li³²³].
      know.how
      会
      'When (I) started first grade, (I) couldn't speak Hanyu.'
      开始读一年级的时候，不会说汉语。

sʏ⁵⁵ so²⁴ sɛi⁴⁴, [pʰi²⁴ŋ²⁴tɕʰi³¹ tɕi⁵⁵ **to³³** lo³¹sɿ²⁴ na²⁴ ma³¹
book study TMP Hanyu CL:TYPE also much hear NEG
书 读 汉语 种 也 很多 听 不
li³²³].
know.how
会
'When (I was) studying, I also couldn't understand much Hanyu.'
上学的时候，也听不懂很多汉语。
(YAY-Erasers)

(1177) [a³³tɕʰa⁵⁵kʰʏ³³ tsʰɿ³¹ma³³ m̩³³ kɯ³²³ ȵɛ²⁴ ta³¹].
that.time daughter-in-law make CSC be.small later
那时候 太太 做 小 后
'(At) that time, women became wives (when) young.'
那时候出嫁的年龄小。

[i²⁴tsʏ²⁴za³¹ tsʰʏ⁴⁴ **to³³** tsʰɿ³¹ma³³ tsʰɿ³³ kɯ³²³ ȵɛ²⁴].
young.man PL also daughter-in-law take CSC be.small
男孩子 们 也 太太 娶 小
'Young men also took wives (when) young.'
男孩子结婚年龄也小。
(YJF-Childhood)

From this pragmatic linking function, *to³³* developed a more overt syntactic linking function. When placed at the end of a clause, it serves to conjoin it with the following clause, much like 'and' does in English, as in (1178). This use is never obligatory, and seems partly to signal to interlocutors that the speaker's turn is not yet over (see § 13.1.1.2). The second clause is not always additive. It may, in fact, present a situation contrary to the first, as in (1179), in which case *to³³* takes on an adversative sense akin to 'but' (see § 13.1.3.2).

(1178) [i³²³tɕa⁵³ ma³¹ tso²⁴] **to³³**,
water NEG EXIST and
水 不 有 也

[ta²⁴to³³ tsʰo³³ tso³²³ ŋa³²³ ma³¹ ta³²³].
still people EXIST be.able NEG be.able
还 人 有 能 不 能
'There was no water, and people weren't able to live (there).'
没有水，也就不能居住人。
(PYX-Dragon Pools)

(1179) ai²⁴ [tsʰo³¹ li²⁴ ja⁴⁴] **to³³** [m̥³³to³¹ kɤ³²³ kɤ²⁴ wa³³ mɛi⁴⁴].
INTJ sing know.how IPFV.EMP also forget finish finish CRS DSC.EMP
哎 唱 会 也 忘记 完 完
'Oh, (I used to) know how to sing, but (I) completely forgot how.'
哎，会唱的，但也全部都忘记了。
(YJF-Dance Parties)

The second clause need not completely rebut the information in the first. It may merely provide a concession — that is, it may offer contrasting information or some other unexpected qualification without entirely negating the main proposition. Thus, *to³³* may link clauses in a concessive construction, with a function more akin to the English 'although' (see § 14.3.1). Often the first clause is presented as a complement of the quotative verb *tɕi³³* 'to say', and may also carry its own emphatic marker, as the example in (1180) illustrates. These additional words are not obligatory but help differentiate the concessive from the adversative construction, though pragmatics alone may suffice. And while Khatso does have a dedicated concessive conditional construction, which presents a condition that may be expected to, but in the end does not, prevent the main proposition (see § 14.4.3), it is routinely replaced by the simple concessive, as (1181) illustrates.

(1180) [xɤ³³ ŋɛi³³ **tɕi⁴⁴** **to³³** [i³³ tɕo³⁵ ma³¹ ɤɤ³⁵ tso²⁴].
scold ASRT say also 3SG then NEG move ITER
骂 说 也 他 就 不 动
'(Although you) scold (him), he doesn't move.'
骂他，他就是不动。
(PRL-Education)

(1181) [pɤ³¹ wa²⁴] **to³³** [xɛi³⁵ tsa³²³ ma³¹ tsa⁵⁵].
dance PFV also still rice NEG feed
娱乐 也 还 饭 不 喂
'(Although we) danced, still (they) wouldn't feed (us).'
跳了也还不给饭吃。
(GCS-Dance Parties)

The concessive construction forms the basis of the universal conditional. The difference is that in the conditional the first clause presents a choice that includes all possible options (see § 14.4.2). If there are only two choices, then the clause may contain a verb and its negation, as in (1182), or two verbs linked by a disjunctive coordinator, as in (1183). If the options are open-ended, then the clause may contain an interrogative pronoun, as in (1184).

(1085) [i³³ li³²³ **ma³¹** li³²³ nɛi³³] **tɕi⁴⁴ to³³** [ŋa³³tsʰɤ³³ ka³²³ wa³⁵].
3SG come NEG come ASRT say also 1PL walk FUT
他 来 不 来 说 也 我们 走
'Whether he comes or not, we will go.'
无论他来不来，我们都要走了。
(KL-Elicitation)

(1183) [i³³ tsʰa³⁵ko³³ tsʰa³⁵ ŋ³³si⁴⁴ ni³¹ka³³ tsʰo³¹ nɛi³³] **tɕi⁴⁴ to³³** [ŋa³³ ma³¹
3SG song sing or dance perform ASRT say also 1SG NEG
他 歌 唱 或 舞 跳 说 也 我 不
ŋ²⁴ka³³ i³³ wa³³].
watch go CRS
看 去
'Whether he sings or dances, I won't go watch.'
无论他唱歌或跳舞，我也不去看了。
(KL-Elicitation)

(1184) [i³³ kɛi³³ **xa³³ni³³** tɕi³³ nɛi³³] **tɕi⁴⁴ to³³** [ŋa³³ kʰua³¹la³¹ i³²³ wa³⁵].
3SG AGT how say ASRT say also 1SG Kunming go FUT
他 怎么 说 说 也 我 昆明 去
'Whatever he says, I'll go to Kunming.'
无论他说什么，我都要去昆明。
(KL-Elicitation)

Thus, the different formulations involving *to³³* all have a common functional thread. *to³³* links a main proposition with another clause containing ancillary information. Since *to³³* may appear in two different positions in a clause, we can take these as different constructions — the clause-linking function likely grammaticalized from the simple adverbial use. This second construction allows for multiple interpretations depending on verbal semantics and discourse context. If the second clause provides additive information, then it is a case of simple clause linking, much like coordination in other languages. But if the second clause contrasts with or even negates the content of the first clause, then a concessive or adversative interpretation is more relevant. Regardless of meaning, however, the two constructions never syntactically integrate their clauses; the linkage is purely pragmatic.

16.2 *ni³²³*

The particle *ni³²³* serves primarily to mark background information. This may be of any form, from simple nouns and noun phrases to adverbs and clauses. Noun phrases marked by *ni³²³* may provide temporal or other explanatory information in discourse, as shown in (1185) and (1186) respectively. Note that regardless of function, *ni*^{323} may trigger tone change in the immediately preceding syllable (see § 3.2.4.1).

(1185) [za^{31}m̥^{31}za^{31} a^{33} tsɛi^{35} ka^{44}]   **ni**^{323},
　　　 girl   that   CL:TMP   from   BKGD
　　　 女孩   那   段   从

　　　 [ɤ^{35} sa^{33} sɿ^{323} n̠ɛ^{323} tsʰɤ^{31}na^{31} wa^{323} sɛi^{31} mɛi^{44}].
　　　 two   three   ten   CL:TMP   stop   PFV   still   DSC.EMP
　　　 二   三   十   年   停止   又
　　　 'Since the time (I was) a girl, (I) stopped for twenty (or) thirty years.'
　　　 从姑娘那个时候起，又停止了二三十年了。
　　　 (WYY-Sewing)

(1186) [no^{53}ma^{33} tɕi^{55}]   **ni**^{323} [tsʰɤ^{44} to^{33} tsʰɤ^{33} ma^{31} kɤ^{53} wa^{33} po^{53}].
　　　 stone   CL:TYPE   BKGD   burn   also   burn   NEG   be.bad   CRS   EPIS.EMP
　　　 石头   种   烧   也   烧   不   坏
　　　 '(That) type of stone, (it can) burn but won't burn up, (see?)'
　　　 那种石头呢，烧也烧不坏了呀。
　　　 (PYX-Dragon Pools)

When a clause is marked by *ni*^{323}, it is usually interpreted as the reason for the following matrix clause, as (1187) illustrates. And although the particle itself has no lexical meaning in Khatso, in this function it is usually translated into Putonghua as *yīnwèi* 因为 and into English as 'because'.

(1187) tsɛi^{35}tsɿ^{35} ma^{31} tso^{323} wa^{33}.
　　　 evidence   NEG   EXIST   CRS
　　　 证据   不   有
　　　 'There's no evidence.'
　　　 没有证据了。

　　　 tɤ^{44} [lɤ^{24} xɛi^{31} no^{53}]   **ni**^{323} [xa^{33}n̠a^{53} tsa^{24}tso^{24} i^{33}]?
　　　 FILL   land   burn   complete   BKGD   where   find   go
　　　 坡   烧   完   哪里   找   去
　　　 'Because (the) land was burned, where (can you) go to find (proof)?'
　　　 被烧了，去哪里找？
　　　 (PYX-Dragon Pools)

However, the construction *ta*^{31} *ni*^{323}, which contains a temporal morpheme meaning 'after', is also employed to mark reason clauses, and often the two are interchangeable (see § 14.1.1). This is likely the bridge between the noun-modifying use of

ni^{323} and its reason-introducing function. Primary events occur after the reasons that bring them about, so the temporal and logical interpretations work hand in hand. Thus, $ta^{31}\ ni^{323}$ may be interpreted either way with only a nuanced difference in meaning, as the phrase in (1188) illustrates.

(1188) [kʰo³³ɕo³²³   mɛi⁴⁴   fa³²³ta²⁴]   **ta³¹ ni³²³**,
       science   CL:GEN   develop   after
       科学   个   发达   以后
       'After science developed,' / 'Because science developed,'
       科学发达以后，/ 因为科学发达，

       [xua³⁵fɛi³²³   no³²³jo³²³   a³³   ko⁵⁵   kɛi³³   ŋ³³   n̪a³³].
       fertilizer   pesticide   that   CL:PL   INS   COP   COP.EMP
       化肥   农药   那   些   用   是
       '(We used) those fertilizers and pesticides, that's right.'
       用那些化肥农药，是吧.
       (PYX-Weeds)

Whether these various functions are a result of grammaticalization or pragmatic flexibility is unclear. Syntactically, they are often identical, since the omission of ta^{31} in the reason interpretation is optional, indicating that this is a single construction. Pragmatically, the difference is so slight, as the example in (1188) above illustrates, as to indicate that context alone drives the two meanings. On the other hand, temporal constructions often grammaticalize into expressions of causation, a pattern found in many languages around the world (Traugott and König 1991: 194–199). The optionality of ta^{31} suggests that it is becoming semantically bleached in the reason interpretation, which implies that grammaticalization is involved. It may be that the new pattern has not yet become fully routinized, placing it somewhere on the continuum between pragmatic inference and the grammaticalization of a separate construction.

16.3 ni^{31}

The primary function of ni^{31} is as a topic marker (§ 10.1). In this use, it may follow any type of word or phrase, from simple nouns to clauses, which establishes a discourse theme about which the following clause provides commentary. The examples in (1189) and (1190) illustrate the pattern. As a result, ni^{31} overlaps somewhat with the topic and temporal marker sei^{44}, though there are key differences. ni^{31} is obligatory in conditional constructions, but sei^{44} can never take part in them. Conversely, one crucial function of sei^{44} is to aid complementation, a use that ni^{31} can never serve. An overview of *sɛi⁴⁴* is presented in § 16.6 below; its role in complementation can be found in Chapter 15.

(1189) [mo⁵⁵ pɤ⁵³ so²⁴ la²⁴ jo³⁵] **ni³¹** [tɕo³⁵ tʰɤ⁵⁵ tɤ⁴⁴ so²⁴ sʅ⁵⁵
      want play learn REL CL:HUM TOP then CL:TMP all learn know
      要   弹   学   位   就   下   都   学   知道
      ta⁵⁵ la³⁵ ŋɛi³³].
      be.type FOC ASRT
      样
      'As for those who want to learn to play, (they) then all learn how, (it's) like that.'
      想学弹的人呢，一下子就都学会了，这样的。
      (YLW-Learning)

(1190) [i²⁴la³¹ sʅ³²³xɯ³⁵ ŋa³³tsʰɤ³¹ n̪ɛ²⁴ za³¹ sʅ³²³xɯ³⁵ tɤ³⁵] **ni³¹**,
      past time 1PL be.small DIM time FOC TOP
      过去 时候 我们 小   时候

      [xa³³n̪a⁵³ li⁴⁴ wa³²³tsʅ³⁵ tɕi³³ tɕi⁵⁵ tsa²⁴tso²⁴ i³³ pa⁵³ ŋa³¹]?
      where in toy this CL:TYPE find go FUT CNT.Q
      哪   里 玩具   这   种   找   去   说
      '(In) the past when we were young, where could (we) go to find those kinds of toys?'
      以前我们小的时候呢，哪里去找这种玩具？
      (HPH-Toys)

As in many Khatso constructions, pragmatics plays a crucial role in determining the relationship between clauses linked by *ni³¹*. If the first clause describes a realis situation, as in (1191), then it may be interpreted as the reason for the event in the matrix clause (see § 14.1.2). The first clause is typically presented as a complement of the quotative verb *tɕi³³* 'say', but unlike the conditional sense of this verb in English, in Khatso it is presented as reported speech, akin to '(they) say'. By contrast, if the first clause is irrealis and does not contain *tɕi³³*, as in (1192), then it is seen as presenting a condition for the realization of following event, thereby creating a conditional construction (see § 14.4.1). Syntactically, these are still topic-comment constructions, but context expands the way they are understood in discourse.

(1191) [tɛi³¹ jo³⁵ tɛi³¹ jo³⁵ tsʰɿ³³ kɯ³³ li³³ ŋɛi³³] **tɕi⁴⁴ ni³¹** tɕo³⁵,
one CL:HUM one CL:HUM marry enter come ASRT say TOP then
一 位 一 位 娶 进 来 说 就
'Since one after another (they) married in (to the family), then,'
一个一个娶进来呢就，

[ŋ³¹ jo³⁵ tsʰɿ³³ kɯ³³ li⁴⁴ ni³¹ tɕo³⁵ ŋ³¹ tsɿ⁵⁵miɛ⁵⁵].
two CL:HUM marry enter come TOP then two CL:FAMGP
两 位 娶 回 来 就 两
'Since two married in, then (they became) two sisters-in-law (of mine).'
娶两个回来呢就是妯娌俩。
(HPH-Family)

(1192) [ti⁵³ tso⁵⁵ tɕɛ²⁴] **ni³¹** [tɕo³⁵ tɤ⁴⁴ kɯ²⁴ta³³ tɛi³³ ma⁴⁴ ma³¹ tso³²³
CL:PCE pull be.tight TOP then all knot this CL:GEN NEG EXIST
点 拉 紧 就 都 结 这 个 不 有
wa³³].
CRS
'If (you) pull (it) tighter, then there won't be this knot.'
拉紧一点呢，这个结就没有了。
(WYY-Sewing)

All of these functions contain a simple temporal logic — the event marked by *ni³¹* generally occurs in time before the following matrix verb. All clauses combined with *ni³¹* thus possess an inherent temporal order, but in certain contexts the simple sequential reading is the relevant one (see § 13.2.4.4). This is most apparent in procedural instructions, as in (1193), where syntactic tail-head linkages are common — that is, where the previous step is repeated in a clause ending in *ni³¹*, followed by the next step.

(1193) i⁴⁴ni³¹ ta³⁵ i³²³tɕa⁵³ kɛi³³ tɛi⁵³ kʰuo⁵³.
later again water INS take be.wet
然后 又 水 用 带 湿
'Later, use water to make (it) wet.'
然后用水弄湿，

[tɛi⁵³ kʰuo⁵³] **ni³¹** kɤ³³ tɤ⁴⁴ kɛi³³ tsɿ³⁵.
take be.wet TOP make CLNK AGT soak
带 湿 做 泡
'Having made (it) wet, let (it) soak.'
弄湿了泡着。
(WYF-Stools)

Thus, the functional expansion of ni^{31} appears to be a result of pragmatic flexibility rather than syntactic innovation through grammaticalization. The various uses all contain the same basic topic-comment structure. Nonetheless, the various pragmatic nuances have become routinized over time. This is especially apparent with the conditional, which can only be conveyed with ni^{31}.

16.4 la^{35}

The particle la^{35} marks focus on a clausal level. That is, it indicates that the clause containing la^{35} brings information that is new to or contrasts with an existing presupposition. Because it marks the entire clause as focal, as opposed to a single element within it, la^{35} always sits between the verb and a small subset of clause-final particles, including the strong assertion particle $\eta\varepsilon i^{33}$, the currently relevant state marker wa^{33}, the epistemic emphatic po^{53}, the discourse emphatic $m\varepsilon i^{44}$ and the affirmative interrogative particle sa^{44}. Thus the link with the preceding idea is pragmatic rather than syntactic; the clauses remain independent.

In discourse, the primary purpose of la^{35} appears to be highlighting contrastive information, as (1194) illustrates, and thus it often has an adversative function (see § 13.1.3.3). Because the meaning depends heavily on context, and its corresponding function in English is mainly conveyed through prosody, there is no simple translation for la^{35}. In its contrastive use, it may be interpreted as 'thus', 'just', 'only', 'like that' or 'instead'. In some instances, a la^{35} clause summarizes a number of other explanatory clauses, as in (1195). Here, the focal information precedes the la^{35} clause, and the latter merely provides an emphatic wrap-up assertion rather than the actual contrastive detail.

(1194) i³²³tso³³ a³³   ma⁴⁴   ɕo³³   tʰɛi³²³ ja³³   tɛi³³ tsɛi³⁵.
       well   that CL:GEN be.clean very   IPFV.EMP this CL:TMP
       井   那   个   干净   很   这   段
       'That well is very clean, now.'
       现在那口井很干净。

i²⁴la³¹ ni³⁵?   [tsa³³   tʰɛi³²³] **la³⁵** ŋɛi³³,   i²⁴la³¹.
past   TOP.Q   be.dirty very   FOC   ASRT   past
以前   脏   很   以前
'In the past? (It) was really dirty, in the past.'
以前呢，很脏的啦。
(PYX-Dragon Pools)

(1195) m̩³¹tsʰɻ⁵³ tɛi³⁵sɻ³⁵ tsɛi³⁵ tsɛi³⁵ ŋ²⁴ka³³ ni³¹ tsɛi³⁵ kv̩³³ ʐɻ⁵³ ma³¹
evening television CL:TMP CL:TMP look TOP CL:TMP do sleep NEG
晚上 电视 段 段 看 段 做 睡 不
sa³³.
be.good
好
'(In the) evening (I) watch television a while, work a while, (when I) can't get to sleep.'
晚上睡不着呢，看一会电视呢，做一会。

[tɕo³⁵ ta⁵⁵ **la³⁵** po⁵³].
then be.type FOC EPIS.EMP
就 样
'(It's) like that, (see?)'
就这么样的嘛。
(WYY-Sewing)

In some cases, the information focused by *la³⁵* does not contrast with a presupposition, but rather provides additional detail. In other cases, it may present a reason for the presupposed activity (see § 14.1.3), or it may cause the *la³⁵* clause to be seen as the effect of an earlier event (see § 14.2.3). There is no syntactic difference in these functions. Rather, discourse context, or perhaps real world knowledge, colors the interpretation. For example, in (1196) old age is cited as the reason for memory loss. In this use, the particle is more aptly translated as 'because' or 'that's why'. Similarly, the second clause in (1197) describes the result of the first, a scenario in which *la³⁵* is better understood as 'so', 'therefore' or 'as a result'.

(1196) tɛi³¹ tsv̩²⁴ to³³ ma³¹ sɻ⁵⁵ wa³³ mɛi⁴⁴, tɛi³³tɕʰa⁵⁵kʰv̩³³ ni⁵³.
everything also NEG know CRS DSC.EMP this.time TOP
什么 也 不 知道 这时候
'(I) don't know anything anymore, these days.'
现在什么也不知道了。

[kv̩³¹ tʰiɛ³³ kv̩³¹ ti³⁵ ta⁵⁵ **la³⁵** wa³³].
old heaven old land be.type FOC CRS
古 天 古 地 样
'Because (I'm) old now.'
成老古人了。
(YJF-Dance Parties)

(1197) ma³¹ mo⁵⁵ pɤ⁵³ so²⁴ la²⁴ tsʰɤ³³ ni³¹,
NEG want play learn REL PL TOP
不　　要　　弹　　学　　　　们

[ma³¹ pɤ⁵³ so²⁴ ta⁵⁵ **la³⁵** ŋɛi³³].
NEG play learn be.type FOC ASRT
不　　弹　　学　　样

'As for those who don't want to learn to play, (they) just don't learn to play (as a result).'
不想学弹的人呢，不学这样的。
(YLW-Learning)

This particle has also given rise to a tone change pattern that may replace *la³⁵* altogether regardless of function (see § 3.2.5). The change in tone may occur in one of two ways. In the first, the tone of the syllable preceding the strong assertion particle *ŋɛi³³*, essentially the position where *la³⁵* would otherwise sit, changes to tone 35. This pattern tends to occur mainly when the changing syllable has a low tone and is a verb or verb-related morpheme such as the adverb *sa²⁴* 'perhaps', the progressive marker *tɤ³³*, the auxiliary *jo³³* 'must', the quotative verb *tɕi³³* 'to say', the copula *ŋ³³*, the existential verb *tso³²³* and the verb *i³²³* 'to go', which often completes serial verb constructions. When the syllable preceding *ŋɛi³³* has a high tone or is not a verb-related morpheme, then it is *ŋɛi³³* itself that changes to tone 35. Examples of each are shown in (1198) and (1199). This pattern does not appear to be a case of tone fusion, but rather an actual change in tone that arose through analogy with *la³⁵* (see § 3.2.5).

(1198) A: xa³³ni³³ nɛi²⁴ xa³³ni³³ fɤ²⁴ tso³²³ ŋa³¹?
　　　how.many CL:ITEM how.many CL:ITEM EXIST CNT.Q
　　　多少　　　姐妹　　多少　　　兄弟　　有

　　　'How many brothers and sisters were there?'
　　　有几个姐妹几个兄弟？

B: [ŋa³³ sɛi⁴⁴ mo³³ sɛi⁴⁴ ni³¹ si³³ nɛi²⁴ **tso³⁵** ŋ³³ po⁵³].
1SG family mother family TOP three CL:ITEM EXIST.FOC ASRT EPIS.EMP
我　　家　　妈　　家　　　　三　　姐妹　　有

'My mother's family, there were (only) three sisters!'
我妈家，只有三个姐妹嘛。
(KL, YJR-Grandfather)

(1199) A: n̥a³²³ka⁵³pʰa³¹   ko⁵⁵   tɕi³³   tɤ³³   ŋ³³   po⁵³.   ŋ⁴⁴   ŋuo³¹?
           n̥a³²³ka⁵³.M   CL:PL say   PROG   ASRT EPIS.EMP   COP   COP.Q
           中村男人   些   说
           '(They) say (they were) n̥a³²³ka⁵³ men, is that right?'
           说的是中村的男的，是吗？

      B: [ma³¹   nɛi³³.   kʰa⁵⁵tsɿ³³pʰa³¹   ko⁵⁵   nɛi³⁵].
           NEG   COP   kʰa⁵⁵tsɿ³³.M   CL:PL   ASRT.FOC
           不   是   下村男人   些
           'No. (They) were kʰa⁵⁵tsɿ³³ men (instead).'
           不是。是下村的男人。
      (KL, PYX-Performing)

Expanding the function of *la³⁵* is not a result of grammaticalization — there is no syntactic difference between the various uses. In each case, *la³⁵* marks a focal clause, but the nature of the focus may vary according to discourse context. Frequently it is contrastive, but it may also summarize other contrastive clauses, or make prominent unexpected reason or effect clauses. The Chinese and English translations suggest that there are different meanings at play, but the underlying construction in Khatso remains unchanged. However, the tone change pattern that optionally replaces *la³⁵* is a separate construction, and thus can be considered a product of grammaticalization. It may have begun as tone fusion, in which the tone of *la³⁵* was attached to that of the preceding syllables as the particle itself was omitted. But now these syllables carry a single tone 35 in this construction; there is no phonetic fusion.

16.5 *tɤ⁴⁴*

While several functions of *tɤ⁴⁴* seem to be related, it may be that they are the result of separate borrowings from Hanyu rather than internal language change, though the evidence is at present inconclusive. The primary function of *tɤ⁴⁴* is to link clauses in a purpose construction (see § 14.6). In this formulation, the matrix clause is first and the dependent purpose clause is second; *tɤ⁴⁴* links the two. An example is shown in (1200). This function overlaps with that of two-event serial verb constructions (see § 8.8.2), and in some instances the two are synonymous. However all arguments must be identical in the verb serializations, while the *tɤ⁴⁴* construction allows for each clause to have a different set of arguments, depending on the verbal semantics. For example, in (1201) the A of the purpose clause is the P of the matrix clause.

(1200) [sɹ³⁵   tʰɛi³¹]   tɤ⁴⁴   [tsɤ³³].
       firewood pick   CLNK   burn
       柴   挑   烧
       '(We) gathered firewood to burn.'
       挑柴烧。
       (YJF-Childhood)

(1201) [ŋa³³   i³³   a³³pʰai³²³]   tɤ⁴⁴   [kʰua³¹la³¹   i³²³]   wa³²³.
       1SG   3SG   arrange   CLNK   Kunming   go   PFV
       我   他   安排   昆明   去
       'I arranged (for) him to go to Kunming.'
       我安排他去昆明了。
       (KL-Elicitation)

When the second clause contains a stative verb, which describes a state brought about by the primary event, it may be interpreted as an effect rather than a purpose, as in (1202). The difference is largely one of intent; the resultant state is usually seen as inadvertant or accidental rather than planned. The *tɤ⁴⁴* construction, then, may be used to express clausal cause and effect relationships (see § 14.2.2).

(1202) nɛi³³   ŋ³¹   pɛi³²³ti³⁵   ni³¹   [ŋ³³]   tɤ⁴⁴   [ma³¹   sʏ³³fʏ²⁴]   ni³¹.
       2SG   FILL   otherwise   TOP   sit   CLNK   NEG   be.comfortable TOP
       你   要不然   坐   不   舒服
       'You, uh, otherwise, (you) will be uncomfortable from sitting.'
       要不然你坐得不舒服了。
       (KL-Doctor)

By contrast, when the first clause contains a stative verb, it conveys the manner in which the event in the second clause is carried out (see § 14.5), as (1203) illustrates. Here the second clause is the matrix clause, though syntactically it behaves like all of the other functions.

(1203) [xo³¹]   tɤ⁴⁴   [zɹ̩⁵³   m̩²⁴   tsɛi³⁵   tsɛi³⁵   kʏ⁵⁵]   tɤ³⁵ wa³³   po⁵³.
       be.soft CLNK   sleep   nap   CL:TMP   CL:TMP   doze   INCP.FOC   EPIS.EMP
       软   睡   瞌   段   段   打
       '(I) now weakly doze off from time to time, (see?)'
       弱地一阵一阵地打瞌睡了呀。
       (WYY-Sewing)

In the purpose and cause and effect functions, the two clauses are generally viewed as sequential, although the two events may overlap in time depending on the semantics of the particular verbs involved. In the manner construction, the two must necessarily occur simultaneously, since one clause describes the way in which the other is performed. This may be why two non-stative clauses linked by *tɤ⁴⁴* may also be interpreted as simultaneous, as shown in (1204). This function is not productive with all verbs, however. In most cases, speakers much prefer to use either the *wa²⁴ xɛi³⁵* or *ni³¹nɛ³²³* constructions to describe concurrent events (see § 13.2.3.1 and § 13.2.3.2 respectively). There is no apparent pattern that explains these limitations. It seems that verbs that may take the simultaneous reading are the exceptions, likely resulting from historically frequent collocations in discourse.

(1204) [ɕi³³   la²⁴ka³³]   **tɤ⁴⁴**   [ɕi³³   tsa³¹]   ŋɛi³³.
       be.accustomed play   CLNK   be.accustomed eat   ASRT
       习惯   玩   习惯   吃
       '(We) would play and eat (there).'
       会在那儿玩在那儿吃。
       (YJF-Dance Parties)

Looking only at the Khatso data suggests that the various functions of *tɤ⁴⁴* result from pragmatic flexibility in discourse. In each case, the syntax is the same — *tɤ⁴⁴* serves as a clause linker, but the exact relationship between clauses is determined through context. However, it is equally likely that the *tɤ⁴⁴* constructions are the result of borrowings from Hanyu. The phonological rules for borrowing are not clear, but it has been noted that tone 44 occurs most often in loanwords (see § 3.1.2). Thus, a particle like *tɤ⁴⁴* may have Chinese origins. And, in fact, the Khatso manner construction mirrors its Chinese counterpart, suggesting that this *tɤ⁴⁴* is borrowed from the Chinese particle *de* 地, pronounced [tɤ] with neutral tone, which makes a stative verb adverbial. Similarly, the cause and effect construction is identical to another Chinese counterpart, which contains a particle *de* 得 that is likewise pronounced [tɤ]. The homophony in Chinese may have thus created homophony in Khatso. The purpose construction *tɤ⁴⁴*, however, may have originated from *dào* 到 'to arrive' in Putonghua, which links a motion clause with a destination clause. This is only one facet of the Khatso construction, which likely expanded its use after it was borrowed from physical destination to intangible goal and then purpose. Placing the dependent clause after the matrix clause is as unusual in Chinese as it is in Khatso, which further points to a potential relationship between the two. Moreover, the Chinese construction is typically interpreted as perfective even without aspectual marking (Li and Thompson 1981: 206), and this is the case in Khatso as well. It is unclear why the Khatso vowel is /ɤ/ rather than /au/, since the diphthong exists in the language as well. If the borrowing hypothesis is correct, then these three functions of *tɤ⁴⁴* are unrelated and homophonous by accident, though perhaps analogy influenced the vowel change in the purpose function. The simultaneous use, however, cannot be explained by language contact — it seems to be an extension of the implied temporal logic of the manner construction. Regardless, without reliable historical linguistic data to decide the matter, either pragmatic flexibility or homophonous loans remains an equally likely explanation for the multifunctionality of *tɤ⁴⁴*.

There are several other morphemes in Khatso pronounced *tɤ⁴⁴*, which do not seem to be related to the clause linker, but may also be loanwords. One is a sentence-final particle, which brings emphasis to a single clause rather than combine clauses. It seems to be borrowed from the nominalizer *de* 的 [tɤ] in the Chinese *shì...de* 是...的 construction (see § 12.6.8). There is also an adverb meaning 'all', which likely comes from the Chinese *dōu* 都. By contrast, the discourse particle *tɤ⁴⁴*, which often begins utterances and roughly means 'then, in that case, so', has no obvious counterpart in Chinese. Two other grammatical particles likewise pronounced [tɤ] in Chinese — the possessive marker 的 and the relativizer 的 — have not been borrowed; Khatso retains native particles for these functions (see § 7.4 and § 7.5 respectively).

16.6 *sɛi⁴⁴*

It is difficult to determine which is the primary function of *sɛi⁴⁴*, the topicalizing or temporal use. In discourse, the particle often has a simple temporal interpretation, as in (1205), providing the time frame for an adjacent clause, much like its counterparts *de shíhou* 的时候 'the time that' in Chinese and 'when' in English (see § 13.2.1). However, in other clauses it marks the topic, which may be a noun or noun phrase as in (1206), without a temporal sense. Thus, at times *sɛi⁴⁴* overlaps somewhat with the more prototypical topic marker *ni³¹*, though the latter is not employed as a general temporal marker, nor is it involved in complementation (see § 16.3). In many cases, speakers say that both temporal and topic senses are present and either interpretation is possible, as (1207) demonstrates.

(1205) [tsʰo³³ɣɤ²⁴ma³³ tsʰɤ³³ ta²⁴to³³ mɛi⁴⁴ la⁵⁴ tʰɛi³²³ wa³²³] [a³³ tsɛi³⁵ tsʰn̩³³]
adult PL also very be.sore very PFV that CL:TMP arrive
大人 们 也 很 心疼 很 那 段 到
sɛi⁴⁴.
TMP
'The adults were very worried, when the time came.'
到那时候了，大人们也都很心疼了。
(GCS-Dance Parties)

(1206) [m̩³¹ kɛi³³ tsʰo³³ kɛi³³] **sɛi⁴⁴**,
horse CONJ person CONJ TOP
马 和 人 和
'As for the horses and men,'
马和人呢，

[wa³²³tɕʰɛ³²³ i³²³tɕa⁵³ mɛi⁴⁴ to³²³ ta³⁵   wa³²³].
completely water   CL:GEN drink   be.able.FOC PFV
完全   水   个   喝   能
'(They) were all able to drink the water.'
全部都喝上水了。
(HPH-Horse Dug Well)

(1207) [sɿ³⁵   tɕi³³]   **sɛi⁴⁴** [nɛi³³tsʰɣ³³ kɛi³³ tɕi³³ tɕi³³ ta³³]?
       firewood   pack   TOP/TMP   2PL   AGT   pack   pack   IPFV.IRR
       柴   装   你们   装   装
'As for packing up the firewood, was it you who packed (it)?' / 'When the firewood (was) packed up, was it you who packed (it)?'
装柴呢，是不是你们装的？ / 装柴的时候，是不是你们装的？
(KL-Dance Parties)

The other functions of *sɛi⁴⁴*, however, do seem to be related to either the temporal or topical uses. For example, since the temporal clause provides a time frame for the second clause, the two logically must be concurrent. Thus, this construction may specifically express simultaneous events, as in (1208); these are outlined more fully in § 13.2.3.3. By contrast, the complementation function stems from the topic use. In this use, the putative complement clause is presented as a topic, about which the clause containing the complement-taking verb provides commentary, as in (1209). There are variations to this construction that indicate that this is not true complementaton, since there is no subordination, but rather an adaptation of the topic-comment structure to convey a complementation-like relationship between clauses (see § 15.1). For example, it is possible to topicalize the clause containing the complement-taking verb rather than the putative complement clause, as in (1210), a reversal of structure not possible with prototypical complementation constructions.

(1208) [i³³   tɕa³²³ ka³²³] **sɛi⁴⁴** [jɛ³³   to³²³].
       3SG   road   walk   TMP   tobacco smoke
       他   路   走   烟   吸
'He walks and smokes.', literally 'When he walks, (he) smokes.'
他走路吸烟。
(KL-Elicitation)

(1209) [na⁵³pɤ³¹   i³²³]   **sɛi⁴⁴**   [na²⁴   kɯ³²³   sa³³   tʰɛi³²³   ja³³].
       night.dance   go   TOP   play   CSC   be.good   very   IPFV.EMP
       跳乐   去   玩   好   很
       'Going dancing is a lot of fun.', literally 'As for going dancing, (it) is a lot of fun.'
       去跳乐很好玩。
       (KL-Elicitation)

(1210) [ŋa³³   tɕɛ³²³ti³⁵]   **sɛi⁴⁴**   [jɛ⁴⁴z̩]³³   so²⁴   wa³⁵].
       1SG   decide   TOP   English   learn   FUT
       我   决定   英语   学
       'I decided to learn English.', literally 'As for my deciding, (I) will learn English.'
       我决定学英语了。
       (KL-Elicitation)

sɛi⁴⁴ also plays a role in manner constructions (see § 14.5), as (1211) illustrates. This is syntactically identical to the complementation strategy just discussed, and thus a logical extension of that function. It is also consistent with the temporal and simultaneous functions, since the manner in which one carries out an activity is necessarily concurrent with the activity itself. As a result, the phrase in (1211) may be interpreted in several ways, as the English translations illustrate.

(1211) [mɛi⁴⁴   pʰi³²³   ja³³]   [ŋa³³tsʰɤ³¹   kɛi³³   kɤ³³]   **sɛi⁴⁴**.
       very   be.slow   IPFV.EMP   1PL   AGT   do   TMP
       很   慢   我们   做
       '(We) do (it) very slowly.', literally '(It) is very slow, when (we) do (it).' or '(It) is very slow, our doing (it).'
       我们做得很慢的。
       (WYY-Sewing)

Thus, the simultaneous, manner and complementation functions of sɛi⁴⁴ are clearly related to the temporal and topical functions. They differ mainly according to verbal semantics and context rather than syntax, and so this seems to be another case of pragmatic flexibility. Whether the primary temporal and topical functions were originally related is unclear. Nuosu, a related Ngwi language, possesses a particle su³³ that has similar functions (Gerner 2013: 98–101), suggesting that a common origin is possible. Or, the Khatso particle may have evolved from a blend of the copula ŋ³³/ŋɛi³³ and the phrase-final adverb sɛi³¹ 'still, yet'. The latter no doubt developed from the Proto-Ngwi *se2 'still, yet' (David Bradley, personal communication). However, as previously mentioned, it has been noted that tone 44 occurs most often in loanwords (see § 3.1.2), and this may be the case here. Khatso has native particles that perform these two functions — ni^{323} is a backgrounding particle that often modifies temporal expressions, and ni^{31} is the more prototypical topic and conditional marker (see § 16.2 and § 16.3 respectively). Perhaps $sɛi^{44}$ was borrowed to bring more prominence to these functions in discourse, such as highlighting a time frame rather than backgrounding it, or emphasizing a topic even more than ni^{31} typically does. It may thus be that the temporal $sɛi^{44}$ originates from the Chinese temporal noun *shí* 时 'when', and the topic $sɛi^{44}$ derives from the Chinese copula *shì* 是, which emphasizes key clausal elements in that language (Li and Thompson 1981:587–592). Although the syllable /shi/ typically becomes /sɿ/ in modern loans, the broad multifunctionality of $sɛi^{44}$ suggests it was likely adopted centuries ago, allowing time for it to evolve during the intervening years. It is common for vowel-less syllables to gain a vowel phrase-finally, and /ɛi/ is often employed for this purpose. For example, the phrase-final form of the native copula $ŋ^{33}$ is $ŋɛi^{33}$ (see § 8.5), and the shape of $sɛi^{44}$ may have become similarly routinized. In addition, it is possible that there was only one loan originally. Perhaps $sɛi^{44}$ was borrowed as a temporal marker, and because of its role in increasing prominence it grammaticalized into a topic marker. Thus, the closely-related functions of $sɛi^{44}$ may be a result of pragmatic flexibility or historical loans. Without more historical data, it is impossible to say for certain.

Appendix A: Grammatical Particles in Khatso

Because Khatso is a pragmatics-based language, and there is little morphology in the language, grammatical particles play a crucial role in organizing discourse into constructions. A list of these particles is presented below with their functions and the sections in which they are described. Also included is their prototypical position within phrases — *non-final* means that a particle may never end a phrase; *final* means that a particle may occur in final position, but does not preclude situations in which it precedes another phrase-final marker. Note that there are tone change patterns that may replace the imperative $jɛ^{24}$ (see § 3.2.4.2) and the focus particle la^{35} (see § 3.2.5).

Table A.1: Grammatical particles in Khatso

Particle	Function	Position	Section
i^{33}	nominalizer	non-final	§ 7.6
ja^{323}	perfective emphatic particle	final	§ 12.6.2
ja^{33}	imperfective emphatic particle	final	§ 12.6.1
$jɛ^{24}$	imperative marker	final	§ 12.2.1
$kɛi^{33}$	agent marker	non-final	§ 10.4
	argument focus particle	non-final	§ 10.1
	nominal conjunction	non-final	§ 7.7.2
	instrumental marker	non-final	§ 10.6.1
	ablative marker	non-final	§ 10.6.2
	pseudo-passive marker	non-final	§ 10.5
	superlative marker	non-final	§ 12.5.5.3
$kɤ^{323}$	nominalizer	non-final	§ 7.6
$kɯ^{323}$	complex stative construction particle	non-final	§ 8.8.1.4
ko^{53}	experiential aspect marker	final	§ 9.2.10
la^{24}	relativizer	non-final	§ 7.5
la^{31}	perfective irrealis aspect marker	final	§ 9.2.6
la^{31}	irrealis question marker	final	§ 12.4.7.4
la^{33}	comparative particle	non-final	§ 12.5
$la^{33}ta^{55}$	causee postposition	non-final	§ 11.2.2.1
la^{35}	contrastive focus marker	non-final	§ 13.1.3.3
	cause-effect clause combining particle	non-final	§ 14.1.3
	reason clause combining particle	non-final	§ 6.3.3

Particle	Function	Position	Section
lɛi³¹	irrealis emphatic particle	final	§ 12.6.4
ma³¹	negative marker	non-final	§ 9.1.1
mɛi⁴⁴	discourse emphatic particle	final	§ 12.6.9
na³¹	epistemic emphatic particle	final	§ 12.6.7
nɛi³³tɕo³⁵	concessive conditional	non-final	§ 14.4.3
ni³¹	conditional marker	final	§ 14.4.1
ni³¹	reason marker	final	§ 14.1.2
ni³¹	sequential event marker	final	§ 13.2.4.4
ni³¹	topic marker	final	§ 10.1
ni³²³	backgrounding particle	final	§ 16.2
ni³²³	reason marker	final	§ 14.1.1
ni³³	adverbial particle	non-final	§ 9.3.4
ni³⁵	topic question marker	final	§ 12.4.7.2
ȵa³³	copular emphatic particle	final	§ 12.6.3
ŋa³¹	content question marker	final	§ 12.4.2
ŋa³³	copular question marker	final	§ 12.4.1
ŋɛi³³	strong assertion particle	final	§ 12.6.5
ŋɛi³⁵	future strong assertion particle	final	§ 9.2.9
pa³⁵	future aspect marker	final	§ 9.2.9
pa³¹	imperative marker	final	§ 12.2.2
pa³¹	solicitative marker	final	§ 12.2.2
pa³²³jɛ²⁴	optative marker	final	§ 12.2.3
pɛi³³	confirmation question marker	final	§ 12.4.7.5
po⁵³	epistemic emphatic particle	final	§ 12.6.6
pɣ³²³	possessive marker	non-final	§ 7.4
sa³¹	'still' question marker	final	§ 12.4.7.1
sa⁴⁴	certain question particle	final	§ 12.4.7.3
sɛi⁴⁴	possessive marker	final	§ 7.4
sɛi⁴⁴	complementation	final	§ 15.1
sɛi⁴⁴	manner linker	final	§ 14.5
sɛi⁴⁴	temporal marker	final	§ 13.2.1
sɛi⁴⁴	topic marker	final	§ 10.1
sɛi⁴⁴	simultaneous event marker	final	§ 13.2.3.3
ta³¹	prohibitive marker	non-final	§ 9.1
ta³¹	rhetorical question particle	final	§ 12.4.7.6
ta³³	imperfective irrealis aspect marker	final	§ 9.2.7

Appendix A: Grammatical Particles in Khatso

Particle	Function	Position	Section
tɤ³³	progressive aspect marker	final	§ 9.2.3
tɤ⁴⁴	stative emphatic marker	final	§ 12.6.8
tɤ⁴⁴	cause and effect linker	non-final	§ 14.2.2
	manner linker	non-final	§ 14.5
	purpose linker	non-final	§ 14.6
	simultaneous event linker	non-final	§ 13.2.3.4
ti³³	progressive aspect marker	final	§ 9.2.3
tsɛi³¹	hearsay particle	final	§ 15.3
tsɤ³¹	continuous aspect marker	final	§ 9.2.4
tso²⁴	iterative aspect marker	final	§ 9.2.5
tsŋ³²³	nominalizer	non-final	§ 7.6
v³²³	reciprocal marker	non-final	§ 12.3
wa³¹	perfective question marker	final	§ 12.4.1
wa³²³	perfective aspect marker	final	§ 9.2.1
wa³³	currently relevant state aspect marker	final	§ 9.2.2
wa³⁵	future aspect marker	final	§ 9.2.9

Appendix B: Khatso Lexicon

This appendix provides a trilingual word list comprising the basic vocabulary of Khatso. Loans from Hanyu are included, since they are an important part of the lexicon, and likely have been for centuries. Each Khatso word is translated into both Chinese and English. See also Appendix A for a list of grammatical particles, and the List of Tables for specific vocabulary items discussed in the grammar, such as numerals and classifiers. A more extensive list can be found at www.khatso.net.

Khatso	Chinese	English
a²⁴kɯ³³lɛi³³tsʰɻ³¹	臭虫	bedbug
a²⁴ko³³	外祖父	maternal grandfather
a²⁴kv³³	螺丝	snail
a²⁴ma³³	妈妈	mother
a²⁴ɳo³¹	哥哥	older brother
a²⁴ɳo³¹ma³³kʰɤ³³	蜘蛛	spider
a²⁴ɳo⁵³	猴子	monkey
a²⁴ŋ³³	奶汁	milk (human & animal)
a²⁴pa³¹	爸爸	father
a²⁴tʰiau³⁵m̩³³	打喷嚏	to sneeze
a³³ŋ⁵⁵	猫	cat
ɕa²⁴	闲	to be not busy, unoccupied
ɕa²⁴tsɻ³¹	箱子	chest, trunk
ɕa³¹	想	to think
ɕa³⁵pʰɤ³²³	下巴	chin
ɕa³⁵tʰiɛ³³	夏天	summer
ɕau⁵³tsʰɻ³⁵	吝啬	to be stingy
ɕɛ⁵³sv³⁵	姓氏	surname
ɕɛ⁵⁵fɤ³⁵	生气	to be angry, furious
ɕɛ⁵⁵tɕi³¹	急躁	to be impetuous
ɕo²⁴	撒（种）	to sow (e.g. seeds)
ɕo²⁴	香	to be fragrant
ɕo²⁴la²⁴	香料	spice
ɕo²⁴sɛi³³	学生	student
ɕo³²³tʰa³²³	学校	school
ɕo²²	修（机器）	to repair (machinery, roads, buildings)
ɕo³³	干净	to be clean
ɕo³³pv³⁵	胸	chest
ɕo⁵⁵sɻ²⁴	老师	teacher

fa³²³o³²³si³³	恶心	to be nauseated
fɛi³⁵	肺	lung
fʏ̬²⁴tsʅ³²³	狮子	lion
fʏ̬²⁴xʏ³³	棚子	shed
fʏ̬³²³li³¹	狐狸	fox
fʏ̬³²³tiɛ³²³	蝴蝶	butterfly
fʏ̬³³	生（孩子）	to give birth, lay (eggs)
fʏ̬³³ma³³	海	ocean, lake
fʏ̬³³sʏ̬²⁴	养活	to support, raise (e.g. animals)
fʏ̬³⁵	埋	to bury
fʏ̬³⁵	熏	to smoke (e.g. meat)
fʏ̬⁵⁵	拧（毛巾）	to wring (e.g. cloth)
fʏ̬⁵⁵	歪	to be crooked
ʏ³¹, zʅ³¹	躺	to lie, recline
ʏ⁵⁵ma³³	孙女	granddaughter
ʏ⁵⁵za³¹	孙子	grandson
ɣa³¹	力气	physical strength, effort
ɣa³¹ɣʏ³¹	力气大	to be strong
ɣa³¹pʰʏ³¹	工钱	wages
ɣa⁵³	鸡	chicken
ɣa⁵³	织	to weave, knit
ɣa⁵³fʏ̬³³	鸡蛋	chicken egg
ɣa⁵³pʰʏ³¹	飞机	airplane
ɣa⁵³sa³¹	鸡肉	chicken (meat)
ɣa⁵⁵	松	to be loose
ɣʏ³¹	大	to be large
ɣʏ⁵⁵ma³³	孙女	granddaughter
ɣʏ⁵⁵za³¹	孙子	grandson
ɣɯ³¹	莲花根	lotus root
ɣɯ³²³	割（肉）	to cut apart (e.g. meat)
ɣɯ³³	摸	to feel, touch
ɣɯ³⁵	鸭子	duck
ɣɯ⁵³	针	needle
ɣɯ⁵³	捉	to catch, grab
i²⁴po⁵³	被子	quilt
i²⁴tsʏ²⁴	男人	man, husband
i²⁴tsʏ²⁴za³¹	小伙子	boy, young man, unmarried man
i³¹kɯ³¹, zʅ³¹kɯ³¹	枕头	pillow
i³¹m̩²⁴tsʰʅ⁵³	今晚	tonight
i³¹ŋ³²³	今天	today
i³¹tsʰʅ³³	头发	hair
i³¹tsʅ³³kɯ³⁵	头	head

i³²³tɕa⁵³	水	water
i³²³tɕa⁵³tʰɣ̩³¹	水桶	bucket
i³²³tso³³	井	water well
i³³	他	3SG
i³³ma³³	女人	woman
i³³sɹ̩³³sɹ̩³³za³¹	绸子	silk fabric
i³³sɹ̩⁵⁵	种子	seed
i³³tsʰɣ³³, i³³tsʰɣ³¹	他们	3PL
i³⁵	脏	to be dirty
i³⁵kɯ³³	勺	spoon
i³⁵sɹ̩³¹	尿	urine
i⁵³	醉	to be drunk
i⁵³xa³³	影子	shadow
i⁵³xa³³	灵魂	soul, spirit
ja³²³tɕɛ³¹	肥皂	soap
ja³²³tsɣ³¹	控制	to control
ja³²³tsʰɛi³²³	火柴	match (for fire)
ja³²³tsʰo³³	洋葱	onion
ja³²³wa³³wa³³	十字镐	pickax
ja³⁵	洗（碗）	to wash (dishes, vegetables, shoes)
jau³³tsɹ̩³¹	肾	kidney
jɛ³¹	（水）流	to flow (of water)
jɛ³²³ŋ²⁴jɛ³¹	发洪水	flood
jɛ³³	烤烟	tobacco
jɛ³³ to³²³	抽烟	to smoke (tobacco)
jɛ³⁵	吞	to swallow
jɛ³⁵tsʰɹ̩³⁵	运气	luck
jɛ⁵³	滑	to be slippery
jo³¹ɣ²⁴	野兽	wild animal
jo³²³	绵羊	sheep
jo³²³fɣ²⁴	蚊子	mosquito
jo³²³kʰɣ³¹tʰɛi³¹ka³³	游泳	to swim, bathe
jo³²³mo³¹	苍蝇	fly
jo⁵³	长（大）	to grow
ka²⁴	敲	to strike, beat
ka³¹	荞	buckwheat
ka³²³	走	to walk, go
ka³²³tɕⁿi³¹	门	door
ka³²³tsɹ̩²⁴	起来	to rise, get up
ka³³	肝	liver
kɣ²⁴za³¹	星星	star
kɣ³¹	跑	to run

kɤ³²³	（太阳）落	to set (of sun)
kɤ³³	捡	to gather
kɤ³⁵	挖	to dig
kɤ⁵³	破	to be torn (clothes), to be broken (things)
kɤ⁵⁵	汗	sweat
kʰa³¹	咸	to be salty
kʰa³¹	苦	to be bitter
kʰa³¹kʰɤ³³	帽子	hat, cap
kʰa³¹si³³	大蒜	garlic
kʰa³¹sɻ³³	鲶鱼	catfish
kʰa⁵⁵tso³¹ma³³	兴蒙女人	Khatso woman
kʰa⁵⁵tso³¹pʰa³¹	兴蒙男人	Khatso man
kʰai³³tsɻ³²³	橡皮擦	eraser
kʰɛi³³	开（车）	to drive (vehicles)
kʰɛi³³sɻ³⁵	开始	to begin
kʰɤ⁵⁵	梳	to comb
kʰɯ³³kʰɯ³³	钩子	hook
kʰo²⁴	拍（桌子）	to slap, pat (e.g. table, insect)
kʰo⁵³	年	year
kʰo⁵³	偿还	to return (item)
kʰo⁵³	赔	to pay for
kʰo⁵³tʰa³¹	年纪	age
kʰua⁵⁵	村子	village
kʰua⁵⁵	宽	to be broad
kʰuo³¹	抽打	to beat, lash
kʰɤ²⁴	空	to be empty
kʰɤ³¹	偷	to steal
kɯ²⁴	硌（脚）	to get hurt when stepping on something hard
kɯ²⁴lo⁵³	角	horn
kɯ³³	跟	to follow
kɯ³⁵	硬	to be hard (texture)
kɯ⁵³	踩	to step on
ko²⁴	烤（火）	to warm oneself by fire
ko³¹ma³³	背	back (of body)
ko³³tsɻ³⁵ȵo³¹	工具	tool
ko³⁵kɯ³²³sa³³	幸福	to be fortunate
ko⁵³	弯	to be crooked
ko⁵³	过	to pass, cross
ko⁵⁵	胶	glue
kua²⁴	灶	stove

kua³¹	嚼	to chew
kua³³ŋa²⁴	乌鸦	crow
kua³⁵miɛ³⁵	面条	noodle
kua⁵³	刮（毛）	to shave
kɣ̩³³li⁵⁵tsʅ³¹	轮子	wheel
la²⁴ka³³	玩耍	to play
la²⁴ta³²³	舌头	tongue
la²⁴tsʰau³⁵	勤快	to be diligent
la²⁴tsɣ²⁴	蜡烛	candle
la³¹	虎	tiger
la³¹xɣ³³	房间	room, bedroom
la³²³	蓝	to be blue
la³²³	锣	gong
la³⁵	晾	to dry in sun, air
la⁵³	手	hand
la⁵³	卷	to roll up, wind (things)
la⁵³ŋ²⁴	手指	finger
la⁵³pʰa⁵⁵	手臂	arm, parts of arm
la⁵³pʰɛi³¹tsʅ³³	肩	shoulder
la⁵³piɛ⁵⁵	戒指	ring (for finger)
la⁵³tɕʰo³¹	右手	right-hand side
la⁵³tsʅ²⁴	手镯	bracelet
la⁵³tsʅ³¹	袖子	sleeve
la⁵³vɣ⁵⁵	左手	left-hand side
la⁵⁵	裤子	trousers
lau³¹sʅ³²³	老实	to be honest
lau³¹tɕa³³	家乡	countryside
lau³¹tsɣ³¹ko³³	祖宗	ancestor
lau³²³	捞	to scoop
lau³³	掏	to take out with hand (e.g. from pocket)
lau³³ti³³	爷爷	paternal grandfather
lau³³zʅ²⁴ma³³mo³¹	蚱蜢	grasshopper
lɛi²⁴	勒	to tie, strap tightly
lɛi²⁴pa³³kɣ²⁴	肋骨	rib
lɛi³²³pɛi³³	颈	neck
lɛi³⁵	晒	to sit in sun
lɛi⁵³	钻（洞）	to drill (holes)
lɣ³¹	涂（漆）	to spread on (e.g. paint)
lɣ³³	迟	to be late
lɣ⁵³	舔	to lick
lɣ⁵⁵	蜕（皮）	to shed (e.g. skin, clothes)

li³²³ ja³³	聪明	to be intelligent
li³²³ti³⁵so³³	花生	peanut
li³²³xo³²³	机灵	to be clever
li³⁵	滤	to strain, filter
li³⁵	脱(脱衣)	to take off (e.g. clothes, shoes)
li³⁵tɕʰɛ²⁴	分开	to separate, divide
li³⁵za³¹	利息	interest (of money)
li⁵³ka⁵³	赶集	to go to market
li⁵⁵la⁵⁵	铃	bell
lia³²³	量	to measure
liɛ³⁵	炼（铁）	to smelt
lo²⁴tsɿ³¹	骡子	mule
lo³¹	龙	dragon
lo³²³	轻	to be light (weight)
lo³⁵	放	to herd (animals)
lo⁵³	够	to be enough
lo⁵⁵	呕吐	to vomit
lv̩²⁴ma⁵³	鹿	deer
lv̩⁵⁵	绿	to be green
m̩²⁴	高	to be tall, high
m̩³¹	马	horse
m̩³¹kɤ⁵⁵	打雷	to thunder
m̩³¹lo⁵³	白天	daytime
m̩³¹lo⁵³ (tɕi³²³)	中饭	lunch
m̩³¹ma²⁴	天气	weather
m̩³¹ma²⁴ xa³³	下雨	to rain
m̩³¹pɤ³²³	坟	grave
m̩³¹pɤ³²³ti³⁵	墓地	cemetery
m̩³¹sɿ³³	风	wind
m̩³¹tʰa³³	天	sky
m̩³¹tsʰɿ⁵³	晚上	evening
m̩³¹tsʰɿ⁵³ (tɕi³²³)	晚饭	dinner
m̩³¹tso³³ma³³	女人	woman, wife
m̩³¹tsɿ³³ma³³	太阳	sun
m̩³¹xa³³	雨	rain
m̩³¹xa³³pa³³	闪电	to lightning
m̩³¹za³¹	小马	foal
m̩³²³wa³¹	犁田	to plow a field
m̩³²³kʰv̩³³ m̩³³	盘田	to plant a field
m̩³²³ti³³	地	earth, land
m̩³²³xo³¹	水田	paddy
m̩³³	碎 (米)	to smash to pieces

m̥³³to³¹	忘记	to forget
m̥³³to³⁵	火	fire
m̥³⁵kʰɤ³¹	烟雾	smoke (N)
m̥⁵³	吹（喇叭）	to blow (air)
m̥⁵⁵	蹲	to squat
ma²⁴sɤ²⁴	竹子	bamboo
ma²⁴tsʅ³³	棍子	rod, stick
ma³¹ kʰa³¹	不咸（淡）	to be unsalted
ma³¹ kuo²⁴	不要紧	to be unimportant
ma³²³ kɯ³²³ na²⁴	饱满	to be full, abundant
ma³²³sɛi³³	壁虱	tick
ma³⁵	溢	to overflow
ma⁵³	堆	to pile
ma⁵³xua³²³	蚂蟥	leech
ma⁵⁵	教	to teach
mau³³liɛ³³	驴	donkey
mɛi²⁴	脉	vein
mɛi³¹	捂（嘴）	to cover (e.g. mouth)
mɛi³³	含（口水）	to hold in mouth
mɛi³⁵	墨	ink
mɛi³⁵	躲藏	to hide (oneself)
mɛi⁵⁵	少	to be few
mɤ³²³	响	to make a sound, be noisy
mɤ³²³sui³¹	墨水	ink
mɤ³³	晕	to be dizzy, drunk
mɤ⁵⁵	尾巴	tail
mi³³	熟	to be ripe, cooked (ready to eat)
mi⁵³	饿	to be hungry
miɛ³¹miɛ³¹	生命	life
miɛ³⁵xo²⁴	浆糊	paste
mo³¹	老	to be old
mo⁵⁵	要	to want
mo⁵⁵i³²³sa³³	好笑	to be funny
na²⁴	听	to hear, listen
na²⁴kɯ³²³ sa³³	好听	to sound good
na²⁴kɤ³²³	好处	benefit (N)
na²⁴kʰɤ³³	鼻子	nose
na²⁴ŋ²⁴	问	to ask
na²⁴po²⁴tɕʰa³¹	耳朵	ear
na³¹	居住	to live, to rest
na³¹tɕi³³ŋ³³	明天	tomorrow
na³²³	疼, 痛	to become ill, to feel ill, to feel pain

na³²³	病	illness
na³²³ŋ²⁴	看病	to see a doctor
na³²³tsʰɿ³¹	药	medicine
na³²³tsʰɿ³¹ tsɿ³¹	打农药	to apply pesticides
na³²³tsʰɿ³¹ xa⁵⁵	熬（药）	to boil (medicine)
na³⁵	深	to be deep
na⁵³	早	to be early
na⁵³	黑	to be black
na⁵³ tsʰo³¹	唱词子	to sing (with lyrics)
na⁵³ma³³	彝族女人	Ngwi (or Yi) woman
na⁵³pʰa³¹	彝族男人	Ngwi (or Yi) man
na⁵³ta⁵⁵	早上	morning
na⁵³ta⁵⁵(tɕi³²³)	早饭	breakfast
na⁵³tɕʰɛ⁵⁵	跳乐	to dance
na⁵⁵	点（火）	to light (a fire)
na⁵⁵ni³¹	耳环	earring
na⁵⁵ta³⁵	传染	to infect
nɛi³¹	闻嗅	to smell, sniff
nɛi³³	你	2SG
nɛi³³	嫩	to be unripe, tender, inexperienced
nɛi³³nɛi³³	奶奶	paternal grandmother
nɛi³³tsʰɤ³³, nɛi³³tsʰɤ³¹	你们	2PL
nɤ²⁴	低	to be low
nɤ³¹	近	to be near
nɤ³⁵	捉弄	to tease, make fun of
nɤ³⁵ŋa³²³	索取	to trick someone out of something
ni³¹	土	dirt, earth
ni³¹na²⁴	嘴巴	mouth
ni³²³tsɿ³¹	呢子	woolen cloth
ni³³ɕɛ⁵⁵	急忙	hurriedly
ni³⁵	系（腰带）	to fasten (belts)
ni⁵⁵	泼（水）	to pour, spill (water)
ni⁵⁵no⁵³	倒掉	to throw out, pour out
no⁵³ma³³	石头	stone
no⁵³o³¹	豌豆	pea
no⁵³tsʰɿ⁵⁵	磨	millstone
no⁵³tsɿ³¹	豆腐	tofu
no⁵³za³¹	黄豆	soybean
nɤ̪³²³	城市	city
nɤ̪³³	点（头）	to nod one's head
nɤ̪³⁵	挤（牙膏）	to squeeze
nɤ̪³⁵	捏	to hold in fist, pinch

ȵa³¹	多	to be many
ȵa³¹	说	to speak, say
ȵa³³	网	net
ȵa³⁵	腻	to be oily, greasy
ȵa⁵³	粘（信）	to paste
ȵa⁵³	赚（钱）	to make (money)
ȵa⁵³i³²³	眼泪	tear (from eye)
ȵa⁵³i³²³ to⁵³	流眼泪	to cry, to let tears flow
ȵa⁵³tsɛi²⁴	眼睛	eye
ȵɛ²⁴	小	to be small
ȵɛ³¹	灭	to extinguish (fire)
ȵɛ³²³	甜	to be sweet
ȵɛ³³	藤子	vine
ȵo³¹	东西	thing
ȵo³¹ m̩³³	做活	to work, make a living
ȵo³⁵	毛	hair
ȵo⁵³	吮	to suck
ŋ²⁴	红	to be red
ŋ²⁴kɯ³²³ sa³³	好看	to be good looking
ŋ²⁴ka³³	看	to see, look, watch
ŋ²⁴mo³²³	看见	to see
ŋ²⁴sa⁵⁵	难看	to be ugly
ŋ²⁴tɕa³³	别人	other
ŋ²⁴tʰɣ⁵⁵	爱, 喜欢	to love, like
ŋ³¹	卖	to sell
ŋ³¹a²⁴ŋ³³	牛奶	cow's milk
ŋ³¹na⁵³	水牛	water buffalo
ŋ³³	是	to be
ŋ³³xa⁵³	时间	time
ŋ³⁵	夹	to grasp (with pincers, chopsticks)
ŋ³⁵ma³³	心	heart
ŋ⁵⁵ɣau³²³	狼	wolf
ŋa³¹	鱼	fish
ŋa³¹tiau³⁵pɣ³²³	蚯蚓	earthworm
ŋa³³	我	1SG
ŋa³³tsʰɣ³³, ŋa³¹tsʰɣ³¹	我们	1PL
ŋa³⁵	鸟	bird
ŋa³⁵ ta³¹	张（嘴）	to open (mouth)
ŋa⁵⁵	借（工具）	to borrow (things)
ŋɣ²⁴	拉（屎）	to defecate
o³¹	菜	vegetable
o³¹ma³³	萝卜	turnip, radish

o³¹ma³³ŋ²⁴	胡萝卜	carrot
o³¹n̠o²⁴	青菜	green vegetables
o³¹piɛ⁵⁵	梳子	comb
o³¹tsa³²³	蔬菜	vegetables
o³¹tsa³⁵i³²³	汤	soup
o³¹tsʰl̩³³	白菜	cabbage
o³²³	鹅	goose
o³³	穴	den, cave, nest
pa²⁴	换	to exchange
pa²⁴tɕa³⁵	螃蟹	crab
pa³¹	薄	to be thin (width)
pa³¹tɛi³⁵	凳子	stool
pa³¹tsʅ²⁴	绑	to bind
pa³³tɕau³³	芭蕉	banana
pɛi³¹to³³	塌毁	to collapse
pɛi³²³	山	mountain
pɛi³²³pʰiɛ⁵⁵	坡	hillside
pɛi³²³tʰa⁵⁵la⁵⁵	兔子	rabbit
pɛi³²³ti³¹ti³³	山顶	mountaintop
pɛi³²³to³⁵	山洞	cave
pɛi³³tɕɛi³³lɛi³³ pa²⁴	打（滚）	to roll around
pɛi³⁵	失败	to lose
pɛi³⁵	蠢	to be stupid
pɛi⁵⁵ɣɯ⁵³	猫头鹰	owl
pɤ³²³	凋谢	to wither and fall
pɤ³²³sa³³tʰa³²³	白糖	sugar
pɤ⁵³	弹（琴）	to play (stringed instruments)
pɤ⁵³ja³³	懒	to be lazy
pʰa³⁵	毛巾	towel
pʰau³³tɕo³²³	球	ball (in sports)
pʰɛi⁵³	肿	to swell
pʰɤ³¹	飞	to fly
pʰɤ³³	辣	to be hot and spicy
pʰɤ⁵⁵	剥（花生）	to peel, shell
pʰi²⁴ŋ²⁴ma³³	汉族女人	Han woman
pʰi²⁴ŋ²⁴pʰa³¹	汉族男人	Han man
pʰi³²³	慢	to be slow
pʰi³²³ko³¹	苹果	apple
pʰi³²³ta³¹	刀	knife
pʰi³³tɕʰɛ³¹	解开	to untie
pʰi³⁵i³²³	唾液	saliva
pʰi⁵³	剖	to cut open

pʰi⁵³	吐（痰）	to spit
pʰo³²³pʰo³²³	外祖母	maternal grandmother
pʰo³⁵	劈（柴）	to split (e.g. firewood)
pʰɤ²⁴	趴	to bend over (something)
pʰɤ³¹kʰa⁵⁵	贵	to be expensive
pʰɤ³¹lo³²³	便宜	to be inexpensive
pʰɤ³¹sa³⁵	毛虫	caterpillar
pʰɤ³³tɕʰɛ³¹	揭（盖子）	to take off cover, lid
pʰɤ³³tɕʰɛ³¹	打开	to open, unfold
pʰɤ³⁵tʂɿ³²³	商店	store (N)
pi³¹tsi³²³	虾	shrimp
pi³⁵	撒（尿）	to urinate
pi⁵³ta²⁴	扁担	shoulder pole
pi⁵⁵	关（门）	to close (e.g. door)
piɛ³⁵	笔	pen
po³¹po³¹	鼓	drum
po³³lo³³tsʰɛi³⁵	菠菜	spinach
po³⁵	翻	to turn something over
po³⁵tsʰa⁵³	爆竹	firecracker
pɤ³¹	蛀虫	moth
pɤ³¹lo⁵³	蚂蚁	ant
pɤ³²³	漂	to float
sa²⁴	小麦	wheat
sa²⁴tʰa³¹	糖	candy
sa²⁴tʰa³¹ɤ³¹tʂɿ⁵⁵	甘蔗	sugarcane
sa³¹	伞	umbrella
sa³¹	肉	meat
sa³¹ko³⁵tʂɿ³¹	皮	skin
sa³¹xo³¹tɤ⁵³	小腿	calf (of leg)
sa³³	富	to be rich
sa³³	扇（风）	to fan
sa³³	缝	to sew
sa³⁵	扫	to sweep
sa⁵³	空气	air
sa⁵³	蒸汽	steam
sa⁵³ tsʰua³¹	喘气	to pant, breathe deeply
sa⁵³tsʰɤ³³, tʂɿ³⁵tsʰɤ³³	汽车	automobile
sa⁵⁵	漏	to leak
sa⁵⁵	穷	to be poor
sa⁵⁵sa⁵⁵za³¹	可怜	to be pitiful
sɛi²⁴	涩	to be astringent
sɛi³¹	桃	peach

sɛi³¹	洒（水）	to pour, spray, sprinkle (water on plants)
sɛi³¹m̩³²³	沙子	sand
sɛi³³	铁	iron
sɛi³³	虱子	louse
sɛi³³m̩³¹ (tsɛi²⁴)	自行车	bicycle
sɛi³³m̩³²³ sɛi⁵³	牙碜	to be gritty (of food)
sɛi³⁵	骟（牛）	to castrate (e.g. livestock, humans)
sɛi³⁵jɛ³²³	寿命	lifespan
sɛi⁵⁵	擦	to wipe, rub
sɤ²⁴	长	to be long
sɤ²⁴	黄	to be yellow
sɤ³¹pʰa³¹	主人	host (N)
sɤ³³	拉	to pull
sɤ⁵⁵	磨（刀）	to sharpen (e.g. knives)
si²⁴si²⁴za³¹	新鲜	to be fresh
si³⁵	信	letter (mail)
si⁵³	杀	to kill
si⁵³ma³³ko³¹	腹	belly, stomach
si⁵³ma³³ko³¹ po³⁵	怀孕	to be/become pregnant
so²⁴	读	to read, study
so²⁴tɤ³⁵	蜷缩	to curl up
so³⁵	切（菜）	to slice (e.g. vegetables)
sʅ²⁴	分（东西）	to divide (things)
sʅ²⁴	吸（气）	to inhale
sʅ²⁴	挑选	to choose
sʅ²⁴liɛ²⁴	梨	pear
sʅ²⁴tɕʰɛ²⁴	分离	to separate
sʅ³¹	血	blood
sʅ³¹sʅ³³	牙齿	tooth
sʅ³³	死	to die
sʅ³³	细	to be fine, thin
sʅ³³sɛi³¹	尸体	corpse
sʅ³⁵	柴	firewood
sʅ³⁵	新	to be new
sʅ³⁵	渴（水）	to be thirsty
sʅ³⁵	试	to try
sʅ³⁵tɕʰa³¹	叶子	leaf
sʅ³⁵tsɤ³²³	树	tree
sʅ⁵⁵	懂	to know, understand
sua²⁴sua³³	刷子	brush (N)
sua³³	(腿）酸	to ache

sua³³tʰa³³ko³²³	番茄	tomato
sua³³tsʰv̩³⁵	醋	vinegar
sua³⁵	算	to calculate
sua³⁵pʰv̩³³	泡沫	foam, bubble
sui³¹ko³¹	水果	fruit
sv̩⁵⁵	字	Chinese character
sv̩⁵⁵pɛi³¹	本子	notebook
ta³¹ma³³	客人	guest
ta³¹tsɿ³³	胆量	courage
ta³³ma⁴⁴tʰi³²³	单独	to be alone
ta³⁵	抱	to hold in arms, embrace
tɕa²⁴	关（羊）	to pen (e.g. livestock)
tɕa²⁴tsɿ³²³	茄子	eggplant
tɕa³¹	蜂	bee
tɕa³¹ɕɛ³²³	聊天	to chat, gossip
tɕa³¹i³²³	蜂蜜	honey
tɕa³²³	路	road
tɕa³³	瘦	to be skinny
tɕa³³kua³³	芦苇	reed
tɕa³⁵tɕʰɛ²⁴, tɕa³⁵tɕʰɛ³²³	价钱	price
tɕa⁵³	冷	to be cold
tɕɛ³¹	紧	to be tight
tɕɛ³¹ŋ²⁴za³¹	洋芋	potato
tɕɛ³²³	脓	pus
tɕɛ³³	满	to be full (location)
tɕɛ³³xua³²³, tɕau³¹xua³²³	狡猾	to be sly
tɕɛ³⁵	菌	mushroom
tɕʰa³¹	河	river
tɕʰa³¹	爬	to crawl, climb
tɕʰa⁵⁵	抓	to grab
tɕʰa⁵⁵	拆（房子）	to dismantle
tɕʰau³³	劁（猪）	to castrate (e.g. pig)
tɕʰau³³tɕʰau³³	匙	spoon
tɕʰɛ³¹	扔	to throw, throw at, throw away
tɕʰɛ³¹	灌溉	to irrigate
tɕʰɛ³³	请	to invite (people)
tɕʰɛ⁵³	完	to finish
tɕʰɛ⁵⁵	踢	to kick
tɕʰi³¹	话	language, speech
tɕʰi³¹n̩a³¹	说话	to speak (language)
tɕʰi³¹tɕa⁵³	谎话	falsehood
tɕʰi⁵³	叮（蚊子）	to bite, sting

tɕʰo³¹	刮（风）	to blow (of wind)
tɕʰo³³tʰiɛ³³	秋天	autumn
tɕi³¹	快	to be quick
tɕi³³ti⁵³	金子	gold
tɕi³⁵tsɿ³¹, tɕɛ³⁵tsɿ³¹	镜子	mirror
tɕi⁵³ka³³	欺骗	to cheat
tɕo³¹tsʰɛi³⁵	韭菜	chives
tɕo³⁵	吓唬	to frighten, threaten
tɕo⁵³	害怕	to be afraid
tɛi²⁴	灯	lamp
tɛi²⁴lo²⁴, tɛi³³lo³³	灯笼	lantern
tɛi³¹	钝	to be blunt (of knife)
tɛi³¹tɕʰau³³	一样	to be the same
tɛi³²³	浅	to be shallow
tɛi³³	追	to chase
tɛi³³pʰau³³	灯泡	lightbulb
tɛi³³tsɛi³⁵	现在	now
tɛi³⁵	指使	to order, instigate
tɛi³⁵	捧	to hold with both hands
tɛi⁵³	炖	to stew
tɛi⁵³	结（果子）	to fruit (e.g. trees)
tɛi⁵⁵	结（冰）	to freeze
tɤ²⁴	云彩	cloud
tɤ²⁴	插（秧）	to insert, plant
tɤ⁵⁵	(肚子)胀	to expand, swell (of stomach)
tɤ⁵⁵	(鱼)游	to swim (of fish, like a fish)
tʰa³¹i³¹	纸	paper
tʰa³²³	弹（棉花）	to fluff (cotton)
tʰa³²³tsɿ³¹	池塘	pond
tʰa³³	扇	to slap (face)
tʰa³⁵	烫（手）	to be hot, scalding; to heat up
tʰa⁵⁵	尖	to be sharp
tʰau³⁵	套	to put a cover on something
tʰɛi³¹	举（手）	to raise (e.g. one's hand)
tʰɛi³¹	抬	to lift, carry with both palms up
tʰɛi³¹	挑	to carry on shoulder pole
tʰɛi³¹ka³³	洗（澡）	to bathe
tʰi²⁴	贴	to paste
tʰi³²³tsɿ²⁴	填（坑）	to fill
tʰi³³tsi³²³	院子	courtyard
tʰiau³³	绣（花）	to embroider
tʰiɛ³²³kua³³	甜瓜	muskmelon

tʰo³¹tsɤ³²³	松树	pine tree
tʰo³²³ŋ²⁴	红铜	copper
tʰo³²³sɤ²⁴	黄铜	brass
tʰo³³	拖	to drag
tʰo³³	衣服	clothing
tʰv̩³³	捅	to poke, dig out
ti³¹	(马蜂)蛰	to sting (of insects)
ti³⁵pɤ³¹	旱地	non-irrigated field
ti⁵⁵	淋	to drench
tiɛ²⁴ta³²³	塔	pagoda
tiɛ³⁵	垫	to place under another thing
tiɛ³⁵ta³³	床单	bedsheet
to²⁴	戳	to poke
to²⁴	指	to point
to³²³	喝	to drink
to³²³	抽（烟）	to smoke (tobacco)
to³³	平	to be flat
to³³tʰiɛ³³	冬天	winter
to³⁵	拄（拐棍）	to lean on (e.g. walking stick)
to³⁵	摞	to pile
to³⁵	撑（船）	to pole (a boat)
to³⁵	点（灯）	to light (lamp)
to⁵³	出	to exit
to⁵³	着（火）	to feed (fire)
to⁵³	补	to mend
tsa²⁴	讨（饭）	to beg for, to look for
tsa²⁴sa³⁵	蚂蚱	locust
tsa²⁴tso²⁴	寻找	to find
tsa³¹	吃	to eat
tsa³¹n̩a²⁴	好吃	to be delicious
tsa³¹sa⁵⁵	难吃	to taste bad
tsa³²³	饭	rice, food
tsa³²³ tsa³¹	吃饭	to eat, to eat rice
tsa³²³ŋ²⁴	乞丐	beggar
tsa³²³za³¹	麻雀	sparrow
tsa³³tsa³³nau³¹nau³¹	垃圾	garbage
tsa³³tsʅ³¹	毯子	blanket
tsa³⁵	债	debt
tsa³⁵	蘸	to dip in liquid
tsa³⁵ tsʰa³³	欠债	to owe a debt
tsa³⁵fv̩³³	绳子	rope
tsa³⁵ko⁵³	蜻蜓	dragonfly

tsa⁵³	（很）挤	to be crowded
tsa⁵³	推	to push
tsa⁵³ɣ³⁵	推动	to promote
tsa⁵⁵	喂	to feed
tsau³¹	找（零钱）	to return (e.g. small change)
tsɛi²⁴	狭窄	to be cramped
tsɛi²⁴	窄	to be narrow
tsɛi²⁴	酸	to be sour
tsɛi³²³	桥	bridge
tsɛi³³	锯子	saw (N)
tsɛi⁵³	花椒	hot pepper
tsɛi⁵⁵i³²³	露水	dew
tsɛi⁵⁵ma³³	锄头	hoe
tsɛi⁵⁵za³¹	柑桔	tangerine
tsɣ²⁴tsɿ³²³	桌子	table
tsɣ³¹	生（熟）	to be raw, uncooked (not ready to eat)
tsɣ³¹	骑	to ride (animals, bicycles, motorcycles)
tsɣ³³	烧（火）	to tend, add to (a fire)
tsɣ³³	相信	to believe
tsɣ⁵³	贼	thief
tsʰa³¹	盐巴	salt
tsʰa³¹tsʰa³³	铁锹	spade, shovel
tsʰa³²³sɿ³³	丝	silk
tsʰa³³	欠	to owe
tsʰa³³	热	to be hot
tsʰa³³xo²⁴to³¹	窗子	window
tsʰa³⁵ko³³	歌	song
tsʰa³⁵ko³³ tsʰa³⁵	唱歌	to sing songs
tsʰa⁵³ ŋ²⁴ka³³	尝	to taste, try
tsʰa⁵³ȵo²⁴	石榴	pomegranate
tsʰa⁵³ŋa³⁵	喜鹊	magpie
tsʰa⁵³xo²⁴	茶壶	teapot
tsʰau³¹	腥	to be fishy-smelling
tsʰɛi²⁴	猜	to guess
tsʰɛi²⁴	短	to be short (length)
tsʰɛi³²³xui³³	尘土	dust
tsʰɛi³³	水稻	rice plant
tsʰɛi³³	伸	to stretch
tsʰɛi³³kʰa³³ (tɛi³²³)	下午饭	evening meal
tsʰɛi³³tsʰɿ³³	大米	white rice
tsʰɛi³⁵	秤	scale (N)

tsʰɛi³⁵lo³¹	积攒	to collect, save
tsʰɛi³⁵tsʅ³¹	油菜	canola
tsʰɛi⁵⁵	插（牌子）	to insert, plug in
tsʰɤ³¹na³¹	停止	to stop
tsʰɤ³¹pʰi⁵³	丢失	to lose
tsʰɤ³¹xua³¹	撒谎	to tell lies
tsʰɤ³³	动物油	lard
tsʰɤ⁵⁵	摘（花）	to pick (e.g. flowers, fruit)
tsʰo²⁴	冲	to rinse
tsʰo³¹	姜	ginger
tsʰo³¹pa³⁵	伙伴	friend
tsʰo³¹to³³	草墩	straw stool
tsʰo³³	人	person
tsʰo³³ɤ²⁴ma³³	成年人	adult
tsʰo³³ȵa⁵³	脸	face
tsʰo³³ɤ³¹sʅ³³	包头巾	headscarf
tsʰo³⁵	枪	gun
tsʰo³⁵	错	to be wrong
tsʰo⁵⁵	剃（头）	to have a haircut, have one's head shaved
tsʰo⁵⁵	盖（房）	to build (e.g. house)
tsʰʅ²⁴	尺子	ruler
tsʰʅ²⁴to³³	答应	to answer, agree, promise
tsʰʅ³¹	狗	dog
tsʰʅ³¹	粪	feces
tsʰʅ³¹	臭	to be stinky
tsʰʅ³¹	洗（衣）	to wash (clothes)
tsʰʅ³¹ko⁵⁵	熊	bear (N)
tsʰʅ³¹sɛi³³	跳蚤	flea
tsʰʅ³¹tso³²³	厕所	restroom
tsʰʅ³¹tsʅ³²³	塞子	cork, stopper
tsʰʅ³²³tsua³³ȵa⁵³	贴瓷砖	to tile
tsʰʅ³³	白	to be white
tsʰʅ³³kɤ²⁴	项圈	necklace
tsʰʅ³³ni³⁵	鞋子	shoe
tsʰʅ³³ȵa⁵³sʅ³¹ko²⁴	脚踝	ankle
tsʰʅ³³ŋ²⁴	脚趾头	toe
tsʰʅ³³pɛi³¹	厚	to be thick (width)
tsʰʅ³³pʰa⁵⁵	脚，下肢	foot, lower limb
tsʰʅ³³ti⁵³	银子	silver
tsʰʅ⁵³	糊	to be overcooked, burnt
tsʰʅ⁵³	羊	goat

tsʰɿ⁵³sa³¹	羊肉	mutton
tsʰɿ⁵⁵	发烧	to have a fever
tsʰɿ⁵⁵	磨（面）	to mill (e.g. flour)
tsʰui²⁴	催	to hurry (someone)
tsʰui³³tʰiɛ³³	春天	spring (season)
tsʰɣ̩³³	粗	to be thick, fat
tsi³²³ma³³, tɕɛ⁵⁵lo³³lo³³	老鹰	hawk, eagle
tsi³⁵sɿ²⁴	安静	to be quiet
tsi⁵³	剪	to cut with scissors
tso²⁴	转（身）	to turn oneself around
tso²⁴kuai³⁵	淘气	to be naughty
tso³¹mo³¹	官	government official
tso³²³	有	to have, to live, there is/are
tso³²³ kɯ³²³ sa³³	舒服	to be comfortable
tso³³	钟	clock
tso³⁵	（饭）凉	to be cool, to cool off (of things)
tso³⁵tʰɣ⁵⁵	着凉	to catch cold
tso⁵³	锁	lock (N)
tso⁵³po²⁴	钥匙	key (of lock)
tso⁵⁵	抽（出）	to take out
tsɿ²⁴	气（人）	to irritate (others)
tsɿ²⁴	着急	to worry (INTR)
tsɿ²⁴	迎接	to meet, welcome
tsɿ³¹	刺	thorn
tsɿ³¹	榨（油）	to press for oil (e.g. plants)
tsɿ³¹	疮	sore, wound
tsɿ³¹pa³³	疮疤	scar
tsɿ³¹tɕa²⁴	自己	self
tsɿ³¹tɕa²⁴tsʰo³³	亲戚	kin
tsɿ³²³	酒	liquor
tsɿ³²³ tsɿ³¹	打架	to fight
tsɿ³²³ xɣ³³	吵架	to argue
tsɿ³³	直	to be straight
tsɿ³³ma³³	芝麻	sesame
tsɿ³⁵	撕	to rip, tear
tsɿ³⁵	柜子	cabinet, chest
tsɿ³⁵	泡	to soak, steep
tsɿ³⁵	痣	mole (of skin)
tsɿ³⁵tsɣ³¹ ta³²³	记得	to remember
tsɿ⁵³	密	to be tightly-structured, dense
tsɿ⁵⁵	借（钱）	to borrow (money)
tsɿ⁵⁵	咳	to cough

tsʅ⁵⁵kʰɣ³¹	布	cloth
tsɣ³²³	筷子	chopsticks
tsɣ³³	盖（被）	to cover (e.g. with quilt)
tsɣ³³	租（房）	to rent
tsɣ⁵⁵	扎（刺）	to prick (of needle, thorn)
tsɣ⁵⁵na³²³	刺痛	to sting
tɣ²⁴	毒	to be poisonous, cruel
tɣ³¹	赌博	to gamble
tɣ³¹tsʅ³³	胃	stomach
tɣ³²³	（路）通	to open, clear (e.g. traffic)
tɣ³²³la⁵³	翅膀	wing
tɣ⁵⁵	皱	to be wrinkled
ɣ̍²⁴	叫	to call, be called
ɣ̍²⁴	喊	to shout
ɣ̍³¹	疯	to be crazy
ɣ̍³¹kɯ³⁵	骨头	bone
ɣ̍³¹tau³⁵	舞蹈	dance (N)
ɣ̍³¹tau³⁵ tɕʰɛ⁵⁵	跳舞	to dance a dance
ɣ̍³²³	拿	to hold, take, pick up
ɣ̍³²³mɣ³³	肠子	intestines
ɣ̍³³	数（数目）	to count
ɣ̍³³kuɛi³³	乌龟	tortoise
va²⁴tsʅ³¹	袜子	socks
vɣ³¹	筛	to sift
vɣ³²³	买	to buy
vɣ³³	圆	to be round
vɣ⁵³	写	to write
vɣ⁵³ li³²³	会写	to be literate
vi⁵³	开（花）	to open (of flowers)
vi⁵³li²⁴	花	flower (N)
wa⁵³	猪	pig
wa⁵³ma³³sɣ²⁴zʅ³¹	彩虹	rainbow
wa⁵³ma³³sʅ³¹tɕa⁵⁵	李子	plum
wa⁵³pʰi³¹tsʅ⁵⁵liɛ⁵⁵	蟋蟀	cricket
wa⁵³sa³¹	猪肉	pork
xa²⁴i³²³ m̩³³	打（哈欠）	to yawn
xa³³	赠送	to give (gifts)
xa³³pa³³ma³³	月亮	moon
xa⁵⁵	煮	to boil
xa⁵⁵	鼠	rat, mouse
xa⁵⁵po³⁵po³⁵	松鼠	squirrel
xɣ³³	房子	house

xɣ³³	骂	to scold
xɣ³³pɛi³³	家	house, home
xɣ³⁵	杏	apricot
xɯ³²³	赢	to win (game, contest)
xɯ³³	染	to dye
xɯ³⁵	恨	to hate
xɯ⁵³	站	to stand
xɯ⁵⁵	馋	to be gluttonous
xo³¹	软	to be soft, mushy
xo³²³tsʰv̩³²³	红薯	sweet potato
xo³³	等	to wait
xo⁵⁵	虫	insect
xo⁵⁵	蛆	maggot
xua²⁴tsa²⁴	忙	to be busy
xua³⁵	画	to paint
xua³⁵	藏	to hide (things)
xua⁵⁵	雪	snow (N)
xua⁵⁵kʰɯ³¹	冰	ice (N)
xua⁵⁵kʰɯ³¹ tɛi⁵⁵	结冰	to freeze, ice up
xua⁵⁵tɛi³³lɛi³³ tsʰi³³	下冰雹	to hail (weather)
xui³²³ɕa³¹	回忆	to recollect
xui³³	灰	to be gray
za³¹	儿子	son
za³¹m̩³¹	女儿	daughter
za³¹m̩³¹za³¹	小姑娘	young girl, unmarried woman
za³¹ni²⁴za³¹	小孩	child
za³¹ni²⁴za³¹ sɣ⁵⁵	带（孩子）	to carry, mind (children)
zɛi³¹	使用	to use
zɛi³¹kɣ³²³	用处	use (N)
zɛi³¹ta³⁵	有用	to be useful
zɣ³²³	柱子	pillar, post
zɻ²⁴	炒（菜）	to stir fry
zɻ²⁴	船	boat
zɻ²⁴	蛇	snake
zɻ²⁴la⁵³tsɻ²⁴	四脚蛇	lizard
zɻ³¹	寺庙	temple
zɻ³¹	远	to be far
zɻ³¹	重	to be heavy
zɻ³¹	野	to be wild
zɻ³¹pɣ³¹	草地	meadow
zɻ⁵³	豹	leopard
zɻ⁵³	压	to press

zɿ⁵³	揉（面）	to knead (e.g. dough)
zɿ⁵³	睡	to sleep
zɿ⁵³kɤ³²³	床	bed
zɿ⁵³ma³³	梦	dream (N)
zɿ⁵³na²⁴ko³²³	打鼾	to snore
zɿ⁵³nɤ̩³¹	睡醒	to wake up
zɿ⁵³pʰiɛ³¹	压扁	to flatten
zɿ⁵³sa³³	睡着	to sleep
zɿ⁵⁵	秧	seedling
zɿ⁵⁵, ɣɤ⁵⁵	滚	to roll
zɤ²⁴tsɿ³¹	褥子	bedding (mattress, quilt, etc.)
zɤ̩³³	大麦	barley

Appendix C: Texts

As described in § 1.8, the analysis of Khatso in this grammar is based on the natural language of everyday speech. This appendix contains two excerpts from audio and video recordings of native speakers made in Xingmeng, which represent different genres of speech. *History* is part of a monologue delivered in Khatso from prepared notes and *Sewing* is a conversation between two seamstresses as they sew. Recordings and additional texts may be found at www.khatso.net.

The excerpts are transcribed using the Santa Barbara transcription method (Du Bois 2013). They follow the conventions for basic transcriptions (Level 2 delicacy), though in places additional detail is included to clarify the text. Each intonation unit (IU) in Khatso is presented on its own line, and the Khatso is translated into Chinese and English on a word-for-word and IU-level basis. A discussion of the IU cues in Khatso is found in § 4.4. Transcription symbols include the following:

;	Speaker label
@	Laughter
[ ]	Overlapping speech
—	Truncation
(( ))	Transcriber notes

C.1 History

A former mayor of Xingmeng, *kʰuɛi⁴⁴ lai³¹tʰua³¹* 奎来团 has a keen interest in the history of the Khatso people and often gives talks on the subject. Typically, the talks are delivered in Chinese, but here he agreed to give the talk in Khatso for the first time. Given the topic, the Khatso spoken in this excerpt contains a great many Chinese loanwords.

na³²³so³⁵	ɕau³³mi³²³	la²⁴	tsɛi³¹kɤ²⁴	ko³⁵tsʰɛi³²³	i³¹ɣɤ²⁴ɣ³³tɕo³³	n̩ɛ³¹.
Southern.Song	eliminate	REL	total	process	one.two.five.nine	CL:TMP
南宋	消灭		整个	过程	一二五九年	年

'The total process of eliminating the Southern Song (was finished in) 1259.'
一二五九年消灭南宋的整个过程。

tɕʰo³³tʰiɛ³³	li⁴⁴	kɛi³³	kɛi³³sɿ³⁵	tsɿ³¹	tsɿ²⁴	ta³¹,
autumn	in	from	begin	fight	rise	after
秋天	里	从	开始	打	起	后

'From after autumn when (they) began to fight,'
从秋天开始打起来以后，

tɕi³¹	ta²⁴	ni³³	tsɿ³¹	tɤ⁴⁴	i³¹ɣɤ²⁴tsʰɿ³¹tɕo³³	n̩ɛ³¹	tsʰɿ³³	ŋ³³.
one	CL:ITEM	ADV	fight	CLNK	one.two.seven.nine	CL:TMP	reach	ASRT
一	直		打		一二七九	年	到	

'(They) continuously fought until 1279.'
一直打到一二七九年。

o³¹,
INTJ
'Yeah,'
哦，

sɛi²⁴kɛi³³	na³²³so³⁵	ɕau³³mi³²³	no⁵³.
until	Southern.Song	eliminate	complete
才	南宋	消灭	掉

'Until (they) completely eliminated the Southern Song.'
才把南宋消灭掉。

sa³³sɿ³²³pa³²³	n̩ɛ³²³	tsɿ³¹	ka³²³	i³³	ŋ³³,
three.ten.eight	CL:TMP	fight	walk	go	ASRT
三十八	年	打	走	去	

'(They) fought thirty-eight years,'

打了三十八年,
sa³³sŋ³²³pa³²³   ȵɛ³²³.
three.ten.eight   CL:TMP
三十八   年
'Thirty-eight years.'
三十八年。

ja⁵³   tɛi³¹   ta²⁴   ni³³,
later   one   CL:ITEM ADV
那么   一直
'Then, continuously,'
那么一直到,

i³¹ɣɤ²⁴tsʰŋ³¹tɕo³³   ȵɛ³¹   tsʰŋ⁴⁴   ta³¹,
one.two.seven.nine   CL:TMP reach   after
一二七九   年   到   后
'Until 1279,'
到了一二七九年呢,

jɛ³²³tsʰau³²³   mɛi⁴⁴   tɕɛ³⁵li³²³   na³⁵.
Yuan.Dynasty   CL:GEN   establish   be.good
元朝   个   建立   好
'(They) established the Yuan Dynasty.'
建立好元朝。

tɕɛ³⁵li³²³   tsŋ²⁴   wa³³.
establish   rise   CRS
建立   起
'(They) established (it).'
建立起来了。

ja⁵³   tɕo³⁵,
FILL   then
       就
'So then,'
那么就,

fɣ³¹pi³¹li³¹,
Kublai.Khan
忽必烈
'Kublai Khan,'
忽必烈,

jɛ³²³tsʰau³²³   tɕɛ³⁵li²⁴   tɕo³⁵,
Yuan.Dynasty   establish   then
元朝   建立   就
'After establishing the Yuan Dynasty then,'
建立元朝后就，

kuo³²³tɤ̩³³   mɛi⁴⁴   tɕo³⁵   pa³³   tɤ⁴⁴   tɛi³³   tsɛi³⁵   pɤ³²³   jɛ³⁵tɕi³³.
capital   CL:GEN   then   move   CLNK   this   CL:TMP   POSS   Yanjing
国都   个   就   搬   这   段   燕京
'(He) then moved the capital to modern Yanjing.'
首都就搬到现在的燕京。

ta³³sʅ³²³   jɛ³⁵tɕi³³   ɣ²⁴   ŋɛi³³.
at.that.time   Yanjing   be.called   ASRT
当时   燕京   叫
'At that time (it) was called Yanjing.'
当时是叫燕京。

kuo³²³tɤ̩³³   mɛi⁴⁴,
capital   CL:GEN
国都   个
'The capital,'
首都，

tɛi³³   tsɛi³⁵   pɤ³²³   pɤ²⁴tɕi³³.
this   CL:TMP   POSS   Beijing
这   段   北京
'Modern Beijing.'
现在的北京。

ŋ³¹.
INTJ
'Uh-huh.'
嗯。

tɛi³³   tsɛi³⁵   pɤ³²³   pɤ²⁴tɕi³³.   ta³³sʅ³²³   sʅ⁴⁴   jɛ³⁵tɕi³³   ɣ²⁴   ŋ³³.
this   CL:TMP   POSS   Beijing   at.that.time   COP   Yanjing   be.called   ASRT
这   段   北京   当时   是   燕京   叫
'Modern Beijing at that time was called Yanjing.'
现在的北京当时是叫燕京。

tɕo³⁵ pa³³ tɤ⁴⁴,
then move CLNK
就   搬
'(He) then moved (it) to,'
就搬到，

pɤ²⁴tɕi³³ i³²³ wa³³,
Beijing   go   CRS
北京   去
'Beijing,'
北京去了，

kuo³²³tɤ³³ mɛi⁴⁴.
capital   CL:GEN
国都   个
'The capital.'
首都。

ja⁵³ tɕo³⁵ jɛ³²³tsʰau³²³ tsʰɛi³²³li³²³ wa³²³,
later then   Yuan.Dynasty   establish   PFV
然后 就   元朝   成立
'So, (he) established the Yuan Dynasty,'
然后就成立了元朝，

pɤ²⁴tɕi³³ ta⁵⁵   ta⁵⁵.
Beijing   be.at be.at
北京   在   在
'At Beijing.'
在北京。

ʐ̩³¹—
one
一
'One—'
一——

ʐ̩³²³ɤɤ²⁴tsʰʐ̩³¹tɕo³³ ɲɛ³¹   tsʰɛi³²³li³²³ ɲɛi³³.
one.two.seven.nine   CL:TMP establish   ASRT
一二七九   年   成立
'(It) was established in 1279.'
是一二七九年成立的。

tsɿ⁴⁴kɤ³³,
FILL
'Then,'
这个,

tsɛi³¹kɤ²⁴   tso³³kuo³²³,
total   China
整个   中国
'All of China's,'
整个中国的,

pɤ³²³   pa³¹tʰɤ³²³   tɛi³³   ma⁴⁴   tɕo³⁵,
POSS   territory   this   CL:GEN then
         版图   这   个   就
'(All) this territory then,'
这个版图就,

tʰo³¹zɿ²⁴   tɤ⁴⁴   fɤ³¹pi³¹li³¹,
unite   STAT.EMP   Kublai.Khan
统一   忽必烈
'Was united, Kublai Khan,'
忽必烈统一,

fɤ³¹pi³¹li³¹   kɛi³³   tʰo³¹zɿ²⁴   tsɿ²⁴   wa³³.
Kublai.Khan   AGT   unite   rise   CRS
忽必烈   统一   起
'Kublai Khan united (it all).'
忽必烈统一起来了。

jɛ³²³tsʰau³²³   tʰo³¹zɿ²⁴,
Yuan.Dynasty   unite
元朝   统一
'The Yuan Dynasty united (it),'
统一元朝,

fɤ³¹pi³¹li³¹.
Kublai.Khan
忽必烈
'(It was) Kublai Khan.'
忽必烈。

tui³⁵	tso³³kuo³²³	pɣ³²³	li³²³sɿ³¹	sa³⁵	jo³⁵	tso³⁵ta³⁵	ko³⁵ɕɛ³⁵.
towards	China	POSS	history	on	have	be.important	contribution
对	中国		历史	上	有	重大	贡献

'(It) was a major contribution in China's history.'
对中国的历史上有重大贡。

ŋ³¹.
INTJ
'Uh-huh.'
嗯。

tso³⁵ta³⁵	ko³⁵ɕɛ³⁵	tso³²³	ja³³.
be.important	contribution	EXIST	IPFV.EMP
重大	贡献	有	

'(It) was a very important contribution.'
有重大贡献的。

sɛi³¹ɕɛ³³,
first
首先
'First,'
首先，

jɛ³²³tsʰau³²³	ta³⁵	tʰo³¹ʐɿ²⁴,
Yuan.Dynasty	be.big	unify
元朝	大	统一

'Yuan Dynasty unified (the country),'
元朝大统一。

pa³¹	tso³³kuo³²³	fɛi³³li³²³	la²⁴	tɕo³²³miɛ³⁵	tɛi³³	ma⁴⁴,
take	China	divided	REL	phase	this	CL:GEN
把	中国	分裂		局面	这	个

'Taking this period of a divided China,'
把分裂中国的这个局面，

tɕɛ³²³sʅ²⁴ wa³³.
end CRS
结束
'(And) ending (it).'
结束了。

C.2 Sewing

The late *wa³¹ ʐɿ²⁴jɛ⁴⁴* 王玉英 (WYY) was a seamstress known for making the intricate button knots that decorate the front of the traditional Khatso woman's jacket. Recorded during a sewing session, this excerpt features *wa³¹ ʐɿ²⁴jɛ⁴⁴* and *kʰuɛi⁴⁴ li²⁴* 奎丽 (KL), also an expert seamstress, chatting about their handiwork.

KL; o⁵³.
     INTJ
     'Oh.'
     哦。

    i³³ ma³¹ mo⁵⁵ tɕi³³ sa²⁴kɛi³³ ma³¹ kɛi³³ tɕi³³ kɯ³¹ tɤ³⁵ ŋɛi³³.
    3SG NEG want say until NEG AGT enter INDR.CAUS PROG.FOC ASRT
    她 不 要 说 才 不 进
    '(If) they say (they) don't want (the backing), (then one) isn't put (in).'
    她说不要才不放的。

    i³³ mo⁵⁵ ja³³ tɕi⁴⁴ ni³¹ kɛi³³ tɕi³³ [kɯ³¹ ti³³ ja³³].
    3SG want IPFV.EMP say TOP AGT enter INDR.CAUS PROG
    她 要 说 进
    '(Only if) they say (they) want (it), (then one) is put (in).'
    她说要的才放的。

WYY;   [xai³²³ja³¹, tɕi³³ tɕi⁵⁵ sa³³]
                                                                     INTJ this CL:TYPE sew
                                                                              这 种 缝

    ŋ³³xa⁵³ sɤ²⁴ wa³³.
    time be.long CRS
    时间 长
    'Oh, (it) will take a while to sew this.'
    哎呀，这种缝的时间长了。

    vɛi³⁵ti³²³ mɛi⁴⁴ sɿ⁴⁴ tɕi³³ tsɛi³⁵ kɛi³³ sa³³ la²⁴ tɕi⁵⁵ ma³¹ ŋ³³
    problem CL:GEN TOP this CL:TMP AGT sew REL CL:TYPE NEG COP
    问题 个 这 段 缝 种 不 是
    wa³³.
    CRS
    'The problem, this piece wasn't sewn recently.'
    问题呢，这个不是现在才缝的了。

sa^{35}—	nɛi^{33}	kɛi^{33}	sa^{33}	la^{24}	tɕi^{55}	ŋ^{33}n̠a^{44}li^{33},
sew	2SG	AGT	sew	REL	CL:TYPE	but
缝	你		缝		种	但是

'Sew— This one you sewed but,'
是你缝的那种的但是，

tɛi^{33}	tɕi^{55}	ma^{33}	lau^{31}kv̩^{31}kv̩^{31}	pv̩^{323}	n̠o^{31}	tɕi^{55}	tv̩^{35}	wa^{33}	mɛi^{44}.
this	CL:TYPE	PART	be.old.fashioned	POSS	thing	CL:TYPE	FOC	CRS	DSC.EMP
这	种		老古董		东西	种			

'This type, the thing is old fashioned.'
这种嘛，是过时了的了。

tɛi^{33}	tɕi^{55}	mo^{55}	ma^{31}	tʰv̩^{55}	[wa^{33}.]
this	CL:TYPE	want	NEG	CL:TMP	CRS
这	种	要	不	下	

'There's no need for this type anymore.'
用不着这种了。

KL;   [tɕo^{35} tɛi^{33} tɕi^{55}] mo^{55} tv̩^{33} wa^{33}.
                                      then   this   CL:TYPE want PROG CRS
                                      就   这   种   要

'(We) want this type.'
就是要这种了。

tsʰo^{33}o^{31}ma^{33}	tsʰɛi^{33}	kɛi^{33}	kv̩^{33}	tv̩^{44},
old.person	PL	AGT	make	STAT.EMP
老人	们		做	

'(It) was made by old people,'
老人们做的，

a^{33}	tɕi^{55}	sa^{24}kɛi^{33}	mo^{55}	tsɛi^{31}.
that	CL:TYPE	until	want	HSY
那	种	才	要	

'(He says he) only wants that type.'
说是那种才要。
((REFERRING TO LINGUIST))

kʰo^{53}tʰa^{31}	n̠ɛ^{24}	la^{24}	tsʰv̩^{33}	ma^{31}	mo^{55}	tsɛi^{31},	jɛ^{33}.
age	be.small	REL	PL	NEG	want	HSY	3SG
年龄	小		们	不	要		他

'(He) says (he) doesn't want (those made by) young people, him.'
他说年轻的人不要。

WYY; tɤ³¹   kʰo⁵³tʰa³¹   n̻ɛ²⁴   la²⁴   tsʰɤ³³   pɤ³²³   tɕi⁵⁵   ni³¹   kv̻³³   kɯ³²³
      FILL age   be.small   REL   PL   POSS   CL:TYPE TOP   make   CSC
            年龄   小   们   种   做
      na²⁴   ja³³   po⁵³.
      be.good   IPFV.EMP   EPIS.EMP
      好
      'Oh, the ones (made by) young people, (they) are good, (you know).'
      那，年轻人的那种也做得好呀。

KL;   kv̻³³   kɯ³²³   ma³¹   na²⁴.
      make   CSC   NEG   be.good
      做   不   好
      '(They) are badly made.'
      做得不好。

      mau³³li⁴⁴mau³³tsau³⁵   ni³³   pʰɤ³¹sa³⁵   ko⁵⁵   la³³   ŋ³³   la³⁵   ŋɛi³³.
      carelessly   ADV   caterpillar CL:PL   CMP   COP   FOC   ASRT
      毛毛糙糙   毛毛虫   些   是
      'Carelessly (done), (they) look like caterpillars.'
      毛毛糙糙的，像毛毛虫。

WYY; @@@.

      tɤ³¹   xa³³jo³⁵   kɛi³³   kv̻³³   la²⁴   tɕi⁵⁵   tɕo³⁵   tɕi³³   ta⁵⁵   la³⁵   ŋ³³
      FILL   who   AGT   make   REL   CL:TYPE then   this   be.type   FOC   ASRT
              谁   做   种   就   这   样
      mɛi⁴⁴.
      DSC.EMP
      'Well, no matter who makes them, (they) will (all) be like that.'
      那谁做的也是这样的。

KL;   ma³¹   ŋ³³   wa³³.
      NEG   COP   CRS
      不   是
      'No.'
      不是了。

      nɛi³³   pɤ³²³   tɕi⁵⁵   jɛ⁵³lɛi³³lɛi³³   ta³³   ja³³.
      2SG   POSS   CL:TYPE   be.very.smooth   be.type   IPFV.EMP
      你   种   滑溜溜   样
      'Yours are really smooth.'
      你的这种滑溜溜的。

WYY; jɛ⁵³lɛi³³lɛi³³ ta⁵⁵ ni³¹ tsi⁵³ jo³³ ja³³.
    be.very.smooth be.type TOP cut.with.scissors must IPFV.EMP
    滑溜溜　　　　 样　　 　　剪　　　　　　　应该
    'The really smooth (ones), (you) must trim (them) with scissors.'
    滑溜溜的呢，要剪的。

KL; ma³¹ tsi⁵³ tso²⁴ kɯ³¹ ta³³.
    NEG cut.with.scissors ITER INDR.CAUS IPFV.IRR
    不　 剪
    '(They) usually don't trim (them)'
    没有剪的。

WYY; ma³¹ tsi⁵³ ta³³ tsɛi³¹ pi⁴⁴li³³ i³³tsʰɤ³¹ [kɛi³³ kv̩³³ sɛi⁵³.]
    NEG cut.with.scissors IPFV.IRR HSY EMP 3PL AGT make TMP
    不　 剪　　　　　　　　　　　　　　 他们　　 做
    '(It's) said (they) don't trim (them), when (they) make (them).'
    听说他们平常做好像不剪。

KL; [ma³¹
    NEG
    不

    tsi⁵³ ta³³.]
    cut.with.scissors IPFV.IRR
    剪
    '(They) don't trim (them).'
    不剪的。

    ma³¹ tsi⁵³ ta³³, ŋ⁴⁴ ŋuo³¹?
    NEG cut.with.scissors IPFV.IRR COP COP.Q
    不　 剪　　　　　　　　　　 是
    '(They) don't trim (them), right?'
    不剪的，是吧。

WYY; ja⁵³ mau³²³to³³ mau³²³to³³ ta⁵⁵ la³⁵ tsɛi³¹ pi⁴⁴li³³.
    later be.prickly be.prickly be.type FOC HSY EMP
    然后　毛刺刺　　　　　　　　 样
    '(It's) said (they look) really prickly.'
    然后听说好像毛刺刺的样子。

KL; ɛi³⁵.
INTJ
'Hey.'
唉。

tɛi³¹ kɣ̍³¹ kɛi³³ la⁵³ ni³²³,
one CL:STRIP INS wind BKGD
一 股 用 绕
'Because wrapping (it) with a thread,'
用一股线绕呢,

kɣ³³ to⁵³ li³³ nɛi³³ pɣ³²³ tɕi⁵⁵ la³³ tɛi³³ni³³ na²⁴ ma³¹ tso³²³.
make exit come 2SG POSS CL:TYPE CMP this.way be.good NEG EXIST
做 出 来 你 种 这么 好 不 有
'Making (them), (they are) not made as well as yours.'
做出来的没有你的这么好。

tɕɛ⁵⁵ sɛi⁴⁴ to³³ tɕɛ⁵⁵ tɣ³³ nɛi³³ pɣ³²³ mɛi⁴⁴ la³³ ni³³,
tack TMP also tack PROG 2SG POSS CL:GEN CMP ADV
钉 时候 也 钉 你 个
'(When) tacking (it), (it's not) tacked like yours,'
钉的时候也不像你钉的,

tɛi³³ni³³ ma³¹ ta⁵⁵ la²⁴².
this.way NEG be.type PFV.IRR.EMP
这么 不 样
'(It's) not like that at all.'
不是这样。

nɛi³³ pɣ³²³ mɛi⁴⁴ li⁵⁵ tso²⁴ ma³¹ li³²³ i³³tshɣ³³ pɣ³²³ tɕi⁵⁵
2SG POSS CL:GEN move ITER NEG know.how 3PL POSS CL:TYPE
你 个 摇 不 会 他们 种
li⁵⁵ tso²⁴ li³²³ ja⁵³
move ITER know.how IPFV.EMP
摇 会
'Yours won't move around, theirs will.'
你的不会摇,他们的会摇。

WYY; xa³³ni³³ li⁵⁵ tso²⁴ pa⁵³ ŋa³¹ lɛi³¹?
how move ITER FUT CNT.Q IRR.EMP
怎么 摇
'How will (they) move around?'
怎么摇的呀？

KL; o²⁴².
INTJ
'Oh.'
哦。

tɕo³³.
INTJ
'Look.'
看。

tɛi³³ni³³ li⁵⁵ tso²⁴ tɤ³³ ŋɛi³³.
this.way move ITER PROG ASRT
这么 摇
'(They) move around like this.'
是这么摇的。

WYY; li⁵⁵ tso²⁴ sɛi⁴⁴ tso⁵⁵ ma³¹ tɕɛ³¹ ŋɛi³³.
move ITER TMP pull NEG be.tight ASRT
摇 拉 不 紧
'When (they) move around, (they) weren't pulled tight.'
摇的是没拉紧。

KL; ŋ³³.
COP
是
'Yeah.'
是。

i³³tsʰɤ³¹ pʏ³²³ tɕi⁵⁵ sɛi⁴⁴ li⁵⁵ tso²⁴ li³²³ ŋɛi³³.
3PL POSS CL:TYPE TOP move ITER know.how ASRT
他们 种 摇 会
'Theirs, (they) will move around'
他们的那种是会摇的。

nɛi³³ pɣ³²³ tɕi⁵⁵ li⁵⁵ tso²⁴ ma³¹ li³²³.
2SG POSS CL:TYPE move ITER NEG know.how
你　　　种　　摇　　　不　会
'Yours won't move around.'
你的那种不会摇。

WYY; ŋa³³ pɣ³²³ tɕi⁵⁵ ni³¹ tso⁵⁵ kɯ³²³ tɕɛ²⁴ ni³²³ tso⁵⁵ tɣ⁵⁵ tɣ³³
1SG POSS CL:TYPE TOP pull CSC be.tight BKGD pull wrinkle PROG
我　　　种　　　　拉　　　紧　　　　拉　皱
ŋ³³ tsɛi³¹.
ASRT HSY
'Mine, because (they) are pulled tight, (they) say (they) are wrinkled'
我的那种呢，说是拉得紧，皱了。

KL; tɛi³³ kɣ²⁴ kɛi³³ ta⁵⁵ ni³¹ tɕo³⁵ ma³¹ tɣ⁵⁵ wa³³.
this CL:STRIP AGT put TOP then NEG wrinkle CRS
这　条　　　　放　　就　　不　皱
'(If) this strip is put (on), then (it) doesn't wrinkle.'
放这条呢，就不皱了。

i³³tsʰɣ³³ pɣ³²³ tɕi⁵⁵ sɛi⁴⁴ li⁵⁵ tso²⁴ li³²³ ŋɛi³³, ŋ³³ n̪a³³.
3PL POSS CL:TYPE TOP move ITER know.how ASRT COP COP.EMP
他们　　　种　　　　摇　　　　会　　　　　是
'As for theirs, (they) will move around, (that) is (right).'
他们的那种会摇的，是的。

References

Aikhenvald, Alexandra Y. 2000. *Classifiers: A typology of noun categorization devices*. Oxford: Oxford University Press.

Aikhenvald, Alexandra Y. and R. M. W. Dixon. 2006. *Serial verb constructions: A cross-linguistic typology*. Oxford: Oxford University Press.

Ameka, Felix K., Alan Dench and Nicholas Evans (eds.) 2006. *Catching a language: The standing challenge of grammar writing*. Berlin & New York: Mouton de Gruyter.

Bái, Bìbō 白碧波. 2012. *Sādūyǔ yánjiū* 撒都语研究 [Sadu language study]. Běijīng: Mínzú Chūbǎnshè.

Bisang, Walter. 2009. On the evolution of complexity: Sometimes less is more in East and mainland Southeast Asia. In Geoffrey Sampson, David Gil and Peter Trudgill (eds.), *Language complexity as an evolving variable*, 34–49. Oxford: Oxford University Press.

Bowern, Claire. 2008. *Linguistic fieldwork: A practical guide*. New York: Palgrave Macmillan.

Bradley, David. 1979. *Proto-Loloish*. London: Curzon Press.

Bradley, David. 1990. The status of the 44 tone in Nosu. *La Trobe University Working Papers in Linguistics* 3.125–137.

Bradley, David. 1995. Grammaticalisation of extent in Mran-Ni. *Linguistics of the Tibeto-Burman Area* 18.1–28.

Bradley, David. 1997. Tibeto-Burman languages and classification. In David Bradley (ed.), *Tibeto-Burman languages of the Himalayas*, 1–72. Canberra: Australian National University.

Bradley, David. 2001a. Language policy for the Yi. In Stevan Harrell (ed.), *Perspectives on the Yi of Southwest China*, 195–213. Berkeley, CA: University of California Press.

Bradley, David. 2001b. Counting the family: Family group classifiers in Yi (Tibeto-Burman) Languages. *Anthropological Linguistics* 43.1–17.

Bradley, David. 2003. Lisu. In Graham Thurgood and Randy J. LaPolla (eds.), *The Sino-Tibetan languages*, 222–235. New York: Routledge.

Bradley, David. 2005a. Sanie and language loss in China. *International Journal of the Sociology of Language* 173.161–178.

Bradley, David. 2005b. Why do numerals show 'irregular' correspondence patterns in Tibeto-Burman? Some Southeastern Tibeto-Burman examples. *Cahiers de Linguistique Asie Orientale* 34.221–38.

Bradley, David. 2012. The characteristics of the Burmic family of Tibeto-Burman. *Language and Linguistics* 13.171–192.

Bradley, David. 2013. Time ordinals in Tibeto-Burman. Paper presented at the 23rd annual meeting of the Southeast Asian Linguistics Society, Bangkok, 31 May.

Bradley, David. 2015. Tibeto-Burman languages of China. In Wolfgang Behr, Gu Yueguo, Zev Handel, C.-T. James Huang and Rint Sybesma (eds.), *Encyclopedia of Chinese Languages and Linguistics*. Leiden: Brill.

Bradley, David and Maya Bradley. 2002. Language policy and language maintenance: Yi in China. In David Bradley and Maya Bradley (eds.), *Language endangerment and language maintenance*, 77–97. London: Routledge Curzon.

Bybee, Joan. 1998. "Irrealis" as a grammatical category. *Anthropological Linguistics* 40.257–271.

Chafe, Wallace L. (ed.) 1980. *The pear stories: Cognitive, cultural and linguistic aspects of narrative production*. Norwood, NJ: Ablex Publishing Corp.

Chafe, Wallace L. 1987. Cognitive constraints on information flow. In Russell S. Tomlin (ed.), *Coherence and Grounding in Discourse*, 21–51. Amsterdam: John Benjamins Publishing Co.

Chafe, Wallace L. 1994. *Discourse, consciousness, and time*. Chicago: University of Chicago Press.

Chen, Yiya and Carlos Gussenhoven. 2008. Emphasis and tonal implementation in Standard Chinese. *Journal of Phonetics* 36.724–46.
Cho, Taehong and Peter Ladefoged. 1999. Variation and universals in VOT: Evidence from 18 languages. *Journal of Phonetics* 27.207–29.
Comrie, Bernard. 1976. *Aspect*. Cambridge: Cambridge University Press.
Comrie, Bernard. 1998. Rethinking the typology of relative clauses. *Language Design* 1.59–86.
Cristofaro, Sonia. 2003. *Subordination*. Oxford: Oxford University Press.
Cristofaro, Sonia. 2012. Descriptive notions vs. grammatical categories: Unrealized states of affairs and 'irrealis'. *Language Sciences* 34.131–146.
Dài, Qìngxià 戴庆夏. 2008. *Yúnnán měnggǔzú kāzhuórén yǔyán shǐyòng xiànzhuàng jíqí yǎnbiàn* 云南蒙古族喀卓人语言使用现状及其演变 [Language use and its evolution among the Yunnan Mongolian Kazhuo people]. Běijīng: Shāngwù Yìnshūguǎn.
Dài, Qìngxià 戴庆夏, Liú Júhuáng 刘菊黄 and Fù Àilán 傅爱兰. 1987. Yúnnán měnggǔzú gāzhuóyǔ yánjiū 云南蒙古族嘎卓语研究 [Yunnan Mongolian Khatso language study]. *Yǔyán Yánjiū* 语言研究 [Studies in Language and Linguistics] 1.151–175.
Dixon, R. M. W. 1979. Ergativity. *Language* 55.59–138.
Dixon, R. M. W. 2004. Adjective classes in typological perspective. In R. M. W Dixon and Alexandra Y. Aikhenvald (eds.), *Adjective classes: A cross-linguistic typology*, 1–49. Oxford: Oxford University Press.
Dixon, R. M. W. 2006. Complement clauses and complementation strategies in typological perspective. In R. M. W Dixon and Alexandra Y. Aikhenvald (eds.), *Complementation: A cross-linguistic perspective*, 1–48. Oxford: Oxford University Press.
Dixon, R. M. W. 2010. *Basic linguistic theory, Vol. II: Grammatical topics*. Oxford: Oxford University Press.
Dixon, R. M. W and Alexandra Y. Aikhenvald. 2000. *Changing valency: Case studies in transitivity*. Cambridge: Cambridge University Press.
Dixon, R. M. W and Alexandra Y. Aikhenvald. 2002. Word: A typological framework. In R. M. W Dixon and Alexandra Y. Aikhenvald (eds.), *Word: A cross-linguistic typology*, 1–41. Cambridge: Cambridge University Press.
Du Bois, John W. 1987. The discourse basis of ergativity. *Language* 63.805–855.
Du Bois, John W. 2013. Representing discourse. Santa Barbara: University of California, Santa Barbara, ms.
Dù, Yùtíng 杜玉亭 and Chén Lǚfàn 陈吕范. 1976. Yúnnán měnggǔzú jiǎnshǐ 云南蒙古族简史 [A brief history of the Yunnan Mongolians]. In *Yúnnán měnggǔzú* 云南蒙古族 [Yunnan Mongolians], 9–14. Hohhot: Inner Mongolia Teacher's College.
Duanmu, San. 1999. Metrical structure and tone: Evidence from Mandarin and Shanghai. *Journal of East Asian Linguistics* 8.1–38.
Dwyer, Arienne M. 2006. Ethics and practicalities of cooperative fieldwork and analysis. In Jost Gippert, Nikolaus P. Himmelmann and Ulrike Mosel (eds.), *Essentials of Language Documentation*, 31-65. Berlin & New York: Mouton de Gruyter.
E-MELD (Electronic Metastructure for Endangered Languages Data). 2006. E-MELD School of Best Practice. Online: http://emeld.org/school.
Fairbanks, Grant, Arthur S. House and Eugene L. Stevens. 1950. An experimental study of vowel intensities. *Journal of the Acoustical Society of America* 22.457–459.
Gāo, Fāyuán 高发元. 2001. *Měnggǔzú: Tōnghǎi Xíngměngxiāng* 蒙古族:通海兴蒙乡 [Mongolians: Tonghai Xingmengxiang]. Kūnmíng: Yúnnán Dàxué Chūbǎnshè.
Garellek, Marc. 2012. Word-initial glottalization and voice quality strengthening. *UCLA Working Papers in Phonetics* 111.92–122.

Gerner, Matthias. 2007. The lexicalization of causative verbs in the Yi group. *Folia Linguistica Historica* 28.145–185.
Gerner, Matthias. 2013. *A grammar of Nuosu*. Berlin & New York: Mouton de Gruyter.
Gippert, Jost, Nikolaus P. Himmelmann and Ulrike Mosel (eds.) 2006. *Essentials of language documentation*. Berlin & New York: Mouton de Gruyter.
Good, Jeff. 2011. Data and language documentation. In Peter Austin and Julia Sallabank (eds.), *Handbook of Endangered Languages*, 212–234. Cambridge: Cambridge University Press.
Gordon, Matthew and Peter Ladefoged. 2001. Phonation types: A cross-linguistic overview. *Journal of Phonetics* 29.383–406.
Haiman, John. 1978. Conditionals are topics. *Language* 54.564-589.
Hāsīěěrdūn 哈斯额尔敦. 1976. Yúnnán měnggǔzú yǔyán chūtán 云南蒙古族语言初探 [A first exploration of the Yunnan Mongolian language]. In *Yúnnán měnggǔzú* 云南蒙古族 [Yunnan Mongolians], 15–18. Hohhot: Inner Mongolia Teacher's College.
Haspelmath, Martin. 1997. *Indefinite pronouns*. Oxford: Oxford University Press.
Hé, Jírén 和即仁. 1989. Yúnnán měnggǔzú yǔyán jíqí xìshǔ wèntí 云南蒙古族语言及其系属问题 [Yunnan Mongolian and the classification question]. *Mínzú Yǔwén* 民族语文 [Minority Languages of China] 5.25–36.
Hé, Jírén 和即仁. 1998. Guānyú yúnnán měnggǔzú kǎzhuóyǔde xíngchéng 关于云南蒙古族卡卓语的形成 [About the formation of Yunnan Mongolian Kazhuo]. *Mínzú Yǔwén* 民族语文 [Minority Languages of China] 4.51–54.
Henderson, Alan, Frieda Goldman-Eisler and Andrew Skarbek. 1965. Temporal patterns of cognitive activity and breath control in speech. *Language and Speech* 8.236–42.
Hopper, Paul J. and Sandra A. Thompson. 1984. The discourse basis for lexical categories in universal grammar. *Language* 60.703–752.
Huáng, Bùfán 黄布凡 (ed.) 1992. *Zàngmiǎnyǔzú yǔyán cíhuì* 藏缅语族语言词汇 [A Tibeto-Burman lexicon]. Běijīng: Zhōngyāng Mínzú Xuéyuàn Chūbǎnshè.
Huáng, Chún 黄淳. 2009. *Měnggǔzú jiǎnshǐ* 蒙古族简史 [Concise history of Mongolians]. Kūnmíng: Yúnnán Rénmín Chūbǎnshè.
Janhunen, Juha A. 2012. *Mongolian*. Amsterdam: John Benjamins.
Jongman, Allard, Wang Yue, Corinne B. Moore and Joan A. Sereno. 2006. Perception and production of Mandarin Chinese tones. In Ping Li, Li Hai Tan, Elizabeth Bates, and Ovid J.L. Tzeng (eds.), *Handbook of East Asian Psycholinguistics, Vol. I: Chinese*, 209–17. Cambridge University Press.
Ju, Namkung (ed.) 1996. *Phonological inventories of Tibeto-Burman languages*. Berkeley, CA: Sino-Tibetan Etymological Dictionary and Thesaurus Project (STEDT), Center for Southeast Asian Studies, University of California.
Kurpaska, Maria. 2010. *Chinese Language(s): A look through the prism of 'The Great Dictionary of Modern Chinese Dialects'*. Berlin & New York: Mouton de Gruyter.
Lama, Ziwo Qiu Fuyuan. 2012. Subgrouping of Nisoic (Yi) languages: A study from the perspectives of shared innovation and phylogenetic estimation. Arlington: University of Texas, ms.
Ladefoged, Peter. 2006. *A course in phonetics*. Boston: Thomson Wadsworth.
Ladefoged, Peter and Ian Maddieson. 2008. *The sounds of the world's languages*. Malden, MA: Blackwell Publishing.
Lai, Catherine, Yanyan Sui and Jiahong Yuan. 2010. A corpus study of the prosody of polysyllabic words in Mandarin Chinese. Paper presented at the Speech Prosody 2010 Fifth International Conference, May 10–14.
LaPolla, Randy J. 1993. Arguments against 'subject' and 'direct object' as viable concepts in Chinese. *Bulletin of the Institute of History and Philology* 63.759–813.

LaPolla, Randy J. 1995. 'Ergative' marking in Tibeto-Burman. In Yoshio Nishi, James A. Matisoff and Yasuhiko Nagano (eds.), *New horizons in Tibeto-Burman morphosyntax*, 189–228. Osaka, Japan: National Museum of Ethnology.
LaPolla, Randy J. 2009. Chinese as a topic-comment (not topic-prominent and not SVO) language. In Janet Xing (ed.), *Studies of Chinese Linguistics: Functional Approaches*, 9–22. Hong Kong: Hong Kong University Press.
Lehmann, Christian. 1988. Towards a typology of clause linkage. In John Haiman and Sandra A. Thompson (eds.), *Clause combining in grammar and discourse*, 181–225. Philadelphia: John Benjamins Publishing Company.
Lewis, M. Paul, Gary F. Simons, and Charles D. Fennig (eds.) 2013. *Ethnologue: Languages of the World*, Seventeenth edition. Dallas, Texas: SIL International. Online: http://www.ethnologue.com.
Li, Charles N. and Sandra A. Thompson. 1976. Subject and topic: A new typology of language. In Charles N. Li (ed.), *Subject and topic*, 459–489. New York: Academic Press.
Li, Charles N. and Sandra A. Thompson. 1981. *Mandarin Chinese: A functional reference grammar*. Berkeley, CA: University of California Press.
Lín, Shèzhí 林舍执. 1976. Língchéng fènghuángde rénmen – Yúnnán měnggǔzú jiǎnjì 凌乘凤凰的人们 一 云南蒙古族简记 [Approaching the phoenix – Brief notes on Yunnan Mongolians]. In *Yúnnán měnggǔzú* 云南蒙古族 [Yunnan Mongolians], 1–8. Hohhot: Inner Mongolia Teacher's College.
Lyons, John. 1977. *Semantics*. Cambridge: Cambridge University Press.
Mǎ, Shìwén 马世雯. 2000. *Měnggǔzú wénhuàshǐ* 蒙古族文化史 [Mongolian cultural history]. Kūnmíng: Yúnnán Rénmín Chūbǎnshè.
Mackerras, Colin. 1988. Aspects of Bai culture: Change and continuity in a Yunnan nationality. *Modern China* 14.51–84.
Maddieson, Ian and Karen Emmorey. 1985. Relationship between semivowels and vowels: Cross-linguistic investigations of acoustic difference and coarticulation. *Phonetica* 42.163–174.
Man, John. 2007. *Kublai Khan: From Xanadu to superpower*. London: Bantam Press.
Matisoff, James A. 1972. Lahu nominalization, relativization, and genitivization. In John P. Kimball (ed.), *Syntax and semantics 1*, 237–257. New York: Seminar Press.
Matisoff, James A. 1973. *The grammar of Lahu*. Berkeley, CA: University of California Press.
Matisoff, James A. 1976. Lahu causative constructions: Case hierarchies and the morphology/syntax circle in a Tibeto-Burman perspective. In Masayoshi Shibatani (ed.), *Syntax and semantics 6: The grammar of causative constructions*, 413–442. New York: Academic Press.
Matisoff, James. 2003. *Handbook of Proto-Tibeto-Burman: System and philosophy of Sino-Tibetan reconstruction*. Berkeley, CA: University of California Press.
Matras, Yaron. 2009. *Language contact*. Cambridge: Cambridge University Press.
Matsumoto, Yoshiko. 1997. *Noun-modifying constructions in Japanese: A frame-semantic approach*. Amsterdam/Philadelphia: John Benjamins.
McGregor, William B. 2010. Optional ergative case marking systems in a typological-semiotic perspective. *Lingua* 120.1610–1636.
Michael, Lev. 2014. The Nanti reality status system: Implications for the typological validity of the realis/irrealis contrast. *Linguistic Typology* 18.251–288.
Mithun, Marianne. 2009. Empirical foundations for grammatical description in the 21st century. Paper presented at the International Symposium on Grammar Writing: Theoretical, Methodological, and Practical Issues, Tokyo, December.
Moravcsik, Edith A. 2003. A semantic analysis of associative plurals. *Studies in Language* 27.469–503.

Moseley, Christopher (ed.) 2010. *Atlas of the world's languages in danger*. Paris: UNESCO Publishing. Online: http://www.unesco.org/culture/en/endangeredlanguages/atlas

Mù, Shìhuá 木什华. 2002. *Kǎzhuóyǔ yánjiū* 卡卓语研究 [A study of Kazhuo]. Běijīng: Mínzú Chūbǎnshè.

Mullaney, Thomas S. 2011. *Coming to terms with the nation: Ethnic classification in modern China*. Berkeley, CA: University of California Press.

Nakayama, Toshihide and Keren Rice (eds.) 2014. *The art and practice of grammar writing*. Honolulu: University of Hawaii Press.

Newman, Paul and Martha Ratliff (eds.) 2001. *Linguistic fieldwork*. Cambridge: Cambridge University Press.

Noonan, Michael. 2007. Complementation. In Timothy Shopen (ed.), *Language typology and syntactic description, Vol. II: Complex constructions*, 52–150. Cambridge: Cambridge University Press.

Ohori, Toshio. 1992. Diachrony in clause linkage and related issues. Berkeley, CA: University of California, ms.

OLAC (Open Language Archives Community). 2009. Online: http://www.languagearchives.org.

Palmer, F. R. 1986. *Mood and modality*. Cambridge: Cambridge University Press.

Payne, Thomas E. 1997. *Describing morphosyntax: A guide for field linguists*. Cambridge: Cambridge University Press.

Payne, Thomas E. and David J. Weber (eds.) 2007. *Perspectives on grammar writing*. Amsterdam: John Benjamins Publishing Company.

Poa, Dory and Randy J. LaPolla. 2007. Minority languages of China. In Osahito Miyaoka, Osamu Sakiyama and Michael E. Krauss (eds.), *The vanishing languages of the Pacific Rim*, 337–354. Oxford: Oxford University Press.

Rice, Keren. 2006. Ethical issues in linguistic fieldwork: An overview. *Journal of Academic Ethics* 4.123–155.

Rybatzki, Volker. 2003. Middle Mongol. In Juha Janhunen (ed.), *The Mongolic languages*, 47–82. London: Routledge.

Schwarz, Henry G. 1984. Some notes on the Mongols of Yunnan. *Central Asiatic Journal* 28.100-118.

Shopen, Timothy (ed). 2007. *Language typology and syntactic description, Vol. II: Complex constructions*. Cambridge: Cambridge University Press.

Silverstein, Michael 1976. Hierarchy of features and ergativity. In R. M. W. Dixon (ed.), *Grammatical categories in Australian languages*, 112–171. Canberra: Australian Institute of Aboriginal Studies.

Sneath, David D. 1999. Some notes on a visit to a 'Mongolian' village in Yunnan, China. *Inner Asia* 1:121–130.

Sūn, Hóngkāi 孙宏开. 2001. Guānyú bīnwēi yǔyán 关于濒危语言 [On endangered languages]. *Yǔyán Jiàoxué Yǔyán Yánjiū* 语言教学语言研究 [Language Teaching and Language Research] 1.1-17

Thieberger, Nicholas and Andrea L. Berez. 2012. Linguistic data management. In Nicholas Thieberger (ed.), *Oxford handbook of linguistic fieldwork*, 90–120. New York: Oxford University Press.

Thomason, Sarah G. 2001. *Language contact: An introduction*. Washington, DC: Georgetown University Press.

Thompson, Sandra A. and Paul J. Hopper. 2001. Transitivity, clause structure, and argument structure: Evidence from conversation. In Joan Bybee and Paul J. Hopper (eds.), *Frequency and the emergence of linguistic structure*, 27–60. Amsterdam: John Benjamins Publishing Co.

Tōnghǎixiàn Xīngměngxiāng 2010 nián tǒngjì niánjiàn 通海县兴蒙乡2010年统计年鉴[Tonghai County Xingmeng Village 2010 Statistical Yearbook]. 2010. Xīngměng: Tōnghǎixiàn Xìngměngxiāng Tǒngjìzhàn.

Traugott, Elizabeth C. and Ekkehard König. 1991. The semantics-pragmatics of grammaticalization revisited. In Elizabeth Closs Traugott and Bernd Heine (eds.), *Approaches to grammaticalization, Vol. I*, 189–218. Amsterdam: John Benjamins Publishing Co.

Vendler, Zeno. 1957. Verbs and times. *The Philosophical Review* 66.143–160.

Wang, Feng. 2005. On the genetic position of the Bai language. *Cahiers de linguistique Asie Orientale* 34.101–127.

Wáng, Lìcái 王立才. 2008. *Yúnnán Tōnghǎi Xīngměng Měnggǔzú Kāzhuóyǔ* 云南通海兴蒙蒙古族喀卓语 [Yunnan Tonghai Xingmeng Mongolian Kazhuo]. Xingmeng: Tonghai Mongolian Nationality Cultural Research and Inheritance Protection Center.

Wu, Gu. 2001. Reconstructing Yi history from Yi records. In Stevan Harrell (ed.), *Perspectives on the Yi of Southwest China*, 21–34. Berkeley, CA: University of California Press.

Wūní, Wūqiě 乌尼乌且, Luó Qū 罗曲, Bái Xìngfā 白兴发, Lǐ Píngfán 李平凡, Zhōu Zhēngāng 周真刚, Sū Liánkē 苏连科, Yáng Yìjié 杨义杰 and Cài Fùlián 蔡富莲 (eds.) 2009. *Yízú jiǎnshǐ* 彝族简史 [A concise history of the Yi nationality]. Běijīng: Mínzú Chūbǎnshè.

Yúnnán měnggǔzú 云南蒙古族 [Yunnan Mongolians]. 1976. Hohhot: Inner Mongolia Teacher's College.

Xǔ, Xiānmíng 许鲜明. 2012. A sketch introduction of the Hlersu language. Paper presented at the 45th International Conference on Sino-Tibetan Languages and Linguistics, Singapore, 26–28 October.

Zhan, Fangqiong and Xiaoman Miao. 2012. A comparative study on Japanese and Chinese NMCs: A semantic and discourse approach. *Rice Working Papers in Linguistics* 3.1–19.

Index

A argument   132, 137, 150, 151, 183, 223, 255, 256, 257, 258, 259, 260, 271, 321, 326, 330, 331, 333, 340, 342, 344, 345, 347, 349, 350, 351–59, 358, 359, 360, 361, 363, 365, 369, 377, 386, 388, 389, 393, 394, 431, 439, 453, 455, 457, 466, 467, 468, 469, 490, 500, 503, 504, 509, 517, 518, 521, 523, 524, 544
adjectives. *See* stative verbs
adverbs   114, 143, 162, 250, 264, 272, 324–39, 343, 347, 446
– and classifiers   189–91, 334
– and clause linking   478–505
– and reduplicated stative construction   250–55
– comparative   337
– day ordinals   327
– degree   325, 335–37
– evidence for class   324, 325, 335, 338
– frequency   330–31
– indefinite   216
– locative   325, 328, 331–32, 363, 365
– manner   150, 325, 333–35
– particle   167, 250, 325, 330, 333, 334, 335, 420, 499
– sentential   325, 338–39, 410, 416, 427, 429, 436, 447, 450, 496, 505, 533–36, 543, 547
– time   183, 190, 222, 299, 325–30, 463–64, 466, 469–71, 475
– word order   325, 326, 330, 331, 333, 335, 338, 347, 350
– year ordinals   327
affixes. *See* suffixes
agency   170, 353, 374, 376, 377, 378, 380, 381, 383
agent   132, 137, 140, 150, 151, 170, 183, 222, 223, 255, 256, 257, 258, 259, 260, 271, 321, 326, 330, 331, 340, 342, 347, 349, 350, 351–59, 358, 351–59, 361, 363, 365, 369, 370, 375, 377, 381, 386, 388, 389, 393, 394, 431, 439, 453, 455, 457, 466, 467, 468, 469, 490, 500, 503, 504, 509, 517, 518, 521, 523, 524, 544
agent marker   32, 116, 215, 222, 234, 235, 244, 256, 258, 259, 344, 351–59, 351–59, 362, 365, 381, 430, 439, 455

Aikhenvald, Alexandra   110, 111, 112, 164, 260, 273
Aktionsart   299
alignment. *See* grammatical relations
ambiguity   120, 137, 179, 208, 222, 235, 244, 250, 255, 256, 258, 259, 267, 271, 288, 301, 321, 344, 347, 348, 351, 352, 353, 354, 355, 356, 357, 358, 369, 371, 373, 375, 376, 377, 378, 380, 383, 431, 437, 480
ambitransitive verbs   242, 260–61, 280
Ameka, Felix   28
animacy   117, 136–41, 141, 142, 146, 147, 148, 154, 166, 170, 173, 175, 176–83, 176, 197, 218, 229, 256, 258, 259, 321, 347, 352, 353, 355, 356, 360, 365, 372, 376, 381, 421, 503
answering questions   201, 292, 308, 316, 398, 402, 404, 406, 410, 411, 413, 416, 435, 444
applicative construction   33, 257, 268, 369–72, 378, 380, 448, 502
arguments   340–68
– core, 33, 133, 137, 146, 147, 150, 166, 199, 215, 216, 222, 223, 224, 226, 227, 230, 235, 240, 241, 244, 253, 255, 257, 258, 260, 265, 266, 267, 340, 342, 344, 345, 359, 369, 372, 374, 375, 377, 380, 386, 402, 418, 419, 424, 446, 508, 517, 528
– oblique   257, 267, 331, 332, 340, 342, 346, 361–68, 402
– shared   273, 287, 345, 352, 372, 380, 422, 446–48, 451, 455, 457, 460, 462, 464, 466, 467, 468, 471, 474, 476, 477, 480, 483, 486, 490, 491, 494, 496, 500, 503, 504, 517, 518, 521, 527, 544
aspect   32, 112, 114, 115, 189, 222, 240, 241, 243, 268, 273, 283, 296–324, 324, 347, 351, 433, 446, 451, 452, 455, 460, 462, 464, 466, 467, 468, 471, 474, 476, 477, 480, 483, 486, 490, 491, 494, 496, 497, 498, 500, 503, 517, 526, 527
– combinations   298, 303, 307, 310, 313, 315, 319, 322
– continuous   32, 97, 285, 294, 297, 298, 303, 307, 311–13, 313, 317, 318, 319, 322, 380, 392, 433, 467, 468, 517

- currently relevant state   97–99, 294, 298, 304–7, 309, 319, 338, 396, 433, 458, 481, 541
- experiential   280, 298, 323–24
- flexibility   297, 300, 306, 313, 320
- future   283, 298, 310, 316, 318, 320–23, 396, 401, 415, 438, 480, 489, 524
- habitual sense   308, 311, 313, 314, 317, 319, 441–43, 467, 477
- imperfective   297, 298, 301, 307–10, 311–13, 313–15, 318, 380, 433–34, 438, 441–43, 441–43
- imperfective irrealis   309, 311, 312, 314, 317–19, 397, 436–37, 491
- inceptive   298, 303, 307, 310, 313, 319–20
- iterative   32, 285, 294, 297, 298, 307, 310, 313–15, 317, 318, 322, 380, 433
- markers   297, 372, 377, 380, 396, 431, 438, 440, 441
- optional use   290, 299, 312, 385, 446
- perfective   241, 298, 300–303, 306, 310, 316, 319, 322, 323, 396, 401, 415–16, 430, 434–35, 438, 464, 474, 477, 489, 504, 519, 546
- perfective irrealis   300, 311, 314, 316–17, 397, 432, 491
- progressive   101, 297, 298, 307–10, 311, 315, 317, 318, 319, 401, 433, 494, 526, 543

auxiliary verbs   268–72, 291, 295, 297, 321, 336, 337, 372, 374, 383, 387, 390, 397, 447, 520, 521, 543

backgrounding   91–99, 92, 211, 311, 366, 462, 471, 472, 473, 478–80, 536–38, 550
Bai Bibo   17
Bai language   15, 17, 22, 23, 24
Bai people   1, 10, 11, 14, 15, 16
beneficiary   140, 347, 369, 371, 372, 378, 380, 383, 502
Berez, Andrea   28
Bisang, Walter   207, 223, 340, 344, 531
borrowing   41, 42, 71, 72, 73, 74, 75, 78, 82, 86, 106, 111, 113, 126, 132, 135, 140, 158–64, 158, 163, 164, 165, 172, 184, 185, 188, 192, 200, 216, 239, 264, 269, 271, 272, 296, 323, 325, 326, 338, 339, 383, 388, 418, 426, 442, 445, 447, 460–61, 463–64, 465, 471, 482–83, 486, 487, 490–91, 493,

497, 499, 504, 505, 506, 511, 520, 521, 531, 544, 546, 547, 549, 554
Bowern, Claire   27, 28
Bradley, David   1, 14, 16, 17, 18, 81, 86, 89, 99, 176, 243, 327, 373, 401, 423, 549
Bradley, Maya   18
Burmese-Ngwi   1, 19
Burmese-Yi. *See* Burmese-Ngwi
Bybee, Joan   316

case marking   255, 256, 344, 347, 348, 351–59
causative constructions   33, 97, 258, 268, 274, 291, 370, 372–84, 391, 448, 521, 545
- and tone change   97, 107
cause and effect constructions   281–85, 372–84, 458, 483–87, 501, 518, 542, 544, 545, 546
certainty   352, 397, 405, 410, 413–15, 415, 416, 436, 513, 514, 530
Chafe, Wallace   27, 120
Chen, Yiya   118
Chinese language. *See* Hanyu *and* Putonghua
Chinese people. *See* Han Chinese people
Cho, Taehong   44
classifiers   32, 112, 113, 114, 117, 128, 131, 164–97, 197, 201, 203, 204, 205, 207, 208, 210, 212, 214, 216, 218, 219, 222, 225, 228, 253, 302, 508
- adverbial   189–91, 334, 387, 391, 428
- and comparative constructions   418, 421, 422, 426
- and demonstratives   141–44
- and interrogative pronouns   146, 153
- and personal names   133
- and place names   135
- and pronouns   138
- collective   129, 139, 142, 153, 154, 173–76
- family group   32, 176–83
- function   165–70
- human   133, 141, 146, 176
- inventory   191–97
- mensural   172–73, 427
- monetary   188–89
- partitive   183
- sortal   170–72
- temporal   165, 166, 183–87, 324, 325, 329, 330, 366, 367, 387, 391
- types   170–97, 191–97
clause combining. *See* clause linking

clause linking   33, 356, 377
- adversative   456–61, 534, 535, 536, 541
- and tone change   92–96
- cause and effect   443, 471, 483–87, 501, 518, 542, 544, 545, 546
- complements. *See* complementation
- concessive   488–90, 495–96, 535, 536
- conditional   344, 480, 491–97, 535, 538, 539, 541
- coordination. *See* clause linking, parallel
- disjunctive   453–55
- juxtaposition   447, 449–51, 451, 478, 516
- manner   486, 498–500, 545, 546, 549
- parallel   447, 449–53, 534
- particles   446, 447, 448, 458, 461, 464, 467, 471, 473, 478, 480, 481, 482, 484, 485, 486, 487, 488, 490, 491, 495, 496, 497, 498, 501, 508, 518, 531–50, 531
- purpose   443, 467, 500–505, 518, 544, 545, 546
- reason   443, 473, 478–83, 537, 539, 542
- resultative   518, 544
- sequential, 469–77, 484, 494, 540, 545
- shared arguments   345, 446–48, 451, 455, 457, 460, 462, 464, 466, 467, 468, 471, 474, 476, 477, 480, 483, 486, 490, 491, 494, 496, 500, 503, 504, 517, 518, 527, 544
- simple   446–77, 536
- simultaneous   464–68, 496, 498, 501, 546, 548, 549
- specialized   478–505
- subject raising   446, 503
- temporal   461–77
- word order   447, 451, 458, 460, 461, 463, 466, 468, 471, 478, 482, 486, 487, 488, 490, 491, 496, 497, 498, 499, 501, 503, 504, 508, 511, 513, 517, 520, 522, 541, 545, 546, 548
clauses   343
- adding arguments. *See* valency
- basic types   385–445
- complement. *See* complementation
- coordination   236, 237, 449–53
- dependent   222–29, 226, 356, 446, 447, 448, 452, 457, 475, 476, 477, 479, 494, 497, 503, 504, 508, 511, 513, 517, 527, 544, 546
- matrix   222, 224, 351, 356, 357, 385, 432, 446, 447, 453, 455, 457, 462, 464, 467, 473, 474, 476, 477, 479, 480, 482, 490, 494, 497, 499, 503, 504, 506, 508, 511, 513, 514, 517, 526, 527, 537, 539, 544, 545, 546
- simple   340–68
- word order   33, 144, 150, 151, 183, 188, 189, 197, 198, 199, 235, 242, 249, 253, 255, 258, 259, 268, 269, 271, 273, 275, 278, 281, 284, 287, 288, 289, 290, 291, 293, 295, 297, 300, 311, 314, 319, 323, 325, 326, 330, 331, 333, 335, 338, 340, 344–47, 347, 352, 354, 355, 361, 363, 365, 369, 374, 377, 380, 386, 387, 390, 399, 400, 410, 416, 417, 418, 419, 424, 433, 437, 447, 451, 469, 481
clitics   112, 164, 241
collocations   86, 90, 117, 152, 165, 203, 216, 239, 240, 242, 247, 248, 249, 250, 251, 264, 309, 468, 497, 531, 546
comparative constructions   213, 235, 236, 417–33, 496–97
complementation   33, 232, 285, 357, 419, 445, 446, 447, 480, 488, 498, 499, 506–30, 535, 538, 539, 548, 549
- optional use   515
complex stative constructions   283, 285, 286–87, 335, 336, 422, 423, 424, 427, 429, 430, 485, 500, 506, 508
compounds   86, 111, 113, 115–17, 126, 157, 166, 169, 184, 186, 198, 204, 205, 211, 230, 239, 250, 373, 389, 418, 457
Comrie, Bernard   226, 299, 346
concessive constructions   488–90, 495–96, 535, 536
conditional constructions   33, 213, 344, 474, 477, 480, 491–97, 535, 538, 539, 541
conjunctions   234–36, 264, 358, 362, 393–94, 418, 420, 424, 446, 447, 449, 453–55, 457, 458, 476, 482, 488, 489, 490
consonants   41–58
- affricates   54
- approximants   56–58
- fricatives   49
- nasals   47–49, 108
- stops   44–47
- VOT   44, 54, 55
coordination   232–38, 403, 449–53, 453–55, 456, 536

copula   32, 101, 153, 243, 253, 261–65, 277, 292, 338, 341, 396, 402, 404–8, 418, 419, 421, 435–37, 455, 457, 525, 543, 549
Cristofaro, Sonia   316, 446

Dai people   7, 10
Dai Qingxia   1, 3, 8, 11, 12–14, 15, 17, 19, 20, 21, 22, 23, 25–26, 41, 42, 52, 53, 61, 62, 71, 74, 77, 80, 82, 84, 86, 107, 108, 115, 126, 372, 394, 445
dative construction   257–59
declarative clauses   316, 385–86, 395, 403, 411, 415, 434, 436, 453, 514
deixis   136–55, 176–83, 274, 275, 276, 331, 334, 364, 525
demonstratives   116, 139, 141–44, 156, 157, 164, 165, 167, 173, 181, 183, 201, 203, 205, 219, 253, 324, 331, 334, 377, 421
Dench   Alan, 28
desiderative construction   271, 374–77, 455, 521
diminutive   117, 184, 198, 250, 333, 366
directional constructions   242, 274–81, 288, 323, 332, 362, 363, 365, 448, 543
discourse   2, 27–29, 29–32, 32, 33, 40, 82, 85, 86, 87, 91, 92–96, 94, 97, 99, 101, 103, 105–6, 108, 111, 112, 119, 120, 121, 126, 128, 129, 130, 132, 133, 135, 136, 137, 138, 140, 141, 143, 146, 149, 150, 151, 154, 157, 158, 161, 164, 165, 168, 170, 179, 180, 183, 189, 197, 200, 201, 203, 204, 205, 208, 214, 217, 223, 225, 228, 233, 239, 240, 241, 250, 258, 262, 265, 266, 290, 295, 297, 299, 301, 305, 310, 313, 320, 325, 329, 331, 334, 335, 339, 340, 341, 344, 345, 347, 350, 352, 354, 355, 357, 358, 359, 360, 366, 369, 375, 384, 385, 386, 387, 388, 390, 393, 406, 408, 409, 413, 419, 425, 427, 433, 434, 435, 438, 439, 440, 441, 443–45, 446, 447, 448, 451, 456, 457, 458, 460, 461, 464, 466, 468, 469, 471, 472, 474, 478, 479, 481, 482, 484, 486, 487, 488, 491, 492, 496, 501, 509, 511, 522, 524, 525, 526, 531, 534, 536, 538, 539, 541, 542, 544, 546, 547, 550, 551
– markers   347, 351, 505, 547
discourse functional framework   2, 27–29, 575
disjunction   236, 403–4, 453–55

ditransitive verbs   244, 257–59, 344, 348, 369, 372, 383, 506
Dixon, R. M. W.   110, 111, 112, 170, 243, 247, 250, 260, 273, 353, 446, 506
double subject. See topic-comment structure
Du Bois, John   27, 28, 120, 170, 353, 575
Du Yuting   10, 11, 16, 17
Duanmu, San   118
Dwyer, Arienne   28

elicitation   27–29, 29–32, 40, 97, 101, 105, 110, 111, 118, 119, 125, 241, 260, 290, 352, 390, 496, 509, 517
embedding   377, 445, 446–48, 451, 452, 455, 457, 460, 466, 467, 468, 474, 476, 480, 500, 503, 506–30, 509, 517, 524
E-MELD   28
Emmorey, Karen   57
emphasis   33, 90, 123, 125, 151, 167, 191, 231, 249, 296, 297, 309, 311, 314, 333, 337, 377, 433–45, 458, 461, 481, 486, 541
– copular   435–36, 458
– discourse   443–45, 458, 541
– epistemic   440–41, 458, 541
– imperfective   307, 308, 321, 338, 432, 433–34, 438, 440, 525
– irrealis   436–37
– markers   490, 491, 525, 535
– perfective   301, 434–35, 440
– rhetorical   295
– stative   441–43, 505, 547
– strong assertion   262, 301, 307, 321, 338, 430, 434, 436–37, 440, 458, 480, 481, 488, 527, 541, 543
epistemicity   316, 397, 403, 405, 409, 410, 413–15, 415, 416, 417, 433, 436, 440–41, 513
– particles   440–41
ergativity. See pragmatic agentivity
Ethnologue   13, 18
Evans, Nicholas   28
existential verb   33, 101, 153, 162, 210, 216, 231, 262, 265–67, 277, 400, 401, 420, 422, 543

Fairbanks, Grant   124
fillers   470, 472, 547

focus   86, 99–102, 134, 244, 357, 358, 404, 430, 438, 439, 440, 447, 456, 458–60, 477, 481–82, 486–87, 541–44
– tone change   99–102, 103

Gao Fayuan   1, 10
gapping   222, 356, 431
Garellek, Marc   59, 108
Gazhuo. *See* Khatso language
generalized noun-modifying clause constructions. *See* relativization
Gerner, Matthias   99, 373, 549
Gippert, Jost   27
Good, Jeff   28
Gordon, Matthew   124
grammatical relations   344–47
grammaticalization   41, 77, 78, 82, 90, 91, 99, 131, 158, 166, 167, 169, 199, 205, 211, 229, 242, 243, 247, 253, 271, 322, 358, 369, 370, 372, 383, 393, 402, 411, 451, 455, 457, 464, 465, 468, 495, 504, 505, 513, 518, 522, 524, 531, 534, 536, 538, 541, 544, 546, 549
Gussenhoven, Carlos   118

Haiman, John   491, 492
Han Chinese people   1, 3, 6, 7, 10, 14, 16
Hani language   24
Hani people   7, 10, 14, 15
Hanyu   1, 3, 4, 8, 12, 13, 16, 21, 23, 24, 25, 26, 29, 32, 40, 41, 53, 63, 71, 72, 73, 74, 78, 82, 86, 106, 111, 113, 126, 132, 135, 140, 158, 163, 164, 165, 172, 184, 185, 186, 188, 189, 192, 200, 216, 239, 264, 269, 271, 323, 325, 326, 339, 388, 418, 425, 426, 447, 456, 460, 461, 463, 465, 471, 482, 486, 487, 490, 491, 493, 497, 499, 504, 506, 511, 520, 531, 544, 546, 550, 554
Hasieerdun   14, 20, 27
Haspelmath, Martin   207
He Jiren   1, 4, 11, 15, 17, 21–22, 23, 24, 42, 61, 65, 77, 86, 108, 115, 126, 160
hearsay   33, 307, 436, 447, 527, 529
Henderson, Alan   124
Himmelmann, Nikolaus   27
Hlersu language   17
homophony   90, 119, 171, 192, 234, 269, 295, 365, 393, 417, 437, 443, 445, 486, 505, 526, 546, 547

Hopper, Paul, 27
Huang Bufan   3, 22, 26
Huang Chun   1, 4, 8, 10, 11, 16, 132
Hui people   6, 7

idiomatic expressions   148, 166, 179, 185, 220, 231, 264, 277, 297, 308, 336, 337, 428, 455, 458, 464, 493, 495, 499
imperatives   96–97, 189, 270, 293–96, 305, 329, 351, 367, 386–93, 390, 523
– tone change   96–97, 313, 381, 387, 390–93
indefinite constructions   156, 167, 169, 207–18, 495
Inner Mongolia   9, 20
instrument   227, 347, 361–62, 381
integration, syntactic   273, 287, 385, 446–48, 448, 449, 451, 452, 455, 457, 458, 460, 462, 464, 466, 467, 468, 471, 474, 477, 480, 482, 483, 484, 486, 490, 491, 496, 498, 500, 503, 504, 506, 517, 518, 524, 528, 536
intensifiers   260, 285, 335–37, 430, 431, 432, 498
interjections   305, 406, 408–9, 409
intonation units   120–25, 290, 327, 344, 443, 451, 453, 469, 482, 524, 575
– cues   32, 121–25
intransitive verbs   140, 242–55, 260–61, 277, 280, 348, 370, 375, 381, 427, 439, 506, 508
irrealis   296, 300, 311, 312, 314, 316–17, 317–19, 320, 397, 398, 415–16, 432, 436–37, 480, 491, 539

Janhunen, Juha   17
Jongman, Allard   118
Ju Namkung   64
juxtaposition   232, 236, 262, 446, 447, 449–51, 451, 478, 516

Katso. *See* Khatso language
Kazhuo. *See* Khatso language
Khatso language   1–2, 4, 8, 12–14, 14–18, 18–19, 20–27
– attitudes towards   12–14, 25–26
– bilingualism   1, 12–14, 26, 40, 41, 126, 239, 482, 487
– borrowing   14–18, 23, 41, 42, 71, 72, 73, 74, 75, 78, 82, 86, 106, 111, 113, 126, 132, 135,

140, 158–64, 158, 163, 164, 165, 172, 184, 185, 188, 192, 200, 216, 239, 264, 269, 271, 272, 296, 323, 325, 326, 338, 339, 383, 388, 418, 426, 442, 445, 447, 460–61, 463–64, 465, 471, 482–83, 486, 487, 490–91, 493, 497, 499, 504, 505, 506, 511, 520, 521, 531, 544, 546, 547, 549, 554
- classification   1, 18–19, 21–22, 22, 24–25
- contact with other languages   1, 12–13, 14–18, 17, 20, 22, 24, 25
- fieldwork   27–29, 29–32, 575
- history   14–18, 21–22, 24–25, 24
- lack of Mongolic influence   1, 14–15, 18, 19, 23, 24
- lack of writing system   2, 4, 11, 13, 26, 110
- methodology   27–29, 40, 41, 57, 59, 67, 68, 69, 71, 73, 75, 575
- previous research   20–27, 41, 42, 52, 57, 61, 62, 77, 82, 86, 107, 108, 115, 116, 126, 132, 160, 372, 394
- primacy of pragmatics   32, 207, 223, 340, 344, 347, 359, 385, 446, 531, 551
- similarity to other Ngwi languages   1, 14, 15, 17, 18–19, 21, 23–25, 32–33, 57, 58, 77, 81, 87–89, 99, 116, 158, 176, 243, 327, 401, 423, 549
- speaker consultants   2, 29–32, 40, 575
- transcription   21, 25, 28, 29, 41, 61, 62, 63, 64, 68, 69, 73, 575
- translation   3, 21, 28, 94, 99, 110, 130, 137, 150, 151, 157, 165, 167, 168, 178, 191, 211, 214, 276, 290, 306, 322, 337, 359, 378, 402, 405, 419, 433, 456, 459, 461, 501, 508, 511, 537, 541, 544, 549
- typology   32–33, 44, 120, 164, 176, 207, 208, 209, 210, 217, 222, 226, 243, 247, 260, 272, 273, 296, 299, 316, 327, 340, 352, 358, 373, 401, 445, 446, 491, 492, 503, 506, 538
- various names of   3–4
- vitality   12–14, 25–26
- website   3, 28, 575
Khatso people   1, 3, 20, 27
- and Inner Mongolia   8, 9, 20, 27
- clothing   8
- cuisine   8
- economy   8, 11
- ethnonyms   4
- festivals   9

- history   5–12, 16, 18
- Mongol heritage   1, 4, 9, 11, 19, 23, 27, 39
- names   29
- population   7, 12
- religion   9
- speaker consultants   29–32, 40, 575
- village. *See* Xingmeng
kin terms   16, 105–6, 139, 176–83, 220
König, Ekkehard   538
Kublai Khan   1, 9, 10, 15, 17
Kui Li   27, 28, 29, 40, 582
Kurpaska, Maria   15

labile verbs. *See* ambitransitive verbs
Ladefoged, Peter   44, 64, 65, 86, 124
Lahu language   115
Lai, Catherine   118
Lalo language   19
Lama, Ziwo Qiu Fuyuan   15, 17, 19
language change. *See* grammaticalization *and* borrowing
language typology   14, 19, 44, 118, 120, 156, 164, 176, 207, 208, 209, 210, 217, 222, 226, 243, 247, 260, 272, 273, 296, 299, 316, 327, 340, 352, 358, 373, 401, 445, 446, 491, 492, 503, 506, 538
- overview of Khatso   32–33
LaPolla, Randy   18, 340, 352, 358, 359
Lawu language   18
Lehmann, Christian   446
Leipzig Glossing Rules   3
Lewis, M. Paul   1, 4, 13, 18
lexicon   554–74
Li, Charles   302, 304, 311, 340, 388, 442, 504, 546, 550
Lin Shezhi   8, 10
Lipo language   19
Lishan Ngwi language   21
Lisu language   17, 19, 24, 89
loanwords. *See* borrowing
locative constructions   135, 149, 150, 198, 221, 242, 265, 266, 324, 325, 328, 331–32, 331, 346, 347, 349, 350, 363–65, 365, 400, 473, 504
Lolo-Burmese. *See* Burmese-Ngwi
Lyons, John   401

Ma Shiwen   9, 10, 16, 132
Mackerras, Colin   17

Maddieson, Ian   57, 64, 65
Man, John   17
Mandarin Chinese. *See* Putonghua
manner constructions   467, 486, 498–500, 545, 546, 549
– adverbs   150, 163, 333–35
– and interrogative pronouns   150, 151
– classifiers   189–91, 226
– reduplicated stative construction   254
– serial verb constructions   285, 286
Matisoff, James   19, 222, 373, 445
Matras, Yaron   17
Matsumoto, Yoshiko   226, 346
McGregor, William   351, 355
methodology   27–29, 29–32, 40, 41, 57, 59, 67, 68, 69, 71, 73, 75, 126, 575
Michael, Lev   316
Ming era   10, 15, 16, 17
Mithun, Marianne   28
modality   268, 272, 390
Mongolian language   1, 14, 17, 18, 19, 20, 23, 24, 25, 39
Mongols   1, 4, 9, 10, 14, 15, 16, 17, 22, 23
Moravcsik Edith, 139
morphology. *See* word structure
Mosel, Ulrike   27
Moseley, Christopher   2, 13
Mu Shihua   1, 4, 10, 14, 15, 16, 18, 19, 23–25, 41, 42, 52, 61, 63, 71, 74, 76, 77, 82, 86, 107, 108, 113, 115, 116, 126, 132, 160, 372
Mullaney, Thomas   18
multifunctionality   32, 33, 91–99, 167, 207, 250, 265, 324, 325, 357, 358, 369–72, 378, 380, 383, 386, 388, 447, 448, 467, 476, 481, 484, 486, 488, 489, 492, 494, 497, 498, 499, 501, 513, 522, 524, 531, 533, 536, 537, 538, 540, 544, 547, 550

Nakayama, Toshihide   28
names   132–36
– personal   132–34, 182, 218, 220, 225
– place   135–36, 242, 266, 363, 364
Nasu language   19
Naxi language   24
negation   162, 199, 207, 214–17, 240, 243, 262, 270, 278, 284, 286, 290–96, 300, 304, 305, 309, 311, 314, 316, 317, 320, 323, 324, 337, 371, 372, 376, 379, 380, 382, 390, 395, 398, 406, 416, 418, 421, 423, 424, 427, 429, 430, 432, 436, 455, 477, 483, 491, 493, 494, 495, 503, 513, 524, 533, 535, 536
Newman, Paul   27
Ngwi languages   1, 4, 14, 15, 16, 17, 18–19, 20, 21, 22, 23, 24, 25, 32–33, 32–33, 57, 58, 77, 81, 86, 89, 99, 116, 158, 176, 243, 327, 401, 423, 549
Ngwi-speaking people   1, 7, 10, 11, 14, 16, 22, 23
Niesu language   23
Nisu language   17
nominalization   32, 116, 201, 229, 250, 253, 443, 445, 508
Noonan, Michael   503, 506
noun phrases   201–38, 261, 366, 402, 404, 406, 411, 415, 416, 417
– word order   33, 147, 153, 165, 183, 184, 185, 191, 197, 198, 201–3, 204, 206, 218, 220, 222, 228, 234, 248, 252
nouns   113, 115, 126–36, 164, 243, 244, 247, 253
– adjectival function   204–5
– adverbial function   299, 324, 327, 331, 347, 365
– and classifiers. *See* classifiers
– common   128–32, 208, 225, 232, 242, 362
– compounds   86, 113, 115–17, 126, 166, 186, 204, 205, 230, 239
– count   161, 165, 170–72, 172, 173
– evidence for class   126, 156–58, 164, 205, 253, 327, 331, 338, 508
– indefinite. *See* indefinite constructions
– mass   161, 165, 172–73, 173
– modified by nouns   204–5
– modified by stative verbs   205–6
– modified by verbs   248, 249, 250, 252
– plural   129, 134, 139, 142, 153, 154, 167, 173–76, 210, 418
– proper   132–36, 182, 232, 242, 363, 364
number   32, 115, 129, 130, 137, 139, 142, 152, 153, 156–200, 207, 210, 228, 388, 421
numerals   114, 128, 129, 130, 138, 139, 142, 156, 157, 158–64, 164, 165, 166, 167, 171, 173, 174, 176, 177, 178, 181, 183, 184, 185, 188, 189, 190, 191, 192, 198, 201, 203, 205, 218, 225, 326, 329, 426
Nuosu language   1, 19, 99, 549

object. *See* patient   P argument
Ohori, Toshio   446
OLAC   28
omission of particles. *See* particles
optative   386, 387, 389

P argument   131, 137, 156, 170, 200, 211, 223, 224, 231, 235, 239, 242, 255, 256, 257, 258, 259, 260, 261, 340, 343, 344, 345, 347, 349, 351, 352, 353, 354, 355, 357, 358, 359, 360, 369, 386, 394, 429, 466, 503, 504, 509, 517, 521, 522, 544
Palmer, F. R.   272
particles   112, 114, 126, 164, 231, 296, 297, 324, 385, 446, 483, 528
– omission   94, 95, 96–97, 101, 103–4, 199, 215, 219, 234, 250, 251, 433, 464, 522
passive. *See* pseudo-passive
patient   131, 137, 156, 170, 200, 211, 223, 224, 231, 235, 239, 242, 255, 256, 257, 258, 259, 260, 261, 340, 343, 347, 349, 351, 352, 353, 354, 355, 357, 358, 359, 360, 369, 386, 394, 429, 466, 503, 504, 509, 517, 521, 522, 544
Payne, Thomas   28, 446
phonemes   40–76
– ŋa^{323}ka^{53} accent   40, 59, 68, 73, 76
– variation   40, 41, 44, 52, 59, 61, 66, 68, 71, 73, 75, 76
phonology   32, 40–76
plural nouns. *See* nouns
Poa, Dory   18
possession   112, 126, 133, 134, 135, 138, 141, 143, 156, 157, 164, 165, 176, 177, 201, 205, 218, 223, 253, 265, 266, 324, 327
pragmatic agentivity   32, 256, 258, 344, 351–59, 359–61
pragmatics   32, 119, 123, 125, 130, 136, 155, 169, 170, 175, 176, 179, 180, 181, 184, 190, 197, 204, 207, 208, 210, 222, 223, 230, 250, 255, 256, 258, 259, 265, 266, 270, 283, 287, 288, 290, 299, 301, 306, 308, 311, 313, 314, 317, 319, 321, 329, 340, 344, 345, 347, 348, 351–59, 359, 360, 367, 369, 371, 373, 375, 376, 378, 383, 385, 387, 388, 390, 401, 411, 415, 429, 430, 431, 433, 438, 439, 440, 441, 443, 446, 447, 448, 449, 450, 451, 452, 453, 455, 458, 459, 460, 464, 466, 473, 474, 477, 484, 486, 488, 489, 491, 494, 499, 501, 502, 508, 516, 521, 525, 526, 529, 531, 533, 534, 535, 536, 538, 539, 540, 541, 542, 544, 546, 547, 549, 551
prohibitive   293–96, 387, 390, 417
pronouns   136–55, 165, 197, 198
– interrogative   144–55, 200, 207, 209, 211, 212, 213, 216, 217, 266, 301, 305, 310, 312, 315, 322, 394, 399–403, 402, 408, 409, 410, 411, 416, 453, 495, 535
– personal   136–41, 161, 163, 166, 179, 182, 183, 203, 218, 219, 220, 225, 229, 250, 252, 253, 387, 393, 525, 529
prosody   49, 60, 66, 92–96, 99, 103, 111, 119, 120–25, 451
pseudo-passive   33, 244, 259, 358, 359, 369
purpose constructions   287, 289, 363, 372, 377, 467, 500–505, 518, 544, 545, 546
Putonghua   1, 2, 3, 4, 8, 9, 10, 11, 12, 13, 15, 17, 19, 20, 21, 22, 23, 24, 25, 26, 28, 29, 32, 39, 65, 72, 73, 81, 82, 94, 110, 118, 126, 158, 168, 171, 172, 178, 184, 186, 188, 189, 192, 226, 239, 264, 323, 326, 339, 340, 359, 361, 388, 402, 425, 439, 442, 445, 447, 456, 460, 461, 463, 465, 471, 482, 486, 487, 490, 491, 493, 497, 499, 504, 506, 508, 521, 537, 544, 546, 547, 550

Qing era   8, 11
quantification   128, 151–54, 156–200, 302, 423, 425, 426
questions   33, 296, 394–417, 433, 514, 524, 526
– and tone change   104–5
– answering   201, 292, 308, 316, 398, 402, 404, 406, 410, 411, 413, 416, 435, 444
– certainty   316, 413–15, 458, 477
– choice   403–4, 453, 454
– confirmation   404, 416, 541
– content   263, 301, 305, 310, 312, 315, 322, 399–403, 403, 411, 437
– echo   104–5, 409–10
– interjection   408–9, 409
– interrogative pronouns   104, 144–55, 166, 184, 187, 306, 310, 312, 315, 322, 416
– irrealis   415–16, 437
– markers   301, 307, 316, 351, 405, 410–17, 455

- polar   210, 250, 263, 271, 279, 284, 287, 292, 301, 305, 310, 315, 316, 317, 318, 322, 324, 371, 372, 377, 379, 382, 383, 395–99, 405, 411, 415, 437, 477, 495, 503, 513
- rhetorical   399, 413, 416–17
- 'still'   410–11
- tag   262, 263, 396, 404–8, 415, 514
- topic marker   411–13

quotative verbs   33, 101, 295, 480–81, 488, 489, 520, 523–30, 535, 539, 543

Qutuoguan   10, 12, 16, 17

R argument   137, 223, 224, 235, 257, 258, 259, 340, 344, 347, 349, 352, 354, 355, 356, 358, 386

Ratliff, Martha   27

reason constructions   289, 376, 473, 478–83, 537, 539, 542

recipient   137, 223, 224, 235, 257, 258, 259, 340, 344, 347, 349, 352, 354, 355, 356, 358, 369, 380, 383, 386, 502

reciprocal constructions   236, 393–94, 420

reduplication   90–91, 95, 111, 162, 166, 167, 172, 230, 250–55, 264, 271, 279, 284, 287, 292, 301, 305, 310, 312, 315, 316, 318, 322, 324, 334, 337, 371, 377, 379, 382, 383, 394, 395–99, 399, 402, 410, 411, 415, 429, 503, 513

reference
- non-specific   131, 156, 168, 169, 207, 210, 211, 217, 257, 303
- specific   130, 132, 133, 168, 207, 209, 222, 228, 303, 445

referents   14, 116, 130, 131, 132, 134, 137, 139, 141, 142, 148, 153, 168, 169, 176, 177, 178, 179, 181, 183, 198, 200, 207, 208, 209, 210, 211, 214, 217, 222, 223, 229, 230, 345, 352, 353, 393, 417, 445

reflexive constructions   140, 257

relativization   32, 33, 127, 133, 135, 138, 139, 143, 156, 157, 164, 165, 201, 205, 206, 210, 216, 222–29, 230, 244, 247, 248, 249, 252, 253, 324, 331, 346, 356, 366, 431, 448, 508

resultative constructions   278, 286, 291, 299, 319, 335, 338, 378, 379, 380, 391, 448, 485, 486, 494, 518, 544, 545

resultative constructions   281–85

Rice, Keren   28

Rybatzki, Volker   15

S argument   132, 137, 150, 151, 183, 223, 224, 231, 241, 242, 243, 244, 260, 271, 321, 326, 330, 331, 333, 340, 344, 345, 349, 350, 351, 358, 361, 363, 365, 388, 389, 439, 453, 455, 457, 466, 467, 468, 469, 490, 500, 503, 504, 508, 518, 544

Sadu language   17, 18, 81

Samei language   23

Samu language   15, 17, 19

Sani Ngwi language   21, 22, 23

Schwarz, Henry   27

semantics   33, 97, 105, 111, 133, 149, 150, 165, 166, 174, 175, 176, 191, 214, 226, 230, 236, 237, 266, 268, 273, 283, 340, 345, 347, 372, 381, 389, 401, 419, 423, 435, 439, 449, 451, 454, 462, 465, 468, 473, 474, 476, 477, 483, 484, 486, 491, 492, 494, 497, 498, 502, 504, 515
- bleached   131, 169, 211, 229, 239, 242, 250, 465, 466, 538
- verbal   32, 119, 255, 258, 277, 282, 287, 288, 322, 340, 341, 344, 352, 353, 356, 362, 369, 372, 446, 448, 478, 498, 506, 508, 509, 518, 531, 536, 544, 545, 549

sentences. *See* clauses

serial verb constructions   33, 90, 101, 222, 268–72, 269, 273–89, 274–81, 291, 297, 323, 347, 363, 380, 397, 422
- and tone change   90
- applicative   369–72
- complex   283, 285, 286–87
- directional   281–85, 288, 323, 448, 543
- manner   285, 286
- one-event   274–87
- resultative   278, 285, 286, 299, 335, 378, 379, 380, 391, 448, 485, 486, 494
- two-event   287–89, 372, 380, 383, 448, 500, 504, 544

Shansu language. *See* Hlersu language

Shopen, Timothy   446

Silverstein, Michael   170, 353

Sino-Tibetan languages   64, 106, 156, 164, 222, 340

Sneath, David   10, 11, 27

solicitative   294, 386, 388, 390, 391

speech, reported   33, 322, 523–30, 539

stative verbs   32, 90, 112, 114, 117, 153, 156, 201, 229, 242–55, 282, 290, 293, 309, 333, 335, 336, 337, 370, 375, 378, 379, 380,

381, 400, 401, 420, 422, 424, 427, 429, 430, 433, 439, 441-43, 465, 486, 498-500, 506, 508, 513, 545
- adjectival function   32, 201, 205-6, 244-50
- adverbial function   324, 546
- complex construction   286-87, 335, 336, 422, 423, 424, 427, 429, 430, 485, 500, 506, 508
- reduplicated construction   90-91, 95, 230, 250-55, 292, 324, 333
STEDT   4
stress   118-19
subject. See S argument and agent
subject raising   446, 503
subordination   273, 287, 377, 385, 445, 446-48, 446, 448, 490, 500, 506-30, 548
suffixes   111, 116-17, 157, 166, 176, 184, 198, 241
Sun Hongkai   18
superlative construction   244, 430-33
syllable structure   32, 41, 42, 46, 47, 48, 49, 50, 51, 52, 55, 56, 57, 59, 61, 62, 63, 67, 69, 70, 74, 77, 78, 86, 102, 103, 108-10, 123, 126
- frequency   109-10
syntactic integration. See integration

tail-head linkage   469, 474, 540
temporal constructions. See time
texts   575-88
Thieberger, Nicholas   28
Thomason, Sarah   17
Thompson, Sandra   27, 302, 304, 311, 340, 388, 442, 504, 546, 550
Tibeto-Burman languages   1, 15, 19, 22, 24, 229, 273, 296, 352, 358, 373, 445
time
- adverbs   222, 325-30, 463-64
- and clause linking   478
- and comparative constructions   430
- and interrogative pronouns   149, 400
- arguments   222, 226, 347, 350, 365-68, 476
- calendar   162, 184, 185, 186, 326
- classifiers   183-87, 189
- indefinite constructions   207-18
- particles   299, 461-63, 493, 499, 508, 513, 517, 537, 547-50
- questions   148

- sequential   287, 288, 289, 469-77, 484, 494, 540, 545
- simultaneous   464-68, 496, 498, 501, 546, 548, 549
tone change   32, 41, 86, 111, 166, 171, 184, 199, 405
- and causatives   107, 373, 374
- and currently relevant aspect   97-99, 381
- and demonstratives   141
- and extended contours   105-6
- and focus   99-102, 103, 310, 438, 440, 456, 458-60, 477, 481-82, 486-87, 527, 543
- and fusion   32, 102-5, 150, 408, 409, 411, 543, 544
- and imperatives   96-97, 313, 381, 387, 390-93
- and non-final phrases   92-96, 311, 342, 411, 450, 452, 458, 464, 473, 474, 475, 479, 480, 488, 491, 496, 533, 537
- and numerals   32, 87-89, 161, 176, 192
- and reduplication   90-91, 250-55
- and verbs 'come', 'go', 90, 269, 275, 276, 277, 288, 397
- marked pattern   91-99, 214, 215, 277
- vocative function   105-6, 525
tone fusion. See tone change
tones   32, 41, 77-107, 108
- duration   81
- frequency   77-80, 82
- minimal octuplets   80
- phonation   81, 84, 85
- sandhi. See tone change
- toneme inventory   77
- variation   86, 107, 91, 132, 136, 141, 161, 163, 166, 171, 184, 326, 482
Tonghai   1, 3, 4, 5, 6, 8, 10, 13, 15, 17, 21, 26
Tonghai Mongolian Nationality Cultural Research and Inheritance Protection Center   26
topic   131, 170, 183, 259, 299, 327, 340-44, 347, 348, 350, 357, 359, 455, 474-76, 491-94, 508, 515, 547-50
- markers   33, 91-99, 92, 213, 259, 311, 340-44, 341, 344, 411-13, 419, 447, 462, 464, 472, 474-76, 480, 491-94, 495, 496, 497, 498, 499, 508, 513, 517, 538-41, 547-50
- optional use   341, 344

topic-comment structure   32, 33, 340–44, 347, 348, 474–76, 491–94, 508, 511, 514, 518, 539, 541, 548
transcription   21, 25, 28, 29, 41, 61, 62, 63, 64, 68, 69, 73, 575
– Santa Barbara method   28, 575
transitive verbs   156, 211, 244, 255, 260–61, 277, 344, 369, 381, 439, 506, 509, 517
translation   94, 99, 110, 130, 137, 150, 151, 157, 165, 167, 168, 178, 191, 211, 214, 276, 290, 306, 322, 337, 359, 378, 402, 405, 419, 433, 456, 459, 461, 501, 508, 511, 537, 541, 544, 549
Traugott, Elizabeth   538
typology. *See* language typology

UNESCO   2, 13
universal constructions   184, 198–200, 231, 495, 535

valency   241, 257, 293, 352, 355, 369–84, 386, 429
Vendler, Zeno   299
verb phrases. *See* clauses
verbs   113, 114, 137, 239–89
– ambitransitive   242, 260–61, 280
– and classifiers   164, 189–91
– auxiliary   268–72, 291, 295, 297, 321, 336, 337, 372, 374, 383, 387, 390, 397, 447, 520, 521, 543
– copula   32, 101, 153, 243, 253, 261–65, 277, 292, 338, 341, 396, 402, 404–8, 418, 419, 421, 435–36, 436–37, 455, 457, 525, 543, 549
– ditransitive   244, 257–59, 344, 348, 369, 372, 383, 506
– evidence for class   239–41, 250, 290
– existential   101, 153, 162, 210, 216, 231, 262, 265–67, 277, 400, 401, 420, 422, 543
– intransitive   140, 242–55, 260–61, 277, 280, 348, 370, 375, 381, 427, 439, 506, 508
– modifiers   241, 268–72, 290–339
– negation. *See* negation
– nominalization   229–32, 250, 253
– quotative   33, 101, 295, 480–81, 488, 489, 520, 523–30, 535, 539, 543
– serial. *See* serial verb constructions
– stative   32, 90, 112, 114, 117, 153, 156, 201, 205–6, 229, 230, 242–55, 282, 290, 293, 309, 333, 335, 336, 337, 370, 375, 378, 379, 380, 381, 400, 401, 420, 422, 424, 427, 429, 430, 433, 439, 441–43, 465, 485, 486, 498–500, 506, 508, 513, 545, 546
– transitive   211, 242, 244, 255, 260–61, 277, 344, 369, 381, 439, 506, 509, 517
– valency. *See* valency
vowels   58–75, 108
– diphthongs   41, 70–74
– monophthongs   58–70
– ɳa^{323}ka^{53} accent   40, 59, 68, 73, 76
– triphthongs   41, 74–75
– variation   40, 59, 61, 63, 66, 68, 70, 71, 73, 75, 76

Wang Feng   15
Wang Licai   4, 26
word classes   126, 239–41, 250, 268, 273, 290, 296, 324, 325, 327, 331, 335, 338, 377
word order
– in clause linking   447, 451, 458, 460, 461, 463, 466, 468, 471, 478, 482, 486, 487, 488, 490, 491, 496, 497, 498, 499, 501, 503, 504, 508, 511, 513, 517, 520, 522, 541, 545, 546, 548
– in clauses   33, 144, 150, 151, 183, 188, 189, 197, 198, 199, 235, 242, 249, 253, 255, 258, 259, 268, 269, 271, 273, 275, 278, 281, 284, 287, 288, 289, 290, 291, 293, 295, 297, 300, 311, 314, 319, 323, 325, 326, 330, 331, 333, 335, 338, 340, 344–47, 347, 352, 354, 355, 361, 363, 365, 369, 374, 377, 380, 386, 387, 390, 399, 400, 410, 416, 417, 418, 419, 424, 433, 437, 447, 451, 469, 481
– in noun phrases   33, 147, 153, 165, 183, 184, 185, 191, 197, 198, 201–3, 204, 205, 206, 218, 220, 222, 228, 234, 248, 252
word structure   77, 110–19, 126, 132, 144, 146, 149, 150, 154, 157, 158, 163, 198, 239, 248, 251, 331, 395, 521
Wu Gu   16
Wuni Wuqie   16

Xingmeng   1, 3, 4, 6, 7, 8, 9, 10, 11, 12, 13, 14, 17, 19, 20, 21, 22, 23, 25, 27, 29–32, 76, 135, 575
– geography   5–8
– historical villages within   4, 6, 10, 12, 40, 135

- history 4, 3–4, 10–11
- photos 34–39
- population 7, 10, 12, 25
- various names 4, 135

Xu Xianming 17

Yi. *See* Ngwi
Yuan era 4, 10, 11, 12, 15, 16, 17
Yunnan 1, 3, 4, 5, 8, 9, 10, 12, 14, 15, 16, 17, 18, 22, 24, 27, 28

zero anaphora 32, 33, 132, 137, 150, 151, 166, 170, 197, 203, 230, 234, 241, 253, 255, 256, 258, 261, 265, 266, 267, 271, 290, 330, 344, 345, 347, 352, 355, 356, 360, 385, 386, 446, 466, 469, 508, 515, 518, 522, 524, 525

Zhan Fangqiong 222

www.ingramcontent.com/pod-product-compliance
Lightning Source LLC
Chambersburg PA
CBHW060451300426
44113CB00016B/2556